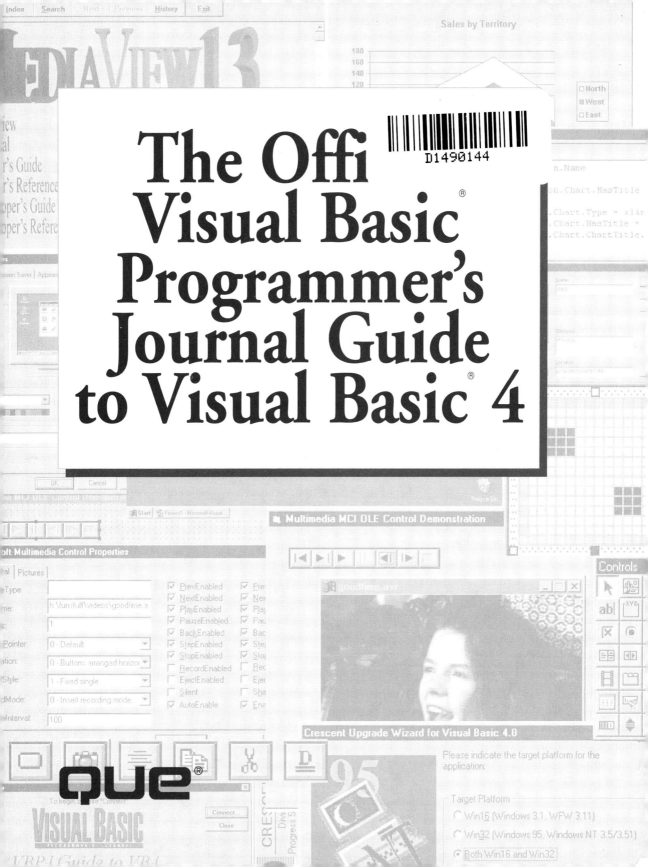

The Official Visual Basic® Programmer's Journal Guide to Visual Basic® 4

The Official Visual Basic® Programmer's Journal Guide to Visual Basic® 4

Daniel Appleman

Chris Barlow

Michiel de Bruijn

Drew Fletcher

Kate Gregory

Roger Jennings

Stan Leszynski

Michael McKelvy

S. Rama Ramachandran

Joe Robison

Ken Schiff

James Schmelzer

Barry Seymour

Jeffrey Smith

Frank Sommer

Scott Swanson

Jonathan Wood

que®

The Official Visual Basic Programmer's Journal Guide to Visual Basic 4

Library of Congress Catalog No.: 95-71420

ISBN: 0-7897-0465-x

98 97 96   6 5 4 3 2 1

Interpretation of the printing code: the rightmost double-digit number is the year of the book's printing; the rightmost single-digit number, the number of the book's printing. For example, a printing code of 96-1 shows that the first printing of the book occurred in 1996.

Screen reproductions in this book were created by using Collage Plus from Inner Media, Inc., Hollis, NH.

Composed in *Stone Serif* and *MCPdigital* by Que Corporation.

Welcome to a Unique Book

Nearly a year ago, the editors of *Visual Basic Programmer's Journal* saw that taking full advantage of Microsoft Visual Basic 4.0 would require a bigger leap in developer understanding than any prior release. So, we approached Que, the leading computer book publisher, about a joint imprint. The result is this book, which we hope will help you get up to speed quickly on the exciting new features in VB4. We've rounded up some of our best, regular magazine authors and columnists to create what we believe is a unique book. Rather than have one author try to cover all aspects of this diverse development environment, we invited a range of prominent VB developers to each examine his or her area of specialty.

This book's goal is to help people who can already program in VB get up to speed on the newest release as quickly as possible, and raise their programming skills to the next level.

When VB first appeared, the leap to event-driven programming confounded some traditional, procedural-oriented programmers. But since then VB has grown in evolutionary steps, adding functionality steadily. The move from VB3 to VB4 is quite different. Although your existing programs can run unchanged, getting the most from VB4 requires learning about classes and three-tier client/server development. Both represent fundamentally new approaches. At the mundane level, workarounds required by shortcomings in VB3 are no longer necessary. For example, if you've ever kludged a way to pass information between forms, you'll be pleased to find that since a form is now an object, you can simply declare a public variable to share data. But at a higher level, creation of objects that can be distributed across networks promises to enable applications that could not be created with desktop tools before.

This book is highly modular. You can read most chapters independently of others, and almost all have code samples on the enclosed CD-ROM to let you try out these new ideas immediately. Speaking for both the editors of *Visual Basic Programmer's Journal* and Que, we hope you enjoy our first joint book. If you have any comments, please feel free to post them on our CompuServe forum (**GO VBPJ**) or our Internet site at **http://www.windx.com**.

James E. Fawcette
Editor and Publisher
VBPJ

Credits

President and Publisher
Roland Elgey

Associate Publisher
Joseph B. Wikert

Editorial Services Director
Elizabeth Keaffaber

Managing Editor
Sandy Doell

Director of Marketing
Lynn E. Zingraf

Senior Series Editor
Chris Nelson

Title Manager
Bryan Gambrel

Acquisitions Editor
Fred Slone

Product Director
Kevin Kloss

Production Editor
Mike La Bonne

Editors
Tom Cirtin
Chuck Hutchinson
Jeff Riley

Assistant Product Marketing Manager
Kim Margolius

Technical Editor
Mark Streger
ABLAZE Business Systems

Technical Specialist
Nadeem Muhammed

Acquisitions Coordinator
Angela C. Kozlowski

Operations Coordinator
Patricia J. Brooks

Editorial Assistant
Michelle R. Newcomb

Book Designer
Ruth Harvey

Cover Designer
Dan Armstrong

Copywriter
Jennifer Reese

Production Team
Steve Adams
Kim Cofer
Joan Evan
Jason Hand
Damon Jordan
Clint Lahnen
Bob LaRoche
Casey Price
Bobbi Satterfield
Mike Thomas
Karen Walsh
Kelly Warner
Todd Wente

Indexers
Carol Sheehan
Brad Herriman

About the Authors

Daniel Appleman is the president of Desaware, a company specializing in add-on components such as SpyWorks, StorageTools, and VersionStamper. He is the author of *PC Magazine*'s *Visual Basic Programmer's Guide to the Windows API, How Computer Programming Works*, and the forthcoming *Visual Basic Programmer's Guide to the Win32 API* from Ziff-Davis Press.

Chris Barlow, in addition to writing a monthly column for the *Visual Basic Programmer's Journal* and speaking at VBITS, Comdex, and TechEd, is the president of SunOpTech®, Inc.

His background includes a combination of entrepreneurial, management, and computer skills. He earned his undergraduate degree from Dartmouth College with Distinction in Economics & Computer Science and, as a student at Dartmouth, worked as a programmer on some of the later enhancements to the BASIC language with its inventors, Drs. Kemeny and Kurtz. He received his MBA from Harvard Business School and worked for Fortune 500 companies in manufacturing and management information systems.

Based in Sarasota, Florida, SunOpTech uses Visual Basic and Visual C++ to develop Windows-based decision support applications for medium- to large-size manufacturing enterprises.

Reach Chris at SunOpTech, Inc., 1500 West University Parkway, Sarasota, FL, 34243; by telephone at 941-362-1271; by fax at 941-355-4497; and on the Internet at **ChrisB@SunOpTech.com**.

Michiel de Bruijn lives in Rotterdam, The Netherlands, and is co-owner of VBD Automatiseringsdiensten, where he is the designer and lead programmer of the Network Communications System, a Windows-based messaging system written almost entirely in Visual Basic. In his spare time, he is a section leader in the VBPJ Forum on CompuServe (**GO VBPJFO**) and tries to help out people in the Microsoft Basic forum (**GO MSBASIC**). For the latter efforts, he received a Microsoft Most Valuable Professional (MVP) Award. Contact Michiel on CompuServe at **100021,1061**, or on the Internet at **mdb@vbd.nl**.

Drew Fletcher works for Microsoft as a program manager on the Visual Basic team. He has been on the Visual Basic team since version 1.0. Before coming to Microsoft, Drew worked for Boeing Computer Services, several startup companies, and as a freelance classical musician.

Kate Gregory has a computer consulting and software development business in rural Ontario, Canada. She works in Visual C++ (specializing in Internet applications), teaches Internet and C++ programming courses, and writes. She has written two other books for Que.

Roger Jennings is a consultant specializing in Windows database and multi-media applications. He is the author of Que's *Unveiling Windows 95; Using Windows Desktop Video,* Special Edition; *Discover Windows 3.1 Multimedia* and *Access for Windows Hot Tips;* and was a contributing author to Que's *Using Windows 95,* Special Edition; *Excel Professional Techniques; Killer Windows Utilities;* and *Using Visual Basic 3.* He has written two other books about creating database applications with Access and Visual Basic, coauthored a book on using Microsoft Visual C++ for database development, is a contributing editor of *Visual Basic Programmer's Journal,* and has written articles for the *Microsoft Developer Network News* and the MSDN CD-ROMs. Roger is a principal of OakLeaf Systems, a Northern California software development and consulting firm; you may contact him via CompuServe (**ID 70233,2161**), on the Internet (**70233.2161@compuserve.com**), or on The Microsoft Network (**Roger_Jennings**).

Stan Leszynski founded Leszynski Company, Inc., in 1982 to create custom PC database applications. Since that time, the firm has created solutions for hundreds of clients, including dozens of applications for Microsoft. The company has also written retail products sold by Microsoft, Microrim, Qualitas, and Kwery with a user base of several million people. Successful products include the OLE calendar controls shipped with Access 2 and Access 95, the 386MAX memory manager, and four R:BASE developer tools. The company currently specializes in Access, Visual Basic, SQL Server, and Visual C++.

Stan's second company, Kwery Corporation, shipped the very first Access add-in—Access To Word—and the first OLE controls for Access—Kwery Control Pak 1.

Stan is the author of *Access Expert Solutions* from Que. He speaks regularly at Access conferences in the U.S., Canada, and Europe, and is consistently one of the top-rated Access speakers.

Michael McKelvy is owner and president of McKelvy Software Systems, a software consulting firm in Birmingham, Ala. He specializes in the development of database applications. Michael has been developing software for business and engineering applications for over 15 years and has written a variety of engineering and financial analysis programs for a number of businesses. Mike is also the author of *Using Visual Basic 4* and the coauthor of Que's *Special Edition Using Visual Basic 4* and *Visual Basic Expert Solutions*. He can be reached by Fax at (205) 980-9816; and on CompuServe at **71477,3513**.

S. Rama Ramachandran is a senior consultant with TechWorks International, a Westport, Connecticut-based Microsoft Solution Provider Partner. He specializes in the design and development of custom, GUI-based, stand-alone, network, and client/server database systems. Rama develops database systems in Visual Basic, MS Access, Visual FoxPro, and PowerBuilder. He has written a number of articles for the *Visual Basic Programmer's Journal*, and has also coauthored Que's *Visual Basic 4.0 Expert Solutions*. He can be reached by phone at (203) 221-1500; Fax, (203) 221-1330; and on CompuServe at **73313,3030**.

Joe Robison, in nearly eight years at Microsoft, has worked on a variety of Microsoft products, including Basic 7.0, PDS, and Microsoft Access. In 1990 he joined a project that eventually became Visual Basic 1.0, and he has worked on every subsequent version. He is currently a program manager working on future products in the Visual Basic group. He can be reached on the Internet at **joero@microsoft.com**.

Ken Schiff is president of Productivity Through Technology, Inc., a consultancy that he started to create and promote obvious, discoverable, and usable software. His varied work experience in several different industries gives him a point of view unique in the development community. A "down in the trenches with dirty fingernails" practitioner, he works with developers from inception, or offers usability inspections on already existing designs. A trainer and teacher by nature, his enthusiasm and passion for good GUI design has made him a popular conference speaker. Ken's clients include some of the largest corporations and commercial software developers in the country, as well as small ISVs, VARs, and system integrators.

James Schmelzer is a consultant with Clarity Consulting, Inc. Jay has architected a number of enterprise client/server solutions with tools such as Visual Basic, PowerBuilder, SQL Server, and Oracle. Jay is coauthor *of Visual Basic 4 Enterprise Development* (Que, ISBN: 0-7897-0099-9).

Barry Seymour has been programming with Visual Basic since it first came out in 1991. He has written numerous client/server programs in Visual Basic, both as an independent contractor and with various San Francisco-based consulting firms, including Vanguard Business Solutions (now Lotus Development Group) and DBSS, Inc. Barry is now a technical marketing specialist at CenterView Software, where he is "product evangelist" for Choreo 1.1, an add-on that vastly simplifies building client/server applications in Visual Basic.

Jeffrey Smith is a consultant with Clarity Consulting, Inc. Jeff holds a degree in biomedical engineering from Northwestern University. He has written articles for several technical journals, *including Visual Basic Programmer's Journal*. Jeff can be reached via the Internet at **jdsmith@claritycnslt.com** and via fax at (312) 266-1006.

Scott Swanson is a product manager working on Visual Basic. He has been writing Visual Basic code since version 1.0. Before that, he spent eight years as a systems engineer and instructor designing, installing, and supporting local area networks and client/server environments.

Frank Sommer is the vice president of VideoSoft Consulting, a company that creates custom Windows applications for its clients using Visual Basic. Frank may be reached on CompuServe at **76002,426** or the Internet at **VBGuy@MSN.com**.

Jonathan Wood lives in Southern California where he writes commercial and custom software in Visual Basic, Visual C++, and assembly language for his own company, SoftCircuits. He writes the Programming Techniques column and an occasional article for the *Visual Basic Programmer's Journal*. He's also section leader for the 16-bit API/DLL section in the VBPJ forum and a Microsoft MVP in the MSBASIC forum on CompuServe. He can be reached in either of these forums at 72134,263.

Trademarks

All terms mentioned in this book that are known to be trademarks or service marks have been appropriately capitalized. Que Corporation cannot attest to the accuracy of this information. Use of a term in this book should not be regarded as affecting the validity of any trademark or service mark.

We'd Like to Hear from You!

As part of our continuing effort to produce books of the highest possible quality, Que would like to hear your comments. To stay competitive, we *really* want you, as a computer book reader and user, to let us know what you like or dislike most about this book or other Que products.

You can mail comments, ideas, or suggestions for improving future editions to the address below, or send us a fax at (317) 581-4663. For the on-line inclined, Macmillan Computer Publishing now has a forum on CompuServe (type **GO QUEBOOKS** at any prompt) through which our staff and authors are available for questions and comments. The address of our Internet site is **http://www.mcp.com** (World Wide Web).

In addition to exploring our forum, please feel free to contact me personally to discuss your opinions of this book. You can reach me on CompuServe at 74201,1064.

Thanks in advance—your comments will help us to continue publishing the best books available on computer topics in today's market.

Kevin Kloss
Product Development Specialist
Que Corporation
201 W. 103rd Street
Indianapolis, Indiana 46290
USA

Contents at a Glance

Contents

5 Database Management Using the ODBC API   107

6 Using Visual Basic as a Multimedia Front-End   137

9 Anatomy of a Client/Server Project   231

17 Creating Visual Basic Naming Conventions 497

Introduction

by Michael McKelvy

Mike is the owner of McKelvy Software Systems, a Birmingham, Alabama-based consulting firm. Mike specializes in the development of database systems and engineering applications. He can be reached by Fax at (205) 980-9816; and on CompuServe at 71477,3513.

Several years ago, Microsoft introduced Visual Basic and set a new standard in program development languages. With Visual Basic, programmers and power users could produce Windows applications more quickly and easily than had ever been possible before. However, like any other tool, users always want more power as they find the limits of the programming language. Each new version of Visual Basic added more features and allowed programmers to create more powerful and complex applications. Visual Basic Version 4 is no exception to this trend.

However, if you are expecting to find that Visual Basic 4 just adds a few features to Visual Basic 3 and makes a few things easier to do, you are in for a big surprise. Visual Basic 4 has been rebuilt from the ground up. It provides you with a host of new features and improves on most of the old features. But, it also changes the ways things were done in the past. These changes are not simply cosmetic changes, but changes in the strategy of creating programs.

Better Capabilities

Although change can be intimidating, and does require you to relearn some of the aspects of programming, these changes provide you with new ways to extend your programming into areas where Visual Basic has never gone before. A few of these changes are as follows:

- Full support for Visual Basic for Applications, Version 2
- Greater OLE support

- New and better client/server tools
- Improved database capabilities

Let's take a brief look at each of these items and how they affect your programming.

A Universal Language

One of the new features of Visual Basic is its support for Visual Basic for Applications (VBA) 2. VBA has been used previously in Excel, but now the same language used in Visual Basic 4 is also used in the latest versions of Excel, Microsoft Project, and Access. This means that the commands you learn to perform a function in one of the products are transferable to the others. This lessens the learning curve for creating integrated applications using these pieces. For example, when I first tried to write a macro in Excel to access some database information, I did not even look at the help file or manuals, I just typed in the same code I was familiar with in Visual Basic 4. I was both pleased and amazed when the code worked.

Objects Are Everywhere

Visual Basic 4 also makes much greater use of objects than was done in Visual Basic 3. Objects are used in the new OCX custom controls, which replace the VBX controls you have used before. The greater use of objects also makes it easier to use parts of other applications to build programs, such as using Word to edit a document, or Excel to chart data.

New to Visual Basic 4 is the capability to create OLE automation servers. This allows you to create reusable components that can be used in any of your applications. Also, these OLE automation servers can be used by any OLE controller application, which means you can extend the capabilities of other applications like Excel or Access.

Finally, you can even extend the capabilities of Visual Basic itself. This is because Visual Basic's development environment is itself an OLE automation server. This means that you can create your own add-ins for task automation, form generators (similar to the Data Form Designer), source code control, or other tasks. And, even if you don't have the desire to create your own add-ins, you will benefit from this capability as third-party vendors will now be able to produce new and more powerful products that can become part of the development environment.

This book provides you with essential coverage of the OLE capabilities of Visual Basic 4. After an introduction to 32-bit OLE, you will find chapters on

OLE automation servers and distributed OLE programming. You will also find chapters devoted to the creation and use of OCX controls, the OLE replacement of the VBX controls used in previous versions of VB.

Enterprise Computing

If you move up to the Enterprise edition of Visual Basic 4, you will find a whole new set of capabilities that allow you to more easily create client/server programs. This edition includes the Remote Data Object (RDO) and Remote Data Control (RDC), which are tuned to work with client/server databases to provide you with better and faster access to the data in these databases. The RDO and RDC work with ODBC client/server databases, and are specifically tuned to work with SQL Server and Oracle databases. The RDO and RDC do for client/server programming what the data control did for database programming.

In addition to the client/server features, the Enterprise edition includes Visual SourceSafe. This product provides Visual Basic 4 with full version control capabilities and facilitates team programming with VB4 on projects by controlling the program source code and keeping up with when and by whom changes are made to a program.

Database Capabilities, Better Than Ever

Visual Basic 3 provided you with the ability to create database applications more easily than ever before. It provided a native database and a data control for easy access. It also provided data access objects for programmatic control of databases.

Although Visual Basic 3 made database applications easier, Visual Basic 4 provides you with the ability to create very powerful and complex database applications. Included with VB4 is a new data control that provides more functionality than the previous version and more bound controls to allow you to perform more database tasks without programming.

In addition to the enhancements to the data control and bound controls, VB4 supports two versions of the JET database engine: 2.5 for 16-bit applications, and 3.0 for 32-bit applications. Each of these versions provides support within Visual Basic for features that were available before only with Access, or not available at all. Visual Basic now fully supports referential integrity, including support for cascading updates and deletes. In addition, the data access objects now give you full programmatic support for the security features of the JET engine. This allows you to provide security administration features within your programs.

If you are using JET Version 3.0, you also have the capability of database replication. This feature allows you to make copies of a database that can be edited by multiple users, then recombined to update the main database. This is a powerful feature for applications that have to support multiple users at multiple sites.

Finally, even with all the improvements in the JET engine, you may still have need to access databases through Open Database Connectivity (ODBC) methods. These methods have also been improved in Visual Basic 4 to enhance your database programming.

Several chapters in this book provide you with information about the new and improved database capabilities in Visual Basic.

New Challenges...and Old

Although all the new features are great, you also want to know how to create applications for today's computing environment. This environment is more complex than ever before. Gone are the days when you needed to worry about only a single user running on a single PC. Now you have to be able to integrate your applications with other programs. You also have to enable your programs to communicate with other programs and users across networks and around the world.

To help you get started in this larger world of communication between applications and users, this book provides several chapters on writing applications that access the Internet or that provide messaging capabilities across a network.

And, as always, there is the old challenge of getting the most out of your application. To help you meet this challenge is a chapter on optimization techniques for getting the most out of your program.

What's Really Special About This Book

If you're like me, you will probably purchase and read several books about Visual Basic to help you learn about various capabilities of the program. So, what's so special about this book? First, it doesn't try to cover everything about Visual Basic. Instead, it targets specific areas that we feel the advanced programmer will want to know more about.

Second, this book was written by a team of authors who worked with Visual Basic for over a year during the beta cycle. These authors have already over-come many of the obstacles that you will face in your transition to Visual Basic 4. Also, most of these authors are the same ones who have been writing the articles that you have enjoyed in the *Visual Basic Programmer's Journal*. What this implies for you is that many of the concepts presented in this book will be further discussed in future issues of VBPJ by the same people who wrote the chapters. It also means that you will be able to find follow-up sup-port through the VBPJ forum on CompuServe (**GO VBPJ**) and through VBPJ's new World Wide Web site (**http://www.windx.com**).

Special Elements

If you are familiar with other Que books, you'll probably notice that some of the elements you have come to expect are not included in this book. This was done so that the voice and style of the magazine authors would still be present in their sections. This book contains the following special elements designed to make it easier to read and to help you find information more quickly:

Tips: Tips are tricks or techniques that help you do your work faster or more efficiently. This is information that is often left out of the user documenta-tion that comes with Visual Basic.

Cautions and Warnings: Cautions tell you of things that could easily cause errors. Warnings let you know about things that have dire consequences such as destroying your data.

Code continuation character (➡): Because some code lines are too long to fit on one line, they wrap to the next line. Code lines that wrap to the next line are indicated by a code continuation arrow.

Code listings: Most of the chapters in this book also include detailed code listings for the subjects being discussed. These listings provide you a basis for creating you own applications in Visual Basic. The listings are also included on the companion CD as well as in the text.

CD-ROM: Includes Limited Edition of Fawcette Technical Publications' VB-CD Quarterly with almost 200M of articles, demos shareware, and example code from the chapters so you don't have to type in long code listings.

Chapter 1

Object-Oriented Programming in Visual Basic 4

by Jonathan Wood

Jonathan Wood lives in Southern California where he writes commercial and custom software in Visual Basic, Visual C++, and assembly language for his own company, SoftCircuits. He writes the Programming Techniques column and an occasional article for the Visual Basic Programmer's Journal. *He's also section leader for the 16-bit API/DLL section in the VBPJ forum and a Microsoft MVP in the MSBASIC forum on CompuServe. He can be reached in either of these forums at 72134,263.*

Since its first release, Visual Basic has been object-based. That is, you create Visual Basic applications by using pre-built objects such as forms, controls, and various system objects (App, Clipboard, Printer, etc.). To use a text box object in your program, for example, you drop a text box control onto a form and then invoke the text box's methods and modify its properties to customize its behavior and appearance.

This makes program development much faster and easier because you use existing objects instead of writing everything yourself. In the case of Visual Basic, this has also meant the availability of a large number of third-party custom controls that can be purchased off-the-shelf and used as objects in your programs.

The computer industry does not consider object-based languages to necessarily be true object-oriented programming languages, however. Object-oriented programming (OOP) refers to more than simply using existing objects during development. OOP refers to a number of design principles and a whole approach to development whereby code is designed as a number of objects.

While Visual Basic does not yet meet all the requirements, Version 4 continues the evolution toward becoming an object-oriented language by allowing you to create your own objects. This ability allows you to gain some of the advantages associated with OOP and can have a significant effect on how you might approach application development.

In this chapter, you will learn about the following:

- What exactly an object is

- New Visual Basic class modules and how they can be used to create your own objects

- How to use Visual Basic's new Collections and how to create your own collection classes

- What serializing is and how to apply it to objects that you create

- New enhancements to form modules and how forms now can behave more like classes

- Object-oriented programming concepts and principles

- How using object-oriented programming can result in real-world benefits for you

What Is an Object?

An *object* is a unit of code and data. It represents a group of related subroutines and variables that can be accessed and manipulated as a single unit. The subroutines for an object define tasks that the object can perform and are called *methods*. The variables for an object are normally used to set and return object attributes. These variables are called *properties*.

If you've worked with Visual Basic, you probably already have a good feel for what an object is. All controls that appear in your application, such as buttons and text boxes, are objects that you work with. For example, to add a new item to a list box control, you invoke the AddItem method for a list box object:

```
List1.AddItem NewItem    'Adds NewItem to the list
```

Similarly, if you want to get the number of items in a list box control, you can read the ListCount property of the list box.

```
nCount = List1.ListCount    'Gets the number of items in the list
```

List boxes are objects that are defined by Visual Basic. They provide functionality that you don't need to write yourself. Visual Basic defines a number of other objects as well. These objects include other controls such as check boxes and radio (option) buttons, and system objects such as the Screen and Err objects.

There is an important distinction to be made here between objects and classes. A class defines an object type. Classes are never used directly within a program. Rather, you must first create one or more instances of a class. Those instances are then the objects that your program will use and manipulate. For example, I've already mentioned list boxes. Visual Basic already defines a list box class. This class determines the characteristics of list box controls. When you place a list box control onto a form, you then have a list box object to use which is an instance of the list box class.

It may help to think of a class as a mold and objects as what are formed by the mold. A mold is not useful in itself except for the sole purpose of forming other objects. Likewise, you do not use classes directly in a program except to declare objects. The objects are what your program will use and manipulate.

In addition to the many predefined objects that you can use in your applications, Visual Basic 4 allows you to write your own objects from scratch. In order to create your own objects, you must first define a new class. This is exactly what Visual Basic's new class modules are used for.

Working with Class Modules

The primary tool for creating your own objects in Visual Basic is the new class module. I suspect that one of the main reasons Microsoft added class modules to Visual Basic was to support the creation of OLE Automation servers. But it certainly wasn't the only reason. Class modules can be used as a powerful tool in regular application design. Class modules allow you to structure and organize program source code in new ways. In addition, because classes tend to keep related code and data together, their functionality can generally be ported to other applications much more easily than traditional source code.

Note that Visual Basic 4 does not allow you to create objects that work like controls. Objects created with class modules have no visible interface and no events. Of course, you can use classes to contain logic associated with controls, but Visual Basic provides no mechanism for automatically linking controls and classes together. Class modules are ideal for data storage algorithms and are well suited for more general data storage and program logic routines.

At first glance, writing code in a class module seems a little like writing code in a standard BASIC module. You can enter any number of subroutines or functions and declare any number of variables. Class subroutines and variables can be declared as *Public* or *Private*. Public subroutines within a class become methods and public variables become properties. Once an object is created by declaring an instance of the class, you can access these methods and properties for that object the same way you access methods and properties for other Visual Basic controls and objects. Subroutines and variables declared within a class module as private can only be accessed by code within that same class module and are not available to other parts of your program.

To demonstrate, let's start with a very simple class for storing information about people. To create the new class, select Class Module from Visual Basic's Insert menu and then name the class CPerson. You can name a class just about whatever you want. Prefixing the name with C (for class) identifies CPerson as being a class name and helps avoid conflict with object names. Of course, you don't need to follow this convention but I'll use it in the examples I present here. You specify the name of a class by setting the Name property in the Properties window (see figure 1.1).

Fig. 1.1
You specify the name of a class by typing the name into the properties window for the class module.

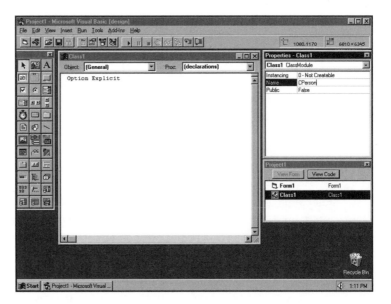

In the code window for the new class, declare class variables to store a name, phone number, and date of birth. Again, by declaring these variables as public, they will become class properties that can be accessed by code outside of the class module. Declare these variables as shown here:

```
Public m_sName As String
Public m_sPhone As String
Public m_DOB As Date
```

I've used another naming convention here. Prefixing variables with m_ (the m stands for member) identifies them immediately as class variables and also helps prevent conflicts with similarly named arguments passed to class methods. Again, it's not a convention that you must follow but is one I'll use in the examples presented here.

You may be thinking that it might just be easier if you always declare *all* class subroutines and variables as Public. That way, you will always be able to access all symbols from anywhere within your program. However, you can make more complex classes easier to use if you make only a few key methods and properties public and keep implementation details of the class private. Also, keep in mind that if you should later decide to improve your class design, private class members are guaranteed not to be used by code outside of the class and can be changed without affecting code that uses the class. As a general rule, fewer public members in a class will result in more of the benefits associated with object-oriented design. This is an important consideration that I'll return to later.

At this point, the declarations in the CPerson class look similar to declarations you might enter in a regular BASIC module. But in order to access these variables from outside the class, things start looking very different indeed. As already discussed, a program cannot work with a class directly. To create an object that you can use to store the information declared in a class, you need to create an instance of the class. This can be done by placing the following statement in a form, BASIC module, or even another class module.

```
Dim person As New CPerson
```

This statement declares a CPerson object named person. If you omitted the New clause, person could be used only after you first set it to reference an existing CPerson object. By including New, the statement actually allocates a new CPerson object. You can now access the properties of the person object the same way you access properties for other objects.

```
person.m_sName = "John Smith"
person.m_sPhone = "555-5555"
person.m_DOB = #10/29/61#
MsgBox person.m_sName
```

At this point, the CPerson class might be starting to look a little like a user-defined type (UDT). A class is similar to a UDT in that you must declare objects of that type before you can use them, and the syntax for accessing property values is identical to the syntax used for accessing members of a UDT. Indeed, you can often use classes instead of UDTs. In fact, Visual Basic has a number of instances where UDTs cannot be used. For example, a variant cannot hold a UDT, and UDTs cannot be passed as arguments to class methods. So you may find cases where it's necessary to use a class instead of a user-defined type.

Of course, classes can do more than user-defined types. UDT variables can only store data and cannot contain subroutines. Classes can contain both data and procedures that operate on that data. To illustrate this, let's add a method to the CPerson class. To add a method to a class, define a public subroutine or function in the class module. Listing 1.1 shows the completed listing for the CPerson class. It includes a method called ShowInfo that displays a message box that lists the current values of class properties.

Listing 1.1 1LIST01.TXT—PERSON.CLS The CPerson example demonstrates a simple class with methods and properties. In addition, the Age property shows how to create read-only properties by using Visual Basic's Property procedures.

```
Option Explicit

'Public properties
Public m_sName As String
Public m_sPhone As String
Public m_DOB As Date

'Read-only property returns approx. age
Property Get Age()
    Age = Year(Date) - Year(m_DOB)
End Property

'Displays information for this instance
Public Sub ShowInfo()
    Dim buff As String

    buff = "Name: " & m_sName & vbCrLf
    buff = buff & "Phone Number: " & m_sPhone & vbCrLf
    buff = buff & "Date of Birth: " & CStr(m_DOB) & vbCrLf
    buff = buff & "Current Age: " & CStr(Age)
    MsgBox buff
End Sub
```

The CPerson class also includes a read-only Age property. This is possible by using Visual Basic's Property Get procedures. You could implement an Age property by just defining another public variable in the class, but this brings up some interesting problems. For one thing, a person's age changes from year to year. Also, we need to make sure the Age property is always in sync with the date of birth property. A Property Get procedure allows code to be associated with property access. The code for the Age property calculates the person's age by using the current date and the date of birth. This also saves memory because the class does not store the age. The age is computed when it's needed.

Visual Basic also provides Property Let procedures, which are used to set property values (and Property Set procedures used for setting the value of properties that are objects). Since the CPerson class does not have a Property Let procedure for the Age property, the Age property is read-only. Attempting to set the Age property results in an error.

In spite of the fact that the Age property is not a true variable, the syntax for accessing the Age property from outside the class is identical to the syntax for accessing other properties. Indeed, code that uses a CPerson object never needs to know how an object implements properties internally.

Designing an object's interface so that it does not reveal the internal implementation of that object is referred to as *abstraction*. Abstraction allows you to create a simple interface to more complex data and is an important technique that can be used when working with objects.

Listing 1.2 shows the code for the Person form. It contains code to test the CPerson object. The form has a button called cmdPushMe. When the button is clicked, an object of type CPerson is created and initialized. The CPerson's ShowInfo method is then invoked to display the object's information.

Listing 1.2 1LIST02.TXT—PERSON.FRM This simple form demonstrates use of the CPerson class

```
    Option Explicit

    Private Sub cmdPushMe_Click()
        Dim person As New CPerson
        Dim nAge As Integer

        'Set public properties
        person.m_sName = "John Smith"
        person.m_sPhone = "555-5555"
        person.m_DOB = #10/29/61#

        'Prove we can access read-only Age property
        nAge = person.Age

        'Have person object display its info
        person.ShowInfo
    End Sub
```

As indicated previously, declaring variables in a class module does not allocate any data. Not until an instance of the class is created is any data allocated. Since objects do contain their own data, one of the advantages of working with them is that, once you have a class written, you can easily create many instances of that class. If several instances of a class are created, each one will have its own set of properties. When code within a class module accesses a class-level variable, it is accessing the variables associated with the particular instance of the object for which the method was invoked. This is a significant advantage over code that is not in a class. If you wrote similar code and declared similar variables in a BASIC module, it may work in a similar fashion. But if you then decided you wanted to track more than one set of data, it would require a major rewrite of the code.

One last issue that I'll just touch upon briefly: although classes do not support events, classes do have two special pseudo events called Initialize, which is called when an instance of the object is created, and Terminate, which is called when an object is destroyed. You may, for example, want to use the Initialize event to initialize class data before an object is used.

Using and Building Collections

Since you can create many instances of a class so easily, you'll probably find yourself writing code to manage groups of objects. So why not write another class to manage those objects? Such a class is called a *collection*.

Visual Basic supplies a number of predefined collections including the Forms and Controls collections. Starting with version 4, Visual Basic also includes a generic collection class that you can use to store your own variables and objects. Collections are a little bit like an array. You can easily write code to iterate through each item in the collection. However, collections differ from arrays in that you can easily insert and delete items.

One thing cool about collections is that, since they store variant data types, they can store data of almost any type including other objects. In fact, you can even have collections store other collections allowing you to create complex data structures. For example, you could write an appointment program, using collections. A master Collection object could contain other collections for each day that has appointments. Each of those collections could contain a list of appointments for that particular day. This would provide a great deal of flexibility and allow you to quickly access a particular appointment.

You declare a `Collection` object the same way you declare any other object.

```
Dim MyCollection As New Collection
```

Items are added and removed from `Collection` objects by using the `Add` and `Remove` methods. Optionally, you can specify a key for the object being added to uniquely identify that object. You can later use the key to quickly locate that item later. If you attempt to add two objects with the same key, Visual Basic generates an error.

```
Dim i As Integer, key As String
key = "MyKey"
coll.Add i, key
coll.Remove key
```

You'll probably want to experiment with `Collection` objects; you'll find them very useful and much more powerful than arrays in cases where items must be inserted and deleted. Of course, this doesn't mean that there's no reason to write your own collections. The `Collection` class works one way. If you need a collection that works another way, you'll need to write it yourself. Class modules can be used to write some very powerful collection classes.

Listing 1.3 shows the `CSparseMatrix` class. A sparse matrix represents a two-dimensional spreadsheet that takes advantage of the fact that many elements within the matrix may be left empty. For example, imagine a 500 by 500 spreadsheet. To represent this spreadsheet by using a two-dimensional array, you would need to allocate 250,000 elements. This could easily take over a million bytes depending on the type of data stored. If only, say, 100 items were added to the spreadsheet, that would be a significant waste of memory.

The `CSparseMatrix` class contains a standard `Collection` object called `m_RowCollection`, which is used to store information for matrix rows. This collection stores other collections, which contain column information for each row that contains data. When an item is added to the matrix, the class first locates the column collection for the specified row, or creates a new column collection if the row doesn't yet exist. Then, the class adds the new item to that column collection.

Once again, this class takes advantage of `Property Get` and `Let` procedures to make the syntax for accessing elements from outside the class exactly the same as for accessing elements in a two-dimensional array. The internal implementation, which saves so much memory by only allocating data for elements actually used, is available by using the same simple syntax you'd use to access a two-dimensional array. Very nice!

Listing 1.3 1LIST03.TXT—SPRSMTRX.CLS The `CSparseMatrix` **class is a collection class. It is also a good demonstration of how a class can use data abstraction to provide a simple interface to more complex data.**

```
Option Explicit

'Private collection to store collections for each row
Private m_RowCollection As New Collection

'Returns the cell value for the given row and column
Public Property Get Cell(nRow As Integer, nCol As Integer)
    Dim ColCollection As Collection
    Dim value As Variant

    On Error Resume Next
    Set ColCollection = m_RowCollection(CStr(nRow))
    'Return empty value if row doesn't exist
    If Err Then Exit Property
    value = ColCollection(CStr(nCol))
    'Return empty value is column doesn't exist
    If Err Then Exit Property
    'Else return cell value
    Cell = value
End Property

'Sets the cell value for the given row and column
Public Property Let Cell(nRow As Integer, nCol As Integer, value As
➥Variant)
    Dim ColCollection As Collection

    On Error Resume Next
    Set ColCollection = m_RowCollection(CStr(nRow))
    'Add row if it doesn't exist
    If Err Then
        Set ColCollection = New Collection
        m_RowCollection.Add ColCollection, CStr(nRow)
    End If
    'Remove cell if it already exists (errors ignored)
    ColCollection.Remove CStr(nCol)
    'Add new value
    ColCollection.Add value, CStr(nCol)
End Property
```

The `CSparseMatrix` class is an excellent example of how data abstraction can be used to create a simple interface to the underlying data structures that can be much more complex. Once you've got the class tested and working, you'll be able to use it again and again and can simply forget about how it was implemented. This also makes it a lot easier to document the class if you plan on writing classes that other people will use because only the simpler, public interface, needs to be explained.

To enforce this abstraction, the class's implementation is kept internal to the class by declaring variables as private. The only public members are the `Property Let` and `Property Get` procedures. Since these property procedures both have the same name, `Cell`, they create the effect of a single public property with this name that can be both written to and read. Property procedures may have arguments. Here, the arguments are the row and column position of the cell you are accessing. This is what makes the syntax exactly the same as accessing items in a two-dimensional array.

Since the internal implementation is kept private, it is easier to make changes within the class. For example, say you decided to change the class to store the information on disk instead of in memory. Only the code within the class module would need to be changed. As long as you maintained the same public interface, code that used the class would not be affected.

Listing 1.4 demonstrates using the `CSparseMatrix` class. The code declares a `CSparseMatrix` object and fills it with a few values and then implements a simple spreadsheet program to browse the matrix.

Listing 1.4   1LIST04.TXT SPRSMTRX.FRM   This form allows you to browse data in a `CSparseMatrix` object. Because of the design of `CSparseMatrix`, this form provides some significant functionality with surprisingly little code.

```
Option Explicit

Private Const CELL_WIDTH = 1000
Private Const CELL_HEIGHT = 255
Private m_Top As Integer, m_Left As Integer
Private Matrix As New CSparseMatrix

'Initialize form
Private Sub Form_Load()
    Dim i As Integer

    'Setup scrollbars for 500x500 grid
    vscScroll.Min = 1
    vscScroll.Max = 500
    vscScroll.LargeChange = (Picture1.ScaleHeight / CELL_HEIGHT)
    hscScroll.Min = 1
    hscScroll.Max = 500
    hscScroll.LargeChange = (Picture1.ScaleWidth / CELL_WIDTH)

    'Enter some values into the spreadsheet
    For i = 1 To 500
        Matrix.Cell(i, i) = CStr(i) & "," & CStr(i)
    Next i
End Sub

'Horizontal scroll
```

(continues)

Listing 1.4 Continued

```
Private Sub hscScroll_Change()
    m_Left = hscScroll
    Picture1.Refresh
End Sub

'Vertical scroll
Private Sub vscScroll_Change()
    m_Top = vscScroll
    Picture1.Refresh
End Sub

'Paint spreadsheet
Private Sub Picture1_Paint()
    Dim x As Integer, y As Integer
    Dim v As Variant

    'Clear existing data
    Picture1.Cls
    'Paint grid lines
    For y = CELL_HEIGHT To Picture1.ScaleHeight Step CELL_HEIGHT
        Picture1.Line (0, y)-(Picture1.ScaleWidth, y), RGB(128,
        ➥128, 128)
    Next y
    For x = CELL_WIDTH To Picture1.ScaleWidth Step CELL_WIDTH
        Picture1.Line (x, 0)-(x, Picture1.ScaleHeight), RGB(128,
        ➥128, 128)
    Next x
    'Show grid data for cells that contain data
    For x = 0 To Picture1.ScaleWidth / CELL_WIDTH
        For y = 0 To Picture1.ScaleHeight / CELL_HEIGHT
            v = Matrix.Cell(m_Top + y, m_Left + x)
            If Not IsEmpty(v) Then
                Picture1.CurrentX = (x * CELL_WIDTH) + 50
                Picture1.CurrentY = (y * CELL_HEIGHT) + 25
                Picture1.Print CStr(v)
            End If
        Next y
    Next x
    'Indicate current scroll positions
    lblTopLeft = "Top: " & CStr(m_Top) & ", Left: " & CStr(m_Left)
End Sub
```

The spreadsheet implemented here isn't much as far as spreadsheets go. It doesn't even allow a user to enter data. But it does present some substantial functionality with a very small amount of easy-to-understand code. Code like this could form the foundation for some pretty significant programs. Figure 1.2 shows the output from the finished program.

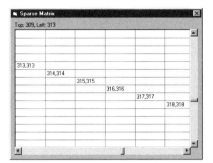

Fig. 1.2
The SPRSMTRX
form demon-
strates use of the
CSparseMatrix
class. The form
creates a simple
spreadsheet that
can be used to
browse the
contents of
the matrix.

Serializing Objects

Serializing is a fancy word that refers to saving objects to disk and reading them back into memory. If you've worked with user-defined types before, you might expect an object to be written to disk like this:

```
Dim person As New CPerson

Open "C:\TEST.DAT" For Binary As #1
Put #1, , person    ' <-- Error - Not allowed!
Close #1
```

But this doesn't work. You can't use Put or Get on an object reference. Each property of an object that needs to be saved to disk must be stored manually. Of course, methods do not need to be saved since they simply become part of your program and there is only one copy of them regardless of how many objects you declare. What makes each object unique is its own copy of class data. The data is what you should save to disk if you want to make the data in your objects permanent.

Keeping with the philosophy of object-oriented programming, an object should know how to save and load itself. In other words, the code to write a particular object to disk should be implemented as a method of that object. If you tried to save the individual properties of an object to disk by using code that was not part of that class module, you wouldn't be able to save private variables. In addition, the code that invokes the serializing methods shouldn't need to know how the class is implemented in order to use it. The goal here is: if you later decide to change the implementation of a class, all required changes to the code should be limited to code within the class module. This way, it is much easier to find all the code affected by the changes.

To demonstrate serializing methods in a class, Listing 1.5 shows the CBitArray class. This class is another collection. This one stores only Boolean values (values that can only be either true or false). It takes advantage of the fact that only one bit is needed to indicate a true or false value. Since there are 16 bits within a single integer, the class creates an array of integers and stores 16 values per integer. Like the CSparseMatrix class, this too results in a significant savings in memory. If, for example, you wanted to store 100,000 Boolean values, a Boolean array would require about 200,000 bytes. The CBitArray class would use only about 6,250 bytes and, although a little work is required to pack 16 values into each integer, Property procedures are used once again to provide abstraction over this complexity. Again, this class makes these memory savings available with no additional work from the code that uses it.

The CBitArray class contains methods called FileRead and FileWrite. These methods take, as an argument, a file number for a file opened for binary mode access. These methods read or write the bit array to the specified file. Of course, you could implement your own classes so that they write to files in text mode instead. The only requirement here is that the read and write methods use a technique compatible with the mode with which the file was opened.

> **Listing 1.5 1LIST05.TXT—BITARRAY.CLS This class demonstrates serialization through the FileRead and FileWrite methods. Because the CBitArray class uses data abstraction to hide the complexity of its implementation, it is only reasonable that code using this class should be able to save it to disk without needing to know how the class works. Using the FileRead and FileWrite methods, the class can, in effect, be told to load and save itself.**

```
Option Explicit

'Private dynamic array to hold data
Private BitArray() As Integer

'Resizes the bit array to hold the number of
'bits specified by nCount
Public Sub RedimArray(nCount As Long)
    ReDim Preserve BitArray(0 To nCount \ 16)
End Sub

'Gets the value of the bit specified by nIndex
Property Get Value(nIndex As Long) As Boolean
    Dim nBit As Long

    nBit = 2 ^ (nIndex Mod 16)
    If nBit = &H8000& Then  'Prevent overflow on high bit
        Value = BitArray(nIndex \ 16) And &H8000
    Else
        Value = BitArray(nIndex \ 16) And nBit
    End If
End Property

'Sets the value of the bit specified by nIndex
Property Let Value(nIndex As Long, bValue As Boolean)
    Dim nBit As Long
```

```
        nBit = 2 ^ (nIndex Mod 16)
        If bValue Then
            If nBit = &H8000& Then   'Prevent overflow on high bit
                BitArray(nIndex \ 16) = (BitArray(nIndex \ 16) Or &H8000)
            Else
                BitArray(nIndex \ 16) = (BitArray(nIndex \ 16) Or nBit)
            End If
        Else
            If nBit = &H8000& Then   'Prevent overflow on high bit
                BitArray(nIndex \ 16) = (BitArray(nIndex \ 16) And Not &H8000)
            Else
                BitArray(nIndex \ 16) = (BitArray(nIndex \ 16) And Not nBit)
            End If
        End If
End Property

'Reads the data from the specified file number
'The file should be open in binary mode
Public Sub FileRead(nFileNum As Integer)
    Dim i As Long

    'Get array size and redimension array
    Get #nFileNum, , i
    ReDim BitArray(0 To i)

    'Read actual data
    For i = 0 To UBound(BitArray)
        Get #nFileNum, , BitArray(i)
    Next i
End Sub

'Writes the data to the specified file number
'The file should be open in binary mode
Public Sub FileWrite(nFileNum As Integer)
    Dim i As Long

    'Save array size
    i = UBound(BitArray)
    Put #nFileNum, , i

    'Save actual data
    For i = 0 To UBound(BitArray)
        Put #nFileNum, , BitArray(i)
    Next i
End Sub
```

The FileRead and FileWrite methods provide an easy way to save instances of
the CBitArray class to disk and read them back. They also keep with the basic
philosophy of object-oriented programming by including methods for performing tasks associated with the particular class. In effect, allowing objects
of this class to save and load themselves to and from disk.

The following code demonstrates the syntax to allocate a CBitArray object and initialize it to hold 100,000 Boolean values. It then sets values 5 and 10,000 to true and writes the bit array to disk by invoking the FileWrite method.

```
Dim Bits As New CBitArray
Bits.RedimArray 100000
Bits.Value(5) = True
Bits.Value(10000) = True
Open "C:\TEST.DAT" For Binary As #1
Bits.FileWrite 1
Close #1
```

Using Forms as Classes

A repeating theme in this chapter has been how you can use Visual Basic class modules to change the way you approach application design. But the enhancements to Visual Basic 4 don't stop with class modules. Form modules have been enhanced to behave more like classes. Visual Basic now allows you to declare form-based subroutines and variables as Private or Public, allowing you to create custom form methods and properties that can be accessed from code outside the form.

This is an important enhancement. Say, for example, you wanted a custom dialog box to retrieve a string from the user. In previous versions of Visual Basic, you had to resort to global variables in order to pass the information entered by the user back to the routine that needed it. Global variables can make programs difficult to maintain because you need to keep track of every place they are used and make sure one piece of code doesn't modify a global variable before another piece of code is done using it. Global variables also require that the functionality you implement must be distributed across several files which makes it harder to port that functionality to projects you may develop in the future.

The enhancements to Visual Basic forms allow you to create form modules that are more self-contained. In fact, one approach might be to simply make forms with only one or two public methods. Code that uses the form needs to interface with only those public methods. Everything else that must be kept track of for the form to operate, including actually loading and unloading the form, can be handled by code and variables within the form module. A form written this way can be copied to other projects very easily since everything is in a single file, and interfacing with the form only requires invoking one or two methods.

Listing 1.6 shows a partial listing for a form that displays a mini-calendar and allows the user to select a date. (The full source listings are on the CD-ROM that comes with this book.) Although the code in this form module is reasonably complex, a Visual Basic project can incorporate its functionality simply by invoking the public GetDate method.

The GetDate method provides the complete interface to the calendar form. Note that calling this method does not automatically cause the form to be loaded. Rather, after some initialization, the GetDate method explicitly loads the form and then determines the result via private variables and then returns the appropriate values to the caller. Since all other subroutines and variables are private, we programmatically enforce that they are not accessed outside the form. If you decide to redesign the calendar form in the future, this means you can safely make assumptions that changes to private procedures and variables will not affect code outside of the form module.

> **Listing 1.6   1LIST06.TXT—CALENDAR.FRM (Partial Listing)**
> **The Calendar form demonstrates how forms now operate more like classes. This form contains only one public member, the method. To use this form in a project, all you need to do is include CALENDAR.FRM in your project file and call GetDate. All the other details, including actually loading the form, are handled by code within the form module.**

```
Option Explicit

'Grid dimensions for days
Private Const GRID_ROWS = 6
Private Const GRID_COLS = 7

'Private variables
Private m_CurrDate As Date, m_bAcceptChange As Boolean
Private m_nGridWidth As Integer, m_nGridHeight As Integer

'Public function: If user selects date, sets UserDate to selected
'date and returns True. Otherwise, returns False.
Public Function GetDate(UserDate As Date, Optional Title) As
Boolean

    'Store user-specified date
    m_CurrDate = UserDate

    'Use caller-specified caption if any
    If Not IsMissing(Title) Then
        Caption = Title
    End If

    'Display this form
    Me.Show vbModal

    'Return selected date
```

(continues)

Listing 1.6 Continued

```
        If m_bAcceptChange Then
            UserDate = m_CurrDate
        End If

        'Return value indicates if date was selected
        GetDate = m_bAcceptChange
End Function

'Form initialization
Private Sub Form_Load()
    'Center form on screen
    Move (Screen.Width - Width) / 2, (Screen.Height - Height) / 2

    'Calculate calendar grid measurements
    m_nGridWidth = ((picMonth.ScaleWidth - _
        Screen.TwipsPerPixelX) \ GRID_COLS)
    m_nGridHeight = ((picMonth.ScaleHeight - _
        Screen.TwipsPerPixelY) \ GRID_ROWS)

    m_bAcceptChange = False
End Sub

'Process user keystrokes
Private Sub picMonth_KeyDown(KeyCode As Integer, Shift As Integer)
    Dim NewDate As Date

    Select Case KeyCode
        Case vbKeyRight
            NewDate = DateAdd("d", 1, m_CurrDate)
        Case vbKeyLeft
            NewDate = DateAdd("d", -1, m_CurrDate)
        Case vbKeyDown
            NewDate = DateAdd("ww", 1, m_CurrDate)
        Case vbKeyUp
            NewDate = DateAdd("ww", -1, m_CurrDate)
        Case vbKeyPageDown
            NewDate = DateAdd("m", 1, m_CurrDate)
        Case vbKeyPageUp
            NewDate = DateAdd("m", -1, m_CurrDate)
        Case vbKeyReturn
            m_bAcceptChange = True
            Unload Me
            Exit Sub
        Case vbKeyEscape
            Unload Me
            Exit Sub
        Case Else
            Exit Sub
    End Select
    SetNewDate NewDate
    KeyCode = 0
End Sub

'Double-click accepts current date
Private Sub picMonth_DblClick()
```

```
        m_bAcceptChange = True
        Unload Me
    End Sub

    ' Select the date by mouse
    Private Sub picMonth_MouseDown(Button As Integer, Shift As Integer,
    _
        x As Single, y As Single)
        Dim i As Integer, MaxDay As Integer

        'Determine which date is being clicked
        i = WeekDay(DateSerial(Year(m_CurrDate), Month(m_CurrDate), 1))
    - 1
        i = (((x \ m_nGridWidth) + 1) + ((y \ m_nGridHeight) *
    GRID_COLS)) - i

        'Get last day of current month
        MaxDay = Day(DateAdd("d", -1, DateSerial(Year(m_CurrDate), _
            Month(m_CurrDate) + 1, 1)))

        If i >= 1 And i <= MaxDay Then
            SetNewDate DateSerial(Year(m_CurrDate), Month(m_CurrDate),
    i)
        End If
    End Sub

    'Continues...
```

The GetDate method takes two arguments. The default date that the form will initially display, and an optional title string that specifies the form's caption. Optional arguments are ones that can be omitted by the calling code. The GetDate method uses the IsMissing function to determine whether a title was specified and assigns it to the form's caption property if it was.

After initialization, the GetDate method loads the form modally with the statement:

```
Me.Show vbModal
```

Since the form is loaded modally, the statement that follows this one is not executed until the form is unloaded. The calendar form unloads if the user double-clicks a date, presses Return or presses Escape. Only if the user double-clicks a date or presses return is the private form variable bAcceptChange set to True. After the form is unloaded, GetDate checks the value of bAcceptChange to determine which value to return to the caller.

Listing 1.7 shows another form that tests the calendar form. Figure 1.3 shows the calendar form in action.

Listing 1.7   1LIST07.TXT—CALTEST.FRM   This form demonstrates using the Calendar form. As shown in the `cmdCalendar_Click` event, the Calendar form can be used with only a single call to `frmCalendar.GetDate`.

```
Option Explicit

'Let user select date from frmCalendar
Private Sub cmdCalendar_Click()
    Dim UserDate As Date

    UserDate = CVDate(txtDate)
    If frmCalendar.GetDate(UserDate) Then
        txtDate = UserDate
    End If
End Sub

'Exit program
Private Sub cmdExit_Click()
    Unload Me
End Sub

'Initialize date on load
Private Sub Form_Load()
    'Default to today's date
    txtDate = Date
End Sub
```

Fig. 1.3
The Calendar form in action. Users can browse the months, and select a date by double-clicking with the mouse.

One last change to form modules that make them more like class modules: forms now have `Initialize` and `Terminate` events, which behave like the same-named events in class modules. Although form modules already have `Load` and `Unload` events, these events do not correspond to the `Initialize` and `Terminate` events. A form's `Initialize` event is called the first time any method or property on the form is accessed. The `Load` event does not occur until the form is actually loaded. The difference is significant because form methods and custom form properties can be accessed without causing the form to be loaded.

Understanding Object-Oriented Programming Concepts

So far, I've presented a number of techniques for using Visual Basic to create your own objects and provided a number of examples to demonstrate these techniques. With this basic understanding under your belt, I'd like to use this section to explore the more conceptual aspects of object-oriented programming.

A number of languages today are considered to be object-oriented. They include C++ (probably the most widely used), Pascal with objects, Smalltalk, and others. The industry has defined several fundamental principles that qualify a language as being object-oriented. These principles include *encapsulation*, *inheritance*, and *polymorphism*. While not all of these principles are fully supported by Visual Basic, it is useful to understand all of them, both for the purpose of fully understanding object-oriented concepts and also for possible insights to features we may see in future versions of Visual Basic.

Encapsulation. Encapsulation simply means to group together. Rather than having a number of logically related subroutines and variables treated as unrelated pieces of code, encapsulation allows you to group them together into a class. Other parts of a program can then treat these subroutines and variables as a single object.

Through encapsulation, much of an object's complexity can be kept internal to that object. Only a few select methods and properties that make up the object's interface need to be available to other parts of a program. Because encapsulation can limit the complexity of the object's public interface, encapsulation lends itself to abstraction. Abstraction is useful because it can be used to provide a simple interface to a more complex implementation and also allows the implementation to change without affecting code that uses the object.

Visual Basic has always provided encapsulation for controls and system objects. Through class modules and new enhancements to form modules, Visual Basic now supports encapsulation in code that you write as well.

Inheritance. Inheritance allows you to base one class on another. For example, say you had a `CAnimal` class that represented animals. It has properties such as `Name`, `Color`, and `Size`, and methods such as `Breathe`, `Walk`, etc. Then suppose the same program needed a `CBird` class to represent birds. Well, since a bird is a type of animal, everything in the `CAnimal` class would be useful in representing a bird. However, a bird is a particular type of animal. It might need new methods such as `Fly` or `Sing`.

One approach would be to create two separate classes, CAnimal and CBird. However, this would make your program larger because you would duplicate a lot of code since everything in the CAnimal class would also be in the CBird class. Inheritance would allow you to create a new class called CBird, and base that class on the CAnimal class. By basing one class on another, the new, or derived, class automatically assumes all the functionality of the base class, and without duplicating any of the code. Any code you added to the new CBird class would then be functionality on top of what is already provided by the CAnimal class.

This example may seem a little silly. I've tried to pick an example that would be easy to describe. Consider that these issues would become much more important for highly sophisticated classes that contained a lot of code.

Visual Basic does not support inheritance. To use the preceding example, you wouldn't be able to inherit the CBird class from the CAnimal class. There are basically three ways you could work around this. You could simply create two separate classes. As already pointed out, this can make your program larger because some of the code would appear in both classes. Still, this would probably be a reasonable approach if the two classes were significantly different. Another option would be to enhance the CAnimal class so that the CBird class would not be necessary. That is, add code to the CAnimal class so that it supported the functionality needed for birds. Unfortunately, this means that *all* CAnimal objects would also have the functionality for the bird class as well. However, this may be a reasonable approach if the two classes were substantially similar.

The third approach would be pseudo-inheritance through containment. Since objects can contain other objects, you could design the CBird class to contain an object of the CAnimal class. The CBird class would then contain all the functionality of the CAnimal class without needing to duplicate any of the code. This is one possible solution but is less than perfect. There are times when containment makes sense. For example, you might expect a CClassRoom class to contain a CTeacher object because it would be reasonable for a classroom to contain a teacher. However, the relationship between CAnimal and CBird is different. One does not contain the other. Rather, a CBird is a type of CAnimal. This subtle difference can make code that would be very simple to write and understand, slightly less so.

Polymorphism. Polymorphism describes the effect of being able to invoke an object's method without knowing the object's exact type, and having the method perform the appropriate action for that particular object. For example, consider these code statements:

```
Dim Obj As Object
For Each Obj In DataCollection
    Obj.FileSave 1
Next Obj
```

This code invokes the `FileSave` method for each object in a collection called `DataCollection`. However, consider that Visual Basic allows collections to store objects of many different types. So what happens when we invoke a method for an object for which we don't know the type? As long as each object in the `DataCollection` collection has a `FileSave` method, there is no error. The `FileSave` method invoked is the one associated with each particular item. Presumably, that method would take the appropriate action for that particular type of object. For example, you may want a program to save its data upon termination. Although different data objects may need to be saved to disk in different ways, as long as each of the objects in the collection has a `FileSave` method, polymorphism allows generic code, such as shown above, to work for all types of objects.

Polymorphism is possible in Visual Basic because Visual Basic allows you to declare generic object types, which can contain references to different types of objects. When you invoke a method on such an object, Visual Basic does not try to resolve exactly which subroutine is being called until the line is actually executed. At that time, Visual Basic determines the object type and the exact code that needs to be called. Of course, if that object doesn't support the named method, a run-time error occurs. So be careful that only appropriate objects will turn up in this type of code.

Visual Basic has come a long way toward providing support for all these principles. It would appear that inheritance is the missing element according to industry standards. Perhaps we'll see true inheritance in the next version of Visual Basic. It would seem a natural next step in the product's evolution. Depending on how it was implemented, inheritance could also mean the ability to inherit from Visual Basic controls. This would allow us to add our own methods and properties to those controls, opening up the door to many new possibilities.

Those are the fundamental principles of object-oriented programming. I've certainly presented a number of buzzwords both in this section and in this chapter as a whole. I guess the next logical question might be, "Why should you really care?" In the next section, we'll explore the real-world benefits these principles provide.

Exploring the Benefits of OOP

I remember my response when I was first exposed to object-oriented programming. I said, "Well, that's nice but I could have done that just fine without objects!" This is a common response I see from others new to the idea of working with objects. After all, it seems that everyone is talking about object-oriented programming these days. With all the hoopla, you'd almost think it eliminates the need for programming altogether!

Certainly, object-oriented programming is not a magic bullet. It's simply an approach to development that you can use to make you a more effective programmer. My goal for this chapter is to go beyond simply explaining what object-oriented programming is; I also want to clearly show how you can benefit from it. This is why I've tried to present examples that you may find useful in your own programs, and why, as each new issue was presented, I tried to discuss how that particular issue may benefit you. In this section, I want to leave you with a summary of these benefits.

Code Reuse. Probably the biggest argument for using object-oriented techniques is to better be able to reuse code that you write. Because well-designed objects contain their own variables and support routines, and Visual Basic class modules are stored in a single file, complex objects can often be used in other applications by simply adding a single file to the project and a couple of lines to the code. This can be a big improvement over the cut-and-paste school of code reuse.

Simplified Data Access. Through data abstraction, it is possible to design objects that provide a reasonably simple interface to more complex data. The preceding CBitArray and CSparseMatrix classes are good examples of this. This also helps code reuse because the code required to use an object tends to be relatively simple.

Isolated Implementation. By keeping class implementation private and being able to enforce that selected variables and subroutines are not accessed outside the class, code implementation within class modules can be modified more easily than with traditional code. You can safely assume that changes to private members will not affect code outside of the class. As long as the public interface is maintained, code that uses an object will not be affected by changing that object's implementation.

Multiple Instances. Because well-designed objects contain their own variables and support routines, creating more instances of an object is usually as simple as just declaring more objects. If you've ever implemented code by using standard subroutines and then decided it would be nice to have the code support multiple items, you can probably see how much easier it would be using objects.

Code Organization. You probably already organize your code by using subroutines and modules. Objects allow you to also organize program code into logically related units. For large projects, this can simplify the development process since program code tends to be organized into more clearly defined units. Also, when program bugs turn up, it's usually easier to determine where the faulty code resides.

Smart Objects Means Simpler Code. Lastly, it is possible to write very simple and generic code for dealing with a collection of objects. Since the basic premise of object-oriented programming is that objects take care of themselves, through polymorphism and other techniques, code that uses objects can invoke common methods without knowing or caring about the type of object or how the object was implemented.

Of course, the specifics of how you design your own objects will affect how many of these benefits you will actually gain. Try to minimize the number of public members within classes that you design. Much of the benefits of object-oriented programming comes from keeping the internal workings of a class private. Of course, you must have some public members to make the functionality available to your program and you should never leave out functionality simply for the sake of reducing the number of public members. However, you should consider how that functionality can be made available with the fewest number of public members possible.

Finally, before you sit down to the keyboard to start coding your next project, carefully consider how you can use objects to model program components. The more accurately you can use objects to represent the things contained within your program, the easier your program will be to write and understand.

Summary

As I've already indicated, object-oriented programming will not solve all of your programming troubles. It's simply a useful tool that can actually have a significant effect on the way you design your applications. By developing code as a collection of distinct units, that code becomes more reusable, and easier to understand and maintain. In an age where software is becoming increasingly complex, it's becoming necessary to continue the trend of isolating program components. In addition to subroutines, modules, and custom controls, we can now add classes to help facilitate this trend.

Chapter 2

Introduction to the Win32 API

by Daniel Appleman

Daniel Appleman is the president of Desaware, a company specializing in add-on components such as SpyWorks, StorageTools, and VersionStamper. He is the author of PC Magazine's Visual Basic Programmer's Guide to the Windows API, How Computer Programming Works, *and the forthcoming* Visual Basic Programmer's Guide to the Win32 API *from Ziff-Davis Press. (Portions of this chapter are excerpted from the book,* The Visual Basic Programmer's Guide to the WIN32 API *by Daniel Appleman, published by* Ziff-Davis Press, *ISBN: 1-56276-287-7, which will be available in the first quarter of 1996)*

Visual Basic has become the most successful Windows software development platform ever for a number of reasons, not the least of which is its incredible extensibility. Perhaps the most important way that Visual Basic can be extended is its ability to provide direct access to the Windows API.

Those who are accustomed to using 16-bit Visual Basic may be somewhat disconcerted by the Visual Basic documentation that describes the conversion process to the 32-bit Visual Basic as a relatively simple matter of loading an existing project, obtaining 32-bit OLE controls to replace VBXs used by the program, and converting any API calls to Win32.

The challenge of replacing VBXs with OLE controls, especially if your VBXs are custom or not from one of the major component vendors, is an interesting subject, and one for a different time. The "simple" process of porting API calls from 16-bit Windows to 32-bit Windows is, unfortunately, not necessarily as simple as some of the Visual Basic documentation might suggest.

Replacing the function declarations are only the first step. Other issues include:

1. Do you want to share source code between 16-bit and 32-bit applications?

2. How do you deal with 16-bit API functions that do not exist under 32-bit Windows?

3. How do you deal with different implementations of the Windows API (say between Windows 95 and Windows NT?)

4. What new functionality is available under 32-bit Windows?

5. How do you handle the fundamental changes to the Windows architecture that occur under 32-bit Windows?

The 32-bit Windows API has many hundreds of new functions, and a number of sometimes subtle changes to take into account. It is not surprising, therefore, that the conversion process can become frustrating on occasion. In fact, it may be made even more frustrating by the attempts to reassure that it is "easy." Yes, some function conversions are well documented and are easy. Many others can be easy and straightforward—given a good understanding at what is really going on—but obtaining that understanding can be a challenge.

This chapter is intended to help you begin that process—whether you are experienced with 16-bit API programming or are completely new at accessing the API from Visual Basic.

Dynamic Link Libraries

An important first step toward using the Windows API is to understand exactly what an API is. In order to do this, you must first understand dynamic link libraries and the process of linking. Linking refers to the process by which external functions are incorporated into an application. There are two different types of linking: *static* and *dynamic*. Static linking takes place during creation of the program. Dynamic linking takes place when the program is running.

Static versus Dynamic Linking

Programming languages are typically extended in two ways. First, most languages provide access to the underlying operating system. In DOS, this is accomplished with interrupt 21 calls to DOS. Second, most languages allow you to create libraries of functions that can be merged into your program. These functions then appear to the programmer as if they were built into the language.

Program modules containing functions are precompiled into object (.OBJ) files. These object files are often grouped into library (.LIB) files by using a program called a librarian (such as LIB.EXE).

When it is time to create a final executable version of an application, a program known as a linker scans your application's object files for references to functions that are not defined. It then searches through any specified library files for the missing functions. The linker extracts any program modules containing the required functions and copies them into the new executable file, "linking" them to your program. This process is known as *static linking* because all of the information needed by your program to access the library functions is fixed when the executable file is created, and remains unchanged (static) when the program is running.

With dynamic linking, program modules containing functions are also precompiled into object (.OBJ) files. Instead of grouping them into library files, they are linked into a special form of Windows executable file known as a *dynamic link library* (DLL). When a DLL is created, the programmer specifies which of the functions included should be accessible from other running applications. This is known as *exporting* the function.

When you create a Windows executable file, the linker scans your program's object files and makes a list of those functions that are not present and the DLLs in which they can be found. The process of specifying where each function can be found is known as *importing* the function.

When your application runs, anytime it needs a function that is not in the executable file, Windows loads the dynamic link library so that all of its functions become accessible to your application. At that time, the address of each function is resolved and dynamically linked into your application—hence the term *dynamic* linking.

Dynamic link libraries typically have the extension .DLL, but this is not a requirement. Visual Basic custom controls and OLE controls are also DLLs (though they have some special features) and use the extension .VBX or .OCX. Windows device drivers are DLLs and typically have the extension .DRV. Some Windows system DLLs use the standard executable extension .EXE—especially in the 16-bit environments.

This latter point is most important—the Windows system itself is ultimately little more than a group of dynamic link libraries that contain functions that can be called from any Windows application, including any Visual Basic application.

Application Program Interface

API is one of those acronyms that seems to be used primarily to intimidate people. An API is simply a set of functions available to an application programmer. The DOS interrupt functions can technically be considered the DOS API. If you write database programs in dBASE, the dBASE functions you use can be considered the dBASE API.

The term is most often used to describe a set of functions that are part of one application but are being accessed by another application. When a Visual Basic program uses OLE Automation to execute an Excel spreadsheet function, you can say that it is accessing the Excel API.

So, the Windows API refers to the set of functions that are part of Windows and are accessible to any Windows application. It is difficult to overstate the significance of this concept. Consider the following example.

Bring up the Windows Program Manager (NT) or Windows Explorer (Windows 95) and invoke the About command from the Help menu. A properties sheet will come up showing information about the system, including the amount of physical memory that is free or available in your system.

Obviously, there is a method within Windows for determining these values. As it turns out, that function is called GlobalMemoryStatus and is exported by Windows (thus, it is part of the API and is available to any Windows application).

Try the following trivial Visual Basic program:

Listing 2.1   2LIST01.TXT—Trivial VB Program

' Create a new project
' In the global module place the following statements:

```
Type MEMORYSTATUS
    dwLength As Long       ' 32
    dwMemoryLoad As Long        ' percent of memory in use
    dwTotalPhys As Long       ' bytes of physical memory
    dwAvailPhys As Long       ' free physical memory bytes
    dwTotalPageFile As Long      ' bytes of paging file
    dwAvailPageFile As Long       ' free bytes of paging file
    dwTotalVirtual As Long       ' user bytes of address space
```

```
         dwAvailVirtual As Long        ' free user bytes
End Type
Declare Sub GlobalMemoryStatus Lib "kernel32" (lpmstMemStat As MEMORYSTATUS)
' In the form_Click event for form1 place the following lines:
Dim ms As MEMORYSTATUS
ms.dwLength = Len(ms)
GlobalMemoryStatus ms
Print "Total physical memory: "; ms.dwTotalPhys
Print "Available physical memory: "; ms.dwAvailPhys
```

Now run the program. When you click anywhere on the form, it will display the physical memory statistics for the system. Almost every aspect of the Windows environment and the API functions associated with it are accessible from Visual Basic.

The Different Flavors of Windows

Between 1991 and 1995, Visual Basic evolved from version 1.0 to 3.0, and Windows evolved from version 3.0 to 3.11. This period saw a dramatic improvement in features and performance in both Windows and Visual Basic, yet the Windows API itself remained fundamentally the same. True, the number of functions increased as Microsoft added new dynamic link libraries to Windows that extended the capability of the operating system. However, the core API remained constant, and you could write your Visual Basic programs to take advantage of the capability provided by the Windows API knowing that your program would run on any Windows system.

In 1995, with the appearance of Visual Basic 4.0, this situation changed. The root of this change lies in this simple, but crucial fact: The Windows API is NOT the same thing as Windows. Or to put it differently: an API is not an operating system. Up until Visual Basic 4.0, Windows programmers did not have to worry about this difference. Windows was essentially a single operating system—from the programmer's point of view the differences between Windows 3.0 and Windows 3.11 were minor. That single operating system had a single API.

Visual Basic 4.0 currently provides support for three different operating systems: Windows 3.x, Windows NT, and Windows 95, and is likely to support additional operating systems soon. As the underlying operating systems have evolved, the Windows API also has evolved. Instead of a single 16-bit API, there is now a 16-bit Windows API called the "Win16" API, and several variations of a 32-bit API as well.

These changes mean that it is no longer possible to write code for a single operating system and API. As long as you are writing pure Visual Basic code, VB hides most of the differences between environments from you. However, in order to preserve compatibility with older operating systems, it also prevents you from taking advantage of many of the new operating system and API features. Once you start accessing the Windows API, it becomes necessary to consider which operating system and API you intend your program to support. In some cases you may need to write functions that perform differently depending on the operating environment. Fortunately, Visual Basic 4.0 contains new features to make this possible.

The following table lists the versions of the Windows API that work with each of the major operating systems available today.

API	Description
Win16	The original Windows 16-bit API. This is the native API for Windows and Windows for Workgroups 3.x. It is also supported by Windows 95 and Windows NT in 16-bit mode. You can access this API from the 16-bit editions of Visual Basic and Visual Basic for Applications.
Win32	The full 32-bit API. This is the native API for Windows NT. You can access this API from any 32-bit edition of Visual Basic or Visual Basic for Applications.
Win32c Windows 95	This is a subset of Win32 that is supported by Windows 95 (the "c" stands for the original code name of Windows 95 which was "Chicago"). You can call any Win32 function under this API, but many of the functions are not implemented—especially those that relate to NT-specific features not built into Windows 95. There may be some operating system-specific API functions in Win32c that are not yet incorporated into the latest implementation of Win32 on Windows NT.
Win32s	This is a smaller subset of Win32 that is supported under Windows and Windows for Workgroups 3.x. It is not supported by Visual Basic 4.0.

The Major Windows DLLs

The core functionality of the Win32 API is divided into three major dynamic link libraries and a number of smaller DLLs as shown in the following table.

DLL Name	Description
KERNEL32.DLL	Low-level operating functions. Memory management, task management, resource handling, and related operations are found here.
USER32.DLL	Functions relating to Windows management. Messages, menus, cursors, carets, timers, communications, and most other non-display functions can be found here.
GDI32.DLL	The Graphics Device Interface library. This DLL contains functions relating to device output. Most drawing, display context, metafile, coordinate, and font functions are in this DLL.
Printer DLLs	Each printer driver has its own dynamic (generally has link library that includes printer setup and the extension .DRV) and control functions.
COMDLG32.	These DLLs provide additional capabilities including DLLLZ32.DLL support for common properties sheets, file compression, and VERSION.DLLand version control.

A Universe of Extension Libraries

You have already seen how Windows is made up of several core dynamic link libraries. One of the curious effects of this operating system architecture is that it makes it possible to change Windows incrementally. When Microsoft wanted to add electronic mail capabilities to the operating system, it did not need to update the entire Windows system, all it had to do was add a new dynamic link library. As it turns out, most of the new features that have appeared in Windows over the past few years have actually taken the form of new DLLs, and with these new DLLs came new extensions to the API. The following table lists some of the most important extension DLLs and the functionality that they provide.

DLL Name	Description
COMCTL32.DLL	This DLL implements a new set of windows controls such as the tree list and rich text edit control. This DLL was initially created for Windows 95, but is now available for Windows NT as well.
MAPI32.DLL	This DLL provides a set of functions that lets any application work with electronic mail.

(continues)

DLL Name	Description
NETAPI32.DLL	This DLL provides a set of API functions for access and control of networks.
ODBC32.DLL	This is one of the DLLs that implements ODBC—Open Database Connectivity. These functions provide a standard API that can be used to work with different types of databases.
WINMM.DLL	This DLL provides access to a system's multimedia capabilities.

The Windows API (be it Win16 or Win32) is evolving rapidly. The complexity and number of functions are growing so quickly that it is nearly impossible to keep up with them. Fortunately, it is not necessary to become an expert in the entire Windows API to use it effectively. It is important to become acquainted with the general architecture of Windows—the fundamental concepts that make it possible to understand the various API functions. It is also important to learn how to read API documentation and function declarations so that you can create the declarations necessary to access those functions from Visual Basic.

Key Concepts

There are a number of fundamental concepts that you must understand before you can truly take advantage of the Win32 API.

Objects

Windows works with many different types of objects. For example, a pen is a graphical object that Windows uses to determine the style, width, and color of lines that are drawn. How you work with these objects depends on the type of object, and it is important that you use them correctly. For example, some objects are exclusive to an application, while others may be shared among applications. Some objects must be deleted after they are created, while others must be left to be deleted by the system.

Handles

Windows, device contexts, program instances, pens, brushes, bitmaps, cursors—these represent some of the most important objects in the Windows environment. They can all be accessed or used in one way or another via Windows API functions. This means that there must be some way to identify these objects and pass them as parameters to a function.

Windows identifies each of these objects with a 32-bit integer known as a *handle* (handles were 16-bit integers under Win16). In the Win32 documentation provided by Microsoft, each handle has a type identifier starting with a lowercase *h*, which is typically used when passing the parameter as a function; for example, a window handle is referred to as hWnd, so the definition of a function like SetFocus that accepts a window handle will typically be SetFocus(hWnd). The following table provides a brief summary of the most important handles, their common type identifiers, and what they are used for.

Object	Identifier	Description
Bitmap	hBitmap	An area in memory that holds image information
Brush	hBrush	Used during drawing to fill areas
Cursor	hCursor	A mouse cursor. An image that can be assigned to represent the mouse position.
Device Context	hDC	Device context
File	hFile	Disk file object
Font	hFont	Represents a text font
Icon	hIcon	An icon. Typically a 32x32 or 16x16 color or monochrome image.
Instance	hInstance	Represents an instance of a running Windows application
Memory	hMem	Refers to a block of memory
Menu	hMenu	Menu bar or pop-up menu
Metafile	hMF hMetaFile	An object in which you can record drawing operations for later playback
Module	hModule hLibModule	Refers to a code module such as a DLL or application module. Often used to access resources within a module such as fonts, icons, cursors, and so on.

(continues)

Object	Identifier	Description
Object (Kernel)	hObject	Win32 defines a number of synchronization objects including events, semaphores, and mutexes. Each of these has a corresponding handle.
Palette	hPalette	Color palette
Pen	hPen	Determines the type of line during drawing
Process	hProcess	Identifies a single executing process. Win32 also provides Thread objects where a process can run multiple threads of execution at once.
Region	hRgn	An area on the window—usually used to specify clipping (the part of the window that can be drawn on)
Window	hWnd hDlg hCtl	Represents a window on the display. hDlg is sometimes used if the window is a dialog box and hCtl if the window is a control—but they are still window handles and can be used interchangeably.

Objects can be created under program control or, in some cases, loaded from existing program modules (application modules or dynamic link libraries). When an object (such as a font, bitmap, or icon) is available to be loaded from a module, it is called a *resource*.

Objects used by the Windows API should not be confused with Visual Basic objects such as forms or controls, or OLE 2.0 objects such as those retrieved by the Visual Basic GetObject command. These objects are manipulated by OLE or by Visual Basic itself and are not part of the core Windows API.

Device Contexts

One of the most important types of objects to understand is the device context—an object required for virtually any graphical operation under Windows, and which will prove essential to taking advantage of the powerful new Win32 drawing functions such as Bézier curves and bitmap rotations.

At any given time when you are drawing under Windows, the area being drawn to has a number of specific characteristics. The size of the area available (window size or page size when printing), the color you are using, the background color, and the type of device (display or printer) are just some of these characteristics. They represent the current drawing context. In Windows, this drawing context is described by an object known as a *device context* (DC). A device context that represents a window on the display screen is sometimes referred to as a *display context*.

A device context describes the characteristics of the current drawing environment for a particular device or window. The following table describes the more important attributes of a device context.

DC Attribute	Description
Background Color	Used for the background of styled lines and hatched brushes, and when converting bitmaps from color to monochrome and vice versa
Bitmap	A DC may have a bitmap selected into it. This bitmap can then be transferred to another DC or to the device.
Brush	Brushes are used for filling graphics objects
Clipping	A clipping region specifies the area within the context that can be drawn on
Coordinate System	The mapping mode (similar to VB scale mode) and coordinate system to use
Font	The font to be used for text output
Pen	Pens are used for all line drawing. Pens have several attributes including width, color, style (solid or dashed).
Pen Position	The current location (start point) for drawing operations
Text Color	Color of text

Windows provides a large set of API functions to get and set device context attributes.

Consider the task of drawing a color line under Windows. The steps are as follows:

1. Get a device context to use for drawing to a window.

2. Determine the start position and use a GDI API function to set the start position for the line (function `MoveTo`).

3. Set the drawing color by selecting a pen of the desired color into the DC.

4. Call the appropriate GDI API function to draw a line (function `LineTo`).

Windows takes care of accessing the display hardware regardless of the type of display being used. If the display is monochrome, Windows automatically converts the line to monochrome. If the display cannot handle the exact pen color you requested, Windows chooses the closest color available.

The real power of this technique comes into play when it is time to print. If you have a function that draws a line to the display, the same function can be used to draw a line to a printer. All that is necessary is to use a printer device context in place of the window device context. This works on more complex tasks as well. You can create a subroutine that draws a pie chart that accepts a device context as a parameter. If you pass it a device context for a window, it will draw the pie chart on the window. If you pass it a device context for a printer, it will draw the pie chart on the printer. You can even arrange things so that the function will automatically scale the pie chart based on the area available for drawing.

Visual Basic provides access to device contexts for forms, picture controls, and the `Printer` object, making it easy to call advanced GDI drawing functions for those objects.

The Visual Basic Windows Interface

As mentioned earlier, all of the functions that comprise the Windows API are located in a set of dynamic link libraries that comprise Windows. Each of these dynamic link libraries has a header that defines which functions in the library can be called by other programs and where they are located in the library. These functions are said to be "exported" from the DLL.

When you write a Visual Basic program, the API functions are called just like VB functions. How does Visual Basic know which functions are API functions and where to find them? This is accomplished by using the `Declare` statement.

The Declare Statement

The Visual Basic `Declare` statement is used to import a DLL function into Visual Basic. It informs VB where a DLL function may be found, and serves to let Visual Basic know what types of parameters a DLL function expects and what values it returns. Once a DLL function is properly declared, it appears to the VB programmer like any other Basic function or subroutine.

The most important consideration with regard to declaring API or DLL functions is that the declaration be correct. The function declaration in Visual Basic must correspond exactly to the DLL function in terms of numbers and types of parameters and the type of value returned. Any errors in this declaration are likely to lead to a fatal exception (or general protection fault), which will, at the very least, cause you to lose all work done in your Visual Basic project since it was last saved.

The syntax for the Visual Basic `Declare` statement is as follows for subroutines that do not return a value:

```
[Public ¦ Private] Declare Sub globalname Lib libname$ [Alias aliasname$]
[(argument list)]
For functions that return a value it is:
[Public ¦ Private] Declare Function globalname Lib libname$ [Alias aliasname$]
[(argument list)]
```

In the `Declare` statement, `globalname` is the name of the function as it will be called from your Visual Basic program. In most cases, this is also the name by which the function is identified in the dynamic link library itself, though as you will see, this is not always the case. If you are defining a function, you should append a type specifier to the name (for example, `globalname%`, `globalname&`, etc.) to indicate the type of value returned by the function. Alternatively, you can add the `AS` *typename* specifier to the end of the function declaration where *typename* is one of `Byte`, `Boolean`, `Integer`, `Long`, `Single`, `Double`, `Currency`, `String`, `Object`, or `Variant`. Note, however, that the Object, Currency and Variant data types are not used by the Win32 API, and that Single and Double results are never returned from API functions.

`libname$` is the name of the dynamic link library that contains the function and specifies to Visual Basic where to look for that function. This is a string type and, thus, must be enclosed in quotes. The name must include the file extension of the DLL unless it is one of the three Windows DLLs (user32, kernel32, or gdi32), in which case no extension is needed. The library name is not case-sensitive.

Here is an example that illustrates the use of the *globalname* and *libname* parameters:

```
Declare Function GetVersion& Lib "kernel32" ()
```

Unicode, ANSI, and Aliases

The next part of the `Declare` statement is the `Alias` term. This option allows you to tell Visual Basic to identify a Windows API or DLL function by a different name within your Visual Basic application. In the Win16 API, this served primarily to allow VB to access functions whose names were not valid in Visual Basic. For example, the _lopen function has a leading underscore, which is legal in C, but not permitted for Visual Basic function names. Also, there are a few Windows API functions such as SetFocus and GetObject which are keywords in Visual Basic. Aliasing is used to define a new function name which VB can use to identify functions whose names would conflict with reserved commands or function names. These cases, fortunately, were few and far between. Even if you include other uses of Alias to promote type safe declarations, only a small fraction of API function declarations under Win16 used the Alias command. With Win32, this is no longer the case.

One of the most significant differences between the Win32 API and the Win16 API relates to the way that functions dealing with text strings are identified. The Win32 API supports three different types of character sets. The first two are the single-byte and double-byte character sets. In a single-byte character set, each text character is represented by one byte, thus the system can support up to 256 characters. In a double-byte character set (DBCS), some byte values are reserved as DBCS "lead bytes," which indicate that the byte that follows should be combined to form a single character. This allows the character set to support over 256 characters, which is crucial for languages such as Japanese, which have hundreds of characters. The Win16 API supports both single- and double-byte character sets.

The third type of character set is actually just one character set called Unicode. It is a wide-character set, meaning that each character is represented by a 16-bit integer. Unicode can have up to 65,535 characters, enough to support all of the characters in all of the languages in use today. The impact of Unicode support on using the Win32 API is far reaching.

To start with, every Win32 API function that uses text must have a way to determine if that text is in DBCS or Unicode format. This poses an interesting challenge. One solution might have been to create a new standard string format that somehow included a character set identifier, but this would have required substantial changes to languages and applications in order to create programs that would run on Win32. Microsoft could also have added a new parameter to each function that used strings to identify the character set, but this would have affected performance and once again posed a compatibility nightmare. Instead, it chose to provide two separate functions for each API function that uses strings. For example, the GetWindowText API function actually exists in two forms: GetWindowTextA and GetWindowTextW, where the A suffix signifies ANSI (the default single-byte character set), and the W suffix signifies "wide" for the Unicode character set. Not every Win32 implementation defines both functions. Windows NT uses Unicode internally, thus, if you call the GetWindowTextA API function, Windows actually calls GetWindowTextW and converts the resulting string into ANSI before returning. Windows 95 does not support Unicode at all—calling GetWindowTextW will lead to an error. Visual Basic always uses the ANSI version of the API. Visual Basic uses Unicode internally, but always converts strings into ANSI before using them as parameters to API or DLL functions defined using the Declare statement. It is possible to access the Unicode functions from Visual Basic, but only if you reference them using a type library.

Accessing the Right Function

The existence of two separate function names for each function poses some problems. Let's say you wanted to retrieve the caption of a window. Under Win16 you would call GetWindowText. Under Win32 you would call GetWindowTextA or GetWindowTextW depending on the character set you wanted to use. Clearly it would be extremely difficult to use the same source code on multiple platforms. To avoid this problem, it is advisable to use the standard Windows API name, while having Visual Basic somehow know that it must call the real API name. The Alias *aliasname$* option in the Declare statement is used when you wish the function to be called in Visual Basic by a name other than the one defined in the dynamic link library. Here is the declaration for the GetWindowText function:

```
Declare Function GetWindowText Lib "user32" Alias "GetWindowTextA" _
(ByVal hWnd As Long, ByVal lpString As String, ByVal aint As Long) _
As Long
```

When you call GetWindowText in your Visual Basic program, Visual Basic will actually call the GetWindowTextA function in the user32 DLL. You could specify GetWindowTextW as an alias, or leave the alias out entirely, depending on the environment. This means that even if you use the GetWindowText function hundreds of times in your program, you would only need to change the declaration once in order to find the correct function on any operating system. Keep in mind, though, that changing the function name is not all that is involved in converting code between platforms. Aliasing can also be used to provide improved type checking for DLL functions that can accept parameters that reflect multiple types.

When you wish to create code that will run on multiple platforms, you will generally use conditional compilation to define two declarations for each API function that you use, one for Win32 and one for Win16.

> **Note**
>
> One important final note: Under the Win32 API, function names within DLLs or the Windows API are case-sensitive. This is a change from Win16.

There are two approaches to ensuring that the case of your function declaration is correct in spite of Visual Basic's tendency to recapitalize variable and function names. The first way is to always use an alias. If Visual Basic changes the capitalization of the function name, it will not affect the name in the Alias statement. The second way is to be careful to declare the function before trying to write code that uses it. One of the nice changes between Visual Basic 3.0 and 4.0 is that VB now coerces the capitalization of names to always match that from the first time the name is declared.

API Call Results

Almost every Win32 API function returns a result. In many cases the result provides information that you requested. For example, the GetFocus function returns a window handle. In many other cases the result tells you whether or not the function succeeded. In most cases a non-zero result (True) indicates success and a zero result (False) indicates failure. Note that the Win32 definition of True (non-zero) does not match the Visual Basic definition (-1). This means that you must compare the result to zero explicitly when testing the result of API functions. For example, you might want to check if a window handle is valid, using the API function IsWindow. Consider the case where the window handle hWnd is valid:

```
If IsWindow(hWnd) then print "It is a window"
```

will print the message, because the condition is True for any non-zero value. However, consider the following code:

```
If not IsWindow(hWnd) then print "It is not a window"
```

will also print the message even if hWnd is a valid window. This is because IsWindow can return the result 1, the inverse of which is &HFFFE (-2) which is also True. The correct way to perform these comparisons is:

```
If IsWindow(hWnd)<>0 then ....
```

or

```
If Not ( IsWindow(hWnd)<>0 ) then ... or
If IsWindow(hWnd)=0 then...
```

When a Win32 API function fails, you can often obtain additional error information by using the `GetLastError` API function. Note that the result of `GetLastError` for some operating systems is not reset when a function succeeds. In other words, you should call it only if the result of an API call indicates that an error occurred. A few functions set an error value even on success to provide additional information. These cases are described in the documentation for the individual functions.

DLL Parameters

In order to understand how to create argument lists for dynamic link libraries, it is necessary to first examine the types of function parameters that DLLs may use. Since dynamic link libraries are typically written in C, they can use a wide variety of parameters that are not supported directly by Visual Basic. The choice of appropriate Visual Basic variable types is not always obvious and an incorrect choice can lead to a fatal exception or runtime error.

Argument Lists

An argument list is a list of dummy parameter names indicating the parameters that are passed to the function. The terms *argument* and *parameter* both have the same meaning in this context. Visual Basic tends to use the term *argument* in its documentation, while Windows uses *parameter*.

The "dummy" variable names in an argument list are merely placeholders—they have no significance outside of the declaration. This means that if you define an argument list like this:

```
ByVal dummy1&, ByVal dummy2&
```

dummy1& and *dummy2&* are not significant outside of this line, nor will they conflict with other variables of the same name elsewhere in the program.

Call by Reference versus Call by Value (Numeric Parameters)

The default calling convention for Visual Basic is *call by reference*. This means that Visual Basic passes to the DLL a pointer to the argument variable itself. The DLL can modify the actual parameter because it has a pointer indicating where in memory the parameter is located.

Call by value is a calling convention in which a copy of the parameter value is passed to the DLL. This is specified for numeric data types by preceding the parameter with the word `ByVal`. Figure 2.1 illustrates the differences between these calling conventions.

Fig. 2.1

CallByValue versus
CallByReference

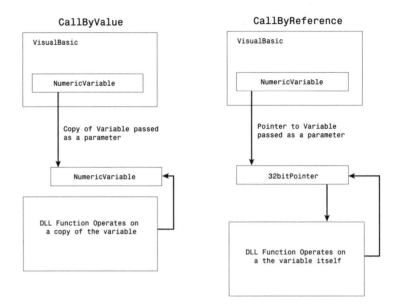

Calling Conventions for String Parameters

Visual Basic is somewhat inconsistent in the use of ByVal with string
variables.

There are two types of strings supported in the interface between Visual Basic
and the DLL. If the ByVal keyword is absent, Visual Basic will pass to the DLL
function a pointer to an OLE 2.0 string (known as the BSTR data type). This
type of string is not generally used by Windows API functions except for
those that are part of the OLE 2.0 API. They may also be supported by other
dynamic link libraries.

Windows API functions expect string parameters to be passed as a pointer to
a null-terminated string; that is, a string of characters, where the end of the
string is identified by a character with the ASCII value of 0. This is the string
format used by the C programming language. When the ByVal keyword is
used with a string parameter, Visual Basic converts the string into C language
format by adding a null-termination character. Because the parameter is a
pointer, the DLL is capable of modifying the string even though the ByVal
keyword is specified. Figure 2.2 shows the differences between the two string
calling conventions.

In some cases, a DLL function is designed to load data into a string that is
passed as a parameter. It is critical that the Visual Basic string variable be
preassigned a string length long enough to hold the data before it is passed as
a parameter to the DLL function. This can be done by using a fixed length
string, or by setting the string length using the String$ function. Additional
issues relating to string parameters will be covered later in this chapter.

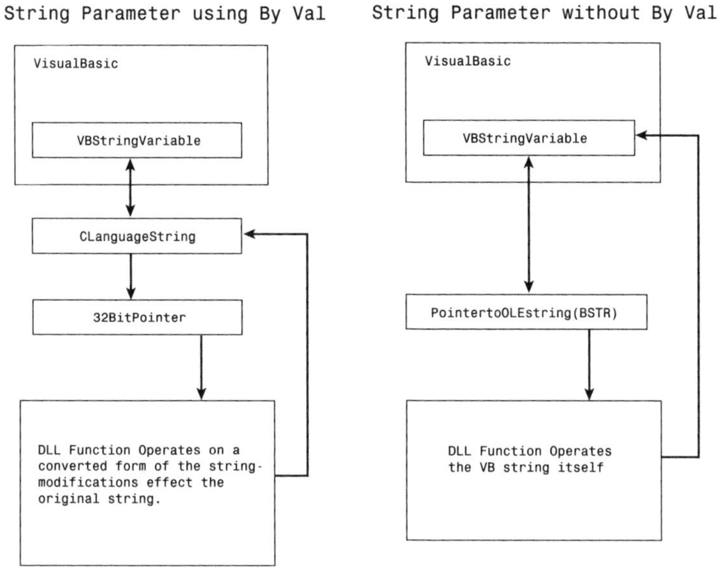

String Parameter using By Val   String Parameter without By Val

```
┌─────────────────────────────┐
│ VisualBasic                 │
│                             │
│   ┌──────────────────────┐  │
│   │ VBStringVariable     │  │
│   └──────────────────────┘  │
│                             │
└─────────────────────────────┘

     ┌──────────────────────┐
     │ CLanguageString      │
     └──────────────────────┘

     ┌──────────────────────┐
     │ 32BitPointer         │
     └──────────────────────┘

┌─────────────────────────────┐
│                             │
│ DLL Function Operates on a  │
│ converted form of the string│
│ modifications effect the    │
│ original string.            │
│                             │
└─────────────────────────────┘
```

```
┌─────────────────────────────┐
│ VisualBasic                 │
│                             │
│   ┌──────────────────────┐  │
│   │ VBStringVariable     │  │
│   └──────────────────────┘  │
│                             │
└─────────────────────────────┘

     ┌──────────────────────┐
     │ PointertoOLEstring(BSTR) │
     └──────────────────────┘

┌─────────────────────────────┐
│                             │
│ DLL Function Operates       │
│ the VB string itself        │
│                             │
└─────────────────────────────┘
```

Fig. 2.2
Calling Conventions for String Parameters

The calling convention specified in the Declare statement must match that expected by the DLL function (this applies to both numeric and string data types). The most common cause of fatal exceptions or "bad DLL calling convention" errors is the failure to include the ByVal keyword when it is needed, or failure to omit it when omission is necessary

Summary of VB Parameter Declarations

The following table summarizes the most common C variable types and how they should be passed as parameters to API functions from Visual Basic.

C Declaration	VB Parameter (Win32)	VB Parameter (Win16)
char chMyChar	ByVal chMyChar As Byte	ByVal chMyChar As Byte
BYTE chMyByte	ByVal chMyByte As Byte	ByVal chMyByte As Byte
short nMyShort	ByVal nMyShort As Integer	ByVal nMyShort As Integer
WORD wMyWord	ByVal wMyWord As Integer	ByVal wMyWord As Integer
int nMyInt	ByVal nMyInt As Long	ByVal nMyInt As Integer
UINT wMyUInt	ByVal nMyUInt As Long	ByVal nMyUInt As Integer

(continues)

C Declaration	VB Parameter (Win32)	VB Parameter (Win16)
BOOL bMyBool	ByVal nMyBool As Long	ByVal nMyBool As Integer
DWORD dwMy DWord	ByVal dwMyDWord As Long	ByVal dwMyDWord As Long
LONG lMyLong	ByVal lMyLong As Long	ByVal lMyLong As Long
float MyFloat	ByVal MyFloat As Single	ByVal MyFloat As Single
double MyDouble	ByVal MyDouble As double	ByVal MyDouble As double
HWND hWnd (window handle)	ByVal hWnd As Long	ByVal hWnd As Integer
HPEN hPen (handle to a pen)	ByVal hPen As Long	ByVal hPen As Integer
HGLOBAL hgbl (Handle to memory block)	ByVal hglbl As Long	ByVal hglbl As Long

Pointers to Numeric Values

Pointers to numeric values include the LPINT, LPSHORT data types, and other pointers to numeric types as defined by the individual DLL functions. It is extremely common for pointers to be used in this way as parameters.

Visual Basic can pass a pointer to a numeric data type simply by not using the ByVal keyword (call by reference). The DLL function can then use this pointer to access the actual variable, and may also modify this variable in some cases. This technique can be used with any numeric data type.

Be very careful, however, that the size of the variable that you are pointing to matches what is expected by the DLL. If you pass a pointer to a VB integer (16-bits) to an API function that expects a pointer to a C integer (32-bits), the API function will go ahead and write data not only into the integer that you provided, but into the next 16 bits of memory. This could cause anything from a tiny data error to a fatal exception, and this type of problem can be notoriously difficult to track down.

Pointers to Structures

A DLL structure is the same as a Visual Basic user-defined type as created with the Type keyword. In many cases it is possible to create a VB user-defined type that exactly matches the structure expected by the DLL. In other cases, that becomes somewhat tricky.

Once you have a compatible VB type definition, it can be passed by reference as a parameter (you cannot pass a user-defined type by value to a DLL).

The issues involved in converting an API structure into a Visual Basic user-defined type range from simple to extremely complex. In general, you will find the structure definitions provided in the WIN32API.TXT file to be correct and sufficient for the most common API calls.

Pointers to Arrays

Some DLL functions accept pointers to arrays of numbers or structures. These can be handled by specifying the parameter data type as that of the array data type and using the call by reference convention. You can then use the first element of the array as the parameter. This passes a pointer to the start of the array.

In cases where the DLL function can modify the contents of the array, it is critical that the array be predefined to be large enough to hold any changes. Refer to the documentation on the specific API function to determine its array size requirements.

The following example shows how to pass the first element of an array to a DLL function:

```
' Declarations is:
Declare Sub SendToDLL Lib "alib.dll" (x%)

' In the subroutine use:
ReDim x(10) As Integer
SendToDLL x(0)
```

Conditional Compilation

Sometimes you may get the impression from the press and advertisements that Microsoft wants everyone to throw out all of its 16-bit software and tools and switch over immediately to pure 32-bit programming. This is probably because (near as I can tell) Microsoft actually does want everyone to throw out all of their 16-bit software and tools and switch over immediately to pure 32-bit programming.

Unfortunately, most programmers will not have the luxury of offering only 32-bit versions of their programs for some time to come—too many computers will continue to run Windows 3.1 and require 16-bit software. Fortunately, Visual Basic does make it possible to not only create both 16- and 32-bit versions of applications, but also to create them out of a common source code base. The language feature that makes this possible is called *conditional compilation*.

The conditional compilation commands, `#if`, `#else`, `#elseif`, and `#endif` look very much like the standard `if`, `else`, `elseif`, and `endif` statements, and work in a similar fashion. The big difference between them lies in when the conditional operation is performed. The conditional compilation commands act on a program once—only during the compilation process. Regular conditional commands are executed while the program is running each time the program is running—they produce actual executable code.

Because the conditional compilation commands execute at compile time, any code that is excluded by these commands is completely thrown away. You can therefore have more than one variable and function with the same name without having to worry about naming conflicts. For example, say you have a variable that is intended to hold the value of a handle. This variable needs to be an integer on Win16, and a long in Win32. You can define this variable as follows:

```
#if Win32
Dim myhandle As Long
#else
Dim myhandle As Integer
#endif
```

With regular conditional commands, Visual Basic would signal an error at compile time, informing you that you have declared a variable with two different types. With conditional compilation, when compiling under Win32, the integer declaration does not exist, so no error occurs. Conditional compilation is most often used to allow you to include both 16- and 32-bit API declarations in one source file. This is shown in the following example.

Example: Determining the Environment

The platform example shown here demonstrates how you can use the Windows API to determine the operating system on which your application is running. It illustrates a situation where the Win32 API is different from Win16 not just in the form of the declaration, but in the functions that are available.

Listing 2.1 2LIST01.TXT—Platform sample program

```
Option Explicit

' Platform sample program
' Copyright (c) 1992-1995 by Desaware
' Constants based on file api32.txt included with
```

```
' the Visual Basic Programmer's Guide to the Win32 API

'-------------------------------------------------

'                Application Global Variables

'-------------------------------------------------


' Holder for version information. Set on form load
Global myVer As OSVERSIONINFO



'------------------------------
'   API Type Definitions
'------------------------------

Public Type SYSTEM_INFO
        dwOemID As Long
        dwPageSize As Long
        lpMinimumApplicationAddress As Long
        lpMaximumApplicationAddress As Long
        dwActiveProcessorMask As Long
        dwNumberOfProcessors As Long
        dwProcessorType As Long
        dwAllocationGranularity As Long
        wProcessorLevel As Integer
        wProcessorRevision As Integer
End Type

Public Type OSVERSIONINFO ' 148 bytes
        dwOSVersionInfoSize As Long
        dwMajorVersion As Long
        dwMinorVersion As Long
        dwBuildNumber As Long
        dwPlatformId As Long
        szCSDVersion As String * 128
End Type


Public Const MAX_DEFAULTCHAR = 2
Public Const MAX_LEADBYTES = 12


#If Win32 Then
Declare Function GetVersion Lib "kernel32" () As Long
Declare Function GetVersionEx Lib "kernel32" Alias "GetVersionExA" _
(lpVersionInformation As OSVERSIONINFO) As Long
Declare Sub GetSystemInfo Lib "kernel32" (lpSystemInfo As SYSTEM_INFO)
#Else   ' Win16 here.
Declare Function GetWinFlags& Lib "Kernel" ()
Declare Function GetVersion& Lib "Kernel" ()

#End If
```

(continues)

Listing 2.1   Continued

```
'-----------------------------------------------------------
'               API constants
'-----------------------------------------------------------

Global Const GFSR_SYSTEMRESOURCES = 0
Global Const GFSR_GDIRESOURCES = 1
Global Const GFSR_USERRESOURCES = 2
Global Const WF_PMODE = &H1
Global Const WF_CPU286 = &H2
Global Const WF_CPU386 = &H4
Global Const WF_CPU486 = &H8
Global Const WF_STANDARD = &H10
Global Const WF_WIN286 = &H10
Global Const WF_ENHANCED = &H20
Global Const WF_WIN386 = &H20
Global Const WF_CPU086 = &H40
Global Const WF_CPU186 = &H80
Global Const WF_LARGEFRAME = &H100
Global Const WF_SMALLFRAME = &H200
Global Const WF_80x87 = &H400


#If Win32 Then
Public Const VER_PLATFORM_WIN32_NT& = 2
Public Const VER_PLATFORM_WIN32_WINDOWS& = 1
#End If


#If Win32 Then

Public Const PROCESSOR_INTEL_386 = 386
Public Const PROCESSOR_INTEL_486 = 486
Public Const PROCESSOR_INTEL_PENTIUM = 586
Public Const PROCESSOR_MIPS_R4000 = 4000
Public Const PROCESSOR_ALPHA_21064 = 21064

Private Sub Form_Load()
    Dim dl&

    #If Win32 Then
        ' Preload version information
        dl& = GetVersionEx&(myVer)
    #End If


End Sub

Private Sub Form_Paint()
    Dim flagnum&
    Dim dl&, s$

    Dim vernum&, verword%
```

```
    #If Win32 Then
        Dim mySys As SYSTEM_INFO
    #End If

    Me.Cls
    Print

    ' Get the windows flags and version numbers
    #If Win32 Then
        myVer.dwOSVersionInfoSize = 148
        dl& = GetVersionEx&(myVer)
        If myVer.dwPlatformId = VER_PLATFORM_WIN32_WINDOWS Then
            s$ = " Windows95 "
        ElseIf myVer.dwPlatformId = VER_PLATFORM_WIN32_NT Then
            s$ = " Windows NT "
        End If
        Print s$ & myVer.dwMajorVersion & "." & myVer.dwMinorVersion _
& " Build " & (myVer.dwBuildNumber And &HFFFF&)
        s$ = LPSTRToVBString(myVer.szCSDVersion)
        If Len(s$) > 0 Then Print s$
        GetSystemInfo mySys
        Print " Page size is " & mySys.dwPageSize; " bytes"
        Print " Lowest memory address: &H" & _
Hex$(mySys.lpMinimumApplicationAddress)
        Print " Highest memory address: &H" & _
Hex$(mySys.lpMaximumApplicationAddress)
        Print " Number of processors: "; mySys.dwNumberOfProcessors
        Print " Processor: ";
        Select Case mySys.dwProcessorType
            Case PROCESSOR_INTEL_386
                Print "Intel 386"
            Case PROCESSOR_INTEL_486
                Print "Intel 486"
            Case PROCESSOR_INTEL_PENTIUM
                Print "Intel Pentium"
            Case PROCESSOR_MIPS_R4000
                Print "MIPS R4000"
            Case PROCESSOR_ALPHA_21064
                Print "Alpha 21064"
        End Select

    #Else
        flagnum& = GetWinFlags&()
        vernum& = GetVersion&()
        verword% = CInt(vernum& / &H10000)

        Print " Running MS-DOS version "; verword% / 256; "."; _
verword% And &HFF
        verword% = CInt(vernum& And &HFFFF&)
        Print " Running Windows version "; verword% And &HFF; "."; _
CInt(verword% / 256)
```

(continues)

Listing 2.1 Continued

```
        If flagnum& And WF_80x87 Then Print _
" 80x87 coprocessor present"
        If flagnum& And WF_CPU086 Then Print " 8086 present"
        If flagnum& And WF_CPU186 Then Print " 80186 present"
        If flagnum& And WF_CPU286 Then Print " 80286 present"
        If flagnum& And WF_CPU386 Then Print " 80386 present"
        If flagnum& And WF_CPU486 Then Print " 80486 present"
        If flagnum& And WF_ENHANCED Then Print _
" Windows 386-enhanced mode"
    #End If


End Sub

' Extracts a VB string from a buffer containing a null terminated
' string
Public Function LPSTRToVBString$(ByVal s$)
    Dim nullpos&
    nullpos& = InStr(s$, Chr$(0))
    If nullpos > 0 Then
        LPSTRToVBString = Left$(s$, nullpos - 1)
    Else
        LPSTRToVBString = ""
    End If
End Function
```

Resources

It is probably glaringly obvious that this one chapter is inadequate to do more than introduce the use of the Win32 API from Visual Basic. It barely covered a few key concepts and the fundamentals of declaring API functions under Win32. You'll need to examine several additional sources to truly take advantage of the vast capabilities that the API makes available.

The Win32 Online Help File WIN32API.HLP

The Win32 Online Help File WIN32API.HLP is included with Visual Basic. This is a good reference to Win32 functionality, though it does not provide any information on using Win32 functions from Visual Basic.

WIN32API.TXT

This is the declaration file for the Win32 API functions that come with Visual Basic. If you have difficulty getting any of the functions declared here to work, be sure to double-check the declaration, as there are a number of errors in the file. For example: every parameter that is declared as `double` in this file should be converted to `single` (the Windows API uses few floating point values, but those it uses are singles, not doubles).

Microsoft Developer's Network CD-ROM

No serious developer should be without this indispensable reference work. It includes not only the latest function references, but complete bug lists as well.

Visual Basic Programmer's Guide to the WIN32 API

The only Win32 API reference designed exclusively for VB and VBA programmers. This chapter should give you a taste of what this book is like—though only a slight taste as it contains but a small fraction of the content of even the introductory chapters.

Summary

For most current Visual Basic programmers, the highest priority initially will relate to porting code from Win16 to Win32. This chapter contains the information that you will need to port the most commonly used functions.

In most cases porting will consist first of taking the appropriate Win32 declarations from the declaration file and copying it into your program. You can use conditional compilation to keep the original 16-bit declarations available. You can then try to run the program, allowing Visual Basic to spot errors which you can then correct. Most of the changes will consist of changing integer variables to longs where necessary. This is frequently all that is necessary in order to make a program run under Win32.

Once you have finished the urgent task of porting to Win32, and have some time to explore, you will find that Win32 contains a vast selection of powerful new functions that can substantially extend the types of operations you can perform using Visual Basic.

Chapter 3

JET 3.0 Database Engine

by Michael McKelvy

Michael McKelvy is the owner of McKelvy Software Systems, a Birmingham, Ala-bama-based consulting firm. Mike specializes in the development of database systems and engineering applications. He can be reached by Fax at (205) 980-9816; and on CompuServe at 71477,3513.

When Microsoft first introduced Visual Basic version 1, it was a good general purpose language, but had no database capabilities built-in. If you wanted to write a database application, you had to use a third-party library of functions or write your own. With version 2, Microsoft added *Open DataBase Connectivity* (ODBC) capabilities to Visual Basic. The ODBC drivers allowed you to perform functions on FoxPro or Paradox (or other) databases. While the use of ODBC was still difficult, at least it was built-in to the product. However, Visual Basic still lacked a native database.

Finally, when Visual Basic 3 arrived, it included Microsoft's *JET* (Joint Engine Technology) database engine. This engine (version 1.1) was shared with Microsoft Access and provided VB programmers with a native database that they could call their own. The JET engine allowed the programmer to use the methods and properties of *Data Access Objects* (DAOs) to access and manipulate database information. These methods and properties allowed you to retrieve data from the database, modify the data, and change the presentation order of the data. You could even modify the structure of the database by creating, modifying, and deleting fields, tables, and indexes. With VB3 and JET 1.1, you finally had an easy way to write database applications.

Two Versions of JET

Even with all its capabilities and ease of use, VB3 and JET 1.1 weren't enough. As programmers, we always want more capabilities, more power, and fewer restrictions on how we create programs. With the release of Visual Basic 4 and JET 2.5/3.0, Microsoft has given programmers many of the things they wanted in a robust database system.

You will notice that I listed the new engine as 2.5/3.0. That's right; there are two versions of the JET engine that come with Visual Basic 4. JET 2.5 is designed for use with 16-bit systems and provides compatibility with Access 2.0 and other 16-bit applications. JET 3.0 is a full 32-bit database system that extends JET's capabilities even further. However, JET 3.0 can only be used with 32-bit operating systems, such as Windows 95 and Windows NT (3.51 or later). In this section, I will discuss the enhancements to the JET engine capabilities that are in version 2.5, the additional capabilities of version 3.0, and a few "gotchas" that you will need to look out for.

JET 2.5

Visual Basic 4 provides you with the capability to use a number of new and enhanced database features that were not available in Visual Basic 3. (Note: Some of these features were available in the JET 2.5 database engine if you used Access 2.0). The following is a list of some of the key new features, (which will be discussed in detail in the remainder of this chapter):

- Engine-level support of referential integrity defined by relations in the database.

- Support for cascading updates and deletions as defined by database relations.

- Engine-level field and table validation. This means that the database engine can actually validate your data entry.

- Full support for Data Definition Language (DDL) queries that allow you to create or modify any database object with a single SQL statement.

- An improved security model that allows you to add, modify, and delete users and groups and their associated database permissions from Visual Basic code. (Previously, security features could only be modified using Access.)

- Support for user-defined properties for many database objects.

- Rushmore™ query optimization that speeds many different types of queries.

■ Support for multiple workspaces, which allows finer control over transaction processing.

JET 3.0

The key new feature that is added for version 3 of the JET engine is database replication. Replication allows you to make copies of a database to be edited or modified by multiple users (for example, people in multiple satellite offices). These multiple copies of the database can then be recombined so that the changes made to the data in any of the databases can be reflected in the master database. In addition, changes to the structure of the master database can be easily copied to all of the replicas.

Which Version Am I Using?

Because there are two versions of the JET database engine with Visual Basic 4, you may be wondering which version you are using. By default, if you are running Visual Basic on a 32-bit system, you are using version 3.0 of the JET engine. If you are running Visual Basic on a 16-bit system, you are running version 2.5 of the JET engine.

For 16-bit systems, you have no choice of versions. You can only use version 2.5. If, however, you are developing applications on a 32-bit system, you can decide whether to use version 2.5 or version 3.0. You can change the JET version by choosing Tools, References.

If you will be converting older applications from Visual Basic 3 to Visual Basic 4, you can choose the Microsoft DAO 2.5/3.0 Compatible library. This library recognizes the older properties, methods, and objects that were supported in JET version 1.1, but are not supported in JET 3.0. This means that you can recompile older code and have it run without major conversions to the data access portions of your code. For all new applications, you should use the Microsoft DAO 3.0 object library. This guarantees that your code will run with new versions of Visual Basic as they are released.

Caveats

As with all programming languages, there are a few things you need to watch out for when developing database applications with the JET 3.0 engine. The biggest thing you need to watch out for in using the JET 3.0 engine is compatibility with other applications. If you will need to share the data in your applications with other programs that use an earlier version of JET (for example, Access 2.0 and Excel 5.0) you will need to make sure that your databases are created as version 2.5 databases. This is accomplished by using the correct version constant in the `CreateDatabase` method, as shown in the following code segment.

```
Dim NewDb As Database, NewWs As Workspace
Set NewWs = DBEngine.Workspaces(0)
filnam = "TEST.MDB"
Set NewDb = NewWs.CreateDatabase(filnam,dbLangGeneral, dbVersion25)
```

Although using a version 2.5 database prevents you from using some of the version 3.0 features, such as database replication, it does maintain compatibility with earlier applications.

Database Objects and Collections

To make it easy for you to work with databases, the JET engine provides you with an object oriented interface to the databases. This interface is the data access object model. In Chapter 4, "Data Access Objects," you will see how these objects are used in programs to manipulate databases. In this section, I explain what some of these objects are, and identify some of the more commonly used properties and methods of the objects. In addition, you'll see how some of the old Visual Basic 3 functions have been replaced by methods of some of the data access objects.

DBEngine

The DBEngine object is used to provide a connection to the JET database engine and to set up system parameters for your program. The DBEngine object contains two methods, CompactDatabase and RepairDatabase, that were previously functions in VB3. The CompactDatabase method is used to recover the empty space left by deleting records from the database. The RepairDatabase is used to fix minor problems that cause database corruption. Both of these methods can only be used on Access databases.

Workspace

The Workspace object is a new object that provides you with greater control and flexibility in your database programming than was available before in the areas of database security and transaction processing. In VB3, if you were working with secured databases, you could only use one user name and password for any application session. To change the user name or use a different database with a different user name, you had to exit your program and restart it. With the Workspace object in VB4, not only can you change user names (using the UserName and Password properties) for the current session on the fly, but you can actually run multiple workspaces in your application, each with a different user name.

With transaction processing, each workspace supports an independent transaction. This means that with multiple workspaces, you can have multiple transactions running at the same time. Previously, you were only able to run a single transaction set at any given time. The transaction processing statements are now methods of the workspace object. To support this, the `BeginTrans`, `CommitTrans`, and `Rollback` commands are now methods of the `Workspace` object.

Other methods of the `Workspace` object that you will use extensively are the `CreateDatabase` and `OpenDatabase` methods. These methods take the place of the functions that were used in VB3. The following code segment shows the difference between using the old function to open a database and using the new method.

```
'*********************************************
' Using the OpenDatabase function (VB3 way)
'*********************************************
Dim OldDb As Database
Set OldDb = OpenDatabase("A:\TRITON.MDB")
'*********************************************
' Using the OpenDatabase method (VB4 way)
'*********************************************
Dim OldDb As Database, OldWs As Workspace
Set OldWs = DBEngine.Workspaces(0)
Set OldDb = OldWs.OpenDatabase("A:\TRITON.MDB")
```

The difference in the look of these two ways to open a database seems minor, but you need to get used to the new method. This is the method that will be supported in future versions of Visual Basic and will be used in Visual Basic for Applications, which is used by other programs.

Database

The `Database` object provides the link to a single JET database or an ODBC connection. The `Database` object allows you to specify the name of the database to which you are connecting, as well as its location and the type of database. You can also use properties of the `Database` object to set the type of access your user will have to the information in the database. You can give a user full access or limit the user to read-only access.

TableDef

The `TableDef` object provides you a connection with the table definition stored in the database. With the `TableDef` object, you can modify the structure of a table by adding and deleting fields and indexes in the table.

Recordset

The `Recordset` object provides you with a connection to the actual data in one or more tables in a database. The `Recordset` object takes the place of the `Table`, `Dynaset`, and `Snapshot` objects that were used in VB3. You can still create recordsets that exhibit the characteristics of a table, dynaset, or snapshot. However, instead of creating these objects directly, you specify the type of recordset you want when you open the recordset. The following example shows the difference between opening a `Dynaset` in VB3 and opening a dynaset-type `Recordset` in VB4.

```
'*********************************************
'Visual Basic 3 method of opening a dynaset
'*********************************************
Dim OldDb As Database, NewDyn As Dynaset
Set OldDb = OpenDatabase("A:\TRITON.MDB")
Set NewDyn = OldDb.CreateDynaset("SELECT * FROM Customers")
'*****************************************************************
'Visual Basic 4 method of opening a dynaset-type recordset
'*****************************************************************
Dim OldDb As Database, NewDyn As Recordset,OldWs As Workspace
Set OldWs = DBEngine.Workspaces(0)
Set OldDb = OldWs.OpenDatabase("A:\TRITON.MDB")
Set NewDyn = OldDb.OpenRecordset("SELECT * FROM
Customers",dbOpenDynaset)
```

QueryDef

A *query* is a SQL statement that performs an action on the database or re-trieves information from the database. The query can be one that is created in your program, or it can be stored in the database itself. The `QueryDef` object allows you to create queries for execution or to be added to the database.

Relations

The `Relation` object allows you to manipulate the relations between tables in a database. A relation tells the database which two tables are related, which table is the parent and which is the child, and the key fields used to specify the relationship. The relations are also used to specify whether referential integrity is enforced between two tables and whether cascading updates and deletes are allowed. Referential integrity will be discussed further in the sec-tion "Data Integrity and Validation" later in this chapter.

User-Defined Properties

Many of the database objects support the use of user-defined properties. These objects are the `Database`, `TableDef`, `QueryDef`, `Index`, and `Field` objects. These user-defined properties are contained in the Properties collection for each of the objects. For each user-defined property, you must specify the name of the property, the type of information (text, number, date) stored in the property, the value of the property, and whether the property is inherited from another object.

Why would you want to use a user-defined property? One use is for the repli-cation of databases. To create a database that can be replicated, you must create a user-defined property for the database that tells the JET engine that replication can be used. You will find a detailed description of this in the database section of Visual Basic's users manuals.

Another use of a user-defined property would be to limit access of people to specific fields in a table. The basic security system in the JET engine only allows you to place limits on access to the database itself or to tables in the database. However, there are a number of situations in which access needs to be restricted to certain fields. In a personnel application, you may want to let everyone view information, such as name, address, and phone number for an employee. However, you would only want certain people to be able to view and/or edit salary information. By creating a user-defined property for the field, you could specify different security levels for the fields in the database. You might also use a user-defined property to keep up with the ID of the last person to modify a database, table, or field.

Data Types

Your programs usually require you to deal with many types of information. The JET engine allows you great flexibility in the types of data that can be stored in a database. These different data types allow the developer a great deal of flexibility in designing a database application. Table 3.1 shows all the different data types available.

Table 3.1 The Data Types Available with the JET Engine		
Name	**Information Stored**	**Size or Range**
Text	Character strings	255 characters maximum
Memo	Long character strings	Up to 1.2G
Byte	Integer (numeric data)	0 to 255
Integer	Integer (numeric data)	−32,768 to 32,767
Long	Integer (numeric data)	−2,147,483,648 to 2,147,483,647
Counter	Long integer, automatically incremented	
Single	Real (numeric data)	-3.4×10^{38} to 3.4×10^{38}
Double	Real (numeric data)	-1.8×10^{308} to 1.8×10^{308}

(continues)

Table 3.1 Continued		
Name	**Information Stored**	**Size or Range**
Yes/No	Logical/Boolean	
Date	Date and time values	
Binary	Binary data	Up to 1.2G
OLE	OLE objects	Up to 1.2G

Data Integrity and Validation

In your database application, you want to make sure that the data going into your database is as accurate as possible. This means that you need to make sure that the data itself is correct (the correct data type and in the proper range) and that the relations between tables are properly maintained as records are added, modified, or deleted. Both of these processes, known as data validation and data integrity, are equally important in ensuring the accuracy of your data. These processes can be implemented within your program using code, or they can be implemented within the database engine itself.

The JET engine provides two forms of data integrity monitoring: primary-key integrity and referential integrity. There are also two key forms of data validation available with the JET engine: field-level validation and record-level validation. These items are discussed later in this section.

In Visual Basic 4, the developer can invoke all these integrity and validation features using the data access objects. The features are determined by setting the properties of the various objects at design time when the database and tables are created. In Visual Basic 3, these features (with the exception of primary-key integrity) could only be set using Microsoft Access.

Primary-Key Integrity

The first type of data integrity is primary-key integrity, which ensures that each record in a table is uniquely identified by a field or combination of fields. Unique keys are essential for properly relating tables. For example, if you make a sale to a customer named John Smith, but have no identifier other than his name, how do you determine which John Smith to send the bill to?

You can implement a primary key in either of two ways. You can define a unique field or combination of fields that is meaningful to you, or you can create a counter field. If you create a counter field, JET automatically creates a new value for the field for each record you add, ensuring the uniqueness of the key. If you define your own field (for example, the first letter of a person's first name plus the person's last names, such as MMCKELVY), you are responsible for making sure that the values are unique and for resolving any conflicts if a new value is not unique. That is, you must provide a program function that generates the key value (or gets an input value from the user) and verifies that the value is unique. If the value is not unique, you must provide a way to change the value and verify its uniqueness.

With either method, JET enforces primary integrity by verifying that the value of the primary key is unique before it allows the addition or updating of a record. If the value is not unique, a trappable error is returned. Your program must be able to handle this error.

Referential Integrity

To relate one table to another, the same value must appear in both tables. In a one-to-many relationship, the table on the one side of the relationship contains the primary key for the table (as described in the preceding section). The table on the many side of the relationship contains a reference to this primary key in a field. This field is known as the foreign key. Figure 3.1 shows the relationship between the Family and Member tables of an application, with the primary and foreign keys labeled.

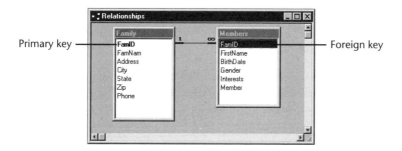

Primary key ⎯⎯⎯⎯

Foreign key ⎯⎯⎯⎯

Fig. 3.1
The foreign key in one table is related to the primary key in another table.

In this relationship, each record in the Family table can be linked to many people in the Member table. However, each person in the Member table can be linked to only one record in the Family table. A one-to-many relationship is often referred to as a parent-child relationship with the primary-key table being the parent table and the foreign-key table being the child table.

Referential integrity is responsible for making sure that the relationship between two tables is maintained. JET supports the following functions of referential integrity:

- When a foreign key is added or changed in a child table, the existence of the key value is verified in the parent table.

- When a new record is added to a child table, a foreign key must be specified.

- When a parent record is deleted or the primary key is changed, JET can either cascade the update or delete through the child tables or reject the operation if there are child records. The choice of behavior is made by the developer.

With Visual Basic 4, you can define the relationships between tables using the data access objects available for relations. With previous versions of Visual Basic and versions of the JET engine before 2.0, referential integrity was either not available or could be set only using Microsoft Access.

Cascading Updates and Deletions

Allowing the cascading of updates and deletions from the parent table to the child tables is a new feature of the JET engine, initially implemented in JET 2.0. Cascading is an optional property of a relationship. You may choose to use cascading updates, cascading deletes, or both. If you choose these options, changes to the parent table are automatically propagated through the child table. For updates, if you change the primary key of the parent table, the related foreign keys in the child table are changed to reflect the new value. For deletions, if you delete a record in the parent table, all related child records are also deleted.

Without cascading, the programmer is responsible for handling conflicts that arise from making changes to a parent record when there are dependent records in a child table. The programmer must either verify that no child records exist before making the change or deletion or let the program make the change when a record is found or an error occurs. If you do not have the cascading options turned on, you get an error when you try to change or delete a record with dependent records in a child table.

Cascading options are set when a relation is created. The options are properties of the Relation object.

> ### Caution
>
> Although cascading is a very useful and powerful method for preserving referential integrity, it should be used with caution—especially cascading deletions. Accidentally deleting a parent record can wipe out quite a bit of data.

Data Validation

Data validation is the process of ensuring that the data input or changed by a user meets certain criteria. Data validation can take several forms, all of which are described in this section.

How Validation Works

The engine-level validation provided by the JET engine uses rules about data fields and tables that are stored in the database itself. When data is changed, the JET engine checks the data against the rule prior to writing the update to the database. If the new data does not conform to the rules, an error message is returned. The rule and the error message are set as properties of the field or table being checked.

You might also use program validation in your application; in this case, the data rules are embedded in the actual program code. These rules check the value of the data against the defined criteria when particular program events occur. A program validation rule might be placed in the data-changed event of an object or the click event code of a command button.

Field-Level Validation

Field-level validation ensures that the information in the field is within a certain range of values. JET supports the use of simple expressions in field-level validation. A simple expression can compare the value of the field to a constant. Additional types of field level validation include the use of user-defined functions or checking for valid entries in another table. Although JET does not support these types of validation at the engine level, they can be programmed into your Visual Basic code.

In addition to setting a validation rule, you can also specify a custom message that is displayed if the validation rule is violated. This message appears in the standard message box when needed. In version 4, field-level validation can be set by setting the optional `ValidationRule` and `ValidationText` properties of the data-access objects. You can also use Microsoft Access or the Data Manager application that comes with Visual Basic. Figure 3.2 shows how the validation rule and text are set using the Data Manager. In Visual Basic, field-level validation expressions are checked when an update method is called.

Fig. 3.2
Validation rules
and violation
messages can be
set for any field.

Error message for failed test ——

Validation expres-
sion returning
True or False

Record-Level Validation

Record-level validation checks the information in a field against data in other
fields of the record, or it checks the results of a combination of fields against
a criterion. For example, you can verify that the ratio of the retail price to the
wholesale price is greater than 25 percent. As with field-level validation, JET
only supports the use of simple expressions for record-level validation. In
addition, only one validation rule can be set for each table. As with field-level
validation, you can enter validation text that provides a custom error message
if the validation rule is violated.

Record-level validation can also be set using the data-access objects or
Microsoft Access. When your program violates the record-level validation, a
message is shown indicating the error. Any text you entered as validation text
is included in the message that appears.

Required Field Validation

The final form of data validation supported by the JET engine is *required field
validation.* With the JET engine, you can specify any field as a required field.
If you specify a field as required, a value *must* exist for it when a record is
added or changed. JET checks each required field for a null value whenever
a record is updated. If you attempt to update a record without a value in a
required field, an error is generated.

Support for Queries

The JET engine supports the use of *Structured Query Language* (SQL) statements
for defining and manipulating data. There are two main groupings of SQL
statements: *Data Manipulation Language* statements, which are used to retrieve
data and to modify the data in tables, and *Data Definition Language* statements, which are used to modify the structure of the databases and their
associated tables.

Data Manipulation Language (DML)

Data Manipulation Language statements allow you to insert, delete, update, and retrieve groups of records in a database. Two basic types of queries are defined: action queries and retrieval queries.

Action Queries

Action queries operate on groups of records. These types of queries let you delete records, insert new records, update fields in records, or create new tables from existing records. JET supports all of these types of action queries. The queries are based on SQL syntax. These queries can be run against an entire table, or you can choose to limit the scope of the queries using the Where clause of the SQL statement. You can run action queries with either a database execute method or a query execute method. Table 3.2 summarizes the action queries supported by the JET engine.

Note

The Execute method is one of the methods associated with the Database and QueryDef objects. Using this method allows you to run a SQL query in your code.

Table 3.2   Action Queries Supported by the JET Engine

Keywords	Function
DELETE...FROM	Removes records from a table based on the selection criteria
INSERT INTO	Appends records to a table from another data source
UPDATE...SET	Changes the values of selected fields
SELECT INTO	Creates a new table from information in other tables

As stated above, the JET engine provides an execute method as part of the Database object and the *QueryDef* object. When it is used, the Execute method tells the engine to process the SQL query against the database. An action query can be executed by specifying the SQL statement as part of the Execute method for a database. An action query can also be used to create a QueryDef. Then the query can be executed on its own. Listing 3.1 shows how both of these methods are used to execute the same SQL statement.

Listing 3.1 3LIST01.TXT—Execute a SQL Statement Using the Database Execute **or Query** Execute Method

```
Dim OldDb AS Database, NewQry AS QueryDef
'*****************************************************
'Define the SQL statement and assign it to a variable
'*****************************************************
SQLstate = "UPDATE Customers SET SalesID = 'EGREEN'"
SQLstate = SQLstate + " WHERE SalesID='JBURNS'"
'*******************************************
'Use the database execute to run the query
'*******************************************
OldDb.Execute SQLstate
'*******************************************
'Create a QueryDef from the SQL statement
'*******************************************
Set NewQry = OldDb.CreateQueryDef("Change Sales", SQLstate)
'*****************************************
'Use the query execute to run the query
'*****************************************
NewQry.Execute
'*****************************************************
'Run the named query with the database execute method
'*****************************************************
OldDb.Execute "Change Sales"
```

Creating a QueryDef allows you to name your query and store it in the database with your tables. You can create either an action query or a retrieval query (one that uses the SELECT statement). Once the query is created, you can call it by name for execution or for creation of a dynaset-type recordset. Listing 3.1 also shows how to create a QueryDef called Change Sales that is used to update the salesperson ID for a group of customers.

Retrieval Queries

Retrieval queries tell the database engine to return a group of records in a recordset of the dynaset or snapshot type for viewing or processing. These queries are SQL SELECT statements that define the fields to be retrieved; the tables in which the fields are located; and the filter criteria for the fields. JET supports standard SQL clauses, such as WHERE, ORDER BY, GROUP BY, and JOIN. In addition, JET supports the new clauses UNION, TOP *n*, and TOP *n*%. JET also supports the use of subqueries, in which the results of one SELECT statement can be used as part of the WHERE clause of another statement. These capabilities of the SELECT statement provide the developer with a lot of flexibility in grouping and manipulating data. Table 3.3 summarizes the clauses of the SELECT statement supported by the JET engine.

Table 3.3 Types of Retrieval Queries and Conditional Clauses Supported by the JET Engine

Keywords	Function
UNION	Creates a recordset containing all records from the defined tables
SELECT...FROM	Retrieves a group of fields from one or more tables subject to the conditional clauses
WHERE *comparison*	A conditional clause that compares an expression to a single value
WHERE...LIKE	A conditional clause that compares an expression to a pattern of values
WHERE...IN	A conditional clause that compares an expression to a group of values
INNER|LEFT|RIGHT JOIN	A conditional clause that combines information from two tables based on identical values in a key field in each table
ORDER BY	A conditional clause that determines the sort sequence of the output recordset
GROUP BY	A conditional clause that combines summary information on records into groups based on the value of one or more listed fields

Data Definition Language (DDL)

Data definition language (DDL) queries are a new feature of the JET engine (versions 2.0 and later). In previous versions of the JET engine, you created tables in a database by defining field and index objects and then adding them to the table definition. With the new DDL queries, you can issue a single command to create, change, or delete a table, and create or delete an index. Table 3.4 summarizes the various DDL queries.

Table 3.4 DDL Queries Used to Modify a Database Structure

Keywords	Function
CREATE TABLE	Creates a new table from a list of field definitions
ALTER TABLE	Adds new fields to a table
DROP TABLE	Deletes a table from the database
CREATE INDEX	Creates a new index for a table
DROP INDEX	Deletes an index from a table

Data definition language (DDL) statements allow you to create, modify, and delete tables and indexes in a database with a single statement. For many situations, these statements take the place of the data access object methods. However, there are some limitations to using the DDL statements. The main limitation is that these statements are supported only for JET databases; remember that data access objects can be used for any database accessed with the JET engine. The other limitation of DDL statements is that they support only a small subset of the properties of the table, field, and index objects. Specifically, you cannot set validation clauses using the DDL statements. If you need to specify properties outside of this subset, you must use the data access object methods.

Defining Tables with DDL Statements

Three DDL statements are used to define tables in a database, as follows:

- CREATE TABLE defines a new table in a database.

- ALTER TABLE changes the structure of the table.

- DROP TABLE deletes a table from the database.

Creating a Table

To create a table with the DDL statements, you create a SQL statement containing the name of the table and the names, types, and sizes of each field in the table. The following code shows how to create a table named Orders.

```
CREATE TABLE Orders (Orderno LONG, Custno LONG, SalesID TEXT (6), _
    OrderDate DATE, Totcost SINGLE)
```

Notice that when you specify the table name and field names, you do not have to enclose the names in quotation marks. However, if you want to specify a name with a space in it, you must enclose the name in square brackets (for example, [Last name]).

When you create a table, you can specify only the field names, types, and sizes. You cannot specify optional parameters, such as default values, validation rules, or validation error messages. Even with this limitation, the DDL CREATE TABLE statement is a powerful tool you can use to create many of the tables in a database.

Modifying a Table

By using the ALTER TABLE statement, you can add a field to an existing table or delete a field from the table. When adding a field, you must specify the name, type, and (if necessary) the size of the field. You add a field by using the ADD COLUMN clause of the ALTER TABLE statement. To delete a field, you only need to specify the field name and use the DROP COLUMN clause of the statement. As with other database modification methods, you cannot delete a field used in an index or a relation. Listing 3.2 shows how to add and then delete a field from the Orders table.

Listing 3.2   3LIST02.TXT—Using the ALTER TABLE Statement to Add or Delete a Field in a Table

```
'***************************************************
'Add a shipping charges field to the "Orders" table
'***************************************************
ALTER TABLE Orders ADD COLUMN Shipping SINGLE
'********************************
'Delete the shipping charges field
'********************************
ALTER TABLE Orders DROP COLUMN Shipping
```

Deleting a Table

You can delete a table from a database using the DROP TABLE statement. The following simple piece of code shows how to get rid of the Orders table.

```
DROP TABLE Orders
```

Use caution when deleting a table; the table and all of its data are gone forever once the command has been executed.

Defining Indexes with DDL Statements

You can use the following two DDL statements with indexes:

- CREATE INDEX defines a new index for a table.

- DROP INDEX deletes an index from a table.

Creating an Index

You can create a single-field or multifield index with the CREATE INDEX statement. To create the index, you must give the name of the index, the name of the table for the index, and at least one field to be included in the index. You can specify ascending or descending order for each field. You can also specify that the index is a primary index for the table. Listing 3.3 shows how to create a primary index on customer number, and a two-field index with the sort orders specified.

Listing 3.3   3LIST03.TXT—Create Several Types of Indexes with the CREATE INDEX Statement

```
'*******************************************
'Create a primary index on customer number
'*******************************************
CREATE INDEX Custno ON Customers (Custno) WITH PRIMARY
'***************************************************************
'Create a two field index with ascending order on Lastname and
'   descending order on Firstname.
'***************************************************************
CREATE INDEX Name2 ON Customers (Lastname ASC, Firstname DESC)
```

Deleting an Index

Getting rid of an index is just as easy as creating one. To delete an index from a table, use the DROP INDEX statement, as shown in the following example.

```
DROP INDEX Custno ON Customers
DROP INDEX Name2 ON Customers
```

These statements delete the two indexes created in Listing 3.3. Notice that you must specify the table name for the index you want to delete.

Security

The tools available for working with secured databases in Visual Basic 4 are greatly improved over those found in VB3. In Visual Basic 3, you could only set up security features using Microsoft Access. The only thing that could be done from within Visual Basic was to specify the user ID and password for a single database when your application started.

What Can Visual Basic 4 Do with Security?

One of the improvements in Visual Basic 4 is that you are no longer limited to a single user ID and password for a session of your application. As was discussed in the section "Workspace," the Workspace object allows you to change user IDs and passwords on the fly as properties of the object. Also, by using multiple workspaces, you can access multiple secured databases with a single application.

The other major improvement in Visual Basic 4 is that you can now administer security features from within your Visual Basic program. This means that you can create new user IDs and user groups; delete user IDs and groups; add or remove IDs from existing groups; and change the permissions of users or groups. All of this can be done using the User and Group objects in the data access model.

Unfortunately, you still cannot initially set up a secured database completely from Visual Basic. The secured database must initially be set up using Microsoft Access. However, once the database is set up, you can perform all of the previously listed functions on the database. All in all, this is a big improvement over previous versions.

What Levels of Security Are Available?

The JET database engine allows you to restrict access of a user or group of users in various ways. You can place restrictions on the entire database, or you can place restrictions on individual tables.

The security features allow you to assign different permissions to each user or group of users for each object in the database. Table 3.5 summarizes the permission levels available for database objects.

Table 3.5 Security Features Available with the JET Engine

Permission Type	User Capability
No Access	No functions may be performed on the database by the user
Full Access	The user may perform any function on the database
Open	Open a database in shared mode so that more than one user can access it at a time
Open Exclusive	Open a database for exclusive use
Read Design	Read database definition objects
Modify Design	Add or change database definition objects
Read Data	Read information in the object
Update Data	Change information but not add or delete records
Insert Data	Insert records but not change data or delete records
Delete Data	Delete records but not change data or insert records
Delete Object	Delete the database object, such as a table or query
Read Security	The user may read the security information for the object
Write Security	The user may modify the security information for the object

For most applications you create, you will only be concerned with specifying the user ID and password for the database to allow the user to perform work with the database. However, if you need to handle the other security functions, the capability is there.

Database Optimization

While the JET database engine is very good at providing you with access to the information in your databases, there are a number of things that you can do in your programs to make the most of JET's capabilities. Some of the optimization methods are part of the design of the database itself, while others are part of the design of your data access program.

Optimizing the Database Design

There are two key aspects of database design that can have a dramatic effect on the performance of your database application: *data normalization* and *indexes*. Data normalization in particular must be carefully considered in the initial design of the database, as a change in the database structure after data has been entered can be very difficult. Indexes, on the other hand, can be added or deleted after the initial design if required.

Data Normalization

Data normalization is concerned with reducing or eliminating redundancy in your data. This is important for several reasons. First, data redundancy wastes space in your database. For example, if you store a customer's name with each order that the customer makes, the name will be repeated in a number of records. A more efficient way to store the data is to link one table with the customer information to the orders table by a customer ID field. If you assume that the customer name fields are 50 bytes long and the customer ID field is 5 bytes long, you save 45 bytes of space for each order record.

Second, storing data in more than one location makes it more difficult to be sure that the data is current. Suppose that in an order entry system you stored the customer's phone number with each order. Then, if the customer's phone number changed, it would have to be changed in each of the order records. If the phone number were only stored in a customer record, it would only have to be changed in one place. An example of the normalized and unnormalized data is shown in figure 3.3.

There are times, however, when it may be necessary to violate the rules of data normalization for the sake of performance. For example, an attendance tracking system I recently built needed to maintain data about each date a person attended an event, but also needed quick access to the last date that a person attended any event. Data normalization requires that the member information be stored in one table and the attendance information be stored in another. However, this would require a search on the attendance table to determine the last attendance date for each person. Depending on the size of the tables, this could be a long search process. An easier way to handle the situation was to also store the last attendance date in the member record. Consequently, with a search of only one table, the user could tell who hadn't attended any events in the past month.

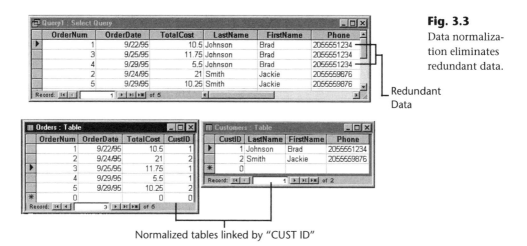

Fig. 3.3
Data normalization eliminates redundant data.

Normalized tables linked by "CUST ID"

Indexes

Indexes are basically specialized tables that contain pointers to the records in the actual data tables. These pointers are arranged in a specific order to make finding a particular record easier than in an unindexed table. An index can be on a single field or on a combination of fields in a table. Aside from the enhanced speed of locating a single record, an index can help speed queries. This is because the Rushmore™ technology used by the JET engine will use available indexes to optimize queries.

What this means for you in the design of your database is that you should create an index for a field that will be used extensively in the processing of queries. There is of course a downside to using too many indexes. Because each index must be updated as records are added, deleted, or modified, having a large number of indexes can cause the processing of records to become quite slow. In addition, a large number of indexes will increase the size of your database, making it less efficient.

Program Optimization

In addition to designing your database for the most efficient possible processing, there are a number of things that you can do within your program to optimize the processing and retrieval of data in a database. This section will list a few of these optimization methods.

First, if you need to find a specific record in a table, use the Seek method instead of the Find method. Because the Seek method requires an index on the field or fields being sought, this method will be faster at locating the record. The drawback is that the method can only be used on table-type recordsets. If you need a recordset that pulls data from multiple tables, the Find method is the only way to locate a specific record.

Another technique is to use an index to change the order of a table instead of using the Sort method. Since the index will typically already exist, this is much faster than the Sort method. However, like the use of the Seek method, an index can only be used on a table-type recordset.

When you are running a query to create a recordset, only include the fields you need instead of including all fields in the table. This creates a smaller recordset, which can be processed much faster. A similar technique is to use the Where clause of SQL statements to limit the number of records retrieved by the query. The smaller the recordset returned by the query, the faster subsequent actions on the recordset can be performed.

Finally, if you are adding or editing a number of records, use transaction processing to speed up the data access. Without transaction processing, the data is written to the disk each time a record is updated. This is obviously a slow process. If you place all the updates inside a transaction, changes and additions are written to the disk only when the transaction is committed. This will make a significant difference in the speed of your program. As an alternative, if your situation lends itself to the use of an action query to modify a group of records, this will be faster than processing each record in the group using program statements.

Summary

The JET database engine provides you with a powerful tool for creating database applications in Visual Basic. This chapter has identified a few of the features that can be used to create efficient and robust applications. I have also talked a little about optimization techniques to help you get the best performance from your applications. See Chapter 4, "Data Access Objects," and Chapter 5, "Database Management Using the ODBC API," for some details of other aspects of database programming in Visual Basic.

Chapter 4

Data Access Objects

by Michael McKelvy

Michael is the owner of McKelvy Software Systems, a Birmingham, Alabama-based consulting firm. Michael specializes in the development of database systems and engineering applications. He can be reached by Fax at (205) 980-9816; and on CompuServe at 71477,3513.

Many of the programs you will be developing in the future will need to be able to store and manage large amounts of information. This type of programming requires the use of a database to provide efficient handling of the data. In Chapter 3, "JET 3.0 Database Engine," I described how the JET engine provided with Visual Basic 4 gives you a robust database system with which to work. In this chapter, I will describe some of the methods used to access and control the information in a JET database.

How Do I Get to My Data?

Visual Basic 4 provides the programmer with two ways to work with database files: the data control (with its associated bound controls) and the data access objects. (*Note:* The data control is the only means available if you are using the Standard Edition of Visual Basic 4.) Each of these means of accessing databases has its advantages. Fortunately, in Visual Basic 4 (unlike in VB3), the data control and the data access objects are not mutually exclusive. They can be used together to take advantage of the strengths of each.

The data access objects (DAOs) provide you, the programmer, with greater control over database functions than the data control. The DAOs also provide you with access to more features than the data control—such as the creation of databases, the modification of the database structure, and the maintenance of security information. For this reason, this chapter will focus on the use of the DAOs. We will not totally ignore the data control, as the chapter will also include a section that describes how to use the two together.

The concept of the data access objects was introduced in Chapter 3, "JET 3.0 Database Engine." Chapter 3 gave you a brief definition of what some of the database objects were. In this chapter, we will cover how the objects are used to build and access a database. We will also concentrate on the differences between how the data access objects are used in Visual Basic 4 and how they were used in Visual Basic 3.

Building a Database

When you want to build a new database for use with Visual Basic 4, you can create it in three ways:

- Using the Data Access Objects
- Using the Data Manager Application
- Using Microsoft Access

Because this chapter is about the DAOs, that way is the only one covered here, but you should know that the other approaches are available to you. The first thing you probably want to know is why you should use the DAOs when the other approaches are available to you. The only advantage to using the DAOs is that they provide the only method of creating databases from within your program. This capability is useful to you for two reasons. First, if you are creating a commercial application for distribution, you can eliminate the need to include the database files on your distribution disks if the program can create them.

Second, and more important, giving your users the ability to create the database files from the program allows them to use databases for series of information. For example, a user could create a separate database for sales information for each year. As another example, an application I am working on uses a database to store information about quality assurance audits of product vendors. This information includes audit checklists, checklist results, and contact information for the audit. The information for each audit needs to be contained in a separate file. Therefore, the program has code to create new database files.

Creating the Database Itself

The first step in creating a database is to create the file itself. This file, when initially created, contains no data, and no definitions of other objects.

The file-creation process simply sets up the physical structure of the file and writes it to the disk. The file creation also serves to set up the database object that is used in the creation of tables, queries, and relations.

If you used the DAOs in Visual Basic 3, you are aware that you used the `CreateDatabase` function to initially create a database. In Visual Basic 4, that has changed. Creating a database is now a method of the `Workspace` object. The syntax of the old function and the syntax for the new method are very similar, as shown in listing 4.1.

Listing 4.1 4LIST01.TXT—The `CreateDatabase` Method

```
'Full syntax of CreateDatabase method
'*********************************
Dim NewDb As Database, NewWs As Workspace
Set NewWs = DBEngine.Workspaces(0)
dbVers = dbVersion25
Set NewDb = NewWs.CreateDatabase("A:\TRITON.MDB",dbLangGeneral,dbVers)
'***********************************************
'Syntax of CreateDatabase function (Old method)
'***********************************************
Dim NewDb As Database
dbVers = dbVersion25
Set NewDb = CreateDatabase("A:\TRITON.MDB",dbLangGeneral,dbVers)
```

The database object name defined in the code can be any valid variable name. Also, in creating the database, you can use a literal name (as shown in the listing), or you can use a string variable to hold the name of the database to be created. Using a variable would allow the user the flexibility of specifying a database name using a text box or common dialog. Using a variable also allows you to create multiple databases with the same structure.

The constant `dbLangGeneral` is a required argument of the `CreateDatabase` method. It specifies the language and code page information for the database. This constant specifies English for the language. Other constants may be used for other languages. These constants are defined in the online help.

The other argument of the `CreateDatabase` method, represented by the variable `dbVers` in the code, is optional. This argument specifies the version of the JET engine to use for the database and whether the database is encrypted. Though the argument is optional, specifying a value is quite important if you will be working with multiple platforms. As was discussed in Chapter 3, Visual Basic 4 comes with two versions of the JET engine, 2.5 and 3.0. If you are using JET 3.0 but want to share data with older applications, you will need to create a version 2.5 database. You do this by setting the value of the `dbVers` argument to the constant dbVersion25. If you do not include the constant, the CreateDatabase method will create a JET 3.0 database if you are working with a 32-bit platform, and a JET 2.5 database on a 16-bit platform.

Note

If you are using the JET 2.5 engine, you cannot create a JET 3.0 database. If you include the dbVersion30 constant, it will be ignored and a JET 2.5 database will be created anyway. No error will occur.

Adding Tables

After you create the database, all you have is a file on a disk. To do anything with the database, you must also create tables in the database. As you recall, tables contain records of related information stored in fields. Defining the fields is part of the creation process for building a table. In addition to the fields, you may also want to create indexes for your tables.

To add a table to your database, you will need to follow these steps:

1. Create the TableDef object to name the table.

2. Set any optional properties for the table.

3. Define the fields for the table.

4. Add the fields to the TableDef object.

5. Add the TableDef to the database.

Each of these five steps will be covered in detail in the following sections.

Defining the TableDef Object

The TableDef object allows you to set the properties for the new table. The following lines of code show how to create a TableDef object and give your table a name:

```
Dim NewTbl As TableDef
Set NewTbl = NewDb.CreateTableDef("Members")
```

If you are working with an Access database, the Name property is the only required property for the TableDef object. If you are working with other types of databases, you may need to set values for the Attributes, Connect, and SourceTableName properties. These properties are set as part of the CreateTableDef method. You will find the complete syntax for the method in the Visual Basic help files.

In Chapter 3, we mentioned that table-level validation could be set for a JET database. Set up table-level validation, validation rules, and validation error messages for a table by setting the values of the appropriate properties (as shown in the following). These statements must follow the `CreateTableDef` method. The table-level validation checks each record as it is modified or added to ensure that it meets the criteria.

```
NewTbl.ValidationRule = "Retail > Wholesale"
NewTbl.ValidationText = "Retail price must exceed wholesale price."
```

Defining the Fields

After the `TableDef` object is defined for the new table, you must define the field objects for the table. A table can contain any number of fields. Each field must be given a name, and the type of data to be stored in the field must be defined. Then, depending on the type of field, you may be required to define other properties. You may also want to set some optional properties, such as field-level validation rules or default values.

For text fields, you must set the `Size` property to specify how long a string the field can contain. The valid entries for the `Size` property of the text field are 1 to 255. If you want to allow longer strings, set the field type to `Memo`.

If you want to create a counter field to give each record a unique ID, you will need to do two things. First, you must set the field type as `Long`. Then you specify the auto-increment setting of the `Attribute` property. This tells the database to increment the value of the field each time a new record is added.

Listing 4.2 shows how the field objects are created and the field properties set for the Retail Items table created previously. The field name, type, and size can be specified as optional arguments of the `CreateField` method. You can also use the `CreateField` method without any arguments and then set all the field properties with assignment statements. Both of these methods are shown in listing 4.2. Any other properties must be set using an assignment statement. As an example of an assignment statement, the listing sets a validation rule for the wholesale price field.

Listing 4.2   4LIST02.TXT—Creating Field Objects and Setting Properties

```
Dim F5 As Field, F6 As Field, F7 As Field, F8 As Field
    Dim F9 As Field, F10 As Field
'Create field objects
    Set F1 = NewTbl.CreateField("MemberNum", dbLong)
    F1.Attributes = dbAutoIncrField
    Set f2 = NewTbl.CreateField("Lastname", dbText, 25)
```

(continues)

> **Listing 4.2   Continued**
>
> ```
>         Set f3 = NewTbl.CreateField("Firstname", dbText, 25)
>         Set F4 = NewTbl.CreateField()
>         F4.Name = "Address"
>         F4.Type = dbText
>         F4.Size = 50
>         Set F5 = NewTbl.CreateField("City", dbText, 30)
>         Set F6 = NewTbl.CreateField("State", dbText, 2)
>         Set F7 = NewTbl.CreateField("Zip", dbText, 5)
>         Set F8 = NewTbl.CreateField("HomePhone", dbText, 10)
>         Set F9 = NewTbl.CreateField("Member", dbBoolean)
> ```

After defining the characteristics of the fields, you need to add the fields to the TableDef object. You do this by using the Append method of the object, as shown in listing 4.3.

> **Listing 4.3   4LIST03.TXT—Adding Fields to the Table Definition**
>
> ```
>     NewTbl.Fields.Append F1
>     NewTbl.Fields.Append F2
>     NewTbl.Fields.Append F3
>     NewTbl.Fields.Append F4
>     NewTbl.Fields.Append F5
>     NewTbl.Fields.Append F6
>     NewTbl.Fields.Append F7
>     NewTbl.Fields.Append F8
>     NewTbl.Fields.Append F9
> ```

Defining the Indexes

For many of your tables, you will also want to define at least one index. *Indexes* set the presentation order of your tables and are used to speed searches and queries. Defining an index with Visual Basic 4 is quite different from the methodology used in Visual Basic 3. The method of creating indexes in Visual Basic 4 is very closely related to the creation of the table. For each index, you must assign a name, define the fields to be included in the index, and determine whether the index is a primary index and whether duplicate values are allowed in the fields that comprise the index key.

To create an index, follow these six steps:

1. Use the CreateIndex method of the TableDef object to create the Index object.

2. Set any optional properties of the index (such as primary or unique).

3. Use the `CreateField` method of the `Index` object to create the field objects.

4. Set any optional properties of the field objects.

5. Append the fields to the `Index` object.

6. Append the index to the `TableDef` object.

For most of your tables, you will want to create a *primary index*. This index is the one typically used to relate the table to other tables in the database. The key fields in a primary index must be unique identifiers for each record. To make an index primary, set the `Primary` property of the index object to `True`. In addition to making sure that the value of the index key for each record is unique, a primary index also ensures that no null values exist for the indexed field.

Sometimes you may need an index, other than the primary index, whose key fields are unique. For this type of index, you would set the `Unique` property of the index to `True`. As an example, you might use this type of index to make sure that you enter a unique Social Security number for each employee in a table.

As you define the fields for the index, you will need to identify the field name for each indexed field. In addition, you may need to set the `Attributes` property of the field object. This property is used to determine whether the sort order of the field is ascending (from A to Z) or descending (from Z to A). The default value is ascending. If you want to sort the field in descending order, set the `Attributes` property to the value of the constant `dbDescending`.

In creating an index, you are not limited to creating an index on a single field. To create a multiple-field index, you just set up multiple field objects with the `CreateField` method. Remember that the order of the fields can have a dramatic impact on the order of your records. The order of the fields in an index is determined by the order in which the fields are appended to the index.

As was the case with the `TableDef`, after you have defined the fields of the index, you add the field objects to the index object using the `Append` method. After you have appended all the fields for your index, you then add the index to the `TableDef` object using its `Append` method. Listing 4.4 demonstrates how to create an index using the data access objects.

Listing 4.4   4LIST04.TXT—Creating Index Objects, Assigning Properties, and Adding Indexes to the Table

```
Dim NewTbl As TableDef, Idx1 As Index, Fld1 As Field
    Dim idx2 As Index, f2 As Field, f3 As Field
    'Set up workspace and database
    Set OldWs = DBEngine.Workspaces(0)
    Set OldDb = OldWs.OpenDatabase(DataName)
    'Create tabledef object
    Set NewTbl = OldDb.TableDefs("Members")
    Set Idx1 = NewTbl.CreateIndex("PrimaryKey")
    Idx1.Primary = True
    Set Fld1 = Idx1.CreateField("MemberNum")
    Idx1.Fields.Append Fld1
    NewTbl.Indexes.Append Idx1
    Set idx2 = NewTbl.CreateIndex("Name")
    Set f2 = idx2.CreateField("LastName")
    Set f3 = idx2.CreateField("FirstName")
    idx2.Fields.Append f2
    idx2.Fields.Append f3
    NewTbl.Indexes.Append idx2
```

Adding the Table to the Database

The final step in creating a database is adding the table or tables to the database. Use the Append method of the database object to accomplish this, as shown in the following code. Note: If the table you are trying to create already exists in the database, an error will occur.

```
NewDb.TableDefs.Append NewTbl
```

Other Structures in the Database

You will probably use two other main objects in a database on a regular basis. These objects are the Relation object and the QueryDef object. These objects are created in your database in a manner similar to that which was used for the TableDef object.

Creating a Relation

A *relation* is what tells the database how the information in two tables is linked. In order to have a relation between two tables, the tables must share a common field such as the ItemID in the inventory example. To create a relation, you must follow these steps:

1. Define a variable for the Relation object using the Dim statement.

2. Create the Relation object using the CreateRelation method of the database object.

3. Define the names of the primary and foreign tables of the relation using the `Table` and `ForeignTable` properties (respectively) of the `Relation` object.

4. Define the key field in the primary table for the relation. Then set the `ForeignName` property of the field to the key field in the foreign table.

5. Define whether referential integrity will be enforced. If it is not to be enforced, you will need to set the `Attributes` property of the relation to the constant `dbRelationDontEnforce`.

6. If referential integrity is enforced, you will need to indicate whether cascading updates and deletions will be supported. You do this by setting the `Attributes` property of the `Relation` object to either `dbRelationUpdateCascade` or `dbRelationDeleteCascade` or the sum of both constants.

7. Append the field to the `Relation` object; then append the `Relation` to the database object.

Listing 4.5 shows how a relation is created by using the data access objects.

Listing 4.5   4LIST05.TXT—Creating a Relation by Using DAOs

```
Dim NewRel As Relation, F1 As Field
    'Set up workspace and database
    Set OldWs = DBEngine.Workspaces(0)
    Set OldDb = OldWs.OpenDatabase(DataName)
    'Create relation object
    Set NewRel = OldDb.CreateRelation("MemberAttend")
    NewRel.Table = "Members"
    NewRel.ForeignTable = "Attendance"
    NewRel.Attributes = dbRelationUpdateCascade + _
      dbRelationDeleteCascade
    Set F1 = NewRel.CreateField("Membernum")
    F1.ForeignName = "Membernum"
    NewRel.Fields.Append F1
    OldDb.Relations.Append NewRel
    OldDb.Close
```

Creating a Query

A *query* is an SQL statement that defines which records are to be retrieved in a recordset. A query may also define an action that is to be performed on a group of records. Queries may be set up in your program and run using the `Execute` method of the database object. However, you can also create a query and store it in the database to be called from your program. The advantage of this approach is that the query will be processed faster as a stored procedure than as a query in a program that must be interpreted prior to being run.

To store a query in your database, you must define it using the QueryDef object. Creating a query in this manner requires two steps. First, you must define a QueryDef object using the Dim statement. Then you use the CreateQueryDef method of the database to define the name and the SQL text of the query. This method automatically stores the query in the database; you don't have to perform any other steps. The following code shows how a query can be created:

```
Dim NewQry As QueryDef
'Create querydef
SQLSel = "Select LastName, FirstName From Members"
Set NewQry = OldDb.CreateQueryDef("NamesOnly", SQLSel)
```

Closing the Database

After you have finished creating your database, or after you have finished using it, you will need to close the database. If you have any recordsets or queries open, you will also need to close them prior to closing the database. The database, recordset, query, and several other data access objects all have a Close method, which accomplishes this purpose. To use the Close method on any of the objects, simply specify the object name and the Close method. The following line of code illustrates this for the database object created at the beginning of this section:

```
OldDb.Close
```

Getting to Your Data

The data access objects are also used to open existing databases and let you get the information from them. In fact, this is the most common use of the DAOs.

The first step in gaining access to the information in a database is to open the database itself. Like the CreateDatabase method described earlier, OpenDatabase is now a method of the Workspace object instead of a function as was the case in Visual Basic 3. However, little has changed about the syntax of the statement. This is illustrated in listing 4.6, which shows the old function and the new method. As with the CreateDatabase method, you should use the OpenDatabase method for all your programming. The old function is still supported, but only for compatibility with existing code.

Listing 4.6   4LIST06.TXT—Using the `OpenDatabase` **Method to Get to the Information in the Database**

```
'*******************************************
'Using the OpenDatabase function (Old way)
'*******************************************
Dim OldDb As Database
Set OldDb = OldWs.OpenDatabase("A:\CHRCHTRK.MDB",False,False)
'*******************************************
'Using the OpenDatabase method (New way)
'*******************************************
Dim OldDb As Database, OldWs As Workspace
Set OldWs = DBEngine.Workspaces(0)
Set OldDb = OldWs.OpenDatabase("A:\CHRCHTRK.MDB",False,False)
```

As you can see from the listing, three arguments may be included in the `OpenDatabase` method. The first argument specifies the name of the database to be opened. It is the only required argument of the method. You can specify a name using either a literal string (enclosed in double quotation marks) or a string variable. The second argument specifies whether the database will be opened for exclusive use (that is, no one else can access the database while you work with it). The value of the second argument must be either `True` or `False`. The third argument specifies whether the database is to be opened as a read-only database, meaning that your program can use the data but cannot modify it. Like the exclusive-use argument, the read-only argument must be either a `True` or `False` value.

The Types of Recordsets

After you have opened the database, you are only part of the way toward accessing your data. To read or use the data, you must also create a recordset that contains the information from the database with which you want to work.

The `Recordset` object, a new object in Visual Basic 4, takes the place of the `Table`, `Dynaset`, and `Snapshot` objects that were present in Visual Basic 3. When you use the `Recordset` object, you have the option of creating it as one of three types of recordsets. They are as follows:

- *Table-type.* Accesses the physical tables in a database that contains the actual data.

- *Dynaset-type.* A set of pointers that provide access to fields and records in one or more tables of a database.

- *Snapshot-type.* A read-only copy of data from one or more tables stored in memory.

Each type of recordset has advantages and drawbacks to its use as you will see.

Table-Type Recordsets

The table-type recordset directly accesses a single table in your database. This means that this recordset can take advantage of any indexes that are defined for the table, and can use the Seek method to find a particular record. Therefore, searches on a table-type recordset will be faster than on a dynaset- or snapshot-type recordset. Some of the advantages to using this type of recordset are as follows:

- You can use or create indexes to change the presentation order of the data in the table during program execution.

- You can perform rapid searches for an individual record using an appropriate index and a Seek command.

- Changes made to the table by other users or programs are immediately available. It is not necessary to "refresh" the table to gain access to these records.

The primary drawback to using a table-type recordset is that it can handle only one table at a time. This means that you cannot use a table-type recordset to retrieve related information from multiple tables. Also with a table-type recordset, you must work with the entire table. You cannot use an SQL statement or a filter to limit the number of records or the fields that are in the recordset.

Dynaset-Type Recordsets

A dynaset-type recordset (dynaset) allows you to work with selected information from multiple tables. This means that you can specify only the fields you need to have included in the recordset. Although you can set up a dynaset to work with just a single table, it is more often used with a stored query or SQL statement to define the information to be included in the recordset. Not only does this capability allow you to specify the fields you want, but it also allows you to specify the presentation order of the records and to include only those records that meet a certain condition, such as "customers living in Florida."

Unlike a table that provides a direct link to the information in a database, a dynaset is actually a set of record pointers that indicates where the data is located in the database. These pointers are set up when the dynaset is created and are updated only for changes made by the current user. When your program makes changes to information in the dynaset, these changes are made in the tables from which the information was derived as well as in the dynaset itself. These changes include additions, edits, and deletions of records.

In addition to the advantages of being able to use multiple tables and being able to limit the fields and records retrieved, a dynaset also allows you to use the Find methods to locate records. The Find methods allow you to easily locate and process every record that meets the search condition. This is in contrast to the Seek method, which is capable of locating only the first record meeting a condition.

Of course, using a dynaset does have drawbacks. The most important of them is that a dynaset does not automatically reflect when records are added or deleted by other users. The dynaset must be explicitly refreshed or re-created to show the changes. This means that if you will be using dynasets in a multi-user environment, you will need to periodically refresh the recordset. The second disadvantage is that you cannot use an index directly on a dynaset. This means that you cannot quickly change the presentation order of a dynaset the way you can a table.

> ### Note
>
> Although indexes are not used directly with a dynaset, the Rushmore optimization technology used by the JET engine will use available indexes to speed up the processing of queries used to create a dynaset.

Snapshot-Type Recordsets

A snapshot-type recordset is very similar to a dynaset. The key difference is that a snapshot is a read-only "picture" of the data in the database at a certain point in time. This means that a snapshot cannot be updated by the user, nor will it automatically reflect changes to the data made by other users. A snapshot supports all the same methods as a dynaset, such as the Move and Find methods.

The key advantage to using a snapshot is speed. A snapshot is stored in your computer's memory. This makes access to the information in a snapshot very fast.

However, storing the data in memory also causes one of the key drawbacks to a snapshot. This drawback is that snapshots should typically be used only for small recordsets (that is, fewer than 200 records). This suggested limit is to avoid running into problems with memory limitations.

Creating a Recordset

To create any of the three types of recordsets in your program, you use the OpenRecordset method of the database object. To identify which type of recordset to create, you specify the appropriate constant as part of the method. These constants are dbOpenTable for a table-type recordset, dbOpenDynaset for a dynaset-type recordset, and dbOpenSnapshot for a snapshot-type recordset. The following code shows how the OpenRecordset method would be used to open a table in a database. The code also shows how you can create a dynaset that retrieves only the first and last names of a person in the Members table.

```
Dim OldWs As Workspace, OldDb As Database, OldTbl As Recordset
Dim OldDyn As Recordset
Set OldWs = DBEngine.Workspaces(0)
Set OldDb = OldWs.OpenDatabase("C:\CHRCHTRK.MDB")
Set OldTbl = OldDb.OpenRecordset("Members",dbOpenTable)
SQLSel = "Select LastName, FirstName From Members"
Set OldDyn = OldDb.OpenRecordset(SQLSel,dbOpenDynaset)
```

The type information for the OpenRecordset method is optional. If you omit the type, Visual Basic will try to create a table-type recordset. However, if the source is something other than a table name (such as a query name or SQL statement), Visual Basic will create a dynaset-type recordset.

In addition to being able to specify the type of recordset to create, the OpenRecordset method has one additional optional parameter. This parameter follows the type parameter, and can be used to specify restrictions on the recordset. These restrictions can set the recordset so that you can only read the information, or so you can modify the information but other users can only read the data. A list of all the options can be found in the online help for Visual Basic.

Accessing the Actual Data

After you open the database and create a recordset, you have access to the information in the database. However, you still need a way to reference the information so that you can display and edit it. To reference any given piece of information in a recordset, you simply specify the name of the field you want. You can do this by specifying the field name within parentheses as shown in the following line of code, which assigns the contents of a field to a variable:

```
famname = OldTbl("LastName")
```

An equivalent method of referencing a field is to use the bang operator (!) between the recordset object name and the field name. The following line of code is equal to the one just shown:

```
famname = OldTbl!LastName
```

Caution

If you use the bang operator, you must use a special form when accessing fields with a space in the name. In this case, the field name must be enclosed in square brackets as shown in this line:

```
itmdsc = ItmTbl![Item Description]
```

To give you an idea how all this would be used in your program, listing 4.7 shows how a membership tracking database would be opened and the information for the first member would be displayed. (*Note:* A couple of functions are used to handle assigning dates to a masked edit control.) The results of this code are shown in figure 4.1.

Listing 4.7   4LIST07.TXT—Retrieving Information from a Database

```
Dim OldWs As Workspace, OldDb As Database, OldTbl As Recordset
Set OldDb = OldWs.OpenDatabase("C:\CHRCHTRK.MDB")
Set TblMember = OldDb.OpenRecordset("Members",dbOpenTable)
'Displays the information for the current member
Dim bkdate As Double, lstid As Long, ShowStr As String
'Place information in text boxes
OldTbl.MoveFirst
txtMember(0).Text = TblMember("LastName")
txtMember(1).Text = TblMember("FirstName")
txtMember(2).Text = TblMember("Address")
txtMember(3).Text = TblMember("City")
txtMember(4).Text = TblMember("State")
txtMember(5).Text = TblMember("Zip")
If TblMember("Member") Then
    chkClient.Value = 1
Else
    chkClient.Value = 0
End If
```

Fig. 4.1
A membership
application
created in Visual
Basic.

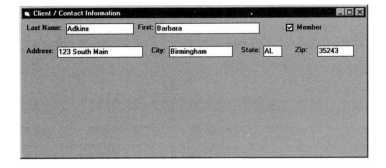

Moving Through a Recordset

You've now seen how to open a database and how to create a recordset.
You have also seen how the information from the fields in a recordset can be
accessed to display the information. However, in order to be useful, the database engine needs to allow you to move to different records in the recordset
and to find specific records.

The JET database engine does this by providing the recordset object with a
series of Move methods for accessing different records. JET also provides the
recordset object with methods to locate specific records. These methods are
the Find methods for use with dynaset- and snapshot-type recordsets, and the
Seek method for use with table-type recordsets.

Move **Methods**

As you would expect, the recordset object contains methods that allow you to
move to the first or last record in the recordset, as well as the records immediately preceding or following the current record. These methods are as follow:

- MoveFirst. Moves the record pointer from the current record to the first
  record in the opened recordset.

- MoveNext. Moves the record pointer from the current record to the
  next record (the record following the current record) in the opened
  recordset. If there is no "next record" (that is, if you are already at the
  last record), the end-of-file (EOF) flag will be set.

- MovePrevious. Moves the record pointer from the current record to
  the preceding record in the opened recordset. If there is no "previous
  record" (that is, if you are at the first record), the beginning-of-file (BOF)
  flag will be set.

- `MoveLast`. Moves the record pointer from the current record to the last record in the opened recordset.

In addition to these methods, the recordset object contains a method and two properties that allow you to move forward or backward a specified number of records, and to move to a specific position in the recordset. These other methods are as follow:

- `Move` *n*. This method moves the record pointer from the current record *n* records down (if *n* is positive) or up (if *n* is negative) in the opened recordset. If the move would place the record pointer beyond the end of the recordset (either `BOF` or `EOF`), an error will occur.

- `PercentPosition`. This property specifies the approximate position in a recordset where a record is located. By setting this property to a value between 0 and 100, you will cause the pointer to move to the record closest to that location.

- `AbsolutePosition`. This property allows you to tell the recordset to move to a specific record. The value of the property can range from 0 for the first record in the recordset to 1 less than the number of records. Setting a value greater than the number of records in the recordset will cause an error. *Note:* The `AbsolutePosition` property is only valid for dynaset- and snapshot-type recordsets.

For many programs, you would assign code to command buttons to use these methods and properties to move through a recordset. Figure 4.2 shows a data-entry form that allows you to use each of the methods and properties to move to a different record. The code for each of the command buttons is presented in listing 4.8. After each of the `Move` methods is invoked, a routine, `ShowMember`, is called to display the new data.

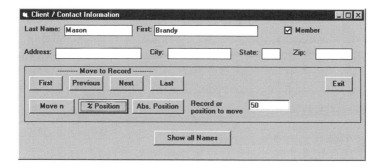

Fig. 4.2
Command buttons allow you to implement the `Move` methods in a data-entry screen.

Listing 4.8   4LIST08.TXT—Code for the Command Buttons Moves You Through a Recordset

```
'Move to first record
TblMember.MoveFirst
Call ShowMember
'Move to previous record
TblMember.MovePrevious
If TblMember.BOF Then TblMember.MoveFirst
Call ShowMember
'Move to next record
TblMember.MoveNext
If TblMember.EOF Then TblMember.MoveLast
Call ShowMember
'Move to last record
TblMember.MoveLast
Call ShowMember
'Move the number of records specified in the text box
rcmov = Val(txtMove.Text)
TblMember.Move rcmov
Call ShowMember
'Move to the percent position specified in the text box
rcmov = Val(txtMove.Text)
If rcmov > 100 Then rcmov = 100
If rcmov < 0 Then rcmov = 0
TblMember.PercentPosition = rcmov
Call ShowMember
'Move to the absolute position specified in the text box
rcabs = Val(txtMove.Text)
If rcabs > TblMember.RecordCount Then rcabs = TblMember.RecordCount
If rcabs < 0 Then rcabs = 0
TblMember.AbsolutePosition = rcabs
Call ShowMember
```

Each of the Move methods and the PercentPosition property can be used with any type of recordset. The AbsolutePosition property cannot be used with table-type recordsets.

Finding a Record

As was stated earlier, the method you use to find a record in a recordset depends on the type of recordset with which you are working. If you are using a dynaset-type or snapshot-type recordset, you will need to use the Find methods to locate a specific record. If you are using a table-type recordset, you will need to use the Seek method to locate the record.

Using the Find Methods

If you are working with dynasets or snapshots, you will use the Find methods to locate specific records in the recordset. The Find methods use a statement such as `"FirstName = 'Mike'"` as the search condition for locating records. These statements are the same as the `Where` clause in an SQL statement, except without the `Where` keyword. You can use four `Find` methods with dynasets and snapshots:

- `FindFirst`. Starting at the top of the database, finds the first record in the recordset with the specified criteria.

- `FindNext`. Starting at the current location in the recordset, finds the next record down with the specified criteria.

- `FindPrevious`. Starting at the current location in the recordset, finds the next record up with the specified criteria.

- `FindLast`. Starting at the bottom of the recordset, finds the last record in the database with the specified criteria.

To determine whether the `Find` method succeeded, you will need to check the `NoMatch` property of the recordset. If `NoMatch` is `True`, then the `Find` method failed to locate a record that matched the search criteria. If the `NoMatch` property is `False`, the search was successful.

Using the `Seek` Method

If you want the absolute fastest way to locate a given record, you will want to use the `Seek` method. However, the `Seek` method has several limitations on its use. In particular, `Seek` can be used only on a table-type recordset; it cannot be used with a dynaset or snapshot. Also, the `Seek` can be used only with an index active, and the search fields of the `Seek` method must match the index fields of the active index. Finally, the `Seek` method will find only the first record that matches the search criteria. You cannot use the `Seek` method to find additional matching records.

To use the `Seek` method, you specify the recordset you are searching, the `Seek` method, the comparison operator to use in the search, and the values of the key fields to be searched. The basic syntax of the `Seek` method is

```
recobject.Seek comparison, fieldlist
```

In this syntax, `recobject` represents the name of the recordset to be searched. The comparison operator can be `<`, `<=`, `=`, `>=`, `>`, or `<>`. The comparison operator must be enclosed in quotation marks. `Fieldlist` represents the list of key values being compared to the fields in the index. These fields must be of the same data type as the fields in the controlling index. Although you are not required to include the same number of key values as there are fields in the index, you *do* have to include a key value for each field you want to search. The following statement shows an example of the Seek method:

```
OldTbl.Seek "=","McKelvy","Mike"
```

This operation assumes that the table has an active index with the LastName and FirstName fields as part of the index.

Manipulating Records

You've seen how to set up your database, how to move from one record to another, and even how to find a specific record. But to be truly useful, your database program will usually need to be able to add, change, and delete records. Fortunately, the recordset object has methods that can handle all these functions. In the data-entry form shown in figure 4.2, we have now added command buttons to add a new record, edit the existing record, or delete the record. These changes are shown in figure 4.3. When either Add or Edit is selected, the screen is set up for data entry/modification. At this point, the command buttons for Save Changes and Discard Changes are shown (see fig. 4.4). The Save Changes button is where the code for adding or editing a record is actually run.

Fig. 4.3

Data-entry form with Add, Edit, and Delete buttons added.

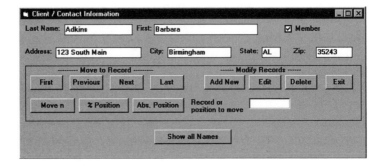

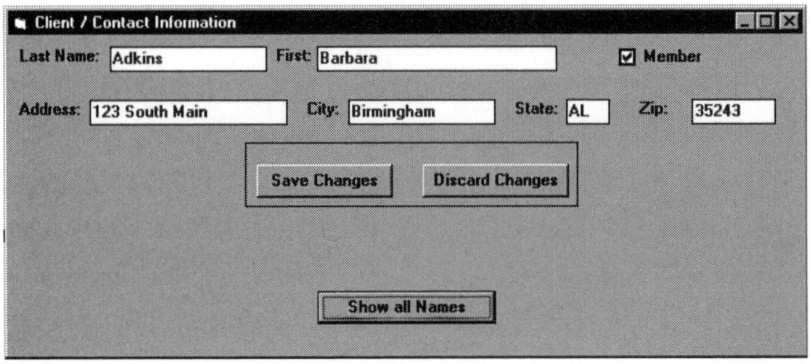

Fig. 4.4

The Save button runs the AddNew or Edit code.

Adding a New Record

Adding a record to a recordset, and to the database, requires that you perform three steps:

1. Use the `AddNew` method to set up a blank record.

2. Assign values to the fields of the record.

3. Use the `Update` method to write the new record to the database.

The `AddNew` method tells the database engine that you will be adding a record to the database. However, `AddNew` only sets up a space in the data buffer for you to assign information to the fields. It is the `Update` method that takes the information from the buffer and writes it to the database. If you do not run the `Update` method, your changes will be lost when you move to another record or run the `AddNew` method again. Listing 4.9 shows how the process of adding a record works.

Listing 4.9   4LIST09.TXT—Using `AddNew` and `Update` to Add a Record to the Recordset

```
'********************************
'Use AddNew to set up a new record
'********************************
TblMember.AddNew
'*********************************************
'Get information in text boxes and place the
information in the recordset fields
'*********************************************
TblMember("LastName") = txtMember(0).Text
TblMember("FirstName") = txtMember(1).Text
TblMember("Address") = txtMember(2).Text
TblMember("City") = txtMember(3).Text
TblMember("State") = Left(txtMember(4).Text, 2)
TblMember("Zip") = Left(txtMember(5).Text, 5)
'*************************************************************
'Use the Update method to add the new record to the recordset
'*************************************************************
TblMember.Update
```

Editing Records

The `Edit` method is the complement of the `AddNew` method. The `Edit` method allows you to make changes to existing records. Like the `AddNew` method, the `Edit` method does not make changes directly to the database. Instead, the `Edit` method copies the information from the current record to the data buffer where you can make changes. To write the changes to the database requires the use of the Update method. Therefore, the steps for using the Edit method are similar to the ones used for the AddNew method:

1. Use the Edit method to copy the information to the data buffer so changes can be made.

2. Assign new values to the fields of the record.

3. Use the Update method to write the record's changes to the database.

As you can see in listing 4.10, the code to edit a record is very similar to the code to add a new record.

Listing 4.10   4LIST10.TXT—Using Edit and Update to Change the Data in a Record

```
'****************************
'Use Edit to access the record
'****************************
TblMember.Edit
'**********************************************
'Get information in text boxes and place the
information in the recordset fields
'**********************************************
TblMember("LastName") = txtMember(0).Text
TblMember("FirstName") = txtMember(1).Text
TblMember("Address") = txtMember(2).Text
TblMember("City") = txtMember(3).Text
TblMember("State") = Left(txtMember(4).Text, 2)
TblMember("Zip") = Left(txtMember(5).Text, 5)
'**************************************************************
'Use the Update method to add the new record to the recordset
'**************************************************************
TblMember.Update
```

Deleting Records

One last function that most programs need to perform is to remove records from the database. This is done with the Delete method. When the Delete method is called, it will remove the current record from the database. There is no confirmation of the deletion. The following lines of code show how the Delete method is used in the membership sample program:

```
'Delete the current record
msgtxt = "Are you sure you want to delete this record?"
retval = MsgBox(msgtxt, 308, "Deletion Confirmation")
If retval = 6 Then
    TblMember.Delete
```

```
    If Not TblMember.EOF Then
        TblMember.MoveNext
    Else
        TblMember.MoveLast
    End If
    Call ShowMember
End If
```

Caution

Once you delete a record, it is gone. You can recover the record only if you issued a `BeginTrans` command before you deleted the record, in which case you can `RollBack` the transaction. Otherwise, the only way to get the information back into the database is to re-create the record with the AddNew method. Also, if you have referential integrity enforced and cascading deletions turned on, deleting a single record can cause the deletion of many other records in other tables.

Combining DAOs with the Data Control

As was stated at the beginning' of this chapter, you can use the data access objects and the data control together in a program. In Visual Basic 4, you can create a recordset using the data access objects and then assign this recordset to a data control. You can also assign the recordset created by a data control to a recordset object. The ability to do this gives you even greater flexibility in your database programming. Listing 4.11 shows how a names list is created with the data access objects and then is assigned to a data control to allow the list to be displayed in a data-bound grid. The results of this listing are shown in figure 4.5.

Listing 4.11   4LIST11.TXT—A Recordset Can Be Assigned to a Data Control

```
'Create the recordset
SQLSel = "Select LastName, FirstName From Members "
SQLSel = SQLSel & "Where Member Order By LastName, FirstName"
Set datRec = OldDb.OpenRecordset(SQLSel, dbOpenDynaset)
'Assign the recordset to the data control
Set datNames.Recordset = datRec
```

Fig. 4.5

A data-bound grid shows the results of the recordset.

Summary

This chapter has given you a look at some of the highlights of using the data access objects. This information should start you on your way to developing database applications using Visual Basic 4.

Chapter 5

Database Management Using the ODBC API

by S. Rama Ramachandran

Rama is a senior consultant with TechWorks International, a Westport, Connecticut-based Microsoft Solution Provider Partner. He specializes in the design and development of custom, GUI-based, stand-alone, network, and client/server database systems. Rama develops database systems in Visual Basic, MS Access, Visual FoxPro, and PowerBuilder. He has written a number of articles for the Visual Basic Programmer's Journal, and has also coauthored Que Publishing's Visual Basic 4.0 Expert Solutions. *He can be reached by phone at (203) 221-1500; Fax, (203) 221-1330; and on CompuServe at 73313,3030.*

Visual Basic Programmers have always had a love-hate relationship with ODBC—Microsoft's Open Database Connectivity. They love the ease with which it allows them to connect to a variety of backends with minimal adjustment of application code. For example, I was able to use the same Visual Basic application with just a few parameter changes to connect to Sybase, SQL Server, or to an Oracle backend. And all this is transparent to my users who have no idea where the data on-screen is coming from. ODBC certainly has made life much easier for programmers who have to deal with database management. However, serious programmers have always hated ODBC because of its sluggish performance—ODBC used to be much slower than native drivers written for each of the above backends. With the arrival of ODBC 2.0, Visual Basic database programmers have been given a new lease on life. At press time, the latest version of ODBC available is 2.10.

In this chapter, you will learn the following:

- What's new with ODBC 2.10

- Step-by-step instructions to connect to and manage ODBC data sources in a typical ODBC API-based application

- How to develop an ODBC API-based SQL Query Builder to provide ad-hoc querying functionality to your users

- How to examine a database by using ODBC catalog functions to obtain a list of tables and their fields for user selection

- How to execute SQL statements and fetch their result sets

Note

Note that the focus of this chapter is not on explaining the ODBC API in detail—that would be the task of an entire book devoted to ODBC API programming. Instead, this chapter describes, by using a very practical example, how to use the ODBC API to manage your database programming tasks. The sample application chosen is one which will expose you to almost all the ODBC API elements, and can be easily incorporated into any VB4 application you are considering.

An ODBC Primer

This section provides a short introduction to ODBC, its emergence as a standard for database connectivity and management, and its architecture. If you are already familiar with the history and architecture of ODBC, you can skip ahead to the next section, "The Life Cycle of an ODBC Application."

The Emergence of ODBC

ODBC has been around since 1992 when the first ODBC SDK was introduced by Microsoft. However, the roots of ODBC go back to 1990, when the SQL Access Group (SAG) released a specification for a standard SQL-based API. SAG, which was made up of a consortium of hardware and software vendors, was determined to work toward resolving interoperability issues between the various database servers proliferating in the market (such as Sybase, Oracle, and DB2). Each of these database servers used its own proprietary interface for communicating with an application, and application developers were forced to rewrite code to match the database against which their applications were being used. Although all of these database servers used Structured Query Language (SQL) for database management, each had its own flavor of SQL as well as proprietary stored procedure structures to contend with. A common application programming interface (API) that could handle these different SQL flavors transparently would definitely be appreciated by the application programming community. The SAG, in 1990, released the specification called SAG CLI (Call Level Interface). This was a library of function calls that supported SQL statements. Microsoft adopted this SAG CLI and extended it further in the development of ODBC. All the SAG CLI functions became the Core API calls within ODBC, and Microsoft further added two sets of function calls, called Level 1 and Level 2, that allowed for extended functionality. You can read about these levels in the next section. ODBC, therefore, is a library of function calls that allow the application programmer to connect to, examine, manipulate, and manage databases through a common, shared API, without having to worry about the backend database server and its idiosyncrasies.

The ODBC Architecture

ODBC simplifies the task for application programmers to connect to and manipulate databases by acting as the middleware between the application (controlled by the application programmer) and the data source (the database server). ODBC itself comprises these three components (see fig. 5.1):

■ The ODBC interface

■ The ODBC driver manager

■ One or more ODBC drivers for one or more data sources.

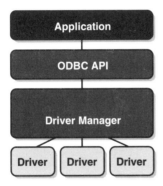

Fig. 5.1
The three components of the ODBC architecture.

The ODBC Interface

The ODBC interface is a collection of function calls, comprising the ODBC API. These function calls allow an application to connect to a database server, execute SQL statements, and retrieve the results. The SQL dialect used in these SQL statements conforms to the SAG CLI specifications. The ODBC interface comprises two types of function calls:

■ **ODBC Core API**—Consists of functions specified in the SAG CLI specifications. These are functions that allocate environment, connect to the data source, prepare and execute SQL statements, assign storage for result sets, and retrieve data from the result sets. Also included are commit/rollback functions and error information retrieval.

- **Extended ODBC API**—Comprises additional functionality over and above the core API function calls. These include function calls to connect to the DBMS by using driver-specific dialog boxes, retrieve catalog (or system table) information, retrieve part of a result set, etc. Also included are functions that allow the usage of scrollable cursors, browsing functions to inspect available data sources, and retrieve information regarding privileges, keys, and procedures. These Extended ODBC API are classified as Level 1 and Level 2 API.

The ODBC Driver Manager

The ODBC driver manager is a dynamic-link library (DLL) that loads the requested ODBC drivers and processes ODBC initializing calls. The ODBC driver manager relies on the ODBC.INI file or the registry entries to map a data source name to a specific ODBC driver in order and load it. The ODBC driver manager acts like a control room, coordinating different application ODBC requests among different backend ODBC data sources via their individual drivers.

ODBC Drivers

ODBC drivers are also dynamic-link libraries that implement backend-specific database function calls on a single data source. The driver contains the information required to translate the standardized ODBC function calls into calls that are understood by a particular backend data source. This obviates the need for the programmer to learn different proprietary function call nomenclature and, by using a single common ODBC API, allows the programmer to implement database management on a variety of different data sources. Obviously, for each data source that needs to be addressed, a driver built specifically for that data-source has to be obtained and used by the programmer.

Apart from the above, the ODBC architecture also includes the "data-sources," which are the physical database management systems, such as SQL Server, Sybase, Oracle, etc. ODBC, therefore, acts as a common standard interface between the programmer and these data sources.

What's New with ODBC Version 2.10

As of press time, the latest version of ODBC was 2.10. This release boasts a number of new features and enhancements. Chief among them are:

- **16- and 32-bit versions** with cross-platform support. ODBC SDK 2.10 is a 32-bit release supporting Windows NT 3.5 on the Intel, Alpha, and MIPS platforms. This results in improved performance visible in your applications. ODBC can now take advantage of the 32-bit environment, including multithreading and asynchronous background processing. You can use a single source code base to create ODBC API-based applications running on 16-bit or 32-bit platforms. Even the 16-bit application performs much better. The ODBC SDK provides complete 32-bit components. In addition, ODBC thunking layers allow 16-bit applications to use 32-bit drivers on Windows NT. Separate thunks also allow 32-bit applications to use existing 16-bit drivers on Win32s. (Note that ODBC SDK 2.10 has not been tested on Win32s. ODBC 2.0 should be used on Win32s.)

- **Enhanced Cursor Library** that now supports dynamic cursors including the ability to perform backward scrolling, absolute or relative positioning within a result set, and the ability to retrieve and update blocks of data. The ODBC SDK provides scrollable result set support to all Level 1 drivers. The cursor library is provided in 16-bit (ODBCCURS.DLL) and 32-bit (ODBCCR32.DLL) binary form.

- **The ODBC installer DLL** now supports high-level installation functions to allow simple and easy administration of ODBC drivers. A set-up program makes function calls to the installer DLL. The installer DLL reads information about the ODBC software to be installed from an installation file, ODBC.INF. The installer DLL records information about installed drivers and translators in the ODBCINST.INI file (or registry). The ODBCINST.INI file is used by the Driver Manager to determine which drivers and translators are currently installed.

- **New 16- and 32-bit ODBC drivers** for Microsoft Access, SQL Server, dBASE, Microsoft Excel, Microsoft FoxPro, Paradox, and Text, and a new 16-bit driver for Btrieve.

The Life Cycle of an ODBC Application

All applications that interact with a data source through the ODBC API have to follow the same basic steps. Core API calls remain the same for all applications. Based on the functionality desired, Level 1 and Level 2 API calls are used. This section describes the groundwork needed before calling ODBC API functions, and also the steps involved in an ODBC application.

ODBC API Fundamentals

Before you begin making ODBC API calls, make sure that you are familiar with making API calls from VB4. Since Visual Basic handles strings and memory variables differently than C or C++, you need to be especially careful or you will encounter the dreaded GPF. Keep the following information in mind when working with the ODBC API.

Porting Code Across 16- and 32-Bit Platforms

All ODBC function names begin with the prefix "SQL," thus making it easier to recognize them in your VB4 code. If you are planning to use your source code for both the 16-bit and 32-bit platforms, you need to include separate declarations for the 16- and 32-bit ODBC API calls, and their associated return values and constants. You can use the new VB4 pre-processor directives `#if..#endif` to segment your code to be compiled for different platforms. The sample application we develop in this chapter, ODBCQry, uses this technique to separate 16- and 32-bit declarations.

Passing String Buffers to the ODBC API

For most of the ODBC functions, you will be using variables that act as buffers, or data stores. These are either Input Buffers via which you will be passing data to the ODBC API, or they may be Output Buffers in which you will expect the ODBC API to return data. Visual Basic handles strings in a format that is different than C or C++ strings. C or C++ strings are long pointers to null terminated data. Visual Basic strings include a header that is used by VB internally, and therefore, is of a different type. As is the case with any API call from VB4, if you are expecting your variable to be returned by the API function call stuffed with data, you need to first initialize the variable and make it sufficiently large enough to hold the data expected. The easiest way of doing this is to use the BASIC *String$* function to stuff your variable with zeros before passing the variable to the API function.

```
Const SQL_MAX_LEN = 256
MyVariable = String$(SQL_MAX_LEN, 0)
```

Binding String Variables to the ODBC API Calls

Some functions, such as SQLBindCol, accept pointers to buffers that are later used by other ODBC functions, such as SQLFetch. In this case, your VB4 program must ensure that the variables are not moved in memory between calls. In order to do so, you will need to allocate memory for your variable, lock the memory space allocated and then copy the contents of the variable in and out of the allocated memory space. You can do this by using the Windows API functions GlobalAlloc, GlobalLock, and hmemcpy to allocate, lock, and retrieve data from memory into Visual Basic strings.

Say we want to bind column 1 of our SQL statement with variable MyVariable, declared as a string. Declare hMemVariable and lpVariable as long variables also. Then use the following code to bind your string variable to a SQL result set column and obtain its data value.

```
' ----- First, allocate memory and get a pointer
    hMemVariable = GlobalAlloc(GMEM_MOVEABLE, Len(MyColVariable))
    lpVariable = GlobalLock(hMemVariable)
    ' ----- Second, bind the column to the memory we allocated.
    iResult = SQLBindCol(ghStmt, 1, SQL_C_CHAR, ByVal lpVariable,_
                        29, lVariableLen)
    ' ----- Third, loop to fetch all records into memory
    iResult = SQLFetch(ghStmt)
    Do While iResult = SQL_SUCCESS Or iResult =
SQL_SUCCESS_WITH_INFO
        ' ----- copy the string from memory to a VB string
        Call hMemCpy(ByVal MyVariable, ByVal lpVariable, lVariableLen)
        ... Process the variable MyVariable
    Loop
    ... more processing if required
    ' ----- Finally, unlock and free memory allocated
    iResult = GlobalUnlock(hMemVariable)
    iResult = GlobalFree(hMemVariable)
```

Handles Used in ODBC Applications

When your program uses the ODBC API, it needs to keep track of three types of handles used consistently within the ODBC Architecture:

- **Environment Handle.** Identifies memory storage for global information. Your application needs to set this handle only once, right in the beginning, before it makes a call to connect to a data source. Use the SQLAllocEnv function to allocate this handle. Since this handle will be used throughout your application, it is better to make it a Public (Global in the VB 3 world) variable. And remember to deallocate it by using the SQLFreeEnv function

  ```
  Public hEnv as long
  if SQLAllocEnv(ghEnv) <> SQL_SUCCESS then
  ... your error management code here
  end if

  ... and at the end of your program

  Dim lResult as long
  lResult = SQLFreeEnv(ghEnv)
  ```

- **One or more Connection Handles.** These identify memory storage for information about a single connection. Your application needs to set this handle before making a request to connect to a data source. Each Connection Handle is linked to the Environment Handle. To do so, you can use the `SQLAllocConnect` function. And when the connection needs to be dropped, you can use the *SQLDisconnect* and *SQLFreeConnect* functions.

- ■ **One or more Statement Handles.** These identify memory storage for a single SQL statement. Your application needs to set them up before making a SQL request. Each Statement Handle is linked with a Connection Handle. You can use the *SQLAllocStmt* and the *SQLFreeStmt* functions to set up and drop these handles.

About ODBC API and Return Values

Most of the ODBC API returns data by using buffers. The return values for most ODBC API calls is an indication of success and failure of the function call. When a function fails, it can return one of a number of different error message indicators. Once a particular step returns a failure code, any subsequent calls to the ODBC API that rely on the successful completion of the prior one will cause an error. Therefore, it is very important, at every step of the way, to check to make sure that our function call was successful. The ODBC API provides a set of function calls to inquire of the ODBC drivers for what error took place, and this can be encapsulated into a custom error display routine. All ODBC function calls should therefore be enclosed within decision statements (an `IF` or a `Select Case`) to allow for suitable branching on success or failure of the call. For example, a call to the `SQLAllocEnv` that returns a successful or unsuccessful value could be made thus:

```
Dim iResult as integer
iResult = SQLAllocEnv(ghEnv)
```

However, in the preceding case, the programmer needs to check the value of `iResult` to ensure that the call returned a successful value. Instead, the above call can be made thus:

```
If SQLAllocEnv(ghEnv) <> SQL_SUCCESS then
... error management code here
End If
```

In our sample application that follows, we always cloak our ODBC API function call within an `IF` statement as shown above.

The Basic ODBC Application

The basic ODBC application that interacts with a data source needs to do the following:

1. Prepare the environment and any handles as needed. The application calls the `SQLAllocEnv` function to initialize the ODBC environment.

2. Connect to the data source by specifying the data source name and other information as needed. If the application knows the details of the data-source name as well as the user ID and password, it can call the SQLConnect function. If the application desires the user to choose from available data-sources and provide the user ID and password, then it can call the SQLDriverConnect function. The Driver Manager then loads the driver DLL and passes the SQLDriverConnect arguments to it.

3. Issue one or more SQL statements that may or may not return a result set. SQL Statements can be executed either by passing a SQL string by using the SQLExecDirect function, or, if the SQL query requires additional parameters and preparation, the application can use SQLPrepare to allocate parameter values, and then call SQLExecute to execute the query. If parameters are to be bound to variables in memory, the application can use the SQLBindParameter call to do so.

4. If a result set is returned, the application can inquire about the result set and fetch the results to perform a transaction—either an edit, delete, or insert. The application can use the SQLFetch function call to obtain one row at a time out of the result set. The application can also query the database for its internal structure, using the ODBC Catalog functions SQLTables, SQLColumns, SQLPrimaryKeys, and SQLForeignKeys.

5. End the transaction by issuing either a commit or a rollback. The application can call SQLTransact to do so.

6. End the connection. The application needs to close the statement handle by calling SQLFreeStmt and then terminate the connection to the driver by calling SQLDisconnect and SQLFreeConnect functions.

7. Free up the environment and any handles that were set up. The SQLFreeEnv frees up the environment handle and all resources associated with it.

Figure 5.2 provides a schematic diagram of the preceding steps.

If you are planning on developing a more sophisticated application, you may be interested in using the ODBC Catalog functions to query the database. In addition, you can also use functions that allow you to manage a query's result set and navigate forward and backward through it adding to or editing the result set. ODBC Catalog functions are the focus of our coming sections, in which we shall see how we can develop an ODBC API-based Query Builder.

Fig. 5.2
The basic steps of
a simple ODBC
application.

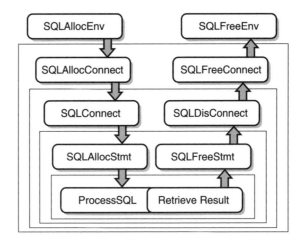

Developing an ODBC API-Based Query Builder

To demonstrate most of the functionality available in the ODBC API, we will be building an ODBC API-based SQL query builder in this chapter. This application, ODBCQry, allows the user to interactively create a SQL Select statement by doing the following:

1. Connect to an ODBC data source.

2. Build a SQL Select statement step-by-step.

The user can specify the following:

1. Which tables to include in the SQL query.

2. Which fields to include from each table.

3. Multiple tables can be selected, and join criteria specified.

4. Filtering information can also be supplied.

The Query builder proceeds to execute the SQL Select statement and, if successful, returns the result set to the user. Since this application is developed in Visual Basic 4.0 and uses only ODBC API calls for database communication, it will not only be an excellent way for you to see the ODBC API in action, but also, with a few modifications, will enable you to provide ad-hoc querying capabilities in your own Visual Basic 4.0 applications.

The Visual Basic Interface

Our Visual Basic 4.0 application, ODBCQry, presents an opening screen (see fig. 5.3) to the user and waits for the user to click connect.

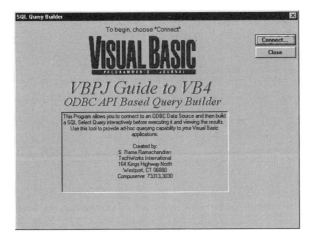

Fig. 5.3
ODBCQry main screen. The user chooses Connect to connect to a data source.

When the user chooses Connect, ODBCQry proceeds to call the SQLAllocConnect and SQLDriverConnect functions to connect to a data source selected by the user (see fig. 5.4).

Fig. 5.4
Driver-specific dialog box that prompts the user to select a data source.

Once a successful connection is achieved, ODBCQry proceeds to display all available tables within the database and presents the Query Builder screen allowing the user to build a SQL select query interactively (see fig. 5.5). The user can choose fields from available tables, and can specify join conditions, and search criteria.

Fig. 5.5
ODBCQry Query
Builder screen.

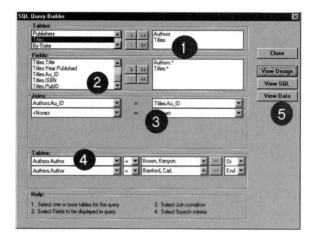

In the ODBCQry Query Builder Server, the user can choose the tables to be included in the query; fields from chosen tables are selected next; join criteria needs to be set (if multiple tables are selected), and optionally, search criteria can be set; the user can choose to see the query results, or the query SQL statement, or return to this design view by using these buttons. At this point, ODBCQry has been building up the SQL Select statement in the background. If users wish to view this SQL statement, they can choose View SQL and see what their SQL Select statement looks like (see fig. 5.6).

Fig. 5.6
ODBCQry SQL
Statement display.

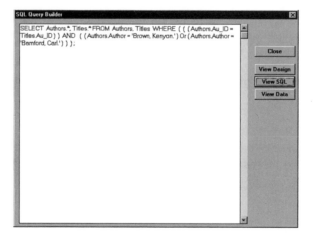

When users choose Run Query, ODBCQry proceeds to prepare and execute the SQL statement. On successful completion of this task, it then proceeds to bring in the result set and display it in a grid-like row and column format. OLE and Memo fields are truncated, and null fields are displayed as <null> (see fig. 5.7).

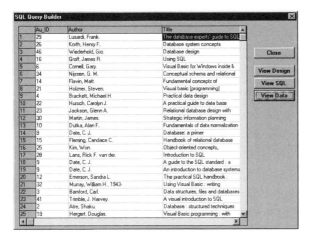

Fig. 5.7
ODBCQry SQL
Query Result set
screen.

Now that we know what ODBCQry does, let us take a look at how it accomplishes its task. The entire source code for ODBCQry is available in the CD-ROM disc accompanying this book. If you wish to see more code than is listed in this chapter, you can browse the code on the CD-ROM.

Setting Up for the Environment

The first step in using the ODBC API is to set up the environment for ODBC API operations. This needs to be done only once per session and, therefore, this is done in the form_load event of the ODBCQry main form. ODBCQry makes a call to the SQLAllocEnv function call to allocate an environment handle. The SQLAllocEnv function is declared as follows:

```
Declare Function SQLAllocEnv Lib "odbc32.dll"  _
     (phenv&) As Integer
```

The single long integer handle argument stores the environment handle allocated. Like most ODBC functions, it returns SQL_SUCCESS on successful completion. SQL_SUCCESS is declared as long integer zero.

Listing 5.1   6LIST01.TXT—ODBCQRY.FRM, the Form_Load event code

```
Private Sub Form_Load()
'------------------------------------------------------------------
' Form_Load
'    Author: S. Rama Ramachandran
'------------------------------------------------------------------
On Error GoTo Form_Load_Err

    ' -- Centers the form
    Me.Move ((Screen.Width - Me.Width) / 2), _
```

(continues)

```
Listing 5.1   Continued
                ((Screen.Height - Me.Height) / 2)


        ' ----- Assign values to global variables
        Quote = "'"      ' Single Quote Chr$(34)
        Endln = Chr$(13) & Chr$(10)

        ' ----- Step Zero: Initialize ODBC environment
        If SQLAllocEnv(ghEnv) <> SQL_SUCCESS Then
            ' -- Call Error Handler
            ShowError "Unable to allocate memory for ODBC operations."_
            & "You may not be able" _
            & "to use all functionality in this demo."
        End If


        ' ----- Set up the screen objects
        SetupControls

        ' ----- By default we are in design mode and not visible
        DisplayDesign False

    ' ----- Error Handlers -----------------------------------------
    Form_Load_Exit:
        Exit Sub

    Form_Load_Err:
        MsgBox Error$, 48, "Error in Routine: Form_Load"
        Resume Form_Load_Exit

    End Sub
```

In the preceding listing, the calls to the procedures SetupControls and DisplayDesign arrange the screen objects.

When the user chooses Connect, ODBCQry makes a call to the ConnectDatabase function, which provides the user with the ability to connect to a data source of choice. Before making the connection, the application has to set up the Connection handle and if the connection is successful, a Statement handle needs to be set up. All this is handled by the ConnectDatabase function, which returns true/false on completion of its task.

The declarations for SQLAllocConnect and SQLAllocStmt are given below:

```
Declare Function SQLAllocConnect Lib "odbc32.dll"  _
    (ByVal henv&, phdbc&) As Integer
Declare Function SQLAllocStmt Lib "odbc32.dll"  _
    (ByVal hdbc&, phstmt&) As Integer
```

In both the preceding functions, the arguments phdbc& and phstmt& represent the long integer handles to the database connection and the statement respectively. Each function relies on the value set up by the previous one.

The SQLDriverConnect function is used to pop up a list of available datasources for the user to select from:

```
Declare Function SQLDriverConnect Lib "odbc32.dll" (ByVal hdbc&, _
    ByVal hwnd As Long, ByVal szCSIn$, ByVal cbCSIn%, ByVal szCSOut$, _
    ByVal cbCSMax%, cbCSOut%, ByVal fDrvrComp%) As Integer
```

In the preceding function, hwnd represents the handle of your calling application's window. szCSIn and szCSOut are the connection string variables.

The *ConnectDatabase* function passes a null string as the argument *szCSIn* to the *SQLDriverConnect* function, instead of passing the name of a connection string. This prompts the ODBC Driver Manager to pop up a list of data sources for the user to choose from. This method is convenient when you wish to provide querying capabilities to any valid ODBC data source for your user.

Listing 5.2 6LIST02.TXT—ODBCQRY.BAS, the ConnectDatabase routine.

```
Function ConnectDatabase() As Integer
'-----------------------------------------------------------------
' ConnectDatabase
'
'   Purpose:
'   Connects to a data source of choice.
'
'   Arguments:
'   None. Returns True/False on Successful/UnSuccessful connection.
'
'   Author: S. Rama Ramachandran
'-----------------------------------------------------------------
On Error GoTo ConnectDatabase_Err

    ' ----- Default value is false
    ConnectDatabase = False

    Dim iResult As Integer
    Dim sConnectString As String
    Dim sConnectStringOut As String
    Dim iBalanceOut As Integer

    sConnectString = "" ' Pass a null string, ask prompt from ODBC
    sConnectStringOut = String$(255, 0) ' Initialize buffer to
                                        ' bring back data
```

(continues)

Listing 5.2   Continued

```
' ----- Connect to a database - or data source name
  ' ----- Step 1 : Allocate a connection handle
  If SQLAllocConnect(ghEnv, ghDBC) <> SQL_SUCCESS Then
      ' ----- Call Error Handler
      ShowError "Unable to allocate a Handle for ODBC connection. " _
      & "Too many connections may be open." _
      & "Please try again later on."
      ' ----- get out
      GoTo ConnectDatabase_Exit
  End If

  ' ----- Step 2 : Connect
  iResult = SQLDriverConnect(ghDBC, w_ODBCQry.hwnd, _
  sConnectString, Len(sConnectString), sConnectStringOut, _
  Len(sConnectStringOut), iBalanceOut, SQL_DRIVER_COMPLETE)
  If (iResult = SQL_ERROR) Or (iResult = SQL_INVALID_HANDLE) _
      Or (iResult = SQL_NO_DATA_FOUND) Then
      MsgBox "Unable to connect to a data source. ", _
          MB_ICONSTOP + MB_OK, APP_NAME
      ' ----- get out
      GoTo ConnectDatabase_Exit
  End If

  ' ----- Step 3 : Get a Statement Handle
  If SQLAllocStmt(ghDBC, ghStmt) <> SQL_SUCCESS Then
      ' ----- Call Error Handler
      ShowError "Unable to allocate a Handle for ODBC " _
      & "SQL Statement." _
      & "Too many connections may be open. " _
      & " Please try again later on."
      ' ----- get out
      GoTo ConnectDatabase_Exit
  End If

  ConnectDatabase = True

' ----- Error Handlers ----------------------------------------
ConnectDatabase_Exit:
    Exit Function

ConnectDatabase_Err:
    MsgBox Error$, 48, "Error in Routine: ConnectDatabase"
    Resume ConnectDatabase_Exit


End Function
```

Once a connection to a data source is successful, ODBCQry proceeds to interrogate the database for its structure, using ODBC Catalog functions, and builds up a list of tables, and a list of fields for each table. The user can now point and click to choose a table and field to include in his SQL Query. We shall see how this is done in the next section.

When we are done with our application, we need to free up the environment handles we set up—the Connection Handle, and the Environment Handle. The code for this is placed in the `Form_Unload` event so that it is called at the very end of the application, when the application closes. The `Form_Unload` event makes calls to the `SQLDisconnect`, `SQLFreeConnect`, and `SQLFreeEnv` functions to drop these handles.

Listing 5.3   6LIST03.TXT—ODBCQRY.FRM, the `Form_Unload` event code

```
Private Sub Form_Unload(Cancel As Integer)
    Dim iResult As Integer
    If ghEnv Then
        ' ----- Free connection and environment - regain resources
        If ghDBC Then
            iResult = SQLDisconnect(ghDBC)
            iResult = SQLFreeConnect(ghDBC)
        End If
        iResult = SQLFreeEnv(ghEnv)
    End If
End Sub
```

Examining a Database Structure

When `ConnectDatabase` returns a successful value, the routine `FillTableList` is called to populate a list box on-screen with all available tables within the database.

This routine uses the ODBC Catalog function `SQLTables` to query the database for its internal structure. The function `SQLTables` is declared as follows:

```
Declare Function SQLTables Lib "odbc32.dll"  _
    (ByVal hstmt&, szTblQualifier As Any, _
    ByVal cbTblQualifier%, szTblOwner As Any, ByVal cbTblOwner%, _
    szTblName As Any, ByVal cbTblName%, szTblType As Any, _
    ByVal cbTblType%) As Integer
```

As you can see in the accompanying listing for routine `FillTableList`, this involves the following steps:

1. Set up a Statement Handle.

2. Call `SQLTables` with null string arguments to get the names of all tables within the database. ODBC now returns a result set with each row containing information on one single table.

3. To find out which column in the result set holds the table names, we can query the details of the result set. To do so, we first get the number of columns in the result set by using the `SQLNumResultCols` function.

Then we walk through each column, using `SQLDescribeCol`, to obtain each column's details. We can then identify the column that contains the table name, which is what we need to list.

4. We then perform a loop of `SQLFetch` function calls to obtain one row at a time out of the result set. For each row fetched, we use `SQLGetData` function to inquire about the contents of a specific column we want—in this case, the column containing the table name. We then populate our list box with this table name to obtain a list of all table names.

5. We then close the result set by freeing our Statement Handle by using `SQLFreeStmt` function call.

The end result of the preceding steps is a list box filled with the names of all our tables. If we wish to isolate certain tables only—for example, no System Tables—we can do so before populating the list box.

Listing 5.4   6LIST04.TXT—ODBCQRY.FRM, the FillTableList routine

```
Private Sub FillTableList()
' ------------------------------------------------------------------
' FillTableList
'
'   Purpose:
'   Fills a list box on screen with a list of
'   tables available in the database
'
'   Arguments:
'   none
'
'   Author: S. Rama Ramachandran
' ------------------------------------------------------------------
On Error GoTo FillTableList_Err

    Const SQL_SYSTEM_TABLE = "SYSTEM TABLE"

    ' ----- Local variables
    Dim iResult As Integer
    Dim iNumColumns As Integer
    Dim i As Integer
    Dim sColName As String
    Dim sTableType As String
    Dim lBalance As Long
    Dim iBalance As Integer
    Dim iSQLType As Integer
    Dim lSQLWidth As Long
    Dim iSQLScale As Integer
    Dim iSQLNullable As Integer

        ' ----- Step 1 : Get a Statement Handle
        If SQLAllocStmt(ghDBC, ghStmt) <> SQL_SUCCESS Then
```

```
        ' ----- Call Error Handler
        ShowError "Unable to allocate a Handle for ODBC " _
        & "SQL Statement." _
        & "Too many connections may be open. " _
        & " Please try again later on."
        ' ----- get out
        GoTo FillTableList_Exit
    End If


    ' ----- Step 2 : Query the database for its list of tables:
    ' ----- Since we need ALL tables,
    ' ----- we pass null string as all arguments
    If SQLTables(ghStmt, ByVal SQL_NULL, 0, ByVal SQL_NULL, 0, _
                ByVal SQL_NULL, 0, ByVal SQL_NULL, 0) <> _
                SQL_SUCCESS Then
        ' ----- Call Error Handler
        ShowError "Unable to obtain Table Information. " _
        & "Table Privileges may not be available."
        GoTo FillTableList_Exit
    End If


    ' ----- Step 3: Not always needed, but it is better to double check
    ' ----- the location of the 'table_name' column within our
    ' ----- result set.
    ' ----- How much info did  we hit
    If SQLNumResultCols(ghStmt, iNumColumns) <> SQL_SUCCESS Then
        ' ----- Call Error Handler
        ShowError "Unable to obtain Table Information. " _
        & "Table Privileges may not be available."
        GoTo FillTableList_Exit
    End If


    ' ----- Which column holds the table name ?
    For i = 1 To iNumColumns
        sColName = String$(SQL_COL_DATA_LEN, 0)
        If SQLDescribeCol(ghStmt, i, sColName, Len(sColName), _
                        iBalance, _
                        iSQLType, lSQLWidth, iSQLScale, _
                        iSQLNullable) _
                        <> SQL_SUCCESS Then
            ' ----- Call Error Handler
            ShowError "Unable to obtain Table Information. " _
            & "Table Privileges may not be available."
            GoTo FillTableList_Exit
        End If
        If Left$(sColName, iBalance) = SQL_TABLE_NAME Then
            Exit For
        End If
    Next i
    ' ----- i now holds our column value : for table name
    ' ----- i+1 holds table type
    ' ----- Get all  table names

    ' ----- Step 4: Loop through all the rows in our result set,
    ' ----- obtaining table_name
```

(continues)

Listing 5.4 Continued

```
        ' ----- get first row
        iResult = SQLFetch(ghStmt)
        Do While iResult = SQL_SUCCESS
            ' ----- What type of a table is this ?
            sTableType = String$(SQL_COL_DATA_LEN, 0)
            If SQLGetData(ghStmt, i + 1, SQL_C_CHAR, ByVal sTableType, _
                          Len(sTableType), lBalance) <> SQL_SUCCESS Then
                ' ----- Call Error Handler
                ShowError "Unable to obtain Table Information. " _
                & "Table Privileges may not be available."
                GoTo FillTableList_Exit
            End If
            If Left$(sTableType, lBalance) = SQL_SYSTEM_TABLE Then
                ' ----- don't add a system table
            Else
                ' ----- Get the Table Name
                sColName = String$(SQL_COL_DATA_LEN, 0)
                If SQLGetData(ghStmt, i, SQL_C_CHAR, ByVal sColName, _
                              Len(sColName), lBalance) <> SQL_SUCCESS Then
                    ' ----- Call Error Handler
                    ShowError "Unable to obtain Table Information. " _
                    & "Table Privileges may not be available."
                    GoTo FillTableList_Exit
                End If
                ' ----- Add our table name to the list box
                lstTables.AddItem Left$(sColName, lBalance)
            End If
            ' ----- get next row
            iResult = SQLFetch(ghStmt)
        Loop

        ' ----- Step 5: Close the Cursor
        If SQLFreeStmt(ghStmt, SQL_CLOSE) <> SQL_SUCCESS Then
            ' ----- Call Error Handler
            ShowError "Unable to obtain Free Resources."
            GoTo FillTableList_Exit
        End If

    ' ----- Error Handlers -------------------------------------
    FillTableList_Exit:
        Exit Sub

    FillTableList_Err:
        MsgBox Error$, 48, "Error in Routine: FillTableList"
        Resume FillTableList_Exit

    End Sub
```

In the same way, when users choose one table to be included in their query, the UpdateFieldList routine populates a different list box with all available columns within the selected table. To accomplish this, the UpdateFieldList routine does the following:

■ Sets up a Statement Handle.

■ Executes a `SQLColumns` function call to obtain information on columns (fields) within a table. The call to `SQLColumns` is very similar to the call to `SQLTables` explained above. ODBC returns a result set with each row containing information on a single column for the table.

■ Loop through the result set obtained from ODBC by using `SQLFetch` to obtain one row at a time, and extract out the column name by using `SQLGetData`. Add column names extracted to the list box.

■ Free the Statement Handle.

Listing 5.5   6LIST05.TXT—ODBCQRY.FRM   Partial listing of the UpdateFieldList routine

```
' ----- For each table in the Output Table list,
' ----- get its columns and populate the other boxes
' ----- Step 1 : Get a Cursor Handle
If SQLAllocStmt(ghDBC, ghStmt) <> SQL_SUCCESS Then
    ' ----- Call Error Handler
    ShowError "Unable to allocate a Handle for " _
    & "ODBC SQL Statement." _
    & "Too many connections may be open. " _
    & " Please try again later on."
    ' ----- get out
    GoTo UpdateFieldList_Exit
End If

' ----- What is our table name
s_Table = Trim$(lstTOutput.List(i))
' ----- Step 2 : Execute a Catalog Call to get
' ----- a list of Columns
' -----          We may not be successful if we do not have
' -----          permissions on this table
If SQLColumns(ghStmt, SQL_NULL, 0, SQL_NULL, 0, s_Table, _
            Len(s_Table), SQL_NULL, 0) <> SQL_SUCCESS Then
    ' ----- Call Error Handler
    ShowError "Unable to obtain Column Information " _
    & "for table " _
    & s_Table & ". " _
    & "Column Privileges may not be available."
Else
    ' ----- We did get a list of columns
    ' ----- add a * for all fields as the first entry
    lstFields.AddItem s_Table & ".*"

    ' ----- column name is in col 4
    ' ----- get each column name for this table
    ' ----- Step 3 : Fetch data from cursor
    ' ----- First row
    iResult = SQLFetch(ghStmt)
```

(continues)

Listing 5.5   Continued

```
Do While iResult = SQL_SUCCESS
    sColName = String$(SQL_COL_DATA_LEN, 0)
    ' ----- Get the Column Name = col 4
    If SQLGetData(ghStmt, 4, SQL_C_CHAR, ByVal
    ➡sColName, _
                    Len(sColName), lBalance) <> _
                SQL_SUCCESS Then
        ' ----- Call Error Handler
        ShowError "Unable to obtain Column Information. " _
        & "Table Privileges may not be available."
        GoTo UpdateFieldList_Exit
    End If
    sColName = Left$(sColName, lBalance)
    sFieldType = String$(SQL_COL_DATA_LEN, 0)
    ' ----- And the Data Type for the column = col 5
    If SQLGetData(ghStmt, 5, SQL_C_CHAR, _
                    ByVal sFieldType, _
                    Len(sFieldType), lBalance) <> _
                SQL_SUCCESS Then
        ' ----- Call Error Handler
        ShowError "Unable to obtain Column Type " _
        & "Information. " _
        & "Table Privileges may not be available."
        'GoTo UpdateFieldList_Exit
    End If


    ' Add field name to fields list box
    lstFields.AddItem s_Table & "." & sColName
    ' ----- and its type
    lstFields.ItemData(lstFields.NewIndex) = _
        CLng(Left$(sFieldType, lBalance))

    ' Add field name to each of the 5 combo boxes
    For k = 0 To 4
        cboxJoinFrom(k).AddItem s_Table & "." & sColName
        cboxJoinTo(k).AddItem s_Table & "." & sColName
    Next k
    ' And to the 3 search criteria field combo boxes
    For k = 0 To 2
        cboxFields(k).AddItem s_Table & "." & sColName
    Next k


        ' ----- get next row
        iResult = SQLFetch(ghStmt)
    Loop
End If
' ----- Step 4 : Close this cursor
If SQLFreeStmt(ghStmt, SQL_CLOSE) <> SQL_SUCCESS Then
    ' ----- Call Error Handler
    ShowError "Unable to Free Resources."
    ' ----- get out
    GoTo UpdateFieldList_Exit
```

Executing a SQL Query and Displaying Results

Once users have chosen the tables and fields in their query, they can also specify join conditions and search criteria. The accompanying CD-ROM contains the full source code for these routines, which use Visual Basic code to accomplish their results. When users are satisfied with their query definition, they can choose to view the Query SQL statement or view the Result set data by running the query. In the background, ODBCQry prepares a SQL statement based on the fields and tables that the user has selected. When it is time to run the query, the routine RunQuery is invoked.

RunQuery prepares and executes the SQL statement and also retrieves and formats the results. It does this by using the following steps:

1. Sets up a Statement Handle.

2. Uses SQLExecDirect to execute the prepared SQL statement.

3. Checks to make sure that a result set was returned by querying ODBC by using the SQLNumResultCols function.

4. Since the names of the fields may not always be available from the SQL statement (e.g., if the SQL statement includes 'SELECT CUSTOMERS.* FROM CUSTOMERS;'), obtains the name of each field returned by looping through each column of the result set and issuing a SQLDescribeCol function to obtain the column (field) name.

5. Loops through the entire result set obtaining one row at a time by using SQLFetch, and obtaining individual column values by issuing SQLGetData. In our sample application, this information is fed into a grid control on-screen to display a row-and-column format of the result set.

6. Frees the Statement Handle, closing our result set.

Listing 5.6   6LIST06.TXT—ODBCQRY.FRM   Partial listing of RunQuery routine

```
' ----- Step 1: Get a Cursor Handle
If SQLAllocStmt(ghDBC, ghStmt) <> SQL_SUCCESS Then
    ' ----- Call Error Handler
    ShowError "Unable to allocate a Handle for ODBC " _
    & "SQL Statement. " _
    & "Too many connections may be open." _
    & " Please try again later on."
    ' ----- get out
    GoTo RunQuery_Exit
End If
```

(continues)

Listing 5.6   Continued

```
' ----- Step 2: Execute our Select Statement
If SQLExecDirect(ghStmt, gsTempSQL, Len(gsTempSQL)) <>  _
    SQL_SUCCESS Then
    ' ----- Call Error Handler
    ShowError "Error executing SQL statement."
    ' ----- get out
    GoTo RunQuery_Exit
End If

' ----- Step 3: Check to make sure we got a result set
If SQLNumResultCols(ghStmt, iCols) <> SQL_SUCCESS Then
    ' ----- Call Error Handler
    ShowError "Error executing SQL statement."
    ' ----- get out
    GoTo RunQuery_Exit
End If

If iCols = 0 Then
    MsgBox "Query Did not return any result set.", _
            MB_OK + MB_ICONSTOP, APP_NAME
    ' ----- get out
    GoTo RunQuery_Exit
End If

' ----- we can only fit in as many cols as the grid will allow
If iCols > GRID_MAX_COLS Then iCols = GRID_MAX_COLS

ReDim AryMaxWidth(0 To iCols) As Integer
ReDim AryColTypes(0 To iCols) As Integer


' ----- Set up the Grid Columns
Grid_Data.FixedRows = 0
Grid_Data.FixedCols = 0

' ----- First, the Column Names themselves
Grid_Data.Rows = 1  ' This clears the grid also
Grid_Data.Cols = iCols + 1     ' We need the first column to hold
                               ' row numbers like a spreadsheet

' ----- Set Column 1 width
AryMaxWidth(0) = 5
Grid_Data.Row = 0
' ----- Populate all other column names
For i = 1 To iCols
    ' ----- move to next column
    Grid_Data.Col = i
    ' ----- Step 4 : Get each Column Name to adorn
    ' ----- the top row of the Grid.
    sColData = String$(SQL_COL_DATA_LEN, 0)
    If SQLDescribeCol(ghStmt, i, sColData, Len(sColData),  _
                      iBalance, _
                      iColType, lColDef, iColScale, iColNullable) _
                      <> SQL_SUCCESS Then
```

```
        ' ----- Call Error Handler
        ShowError "Error fetching Column information."
        ' ----- get out
        GoTo RunQuery_Exit
    End If
    ' ----- Place the Column Name
    Grid_Data.Text = Left$(sColData, iBalance)
    ' ----- And remember this width for later
    If lColDef > AryMaxWidth(i) Then
        If lColDef > MAX_COL_WIDTH Then
            ' ----- probably an OLE object or picture, binary field
            ' ----- we are not going to display data anyway, so
            ' ----- just make it as wide as the column name or
            ' ----- "(longbinary)" whichever is more
            AryMaxWidth(i) = iBalance
            If iBalance < Len("(longbinary)") Then
                AryMaxWidth(i) = Len("(longbinary)")
            End If
        Else
            AryMaxWidth(i) = lColDef
        End If
    End If
    ' ----- Also, remember the col type for later
    AryColTypes(i) = iColType

Next i

' ----- Move to Row 1 in the Grid
irow = 1
' ----- Step 5: Fetch all the data
' ----- First row
iResult = SQLFetch(ghStmt)
Do While iResult = SQL_SUCCESS
    ' ----- Get all columns for this row and
    ' ----- populate it into the Grid
    Grid_Data.Rows = irow + 1

    Grid_Data.Row = irow
    ' ----- row number
    Grid_Data.Col = 0
    Grid_Data.Text = Format$(irow, "#,##0")
    ' ----- For each col, get the data
    For i = 1 To iCols
        ' ----- Add data to Grid
        Grid_Data.Col = i

        If AryColTypes(i) = SQL_LONGVARBINARY Or AryColTypes(i) _
                        = SQL_VARBINARY Then
            ' ----- we cannot get these data types here.
            ' ----- They may be
            ' ----- OLE objects or pictures or whatever
          Grid_Data.Text = "(longbinary)"
        ElseIf AryColTypes(i) = SQL_LONGVARCHAR Then
          Grid_Data.Text = "(memo)"
        Else
            sColData = String$(SQL_COL_DATA_LEN, 0)
```

(continues)

```
Listing 5.6  Continued
                         If SQLGetData(ghStmt, i, SQL_C_CHAR, ByVal sColData, _
                                       Len(sColData), lBalance) <>  _
                                       SQL_SUCCESS Then
                             ' ----- Call Error Handler
                             ShowError "Unable to obtain Data."
                             'GoTo RunQuery_Exit
                         End If
                         If lBalance = SQL_NULL_DATA Then
                           Grid_Data.Text = "(null)"
                         Else
                           Grid_Data.Text = Left$(sColData, lBalance)
                         End If
                         ' ----- And remember this width for later
                         If lBalance > AryMaxWidth(i) Then
                             If lBalance > MAX_COL_WIDTH Then
                                 AryMaxWidth(i) = MAX_COL_WIDTH
                             Else
                                 AryMaxWidth(i) = lBalance
                             End If
                         End If
                     End If
                Next i
                ' ----- Next row
                irow = irow + 1
                If irow > GRID_MAX_ROWS Then
                    ' ----- we've filled up our grid
                    Exit Do
                End If
                iResult = SQLFetch(ghStmt)
        Loop

        ' ----- Step 6 : Close this cursor
        If SQLFreeStmt(ghStmt, SQL_CLOSE) <> SQL_SUCCESS Then
            ' ----- Call Error Handler
            ShowError "Unable to Free Resources."
            ' ----- get out
            GoTo RunQuery_Exit
        End If
```

Error Handling and Graceful Exits

The ODBC API contains function calls to inquire about errors that take place within your application. In our sample application, at every call to an ODBC API function, we check to see if the function returned SQL_SUCCESS, indicating successful function call execution. If not, we call the routine ShowError and pass to it an additional explanatory message from our application. The ShowError routine displays our message and asks the users if they wish to view even the ODBC error details.

Listing 5.7 6LIST07.TXT—ODBCQry.BAS The ShowError routine

```
Sub ShowError(ByVal sMsg As String)
    Dim iPointer As Integer
    iPointer = Screen.MousePointer
    Screen.MousePointer = 0    ' default
    Select Case MsgBox("An ODBC Error has taken Place." _
        & Endln & Endln _
        & sMsg & Endln & Endln _
        & "Do you wish to view the error details?", _
        MB_ICONQUESTION + MB_YESNO, APP_NAME)
        Case IDYES
            w_ODBCError.Show 1
        Case IDNO
    End Select

    Screen.MousePointer = iPointer
End Sub
```

If the user answers yes, the routine brings up the modal window w_ODBCError. In the Form_Load event of w_ODBCError, a call to the routine ShowErrorDetails is made, which gathers error information from ODBC. The routine ShowErrorDetails accomplishes this by making frequent calls to SQLError routine till all error messages are retrieved. It then places these error strings into a text box on screen (txtErrorDetails) for the user's perusal.

Listing 5.8 6LIST08.TXT—ODBCErr.FRM The ShowErrorDetails routine

```
Private Sub ShowErrorDetails()
'-------------------------------------------------------------
' ShowErrorDetails
'
'   Purpose:
'   Displays ODBC error message
'
'   Arguments:
'   none
'
'   Author: S. Rama Ramachandran
'-------------------------------------------------------------
Dim sSQLState As String
    Dim lNative As Long
    Dim sErrorMsg As String
    Dim iErrorMsgMax As Integer
    Dim iErrorMsg As Integer
    Dim iResult As Integer

    ' ----- initialize string variables
```

(continues)

Listing 5.8   Continued

```
            sSQLState = String$(SQL_COL_DATA_LEN, 0)
            sErrorMsg = String$(SQL_COL_DATA_LEN, 0)
            iErrorMsgMax = Len(sErrorMsg)
            iErrorMsg = iErrorMsgMax
            lNative = 0
            txtErrorDetails = "ODBC Error Message:"

            ' ----- call Function repeatedly till we get all error messages
            Do
                iResult = SQLError(ghEnv, ghDBC, ghStmt, sSQLState, lNative, _
                                   sErrorMsg, iErrorMsgMax, iErrorMsg)
                If iResult = SQL_SUCCESS Or _
                   iResult = SQL_SUCCESS_WITH_INFO Then
                    If iErrorMsg > 0 Then
                        txtErrorDetails = txtErrorDetails & Endln _
                        & Left$(sErrorMsg, iErrorMsg)
                    End If
                End If
            Loop Until iResult <> SQL_SUCCESS
        End Sub
```

Summary

As you can see, we have carried out a whirlwind tour of the ODBC API. We
managed to glimpse briefly at the power and ease of using the ODBC API.
The only way you can master it fully is by practice. The sample application
we built in this chapter can benefit from your improvements. It is not very
robust and you can modify it to include better error checking. Also, we did
not use many custom controls—for example, a tab interface would make the
application slicker and would ease the switching between the different
views—design, SQL, and query results. Also, in this application we displayed
the query results in a row-col format in a grid control. You may want to display the results differently. The FillTableList and UpdateFieldList routines
that return a list of available tables and fields, respectively, can be made generic functions to return the list either in a list box, or in a combo box or in
an array. You can use the application any way you want.

You can round out your knowledge on the ODBC API and use it in your applications. To do so, you should also review the material in the following
chapters of this book:

- For more information on using the 32-bit Windows API calls, see
  Chapter 2, "Introduction to the Win32 API."

■ For more information on using the Data Access Objects (DAO) of the JET Engine to link to ODBC data-sources, see Chapter 4, "Data Access Objects."

■ For more information on developing client/server applications and the scope of ODBC usage, see Chapter 9, "Anatomy of a Client/Server Project."

■ And for general tips on optimizing your code and applications, see Chapter 14, "Put Your Code into Overdrive."

Chapter 6

Using Visual Basic as a Multimedia Front-End

by Roger Jennings

Roger Jennings is a consultant specializing in Windows database and multimedia applications. He is the author of Que's Unveiling Windows 95; Using Windows Desktop Video, *Special Edition;* Discover Windows 3.1 Multimedia *and* Access for Windows Hot Tips; *and was a contributing author to Que's* Using Windows 95, *Special Edition;* Excel Professional Techniques; Killer Windows Utilities; *and* Using Visual Basic 3. *He has written two other books about creating database applications with Access and Visual Basic, coauthored a book on using Microsoft Visual C++ for database development, is a contributing editor of* Visual Basic Programmer's Journal, *and has written articles for the* Microsoft Developer Network News *and the MSDN CD-ROMs. Roger is a principal of OakLeaf Systems, a Northern California software development and consulting firm; you may contact him via CompuServe (ID 70233,2161), on the Internet (70233.2161@compuserve.com), or on The Microsoft Network (Roger_Jennings).*

Windows 95 offers enhanced multimedia capabilities, including the Audio and Video Compression Managers, AutoPlay for CD-ROMs, Plug and Play installation of multimedia devices, and a new 32-bit CD-ROM File System (CDFS). Although much of the multimedia software pipeline in Windows 95 remains in the 16-bit camp, there's no question that multimedia productions play better under Windows 95 than under its predecessors. Unfortunately for multimedia developers, the major new features of Visual Basic 4 are almost exclusively targeted to database developers. As an example, Visual Basic 4's Multimedia MCI OLE Controls (Mci16.ocx and Mci32.ocx) are straight-ahead ports of the venerable MCI.VBX, which hasn't changed significantly since the days of the Professional Extensions for Visual Basic 1.0. Clearly, upgrading multimedia features wasn't high on Microsoft's feature priority list for Visual Basic 4.

If you want to apply Microsoft's "Designed for Windows 95" logo to your Visual Basic 3 multimedia production, you must port it to 32-bit Visual Basic 4 and follow the rest of Microsoft's logo guidelines that apply to multimedia. The majority of commercial Visual Basic multimedia applications are designed for the consumer market; consumers currently are adopting Windows 95 and Pentium-class PCs at a much faster pace than business users. Thus, the "Designed for Windows 95" logo is likely to play an important role in the success of commercial multimedia titles in 1996 and beyond. Fortunately, high-performance 32-bit multimedia OLE Controls are on their way from third-party custom control suppliers; in some cases, only 32-bit versions of these controls are available. 32-bit multimedia OLE Controls also have an important role to play in a future version of the Blackbird toolset for The Microsoft Network.

What's more important for Visual Basic 4 multimedia developers is the new video technology that was announced about the same time Microsoft released Visual Basic 4. Microsoft DirectDraw to speed display of animated images had just become available as part of the Windows Game SDK when this book was written. Intel's Indeo Video Interactive (Indeo 4), which competes with MPEG-1 for full-screen, full-motion video but doesn't require hardware assistance for decoding, also arrived as an SDK. Sony Corporation's September 1995 announcement of consumer digital video (DV) camcorders with IEEE 1394-1995 (FireWire™) digital audio and video input/output portends video image quality that rivals professional videotape formats, such as Sony's Betacam SP and Panasonic's MIII. Zoom Video promises to greatly improve the performance of full-motion video in both laptop and desktop PCs.

This chapter provides an overview of the multimedia capabilities of the professional version of Visual Basic 4, including the Media Control Interface and the Mci16.ocx and Mci32.ocx OLE Controls, and a description of how to use some of the third-party multimedia OLE Controls available when this book was written. The chapter closes with projections of the effect of important new video technologies on Visual Basic 4 multimedia applications.

Understanding the Media Control Interface

The Media Control Interface (MCI), which originated back in the original OS/2 days when Microsoft and IBM were friends, has undergone little change over the years. Microsoft calls MCI a "mid-level" interface; the MCIWnd window class is called "high-level," and some devices, such as MIDI (Musical Instrument Digital Interface) and Joystick, use "low-level" calls. This chapter concentrates on mid-level MCI, because MCI is the easiest method of controlling multimedia devices with Visual Basic 4. MCI is slower than using low-level function calls, but unless you're involved with synchronizing audio and video content, MCI commands usually are adequate for Visual Basic 4 multimedia applications.

MCI in Windows 95 and Windows NT 3+ is implemented by WinMM.dll. The Windows 95 and Windows NT versions add a thunking layer to the original 16-bit MMSystem.dll of Windows 3.1+ for 32-bit compatibility. One of the principal multimedia enhancements to Windows 95 is the Advanced page of the Control Panel's Multimedia Properties Sheet shown in figure 6.1. The Media Control Devices category includes a Registry entry for each MCI device installed with Windows 95, plus related multimedia devices installed by Win16 and Win32 applications. The QTWVideo device that appears in figure 6.1 is Apple Computer's QuickTime for Windows; QTWVideo is not an MCI device, but QTWVideo does qualify as a Media Control Device.

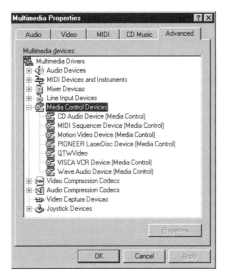

Fig. 6.1
Media Control Devices installed by Windows 95, plus Apple Computer's QuickTime for Windows.

Figure 6.2 shows Windows 95's Registry Editor displaying the Registry hives under the HKEY_LOCAL_MACHINE\System\Current\ControSet\control\ MediaResources branch. All MCI and related device drivers register in the ...\mci hive. The MCI VISCA VCR Device for Sony Hi8 VISCA (VIdeo System

Control Architecture) devices, for example, is implemented by the 16-bit MCIVisca.drv. Third-party suppliers of video editing applications usually write their own VCR drivers. Multi-Media Computing Solutions, Inc. wrote its own VISCA driver for VideoMagician, a commercial Visual Basic 3 video editing application used by many commercial video makers.

Fig. 6.2
Windows 95
Registry entries for
the VISCA VCR
device driver.

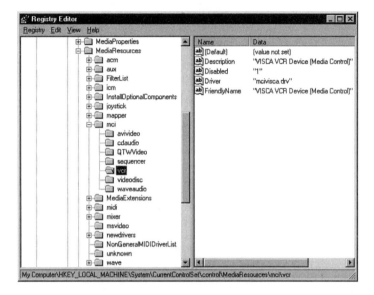

> **Note**
>
> Sony announced in September 1995 the discontinuance of its VISCA product line, which consisted of the CVD-1000 (Hi8) and DVD-500 (8-mm) Vdeck VCRs, plus the CI-1000 Vbox computer interface. Tens of thousands of these devices for conventional linear video editing have been sold worldwide, so there is some life left in applications that use the VISCA device control protocol. In its VISCA announcement, Sony stated that the firm now will concentrate on the new DV recording format, described in the "Consumer Digital Video Camcorders and VCRs" section near the end of this chapter, for desktop video (DTV) production.

The following sections describe the architecture of the MCI, MCI command string syntax, and execution of the `mciSendString()` function from VBA code.

The Architecture of MMSystem.dll and MCI Drivers

The Media Control Interface is a layered, hardware- and platform-independent API for manipulating multimedia data that involves digital audio and moving images. Figure 6.3 illustrates the flow of commands and data through the six layers required to implement most multimedia functions. Applications typically call the `mciExecute()`, `mciSendCommand()`, or `mciSendString()` functions of Windows 95's WinMM.dll to initiate or terminate a multimedia function. The device type, which is serviced by an MCI device driver, is determined by explicit reference in the function's argument(s) or, if files are used, by association of a file type with a device. Figure 6.3 shows three device types, *vcr*, *waveaudio*, and *digitalvideo*, which require the MCIVisca.drv, MCIWave.drv, and MCIAVI.drv drivers, respectively. The *vcr* device is designed only to control VCRs and camcorders; no multimedia data is associated with the *vcr* device. The *waveaudio* and *digitalvideo* devices are file-oriented, using waveform audio (.wav) and audio-video interleaved (.avi) files, respectively, as data source or destination.

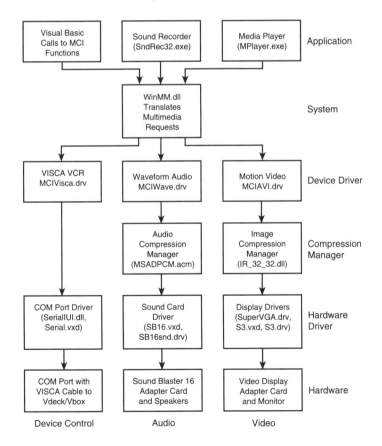

Fig. 6.3
Architecture of Windows 95's MCI command and data flow for digital audio/video reproduction and VCR device control.

Note

As noted earlier in the chapter, WinMM.dll is the Windows 95 and Windows NT version of Windows 3.1's MMSystem.dll. Both Windows 95 and Windows NT install MMSystem.dll for compatibility with 16-bit multimedia applications. The 32-bit multimedia applications, however, must call MCI functions in WinMM.dll. Visual Basic prototype declarations for the MCI functions of WinMM.dll appear in the "Using the Simple *mciExecute( )* Function" and "Expanding Capabilities with *mciSendString( )*" sections that follow. The MCI function prototype declarations in the WinMMSys.txt file for the Windows API Viewer included with Visual Basic 4 are for 16-bit applications only.

Table 6.1 lists the valid MCI device types specified by the "Multimedia" section of the Win32 SDK, the file name of the corresponding device driver included with Windows 95, where applicable, and the device type description. With the exception of the *vcr* and *videodisc* drivers, the MCI device drivers supplied with Windows 95 also are included with Windows NT 3.5+. MCI Device types that use files are identified with an asterisk (*). The most commonly used devices today are *waveaudio*, *sequencer*, and *digitalvideo* because only a sound card is required for playback.

Table 6.1   MCI Device Types Defined by the Win32 Software Development Kit

MCI Device Type	Window 95 Driver	Description
*animation**	None	Animation device
cdaudio	MCICDA.drv	CD audio player
dat	None	Digital-audio tape player or recorder
*digitalvideo**	MCIAVI.drv	Digital video in a window (not GDI-based)
other	None	Undefined MCI device
overlay	None	Overlay device (analog video in a window)
*scanner**	None	Image scanner
*sequencer**	MCISeq.drv	MIDI sequencer
vcr	MCIVISCA.drv (Sony VISCA)	Video-cassette recorder or player

MCI Device Type	Window 95 Driver	Description
videodisc	MCIPionr.drv (Pioneer LaserDisc)	Videodisc player
waveaudio*	MCIWave.drv	Audio adapter (sound) card or peripheral

All *digitalvideo* data is compressed because the data rate of an uncompressed video stream, about 30 MBps (Megabytes per second) or more, exceeds the capabilities of today's (and probably tomorrow's) PCs. Handling compressed video files requires a codec (*coder-dec*oder); Windows 95's Image Compression Manager (IMC) automatically selects the proper codec for the .avi file in use. The most popular digital video codecs when this book was written were Radius, Inc.'s Cinepak (iccvid.dll) and Intel Corp.'s Indeo 3.2 (IV32_32.dll), 32-bit versions of these two codecs, plus Microsoft Video 1 (MSVidC32.dll), and Microsoft RLE (MSRLE32.dll). RLE (run-length encoding) is used primarily for animation files that have large areas of solid color. Cinepak and Indeo 3.*x* codecs are limited to one quarter-screen (320- by 240-pixel) images, unless you have a Windows graphics accelerator card with video acceleration (interpolation) to deliver full-screen images. Intel's Indeo 4 (Indeo Interactive) is likely by early 1996 to become a major player in video compression for CD-ROM delivery because Indeo 4 running on Pentium-class PCs can deliver full-screen, full-motion video.

> **Note**
>
> The codecs discussed in the preceding paragraph are software-only codecs designed primarily for video playback from double-speed or faster CD-ROMs. A variety of hardware-assisted codecs for video capture to .avi files with real-time compression are available. The Intel Smart Video Recorder Pro and Creative Labs's Video Blaster RT300, which incorporate the Intel i750 video processor chip, use the Intel YVU9 and YVU9C (raw video) formats for one quarter-screen .avi capture files. Video capture cards with hardware assisted Motion-JPEG capture and playback presently dominate the full-screen video capture market.

Use of compressed *waveaudio* data is relatively uncommon in commercial multimedia titles, because conventional (uncompressed) 8-bit, 22.05-kHz (0.022 MBps) monaural digital audio is required to support legacy 8-bit sound cards, such as Creative Labs's original Sound Blaster and Media Vision's Thunderboard cards.

MCI Command Strings

MCI command strings are simple, structured English sentences that describe an action to be performed by an MCI device. All MCI devices are expected to support a standard set of commands, such as **open**, **play**, **stop**, and **close**. The general syntax of MCI command strings is

```
command device_id [argument(s)]
```

The following list briefly describes the three elements of an MCI command string:

- The *command* usually is a verb, such as **open**, **close**, **play**, **stop**, or **eject**. Nouns, such as **capabilities**, **info**, and **status**, also are used. The device type determines the commands supported, but all devices are expected to support a simple set of commands. (MCI commands are set in bold monospace type in this chapter.)

- The *device_id* is a path and file name for MCI devices that use files, the device type name, or an alias for the instance of a device. The path and file name must be enclosed within double quotation marks.

- Some commands accept *argument(s)*, such as **from** i **to** j, where i and j represent a beginning and ending time or track, expressed as signed **Long** integers. Arguments also can be a **String** variable or a rectangle defined by an ordered list of four signed **Integer** values, separated by spaces, that define the position and size of a window. (Key words, or flags, used in arguments also are set in bold type.)

The following set of MCI commands plays track six of an audio CD inserted in a CD-ROM drive:

```
open cdaudio
set cdaudio time format tmsf
play cdaudio from 6 to 7
close cdaudio
```

The **time format** tmsf argument sets the data returned by a **status** cdaudio **position** command to tracks:minutes:seconds:frames format.

The following MCI commands play the first 10,000 samples of The Microsoft Sound.wav file, which is included with Windows 95:

```
open "c:\windows\media\TheMic~1.wav" type waveaudio alias tms
set tms time format samples
play tms from 1 to 10000 wait
close tms
```

The **type** waveaudio argument is optional for registered media file types, such as .wav, .mid, and .avi. The **alias** *alias_name* statement lets you substitute a short name for the full path and file name of the device. Background play of MCI devices is the default; control returns to your application immediately after issuing the **play** command. If you add the **wait** argument, control returns to your application after play completes.

This set of MCI commands plays most of Clouds.mid, the MIDI background music for the Windows 95 "Easter Egg" that lists the members of the Microsoft Windows 95 team:

```
open "c:\windows\media\clouds.mid" alias clouds
set clouds time format song pointer
play clouds from 1 to 1000
```

The song pointer format is the default for .mid files, so the second line of the preceding set of commands is optional. You can determine the default time format for a device with the **status** *device_name* **time format** command. To replay Clouds.mid without closing and opening the device, you can reposition the MIDI song position pointer (SPP) to the beginning of the file with a **seek** clouds **to** start command and then issue a **play** clouds command.

The "MCI Command String" chapter of the Media Control Interface documentation included in the Win32 SDK defines a standard set of commands and a subset of arguments for each MCI device type. A complete listing of the commands applicable to each device type is beyond the scope of this chapter. You need the documentation for the Win32 SDK, included on the Microsoft Developer Network Level I CD-ROM to use MCI command strings for all but the simplest multimedia operations.

Using the Simple `mciExecute()` Function

The easiest method of executing MCI command strings is to use the mciExecute() function of WinMM.dll. MCIExecute() accepts a single MCI command string as its sole argument and, as its name implies, executes the command. Following is the 32-bit VBA function prototype declaration for mciExecute():

```
Declare Function mciExecute Lib "winmm.dll" _
    (ByVal lpstrCommand As String) As Long
```

The mciExecute() function doesn't return **String** variables, so there is no "mciExecuteA()" function and no alias is required. The 16-bit version is declared as follows:

```
Declare Function mciExecute Lib "mmsystem" _
    (ByVal lpstrCommand As String) As Integer
```

A typical `mciExecute()` function call appears as follows:

```
Dim mciCommand As String
Dim mciError As Long

mciCommand = "open " & Chr$(34) & _
    "c:\windows\media\tada.wav" & Chr$(34)
mciError = mciExecute(mciCommand)
```

If an error occurs, `mciExecute()` returns 0 and posts an error message, such as that shown in figure 6.4, describing the problem. The error message shown in figure 6.4 results from an incorrect path specification. Error messages from WinMM.dll include the MMSYSTEM prefix; error messages from Windows 3.1+'s MMSYSTEM.DLL begin with the error number.

Fig. 6.4

An error message posted by WinMM.dll as a result of an incorrect path to a .wav file.

Expanding Capabilities with `mciSendString()`

The `mciExecute()` function is quite simple to declare and use, but it has serious limitations in other than trivial multimedia applications. The `mciSendString()` function includes the capability to return information requested from a device in the form of a return **String** variable, to report the type of error encountered, and to provide a window handle for a callback function that's activated by the **notify** argument. MCI also provides the `mciGetErrorString()` function to return a description of the error based on the **Long** value returned by `mciSendString()`. Visual Basic 4 can't handle callback functions directly, so you set the value of the callback window handle to 0. Following are the 32-bit function declarations for using `mciSendString()`:

```
Declare Function mciSendString Lib "winmm.dll" _
    Alias "mciSendStringA" _
    (ByVal lpstrCommand As String, _
    ByVal lpstrReturnString As String, _
    ByVal uReturnLength As Long, _
    ByVal hwndCallback As Long) As Long

Declare Function mciGetErrorString Lib "winmm.dll" _
    Alias "mciGetErrorStringA" _
    (ByVal dwError As Long, _
    ByVal lpstrBuffer As String, _
    ByVal uLength As Long) As Long
```

WinMM.dll's `mciSendString()` and `mciGetErrorString()` functions return **String** variables, and thus the ANSI version of the functions is aliased to the standard function name in the preceding declarations. The equivalent 16-bit function calls to MMSystem.dll are as follows:

```
Declare Function mciSendString Lib "mmsystem" _
  (ByVal lpstrCommand As String, _
   ByVal lpstrReturnString As String, _
   ByVal uReturnLength As Integer, _
   ByVal hWndCallback As Integer) As Long

Declare Function mciGetErrorString Lib "mmsystem" _
  (ByVal wError As Long, _
   ByVal lpstrBuffer As String, _
   ByVal uLength As Integer) As Integer
```

You can use the conditional compilation directive structure, **#If** Win32 **Then** ... **#Else** ... **#End If**, to write common code for both 16-bit and 32-bit Visual Basic applications. Enclose the preceding function prototype declarations between the compiler directives; then declare the appropriate variable data types with the following code:

```
Public mciCommand   As String
Public mciReturn    As String * 256
Public mciErrString As String * 256
Public mciError     As Long

#If Win32 Then
    Public mciReturnLen As Long
    Public mcihWnd      As Long
    Public mciErrLen    As Long
    Public mciErrResult As Long
#Else
    Public mciReturnLen As Integer
    Public mcihWnd      As Integer
    Public mciErrLen    As Integer
    Public mciErrResult As Integer
#End If
```

Figure 6.5 shows a simple form, mciDemo, that lets you enter MCI command strings in a text box and displays the return string or error string in two label controls. A history list box displays MCI commands that have executed or that resulted in an error. The source code for mciDemo.vpj, which you can compile either as a 16-bit or a 32-bit mciDemo.exe file, is included on the accompanying CD-ROM. Type the MCI command string in the text box, click the Execute or Send String button, and mciDemo sends the command string to WinMM.dll or MMSytem.dll.

Fig. 6.5

Playing the
Clouds.mid MIDI
file with the 32-bit
version of the
Visual Basic 4
mciDemo
application.

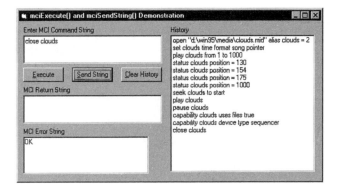

Following is the code for the cmdSend_Click event subprocedure that calls the
mciSendString() function and, if necessary, the mciGetErrorString() function:

```
Private Sub cmdSend_Click()
    'Executed on clicking Send String button
    lblReturn.Caption = ""
    lblError.Caption = ""
    mciReturnLen = Len(mciReturn) - 1
    mciErrLen = Len(mciErrString) - 1
    mciCommand = txtCommand.Text
    mcihWnd = 0
    mciError = mciSendString(mciCommand, mciReturn, _
        mciReturnLen, mcihWnd)
    lblReturn.Caption = Left$(mciReturn, (mciReturnLen - 1))
    If mciError > 0 Then
        'An error occurred
        mciErrResult = mciGetErrorString(mciError, _
            mciErrString, mciErrLen)
        lblError.Caption = LTrim$(Str$(mciError)) & "  " & _
            Left$(mciErrString, (mciErrLen - 1))
        lstHistory.AddItem mciCommand & " Err: " & _
            mciError
    Else
        'Command executed
        lblError.Caption = "OK"
        If Val(lblReturn.Caption) > 0 Then
            'Return string with numeric value
            lstHistory.AddItem mciCommand & " = " & _
                lblReturn.Caption
        Else
            If Len(RTrim$(lblReturn.Caption)) > 0 Then
                'Return string with text content
                lstHistory.AddItem mciCommand & " " & _
                    lblReturn.Caption
            Else
                'No return string
                lstHistory.AddItem mciCommand
            End If
        End If
    End If
End Sub
```

> **Note**
>
> The mci tag, rather than data type tags specified by the Leszynski Naming Conventions for Visual Basic 4, is used to identify variables associated with MCI commands in the preceding code example. The mci tag is used for two reasons: It makes variables associated with the mci...() functions more evident; and several numeric arguments of the mci...() functions change from **Integer** to **Long** data types, depending on the bitness of the .exe file.

Using the Multimedia MCI OLE Controls

WinMM.dll and MMSystem.dll include the message-based mciSendCommand() function that is used primarily by C and C++ programmers. The Win32 function call has the following C syntax:

```
mciSendCommand(wDeviceID,          // device identifier
    MCI_PLAY,                      // command message
    0,                             // flags
    (DWORD)(LPVOID) &mciPlayParms);  // parameter
```

Each command has a corresponding MCI_... constant, such as MCI_PLAY shown in the preceding example. Figure 6.6 shows a few of the constants for the sequencer device in the upper list box of the API Viewer and the most commonly used MCI constants in the lower list box. Depending on the particular command, flags and/or parameters may be supplied and/or returned. The mciSendCommand() function is faster than mciSendString() because there's no need to parse the command string prior to execution. Although it's possible to use mciSendCommand() in Visual Basic 4 applications, most developers opt for the simpler mciSendString() approach.

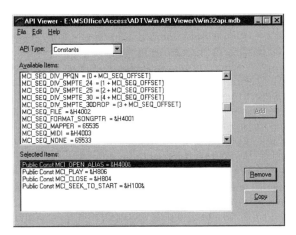

Fig. 6.6
Visual Basic 4's API Viewer displaying sequencer device constants in the upper list box and commonly used MCI constants in the lower list box.

The Multimedia MCI OLE Controls included with Visual Basic 4, Mci16.ocx and Mci32.ocx, simplify creating Visual Basic 4 multimedia applications by eliminating the need to declare mci...() function prototypes and to call the function within VBA code. As mentioned earlier in this chapter, these two controls are derived from Visual Basic 3's MCI.VBX; no new features are implemented in the two .ocx versions. Both MCI OLE Controls use the mciSendCommand() function, and they implement the notify callback function as an event. Thus, the Done or PlayCompleted event triggered by Mci16.ocx and Mci32.ocx makes it easy for your application to determine when the MCI play command completes execution. (A *ButtonCompleted* event is associated with each button of the MCI OLE Controls.) A StatusUpdate event lets you keep the user informed of the progress of, for instance, a play operation at intervals determined by the value of the control's UpdateInterval property.

Figure 6.7 shows the design of a form that provides a quick and easy way to play an .avi file with the Mci32.ocx OLE Control. The MCI OLE Controls' Property Sheet provides a General page in which you set the most important property values for the Control. You enter the path and file name of the .avi file to play in the FileName text box. You can't record or eject an .avi file, so these two buttons are disabled and made invisible. The *digitalvideo* device supports the balance of the buttons: Beginning of File (Previous), End of File (Next), Play, Pause, Back, Step, and Stop. Back and Step are equivalent to the jog control on a VCR, allowing you to pause and then step one frame at a time through a video clip. You can set the number of frames to step forward or backward by setting the Frames property of the control (**Long** data type).

Fig. 6.7
Setting the properties of a Multimedia MCI Control to play an .avi file.

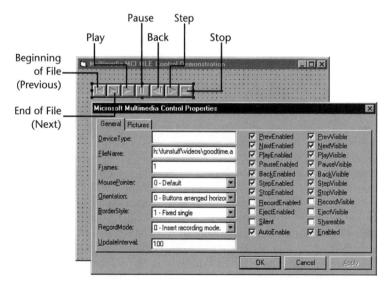

You need only add one line of code, `mciControl.Command = "Open"`, to the `Form_Load` event stub to open the specified file. Clicking the Play button starts the video clip in its default one quarter-screen (320- by 240-pixel) window. Click the Pause button and then the Back or Step button to step frame-by-frame through the clip. Figure 6.8 is a screen capture from Goodtime.avi in Pause mode.

Fig. 6.8
A frame from the Goodtime.avi file on the Windows 95 CD-ROM. (Video clip courtesy of Geffen Records, Inc.)

Many of the properties of the MCI Multimedia control, such as `Command`, `Position`, `Frames`, and `TimeFormat`, are available only at runtime. You can add a label to display the current frame number or the elapsed time in milliseconds by setting the value of the `TimeFormat` property to 3 (frames) or 0 (milliseconds) and then getting the value of the `Position` property at a specified `UpdateInterval` property value. A progress bar or slider control also is useful to provide an indication of the current play position and playing time remaining. Figure 6.9 shows a status bar, plus Position and Length labels, added to the basic form shown in figure 6.8.

Fig. 6.9
Adding a progress bar and labels for position indication to the basic Multimedia MCI control form. (Video clip courtesy of Geffen Records, Inc.)

The following simple event subprocedure opens a specified .avi file and sets the property values required for the display:

```
Private Sub Form_Load()
    'Open .avi file, set TimeFormat and initialize controls
    mciControl.Command = "Open"
    mciControl.TimeFormat = 0                    'Milliseconds
    pgbPosition.Max = mciControl.Length \ 100 'Progress bar
    lblLength.Caption = Format$((mciControl.Length / 1000), _
        "###0.0")                                'Length label
End Sub
```

The following code in the StatusUpdate event handler passes position information to the Position label and the progress bar:

```
Private Sub mciControl_StatusUpdate()
    lblPosition.Caption = Format$((mciControl.Position / _
        1000), "###0.0")
    pgbPosition.Value = mciControl.Position \ 100
End Sub
```

> **Note**
>
> Depending on the speed of your PC's processor, adding code to the StatusUpdate event handler can cause the video to skip frames or even can result in audio breakups (sound pauses). PCs using 80486DX2/66 processors may experience audio breakups with UpdateInterval values of 100 ms or less. If you experience a video playback problem, increase the value of the UpdateInterval property to 1000 ms or more.

One of the primary problems with the Multimedia MCI OLE Controls is the inability to control the position and focus of the floating video window. The video window usually appears at the upper left of your display and easily becomes obscured by other windows. The 32-bit MCIWndX OLE Control, described later in this chapter, solves this problem by providing its own window for playing .avi video clips. Mci16.ocx and Mci32.ocx are quite suitable, however, for applications that play .wav files or audio CD tracks, and for tape deck control applications using the *vcr* device. As an example, you can combine a multiline text box with a Multimedia MCI OLE Control to create a simple application for transcribing dialog or narration from Hi8 video source material played by a Sony Vdeck or a Hi8 VCR with timecode capability, such as the Sony EV-S7000, using a Vbox to convert VISCA to Sony's LANC protocol.

Taking Advantage of Other Multimedia OLE Controls

The limitations of multimedia delivery using Visual Basic custom controls and low-cost multimedia authoring systems have spawned thriving freeware, shareware, and commercial markets for multimedia OLE Controls. The following sections describe two new OLE Controls, MCIWndX.ocx and MV13(32).ocx, developed by Microsoft and the commercial 16-bit and 32-bit MediaDeveloper OLE Controls offered by Lenel Systems International, Inc.

MCIWndX.ocx, a 32-Bit OLE Control for Playing Video Clips

Microsoft includes the MCIWndX.VBX custom control with the Video for Windows 1.1e SDK that's on the MSDN Level I CD-ROM. The MCIWndX.VBX custom control is designed specifically for playing video clips or animations in a sizable window contained in a Visual Basic form. In addition to solving the floating window problem of Visual Basic 4's Multimedia MCI OLE Controls, MCIWndX.VBX provides a number of added features that aid in playing video clips, especially from within Visual Basic multimedia applications. In late 1995, Microsoft's Simon Bernstein developed a 32-bit MCIWndX OLE Control based on the original 16-bit MCIWndX.VBX design. When this book was written, MCIWndX.ocx was in the beta test stage. Both MCIWndX.vbx and MCIWndX.ocx use the `MCIWnd` window class and the `MCIWnd...()` functions to create and manipulate the `MCIWnd` instance. The following list describes the features of MCIWndX.ocx:

- A sizable `MCIWnd` window in which to play .avi files. You can set the window size and location on a form with the conventional `Width`, `Height`, `Left`, and `Top` properties. Setting the `AutosizeWindow` property to **True** forces the dimensions of the window to the size of the video clip; setting `AutosizeMovie` to **True** scales the video image to fit the size of the window.

- An `MCIWnd` playbar that includes a play/stop button, menu button, and slider control for setting playback position. Left-clicking the menu button or right-clicking the video window opens a pop-up menu that offers choices to change the size of the window (half, normal, or double), change the playback speed or volume, open or close a file, copy an image to the Clipboard, configure your video properties, and issue `mciSendString()` commands. MCIWndX.ocx's capability to copy a still frame to the Clipboard isn't available in the .VBX version. You can make the playbar disappear by setting the `Playbar` property to **False** and disable the pop-up menu by setting the `Menu` property to **False**.

■ A `Command` property that lets you execute an MCI command string and the `ErrorString` property that returns the text of an error encountered when attempting to execute an MCI command string.

■ A handle to the `MCIWnd` window that lets you use the `MCIWnd...()` functions for low-level chores not supported by MCIWndX.ocx or the MCI command strings. This feature is unique to the OLE Control version. The "Introduction" chapter of the "Multimedia" section of the Win32 SDK documentation on the MSDN Level I CD-ROM describes the `MCIWnd...()` functions in detail.

■ Automatic display of the Windows 95 common file Open dialog. Setting the value of the `File` property to ? lets you select the .avi file to play in the Open dialog after opening the form.

Unlike the Multimedia MCI OLE Controls, you don't need to issue the `Open` command in the `Form_Load` event handler to display the MCIWnd window. It's a good idea, however, to size and position the window to correspond to the dimensions of your .avi file on loading the form if you specify a particular .avi file as the `File` property value. The following code scales and positions the window for 320- by 240-pixel .avi files:

```
Private Sub Form_Load()
    'Set up the window and start playing the file
    mciWndX.Width = Screen.TwipsPerPixelX * 320
    mciWndX.Height = Screen.TwipsPerPixelX * (240 + 28)
    mciWndX.Left = (Me.Width - mciWndX.Width) \ 2
    mciWndX.Top = (Me.Height - mciWndX.Height) \ 3
    mciWndX.TimeFormat = "frames"
    mciWndX.Command = "Play"
End Sub
```

Note

Microsoft's documentation for the `MCIWnd` window class states that, for best performance, the window instance should be aligned on an even four-pixel boundary. A test program that moves the image to the right and down in one-pixel increments every two seconds did not disclose a performance difference at different pixel boundaries. Add the statements

```
mciWndX.Left = mciWndX.Left + Screen.TwipsPerPixelX
mciWndX.Top = mciWndX.Top + Screen.TwipsPerPixelY
```

> to the `mciWndX` `PositionChange` event handler to test whether window positioning affects performance in your application. You can use the `Left`, `Top`, `Width`, and `Height` properties of a window without a border, combined with variations in the value of the `TimerFreq` property to manipulate digital video images overlaid on a background bitmap.

The extra 28 pixels added to the `Height` property accommodate the playback bar. Figure 6.10 shows MCIWndX.ocx playing a video clip with the pop-up menu active. You can use MCIWndX.ocx to play any type of multimedia device for which you have the appropriate hardware and driver. You also can set the `Record` property to **True** to enable recording of *waveaudio* (but not *digitalvideo*) files.

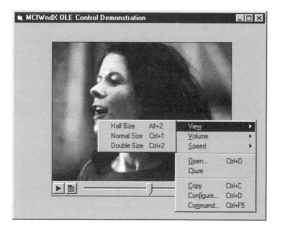

Fig. 6.10
MCIWndX.ocx's window with the MCIWnd standard playbar and pop-up menu. (Video clip courtesy of Geffen Records, Inc.)

Note

Watch for availability of the final version of MCIWndX.ocx in the VBPJ Forum, MSBASIC Forum and the Windows Multimedia (WINMM) Forums on CompuServe. It's a good bet that MCIWndX.ocx also will accompany the release of Microsoft's DirectVideo SDK on an MSDN Level I CD-ROM.

Creating Visual Basic Multimedia Applications with MediaView 1.3

Microsoft's Multimedia Viewer 1.0 (usually just called Viewer) was part of the first Multimedia Development Kit (MDK) that Microsoft released in 1991 in conjunction with the Multimedia Extensions for Windows 3. Microsoft designed Viewer for creating multimedia titles for distribution on diskette and CD-ROM. Microsoft updated Viewer to version 2.0 after the release of Windows 3.1. Viewer 2.0 provides a user interface, navigation features, data management, and file I/O management for .MVB files and subfiles. Viewer's .MVB files and their compilation are closely related to WinHelp 3.1+ .HLP files, but Viewer offers the advantage of full-text, indexed searches. Like Windows help files, you create .MVB file content in Word 2.0+, save the files in rich-text format (.RTF), and then compile the files with the Viewer 2.0 compiler.

All Viewer 2.0 titles have a similar look and feel, often called the "Viewer look," because Viewer 2.0 provides its own standard user interface and a rigid built-in navigation system. MediaView, Microsoft's replacement for the venerable Viewer product, eliminates Viewer's built-in user interface and navigation features in favor of a custom UI and navigation system you create with Visual Basic or Visual C++ executables. Windows 95's 32-bit WinHelp system is, in essence, a custom UI and navigation system that shares many of the features of MediaView, including full-text searching of indexed .hlp files. Microsoft representatives stated at the Multimedia Bootcamp held in late 1994, "There will never be a 32-bit version of Viewer." If you want the full Windows 95 look and feel for Visual Basic 4 multimedia titles, you need to use MediaView 1.3.

> ### Note
>
> MediaView 1.4 (also called MSNView or On-Line MediaView), which is available only to independent content providers (ICPs) for The Microsoft Network, provides extensions, such as Download/Run, that are specific to MSN. (Windows 95 includes Mosview.exe, a simple viewer for MediaView files downloaded from MSN.) At the Microsoft Interactive Media Conference held in July 1995, Microsoft promised a "client-server" version of MediaView for MSN. Future versions of MediaView, scheduled for release in 1996, will support OLE Controls and let you host MediaView HGML titles on the Internet. There's also a 32-bit version of MediaView in the works for the Apple Macintosh.

You can create simple Visual Basic 4 viewers with Alex Lynch's shareware 16-bit and 32-bit OLE Controls for MediaView, MV13.ocx and MV1332.ocx, that you can download as MV13OCX.ZIP from Library 3, MediaView, of the WINMM forum on CompuServe. MV13.ocx and MV1332.ocx don't provide access to the full functionality of the MediaView API, but you're likely to find these two OLE Controls satisfy 90 percent or more of your multimedia viewer requirements. Figure 6.11 shows a simple Visual Basic 4 form with a standard set of MediaView navigation buttons and the 32-bit MediaView 1.3 OLE

Control added. Both of the MediaView OCXs have a complete Properties Sheet with several tabbed pages for setting basic property values.

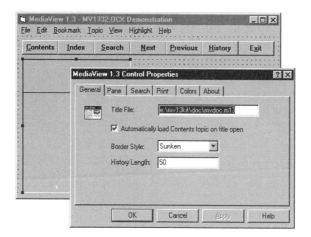

Fig. 6.11

The Properties Sheet of the MediaView 1.3 OLE Control.

Programming the MV1332.ocx control (named ocxMV13 in this example) requires reference to the MV13ocx.hlp file, included in MV13OCX.ZIP, which provides the documentation for the control's properties, methods, and events. The three primary navigation methods are JumpContents, JumpNext, and JumpPrevious, which you invoke with the Contents, Next, and Previous buttons (see listing 6.1 and fig. 6.12). Enabling of the Next and Previous buttons is controlled by the return value of the IsNextTopic and IsPrevTopic properties, which you test in the handler for the TopicEnter event. Once you've written the basic navigation code, you can move to any topic in the .m13 file. Figure 6.12 shows the full-screen presentation of the opening topic of the MediaView 1.3 help file, Mv13doc.m13, from Microsoft's JumpStart CD-ROM.

Listing 6.1   6LIST01.TXT—Code for the Basic Navigation Commands for the MediaView 1.3 OLE Control

```
Option Explicit

Public fToContents As Boolean
Public fIsFullscreen As Boolean
Private Sub Form_Load()
   'Set True for constant full-screen display
   'Set False for small contents window
   fIsFullscreen = True

   'Expand form to full screen
   Me.Left = 0
   Me.Top = 0
```

(continues)

Listing 6.1 Continued

```
      Me.Height = Screen.Height
      Me.Width = Screen.Width
      If fIsFullscreen Then
         ocxMV13.Left = 20
         ocxMV13.Width = Screen.Width - 150
         ocxMV13.Height = Screen.Height - 1285
      End If
   End Sub

   Private Sub cmdContents_Click()
      'Provides for small contents window
      fToContents = True
      If Not fIsFullscreen Then
         ocxMV13.Width = 2895
         ocxMV13.Height = 3495
         ocxMV13.Top = 600
         ocxMV13.Left = 120
      End If
      ocxMV13.Object.JumpContents
   End Sub

   Private Sub ocxMV13_TopicEnter(ByVal Addr As Long, _
         ByVal TopicTitle As String)
      If ocxMV13.IsPrevTopic Then
         cmdPrevious.Enabled = True
      Else
         cmdPrevious.Enabled = False
      End If
      If ocxMV13.IsNextTopic Then
         cmdNext.Enabled = True
      Else
         cmdNext.Enabled = False
      End If
   End Sub

   Private Sub cmdNext_Click()
      ocxMV13.Object.JumpNextTopic
   End Sub

   Private Sub cmdPrevious_Click()
       ocxMV13.Object.JumpPrevTopic
   End Sub
```

One of the advantages of MediaView is that you can take advantage of Visual Basic 4's and third-party OLE Controls in pop-up forms that take advantage of additional MediaView functions. A history form is the simplest to implement with MV1332.ocx's History List properties (see listing 6.2 and fig. 6.13). MediaView files aren't yet object enabled, so you must deal with arrays of topic names and addresses, instead of collections and member objects.

The Form_Load event handler for frmHistory iterates the HistoryTitle and HistoryAddr(ess) arrays, which have HistoryCount elements, and loads the List and ListData items of the lstHistory list box with the array values. When you select a lstHistory item and click the Jump button, or double-click a lstHistory item, the JumpAddr(*Index*) method causes a jump to the topic specified by the selected HistoryAddr value.

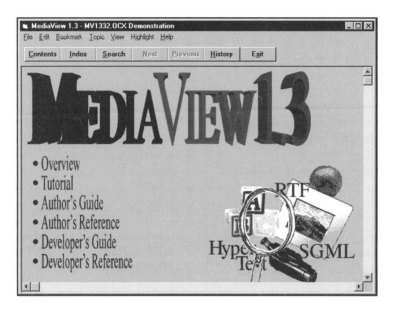

Fig. 6.12
The MediaView demonstration form displaying the first topic of the Mv13doc.m13 help file from Microsoft's JumpStart CD-ROM.

Listing 6.2   6LIST02.TXT—Code for Creating a MediaView History List Box in a Pop-up Form

```
Option Explicit

Private Sub Form_Load()
    'Load History list box with history titles and addresses

    Dim lngCtr As Long

    cmdJump.Enabled = False
    lstHistory.Clear
    For lngCtr = 0 To frmMain!ocxMV13.HistoryCount - 1
        If Len(frmMain!ocxMV13.HistoryTitle(lngCtr)) > 0 Then
            lstHistory.AddItem
                frmMain!ocxMV13.HistoryTitle(lngCtr)
            lstHistory.ItemData(lstHistory.ListCount - 1) = _
                frmMain!ocxMV13.HistoryAddr(lngCtr)
        End If
    Next lngCtr
End Sub
```

(continues)

Listing 6.2 Continued

```
Private Sub lstHistory_Click()
    'If a selection, enable the Jump button
    If lstHistory.ListIndex > -1 Then
        cmdJump.Enabled = True
    End If
End Sub

Private Sub cmdJump_Click()
    'Jump to the topic selected in the list box
    frmMain!ocxMV13.Object.JumpAddr _
        (lstHistory.ItemData(lstHistory.ListIndex))
    Unload Me
End Sub

Private Sub lstHistory_DblClick()
    'Same as clicking the Jump button
    cmdJump_Click
End Sub

Private Sub cmdClose_Click()
    Unload Me
End Sub
```

Fig. 6.13

A pop-up form with a history list box added to the basic MediaView form.

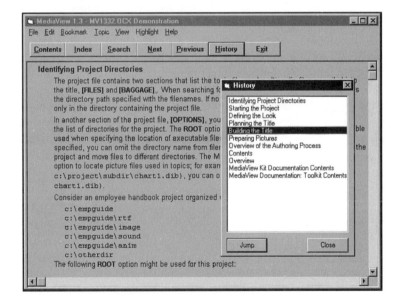

Lenel MediaDeveloper Controls

Lenel Systems International, Inc. (Fairport, NY) has been in the forefront of Windows multimedia development tools since the early days of Windows

3.1. Lenel was first out of the gate in 1994 with a full set of 16-bit multimedia OLE Controls for Access 2.0, which was the only OLE Control container application at the time. In 1995, Lenel released updated 16-bit and 32-bit MediaDeveloper OLE Controls for digital audio, digital video, bitmapped images, animations, and overlay video. The new MediaDeveloper controls are aimed at multimedia title developers who need a richer set of properties and methods than those offered by Visual Basic's MCI control or MCIWndX derivatives. As an example, the Lenel 32-bit digital video control (L_dvid32.ocx) provides the following unique features:

- A grafted Control menu with submenus for media control operations, such as play, stop, rewind, and fast forward, plus a floating toolbar for media navigation. Your form needs a menu bar in which to graft the Control menu. You set the form's `NegotiateMenu` property to **True** (the default) and then set the relative position of the menu bar choices with the `NegotiatePosition` property in the Menu Editor.

- Scaled thumbnail images in Windows DIB (Device-Independent Bitmap) format (`CreateDIBThumbnail` method) that you can copy to the Clipboard (`CopyToClipboard` method) or save to a file (`SaveFormatAs` method). Lenel's Gallery OLE Control lets you display multiple titled thumbnail images in a single control with point-and-click activation of the corresponding original file. Thumbnail images are especially useful in creating multimedia database tables that include a field with pointers to the corresponding source files.

- Automatic saving of still images to files (`Save` and `SaveAs` methods) in a variety of common graphics formats, including .dib, .bmp, .jpg, .pcx, .tif, and .gif files. The file extension you select determines the graphics format. You also can capture the image as a Windows metafile (`GetMetafile` method).

- Support for a variety of digital video file formats, such as Windows (.avi), QuickTime (.mov, .jpg, .pic), MPEG-1 (.mpg), and Intel DVI (.avs). You need the appropriate hardware and/or drivers for each file format.

- Selectable colors for each edge of the frame surrounding the video window and the ability to specify the frame width.

Many of the properties, methods, and events of the L_dvid32.ocx are shared across the 16-bit and 32-bit versions of the other Lenel MediaDeveloper controls. Figure 6.14 shows the Attributes page of the Properties Sheet for the

Lenel L_dvid32.ocx control. The Property Sheet pages for other MediaDeveloper controls use the same general format. Figure 6.15 shows the Control menu grafted to a standard menu bar. The `NegotiatePosition` property value of the File, Edit, and View menu choices is set to Left and the Help menu value is set to Right. Thus, the Control menu appears between the View and Help menu choices.

Fig. 6.14

The Attributes page of the Properties Sheet for the Lenel MediaDeveloper digital video OLE Controls.

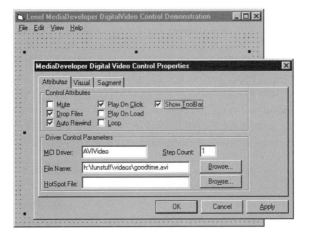

Fig. 6.15

The optional Control menu choice added by the MediaDeveloper digital video control. (Image courtesy of Geffen Records, Inc.)

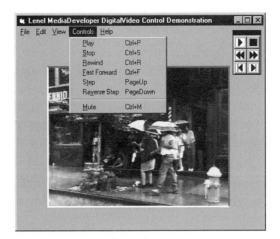

> **Note**
>
> The lack of an underscore to indicate the accelerator key for the Control menu is an artifact of Microsoft's Control menu feature, not of the MediaDeveloper controls. Although the underscore does not appear, Alt+C opens the Control menu.

Listing 6.3 shows the 32-bit VBA code required to capture to the Clipboard full-size and thumbnail images of the current video frame in three sizes: 80-by-60, 120-by-90, and 180-by-160 pixels. The Edit menu offers Copy Image, Copy Thumbnail 80×60, Copy Thumbnail 120×90, and Copy Thumbnail 180×120 choices. The vbCFDIB constant, defined by the ClipBoardConstants class of the VB - Visual Basic objects and procedures type library, corresponds to the Windows CF_DIB Clipboard constant. Figure 6.16 shows examples of full-size (320 by 480 pixels for .avi files) and scaled thumbnail images in each of the three sizes.

Listing 6.3   6LIST03.TXT—Code for Capturing with the MediaDeveloper L_dvid32.ocx Control Full-Size and Thumbnail Images from Individual Video Frames

```
Option Explicit
Private fCopy As Boolean
Private hDIB As Long

Private Sub mnuEditCopyImage_Click()
    hDIB = ocxLenelDV.GetDIB
    fCopy = ocxLenelDV.CopyToClipboard(hDIB, vbCFDIB, True)
End Sub

Private Sub mnuEditCopyTN80_Click()
    '80 x 60 Thumbnail
    Call CopyThumbnail(80, 60)
End Sub

Private Sub mnuEditCopyTN120_Click()
    '120 x 90 Thumbnail
    Call CopyThumbnail(120, 90)
End Sub

Private Sub mnuEditCopyTN180_Click()
    '180 x 120 Thumbnail
    Call CopyThumbnail(180, 120)
End Sub

Private Sub CopyThumbnail(intX As Integer, intY As Integer)
    hDIB = ocxLenelDV.CreateDIBThumbnail(intX, intY)
    fCopy = ocxLenelDV.CopyToClipboard(hDIB, vbCFDIB, True)
End Sub
```

Fig. 6.16
Quarter-screen
(320-by-240) and
thumbnail images
captured from
multiple video
frames. (Images
courtesy of Geffen
Records, Inc.)

Taking Advantage of New Digital Video Technology for Multimedia

This chapter was written during a major turning point in digital video for multimedia applications. In September 1995, Sony and Panasonic introduced high-end camcorders using the new consumer Digital Video (DV) format; a month later, Japan Victor Co. (JVC) and Sharp Electronics also announced DV products. On October 12, Intel released 16-bit and 32-bit versions of its new Indeo Video Interactive (IVI, Indeo 4.1) scalable codec designed specifically for Pentium PCs, but usable with faster 80486-based computers. Microsoft's Halloween trick-or-treat was the Windows 95 Game SDK, minus DirectVideo, but with all the other DirectX APIs in place. Although these new multimedia products aren't targeted specifically to users of Visual Basic 4, the new video hardware and software will have a major impact on the quality of video content included in the multimedia titles you develop with Visual Basic 4. The following three sections describe these three new multimedia-related technologies.

Consumer Digital Video Camcorders and DVCRs

Recording-quality video content for multimedia applications requires camcorders that use one of the professional video formats, such as Sony Betacam SP or Panasonic MII component (YCrCb) analog video, or the common digital video formats: Digital Betacam, D-1, D-3, or D-5. High-quality Hi8 footage shot with $6,000 to $7,000 camcorders, like the Sony EVW-300 series, often is acceptable, but you should not expect a conventional consumer camcorder to deliver usable content for a CD-ROM title. The garbage in, garbage out (GIGO) adage is especially applicable to digital video formats for CD-ROM distribution, such as Indeo, Cinepak, or MPEG-1, where interframe compression is used. If your analog video source material isn't virtually perfect, image quality at today's double-speed CD-ROM data rates goes to pot.

New "consumer" camcorders that use the Digital Video recording format make high-quality video acquisition accessible to multimedia producers on a tight budget. The Sony DCR-VX1000, a $4,199 (list price, $3,600 to $4,000 street price) DV camcorder with three 410,000-pixel CCD sensors (see fig. 6.17), delivers analog S-video output with 500 lines of theoretical horizontal resolution. A luminance sampling rate of 13.5 MHz, 1.5-MHz chrominance bandwidth, and signal-to-noise ratio (SNR) of > 54 dB provides video quality that's almost indistinguishable from the Betacam SP and MII component formats. One-hour DV minicassettes ($2.25 \times 2 \times 0.5$ inches) are about the same size as an audio microcassette; the tape itself is only .25 inch (6.35 mm) wide.

Fig. 6.17
The Sony DCR-VX1000 3-CCD Digital Video camcorder. (Courtesy of Sony Corporation)

Although the video signal is compressed about 5:1 by a process similar to the Motion-JPEG codec used by high-end digital video capture cards, compression artifacts are only visible to a trained observer with very good eyesight. The proof that the DV format can deliver "broadcast quality" video is Panasonic Broadcast & Television Systems Company's DVCPRO product line, which is designed for broadcast ENG (electronic news gathering) and EFP (electronic field production) work. Although DVCPRO uses a different tape cassette and offers professional digital video (D-1) and serial digital audio

(AES/EBU) outputs, the video and audio signals are recorded in the consumer DV format, but at a different track spacing. DVCPRO adds an audio cue track and linear timecode (LTC) to aid in the editing process.

Note

The Sony DCR-VX1000 and its single-CCD companion (DCR-VX700) record 12-bit, non-linear, 32-kHz stereo digital audio channels. Although the high frequency response of this recording format doesn't match that of 16-bit, linear, 48-kHz recordings with the Panasonic consumer and DVCPRO products, reproduction of frequencies above 15 kHz is not essential for most multimedia footage. For more information on the Sony DV camcorders, visit Sony's Digital Handycam Web page at `http://www.sel.sony.com/SEL/consumer/camcorder/digital.html`.

What's more significant about the Sony DCR-VX series camcorders is their IEEE-1394 digital input/output connectors. The IEEE-1394 High Performance Serial Bus, called the "Multimedia Connection" by the 1394 Trade Association, sometimes is referred to as the FireWire bus. (FireWire is Apple Computer, Inc.'s trademark for its implementation of IEEE-1394.) The advantage of digital I/O is that there is no loss of quality (called *generation loss*) when making successive copies of DV tapes. Better yet, you don't go through the digital-to-analog and analog-to-digital conversion process when capturing DV video and audio data to your fixed disk for non-linear video editing with applications such as Adobe Premiere; it's digital all the way. Capturing full-motion video requires fixed disks with a minimum sustained data transfer rate of 3.5 M/sec, well within the capabilities of today's fast SCSI drives designed specifically for audio/video applications. Although no digital video capture cards with IEEE-1394 inputs were available when this book was published, you can expect announcements of several such cards based on Texas Instruments' PCILynx 1394-to-PCI chipset and similar architectures at the Spring 1996 National Association of Broadcasters convention.

Note

The accompanying CD-ROM contains three "white papers" in Microsoft Word 6.0 format that describe the DV format (Dv_formt.doc), the IEEE-1394 High Performance Serial Bus (Dv_1394.doc), and forthcoming IEEE-1394 adapter cards for DV gear (Dv_adapt.doc). These files are located in the \\CODE\CH6 folder of the CD-ROM. Updated versions of these papers will appear from time to time in the Premiere Library of the Adobe Applications Forum (GO ADOBEAPP) on CompuServe. You can obtain additional up-to-date information on the IEEE-1394 High Performance Serial

Bus from the 1394 Trade Association Web page at `http://www.skipstone.com`. Skipstone, Inc. is the "central supplier of technology and products for the IEEE-1394 serial bus." Information on Texas Instruments' IEEE-1394 product line is available from `http://www.ti.com/sc/1394`.

Intel Indeo Video Interactive

The folks who bring you digital video content on CD-ROMs have long sought a software-only playback codec that delivers higher quality images than those available from the most popular Video for Windows 1.1e codecs, Indeo 3.2 and Cinepak. MPEG-1 compression, which requires hardware-assisted playback for full-screen (640-by-480-pixel), full-motion (29.97-frames/second) images and hi-fi sound from CD-ROMs, costs users an additional $200 to $300 for an MPEG-1 decoder card. Compaq Computer Corporation has announced multimedia PCs with on-board MPEG-1 decoder chips and, by the time you read this book, Microsoft is likely to have released a software-only MPEG-1 decoder for Pentium-based PCs acquired from a third-party developer.

Intel's new scalable Indeo Video Interactive (IVI) codec, which uses wavelets compression for software-only video and audio playback, is intended to challenge MPEG-1 (at least on Pentium PCs). If you're a member of The Microsoft Network, you've seen wavelets compression in action; MSN uses wavelets compression for progressive rendering of graphic images. When you're playing back IVI video, the resolution of the image improves as your CPU horsepower increases. It's not surprising that Intel gives away the 16-bit and 32-bit versions of IVI, when you consider that you need a 90-MHz or faster Pentium to obtain optimum video quality.

In addition to scalability, the IVI codec offers the following unique features:

- The capability to chroma-key (also called *blue-screen*) motion video on a still bitmap background image. You shoot your video against a deep blue (*chroma blue*) background and set chroma blue as the transparent "color." The bitmap background appears in the transparent region. (Chroma-keying is how TV weatherpersons appear to be superimposed on weather maps.)

- In many cases, especially PC games, you need to display only a particular region of the video image. The IVI codec provides a feature called *local decode* that lets you establish a movable viewport for the on-screen display.

- Unlike existing codecs, IVI lets you apply special effects to the video image during playback. Brightness, contrast, and saturation can be changed by player software to emulate, for instance, different lighting conditions.

- Traditional software-only video decoders drop frames when your PC can't keep up with the decoding process for the video data stream. Today's Indeo 3.2 and Cinepak one quarter-screen (320-by-240-pixel) video delivers a maximum of about 15 frames per second (fps) from a double-speed CD-ROM. IVI, which uses a more efficient bi-directional compression algorithm (similar to MPEG-1 B-frame encoding), can deliver 24 fps. Instead of dropping frames, which can be very distracting to the viewer, the images simply lose sharpness if the viewer's PC can't keep up with the decoding chores.

> **Note**
>
> You can download the 16-bit and 32-bit Intel IVI codecs and a set of white papers that describe in detail Indeo 4.1's new features from the Multimedia library of the Intel Architecture Forum (GO INTELA) on CompuServe. The same files are available from Intel's Web site, **http://www.intel.com**.

The Microsoft Windows Game SDK

Microsoft is targeting PC game producers as a driving force behind the universal adoption of Windows 95 in the consumer market. Sales of game cartridges for dedicated players still exceed PC game sales by a wide margin. To attract game producers to Windows 95 platforms, Microsoft developed the 32-bit Windows Game SDK, which includes the following elements:

- *DirectDraw* for accelerating rendering of bitmapped graphic images. DirectDraw is the successor to the DCI (Display Control Interface) technology originally intended to be included in Windows 95. To get the most out of DirectDraw, you need 32-bit video drivers that incorporate a DirectDraw Hardware Abstraction Layer (HAL) for your Windows graphics accelerator card. Even if you don't have an updated driver, the DirectDraw Hardware Emulation Layer (HEL) can substitue for missing hardware and/or driver features.

- *DirectSound* is the audio counterpart to DirectDraw. DirectSound also provides an HEL to perform in software DirectSound functions that are missing in sound card hardware and/or the sound card's HAL, if present. The most useful feature of DirectSound is its low-latency wave-form audio mixing capabilities. (Anyone who has used or tried to use Wavemix.dll will appreciate DirectSound's mixer.) When this book was published, you couldn't use DirectSound with .avi files; Microsoft's forthcoming DirectVideo API is likely to overcome this limitation.

- *DirectPlay* is designed for creating multiplayer games, where the players are connected by a serial communication link, such as the Internet or a commercial online service provider.

- *DirectInput* provides optimized access to digital and analog joysticks. DirectInput HAL drivers deal with joystick type, calibration data, and other hardware-specific features.

- *DirectSetup* to streamline installation operations for PC games running under Windows 95.

What's missing from the preceding list of DirectX APIs is *DirectVideo*, the long-awaited enhancements to the scaled-back version of Video for Windows (VfW 1.1e) that shipped with retail Windows 95. Fortunately 32-bit Windows video codecs automatically utilize DirectDraw features, if a DirectDraw driver is installed on the user's PC. Initial indications are that DirectDraw improves the performance of VfW 1.1e, but 32-bit DirectVideo is likely to offer considerably better video playback performance with the next round of Windows graphics accelerator cards that support the forthcoming industry standard for ZoomVideo (ZV). ZoomVideo bypasses the PC's bus and permits direct video transfer to a frame buffer on the graphics adapter card by yet another flavor of "over-the-top" feature connector.

The DirectX APIs are based on Microsoft's Common Object Model (COM), one of the subjects of the next chapter. Each of the DirectX APIs has its own object interface, such as `IDirectDraw` or `IDirectSound`, which is derived from the `IUnknown` interface. `IDirectDraw`, for example, abstracts the graphics display adapter card and creates a `DirectDrawSurface` object to represent video RAM and `DirectDrawPalette` object for hardware palettes. Similarly, `IDirectSound` creates the `DirectSoundBuffer` object that abstracts the resources of a sound card. The initial set of DirectX APIs are for Windows 95 only; it's likely that DirectX APIs for Windows NT 3.51+ will be available by the time you read this book.

Summary

Despite the lack of exciting new multimedia features in the Visual Basic 4 package, Microsoft developers and third-party OLE Control publishers are introducing a variety of new 32-bit multimedia controls for Visual Basic and other OLE Control container applications. At the same time, consumer electronics firms are introducing digital camcorders that promise to bring professional-quality video acquisition to a price point that's affordable by multimedia producers without millon-dollar budgets. As Pentium PCs with hardware video acceleration become more prevalent, software MPEG-1 and Intel Interactive Video codecs will provide multimedia and PC game aficionados with low-cost playback at full VGA resolution and acceptable frame rates. When Microsoft releases the DirectVideo API and adapter card manufacturers climb on the DirectX bandwagon, you can expect a major boost to the use of digital video by Visual Basic multimedia developers.

Chapter 7

Introducing 32-Bit OLE 2.1

by Roger Jennings

Roger Jennings is a consultant specializing in Windows database and multimedia applications. He is the author of Que's Unveiling Windows 95; Using Windows Desktop Video, *Special Edition;* Discover Windows 3.1 Multimedia *and* Access for Windows Hot Tips; *and was a contributing author to Que's* Using Windows 95, *Special Edition;* Excel Professional Techniques; Killer Windows Utilities; *and* Using Visual Basic 3. *He has written two other books about creating database applications with Access and Visual Basic, coauthored a book on using Microsoft Visual C++ for database development, is a contributing editor of* Visual Basic Programmer's Journal, *and has written articles for the* Microsoft Developer Network News *and the MSDN CD-ROMs. Roger is a principal of OakLeaf Systems, a Northern California software development and consulting firm; you may contact him via CompuServe (ID 70233,2161), on the Internet (70233.2161@compuserve.com), or on The Microsoft Network.*

Object Linking and Embedding has come a long, long way from its beginnings as a built-in element of early versions of Microsoft PowerPoint. Subsequently, 16-bit Microsoft Office applications for Windows 3 adopted OLE 1.0 as their primary method of inter-process communication, supplementing Clipboard copy-and-paste applications and DDE. Windows 3.1 added OLE 1.0 services (provided by OLECLI.DLL and OLESVR.DLL) as a basic component of the Windows graphical user interface. In 1993, Microsoft introduced 16-bit OLE 2.0, which added a variety of new features to OLE 1.0 through a collection of seven DLLs stored in \WINDOWS\SYSTEM. The most important of the OLE 2.0 additions were in-place activation and editing of embedded objects, nested embedded objects, the ability to drag and drop objects into compound documents, and OLE Automation. In just a couple of years, OLE Automation has proven to be the most important feature of OLE 2x.

Visual Basic 3 provided the MSOLE2.VBX custom control and a helper DLL, MSOLEVBX.DLL, to provide basic OLE 2.0 container capabilities. Visual Basic 3 also supported the client side of OLE Automation with its `CreateObject` and `GetObject` functions. At the time of Visual Basic 3's release, there were no commercial OLE Automation server applications, which explains the lack of real-world OLE Automation code examples in the Visual Basic 3 *Programmer's Guide*. Visio Corporation (then Shapeware) introduced the first OLE Automation server; Microsoft quickly followed with Excel 5.0, Word 6.0, and Project 4. Access 2.0, an OLE Automation client, included support for a prototype version of today's OLE (Custom) Controls.

Windows 95, Windows NT 3.51, and 32-bit OLE 2.1 eliminate many of the problems associated with the initial implementations of 16-bit OLE 2.0. The most vexing problem for users of OLE 2.0 has been `Out of Memory` messages when attempting to link or embed objects created with Microsoft Office mega-apps, such as Word and Excel. The 32-bit OLE 2.1 also promises improved performance as applications are upgraded and tuned to take full advantage of 32-bit operating system features, such as multithreading and (under Windows NT 3.51+) symmetrical multiprocessing. Ultimately, Network OLE will eliminate the single-workstation orientation of OLE 2.1.

This chapter provides an overview of Visual Basic 4's role as an OLE 2.1 client application. All the examples in this chapter are 32-bit, because the future of OLE is inexorably tied to Microsoft's 32-bit operating systems. The majority of the examples, however, are equally applicable to 16-bit Visual Basic applications and 16-bit OLE 2.0 servers. The chapter begins with a definition of important OLE 2x terms, explains the registration of OLE servers in the Windows 95 and Windows NT Registry, goes on to describe how to use the OLE container control and insertable object controls in a variety of scenarios, and concludes with an introduction to the client side of 32-bit OLE Automation.

Defining OLE 2.1 Terms

Getting a grip on OLE 2.1 requires an updated glossary of OLE terminology. Following are definitions of the most important of the current OLE 2x buzzwords:

- *Component Object Model* (COM) is Microsoft's infrastructure for code modules (called *objects*) that are independent of programming languages and computer platforms. COM is oriented to C++ programming on Intel PCs, but Windows NT 3.51+ also supports COM on MIPS, DEC Alpha, and PowerPC RISC systems. COM defines a set of *interfaces*, implemented as a virtual table (`Vtbl`), that points to entries in member function tables. COM requires that all objects support the `IUnknown` interface, which has `AddRef`, `Release`, and `QueryInterface` member functions. The `AddRef` and `Release` functions maintain a count of the number of instances of the object in use. The `QueryInterface` function returns information on the capabilities of the object. COM is implemented by Compobj.dll under Windows 95 and Compob32.dll under Windows NT. OLE is Microsoft's high-level COM implementation.

- *OLE Documents* allow an application to share data created by another OLE-enabled application. A document that contains data created within another application is called a *compound document*, which can be stored in a *compound file*. (OLE 1.0 called compound documents *destination documents*.) Data can be embedded in an OLE Document or created by a link to a file containing the data. Embedded data is contained entirely within the OLE Document, whereas linked data relies on an external file. Monikers (`IMoniker` interface) identify and manage references to embedded or linked OLE objects, including their data element(s). Uniform data transfer allows objects that implement the `IDataObject` interface to pass data via the Windows Clipboard, through OLE drag-and-drop methods, and within a compound document.

- *Container applications*, previously called *OLE client applications*, are capable of displaying and manipulating OLE Documents. The 16-bit and 32-bit versions of Microsoft Excel, Word, Access, PowerPoint, Project, and Visual Basic 4 are OLE container applications.

- *Local servers* are executable applications that are capable of embedding or linking objects within a container application's OLE Document. Local servers, as the name implies, must reside on the same computer as the container application. Local servers are classified as *full servers*, which provide both linking and embedding capabilities, and *mini-servers*, which only can embed data in a compound document and don't open or save files. Most container applications are local servers; however, neither Visual Basic 4 or Access are local servers. Microsoft Graph 5.0 is an example of a mini-server.

- *Automation servers* expose *programmable objects* for manipulation by client applications that include an (OLE) Automation-compliant programming language, such as VBA. The Automation client usually is, but need not be, an OLE container application. An Automation server can be implemented as an *in-process* .dll, which shares the same address space as the Automation client, or an *out-of-process* .exe, which uses

LRPCs (Lightweight Remote Procedure Calls) to communicate with the Automation client. Access 95 and Schedule+, although not local servers, are automation servers. Visual Basic 4 is capable of creating both in-process and out-of-process local Automation servers as well as remote Automation servers.

■ *OLE Custom Controls*, are a special class of in-process Automation server that also expose events. You can add an OLE Control to any container application, but events exposed by the control are accessible only to container applications such as Visual Basic 4 and Access 2.0/95, which are specifically designed to act as OLE Control containers. Future versions of Microsoft Office applications, plus authoring applications for The Microsoft Network and the Internet (codenamed Blackbird during the beta cycle), are expected to support OLE Controls. Chapter 11, "VBX versus OCX," describes OLE Controls in detail.

■ *Remote Automation servers*, also called *Remote Automation Objects* (RAOs), are *out-of-process* Automation servers that communicate via Remote Procedure Calls (RPCs) with networked Automation clients. Visual Basic 4 is the first programming language to be capable of creating RAOs. RAO technology in Visual Basic 4 is the precursor to Network OLE. One of the most important applications for RAOs is developing three-tier client/server database applications, where an RAO (called a *LOBject* for Line-of-Business object) is used in the middle tier to implement business rules. RAOs are one of the subjects of Chapter 18, "Using Remote Data Objects."

One of the objectives of COM is to create *component applications*, which are made up of a combination of local servers, plus in-process or out-of-process automation servers to implement high-end features. The mega-apps that comprise the Microsoft Office software suite are logical candidates for componentizing. As an example, you might want to incorporate only the basic functionality of an Excel worksheet or use Word as a minimal word processor in a Visual Basic application. Although you don't need all the features of either Excel or Word, the present versions of these Microsoft productivity applications are monolithic. Large, monolithic applications require a long time to load and consume resources big time. Componentizing best-selling applications raises the specter of licensing individual pieces of highly profitable mainstream software; thus, it may be some time before you see "pieceware" versions of Microsoft productivity applications.

> **Note**
>
> To qualify for use of Microsoft's trademarked "Designed for Windows 95" logo, 32-bit Windows applications must support OLE 2x containers, objects, or both containers and objects. This requirement, which does not apply to utilities or applications that run exclusively in full-screen mode, is sure to increase the number and variety of OLE servers and, to a lesser extent, OLE container applications. The level of required OLE support depends on whether an application uses files. Applications that use files must support OLE drag and drop. Support for in-place activation, compound files, and OLE Automation is "strongly recommended," but not mandatory.

Interoperating with 16-Bit and 32-Bit OLE Applications

OLE 2.1 running under Windows 95 and Windows NT provides support for interoperability of 16-bit and 32-bit by a process called *thunking*. Following are the rules for using 16-bit and 32-bit OLE objects with container applications:

- 32-bit OLE 2x container applications can embed or link objects created by 16-bit OLE local servers, including OLE 1.0 servers.

- 16-bit OLE 1.0 container (client) applications cannot embed or link objects created by 32-bit OLE 2x local servers. 16-bit OLE 2.0 containers can (or should be able to) embed or link objects created with 32-bit OLE 2x local servers by thunking.

- 32-bit OLE 2x clients can call 16-bit out-of-process Automation servers, and vice versa. All Automation servers are OLE 2x objects. Out-of-process servers that have custom interfaces, however, must have the same "bitness."

- In-process OLE .dlls and OLE Controls must have the same "bitness." Thus, separate 16-bit and 32-bit versions of OLE Controls are provided with Visual Basic 4.

> **Note**
>
> Windows 3.1+, Windows 95, and Windows NT 3.5+ use different thunking processes (Universal, Flat, and Generic, respectively.) For further information on the thunking process for OLE 2x operations, see the "Thunk Layer Operation" chapter of the *OLE Programmer's Reference* in the Win32 SDK.

Registering OLE Servers

All OLE servers, including Automation servers and OLE Controls, must be registered before you can use them. Windows 3.1+ registers OLE servers in its registration database, REG.DAT. Windows 95 and Windows NT use the Registry (System.dat), a more robust version of REG.DAT, to store information about the location and capabilities of OLE servers. Well-behaved OLE servers of all types are self-registering on installation and should de-register themselves as part of the uninstall process required for compliance with the "Designed for Windows 95" logo guidelines. All OLE servers aren't likely to be well-behaved, so you should be familiar with methods of checking, editing, and deleting registry entries. The following two sections describe how to use Windows 95's Registry Editor and the Regsvr32.exe application.

Using Windows 95's Registry Editor

Familiarity with the Windows 95 and/or Windows NT registry is a must for 32-bit Visual Basic 4 developers. As an example, if you manually move an OLE server's executable file (instead of uninstalling and reinstalling the application), you must alter the contents of the Registry to reflect the new well-formed path to the server. You launch Windows 95's Registry Editor, Regedit.exe, from the \Start\Programs\Accessories\System Tools menu. Unlike Windows 3.1's REGEDIT.EXE, you do not need to specify verbose mode with a /v command-line switch to display detailed Registry entries. Windows 95's Registry Editor uses the Explorer model to display the hierarchy of Registry entries, which is much more complex than that of Windows 3.1+'s REG.DAT.

OLE 2 server registration takes place in the HKEY_CLASSES_ROOT\CLSID hive of the Registry. CLSID (Class ID) is a 32-character GUID (Globally-Unique IDentifier) that uniquely identifies each OLE 2 server. To check the registration data for an OLE server, launch the Registry Editor and choose Edit, Find to open the Find dialog. Type the executable file name, including the extension, in the Find What text box and click the Find Next button. Press F3 to bypass file extension association entries until Regedit reaches the . . .\CLSID hive. Figure 7.1 shows the primary LocalServer32 entry for Excel 95 (version 7.0), Microsoft Excel Sheet. If the entry does not point to the current location of the server, double-click the string ("AB") icon to open the Edit String dialog. Edit the Value Data string as required to specify the new location for both the 32-bit LocalServer32 and 16-bit LocalServer values, unless you want to use Excel 5.0 for testing 16-bit container applications.

In addition to the CLSID for Excel 95's Sheet object (ProgID = Excel.Sheet.5), there are successive CLSID entries for Excel Chart (ProgID = Excel.Chart.5), and Application objects, each of which points to *d*:*path*\excel.exe. ProgID is an abbreviation for Programmatic ID, the name of the object used with Visual Basic's **CreateObject**() function for creating an instance of an Automation server object. Launching Excel 95 as an Automation server requires adding the /Auto command-line parameter to preclude its window from appearing and to prevent addition of the Microsoft Excel item to the taskbar. If you change the location of a server, you need to alter each incidence of the server location string in the Registry. Unfortunately, the Registry Editor doesn't have an Edit, Replace menu choice.

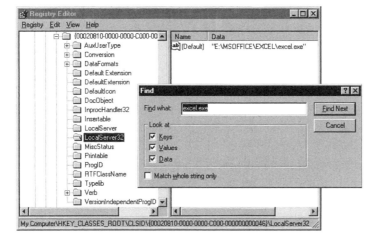

Fig. 7.1

The path to and name of Excel 95's executable file for registration of the Excel.Sheet.5 object.

> **Note**
>
> Windows 3.1+'s REGEDIT.EXE (opened with the /V parameter for verbose mode) and Windows NT's 3.5's Regedt32.exe use similar entries to specify the location of OLE servers. Only Windows 95's Regedit.exe, however, includes the full-featured Edit, Find feature described in this section. You must manually locate entries for server registration in Windows 3.1+ and Windows NT 3.5+. The hierarchy of Registry hives in Windows NT is quite similar to that of Windows 95.

Registering and Unregistering OLE Servers with Regsvr32.exe

Regsvr32.exe, which is included with Visual Basic 4, is a command-line application that adds, updates, or deletes registry entries for OLE servers, including OLE Controls. You must use Regsvr32.exe to install OLE Controls that don't come with an installation application; many shareware and freeware OLE

Controls don't include a setup feature. To register an OLE server, use the following syntax in the Open text box of Windows 95's Run dialog:

```
regsvr32.exe d:\path\oleserver.ext
```

The preceding syntax example assumes that Regsvr32.exe is located in the \Windows, \Windows\System, or another folder on the current DOS path. Figure 7.2 shows the message box that appears when registration of an OLE Control, in this case the Lenel MediaDeveloper L_dvid32.ocx described in the preceding chapter, is successful. The conventional location for Regsvr32.exe, OLE Controls, and Automation servers you create with Visual Basic 4 is the \Windows\System folder.

Fig. 7.2

The message box indicating successful registration of an OLE Control with Regsvr32.exe.

If you want to remove an OLE 2x server or intend to move an OLE 2x server to a new location, take advantage of Regsvr32.exe's capability to unregister a server. The server must be present for unregistration to work, so don't delete or move the server's file until you execute the following command line:

```
regsvr32.exe /u d:\path\oleserver.ext
```

Figure 7.3 shows the somewhat strange message you receive when unregistering a server. You can repeatedly register and/or unregister servers with no ill effects. Unregistering a server you move to a new location is useful to ensure that all the registration data is updated.

Fig. 7.3

The message box that appears after unregistering an OLE Control with Regsvr32.exe.

Using Visual Basic 4 to Create OLE Container Applications

Like Visual Basic 3, Visual Basic 4 includes an OLE container control. Unlike Visual Basic 3's MSOLE2.VBX, Visual Basic 4's OLE Control is intrinsic; it automatically appears in the toolbox when you launch Visual Basic 4. The OLE container control is a "wrapper" object that provides a set of properties, methods, and events, which are applicable to a wide variety of embedded and linked objects. The following sections describe the features of the OLE container control and how to use the OLE container control to embed or link a variety of OLE objects.

Working with the OLE Container Control

Visual Basic 4's OLE container control is capable of displaying and manipulating documents created by any OLE full server or mini-server, including OLE 1.0 servers. Adding an OLE container control to a Visual Basic 4 form is similar to creating a compound document with any other OLE container application, such as Microsoft Excel or Word. In the case of Visual Basic 4, the form, rather than an Excel worksheet or Word document, is the container document. An Access 2.0/95 form with an unbound object frame control also is a container document. When you add an OLE container control to a Visual Basic form, the standard OLE 2.0 Insert Object dialog appears, as shown in figure 7.4. The Object Type list displays each OLE local server registered by your computer. The following two sections describe how to embed or link documents with the OLE container control.

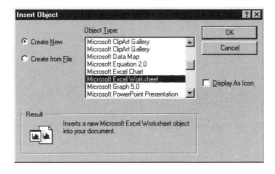

Fig. 7.4

The Insert Object dialog that appears when adding an OLE container control to a Visual Basic 4 form.

Embedding Objects in the OLE Container Control

To create a new (empty) embedded instance of an object, with the Create New option selected, pick the server to create the object from the Object Type list and click OK. Alternatively, you can double-click the Object Type item.

An empty Excel 95 worksheet embedded in a form with the OLE container control initially appears, as shown in figure 7.5. The empty worksheet object is activated for in-place editing, superimposed over the *presentation* of the object. The presentation of an OLE object is a static Windows metafile that displays an object's data when the object is not activated. In design mode, the embedded object grafts all or a part of its menu structure to the form; embedded objects don't display the server's File menu choice. Menus grafted from OLE servers don't appear in run mode unless you add a menu bar to your form and set the NegotiateMenus property of the form to **True** (the default).

Fig. 7.5

Embedding an empty Excel worksheet in a form results in an activated object superimposed over the presentation.

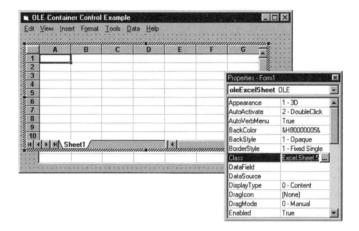

To activate the worksheet object, double-click the presentation surface. Alternatively, with the mouse pointer over the presentation surface, click the right mouse button to open a pop-up menu that displays the verbs applicable to the object. Most servers offer Edit and Open choices; Edit activates the object in place, and Open opens the server's window. Figure 7.6 illustrates an Excel worksheet activated in run mode. A menu bar with a single File menu choice is added to the form to enable grafted menu negotiation. (The "Lenel MediaDeveloper Controls" section of chapter 6, "Using Visual Basic as a Multimedia Front-End," describes the menu grafting and negotiation process for OLE Controls. Excel's row and column headers, scroll bars, and sheet tab(s) appear as frame adornments. You must provide a margin at the top and to the left of the OLE container control to accommodate Excel's frame adornments. You can enter data in the empty activated worksheet and use many of Excel's grafted menu choices to manipulate the embedded object. The eight sizing handles allow you to adjust the size of the activated object within the limit of the size of the OLE container control. Pressing Esc deactivates the object and displays its presentation in the OLE container control (see fig. 7.7).

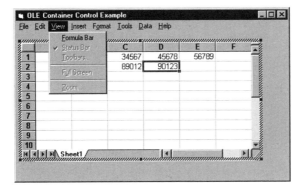

Fig. 7.6
An embedded
Excel worksheet
object with grafted
menus activated
for editing.

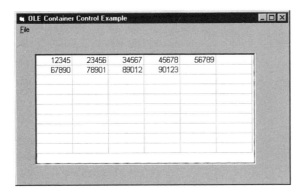

Fig. 7.7
The inactive
presentation of an
Excel 95 worksheet
after entering data
in the activated
state.

Tip

If you want to activate the OLE object when your form opens, apply the appropriate
DoVerb (vbOLE*Constant*) method to the object in the Form_Activate event
handler. The DoVerb method is one of the subjects of the "Properties and Methods
of the OLE Container Control" section, later in this chapter. Activating the control
from the Form_Activate event, rather than the Form_Load event, displays the form
and the presentation of the object while the server loads. Depending on the speed of
the user's PC and free system resources available, opening the object's server can
take an appreciable amount of time.

Note

The OLE 2x specification's state diagram for embedded objects requires that a single click outside the surface of the activated object must deactivate the object. Clicking the surface of the form (outside the OLE container control) doesn't deactivate the object in run mode. If your form contains one or more controls in addition to the OLE container control, you can use the Form_Click event handler to apply the SetFocus method to another control. If you don't want another control to appear on your form, add to the form a small PictureBox control with no border and a ForeColor value that matches the ForeColor property value of your form. Apply the SetFocus method to the PictureBox and then to the OLE container control, as in the following example:

```
Private Sub Form_Click()
    picEmpty.SetFocus
    oleExcelSheet.SetFocus
End Sub
```

You also can embed an object based on data contained in a server file. When the Insert Object dialog appears upon adding an OLE container control to a form, click the Create from File option button to display the file version of the Insert Object dialog. Click the Browse button to select in the Browse dialog the file that contains the data. The file extension association contained in the HKEY_LOCAL_MACHINE\ROOT hive of the Registry identifies the appropriate server for the document. Figure 7.8 illustrates selection of a Word 95 document. (Although Word 95 is version 7.0, Word objects are classified as Microsoft Word 6.0 documents to maintain backward compatibility with 16-bit Word 6.0 and 32-bit Word for Microsoft NT.) When you click OK, the upper-left corner of your document appears in Word's Page Layout presentation. (Normal and Outline view are not available when embedding Word documents.)

Fig. 7.8
Creating an embedded Word 95 document from a file.

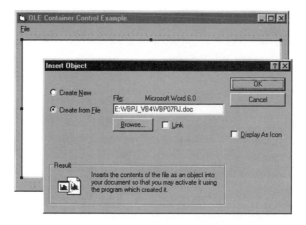

When you activate the Word object, either by double-clicking the OLE container or by a `Form_Activate` event handler, Word's toolbars appear as sizable floating toolbars and the Word menu is grafted to your form's menu, as shown in figure 7.9. Unlike Excel, Word 95 doesn't provide frame adornments for navigating the document; you must use the cursor positioning keys to maneuver to a specific location in the Word document.

> **Note**
>
> The OLE container control exhibits several anomalies with embedded Excel 95 worksheets. For example, Word's toolbars appear as floating toolbars after you activate an embedded Word 95 document object, but Excel 95's toolbars do not appear on activation. Although the Formula Bar choice appears when you open Excel's View menu, the Formula Bar does not appear, except for a brief flash below the menu bar. Activating embedded Excel 95 worksheets created from .xls files results in peculiar appearance in the OLE container, especially if Excel's `AutoFormat` method has been applied to the worksheet. One of the problems with activating in Visual Basic 4 Excel 95 worksheets based on files is described in the Microsoft Knowledge Base document Q129793, "BUG: Excel Displays Only First Column in Embedded Worksheet."

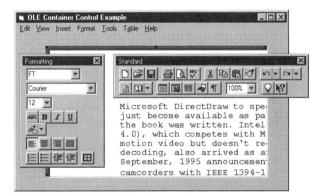

Fig. 7.9
An activated Word 95 document with grafted menus and floating toolbars.

The extent to which you can manipulate activated embedded document objects within the OLE container control is dependent on capabilities contributed by the server. Each OLE 2x server has its own set of features and idiosyncrasies when used to embed objects in compound documents. Idiosyncrasies, in particular, confuse users who expect the embedded object to behave in an OLE container control exactly as the object behaves when opened in its server application or when inserted as an object in a conventional container document. Thus, you're likely to find that opening the server's window, rather than in-place activation, is the better design approach, especially when dealing with documents based on files. Substitute the vbOLEOpen constant for vbOLEUIActivate as the argument of the DoVerb method in your Form_Activate event handler to open the server's window.

Linking Objects to the OLE Container Control

When you embed an object with an OLE container control, the object's data is contained in the form. Other applications cannot access the embedded data, other than by Clipboard operations with an active instance of the object. When you compile a project, the embedded data is incorporated in the project's .exe file. Very large embedded objects, such as spreadsheets with many rows and column, full-screen color bitmaps, or multimedia (.wav and .avi) files, can have a profound effect on the .exe file's size. The solution to these problems is to link the file to the OLE container object. Linking only embeds a pointer file; like embedding an object from a file, the file extension determines the OLE server that is used to open the file. The linked file may be located on a server, and you can create a link to a part of a file, such as a range of cells in an Excel worksheet, a paragraph of a Word document, or a particular segment of a multimedia file.

Creating an object linked to an OLE container control is similar to embedding an object from a file. Select the Create from File option, select the file that contains the data you want to link, and mark the Link check box (see fig. 7.10). Click OK to create the link. When you run your form, the presentation appears as shown in figure 7.11. Double-click the surface of the OLE container control to open Excel 95's window, or use the right mouse button to display the pop-up verb menu; choosing either Edit or Open from the verb menu launches Excel 95 and displays Excel's window.

Fig. 7.10

Creating a link to an Excel 95 workbook file.

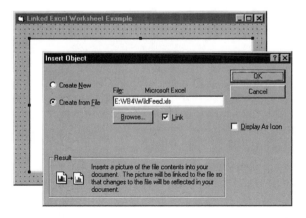

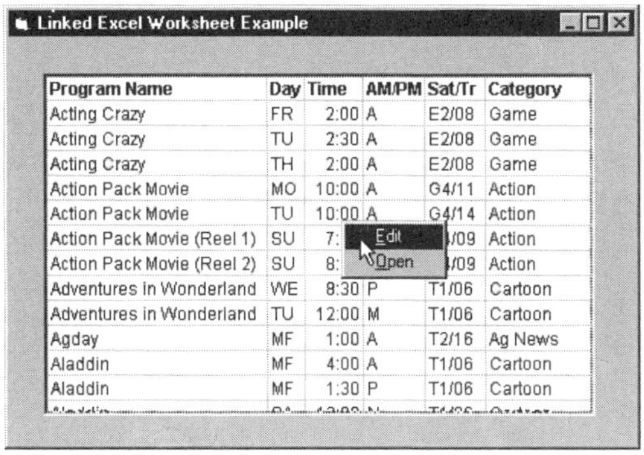

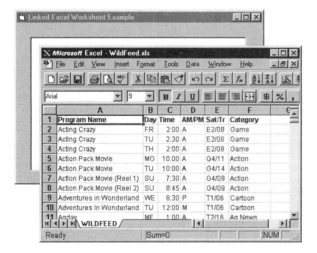

Fig. 7.11
The presentation
of a linked Excel
95 spreadsheet
with the pop-up
verb menu active.

By default, the server opens in a normal window of modest dimensions (see fig. 7.12). All the server's menu choices are available when you open the server's main window, including the File menu, so you don't need to include a menu bar on your form.

Fig. 7.12
Excel 95's main
window displaying
data in a linked
workbook file.

When you create a link to a file, the path to and name of the file appears as the value of the SourceDoc property. 32-bit Visual Basic 4 supports long file names and Uniform Naming Convention (UNC) for files located on servers. Thus, you can use \\ServerName\ShareName\FileName.ext as the value of the SourceDoc property. UNC file names eliminate Invalid link messages when server shares are mapped to workstation drive letters, which may change from user to user.

You can specify a subset of the data in the linked file to appear in the presentation window by specifying a data identifier in the SourceItem property text box. For Excel spreadsheets, you use row-column (R#C#:R#C#) syntax or a named range; Word documents use Bookmarks to specify a particular block of text. An alternative method is to open the file in the server's window, select the cells or text you want to link, and copy the selection to the Clipboard. Right-click the OLE container control, and choose Delete Object from the pop-up menu; then open the pop-up menu again, and choose Paste Special to open the Paste Special dialog. Select the Paste Link option (see fig. 7.13), and click the OK button to re-create the link. When you open the server's window, the selected cells or text are selected automatically (see fig. 7.14).

Fig. 7.13

Using the Paste Special dialog to link a range of Excel 95 worksheet cells to an OLE container control.

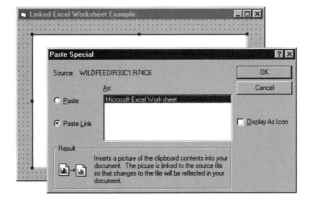

Fig. 7.14

The linked range of cells is selected when you open Excel 95's window from the OLE container control.

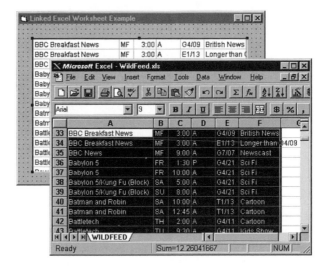

> **Note**
>
> When you change a link by typing a new value for the SourceDoc property or alter the value of the SourceItem property, a Delete Current Link message box appears. Click Yes to delete the existing link; then right-click the container control to open the pop-up menu. Choose Create Link to re-create the link to the new file and/or data item. If you want to change only the SourceItem property, delete the data item extension (such as !R1C1:R12:C6) from the SourceDoc value; then retype the data item identifier in the SourceItem property text box.

Properties and Methods of the OLE Container Control

The preceding sections describe the most commonly used properties and methods of the OLE container control. Online help for the OLE container control provides (in most cases) the information you need to set property values and apply methods programmatically. Following are some of the changes to OLE container control methods and properties between Visual Basic 3 and 4:

- The Action property of the Visual Basic 3 OLE container custom control is replaced by methods of the Visual Basic 4 OLE container control. The Action property is retained for backward compatibility; new OLE applications should use the methods that correspond to the 14 Action constants. (Search online help for the Action property of the OLE container control for the methods.)

- The Verb property of Visual Basic 3 is replaced with the DoVerb method, although you can still use the Verb property and its numeric arguments with existing code. The syntax of the DoVerb method is oleName.DoVerb(vbOLEConstant), where vbOLEConstant is one of seven intrinsic constants whose value ranges from 0 to –6. The vbOLEHide constant (–3) hides the server's window after you choose the Open option of an embedded control or apply the DoVerb method with the vbOLEOpen (–2) constant. When the server is hidden, the presentation of the object is hatched with diagonal lines. Using the vbOLEShow constant (–1) activates an embedded object in-place, as does vbOLEUIActivate (–4).

- The Zoom and Stretch values of the SizeMode property seldom are useful in real-world applications other than displaying bitmapped and vector images. Large spreadsheets or other documents are illegible when Zoomed or Stretched. Using the AutoSize value, which causes the control to fit its content, often makes the size of the OLE container control larger than the form.

■ OLEDropAllowed is a new property that, when set to **True**, enables the OLE container control to act as a target for OLE drag-and-drop operations. OLE drag and drop is the subject of the next section.

Implementing OLE Drag and Drop with the OLE Container Control

To obtain the right to apply Microsoft's "Designed for Windows 95" logo to an application that uses files, the application must support the OLE drag-and-drop feature of Windows 95. OLE drag and drop lets you drag the icon of a file that's supported by a local OLE server from My Computer or Explorer and drop it on the surface of an OLE container control. The new object created by the drag-and-drop process replaces the object, if any, in the OLE container control. If you drag a desktop shortcut to a file supported by an OLE server, an icon representing the shortcut appears in the OLE container control. You double-click the shortcut to open the server's window to edit the shortcut's file.

To enable an OLE container object as an OLE drag-and-drop target in run mode, set the value of the OLEDropAllowed property to **True** (the default is **False**) and set the value of the OLETypeAllowed property to Linked (only), Embedded (only), or Either (0, 1, or 2, respectively). In design mode, you can use the OLE container control as an OLE drop target without setting OLEDropAllowed to **True**. Figure 7.15 shows a linked Excel 95 worksheet created by dragging the Dtv_toc.xls file icon from Windows' Explorer to an OLE Control container in run mode.

Fig. 7.15

A linked Excel 95 worksheet in an OLE container control created by dragging a file icon from Windows' Explorer.

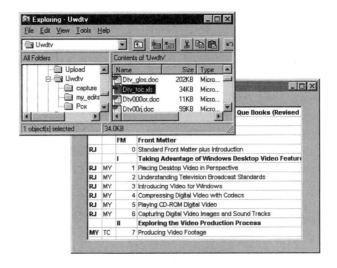

> **Note**
>
> The presentation of a link that you create in run mode does not appear when you return to design mode. To make the presentation appear in design mode, right-click the OLE container control and choose Create Link from the pop-up menu.

Binding the OLE Container Control to an OLE Object Field

Like many of Visual Basic 4's other OLE Controls, the OLE container control is data-enabled, letting you display OLE objects linked to or embedded in OLE Object fields of Access tables. Visual Basic 3's OLE Control was not data-enabled, so displaying objects contained in Access OLE Object fields involved a substantial amount of code to deal with Access's "OLE wrapper." When you bind the OLE container control to an OLE Object field, the control behaves much the same as Access's bound object frame control. For most Visual Basic 4 developers, displaying OLE Objects in tables of .mdb files is the most common application for the OLE container control.

To bind a Visual Basic 4 OLE container control to a field of Access's OLE `Object` type, add a Data control to a form, set the value of the `DatabaseName` property to point to an Access .mdb file, such as Northwind.mdb, that contains a table with an OLE Object field, and then choose the table with the OLE Object field as the `RecordSource` of the Data control. Add an OLE container control to the form; then click Cancel when the Insert Object dialog appears to create an empty control. Connect the `DataSource` property of the OLE container control to the Data control, and select the OLE Object field for the `DataField` property. Figure 7.16 shows a simple form that displays the contents of the Photo, Notes, LastName, and FirstName fields of Northwind.mdb's Employees table. No code is required to create the form shown in figure 7.16. Double-clicking the bitmapped presentation opens the Windows Paint application to let you edit the image.

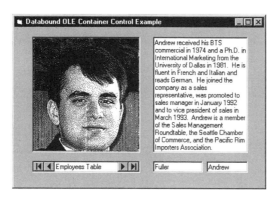

Fig. 7.16
A simple form to display bitmapped images contained in an Access OLE Object field.

Writing and Reading OLE Data Files

Embedded OLE objects you create or modify in OLE container controls in run mode are not persistent; the content is lost when you return to design mode or close your executable application. You can save the presentation and data of an embedded OLE object or the presentation and link pointer of a linked OLE object with the OLE container's SaveToFile method. The following code saves an embedded OLE object in an OLE container named oleExcelSheet to the Sheet1.ole file when you choose File, Save from the form's menu:

```
Private Sub mnuFileSave_Click()
    Dim intFileNum As Integer
    intFileNum = FreeFile
    Open "Sheet1.ole" For Binary As #intFileNum
    oleExcelSheet.SaveToFile intFileNum
    Close #intFileNum
End Sub
```

The file is saved in OLE stream format. Reading the data from an OLE file created by the preceding subprocedure and updating the presentation requires use of the ReadFromFile method, as in the following example:

```
Private Sub mnuFileOpen_Click()
    Dim intFileNum As Integer
    intFileNum = FreeFile
    'Open the file
    Open "Sheet1.ole" For Binary As #intFileNum
    oleExcelSheet.ReadFromFile intFileNum
    Close #intFileNum
    'Update the presentation
    oleExcelSheet.DoVerb (vbOLEUIActivate)
    picEmpty.SetFocus
    oleExcelSheet.SetFocus
End Sub
```

The last three lines of code update the static presentation to display the data from the file by momentarily activating the embedded Excel worksheet object. The picEmpty picture box control serves as a control to which focus is set temporarily to deactivate the OLE container control.

Insertable Objects

As noted in the "Working with the OLE Container Control" section earlier in the chapter, Visual Basic 4 forms are OLE containers. You can prove this by embedding an *insertable object* directly in a form, rather than into an OLE Control. Visual Basic 4's online help defines an insertable object as "[a]n object of an application, such as a Microsoft Excel Worksheet, that is a type of custom control." Visual Basic 4 forms are simple OLE containers that support operations such as grafted menus (menu negotiation) and in-place activation, but most insertable objects don't provide a window to display the object's presentation.

You can add buttons representing insertable objects to Visual Basic 4's toolbox from the Custom Controls dialog. Marking only the Insertable Objects check box results in a list of objects identical to those in the Object Type list of the Insert Object dialog (see fig. 7.17). Like OLE Controls, the items you check are appended to the toolbox when you click the OK button. The default name of an insertable object is derived from its object type: Excel objects are Sheet1 or Chart1, and a Media Player object is named mplayer1.

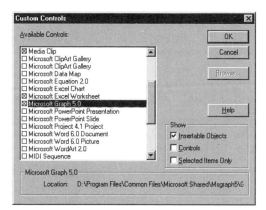

Fig. 7.17

The Custom Controls dialog displays a list of Insertable Objects that you can add to Visual Basic 4's toolbox.

Insertable objects that support in-place activation, such as Excel Worksheet and Chart objects, graft their menus to Visual Basic 4 menu bars when activated. Figure 7.18 shows insertable Media Player and Excel Chart objects added to a form; the Chart object is activated for editing. Unlike OLE Controls, insertable objects have only a generic property set and a few events that are common to all control objects. Insertable objects do not support methods, except two generic methods, SetFocus and Move. Insertable objects created by OLE Automation servers, however, have an Object property that you can use to program the insertable object. Thus, the primary application for today's insertable objects is to provide a visual presentation for programmable objects. Programming objects exposed by OLE Automation servers is the subject of the remaining sections of this chapter.

Fig. 7.18
An insertable Excel
Chart object
activated for
editing in place.

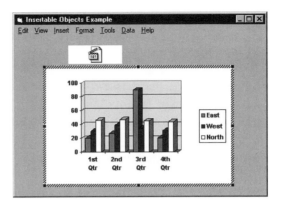

Creating Integrated Applications with OLE Automation Servers

OLE 2.0 introduced the concept of OLE servers that expose programmable objects for manipulation by OLE Automation client applications. An OLE Automation client need not be a container application, because an invisible instance of the OLE Automation server handles manipulation of its programmable objects. Any application that incorporates VBA is an OLE Automation client, and all members of the Professional Edition of Office 95 are OLE Automation servers. (Microsoft Word 6.0 and Word 95 are not full-fledged OLE Automation servers, but the Word.Basic object exposed by these versions of Word lets you manipulate Word documents with Word Basic commands.) An OLE Automation server need not be an OLE full server; Access 95 is an example of an OLE Automation server that cannot contribute objects to a compound document created by an OLE container application because Access 95 is not an OLE 2x full server or mini-server.

Excel 5.0 was the first product to incorporate VBA as an application programming language and to expose objects as an OLE Automation out-of-process server. Visual Basic 3, which predated the retail release of Excel 5.0, was the first OLE Automation client. Today, most of Microsoft's software offerings to the business community are OLE Automation servers or are in the process of being updated to expose programmable objects. Microsoft's competitors, such as Novell and Lotus, were adding OLE Automation to their forthcoming 32-bit productivity software suites when this book went to press. When Microsoft releases the next major upgrade to Windows NT 3.51+, presently code-named Cairo, 32-bit OLE Automation will become a basic component of the Windows operating system.

The following sections discuss the basics of programming predefined hierarchies of objects exposed by commercial full-server applications. As noted in the "Defining OLE 2.1 Terms" section near the beginning of this chapter, Visual Basic 4 lets you create your own in-process and out-of-process local Automation servers, plus remote Automation servers. Chapter 19, "Remote Automation," discusses out-of-process servers that you can access over a network.

Exposing Object Properties and Methods with Type Libraries and References

The Microsoft OLE 2.0 *Programmer's Reference* defines properties of programmable objects as "member function pairs that set or return information about the state of an object, such as whether or not an object is visible." Methods are single member functions "that perform an action on an object, such as resizing it or causing it to evaluate member data." OLE Automation interfaces provide access to the collection of member functions through the IDispatch, IEnumVariant, ITypeLib, and ITypeInfo interfaces. The IDispatch and IEnumVariant interfaces access to individual objects and object collections, respectively. ITypeLib supplies information about the objects exposed by the Automation server, and ITypeInfo provides details about the properties and methods of each object. The purpose of ITypeLib and ITypeInfo interfaces, which are not mandatory, is to assist object programmers by providing information about the exposed objects with object browsers.

VBA introduced the use of references to type libraries supplied with OLE Automation servers. Type libraries for out-of-process servers use .olb and .tlb extensions; many in-process OLE DLLs, such as DAO3032.dll, have self-contained type libraries. (Most OLE Controls use .oca type libraries to speed loading of the control.) VBA also adds an object browser that lists the exposed objects, plus the properties and methods of each object. Another advantage of using a type library is that the Visual Basic interpreter/compiler checks the syntax of your OLE Automation code in design mode. Visual Basic 3 and Access 2.0 detect errors in OLE Automation source code only when the code is executed in run mode.

To make a type library visible in Visual Basic 4's object browser and accessible by the VBA interpreter/compiler, you create a reference to the type library in the References dialog that opens when you choose <u>T</u>ools, <u>R</u>eferences. The names and locations of type libraries appear in Registry entries. Figure 7.19 shows the References dialog listing type libraries in the Available References list. To make a type library accessible to Visual Basic 4 and the object browser, you must mark the check box to the left of the library name and then click OK to close the References dialog.

Fig. 7.19
VBA's References
dialog listing the
type libraries of
installed OLE
Automation
servers and
insertable control
objects.

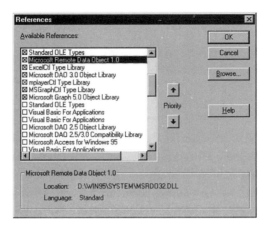

Visual Basic creates some references, such as those for insertable object controls, automatically. You must add references to object libraries of applications such as Microsoft Excel, Access, Word, and Project manually. (Word 95's Word95 Objects for ACCESS type library exposes only the few methods of the Word95Access object needed for mail-merge applications.) Once you've added references to the server applications you plan to use, information contained in the referenced type libraries is accessible from the object browser. Objects contained in your current Visual Basic 4 project appear as the default entry in the Libraries/Modules drop-down list of the object browser. To display the objects, methods, properties, and constants defined in an OLE Automation type library, open the Libraries/Modules list and pick the appropriate library. Figure 7.20 shows the extraordinary syntax for the ChartWizard method of the Chart object of the MSGraph5 OLE Automation mini-server. Clicking the ? button displays the help file for object, method, or property. (The ChartWizard method, which is used by Access 95 and Excel 95, is not documented in the online help file for Microsoft Graph 5.0, but The Excel 95 VBA help file has a topic that covers the ChartWizard method).

Fig. 7.20
VBA's object
browser displaying
the syntax of the
ChartWizard
method of
MSGraph5's
Chart object.

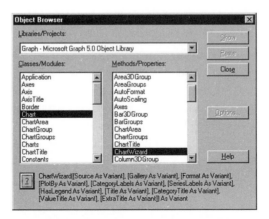

> **Note**
>
> Special type libraries for insertable objects used as controls contained in Visual Basic 4 forms are temporary type library files named VB####.tmp, which are stored in your \Windows\Temp folder. #### represents an arbitrarily assigned four-character hexadecimal number. As an example, the type library for an insertable Graph object (named MSGraphCtrl) might be VB4290.tmp. Type libraries for insertable objects expose the standard set of properties and methods applicable to all Visual Basic 4 controls that are created from insertable objects. A .tmp control type library does not enumerate the object(s) exposed by the OLE Automation server.

Unlike OLE Controls, programmable OLE objects do not expose events. If you link or embed a programmable object in an OLE container control, events such as Updated are triggered by the control, not by the server object contained in the control. All arguments and return values of methods and properties for exposed objects are of the **Variant** data type for compatibility with the IEnumVariant interface.

Creating and Manipulating Programmable Objects

The easiest way to experiment with programmable OLE objects is to add an insertable object or OLE container control to a form and then write code in the debug window to manipulate the control's Object property. An Excel Sheet object linked to an OLE container control or an MSChartCtl insertable object control is a good starting point for learning the basics of OLE Automation client programming. Figure 7.21 illustrates use of the debug window to modify the default chart that appears when you add an MSChartCtl control to a form. You gain access to the programmable aspects of the control through the Chart1.Object.Application.Chart object. The presentation of the insertable chart object changes as you alter the values of the Chart object's properties in the debug window.

To minimize the amount of typing necessary to refer to the Chart object, create a pointer to the Chart object by declaring an object variable in the declarations section of your form and then setting a pointer to the Chart object in the Form_Load event handler, as in the following example:

```
Option Explicit
Private chtTest As Object

Private Sub Form_Load()
    Set chtTest = Chart1.Object.Application.Chart
End Sub
```

Fig. 7.21
Obtaining and
setting property
values of an
`MSChartCtl` object
in the debug
window.

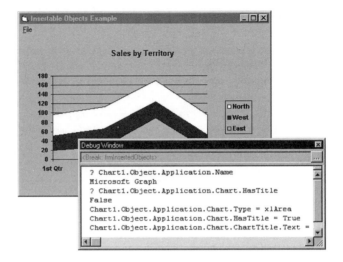

After creating a pointer to the `Chart` object, you use the new object variable in statements such as those shown in figure 7.22. The last five statements in the debug window of figure 7.22 are equivalent to the `With...End With` structure in the following code:

```
Private Sub Form_Load()
    Set chtTest = Chart1.Object.Application.Chart
    With chtTest
        .HasTitle = True
        .ChartTitle.Text = "Sales by Territory"
        .ChartTitle.Font.Size = 18
        .ChartTitle.Font.Italic = True
        .Type = xlBar
    End With
End Sub
```

Note

Documentation for the objects, methods, and functions of Graph5.exe in the MSGraph.hlp file is limited, to be charitable. Excel 95's online help has substantially more information on the object hierarchy of MSGraph5, plus the properties and methods of MSGraph5 objects. Type **Chart Object** in the Index page of Help Topics: Microsoft Excel dialog to display the starting point for `Chart` objects. MSGraph5 is of limited utility as a Visual Basic 4 graphing tool because you cannot gain direct access to the `Datasheet` object that stores data values for the `Chart` object. Graph5.exe expects source data from a specified range of an Excel worksheet or from an application, such as Access, in Excel's native BIFF format.

Getting and setting the cell values of an Excel `Sheet` object linked to an OLE container control uses a similar approach. Setting a pointer to a `Sheet` object exposed by Excel requires the following code:

```
Option Explicit
Dim xlsTOC As Object

Private Sub Form_Load()
    Set xlsTOC = _
        oleExcelLink.Object.Application.Workbooks(1).Sheets(1)
End Sub
```

Examples of getting and setting the properties of a Sheet object in the debug window appear as shown in figure 7.22. Changes to cell values are reflected in the presentation. To close the invisible instance of Excel, you apply the `Quit` method to the `Application` object, which causes a Save changes? message box to appear, if you make changes to the `Sheet` object. You can bypass saving changes and the message box by executing `xlsTOC.Parent.Saved = True` to clear the dirty flag prior to executing `xlsTOC.Application.Quit`.

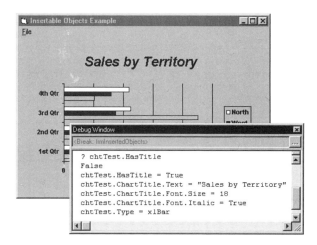

Fig. 7.22
Setting `Chart` properties with an object variable that points to the `Chart` object.

Using VBA's `CreateObject` and `GetObject` Functions

If you don't want to display an object's presentation on your form, you can create object variables with the **CreateObject** or **GetObject** function. To use either of these functions, first declare an object variable in the declarations section of a form or module. **CreateObject** is related to inserting an empty object of a type chosen in the Insert Object dialog, and **GetObject** parallels the Insert from File option of the Insert Object dialog. The generalized syntax of these two functions is:

```
Set objVariable = CreateObject("AppName.ObjType")

Set objVariable = GetObject(["d:\path\filename.ext"], ["AppName.ObjType"])
```

The *AppName.ObjType* argument consists of the application name and the object type you want to create or open, such as Word.Basic for Word 6.0/95 or Excel.Sheet for Excel 5.0/95. The *AppName.ObjType* argument is optional for the **GetObject** function if the file extension specifies, through an association entry in the Registry, the particular object type you want. In most cases, you don't need to use the second object. If you omit **GetObject**'s *d:\path\filename.ext* argument, you must provide the *AppName.ObjType* argument for an open instance of the application and object type.

The following code example populates a list box, lstFeeds, with the first 100 unduplicated items from a list of satellite wildfeeds (unscheduled programming) contained in a Wildfeed.xls file. The program names appear in column A of the worksheet, beginning at row 2.

```
Option Explicit
Private xlsFeeds As Object

Private Sub Form_Activate()
    Dim intCtr As Integer
    Dim strProgram As String

    lstPrograms.Clear
    Set xlsFeeds = GetObject("e:\vb4\wildfeed.xls")
    For intCtr = 2 To 101
        strProgram = xlsFeeds.Range("A" & CStr(intCtr)).Value
        If lstPrograms.ListCount = 0 Then
            lstPrograms.AddItem strProgram
        ElseIf lstPrograms.List(lstPrograms.ListCount - 1) _
            <> strProgram Then
            lstPrograms.AddItem strProgram
        End If
        lstPrograms.Refresh
    Next intCtr
    xlsFeeds.Parent.Saved = True
    xlsFeeds.Application.Quit
    Set xlsFeeds = Nothing
End Sub
```

Adding the preceding code to the Form_Activate event handler and executing the lstPrograms.Refresh statement in the **For...Next** loop lets you watch the list box fill with the entries as they are retrieved from the Wildfeeds worksheet. Setting xlsFeeds to **Nothing** frees resources associated with the xlsFeeds object.

> **Tip**
>
> If you're performing complex operations on another application's programmable objects and the application supports VBA, you can speed operation of your client application by writing a VBA function in the server application and calling the function from your Visual Basic 4 code. Communication with out-of-process servers is by Lightweight Remote Procedure Calls (LRPCs), which are very slow in comparison to execution of VBA code contained in a server application module. Writing as much VBA code as possible in the server application makes the testing process easier and faster, too. The Run method of Excel's Application object lets you execute from Visual Basic 4 a function written in Excel VBA. For more information on the Run method, search Excel 95's online help.

Expanding Your Use of Visual Basic 4 to Create OLE Automation Client Applications

Getting the most out of integrated applications requires familiarity with the hierarchies of objects exposed by OLE Automation servers. Excel 95 exposes more than 100 objects and object collections. The Word.Basic pseudo-object lets you use a multitude of sometimes-arcane Word Basic commands. (VBA's capability to use named arguments makes dealing with Word Basic commands much easier than Visual Basic 3 code.) Publishing limitations preclude adding code examples to this chapter for all of today's OLE Automation servers, but the preceding examples should serve to get you started writing VBA code to create large-scale integrated productivity applications.

Summary

Microsoft is betting the future of its Microsoft Office productivity software suite, the BackOffice server suite, and upgrades to the Windows 95 and Windows NT operating systems on the Component Object Model and 32-bit OLE 2.1+. This chapter emphasizes use of Visual Basic 4's 32-bit OLE container control in conjunction with OLE Automation objects exposed by Excel 95 and Word 95. As Windows 95 and Windows NT 3.51+ gain momentum, virtually all mainstream Windows applications will include OLE full server and Automation features. Today's OLE mega-servers are heavy-hitters in the resource department; future versions are likely to be replaced by fully componentized applications that let you pick the feature set you need for your Visual Basic 4+ OLE client applications. When members of Microsoft Office 95, the Blackbird authoring tools for MSN and the Internet, and other best-selling software are upgraded to include OLE Control container features, the market for 32-bit OLE Controls will expand by at least an order of magnitude. As this chapter demonstrates, however, you can use today's OLE full server, mini-servers, and Automation severs, both in-process and out-of-process, to create useful 32-bit OLE 2.1 component applications with Visual Basic 4.

Chapter 8

Programming MAPI

by Chris Barlow

In addition to writing a monthly column for the Visual Basic Programmer's Journal *and speaking at VBITS, Comdex, and TechEd, Chris Barlow is the President of
SunOpTech®, Inc.*

*His background includes a combination of entrepreneurial, management, and com-
puter skills. He earned his undergraduate degree from Dartmouth College with Distinction in Economics & Computer Science and, as a student at Dartmouth, worked
as a programmer on some of the later enhancements to the BASIC language with its
inventors, Drs. Kemeny and Kurtz. He received his MBA from Harvard Business
School and worked for Fortune 500 companies in manufacturing and management
information systems.*

*Based in Sarasota, Florida, SunOpTech uses Visual Basic and Visual C++ to develop
Windows-based decision support applications for medium- to large-size manufacturing enterprises.*

*Reach Chris at SunOpTech, Inc., 1500 West University Parkway, Sarasota, FL,
34243; by telephone at 941-362-1271; by fax at 941-355-4497; and on the
Internet at ChrisB@SunOpTech.com.*

Message-enabled applications are mushrooming and it is becoming a requirement for programmers to understand how to enable their applications to
send and receive messages.

The Growth of Messaging

In this chapter, we'll learn how to use the Messaging Application Program
Interface (MAPI) built into Microsoft Windows. We'll also learn how to do
the following:

■ Send and receive messages with MAPI

■ Create our own MAPI Class module

■ Finish with our own MAPI OLE Server

Direct Access Architecture

Computers can share information with each other in two ways: *direct access* and *messaging*.

Until recently, most software development focused on direct access information exchange. The most common example of this is reading a database from a server that has been redirected to a network drive on the client computer. However, many programmers are now realizing that messaging architecture results in more robust applications.

If you think back to the early days of software development, programmers were writing applications for stand-alone mainframe computers. The programmers had to focus only on the one computer; they knew that their application would be the only one running on the computer and that it would run from start to finish. As they wrote their application they knew that a file on a tape or disk drive would be available on the computer and that their program would be the only program accessing that file. Unfortunately, today many programmers still think this way!

I was a student at Dartmouth College in 1969 when John Kemeny and Tom Kurtz were working on some of the later enhancements to the BASIC programming language that they had developed in the early 1960s. The development of BASIC was driven by the invention of timesharing by a Dartmouth student. Timesharing was the first time that multiple terminals could share a single computer.

The terminals we used are not what you are used to! They printed each character on a roll of paper rather than displaying it on a screen. Because it took several seconds for the user to type a line and press the carriage return key, the computer spent most of its time waiting for terminal input. Timesharing was a supervisor program that ran on the mainframe computer and allowed the computer to process the input from one terminal while the other terminals were printing or waiting for input. Then the supervisor program would save all the code and data from that terminal and switch to process the input from another terminal. I remember the celebration we had when, for the first time, we had over 100 terminals connected to a single computer.

Today this concept of sharing time on a computer sounds normal to us. After all, Microsoft Windows is really a "supervisor program" that runs on our PCs and switches to process the input from one window or another. But this concept was so revolutionary in the 1960s that General Electric hired the student who invented it to help develop the GE Timesharing Network.

Timesharing from a terminal was the first time programmers could be interactive with a computer. Before timesharing, programmers would submit a stack of computer punched cards with their program source code and wait for several hours for their turn to compile their program on the computer. Then they would receive a huge printout of the program listing and its errors so they could punch up some new cards with the corrections and go through the process again. With timesharing, users could type their program directly into the computer from the terminal. It was this interactive programming development environment that drove the development of BASIC with its interpretive line-oriented compiler, line numbers, GOTO, etc.

The single direct access model of programming continued with the first PCs. In DOS, on a stand-alone PC, there was no need to worry about interacting with another program or another computer. However, the popularity of local area networks (LAN) forced developers to rethink this single-use strategy.

Unfortunately, the LAN developers "solved" this problem by adding network software which would redirect a drive on another computer to a drive letter on their computer. This way, the program could pretend that the data was still on their computer. To deal with the possibility of multiple users of files, the LAN developers provided a locking program, SHARE, that could lock a data file and not allow others to access it. This way, the application program could, again, pretend that it was the only program using the file.

This obsolete software architecture of direct access via shared network files continues today. The problems with this architecture have become more obvious as modern business has evolved to enterprises.

Over the past few years, some companies have begun to think of themselves as an "enterprise" with distributed multiple branch offices. These distributed offices must constantly share information to effectively serve their customers.

More recent is the growth of the "virtual enterprise," which joins a company and its vendors and distributors under a single information umbrella so that they appear to the customer as one organization.

This change has placed a huge demand on MIS departments to come up with creative solutions through reengineering. Unfortunately, the solution of most software developers has been to continue the deception of direct access by creating expensive, hardware intensive, wide area networks (WAN) with automatic routers that make a long-distance connection anytime a program requires one. This allows the programs to continue to pretend that the data file is available on one of their disk drives.

However, this "solution" has not made it any easier for enterprise people who often must do their jobs from laptop computers in remote sites. Direct access architecture generally requires heterogeneous networks and begins to break down as different types of hardware and networks need to be connected.

I believe this basic shift to distributed enterprise organizations and the growth in mobile computing requires a rethinking of this direct access architecture and a redesign of applications to share information via a messaging architecture.

Note that I'm not suggesting that we use the currently popular client/server model where the MIS department spends years trying to set up a few tightly controlled, highly structured servers and to implement custom designed client access software throughout the organization. We all know the horror stories of large client/server implementations.

Rather I'm suggesting a set of applications throughout an organization that use messaging as their access method to publish just their own small piece of the organization's prime data. The data is developed and maintained by each of the departments that cooperate to provide links to the other related messaging servers.

Messaging Architecture

At SunOpTech®, we have used this messaging model extensively for the past five years to design robust manufacturing scheduling systems. Ken Henderson, Bob Koski, and I hold a software patent, #07/986,727 from the United States Patent Office for *Decentralized Distributed Asynchronous Object Oriented System and Method of Electronic Data Management, Storage, and Communication,* which we call the ObjectBank®.

We have seen how easy it is to develop effective software once the programmer begins to think about messaging rather than direct access. Messaging gives great flexibility to a distributed enterprise because it is inherently cross-platform and not dependent on a particular type of hardware or software.

There are two basic types of message exchange between computers: *synchronous* and *asynchronous*.

Synchronous message exchange requires some interconnection of the computers and usually relies on a network transport system like TCP/IP. Web Browsers on the Internet are good examples of this type of transfer mechanism. In a synchronous message exchange, the client application usually stops and waits for a return message from the server computer as when a Web browser displays the message `Connecting to www.sunoptech.com` and waits for a response from the Web server.

Asynchronous message exchange, on the other hand, does not require that the two computers be able to establish a real-time communication link. Rather, the application sends a message and then resumes its activities. It receives a response at some later time, perhaps seconds or days from when it sent the original message, and completes whatever processing is necessary. The strength of this model is that the information exchange does not require a real-time connection. The program does not lock up or stop processing while waiting for information but continues with other tasks.

A real advantage of the asynchronous model is that it provides the ultimate flexibility with a single program architecture. If the computers are directly connected on a network the message response can be received almost instantaneously. In this mode it is difficult to tell the difference between synchronous and asynchronous application architecture by looking at the response time. In fact, a messaging application can respond almost as quickly as a direct access application when the computers are interconnected.

Programmers can write their application by using only the asynchronous model. If the computers are not connected, as in a user operating a laptop on an airplane, the program will create messages and continue processing while it waits for a response. But, if the computers are interconnected, the program will operate nearly as quickly as using synchronous messaging or even a direct access model.

In today's world of interconnected computers, designing your software by using an asynchronous architecture allows your application to operate as effectively with a laptop in a hotel room as it does with your PC in the office.

MAPI—Messaging Applications

MAPI stands for Messaging Application Programmer Interface but deals only with asynchronous messaging. Not every application can fit easily into the asynchronous model. For example, ordering items from a telephone order department would seem to require at least a synchronous if not a direct access model. However, smart business reengineering can change this requirement. For example, suppose that the customer could receive information on sale items and respond with an order or request for more information via an e-mail system? It might be possible to provide better service to the customer and eliminate the order entry person. Let's examine some of the common categories of messaging applications.

E-Mail Applications

Everyone recognizes e-mail as the most common form of asynchronous messaging. Most e-mail is just a close imitation of the U.S. Mail system—one person types a message and e-mails it to another person at an address where it sits until the person "opens" his or her mail and reads the message.

Most e-mail systems let you attach files to messages so that a spreadsheet, word processing program, or even an EXE file can be sent with the e-mail message. However, this type of e-mail generally relies on the client software delivered with the mail system to create and send the message.

Developers are beginning to "mail-enable" their applications. Some programs simply emulate the e-mail client's ability to let the user create and send a message. Most spreadsheet programs now allow users to e-mail their spreadsheet. Some programs, such as Microsoft Office applications, have even added a "routing" capability, even though this is not supported by Microsoft Mail v3.

However, there are some interesting applications where either the sender or the receiver of the mail message is not a human but a computer program.

Report Distribution Applications

The largest category for automated mail senders is report distribution, where documents are sent in response to a request by a recipient or initiated by the sender. List server programs are the most common example of this category.

For example, if you send an e-mail message to *listserv@listserv.tamu.edu*, with the subject blank and the first two lines of the body of the message:

- sub VISBAS-L <your name goes here>
- set VISBAS-L digests

then your mail message will be received by the list server program and your e-mail address added to a database. Periodically, the list server will send you a report of all Visual Basic-related messages in this list.

Database Query Applications

Another interesting use of this asynchronous messaging architecture is the ability to query information from a database on another computer.

SunOpTech's ObjectBank system watches its e-mail address for withdrawal queries from the ObjectTeller program and responds with an e-mail message containing the requested objects.

Microsoft's SQLServer 6.0 supports database queries sent via e-mail. SQLMail operates as a MAPI client, including extended stored procedures so that you can e-mail a SQL query to the e-mail address monitored by a SQLServer database. It will process the query and return the result set to you via e-mail.

Inter-Application Communication Applications

I think the really interesting applications are those where both the sender and the receiver are computer programs.

For example, in SunOpTech's ObjectJob manufacturing system, new jobs arrive in a department's scheduling queue via e-mail from a customer or another department. The Cube Scheduling System monitors this e-mail address, receives the order, and sends e-mail messages to all the required Resource Objects requesting information on their availability. The Resource Objects monitor their own e-mail address and respond to availability requests with a rich response detailing their availability, flexibility, and possible conflicts.

In this system, the use of the asynchronous messaging model allows the Cube Scheduling System to properly schedule jobs that use both local resources within the department and resources provided by vendors in remote locations without regard to the location of the Resource Objects.

If the exciting concept of developing software by using the messaging model is not enough, there is one more compelling reason to learn how to program by using MAPI: it is a Windows 95 logo requirement for an application to support a simple send mail menu item using Common Mail Calls.

Before we see how easily you can mail-enable your applications by using MAPI with Visual Basic 4, let's take a closer look at what MAPI really is.

MAPI—Messaging Application Program Interface

MAPI is part of Microsoft's WOSA and seems to have won the battle with Lotus Corporation's VIM to be the universal messaging API. Lotus has announced that its Notes product will have a MAPI interface. The alternative Common Mail Calls (CMC) API, the X400 standard, can also be used but is modeled very closely on MAPI.

Forms of MAPI

There are actually three forms of MAPI. The first, and only fully released, form is Simple MAPI. It lets you send mail, work with the address book, and read mail from the folder defined as the inbox. We'll focus on Simple MAPI in this chapter because it lets you mail-enable an application. Soon to be released MAPI 1.0 lets you access other folders in the mail system. Extended MAPI lets you create a MAPI service provider such as Microsoft Mail or CompuServe's MAPI driver.

MAPI's Role in Development

The role of MAPI and the other messaging APIs is to provide the link between messaging client programs, like you will write after reading this chapter, and the service providers such as Microsoft Mail 3.2, Lotus Notes, and CompuServe.

Yes, CompuServe has a MAPI interface (GO MAPI on CIS) that allows you to use your standard MSMail client (or your own MAPI program!) to send and receive e-mail on CompuServe. If you're interested in working with the sample code in this chapter but don't have an e-mail system on your network, you can download CompuServe's MAPI driver and test your MAPI programs via CompuServe.

It seems certain that more and more vendors will add MAPI support to their systems.

Writing MAPI Applications

To write mail-enabled applications, you'll need your own MAPI application, the MAPI DLL's included with most versions of Windows, and a MAPI Service Provider like MSMail or CompuServe.

Providing the simple mail support required for Windows 95 is actually very easy. As a Visual Basic 4 programmer, you have three alternatives:

- Use the MAPI Session and Message controls (in their VBX or OCX form) included with Visual Basic

- Make direct calls to the MAPI or MAPI32 DLLs

- Use an OLE Automation interface to MAPI

Microsoft does its usual excellent job in its Visual Basic 4 samples, tutorial, and help files to explain the use of the MAPI controls. These controls provide a relatively easy method to mail-enable an application, although they have some weaknesses.

The MAPI controls seem too complicated for the simple tasks of enabling your application to send a file attached to an e-mail message. Yet they don't appear to be robust enough for the more complex job of creating a mail-centered application. The MAPI VBX controls do have a real weakness; if you build an EXE with these controls and try to run it on a system that does not have MAPI present, you won't just get an error message—your application won't even load!

In the rest of this chapter we'll learn how to use the functions in the MAPI DLL, then we'll create a MAPI class to encapsulate our MAPI functionality, and finally we'll develop our own OLE automation interface to MAPI.

Adding a Send Mail Menu Item

Let's begin by adding the capability to your program to mail a message. The MAPI DLL is pretty smart! If you call one of the functions and you're not logged on to the mail system, then the MAPI DLL will perform the logon by using the user name and password defaults set up in MSMAIL.INI.

The MAPI DLL's have their own standard dialogs for creating and sending messages. These dialogs provide the full capability to access the service provider's address book and attach files to messages.

The first step is to create a new project, called Mapi1, for our mail-enabled application. Add a module to the project and call it MAPI.BAS. Then add this function declaration for SendDocuments to a module in your application. The function lets us pass parameters for the files we would like to attach to the mail message, but as null parameters are passed, the function will display a dialog:

```
Declare Function MAPISendDocuments Lib "MAPI.DLL" (ByVal UIParam&,
➥ByVal DelimStr$, ByVal FilePaths$, ByVal
FileNames$, ByVal Reserved&) As Long
```

Now, on Form1 add a File menu item and under it a SendMail menu item called mnuSendMail. In the mnuSendMail_click event add the following code:

```
dim rc&
rc = MAPISendDocuments(0&, 0&, vbNullChar, vbNullChar, 0&)
```

Now run your application and click the File|SendMail menu item and you should see MAPI's Edit dialog that allows you to type a message, choose a recipient from the address book, and attach files before sending the message (see figure 8.1). That's all there is to it!

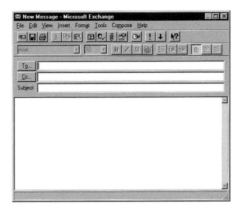

This function call also lets you attach one or more of your application's
data or document files to the mail message before displaying the dialog.
Try changing the line of code to:

```
rc = MAPISendDocuments(0&, ",", "c:\autoexec.bat,c:\config.sys",
➥"autoexec,config", 0&)
```

Now when you click the menu item, you'll see that the AUTOEXEC.BAT and
CONFIG.SYS are already attached to the message. You could do the same
with your own application's files.

MAPI Types

The MAPISendDocuments function lets you easily send a message and files from
your application. But if you want to add more functionality, you need to
understand a few more functions and the three MAPI structures or User
Defined Types:

- MAPIMessage—Stores information about the MAPI message

- MAPIFile—Stores information about files attached to a MAPI message

- MAPIRecip—Stores information about senders and receivers of MAPI
  messages

When you call some of the MAPI functions, you'll need to pass these structures to pass information to MAPI.

The MAPIMessage structure contains the information about a single message:

```
Type MapiMessage
    Reserved As Long
    Subject As String              'the subject of the message
    NoteText As String     'the text of the message
    MessageType As String 'can be a custom type but usually null
    DateReceived As String
    ConversationID As String
```

```
        Flags As Long
        RecipCount As Long        'number of recipients
        FileCount As Long             'number of attached files
    End Type
```

The last two fields in the structure contain the number of MAPIRecip and
MAPIFile structures attached to this message. You can have multiple recipients to a message with each recipient having a `RecipClass` variable, as shown
below, that indicates whether the name should appear on the To, CC, or BCC
line of the message.

```
    Type MAPIRecip
        Reserved As Long
        RecipClass As Long      'used to identify To, CC, BCC
        Name As String              'email name
        Address As String           'email address
        EIDSize As Long
        EntryID As String
    End Type
```

The MAPIFile `PathName` variable gives the fully qualified path for the attached
file while the `FileName` contains just the name. The `Position` variable tells
where the icon for the file appears in the body of the message. The `FileType`
variable allows for the attachment of `OLE` objects to MAPI messages.

```
    Type MapiFile
        Reserved As Long
        Flags As Long
        Position As Long        'position within the NoteText of the message
        PathName As String      'full path to the file
        FileName As String      'the filename to display under the icon
        FileType As String      'file or ole object
    End Type
```

MAPI Functions

There are only 11 functions in Simple MAPI that fall into four main categories:

Function	Category
MAPILogon MAPILogoff	Logon and LogOff:
MAPISendDocuments MAPIDelete-mail MAPISendMail MAPISave-mail (BMAPISave-mail)	Sending Mail:
MAPIFindNext (BMAPIFindNext) MAPIReadMail (BMAPIReadMail)	Reading Mail:
MAPIAddress (BMAPIAddress) MAPIDetails MAPIResolveName (BMAPIResolveName)	Choosing Recipients:

Notice that several of the functions have BMAPI functions to use with Visual Basic instead of the regular functions. This is because the primary functions may need to change the number of recipients or files attached to a message and use complex C pointers. Because MAPI cannot change the number of items in the arrays used to hold the MAPIRecip and MAPIFile structures, these special routines handle the way Visual Basic works with strings. These special routines are in the VBAMAPI DLL on the CD-ROM.

As you look through the declarations for these functions, you'll notice that most include a `Session` parameter. For example, the `Logon` function establishes a session with the mail system. If the `Logon` is successful, then the `Session` parameter will contain a handle to a mail session that can be passed to subsequent functions. It isn't necessary to explicitly log on to the mail system. Most of these functions will log on, perform their function, then log off.

Send the Mail

The next step is to expand our application so that it can send a message with multiple attachments to multiple recipients by using the `MAPISendMail` function. Let's code a simple example so you can see the way this is done.

Add a Send button to your `Form1` and insert this code:

```
Private Sub butSend_Click()
Dim rc&
Dim Msg As MapiMessage
Dim Recip(0 To 1) As MAPIRecip
Dim Files(0 To 1) As MapiFile
```

This creates an instance of the `Message` type and arrays for two recipients and attachments. Now assign a message subject and body of the message. Notice how I leave two characters in front of the body of the message for the two attached file icons. If you do not do this, then part of your text will be overwritten!:

```
Msg.Subject = "Test message"
Msg.NoteText = "..This is a test message with 2 recips and 2 files"
Msg.RecipCount = 2
Msg.FileCount = 2
```

Now complete the recipient and file information. I'll use RecipClass of MAPI_TO for the person I am sending To and MAPI_CC for the person receiving a copy. Some MAPI system also support a third RecipClass of MAPI_BCC for a blind copy:

```
Recip(0).Name = "Joe Maffei"
Recip(0).RecipClass = MAPI_TO 'This means this is the To:
Recip(1).Name = "Jim Maffei"
Recip(1).RecipClass = MAPI_CC 'This means this is the CC:
Files(0).PathName = "c:\autoexec.bat"
```

```
Files(0).FileName = "autoexec"
Files(0).Position = 0
Files(1).PathName = "c:\config.sys"
Files(1).FileName = "config"
Files(1).Position = 1
```

Note that you must have the valid e-mail name for each of these recipients. If the exact name is not known, the MAPIResolveName function can be used to determine the correct name and address.

Finally, call the `SendMail` function with the proper arguments. Notice how we pass the first element in the recipient and file arrays to MAPI:

```
rc = MAPISendMail(Session:=0&, UIParam:=0&, Message:=Msg, _
    Recipient:=Recip(0), File:=Files(0), Flags:=0&, Reserved:=0&)
```

Read the Mail

Reading mail from MAPI is a two-step process. The first step is to use the `MAPIFindNext` function to get the first message's unique `MessageID` by passing a null character in the `SeedMessageID` parameter, then call the `MAPIRead` function with the found `MessageID` to retrieve the message. After the message is read, your procedure loops back and that message's `MessageID` is passed as the `SeedMessageID` to the `FindNext` function to get the next message.

The `FindNext` function is quite versatile. This function allows an application to find all messages or just unread messages of a given `MessageType`. `MAPIFindNext` looks for messages in the folder in which new messages of the specified type are delivered. You'll need to call `MAPILogon` and establish a session before calling `MAPIFindNext`.

The `MAPIReadMail` function fills the `MapiMessage`, `MAPIRecip`, and `MAPIFiles` types. File attachments are saved to temporary files. The function provides options through the `Flag` parameter to retrieve only the "envelope information" rather than the complete message and whether to mark the message as read.

Let's write a simple procedure to retrieve all the messages in your inbox. First, add a Read button and a list box to `Form1`, as shown in figure 8.2. Then add this code to set up the variables you'll need and log on to the mail system:

```
Private Sub butRead_Click()
Dim rc&, Sess&, MsgID$
Dim i As Long
Dim Msg As MAPIMessage
Dim Orig As MAPIRecip
ReDim recips(0) As MAPIRecip
ReDim Files(0) As MAPIFile
MsgID = Chr$(0) & Space(128)
rc = MAPILogon(UIParam:=0&, User:=vbNullChar, Password:=vbNullChar, _
    Flags:=0&, Reserved:=0&, Session:=Sess)
```

Then, if the MAPILogon function succeeded and returned a MAPI session in the Sess variable, we can create the FindNext—ReadMail loop and display the originator's name and message subject in the list box. Once MAPIFindNext returns a value in rc other than 0 there are no more messages and the procedure can log off and exit:

```
Do While rc = 0
    rc = MAPIFindNext(Session:=Sess, UIParam:=0&, _
        MsgType:=vbNullString, SeedMsgID:=MsgID, Flag:=0&, _
        ➥Reserved:=0&, MsgID:=MsgID)
  If rc = 0 Then
        rc = MAPIReadMail(Session:=Sess, UIParam:=0&, _
          MsgID:=MsgID, Flags:=0&, Reserved:=0&, Message:=Msg, _
          Originator:=Orig, Recips:=Recips(), Files:=Files())
        List1.AddItem Orig.Name & vbTab & Msg.Subject
    End If
Loop
rc = MAPILogoff(Session:=Sess, UIParam:=0&, Flags:=0&, Reserved:=0&)
End Sub
```

Creating a MAPI Class

We've been able to experiment with sending and receiving messages by using some very simple procedures. You could build a mail-enabled application with these procedures but it would be good software design practice to write these procedures as encapsulated reusable procedures. Visual Basic 4's new class modules are ideal for MAPI functionality. We should be able to develop some properties, like Subject, and methods, like SendMail, that encapsulate our MAPI procedures into a class we can reuse in any of our projects.

Create a new project called MapiClass and insert a module and a class module. Name the module MAPI, name the class MAPIClass, and save the project in a new subdirectory as MapiClas.

MAPI Class Properties

Load the MAPI module with the MAPI type definitions, function declarations, and constants as shown in Listing 8.1. Then we'll create the following properties in the MAPIClas class module:

```
Public Session As Long
Public User As String
Public Password As String

Public MessageType As String
Public Subject As String
Public NoteText As String
Public MessageID As String
Public Recipients As New Collection
```

```
Public Attachments As New Collection
Private sOrigName$
Private sOrigAddr$
```

The last two variables are for the Originator of the messages that we read from the mail system. They are private variables for the "read-only" public variables OrigName and OrigAddress. These read-only variables are exported from the MAPIClass through Property Get procedures because we don't want the user to be able to change the originator information about a message. Next, we'll create a class module to hold the data for the message recipients and attached files. Insert a class module, name it Recipient and add the following properties:

```
Public RecipClass As Long
Public Name As String
Public Address As String
```

Then insert a class module, name it Attachment and add the following properties:

```
Public Flags As Long
Public Position As Long
Public PathName As String
Public FileName As String
Public FileType As String
```

Send Documents Method

Now that we have our properties defined, it's time to start adding methods. I always write VB code incrementally and test each function as I write it, so let's start by adding the SendDocuments method by using the MAPI SendDocuments function that we used above. Add the following code to the MapiClass module:

```
Public Function SendDocuments() As Long
SendDocuments = MAPISendDocuments(0, 0, vbNullChar, vbNullChar, 0)
End Function
```

Now copy the menu structure we used in the MAPI1 project to add a SendMail menu item under the File menu and add this code to create MyMapi as an instance of your MAPIClass and call the SendDocuments method. Because we'll create MyMapi in the declarations section of the form, this instance of our MAPIClass will be available to all procedures in this form:

```
Option Explicit
Dim MyMapi As New MAPIClass

Private Sub mnuSend_Click()
MyMapi.SendDocuments
End Sub
```

When you run this, you'll see the standard MAPI send dialog appear. Neat! Now that we know our class is working, let's begin to add more methods to our MapiClass and test as we go along.

Logon/Logoff Methods

The Logon and Logoff methods are easy and we'll make sure they send the Session property. We have not set the User and Password properties, but if they are null, then the MAPILogon function uses the default User and Password for our mail system.:

```
Public Function Logon() As Long
Logon = MAPILogon(0&, User, Password, &H1000, 0&, Session)
End Function

Public Function Logoff() As Long
Logoff = MAPILogoff(Session, 0&, 0&, 0&)
Session = 0
End Function
```

Send Mail Method

Now, let's add the SendMail function. That will give us full access to the message subject and body and the ability to add recipients and attachments to the message. Note that we've defined a Recipients collection to hold Recipient objects. We'll want methods to add and remove Recipient objects from this collection in our MapiClass:

```
Public Function RecipientAdd(Name$, RecipClass&) As Recipient
Dim Recip As New Recipient
Recip.Name = Name$          'first set the name
Recip.RecipClass = RecipClass     'then set the class
Recipients.Add Recip, Name$       'then add to the collection
Set RecipientAdd = Recip   'and return the new Recip object
End Function

Public Function RecipientRemove(Name$) As Integer
Recipients.Remove Name$    'remove this name from the collection
RecipientRemove = True
End Function
```

Notice how the RecipientAdd method is defined as Recipient so it passes a pointer to the new Recipient object back to the caller. Now copy these and create similar routines for the Attachments collection:

```
Public Function AttachmentAdd(FileName$, PathName$, Position&) As
➥Attachment
Dim Attach As New Attachment
Attach.FileName = FileName
Attach.PathName = PathName
Attach.Position = Position
Attachments.Add Attach, PathName
Set AttachmentAdd = Attach
End Function
```

```
Public Function AttachmentRemove(FileName$) As Integer
Attachments.Remove FileName
AttachmentRemove = True
End Function
```

Unfortunately, we cannot pass these collections to MAPI. MAPI expects to receive dynamic arrays of these types, so we'll need private procedures to convert from our collections to arrays and back again. For now we'll just default some of the Flag and other properties. Obviously, for a complete solution, we should have properties in our Recipient and Attachment objects for all the fields in the MAPI types:

```
Private Sub RecipToArray(Recip() As MAPIRecip)
Dim i&
ReDim Recip(0 To Recipients.Count - 1) As MAPIRecip
For i = 1 To Recipients.Count
    Recip(i - 1).RecipClass = Recipients(i).RecipClass
    Recip(i - 1).Name = Recipients(i).Name
    Recip(i - 1).Address = Recipients(i).Address
    Recip(i - 1).EntryID = ""
    Recip(i - 1).Reserved = 0&
    Recip(i - 1).EIDSize = 0&
Next
End Sub

Private Sub RecipFrArray(Recip() As MAPIRecip)
Dim i&
Set Recipients = New Collection
For i = LBound(Recip) To UBound(Recip)
    RecipientAdd Recip(i).Name, _
        Recip(i).RecipClass, Recip(i).Address
Next
End Sub
```

Copy the procedures and modify them to link the Files array to the Attachments collection and we're ready to write the SendMail method. We'll assume that the user has first set the Subject and NoteText properties and added recipients and files to the appropriate collections. The first step will be to dimension variables of each of the MAPI types:

```
Public Function SendMail() As Long
Dim Msg As MAPIMessage
ReDim Recip(1) As MAPIRecip
ReDim Files(1) As MAPIFile
```

Then we'll call our private routines to copy the Recipients and Attachments collections to the arrays and we'll set the Count properties in the message:

```
If Recipients.Count Then
    RecipToArray Recip()
Else
    Exit Function
End If
Msg.RecipCount = Recipients.Count
```

```
        If Attachments.Count Then
            AttachToArray Files()
        End If
        Msg.FileCount = Attachments.Count
```

Finally, we can complete the rest of the fields in the MAPI message structure and call the `MAPISendMail` function:

```
        Msg.Reserved = 0&
        Msg.Subject = Subject
        Msg.NoteText = Space$(Msg.FileCount + 5) & NoteText
        Msg.MessageType = MessageType
        Msg.DateReceived = ""
        Msg.ConversationID = ""
        Msg.Flags = 0&
        SendMail = MAPISendMail(Session, 0&, Msg, Recip(0), Files(0), 0&, 0&)
        End Function
```

Let's write a small procedure to test this method. Add some text boxes to the form for the recipient, subject, notetext and attached file name so the form looks something like figure 8.2.

Fig. 8.2

A sample form created to test the MAPI Class.

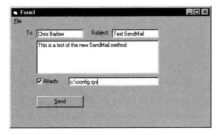

Then add a Send button and insert this code:

```
        Private Sub butSend_Click()
        MyMapi.Subject = txtSubject
        MyMapi.NoteText = txtNoteText
        MyMapi.RecipientAdd txtTo, 1, ""
        If chkAttach = 1 Then _
            MyMapi.AttachmentAdd txtAttach, txtAttach, 1
        MsgBox "SendMail Method returned: " & MyMapi.SendMail
        End Sub
```

You're starting to see the benefits of encapsulating the MAPI function calls in a class—this code is quite easy to follow!

Before we turn to methods to read the mail, I suggest we add one additional method to send mail. The `SendDocuments` method provides a simple way to pop up the Send dialog, and the `SendMail` method gives us full control over the message mailing process but requires setting a number of properties and adding items to collections. In designing a class module, I find it convenient to provide some additional "wrapper" functions to handle the most common tasks.

For example, the e-mail task I program most often is to send a file as an attachment to a message to a known recipient. I don't want a dialog displayed, as in the `SendDocuments` method, but I don't want to write the extra lines of code required to set up for the `SendMail` method. So, let's create a `SendFile` method to perform this common task. We'll provide arguments for a single recipient and a single attached file. It will set up the class properties then call the `SendMail` function:

```
Public Function SendFile(SendTo$, PathName$, Subj$, Text$) As Long
RecipientAdd SendTo, 1, ""
AttachmentAdd PathName, PathName, 1
Subject = Subj
NoteText = Text
SendFile = SendMail
End Function
```

Read Mail Methods

Let's create a `MoveFirst` method that will find and read the first message in our inbox. As usual, we'll define the variables and log on:

```
Public Function MoveFirst(Optional Unread As Variant) As Long
Dim Msg As MAPIMessage
Dim Orig As MAPIRecip
ReDim Recip(1) As MAPIRecip
ReDim Files(1) As MAPIFile
Dim rc&, i%, nRecips&, nFiles&, Flags&
MessageID = Space$(128)
If IsMissing(Unread) Then Unread = False
If Unread Then Flags = MAPI_UNREAD_ONLY
rc = MAPILogon(0, vbNullChar, vbNullChar, 0, 0, Session)
```

Notice that we can pass an optional parameter to this method to move to the first unread message. If the logon was successful, then we'll call `FindNext` with a null `SeedMessageID` to find the first message, then read the message by using `MAPIReadMail` to fill the MAPI structures:

```
If rc = SUCCESS_SUCCESS Then
    If MAPIFindNext(Session, 0, vbNullString, vbNullChar, _
        Flags&, 0, MessageID) = SUCCESS_SUCCESS Then
        If MAPIReadMail(Session, 0, MessageID, 0, 0, Msg, Orig, _
            Recip(), Files()) = SUCCESS_SUCCESS Then
```

Now we have the first message, so we'll move the data from the MAPI structures to our class properties:

```
                RecipFrArray Recip()
                If Msg.FileCount Then AttachFrArray Files()
                Subject = Msg.Subject
                NoteText = Msg.NoteText
                sOrigName = Orig.Name
                sOrigAddr = Orig.Address
            End If
        End If
    MAPILogoff Session, 0, 0, 0
```

```
    End If
    MoveFirst = rc
End Function
```

Let's test our `MoveFirst` method. Add a MoveFirst button to the form with this code:

```
Private Sub butMoveFirst_Click()
MyMapi.MoveFirst
txtSubject = MyMapi.Subject
txtNoteText = MyMapi.NoteText
txtTo = Recipients(1).Name
txtAttach = Attachments(1).PathName
End Sub
```

If you look at the complete listing of the MapiClass in Listing 8.2, you'll see that the `MoveNext` method is almost the same as the `MoveFirst` method. Since we've saved the `MessageID` in our class it can be passed to the `FindNext` function call and the next message will be returned. Add a MoveNext button to the form and copy the code from the MoveFirst button and make sure this method works.

Address Book Methods

The last set of MAPI functions deals with choosing recipients by using the address book. We'll create a simple `Address` method that will convert the current Recipients collection to the `MAPI` array and pass that array to the `MAPIAddress` function. This will pop up a standard MAPI address dialog that allows the user to select recipients from the address book. When the recipients are returned in the `Recip` array, we use our `RecipFrArray` function to move them to our Recipients collection.

```
Public Function Address() As Long
Dim Info&, nRecips&, rc&
ReDim Recip(1 To 1) As MAPIRecip
nRecips = Recipients.Count
If nRecips Then RecipToArray Recip()
rc& = MAPIAddress(Session, 0&, "", 3&, _
    "", nRecips, Recip(), 0&, 0&)
If rc& = SUCCESS_SUCCESS Then
    Do While Recipients.Count
        Recipients.Remove 0
    Loop
    If nRecips > 0 Then
        RecipFrArray Recip()
    End If
End If
End Function
```

The MAPI function `ResolveName` checks a recipient name to make sure there is a valid unambiguous address. If the name could match more than one address, MAPI can show a dialog so the user can select the correct name.

We'll create a `CheckNames` method that will cycle through all recipients and resolve their addresses:

```
Function CheckNames() As Long
Dim i%, nRecips&, rc&
ReDim Recip(1) As MAPIRecip
nRecips = Recipients.Count
If nRecips Then RecipToArray Recip()
For i = 1 To nRecips
    rc& = MAPIResolveName(Session, 0, Recip(i).Name, MAPI_DIALOG, 0, Recip(i))
Next
RecipFrArray Recip()
End Function
```

We'll complete the address book methods with the `MAPIDetails` function, which displays a dialog of detailed address book information about a recipient:

```
Public Function Details(Name$) As Long
Dim i%, rc&
Dim Recip As MAPIRecip
Recip.Name = Name
rc& = MAPIResolveName(Session, 0, Name, MAPI_DIALOG, 0, Recip)
rc& = MAPIDetails(Session, 0, Recip, 0, 0)
End Function
```

We've created a fairly complete MAPI class that encapsulates the main functionality of the MAPI DLL into an easier-to-use set of properties and methods. Anytime we need to write a mail-enabled application we can simply include this class in our project and have all this functionality. Of course, this will expose the class's source code to every project and most programmers have trouble keeping their hands off a piece of source code! They'll tweak it a bit with a new project and end up breaking a dozen old projects! We would really like to encapsulate this functionality even further so that its functions could be used without exposing the source code.

Creating a MAPI OLE Server

Using our `MAPIClass` to create an `OLE Server` will allow us to distribute the class as an EXE that can be used through OLE Automation. We'll just zip through what we need to do to convert our class to a server.

The steps are quite easy. First, save the current `MAPIClass` module with a new name—MAPIVB4. Also, save the project as MAPIVB4. Then remove the `Form` from the project—as an OLE Server we won't have any visible user interface so we won't need a form. Insert a module, name it `Mainmod.Bas`, and add a single empty `Sub Main` procedure.

In the Tools, Options dialog on the Project tab, make sure the startup is Sub Main, the Project Name is MAPIVB4, and the Start Mode is OLE Server. Then change the properties of the MAPIVB4 class module to Public, Creatable Multiuse. Also make sure that the Recipient and Attachment class modules are public (see fig. 8.3).

Fig. 8.3
These options tell Visual Basic to register your OLE Server.

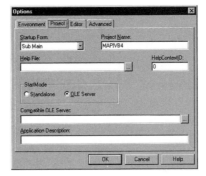

Now run this project. You won't see any user interface, but your OLE Server should be started. Let's test it and see if we can really reach it through OLE Automation. The easiest way to test it is to fire up another instance of VB4, remove the default Form1 and add the Form1 from our MAPIClas project. Remember, this form was our user interface when we were using the class module embedded in the project. If we start a new project containing only this user interface form, and it works, then it must be operating through OLE Automation!

You'll need to refer to the MAPIVB4 server in the Tools, References menu item. See figure 8.4.

Then run this project and try the Send button—mine works fine!

Fig. 8.4
You must reference your OLE Server so Visual Basic can find its properties and methods.

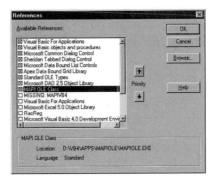

Summary

You should be starting to feel comfortable with messaging and accessing MAPI by using OLE. Experiment with the sample code from this chapter and see if you can write your own messaging application.

Listing 8.1   8LIST01.TXT—MAPIMessage

```
Option Explicit

'**************************************************
'   MAPI Message holds information about a message
'**************************************************

Type MAPIMessage
      Reserved As Long
      Subject As String
      NoteText As String
      MessageType As String
      DateReceived As String
      ConversationID As String
      Flags As Long
      RecipCount As Long
      FileCount As Long
End Type


'************************************************
'   MAPIRecip holds information about a message
'   originator or recipient
'************************************************

Type MAPIRecip
      Reserved As Long
      RecipClass As Long
      Name As String
      Address As String
      EIDSize As Long
      EntryID As String
End Type


'****************************************************
'   MapiFile holds information about file attachments
'****************************************************

Type MAPIFile
      Reserved As Long
      Flags As Long
      Position As Long
      PathName As String
      FileName As String
      FileType As String
End Type
```

(continues)

Listing 8.1 Continued

```
'***************************
'   FUNCTION Declarations
'***************************

Declare Function MAPILogon Lib "MAPI.DLL" (ByVal UIParam&, ByVal
➥User$, ByVal Password$, ByVal Flags&, ByVal Reserved&, Session&)
➥As Long
Declare Function MAPILogoff Lib "MAPI.DLL" (ByVal Session&, ByVal
➥UIParam&, ByVal Flags&, ByVal Reserved&) As Long
Declare Function MAPIDetails Lib "MAPI.DLL" (ByVal Session&, ByVal
➥UIParam&, Recipient As MAPIRecip, ByVal Flags&, ByVal Reserved&)
➥As Long
Declare Function MAPIDeleteMail Lib "MAPI.DLL" (ByVal Session&,
➥ByVal UIParam&, ByVal MsgID$, ByVal Flags&, ByVal Reserved&) As
➥Long
Declare Function MAPISendDocuments Lib "MAPI.DLL" (ByVal UIParam&,
➥ByVal DelimStr$, ByVal FilePaths$, ByVal FileNames$, ByVal
➥Reserved&) As Long

Declare Function MAPIResolveName Lib "VBAMAPI.DLL" Alias
➥"BMAPIResolveName" (ByVal Session&, ByVal UIParam&, ByVal
➥UserName$, ByVal Flags&, ByVal Reserved&, Recipient As MAPIRecip)
➥As Long
Declare Function MAPIFindNext Lib "VBAMAPI.DLL" Alias
➥"BMAPIFindNext" (ByVal Session&, ByVal UIParam&, MsgType$,
➥SeedMsgID$, ByVal Flag&, ByVal Reserved&, MsgID$) As Long
Declare Function MAPIAddress Lib "VBAMAPI.DLL" Alias "BMAPIAddress"
➥(ByVal Session&, ByVal UIParam&, Caption$, ByVal EditFields&,
➥Label$, RecipCount&, Recipients() As MAPIRecip, ByVal Flags&,
➥ByVal Reserved&) As Long
Declare Function MAPISaveMail Lib "VBAMAPI.DLL" Alias
➥"BMAPISaveMail" (ByVal Session&, ByVal UIParam&, Message As
➥MapiMessage, Recipient As MAPIRecip, File As MapiFile, ByVal
➥Flags&, ByVal Reserved&, MsgID$) As Long
Declare Function MAPISendMail Lib "VBAMAPI.DLL" Alias
➥"BMAPISendMail" (ByVal Session&, ByVal UIParam&, Message As
➥MapiMessage, Recipient As MAPIRecip, File As MapiFile, ByVal
➥Flags&, ByVal Reserved&) As Long
Declare Function MAPIReadMail Lib "VBAMAPI.DLL" Alias
➥"BMAPIReadMail" (ByVal Session&, ByVal UIParam&, ByVal MsgID$,
➥ByVal Flags&, ByVal Reserved&, Message As MapiMessage, Originator
➥As MAPIRecip, Recips() As MAPIRecip, Files() As MapiFile) As Long

 'MAPI
Global Const MAPI_ORIG = 0              '// Recipient is message
                                           originator
Global Const MAPI_TO = 1               '// Recipient is a primary
                                           recipient
Global Const MAIL_LONGDATE = 0
Global Const MAIL_LISTVIEW = 1

Global Const Mapi_ATT_FILE = 0         'Attachment Type: data File
```

```
'********************************
'   MAPI.DLL CONSTANT Declarations
'********************************
'

Global Const SUCCESS_SUCCESS = 0
Global Const MAPI_USER_ABORT = 1
Global Const MAPI_E_FAILURE = 2
Global Const MAPI_E_LOGIN_FAILURE = 3
Global Const MAPI_E_DISK_FULL = 4
Global Const MAPI_E_INSUFFICIENT_MEMORY = 5

Global Const MAPI_CC = 2                 '// Recipient is a copy recipient
Global Const MAPI_BCC = 3                '// Recipient is blind copy recipient
Global Const MAPI_E_BLK_TOO_SMALL = 6
Global Const MAPI_E_TOO_MANY_SESSIONS = 8
Global Const MAPI_ATT_EOle = 1           'Attachment Type: embedded OLE Object
Global Const MAPI_ATT_SOle = 2           'Attachment Type: static OLE Object
Global Const MAPI_E_TOO_MANY_FILES = 9
Global Const MAPI_E_TOO_MANY_RECIPIENTS = 10
Global Const MAPI_E_ATTACHMENT_NOT_FOUND = 11
Global Const MAPI_E_ATTACHMENT_OPEN_FAILURE = 12
Global Const MAPI_E_ATTACHMENT_WRITE_FAILURE = 13
Global Const MAPI_E_UNKNOWN_RECIPIENT = 14
Global Const MAPI_E_BAD_RECIPTYPE = 15
Global Const MAPI_E_NO_MESSAGES = 16
Global Const MAPI_E_INVALID_MESSAGE = 17
Global Const MAPI_E_TEXT_TOO_LARGE = 18
Global Const MAPI_E_INVALID_SESSION = 19
Global Const MAPI_E_TYPE_NOT_SUPPORTED = 20
Global Const MAPI_E_AMBIGUOUS_RECIPIENT = 21
Global Const MAPI_E_MESSAGE_IN_USE = 22
Global Const MAPI_E_NETWORK_FAILURE = 23
Global Const MAPI_E_INVALID_EDITFIELDS = 24
Global Const MAPI_E_INVALID_RECIPS = 25
Global Const MAPI_E_NOT_SUPPORTED = 26

Global Const MAPI_UNREAD = &H1
Global Const MAPI_RECEIPT_REQUESTED = &H2
Global Const MAPI_SENT = &H4


'*********************
'   FLAG Declarations
'*********************

Global Const MAPI_LOGON_UI = &H1
Global Const MAPI_NEW_SESSION = &H2
Global Const MAPI_DIALOG = &H8
Global Const MAPI_UNREAD_ONLY = &H20
Global Const MAPI_ENVELOPE_ONLY = &H40
Global Const MAPI_PEEK = &H80
Global Const MAPI_GUARANTEE_FIFO = &H100
Global Const MAPI_BODY_AS_FILE = &H200
Global Const MAPI_AB_NOMODIFY = &H400
Global Const MAPI_SUPPRESS_ATTACH = &H800
Global Const MAPI_FORCE_DOWNLOAD = &H1000
```

(continues)

Listing 8.1   Continued

```
Global Const MAPI_OLE = &H1
Global Const MAPI_OLE_STATIC = &H2
```

Listing 8.2   2LIST02.TXT—Option Explicit

```
Option Explicit

Public Session As Long
Public User As String
Public Password As String

Public MessageType As String
Public Subject As String
Public NoteText As String
Public MessageID As String

Public Recipients As New Collection
Public Attachments As New Collection

Private sOrigName$
Private sOrigAddr$
Public Property Get OrigName()
    OrigName = sOrigName
End Property
Public Property Get OrigAddress()
    OrigAddress = sOrigAddr
End Property

Public Function AttachmentAdd(FileName$, PathName$, Position&) As
➥Attachment
Dim attach As New Attachment
attach.FileName = FileName
attach.PathName = PathName
attach.Position = Position
Attachments.Add attach, PathName
Set AttachmentAdd = attach
End Function
Public Function AttachmentRemove(FileName$) As Integer
Attachments.Remove FileName
AttachmentRemove = True
End Function
Private Sub AttachToArray(Files() As MAPIFile)
Dim i&
ReDim Files(0 To Attachments.Count - 1) As MAPIFile
For i = 1 To Attachments.Count
    Files(i - 1).FileName = Attachments(i).FileName
    Files(i - 1).PathName = Attachments(i).PathName
    Files(i - 1).Position = Attachments(i).Position
    Files(i - 1).FileType = Mapi_ATT_FILE
    Files(i - 1).Reserved = 0&
    Files(i - 1).Flags = 0&
```

```
Next
End Sub
Private Sub AttachFrArray(Files() As MAPIFile)
Dim i&
Set Attachments = New Collection
For i = LBound(Files) To UBound(Files)
    AttachmentAdd Files(i).FileName, _
        Files(i).PathName, Files(i).Position
Next
End Sub
Public Function Logon() As Long
Logon = MAPILogon(0&, User, Password, &H1000, 0&, Session)
End Function
Public Function Logoff() As Long
Logoff = MAPILogoff(Session, 0&, 0&, 0&)
Session = 0
End Function
Public Function RecipientAdd(Name$, RecipClass&, Address$) As
➥Recipient
Dim Recip As New Recipient
Recip.Name = Name
Recip.RecipClass = RecipClass
Recipients.Add Recip, Name
Recip.Address = Address
Set RecipientAdd = Recip
End Function
Public Function RecipientRemove(Name$) As Integer
Recipients.Remove Name
RecipientRemove = True
End Function
Private Sub RecipToArray(Recip() As MAPIRecip)
Dim i&
ReDim Recip(0 To Recipients.Count - 1) As MAPIRecip
For i = 1 To Recipients.Count
    Recip(i - 1).RecipClass = Recipients(i).RecipClass
    Recip(i - 1).Name = Recipients(i).Name
    Recip(i - 1).Address = Recipients(i).Address
    Recip(i - 1).EntryID = ""
    Recip(i - 1).Reserved = 0&
    Recip(i - 1).EIDSize = 0&
Next
End Sub
Private Sub RecipFrArray(Recip() As MAPIRecip)
Dim i&
Set Recipients = New Collection
For i = LBound(Recip) To UBound(Recip)
    RecipientAdd Recip(i).Name, _
        Recip(i).RecipClass, Recip(i).Address
Next
End Sub
Public Function SendDocuments() As Long
    SendDocuments = MAPISendDocuments(0, 0, vbNullChar, _
    ➥vbNullChar, 0)
End Function
Public Function SendMail() As Long
```

(continues)

Listing 8.2 Continued

```
Dim Msg As MAPIMessage
ReDim Recip(1) As MAPIRecip
ReDim Files(1) As MAPIFile
If Subject = "" Then Exit Function
If Recipients.Count Then
    RecipToArray Recip()
Else
    Exit Function
End If
Msg.RecipCount = Recipients.Count
If Attachments.Count Then
    AttachToArray Files()
End If
Msg.FileCount = Attachments.Count
Msg.Reserved = 0&
Msg.Subject = Subject
Msg.NoteText = Space$(Msg.FileCount + 5) & NoteText
Msg.MessageType = MessageType
Msg.DateReceived = ""
Msg.ConversationID = ""
Msg.Flags = 0&
SendMail = MAPISendMail(Session, 0&, Msg, Recip(0), Files(0), 0&, 0&)
End Function


Public Function MoveFirst(Optional Unread As Variant) As Long
Dim Msg As MAPIMessage
Dim Orig As MAPIRecip
ReDim Recip(1) As MAPIRecip
ReDim Files(1) As MAPIFile
Dim rc&, i%, nRecips&, nFiles&, Flags&
MessageID = Space$(128)
If IsMissing(Unread) Then Unread = False
If Unread Then Flags = MAPI_UNREAD_ONLY
rc = MAPILogon(0, vbNullChar, vbNullChar, 0, 0, Session)
If rc = SUCCESS_SUCCESS Then
    If MAPIFindNext(Session, 0, vbNullString, vbNullChar, _
        Flags&, 0, MessageID) = SUCCESS_SUCCESS Then
        If MAPIReadMail(Session, 0, MessageID, 0, 0, Msg, Orig, _
            Recip(), Files()) = SUCCESS_SUCCESS Then
            RecipFrArray Recip()
            If Msg.FileCount Then AttachFrArray Files()
            Subject = Msg.Subject
            NoteText = Msg.NoteText
            sOrigName = Orig.Name
            sOrigAddr = Orig.Address
        End If
    End If
    MAPILogoff Session, 0, 0, 0
End If
MoveFirst = rc
End Function


Public Function MoveNext(Optional Unread As Variant) As Long
Dim Msg As MAPIMessage
```

```
Dim Orig As MAPIRecip
ReDim Recip(1) As MAPIRecip
ReDim Files(1) As MAPIFile
Dim rc&, i%, nRecips&, nFiles&, Flags&
If IsMissing(Unread) Then Unread = False
If Unread Then Flags = MAPI_UNREAD_ONLY
rc = MAPILogon(0, vbNullChar, vbNullChar, 0, 0, Session)
If rc = SUCCESS_SUCCESS Then
    If MAPIFindNext(Session, 0, vbNullString, MessageID, _
        Flags&, 0, MessageID) = SUCCESS_SUCCESS Then
        If MAPIReadMail(Session, 0, MessageID, 0, 0, Msg, Orig, _
            Recip(), Files()) = SUCCESS_SUCCESS Then
            RecipFrArray Recip()
            If Msg.FileCount Then AttachFrArray Files()
            Subject = Msg.Subject
            NoteText = Msg.NoteText
            sOrigName = Orig.Name
            sOrigAddr = Orig.Address
        End If
    End If
    MAPILogoff Session, 0, 0, 0
End If
MoveNext = rc
End Function


Public Function Address() As Long
Dim Info&, nRecips&, rc&
ReDim Recip(1 To 1) As MAPIRecip
nRecips = Recipients.Count
If nRecips Then RecipToArray Recip()
rc& = MAPIAddress(Session, 0&, "", 3&, _
    "", nRecips, Recip(), 0&, 0&)
If rc& = SUCCESS_SUCCESS Then
    Do While Recipients.Count
        Recipients.Remove 0
    Loop
    If nRecips > 0 Then
        RecipFrArray Recip()
    End If
End If
End Function


Public Function CheckNames() As Long
Dim i%, nRecips&, rc&
ReDim Recip(1) As MAPIRecip
nRecips = Recipients.Count
If nRecips Then RecipToArray Recip()
For i = 1 To nRecips
    rc& = MAPIResolveName(Session, 0, Recip(i).Name, MAPI_DIALOG,
    ➥0, Recip(i))
Next
RecipFrArray Recip()
End Function
Public Function Details(Name$) As Long
Dim i%, rc&
Dim Recip As MAPIRecip
```

(continues)

Listing 8.2 Continued

```
Recip.Name = Name
rc& = MAPIResolveName(Session, 0, Name, MAPI_DIALOG, 0, Recip)
rc& = MAPIDetails(Session, 0, Recip, 0, 0)
End Function

Public Function SendFile(SendTo$, PathName$, Subj$, Text$) As Long
RecipientAdd SendTo, 1, ""
AttachmentAdd PathName, PathName, 1
Subject = Subj
NoteText = Text
SendFile = SendMail
End Function
```

Chapter 9

Anatomy of a Client/ Server Project

by Barry Seymour

Barry Seymour has been programming with Visual Basic since it first came out in 1991. He has written numerous client/server programs in Visual Basic, both as an independent contractor and with various San Francisco-based consulting firms including Vanguard Business Solutions (now Lotus Development Group) and DBSS, Inc. Barry is now a Technical Marketing Specialist at CenterView Software, where he is "product evangelist" for Choreo 1.1, an add-on which vastly simplifies building client/server applications in Visual Basic.

Client/server has been the buzzword in programming for the past seven years or so, but only in the past three years has it truly come into maturity on the desktop. With Windows 3.0, 3.1, and now Windows 95, a powerful operating system has become commonplace. What naturally followed was more powerful tools to build programs for that environment.

When Visual Basic came out in 1991 (only two floppy disks, remember?), it was positioned as an easy-to-use tool that would enable the average programmer to write simple Windows programs without having to master C or C++ programming. As time went on and Windows programs become more popular, many developers turned to VB to quickly and efficiently develop the kinds of applications the world was clamoring for.

In large part, Visual Basic succeeded because of its extensibility. If "you couldn't do that in Visual Basic," chances were someone would come up with a VBX so you could. If not a VBX, then a DLL could be used to provide functionality not present in the standard Visual Basic package—all you needed to do was get a C programmer to tell you how to use the darn things. It was only natural that sooner or later more programmers would start using Visual Basic for their application development efforts.

Early efforts at adding client/server functionality to Visual Basic centered around quick ports to talk to DBLibrary. VBSQL.VBX was the first instance of this, providing a simple way to jack in all the functionality of what was then the most common way of getting at a server—the WDDBLIB.DLL API. Later, bound controls provided even easier ways to include this functionality in your programs, still through DBLibrary.

In 1993, Microsoft's ODBC (Open Database Connectivity) emerged as a clear standard for database development. For better or for worse, Microsoft had succeeded in getting this common standard adopted for client/server development. The concept was that ODBC would provide an additional layer between the programmer's code and whatever API was needed to talk to the database. This layer would use common calls which applied to all supported platforms. Theoretically, a programmer could use ODBC to talk to SQL Server, then just change the ODBC driver and use the same program to talk to Oracle, FoxPro, or any other platform which had an ODBC driver. The reality was a bit different: some back-end databases provided functionality not supported by ODBC and others provided similar features with differing implementations.

While the promise of seamless cross-platform support wasn't completely achieved, much of the computing world standardized on ODBC. Bound controls and third-party drivers started showing up with ODBC-compliant underpinnings and Microsoft started building more database power into Visual Basic itself, evolving it into one of the dominant platforms for client/server program development.

With Visual Basic 3.0, Data Access Objects (DAO) became part of the VB vernacular. Object-orientation was spreading from the design environment into these new controls and concepts which were supposed to make it easier to program database applications. VB 3.0 also introduced support for the JET Engine, which was used by Microsoft Access 1.0/1.1 to perform it's database tasks. Now two major platforms shared a file format, further enhancing the position of each.

Visual Basic 4.0 further evolves this object-oriented model and places it atop a newer, faster version of the JET engine built for 16- and 32-bit environments. This latest version of JET is an object-oriented collection of collections. The DBEngine object contains Workspaces, Workspaces contain Databases, Databases contain Tables, Tables contain Fields, and so on. The level of complexity has gone up, but so has the capability to re-use code by objectifying all the relevant components of database access.

Through all this evolution and revolution, however, one thing has remained constant. Client/Server programming has always represented the need to reach out beyond the immediate programming environment, to look beyond the immediate desktop and into something larger, whether it be the neighborhood LAN or a worldwide WAN-based enterprise.

Now programmers have much more to take into consideration; the complexities of their own program, the requirements and capabilities of the server, and the needs of other front-end programs which may be working with the same database. Add to this the fact that you're in a full-blown multiuser environment and the level of complexity increases rapidly.

In this chapter, we'll do the following:

- We'll go through the whole process in miniature

- We'll not only write a Visual Basic program, but also look at the design of the database itself and how its structure affects its usage in a multiuser environment

- We'll look at what our server platform (in this case, the newly released Microsoft SQL Server 6.0) has to say in how things get written and where the processing actually gets done

- We'll discover that how we access our data and how much of it we get in one chunk becomes critical

- We'll see how we can modularize parts of our program to make them available to other applications and even other platforms

More Than Just Visual Basic Programming

A client/server development effort is far more than just the front-end programming tool—in this case Visual Basic. By its very name one can infer that in Client/Server computing there's a client and there's a server. However, one must also take into account the fact that there will be multiple clients and there could be multiple servers. The LAN, the transport medium for much of our programmatic activity, must also occupy a central part of our considerations as we design and code.

Take for example a typical client/server architecture, as shown in figure 9.1.

Here we have three different clients using three different software packages working with data from the same database. The first system is doing data entry, adding, updating, and deleting data. The second PC is using a spreadsheet to perform decision support, while the third client is using a word processor to perform mail merge against the data in the database.

Fig. 9.1

A typical client/ server architecture.

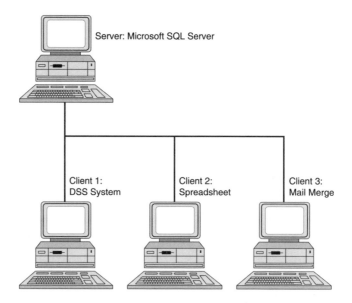

Server: Microsoft SQL Server

Client 1: DSS System

Client 2: Spreadsheet

Client 3: Mail Merge

Not only is each PC performing a different function, but also each is operating under different sets of assumptions. Clients 2 and 3 assume the data is static and won't change in the middle of their operations, while Client 1 is actively engaged in changing that very data. Client 2 is actively performing its own set of calculations on the data to perform various "what if" scenarios, while Client 3 is getting a copy of data to prepare form letters.

For this reason it's imperative to lift your programming sights beyond your own CPU and look at the larger picture when designing or programming a client/server system. You'll be dealing with multiple front ends, possibly several back ends and a number of differing expectations and requirements from the various clients who will be using your system.

Multiples

Unlike a typical stand-alone application, your client/server program will have to deal in multiples; multiple users, multiple applications, multiple platforms, and (in development at least) multiple developers. The interaction of these many considerations requires you to consider multiple solutions.

Many users will be using your application at the same time. In a database-centric program this introduces a number of risks, the most fundamental of which is that two users may try to modify the same data at the same time. Client/server database applications deal with this problem by *locking*, the process of preventing changes to a record by more than one user at a time. For example, if user A is modifying a record, it is locked so user B cannot change it.

Mechanisms at both the client and the server may be used to implement locking, but most often a combination of the two is used. Server-side software provides consistent, centralized protection of data, but usually it is up to the application running on the client side to assist the user around the conflict, usually in the form of error messages and input validation.

How you implement this protection depends on both the client- and server-based components you are using and how well they interact, both with each other and with the user. After all, it will take the intelligent cooperation of server, client, and user to resolve these kinds of data-access issues.

Not only will multiple users be accessing the data in your client/server system, but also they will be doing so from different applications and multiple platforms, further complicating the design decisions you must make. Issues of error handling, record locking, and such may require different solutions in different applications. Some programs may do a better job of validating input, handling errors, and preserving data integrity at the client end, while others may have to rely more heavily upon the server for such functions. Programs running on Windows may be more capable of communicating with Windows-based server software than programs running on a MacIntosh or UNIX machine. As you assess the sum total of all the tools you will be using, you'll have to decide what functions should be centralized at the server and what functions can be handled (in various ways) by the client software packages you have chosen.

With projects of this size, you may have help in the form of a programming team. Unfortunately, this introduces another level of complexity. The traditional VB programming model assumes a single developer working on a single project, with full control over all the files in that project. Client/server development efforts can easily involve teams of programmers, requiring more coordination of effort and more modularity in the design of your programs. Fortunately, Visual Basic 4.0, Enterprise Edition also includes Visual SourceSafe, a complete and integrated version control program which makes it easier to integrate your Visual Basic development into a team programming situation.

Why Client/Server?

The client/server programming model is the natural outgrowth of evolution, both of the processing power and connectivity of personal computers and of the changing climate in corporate computing. When personal computers first became a significant presence on the corporate desktop in the early 1980s, business computing began a shift away from centralized mainframe computers towards individual machines working alone. As local area networks increased in speed and power, computers moved more towards sharing their data and work with each other. Database applications began sharing data on the LAN, often from one centralized location. This "file-server" model made it possible to share one set of data between many machines, resulting in greater efficiency in data storage and greater consistency in the data.

While file-server systems were an improvement, they still functioned essentially as stand-alone systems; the only change was that the disk containing the data was somewhere else on the LAN. When a program had to fetch data, it usually brought the entire data set over the network line to the workstation, resulting in increased network traffic and a decrease in LAN performance for everyone else.

Client/server computing solves this problem by splitting the processing between the server and the client. Thus, a database program requesting a list of all clients named "Smith" in a certain city would send its request to the server, which would filter and send back only the data which was requested. This results in less network traffic and better performance for other users on the LAN.

Since the server has the capacity to "think" and process for itself, it makes sense to place functionality within the server engine whenever possible. A programming language, usually some variant of SQL (Structured Query Language), is provided to allow the user to manipulate the database. *Stored procedures* written in this language can perform standardized or custom-designed functions. These stored procedures, along with *triggers* and *rules*, allow you to embed functionality in the database engine itself, allowing the server to intelligently protect the nature of its data according to rules set by the designer of the system. Newer versions of server software allow you to embed these rules right into the structure and design of the tables of your database.

This model is the most common example of *distributed processing*, whereby the CPU on both ends of the wire shares the work load, reducing traffic on the LAN itself. Later in this chapter, we'll see more instances of server-side processing which can help the performance and robustness of our database application.

Data Access—a Whirlwind Tour

How you get at your data has a direct and measurable influence on the speed of your application. Very often the single most significant factor in the performance of your application is the speed at which it obtains data from the server.

ODBC and the JET Engine

For the purposes of this chapter, we'll be using ODBC and the JET engine provided with Access and Visual Basic. Visual Basic 4.0 has two versions of the JET engine, one for 32-bit systems and one for 16-bit systems. Since we're developing on a Windows 95 PC and desire the performance benefits that the 32-bit version of JET provides, we'll be using JET 3.0, the 32-bit version.

Note that Visual Basic installs 32-bit ODBC drivers for SQL Server; you can add additional ODBC drivers to your system by using the ODBC applet in the Control Panel.

Data Source Names

When working with ODBC database drivers you must create a *data source name,* an entry in ODBC.INI, or the Windows registry which collects the name of the database driver, the name of the server, and other login information into one logical entity. To create a Data Source Name, open the ODBC applet in the Control Panel, specify the ODBC driver to use and enter the information required to connect to the database—server name, user ID, password, and database name.

When you write an ODBC application, you must include the data source name in its connect string. You can also override the user ID, database, and password settings in the connect string if you wish.

The Data Control and Data Access Objects

Visual Basic's Data Control makes it easy to write simple database applications. You specify the connect string, type in the `RecordSource` property (the name of the database table to use) and then bind data-aware controls (usually text boxes) to the data control for display and editing. This works for simpler interfaces, as it provides a simple, easy-to-understand framework for building the application and responding to conventional events such as moving through results sets and updating data.

The Data Control is appealing at first glance and certainly has its uses, but once your application passes a certain threshhold of complexity you'll need the increased power and performance provided by *data access objects* (DAO). Data access objects allow you to refer to database data programmatically by treating them as separate discrete objects. Visual Basic 4.0 extends this metaphor to its logical conclusion by making all data access objects part of an object hierarchy. Once you understand the "lay of the land," it becomes easier to conceptualize and code against these structures. The DBEngine object contains the Workspaces collection; each Workspace contains a Database collection, each Database contains Tables, Indexes, Users, and so on.

Objects and collections provide different types of containment relationships: Objects contain zero or more collections, all of different types; and collections contain zero or more objects, all of the same type. Although objects and collections are similar entities, the distinction differentiates the two types of relationships.

Remote Data Objects

With *Remote Data Objects* (RDO) and the RemoteData control, your applications can access ODBC data sources directly without using a local query processor. The result can be significantly faster performance and greater flexibility when accessing server-side databases. Although you can access any ODBC data source with RDO and the RemoteData control, these features are designed to take advantage of database servers like Microsoft SQL Server and Oracle that use sophisticated query engines.

Using RDO, you can create simple cursor-less result sets or more complex cursors. You can also execute stored procedures that return result sets. You can also limit the number of rows returned and monitor all of the messages and errors generated by the remote data source without compromising the executing query. RDO also permits either synchronous or asynchronous operation, so your application doesn't need to be locked while lengthy queries are executed.

Note that RDO and the RemoteData control are features of the Visual Basic, Enterprise Edition. You cannot develop code or use the RDO object library or RemoteData control in the Professional or Standard Editions of Visual Basic.

For this reason, this chapter deals with DAO and the data control only. We'll explore various techniques for using data access objects to fetch result sets and we'll use the data control to deal with various sets of detail data for addresses and events.

SQL Server 6.0

Microsoft SQL Server 6.0 contains a host of new, advanced features, including an enhanced implementation of the Transact-SQL programming language. One of these new features is the ANSI-SQL compliant WHILE statement, allowing Transact-SQL programmers to write loops within stored procedures. The WHILE clause has made it possible to create stored procedures within the CSCM database which populate various database tables with test records. The RepopContact, RepopAddress, and RepopCAAssoc stored procedures create 5,000 Contacts, 5,000 Addresses, and 5,000 records in ContAddrAssoc, which link them together. Using these stored procedures, you can fill your database with enough data to test performance at a realistic level.

SQL Server 6.0 also features better performance through use of multi-threading under Windows NT. This is not a feature you need to be aware of to benefit from—it happens automatically.

The Project Specification

So now that we know what our client/server system *can* do, let's figure out what it *should* do. While this chapter is not intended to be a treatise on how to design applications, some mention will be made of the project specification, the document you will create as a blueprint for your application.

Client/server applications with multiple users are invariably complex. The system you are creating will most likely have a centralized server component augmented by client components of varying capabilities meeting various needs. The question of what goes where is central to this effort. The perceived needs of the project are also likely to change as the project develops. Perhaps the order-processing department may determine that it needs to do mail merge for shipping labels as well as form letters, or a change in the way quarterly reports are calculated may require a change in the structure of the database itself. While such changes are often inevitable, the creation of the project specification can help "lock down" a picture of the application as first designed. As changes occur, they can be more accurately tracked against the "base model," the original design. Additionally, it is hoped that the research performed in creating the product spec would minimize these surprises.

For this chapter, our project specification will be a simple one. The program we develop will be named the "Client/Server Contact Manager," or CSCM. The program will provide the following functionality:

- A database of contacts, i.e., people, will be displayed to the user through an on-screen form, which will let the user add, delete, and/or update records.

- Fully editable information on the addresses of these contacts will be displayed, allowing the user to associate more than one address with a contact, and more than one contact with any given address.

- Event scheduling capabilities for each contact will be provided, allowing the user to record timestamped events.

In addition, a simple set of referential integrity rules and business rules will be implemented:

1. A contact can have one, many, or no addresses.

2. An address must have *at least* one contact.

3. If a contact is deleted and its addresses are orphaned, the addresses must be deleted as well in order to enforce step 2.

How Does Your User Work?

Determining what your program does and determining how the users do their work are two different things, yet they must come together in your program. Not only must your application meet the criteria in the project specification, but also it must reflect the real world the user lives and works in. This means talk to the users and understand how they intend to use the product you're building for them. Some questions might include:

- What does the user do?

- How is the user doing it now?

- What does the user *really* need to do?

- How can your application help the user do it faster and more efficiently?

This chapter is not intended to be a treatise on software design. Suffice it to say that a thorough understanding of the user's job and work flow is essential to design software which supports that work flow as effectively as possible.

What Will the User Do?

For the purposes of this chapter, it will be assumed that a survey of the prospective users of the program has been performed and that the following conclusions have been drawn:

1. Most users will use the system to locate contacts, either to call them, to review the current status of the contact, or to view the events and appointments associated with that contact.

2. Some users will use the system to respond to incoming calls, so it is imperative that they be able to locate an individual contact quickly and efficiently.

3. Since it is anticipated that the program will be used continuously throughout a standard workday, it will have a small "footprint" and low RAM requirements so it can be left open without significantly affecting other programs.

Software and Hardware Requirements

If your user has expectations of how fast your software will run, you should temper them by specifying the minimum platform required. We have the following minimum requirements:

Workstation Hardware	**Server Hardware**
486/66 with 8M RAM minimum	486/66 with 24M RAM (minimum)
VGA or Super VGA	Pentium 60 or more with 32M
Fast NIC	RAM (preferred)
	OS: Windows NT Server 3.51
	500M Hard disk (minimum)
	Fast NIC
Workstation Software	**Server Software**
OS: Windows 95	Database: SQL Server 6.0
Programming: Visual Basic 4.0	LAN: Windows NT Network

For this application, Windows 95 or Windows NT will run on the client workstation, while Windows NT will run on the server. The 32-bit Windows 95 and Windows NT operating systems are better at memory and resource management than the DOS/Windows combination previously used, and support the 32-bit version of Visual Basic 4.0. Windows NT is required to run Microsoft SQL Server. Although you can run Windows NT and SQL Server with as little as 16M of RAM, this is the bare minimum configuration. At least 24M of RAM on the server is preferable for this application.

Referential Integrity, Rules, and Data Validation

Within any relational database there are rules which ensure that the data makes sense. For example, if an orders table is linked to a clients table, it makes sense that there cannot be an order without a client to place it. If a database is internally consistent in this regard it is said to have *referential integrity*. The "cross-references" within the database tables (in this case between the orders table and the clients table) are correctly maintained. Since client/server databases have the ability to do their own processing, it makes a lot of sense to have the database engine enforce referential integrity wherever possible. If a user attempts to delete a client who has outstanding orders, that deletion should be prevented and the user informed of the error.

Similarly, there may be rules which the database should follow to ensure it correctly reflects the nature of the business process the database is supporting. Let's say our hypothetical business does not allow a client to place any more orders if that client's outstanding balance is higher than $5,000. You should then code the database to reject any orders which match this criteria. While such rules are not necessary to maintain referential integrity, they are necessary to the business using the database. These rules are called *business rules*, and you should have a good knowledge of them as you design both your database system and the application(s) which will use it.

Finally, there are some sorts of data which are considered inherently incorrect by the system. A product price cannot be a negative number, for example, state abbreviations cannot have more than two letters, and so on. The process of screening out "bad" information is called *data validation*.

The reason it is mentioned here is that some data validation can and should be performed on the server. This central location ensures that bad data is filtered out regardless of the application being used to enter it. It is also possible that writing the code in a single place (the server) can make it unnecessary to write it again in one or more of the client applications.

On the other hand, it is often easiest to implement data validation on the client, i.e., the application you're writing. Your program can more readily interact with the user, pointing out incorrect entries and providing informative messages to help the user enter correct data. These two factors mean that you may be required to implement data validation both on the client and the server; server-side implementation ensures that data is kept valid regardless of the application accessing the database, while client-side implementation lets your program be more helpful and proactive in assisting the user.

Enforcing the Rules

There are a number of ways SQL Server can ensure that referential integrity is maintained, business rules are not broken, and data entered into the database is valid. With previous versions of SQL Server you had *rules* and *triggers*; with SQL Server 6.0 you also have *constraints*.

Rules

A *rule* specifies the acceptable values that can be inserted into a table column. Rules can be created by using a range, a list, or a pattern to determine acceptable values. For example, a rule could specify that a product cost must fall within a specified range, say $1,000 to $5,000. Any value outside that range would be automatically rejected by the database. A *list rule* would specify a list of values which would be acceptable, while a *pattern rule* would specify a pattern which the data must match. For example, the following Transact-SQL code creates a rule to follow a pattern of any two characters followed by a hyphen, any number of characters (or no characters), and ending with an integer between 0 and 9:

```
CREATE RULE pattern_rule @value LIKE '_ _-%[0-9]'
```

Triggers

Triggers are a type of stored procedure executed in response to a table event. The three types of triggers are *insert triggers*, *update triggers,* and *delete triggers*. As their names imply, these triggers are called when a record is inserted, updated, or deleted in the database. Triggers are often used for enforcing business rules and data integrity and are useful to ensure appropriate actions when cascading deletions or updates need to occur. Triggers are usually very fast; the time involved in running a trigger is spent mostly in referencing other tables, which may be either in memory or on disk.

In this application, we will see how a delete trigger helps us maintain referential integrity and prevent orphaned address records from cluttering up the address table. Our delete trigger will delete other records according to a predefined set of conditions.

While rules and triggers are supported by all versions of Microsoft SQL Server, a better method might be to use constraints.

Constraints

Rules and triggers have been commonly used in earlier versions of SQL Server to enforce complex business rules and referential integrity. SQL Server 6.0 provides *declarative referential integrity* (DRI) capabilities through the CREATE TABLE statement. DRI refers to the process of building the implementation and enforcement of these kinds of rules directly into the definition of the table itself. Rather than create a rule for a table, you can create table- and column-level CHECK constraints as described with the CREATE TABLE. You can enforce referential integrity across tables by defining foreign key constraints in the table.

Using constraints is the preferred method of restricting column data because multiple constraints can be defined on a column or multiple columns, while a column or user-defined datatype can have only one rule bound to it. Constraints also cannot be removed from a table after creation, as a rule could be. Later, we'll see how constraints are used to ensure that only good data is entered into the database.

The Database and the Schema

The *schema* is the map of all database tables in our database. This map can indicate a number of things about the database depending on the notation you use and the information you include. In our example, the schema will show the columns contained in each table and the way in which those columns are used to link one table to another.

There are a number of tools available on the market which let you graphically create and modify schemas. Many of the tools can import database, table, and column information from an existing table or generate a script for your database engine which, when run, will create the tables you have designed. Among these tools are Microsoft Access 2.0, ERWin ERX, and others.

If the tables in our CSCM database had been designed in an MDB file by using Microsoft Access (not such an unlikely possibility), the Relationships window would display the links between the major tables in the database as shown in figure 9.2.

Fig. 9.2
The CSCM Schema.

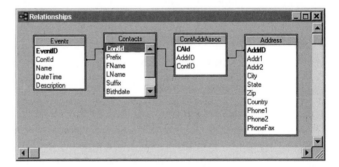

This way of looking at the tables in the database and their relationship to each other is typical of many CASE tools used to design databases. The tables are shown as separate objects with their field names listed; any joins between tables are indicated by the arrow lines which point from key field to key field.

The Contact table is central to the Schema. Each contact can have one or more events, which are linked to the contact by the ContID field in the Events table, referred to as Events.Contid. This is known as a *one-to-many relationship*; one Contact can have many events but each event can only have one Contact. Data of this nature can often be displayed and edited in what is called a *master-detail form*. In this case, such a form would display information on a single contact at the top of a window (the master information) with information about all events (the detail information) shown at the bottom. Our application will follow this model.

Contacts are linked to Addresses by way of the ContAddrAssoc table. Using the ContAddrAssoc table in this fashion allows one Contact to have many Addresses and one Address to have many Contacts. The Contact's ConID field is located in the ContractAddrAssoc table, each record of which also contains an AddrId field. That field in turn is used to look up the Address it represents in the Address table. This is called a *many-to-many relationship* and is defined and maintained by way of a *three-table join* between the Contact, ContAddrAssoc, and Address tables.

Creating the Database

The source code in the CD-ROM provided with this book contains a Transact-SQL script you can run to create the CSCM database in a Microsoft SQL Server 6.0 database and to create the preceding tables within it. The text file CSCM.SQL contains all the commands required to create all the tables in the CSCM database. It also creates all indexes and stored procedures in the table.

Before you do create the database you may wish to create new database devices for it; these are separate physical files managed by SQL Server which store data from one or more databases. The recommended solution is to create two separate files, one for the database and one for the log. CSCMDATA.DAT should be a 20M data file, while CSCMLOG.DAT should be a 10M data file. You should use SQL Server Enterprise Manager to create these database devices, then create the CSCM database. After that you can load the CSCM.SQL script into ISQL/W and run it to create all database tables, indexes, triggers, and stored procedures.

After running this script you will have several stored procedures available to you which you can run to populate the database with test data. These stored procedures are RepopAddress, RepopContact, and RepopCAAsoc. Each stored procedure requires a parameter which tells them how many records to create; you should use the same value for all three stored procedures.

While the data created by these stored procedures is not "pretty," it will serve the purpose of filling your database with enough test records to evaluate its performance under high stress conditions.

The next step is to connect the CSCM application to the database. The CSCM application itself contains a module (CreateMDB) which will create a local database file named CSCM.MDB. This MDB file contains tables which in turn have attachments to the corresponding tables in the CSCM SQL Server database. You can use the CreateMDB procedure as a template to write your own Visual Basic code which will create other MDB files if you wish.

For the sake of brevity and clarity, we will examine sections of the CSCM.SQL script separately, both to understand the structure of each table and to become familiar with Transact-SQL, the language used to create these structures.

The Contacts Table

Here is the portion of the script which creates the Contact table. Note that the CREATE TABLE command indicates the names and datatypes of every column in the table.

```
CREATE TABLE Contact
(
    ContId int IDENTITY (1001, 1) NOT NULL ,
    Prefix varchar (15) NULL ,
    FName varchar (30) NULL ,
    MName varchar (20) NULL ,
    LName varchar (30) NULL ,
    Title varchar (15) NULL ,
    Company varchar (30) NULL ,
    Note varchar (255) NULL ,
    CONSTRAINT PK_Contact_1__12 PRIMARY KEY  CLUSTERED
    (ContId      ),
    CONSTRAINT UQ_Contact_1__12 UNIQUE  NONCLUSTERED
    (ContId     )
)
GO
```

There are some keywords here which may need explaining. First is the use of the NULL and NOT NULL statements for each field in the table. This tells SQL Server what fields must be filled in and which ones can be left empty, or null. Each Contact record must have a ContId (contact ID) but all other fields are optional; hence the only field which is NOT NULL is ContId.

There are also a few keywords in this CREATE TABLE statement, which are new to SQL Server 6.0. First is the IDENTITY keyword, which tells SQL Server that the values in the ContID field uniquely identify each row within the table. You can use this feature to have SQL Server automatically generate unique sequential numbers for `ContId`. In this case, the first Contact record created in the table will be given a `ContId` of 1001; that value will automatically increment by one with each new record added, ensuring each record has a unique, sequential contact id number.

Note also the `CONSTRAINT` keyword, which is used twice. The first indicates an index on the `ContId`, which is specified as this table's primary key. This constraint indicates that the primary key `ContID` is indexed by a *clustered index,* an object where the physical order of rows as stored on disk is the same as the indexed order of the rows. By definition, only one clustered index is permitted per table. Since SQL Server automatically provides a sequential value for the contact id of each new record created (as described above), a clustered index is a good way to index this table for speedy access. This clustered index does not require a separate statement to create it; the index is created by default whenever a field is designated the primary key for a table.

The second use of the `CONSTRAINT` keyword is used to specify that each Contact ID must be unique within the table. Having this field specified as unique makes it possible for Visual Basic 4.0 to open updatable recordsets for this table.

Here is the statement which creates indexes for the Contact table called `idxContact`. The `idxContact` index uses the contact's name and company information, making searches or sorts go faster when using these fields. The `idxPrimaryContact` index makes it faster to find a Contact using the `ContID` field.

```
CREATE   INDEX idxContact ON dbo.Contact(LName, FName, MName, Company)
GO

CREATE   INDEX idxPrimaryContact ON dbo.Contact(ContId)
GO
```

The Address Table

Here is the SQL statement in CSCM.SQL, which creates the Address table.

Listing 9.1 9LIST01.TXT—Create Table Address

```
(
    AddrID int IDENTITY (1001, 1) NOT NULL ,
    Addr1 varchar (50) NOT NULL ,
    Addr2 varchar (50) NULL ,
    City varchar (30) NOT NULL ,
    State char (2) NOT NULL ,
    Zip varchar (20) NULL ,
    Country varchar (15) NULL ,
```

(continues)

Listing 9.1 Continued

```
        Phone1 varchar (15) NULL ,
        Phone2 varchar (15) NULL ,
        PhoneFax varchar (15) NULL ,
        CONSTRAINT PK_Address_1__10 PRIMARY KEY  CLUSTERED
        (AddrID),
        CONSTRAINT UQ_Address_2__12 UNIQUE  NONCLUSTERED
        (AddrID)
    )
    GO
```

Notice here that we have more NOT NULL fields; any address entered must not only have an AddrId (address ID), but at the very least, City and State must also be filled in.

Note again the IDENTIY nature of AddrId. This works the same way as in the Contact table, seeding the first new record of the table with an AddrId of 1001 and automatically incrementing the value by one with each succeeding record created. There is also a Constraint mandating that each Address ID should be unique.

We also add two indexes to the Address table to make it easier to look up addresses by city, state, and zip or by Address ID.

```
CREATE  INDEX idxAddress ON dbo.Address(City, State, Zip)
GO

CREATE  INDEX idxPrimaryAddr ON dbo.Address(AddrID)
GO
```

The Events Table

Here are the create statements for the Events table.

```
CREATE TABLE Events
(     EventID int IDENTITY (1001, 1) NOT NULL ,
      ContID int NOT NULL ,
      Name varchar (30) NOT NULL CONSTRAINT DF_Events_Name_4__12
      ➥DEFAULT ('New Event'),
      EventDateTime datetime NOT NULL ,
      Description varchar (255) NOT NULL ,
      CONSTRAINT PK___2__12 PRIMARY KEY  CLUSTERED
      (EventID),
      CONSTRAINT constEventId UNIQUE  NONCLUSTERED
      (EventID))
    GO
```

This is a smaller table, but note that the `EventID`, `ContID`, `Name`, and `DateTime` fields *must* be filled in. While not necessarily required by SQL Server, our business rules state that any event entered into the database must have at least these pieces of information or else the event record will be considered meaningless. Again, each event ID must be unique within the table.

We also create an index on the Events table to make it quicker to sort on and search by an event's date/time stamp.

```
CREATE INDEX idxEventTimes ON dbo.Events(EventDateTime)
```

The ContAddrAssoc Table

Lastly, we create the ContAddrAssoc table, the table which makes it possible to establish a many-to-many relationship between the Contact table and the Addresses table:

```
CREATE TABLE ContAddrAssoc
(
    CAId int IDENTITY (1001, 1) NOT NULL ,
    AddrID int NOT NULL ,
    ContID int NOT NULL ,
    CONSTRAINT PK_ContAddrAssoc_1__10 PRIMARY KEY  CLUSTERED
    (CAId),
    CONSTRAINT UQ_ContAddrAssoc_1__12 UNIQUE   NONCLUSTERED
    (CAId, AddrID,    ContID)
)
```

This is an even smaller table, containing only three fields, but all three are required for the record to have meaning. The unique identifier `CAID` is the `IDENTITY` field for the table, while each record must also have a `ContId` and and `AddrID` to correctly link records from each table. Note here that each record in the table must have a *unique* combination of `CAID`, `CONTID`, and `ADDRID`.

Two Indexes are created, making it possible for SQL Server to provide information from the joined Contact and Address tables more rapidly.

```
CREATE  INDEX idxContAddr ON dbo.ContAddrAssoc(AddrID, ContID)
GO

CREATE  INDEX IdxPrimaryCA ON dbo.ContAddrAssoc(CAId)
GO
```

Rules

For our application to work intelligently, we must apply rules which make the database support real-world business processes. Whether these rules are implemented and enforced at the client side or the database server, they must first be listed, examined, and understood.

These rules are arbitrary to our particular application; your application will most likely have different (and more complex) rules; what those rules are depends on the processes the application will support.

Rule 1: A Contact can have one, many, or no Addresses

It is possible that our fictional business can get the name and company of a contact but not an address or phone number. The system will allow a user to enter this information even though it may not be considered to be complete. If one or more addresses are obtained later for this Contact, they may be added to the database and associated with the Contact.

It is also possible to design the database to clean itself up automatically. For example, if a Contact is deleted from the database, it might be convenient to automatically delete that Contact's Addresses as well. However, if these Addresses are associated with other Contacts, this would be a bad idea. Our best solution will be to write a stored procedure which would delete any related Addresses for a Contact, but *only* if those Addresses were no longer associated with any other Contact. In the following section, we'll see how the CSCM database does this.

Rule 2: An Address must have at least one Contact

No Address can be created in the database unless it can be linked to an existing Contact. This rule is best enforced at the client side by designing the application in such a way that it is impossible to create or link an Address without selecting a Contact first.

Note that an insert trigger on the Address table would *not* be a good way to enforce this rule. The CSCM application must first create an Address, then create a link to a Contact through the ContAddrAssoc table. If a trigger prevents an unlinked Address, then the CSCM application would be unable to create that new Address before linking it to a Contact. This is one rule which can only be enforced from the client application.

Rule 3: An Event must have one and only one Contact

As with Addresses, you create events by associating them with Contacts, so you have to look up or create a Contact before you can define an event. Conversely, if a Contact is deleted, all of the events for that Contact should be deleted as well. The DRI rules for the Contact table help prevent "orphaned" events, since the ContID field is a required (NOT NULL) field.

Enforcing the Rules

An efficient and automatic method of handling the preceding scenario is by using a *trigger*. Triggers are stored procedures which fire off automatically in response to insertions, deletions, or updates within a database. It logically follows, then, that the three types of triggers are called *insert* triggers, *delete* triggers, and *update* triggers.

This function is performed by the trigger `tr_DelOrphanAddr`, which fires off whenever a record is deleted from the ContAddrAssoc table.

```
CREATE TRIGGER tr_DelOrphanAddr ON dbo.contaddrassoc
FOR DELETE
AS
IF NOT EXISTS
(SELECT * FROM CONTADDRASSOC WHERE ADDRID = (SELECT ADDRID FROM DELETED))
DELETE FROM ADDRESS WHERE ADDRID = (SELECT ADDRID FROM DELETED)
GO
```

This trigger ensures that no Addresses are left orphaned in the database. If Contact A is unlinked from Address B, and Address B is not linked to any other Contact, then `tr_DelOrphanAddr` deletes Address B from the Addresses table.

Views

Views are virtual tables which provide a simplified look at complex data. A single view may appear as a single table to an application or user, yet it actually may be comprised of multiple tables joined together according to the requirements of the database schema. The tables behind a view are called *base tables*.

The CSCM database uses several views to provide quick access to related data. Since the database joins are defined in the view, the work of joining the table data meaningfully is performed by the server. The advantage is quick, simple access to otherwise complex data. There are three views: `AddressList`, `EventView`, and `LookupView`, and they are defined in CSCM.SQL:

```
CREATE VIEW AddressList AS
Select contaddrassoc.contid, address.*
from contaddrassoc, address
where contaddrassoc.addrid = address.addrid
```

This view makes it possible to quickly look up Contacts by using Address information only.

The `EventView` view lets the CSCM database quickly return a list of events associated with a Contact.

```
CREATE VIEW EventView AS
select EventID, eventdatetime, contact.*
from contact, events
where contact.contid = events.eventid
```

Lastly, the `LookupView` is used to quickly look up Contacts by using Address *or* Contact information, or a combination of both.

```
CREATE VIEW LookupView AS
Select c.*, a.addrid, a.city, a.state, a.zip
From contact c, contaddrassoc ca, address a
where c.contid = ca.contid and ca.addrid = a.addrid
```

To ensure that a view can be updated, you must create a unique index in your local table. Views themselves cannot support indexes as tables can, so your indexing must be done on the local table which is attached to the view. There may also be times when a view cannot or should not be updated, in which case you'll have to execute SQL code (using `SQLPassThrough`), which acts directly on the base tables of the view. After the commands are complete, you can refresh your picture of the view to see the changed data.

The Client Server Contact Manager

Now that we have a functional specification and an idea of how the user will be using the program we can develop a prototype which will give the users an idea of how the program will look and feel. In our case, the CSCM will have a main section on top and a tab section at the bottom.

Design Overview

The interface to CSCM has been designed to make it easy for the users to quickly access the information they need. The program has been designed on the assumption that the primary use of the program will be to deal with calls as they come in or to quickly locate individual people in the database. For that reason, there's only one window and it is Contact-centric (see fig. 9.3). The window is also of a fixed size to minimize considerations about control placement and other sizing issues, which are outside of the scope of this chapter.

Fig. 9.3
The Client Server
Contact Manager.

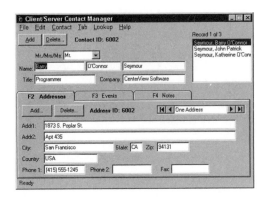

Looking up a Contact is simple—click the Lookup menu and choose the method to use: name, company, city, state, or zip. The menu also offers the option to locate a specific Contact by Contact ID or to locate all the Contacts at a given Address (presuming you know the Address ID). Lastly, the Lookup menu allows you to look up Contacts who have events within a given date range.

Query By Form (QBF) is a common technique used in database applications, especially client/server ones. In QBF the data entry form is cleared and the user enters search criteria directly into it. This allows the user to enter any possible combination of field information to define the search. After the search is initiated the results are returned to the data entry form.

For the sake of simplicity (this is a simple application after all) the concept of Query By Form (QBF) has not been implemented here.

Connecting to the Database

As mentioned above, CSCM will use the Jet database engine and Data Access Objects to access SQL Server 6.0 ODBC drivers installed on the system. The most efficient way to do this is to create a local database (MDB) file, then attach tables from the SQL database to it. Performance is better when this technique is used because information about the database structure itself is cached locally in the MDB file (and often in disk cache memory). If a local database file were not used, the system would be forced to obtain information on the database structure with every query issued. As we'll see later, CSCM performs a check upon startup to see if the database file is present; if it isn't the program creates it.

The Main Form

The main section contains a list box listing every client in the current result set. As a client name is clicked, the record is displayed in the text boxes of the main section. The addresses of that contact are then fetched and placed in an address tab at bottom. Each address is fetched and displayed when the user clicks the data control.

The Sheridan 3D Tab Control (provided with Visual Basic 4.0) is used to provide three tabs at the bottom of the window. Here will be displayed information about addresses, events, and notes for the contact. This control is named *tabEvents*.

A note about the Sheridan Tab Control; at the time of this writing, a known bug existed which prevents you from changing the tab property of the tab control while the form is invisible. For this reason the `tabEvents.Tab` property must be set to 1 in design mode before you run the application. In the Form_Load Event for frmContact is some code which pops up an error message and ends the program if tabEvents.Tab is not 1. Make sure you set this property correctly before generating an EXE file!

The *Addresses Tab* (see bottom of fig. 9.3) displays all Addresses for the Contact. Based on our referential integrity rules, there are four things you can do in this tab:

1. Create a new address for the current contact.

2. Link an existing address to the current contact.

3. Edit the current address.

4. Unlink or "drop" the current address from the current contact. Note that if this is the only Contact the Address is associated with, dropping the address will delete it.

The Events tab displays a list box of all events associated with the contact, arranged in reverse chronological order by date and time, newest on the top, as shown in figure 9.4.

Fig. 9.4

The Client Server Contact Manager Events tab.

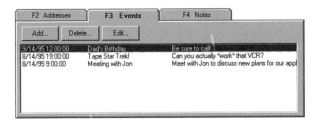

Using this list, the user will be able to add, edit/review, and delete events. A separate modal properties sheet will be used for the review and edit functions.

The *Notes tab* (see fig. 9.5) will display a single multiline text box, which will contain notes for the user. This is the Note field in the Contact table, a field of type VarChar(255). For the purposes of this application, 255 characters is deemed sufficient to keep notes on a Contact.

If you were to use the SQL Server TEXT datatype for this field, the attached table would treat the column as being of the MEMO datatype. Updates to this sort of field can be significantly slower, even if only a small amount of text is actually stored.

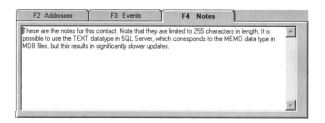

Fig. 9.5
The Client Server
Contact Manager
Notes tab.

The Event Properties Sheet

All events for a Contact are displayed in a list in the second tab. This list shows all events in reverse chronological order. When the user double-clicks an existing event the Event properties sheet appears, displaying information about the event (see fig. 9.6).

Fig. 9.6
The Client Server
Contact Manager
Events properties
sheet.

If the event is an Appointment which has not yet come to pass, it may be edited or deleted. The Event properties sheet gives the user the opportunity to edit the date or time or to change the description and text of the appointment. If the time of the event has passed it can only be viewed.

Menus

The CSCM will have a set of menus (see fig. 9.7), which will facilitate the operation of the program. Wherever possible, keyboard shortcuts will be provided, making it easier for touch typists to perform all functions without requiring the mouse. This sort of functionality is especially helpful to operators performing large amounts of data entry.

Fig. 9.7.
The File, Edit, and
Contact menus.

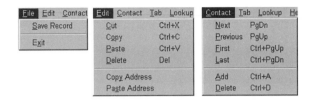

The **File** menu provides options for logging on, printing, and exiting from the program. It also provides a Save command, which allows the user to save changes to the current record without leaving it.

The **Edit** menu allows for text box editing; it also provides copy and paste commands for individual addresses, making it easier to assign one address to several Contacts. Just locate the Address, copy it, locate the other Contact, and click "Copy Address" to link that Address to the contact.

The **Contact** menu provides a means for navigating the list of Contacts and for adding and deleting a contact.

The **Tab** menus (see fig. 9.8) provide tab selection capabilities and tab-specific functions via the keyboard. The active tab is indicated with a checkmark and can be changed by clicking the mouse on the menu item, using access keys, or the shortcut keys F2, F3, and F4 as indicated. As the active tab is changed, the available entries in the Tab menu change to provide only those functions which are appropriate for the tab. Note the use of function keys to switch between tabs, again supporting the touch typist.

Fig. 9.8
The Tab menu in
each of its three
configurations.

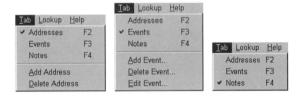

The **Lookup** menu facilitates the various searches CSCM provides, and the **Help** menu provides access to the CSCM help system and the about screen (see fig. 9.9).

Fig. 9.9
The Lookup and
Help menus.

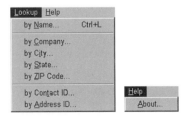

Writing the Code

Now that we know how the user interface works, it's time to look under the hood at the code doing the work. Before the user ever gets to touch a key or mouse button, the application jumps through a number of hoops to ensure that it's ready.

Initializing the Application

When the application is first run, a number of initialization routines are performed to set up "public" variables (note they're not "global" anymore!) and to initialize the database connection via the local database file.

The Main sub in CSCM.BAS is our starting point. Using a Sub Main is helpful in that it can be used to initialize the program without the overhead of forms loading and displaying. One of the first actions the procedure takes is to load a splash screen. This makes it feel like the program is starting quickly, even though it may take a few seconds to establish a valid database connection and load the main form. The ShowSplash sub quickly loads and shows the splash screen, using its single parameter to determine if the form's OK button should be displayed or not. (This sub is also called from the About submenu in the Help menu.)

Listing 9.2   9LIST02.TXT—ShowSplash sub

```
Sub Main()
   Dim x As Integer, f As Form
   ChDir App.Path

   ShowSplash False 'show splash/about form

   Select Case UCase$(Command$)
      Case "RECREATE"
          On Error Resume Next
          Kill "CSCM.MDB"
          On Error GoTo 0
          CreateMDB
      Case "" 'do nothing
      Case Else
          Beep
          MsgBox "Command Line string '" & Command$ & "' is not supported."
   End Select

   Screen.MousePointer = 11
   DoEvents

   Load frmContact
   Set f = frmContact
```

(continues)

Listing 9.2   Continued

```
      InitGlobals
      If InitContactDB() = False Then ShutDown

      ClearForm frmContact   'clear all controls
      Unload frmAbout
      f.Show
      f.Refresh
      DoEvents
      Screen.MousePointer = 0
      LookupByName

  End Sub
```

The `InitContactDB` function initializes the connection to the database.

Listing 9.3   9LIST03.TXT—InitContactDB()

```
  Function InitContactDB() As Integer
     'initialize the database
     Dim msg As String

     ChDir App.Path
     Err.Clear
     If Dir$("CSCM.MDB") = "" Then CreateMDB ' if this fails,
     ➥program ends
     On Error Resume Next
     Set DB = OpenDatabase("CSCM.MDB")

     Err.Clear
     Set rsContactSet = DB.OpenRecordset("Contact")
        If Err.Number <> 0 Then
        msg = "Error " & Err.Number & ": "
        If Err.Description = "" Then
          msg = msg & "Unknown Error."
        Else
          msg = msg & Err.Description
        End If
        MsgBox msg, vbExclamation
        InitContactDB = False
     Else
        InitContactDB = True
     End If
  End Function
```

Note the call to `CreateMDB()`; if the local database file doesn't exist, this procedure creates it. Note also the option to force CSCM to rebuild the CSCM.MDB file in `Sub Main`. If the word RECREATE is appended to the command line, the application will delete and rebuild the file by using `CreateMDB`.

Listing 9.4   9LIST04.TXT—SubCreateMDB()

```
Sub CreateMDB()
    Dim r As Integer ' results
    Dim Td As TableDef, qd As QueryDef
    Dim TableNam(6) As String, x As Integer

    Dim Param As String, QDString As String
    'dimension parameter and querydef strings

    On Error GoTo CreateMDBFail

    'initialize your DBEngine Workspace...
    Set WS = DBEngine.Workspaces(0)

    ChDir App.Path
    If Dir$("CSCM.MDB") <> "" Then ' just in case CreateMDB is
    ➥called in error...
        If MsgBox("Overwrite existing CSCM.MDB?", vbQuestion +
        ➥vbYesNo) = vbNo Then
            Exit Sub
        Else
            DB.Close
            Set DB = Nothing
            Kill "CSCM.MDB"
        End If
    End If

    If SplashVisible Then
        frmAbout.lblStatus = "Creating CSCM.MDB data file..."
        frmAbout.lblStatus.Visible = True
        frmAbout.lblStatus.Refresh
    End If

    ' Create a new CSCM.MDB file
    Set DB = WS.CreateDatabase("CSCM.MDB", dbLangGeneral, dbVersion11)
    DB.QueryTimeout = DB.QueryTimeout

    '======= CREATE TABLEDEFS ===============================
    If SplashVisible Then
        frmAbout.lblStatus = "Attaching tables from SQL Server..."
        frmAbout.lblStatus.Refresh
    End If

    'use an array of table names to simplify the code
    'needed to create and attach tables...
    TableNam(0) = "Contact"
    TableNam(1) = "Address"
    TableNam(2) = "Events"
    TableNam(3) = "Types"
    TableNam(4) = "ContaddrAssoc"
    TableNam(5) = "LookupView"
    TableNam(6) = "AddressList"
```

(continues)

Listing 9.4   Continued

```
For x = 0 To 6
    Set Td = DB.CreateTableDef(TableNam(x))
    Td.Connect = "ODBC;DSN=CSCM;UID=" & LOGINID &
    ➥";PWD=;DATABASE=CSCM;"
    Td.SourceTableName = TableNam(x)
    DB.TableDefs.Append Td
Next x

If SplashVisible Then
    frmAbout.lblStatus = "Attaching Query Definitions..."
    frmAbout.lblStatus.Refresh
End If

If SplashVisible Then
    frmAbout.lblStatus = "CSCM.MDB data file was created
    ➥successfully!"
    frmAbout.lblStatus.Refresh
End If

'Create unique indexes on attached views so they can return
➥updatable result sets
DB.Execute "CREATE UNIQUE INDEX  idxAddr on AddressList
➥(AddrId)", dbFailOnError
DB.Execute "CREATE UNIQUE INDEX  idxContId on LookupView
➥(ContId)", dbFailOnError
DB.Execute "CREATE UNIQUE INDEX  idxEvent on Events(EventId)",
➥dbFailOnError

'note we don't close the database!

Exit Sub

CreateMDBFail:
    Beep
    MsgBox "Error Creating CSCM.MDB:" & Err.Description & _
    " Please contact technical support.", vbCritical + 4096
    ShutDown
End Sub
```

Note the use of constants for LOGINID and PWD (password). In this application they are hard-coded to SA and null password respectively, but you might wish to use the registry or INI files to store and read these values.

Note also that the names of the local tables match the names of the tables in the SQL Server database we're attaching to. This will make it easy later to modify the application so the user can import data to the local MDB file and work "off-line" without requiring a server connection. If you were to implement this feature you'd have to write routines to import data from the server and to selectively update any changes the user might have made upon reconnecting.

Fetching Contact Records

Once the form is initialized, the database connection is made, and the splash screen dismissed, it's time to fetch some data. To save the user an unnecessary step, the public function LookUpByName() is automatically called after all these procedures have completed. This sub loops until the user selects a valid result set or cancels the operation.

Listing 9.5 9LIST05.TXT—SubLookUpByName()

```
Sub LookupByName()
 'This requires different handling, which is why it's not
 'in the mnuLookupSub menu array

 Dim x As Integer, f As Form, Qry As String, msg As String
 On Error Resume Next

 Do ' this until you cancel or get a result set!
     Screen.MousePointer = 0
     frmLookup.Show vbModal
     If frmLookup.Tag = frmLookup.btnOK(1).Caption Then GoTo GetOut
     If Trim(frmLookup.txtLookup(0)) = "" And
     ➥Trim(frmLookup.txtLookup(1)) = "" Then GoTo GetOut

     Screen.MousePointer = 11
     frmContact.Refetch = True

     Qry = "Select * from Contact where Lname like '" &
     ➥Trim(frmLookup.txtLookup(0)) _
     & "*' and FName Like '" & Trim(frmLookup.txtLookup(1)) & "*'
     ➥order by lname, fname, mname"

     Set rsContactSet = Db.OpenRecordset(Qry, dbOpenDynaset,
     ➥dbSeeChanges)

     If rsContactSet.RecordCount Then
         FillList "Contact" ' this fills the list by cloning the
         ➥recordset
         Exit Do
     Else
         msg = "No records match the search request you entered. "
         msg = msg & "Query was " & LF & LF & QT & UCase$(Qry) &
QT & LF & LF
         msg = msg & "Try again?"
```

(continues)

Listing 9.5 Continued

```
            If MsgBox(msg, vbQuestion + vbYesNo) = vbNo Then GoTo
            ➥GetOut
            'the current recordset is left intact.
        End If
        DoEvents
        frmContact.txtContact(2).SetFocus
    Loop
    Screen.MousePointer = 0
Exit Sub

GetOut:
    frmContact.Refetch = False
    Unload frmLookup
    Screen.MousePointer = 0
    On Error GoTo 0
    Exit Sub
End Sub
```

This sub uses a separate form to ask for two fields—last name and first name—upon which to base its query. Only part of either of the two fields is absolutely required by the routine, but the more information the user enters, the narrower the search criteria will be and the faster the results will return to the workstation.

The form frmLookup is used to gather the data, storing "OK" or "Cancel" in its tag to indicate the resultant user action. If "OK," the name information is incorporated into a SQL Query, which is executed to populate the public recordset variable rsContactSet. That recordset is then cloned, and the clone used to fill the result set list at the top right corner of the form. This list allows the user to quickly scroll through all names returned by the query to find the Contact desired.

In figure 9.10, you see what would happen if a user queried our test database looking for everyone with a last name like "10." If users were to look up "Smith" without specifying a first name they'd probably get more than the usual amount of records. This result set list allows them to quickly scroll to the record desired without fetching all the intermediate data.

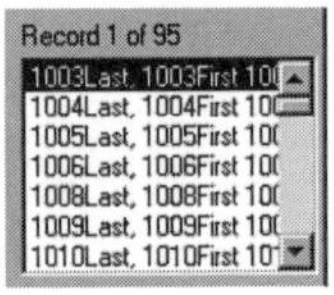

Fig. 9.10
The Result Set List displaying the first of 95 records fetched.

This is about as large a result set as you should try to get. A recordset containing more than 100 records requires two connections: Visual Basic uses one connection to fetch the key values from the server and another to fetch the data associated with those keys for the records visible on-screen. Other dynasets can share the second connection, but can't share the first because all key values might not have been retrieved from the server. Thus, a recordset of 300 records would require four connections.

> **Note**
>
> Since our database was automatically populated with meaningless test records (5,000 in all) for testing purposes, the names shown in the preceding list don't mean a lot, but the concept is still valid.)

Once the desired record is clicked, the appropriate record is retrieved from the result set rsContacts and displayed in the window. This is achieved through the lstContacts_Click event procedure.

Listing 9.6   9LIST06.TXT—PrivateSub1stContacts_Click()

```
Private Sub lstContacts_Click()
   If Not lstContacts.Enabled Then Exit Sub ' prevent accidental
   ➥activation
   If lstContacts.ListIndex = -1 Then Exit Sub
   Dim ContID As Long, LBox As Control, lbl As Label
   Dim Qry As String

   If lstContacts.ItemData(lstContacts.ListIndex) =
   ➥Val(txtContact(0)) Then
     'the current contact was clicked
     If Refetch = False Then Exit Sub
        'no need to refetch unless form-level var 'Refetch' is True.
   Else ' a new contact was clicked. Save the current one before leaving
     UpdateContact
   End If

   'if you get this far, proceed with fetching and displaying
   'the selected contact.

   'set object variables to point to the relevant controls
   Set LBox = frmContact.lstContacts
   Set lbl = frmContact.lblContact(0)

   'This activates the record...
   rsContactSet.AbsolutePosition = LBox.ListIndex
```

(continues)

Listing 9.6   Continued

```
'load data to show the current contact record
For x = 0 To 7
    If Not IsNull(rsContactSet.Fields(txtContact(x).DataField)) Then _
    txtContact(x) = rsContactSet.Fields(txtContact(x).DataField) _
    Else txtContact(x) = ""
Next x
ContactChanged = False ' set public form-level var

lblContact(0) = "Contact ID: " & rsContactSet!ContID
lblResultSet = "Record " & lstContacts.ListIndex + 1 & " of " &
➥lstContacts.ListCount

Screen.MousePointer = 0
Me.Refresh

'reinitialize the TabFetched() array
For x = 0 To 2: TabFetched(x) = False: Next x

'now fetch data for the current tab..
FetchTab tabDetails.Tab

'update the navigation menu
mnuContactSub(0).Enabled = lstContacts.ListIndex <
➥lstContacts.ListCount - 1 ' Next contact
mnuContactSub(1).Enabled = lstContacts.ListIndex > 0 ' previous
➥contact
mnuContactSub(2).Enabled = lstContacts.ListIndex > 0 ' First
➥contact
mnuContactSub(3).Enabled = lstContacts.ListIndex <
➥lstContacts.ListCount - 1 ' Last contact
Stat "Ready"
End Sub
```

The AbsolutePosition property of the recordset (a new VB 4.0 feature) is used to fetch the record which corresponds to the list entry clicked. The record data is then copied into the text boxes and the navigation menus updated.

Fetching Details

CSCM works on a principle of *cascading queries*. Data is not fetched until the program actually needs it. For example, near the end of the lstContacts_Click procedure, you'll see a call to FetchTab, a procedure which evaluates which tab is active and fetches data *only* for that tab. Fetchtab is also called whenever a new tab is clicked, unless the data for that tab has already been fetched. A double-click on the current tab will refetch its data regardless of the current state of the data displayed in the tab.

Listing 9.7   9LIST07.TXT—SubFetchTab(TabNoAsInteger)

```
Sub FetchTab(TabNo As Integer)
    Dim x As Integer, MP As Integer
    MP = Screen.MousePointer ' save this
    Dim rs As Recordset

    Screen.MousePointer = 11

    If TabFetched(TabNo) Then Exit Sub
    Select Case TabNo
        Case 0 ' addresses
            FetchingAddr = True
            dtaAddress.Enabled = False
            Qry = "Select * from AddressList where contid = " _
            & lstContacts.ItemData(lstContacts.ListIndex)

            dtaAddress.RecordSource = Qry
            dtaAddress.Refresh

            On Error Resume Next
            dtaAddress.Recordset.MoveLast
            If Err.Number = 3021 Then ' no records!
              dtaAddress.Caption = "No Addresses"
              dtaAddress.Enabled = False
              btnAddress(1).Enabled = False ' delete button
              mnuEditAddr(0).Enabled = False ' edit¦copy address
            Else
              dtaAddress.Enabled = True
              'Use MoveLast to get a count of the Address records returned.
              'Do not do this if you have large result sets of addresses.
              dtaAddress.Recordset.MoveFirst
              btnAddress(1).Enabled = True ' delete button
              mnuEditAddr(0).Enabled = True ' edit¦copy address
            End If
            On Error GoTo 0

            'set public and form-level status flags
            AddressChanged = False
            Refetch = False ' reset form-level var
            FetchingAddr = False ' ditto
            If CopiedAddr.AddrId <> 0 Then mnuEditAddr(1).Enabled = True

        Case 1 ' events
            GetEventRecordSet Val(txtContact(0))

        Case 2 ' notes
            'nothing to do here yet.

    End Select
    Screen.MousePointer = MP ' restore prior mousepointer
    TabFetched(TabNo) = True

End Sub
```

This sub evaluates which tab is active and checks an array of form-level flags to see if the data requires fetching. If the Address data requires fetching, the RecordSource property of the data control dtaAddress is updated and its recordset refreshed; bound controls handle the rest. If the Events tab is active, the GetEventRecordSet sub is called which fetches all events for the current Contact and places them in a list.

Listing 9.8   9LIST08.TXT—Sub GetEventRecordSet(ContID As Long)

```
Sub GetEventRecordSet(ContID As Long)
    Dim Qry As String, Temp As String
    Dim x As Integer ' looping var
    Dim c As Control

    Set c = frmContact.lstEvents
    Screen.MousePointer = 11
    DoEvents
    frmContact.lstEvents.Clear

    'build the query string based on the parameters assembled
    Qry = "Select * from Events where contid = " &
➥frmContact.txtContact(0)
    Qry = Qry & " order by EventDateTime DESC"

    'We only need this data to fill the listbox, so dbForwardOnly
➥makes sense.
    Set rsEventSet = Db.OpenRecordset(Qry, dbOpenDynaset,
➥dbSeeChanges)

    If rsEventSet.RecordCount = 0 Then
        frmContact.lstEvents.AddItem "No Events"
        frmContact.btnEvent(1).Enabled = False
        frmContact.btnEvent(2).Enabled = False
        Screen.MousePointer = 0
        Exit Sub
    End If

    ' if you get this far, fill the list.
    rsEventSet.MoveFirst

    Do While Not rsEventSet.EOF
        Temp = rsEventSet.Fields("EventDateTime") & TB _
        & rsEventSet.Fields("Name") & TB _
        & rsEventSet.Fields("Description")

        'trim trailing linefeeds
        While Right$(Temp, 1) = Chr$(13) Or Right$(Temp, 1) =
➥Chr$(10)
          Temp = Left$(Temp, Len(Temp) - 1)
        Wend

        c.AddItem Temp
        c.ItemData(c.NewIndex) = Val(rsEventSet.Fields("EventID"))
        rsEventSet.MoveNext
```

```
      Loop
      c.ListIndex = -1
      frmContact.btnEvent(1).Enabled = False
      frmContact.btnEvent(2).Enabled = False

      Screen.MousePointer = 0
   End Sub
```

Working with Addresses

As mentioned earlier, it is possible for a Contact to have one, many, or no
Addresses. The CSCM application uses the data control to fetch recordsets of
Addresses; once those records are fetched, the data control automatically
handles the display and updating of existing Addresses. However, the user
also needs the ability to add or delete Address records as well, which is where
the btnAddress() button array comes into play.

This control array of two buttons lets the user add either a new or an existing
Address to the Contact. The logic these controls use is best understood by
reviewing the code:

Listing 9.9   9LIST09.TXT—Private Sub btnAddress_Click(Index As Integer)

```
   Private Sub btnAddress_Click(Index As Integer)
    Select Case Index
    Case 0 ' add / save
      If btnAddress(0).Caption = "Add..." Then
        AddressAdd
      ElseIf btnAddress(0).Caption = "Create" Then
        AddressCreate
      End If

    Case 1 ' delete/discard
      If btnAddress(1).Caption = "Delete..." Then
        AddressDelete
      ElseIf btnAddress(1).Caption = "Discard" Then
        AddressDiscard
      End If
    End Select
   End Sub
```

Notice the terminology used in naming the called subs. To "Add" an Address
involves linking an existing Address; to "create" one creates a new Address
record; to "delete" an Address means to erase an existing record; and to
"discard" an Address refers to throwing away Address information without
saving it in the first place.

The AddressAdd sub in turn calls PickExistingAddr, which lets the user enter a zip code for the Address to add. At that point, a pick list is displayed showing all Address records in the database at that zip code. If the desired Address is in that list, the user can select it, at which point it will be associated with the Contact. If the Address is not in the list, the user can click the New button to create a new address.

Listing 9.10   9LIST10.TXT— Sub AddressAdd()

```
Sub AddressAdd()
 Dim NewAddrID As String, SQL As String, rs As Recordset, msg As
 ➥String

 NewAddrID = PickExistingAddr() ' offer user the option to pick an
 ➥existing address
 Select Case NewAddrID
   Case "New"

     dtaAddress.Recordset.AddNew
     txtAddress(x) = txtContact(0) 'save contact id
     btnAddress(0).Caption = "Create"
     btnAddress(1).Caption = "Discard"
     txtAddress(1).SetFocus

   Case "Cancel", ""
     Exit Sub

   Case Else ' user specified an existing zip code.

     ' NewAddrID contains An address Id to link to this contact.
     SQL = "INSERT INTO CONTADDRASSOC (CONTID, ADDRID) VALUES ("
     SQL = SQL & txtContact(0) & ", " & NewAddrID & ")"
     Db.Execute SQL
     'NOTE we use this technique because dtaAddress is looking at a
     'VIEW. We need to update the source table, then refresh the
     ➥query.
     'Also note that if this fails, it'll be because an association
     'already exists. This is NOT a problem!

     DoEvents

     'refetch the address list for this contact
     TabFetched(0) = False
     FetchTab 0

     'find the address you just added
     dtaAddress.Recordset.FindFirst "AddrId = " & NewAddrID

   End Select
End Sub
```

If users decide to create a new Address, an empty record is created for them to fill in. When they click the "Create" button, the `AddressCreate` sub is executed:

Listing 9.11   9LIST11.TXT—The AddressCreate Sub

```
Sub AddressCreate()
  'EVEN THOUGH we created a new record using dtaAddress.AddNew,
  'we can't perform an update using the .Update method since
  'dtaAddress is looking at a view. For that reason we use the
  'values in the address textboxes to create a SQL server statement
  'which inserts the record. We then refetch the address set.

  Dim NewAddrID As String, SQL As String, rs As Recordset, msg As String

  SQL = "INSERT INTO ADDRESS ("
  For x = 1 To 9 ' get the datafields
    SQL = SQL & txtAddress(x).DataField
    If x < 9 Then SQL = SQL & ", "
  Next x
  SQL = SQL & ") VALUES ("

  For x = 1 To 9 ' get the datafields
    SQL = SQL & QT & Trim(txtAddress(x).Text) & QT
    If x < 9 Then SQL = SQL & ", "
  Next x
  SQL = SQL & ")"

  Stat "Creating Address..."
  Db.Execute SQL, dbSQLPassThrough

  'now we should have only ONE address in the Address table
  'which isn't associated with a contact. Find it's AddrID
  Stat "Linking Address..."

  SQL = "Select Addrid from ADDRESS where "

  For x = 1 To 9 ' get the datafields
    SQL = SQL & txtAddress(x).DataField & " = "
    If Trim(txtAddress(x).Text) = "" Then
      SQL = SQL & " null "
    Else
      SQL = SQL & QT & txtAddress(x).Text & QT
    End If
    If x < 9 Then SQL = SQL & " AND "
  Next x

  Set rs = Db.OpenRecordset(SQL, dbOpenSnapshot)

  If rs.RecordCount Then ' we found the address! link it.
    SQL = "insert into contaddrassoc (ADDRID, CONTID) values ("
    SQL = SQL & rs.Fields("Addrid") & ", " & txtContact(0) & ")"
    Db.Execute SQL, dbSQLPassThrough
```

(continues)

Listing 9.11 Continued

```
            'Refetch the data
            TabFetched(0) = False
            FetchTab 0

            'locate the address you just created
            dtaAddress.Recordset.FindFirst "addrid = " & rs.Fields("Addrid")

        Else
          Beep
          MsgBox "Unable to find new, unlinked address just created."
        End If

        btnAddress(0).Caption = "Add..."
        btnAddress(1).Caption = "Delete..."

    End Sub
```

AddressDiscard merely calls FetchTab to refresh the Address tab without saving data. If the user elects to delete an existing Address, the AddressDelete sub is called.

Listing 9.12 9LIST12.TXT—The AddressDelete Sub

```
    Sub AddressDelete()
    'This sub simply issues a call to delete the link in ContAddrAssoc
    'joining the Address and Contact tables.
    'On the Server side, there is a delete trigger on ContAddrAssoc
    'which will in turn delete the address record if it is no longer
    'associated with any contacts.

      msg = "If you unlink this Address from this Contact "
      msg = msg & "and no other Contacts are linked to this Address "
      msg = msg & "then the Address will be DELETED from the database."
    ➥& LF & LF & "Continue?"
      Beep
      If MsgBox(msg, vbYesNo + vbQuestion) = vbNo Then Exit Sub

      Screen.MousePointer = 11
      SQL = "delete from contaddrassoc where contid = " &
      SQL = SQL & txtContact(0) & " and addrid = " & txtAddress(0)

      Db.Execute SQL, dbSQLPassThrough + dbSeeChanges
      TabFetched(0) = False
      FetchTab 0 ' refresh the address list
      Screen.MousePointer = 0
    End Sub
```

One brief suggestion on naming conventions: All subs relating to the management of Address records start with the same word—Address. This makes them all appear next to each other in the drop-down list boxes of the Visual Basic code editor. You may wish to adopt this sort of naming technique in your own applications.

Working with Events

CSCM lets you do three things with events: create them, edit them, or delete them. The frmEvent form is used for creating and editing individual event records, while deleting events is achieved either through executing Transact-SQL statements directly or by deleting recordset records within a transaction.

Whenever an event description is double-clicked in the main form, the frmEVent form displays the selected record for editing; if the Add button is clicked, the form displays data for a new record, which is added to the recordset when the user clicks OK.

The interesting thing about frmEvent is that it contains *public* procedures, a new capability for forms in Visual Basic 4.0. The sub's EditEvent and NewEvent are declared as being public and are located in the General Section of frmEvent. When the user clicks the Add or Edit button on frmContact, the corresponding method is called in the frmEvent form, as shown below in the btnEvent_Click sub. Note the call to frmEvent.EditEvent in Case 0 and the call to frmEvent.NewEvent in Case 2. These procedures obtain information from the frmContact form to perform their functions.

Listing 9.13   9LIST13.TXT—Private Sub btnEvent_Click(Index As Integer)

```
Private Sub btnEvent_Click(Index As Integer)
    Dim msg As String, SelCount As Integer, x As Integer

    lstEvents.SetFocus
    Select Case Index
        Case 0 ' add
            frmEvent.Center ' calls the "Center" sub in frmEvent!
            frmEvent.NewEvent ' calls the "NewEvent" sub in frmEvent!
            frmEvent.Show vbModal

        Case 1 ' delete
            SelCount = 0
            For x = 0 To lstEvents.ListCount - 1
              If lstEvents.Selected(x) Then SelCount = SelCount + 1
            Next x
```

(continues)

Listing 9.13   Continued

```
                    Case 0 ' No record selected! This shouldn't happen.
                    Beep
                    MsgBox "Error: No record is selected for deletion!", _
                    ➥vbExclamation
                    Exit Sub

                Case 1  ' a single event was selected
                    msg = "The current event is " & LF & LF
                    msg = msg & QT & rsEventSet.Fields("Name") & QT & LF & LF
                    msg = msg & "Are you sure you want to delete this event?"
                    Beep
                    If MsgBox(msg, vbQuestion + vbYesNo, "Delete Event") _
                    ➥= vbNo Then Exit Sub
                    msg = "DELETE FROM EVENTS WHERE EVENTID = " & _
                    ➥rsEventSet.Fields("EventID")
                    DB.Execute msg

                Case Else ' more than one selected
                    msg = "Delete these " & SelCount & " Events?"
                    Beep
                    If MsgBox(msg, vbQuestion + vbYesNo, "Delete Events") _
                    ➥= vbNo Then Exit Sub
                    Screen.MousePointer = 11

                    DBEngine.Workspaces(0).BeginTrans ' begin a transaction
                    x = 0
                    Do While x < lstEvents.ListCount
                      If lstEvents.Selected(x) Then
                        rsEventSet.AbsolutePosition = x
                        rsEventSet.Delete
                        lstEvents.RemoveItem x
                        lstEvents.Refresh
                      Else
                        x = x + 1
                      End If
                    Loop
                    DBEngine.Workspaces(0).CommitTrans ' Commit the
                    ➥transaction
                    Screen.MousePointer = 0

                End Select
                GetEventRecordSet Val(txtContact(0))

            Case 2 ' edit
                frmEvent.Center
                frmEvent.EditEvent 'edits the currently selected event
                frmEvent.Show vbModal
        End Select
    End Sub
```

When deleting events, the sub uses one of two methods. If only a single event is selected for deletion, a simple Transact-SQL statement is executed. If more than one event is selected, however, the sub cycles through the event list on frmContact, deleting each selected record from rsContactSet. Performance for this operation could be improved by nesting this loop inside a transaction, which is started with the BeginTrans method of DBEngine.WorkSpaces(0) and closed by the CommitTrans method.

> **Note**
>
> The new JET 3.0 engine would probably nest these delete operations inside a transaction anyway, given the rapid nature of their execution. The BeginTrans and CommitTrans methods are shown here for illustrative purposes only.)

The public sub EditEvent in the event properties sheet determines the EventID to be edited by looking at the ItemData property of the currently selected lstEvent item.

Listing 9.14 9LIST14.TXT— Public Sub EditEvent()

```
    Public Sub EditEvent()
        'This edits the current event in rsEventSet.
        'get current values into textboxes
        Dim x As Integer

        txtEvent(0) = rsEventSet.Fields("EventID")
        txtEvent(1) = Format$(rsEventSet.Fields("EventDateTime"), EVENTDATEFORMAT)
        txtEvent(2) = Format$(rsEventSet.Fields("EventDateTime"), EVENTTIMEFORMAT)
        txtEvent(3) = rsEventSet.Fields("Name")
        txtEvent(4) = rsEventSet.Fields("Description")
        Me.Caption = "Edit Event"
        btnOK(0).Enabled = False
    End Sub
```

The NewEvent Sub simply fills in the form with information derived from the current date and time and displays the form.

```
    Public Sub NewEvent()
        txtEvent(0) = frmContact.txtContact(0)
        txtEvent(1) = Format$(Now, EVENTDATEFORMAT)
        txtEvent(2) = Format$(Now, EVENTTIMEFORMAT)
        txtEvent(3) = "New Event"
        txtEvent(4) = "New Event Created on " & txtEvent(1) & " at " &
        ➥txtEvent(2) & ". "
```

```
        Me.Caption = "New Event"
        If Me.Visible Then
            txtEvent(3).SetFocus
            Sel
        End If
    End Sub
```

The public nature of these procedures means that they can be called from outside the form.

There is some data validation code in frmEvent. Rather than rely on masked edit controls, a simple piece of code in the LostFocus Event serves to ensure correct data. Only the date and time fields are validated by using VB's Format$ statement.

Listing 9.15 9LIST15.TXT—The LostFocus event for txtEvent.
Private Sub txtEvent_LostFocus(Index As Integer)

```
    Dim Temp As String, d As Variant
    On Error GoTo txtEventError
    Select Case Index
        Case 1 ' date
            d = DateValue(txtEvent(1).Text)
            If d < 0 Then GoTo txtEventError ' really old dates are
            ➥disallowed!
            txtEvent(1) = Format$(d, EVENTDATEFORMAT)

        Case 2 ' time
            d = TimeValue(txtEvent(2).Text)
            txtEvent(2) = Format$(d, EVENTTIMEFORMAT)
    End Select
    On Error GoTo 0
Exit Sub

txtEventError:
    txtEvent(Index) = UCase$("INVALID " &
    ➥Mid$(lblEvent(Index).Caption, 2, 4) & "!")
    Exit Sub
End Sub
```

Working with Notes

The notes field of this form actually requires no special handling at all. It's simply another field of data which is fetched along with the "master" Contact information. It is worth noting, however, that all text boxes are set to hold only as much data as their related database columns will allow. This function is performed in the SetLengths sub:

Listing 9.16   9LIST16.TXT—The SetLengths sub

```
Sub SetLengths()
'This makes sure all textboxes can only accept values
'which aren't too large.

 Dim f As Form, x As Integer
 On Error GoTo SetLengthsErr

 Set f = frmContact

 'setup contact fields
 For x = 0 To 7
   f.txtContact(x).MaxLength = rsContactSet.Fields(f.txtContact(x).DataField).Size
 Next x

 'setup address fields
 For x = 0 To 9
   f.txtAddress(x).MaxLength = f.dtaAddress.Recordset.Fields(f.txtAddress(x)
   ➥.DataField).Size Next x

Exit Sub

SetLengthsErr:
  Exit Sub ' just get out without asking questions...

End Sub
```

Deleting Contacts

When it comes time to delete a Contact, there are two methods we could use. The easiest would be to execute SQL commands to delete records from the Contact and ContAddrAssoc tables by using the Contact ID as a parameter. The program could then remove the record from the recordset, remove the Contact from the result set list, and be ready to continue. Since we have a delete trigger on the ContAddrAssoc table, that would also take care of any orphaned Addresses left behind. However, this would do nothing to delete records from the Events table.

We could use a delete trigger on the Contact table to clean up orphaned events. The CSCM database does have such a trigger:

```
CREATE TRIGGER tr_DeleteEvents ON dbo.Contact
FOR DELETE
AS

DELETE FROM EVENTS WHERE CONTID = (SELECT CONTID FROM DELETED)
GO
```

At this point, deleting a Contact becomes such an involved process that you might want to think about using a stored procedure to perform the job. This ensures that everything gets deleted that should be deleted to maintain referential integrity. While this is strictly not required (the delete triggers delete everything which must be deleted), this gives us the opportunity to explore how to run stored procedures on the server.

The stored procedure will be called sp_DelContact and will take ContID as its only paremeter. We can examine CSCM.SQL to see how this trigger is created:

```
create procedure sp_DelContact (@ContID int) as

delete from contaddrAssoc where contid = @ContId
/* this deletes addresses as well, if warranted... */

delete from contact where contid = @contid
/* This deletes the contact. */

/* Note we don't have to delete the Contact's Events, since
   the Delete trigger on the Contact table has already
   done so.
*/
GO
```

Once the stored procedure is written and functional, we use the ExecSQL function to execute it.

Listing 9.17   9LIST17.TXT—The ExecSQL sub

```
Public Function ExecSQL(SQL As String) As Integer

  Dim QD As QueryDef
  On Error GoTo ExecSQLErr

  Set QD = Db.CreateQueryDef("")
  QD.Connect = Db.TableDefs(0).Connect
  QD.SQL = SQL
  QD.ReturnsRecords = False
  QD.Execute dbFailOnError + dbSQLPassThrough

  ExecSQL = True

Exit Function

ExecSQLErr:

  MsgBox "Error " & Err & ": " & Err.Description, vbExclamation,
  ➥"ExecSQL Error"
  ExecSQL = False
  Exit Function
End Function
```

Lastly, the `ContactDelete` sub actually deletes the Contact and updates
`frmContact`:

Listing 9.18   9LIST18.TXT—The ContactDelete sub

```
Sub ContactDelete()
  Dim x As Integer, SQL As String, ContID As Long, r As Integer

  Beep
  If MsgBox(QT & txtContact(2) & " " & txtContact(4) & QT & LF & LF
  ➥& "Are you SURE you want to delete this contact from the
  ➥database?", _
  vbQuestion + vbYesNo) = vbNo Then Exit Sub

  x = lstContacts.ListIndex ' save the place of the contact to delete...

  Stat "Deleting Contact " & ContID & ", " & QT &
  ➥lstContacts.List(x) & QT

  ' execute stored procedure to delete the contact
  Stat "sp_delcontact " & txtContact(0)
  r = ExecSQL("sp_delcontact " & txtContact(0))

  If r = True Then
    Stat "Refreshing records..."
    rsContactSet.Requery

    If rsContactSet.RecordCount = 0 Then
      lblContact(0) = ""
      lblResultSet = ""
      lstContacts.Enabled = False
      lstContacts.Clear
      Beep
      MsgBox "There are no records left in the current result
      ➥set.", vbInformation
      LookupByName
    Else ' there are records left...
      'force an intelligent select of a lstcontact entry to fetch
      ➥another record.
      lstContacts.Enabled = False
      lstContacts.RemoveItem x
      lstContacts.Enabled = True
      rsContactSet.MoveLast

      Select Case x
        Case 0: lstContacts.ListIndex = 0
        Case lstContacts.ListCount: lstContacts.ListIndex =
        ➥lstContacts.ListCount - 1
        Case Else: lstContacts.ListIndex = x
      End Select
    End If
  End If
```

(continues)

Listing 9.18   Continued

```
        Stat "Ready"

    End Sub
```

You may wish to also check the other Contact-related subs in `frmContact`; `ContactAddNew`, and `ContactDiscardNew`.

Summary

Writing a client/server application can require a complex balance of what is easy to write versus what executes quickly. More often than not, a combination of these techniques applies. Usually it's a good rule of thumb to place processing on the server whenever possible, both to take advantage of the efficient SQL Server engine and to offload work to a machine which is presumably more powerful than most. On the other hand, certain functions like data validation may best be performed on the client side, although duplicate functionality should be created for the server as well to protect against data access from other, less structured methods.

Whatever methods you use, you'll usually find that there are no pat answers; the solution or solutions you choose will depend upon the challenges you face and the needs of the program and its users. The more broad-based your knowledge set, the better qualified you'll be to select the solution which best meets your needs. Solutions can range from low-level API-based procedures through the ODBC API, the Data Control, Data Access Objects (Pro or Enterprise Edition only), Remote Data Objects (Enterprise Edition only), or any number of a host of available third-party custom controls. Most likely, you'll be using a combination of all of these things to achieve optimal solutions for your program.

Chapter 10

Visual C++

by Kate M. Gregory

Kate has a computer consulting and software development business in rural Ontario, Canada. She works in Visual C++ (specializing in Internet applications), teaches Internet and C++ programming courses, and writes. She has written two other books for Que.

There are times when even the most ardent Visual Basic programmer needs to turn to Visual C++. The classic reason is to get faster execution from the critical parts of your application, but you may also want to access an existing library of C functions or create your own custom controls.

In this chapter, you'll learn how to do the following:

- Gather C functions into a DLL

- Use a DLL from Visual Basic

- Build an OCX Custom Control

- Use an OCX in Visual Basic

Creating Your Own DLL

A DLL is, of course, a *Dynamic-Link Library*, a reusable, dynamically loaded set of functions. Using a DLL lets many applications share the same utility functions: most of Windows is gathered up into a collection of DLLs that are collectively called the Windows API. There are many different reasons for using a DLL, but they boil down to two main reasons: either to use code that someone else has written, or to call fast C or C++ code from within Visual Basic. The following are examples:

- You can use the functions in the readily available CARDS.DLL to handle the work of drawing the faces and backs of a deck of cards, rather than writing those routines yourself.

- You can take advantage of an existing investment in a C library of mathematical functions or graphics routines. Whether you bought the library or developed it in-house, you want to be able to use it in all of your applications, including your Visual Basic work.

- You can write a few critical functions in C++ for speed and call them from your Visual Basic application.

- You can use the power of threading to move some slow process, such as printing or file I/O, into the background. You can use the multitasking features of Windows 95 and NT in C or C++ functions.

If the C or C++ functions you want to use are not already provided as a DLL, you can gather them up into one quite easily. For this chapter, I've written some very simple functions and gathered them into a DLL just to show how it's done. In real life, the functions you'd gather together would be far more significant than these. The example functions will perform simple statistical analysis on an array of `double` numbers. You'll code two functions: one that determines the mean of the numbers and the other that determines the standard deviation. You could easily expand this into a real statistical package if you don't already have one.

Here's how it's done. Start up Visual C++ and choose File, New. From the list that appears, choose Project Workspace and click OK, or double-click Project Workspace. Click Dynamic-Link Library in the list at the left of the dialog, and fill in a project name at the top. Figure 10.1 shows this dialog as I completed it with the project name `stats`.

Fig. 10.1
The first step in creating a DLL is running AppWizard.

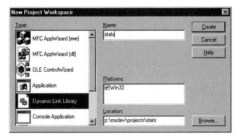

After you click Create on this first AppWizard dialog, something rather surprising happens: the application is created. Normally AppWizard asks several screens worth of questions and gives you a final Create/Cancel choice, but when it comes to DLL creation, it just does it. Not that it does much. It doesn't make any source files or generate any code for you, but it does create an empty project and set some parameters.

The first step is to get an empty file to put your code in. Click the New Source File button at the far left of the Standard toolbar to get a blank file. Choose File, Save As and name it STATS.CPP.

Next, you need to actually add code to STATS.CPP. First add `Mean()`, which takes an array of numbers and the count of entries in the array, and returns the simple average or mean. The code is simple enough: go through the array adding up a running total, then divide by the number of entries in the array. But before you can code the function, you need to declare it. Declaring a function that will go into a DLL has a few special requirements. The declaration looks like the following:

```
extern "C" __declspec( dllexport ) double WINAPI
            Mean( double* numbers, int count);
```

The following are the five important components to this declaration:

- `extern "C"`

- `__declspec( dllexport )`

- `double`

- `__stdcall`

- `Mean(double* numbers, int count)`

The declaration starts with `extern "C"` to instruct the linker to treat this as a C function even though the source file is STATS.CPP. You do this to prevent C++ *name decoration*: the adjustment of function names by the C++ compiler. Although as you'll see in a moment, you can't prevent it all, but you can reduce it.

The `__declspec` is a Microsoft-specific language extension. It defines a *storage class* for your function. Some storage classes, such as `static` and `extern`, are part of the C++ language. Microsoft has added a number of other storage types to the language, including `dllexport`. This modifier identifies functions that will be exported in a DLL, and takes care of generating the extra information that the linker needs to create the DLL.

`double` is simply the return type from the function.

`__stdcall` is a DLL-related keyword that defines the way that the calling program and the DLL share responsibility for the stack. It ensures that the DLL cleans up the stack because Visual Basic can't. Unfortunately, it brings with it some name decoration. The name you've chosen, `Mean`, becomes `_Mean@8` inside the DLL. The _ and the @ are put around the original name, and then a number is added: it's the total length (in bytes) of the parameters being passed. Mean takes a pointer-to-double and a long, each of which are four bytes long for a total of eight.

> **Note**
>
> If you've done this before, you might wonder why you don't use the _pascal keyword. It's obsolete in Visual C++ 4.0 and has been replaced with __stdcall.

Finally, declare the function name and its arguments in the usual C/C++ way. Then repeat the keywords when you define it, like this:

```
declspec( dllexport ) double __stdcall Mean( double* numbers, int count)
{
    double total = 0;
    for ( int i = 0; i < count; i++)
    {
        total += numbers[i];
    }
    return total/count;
}
```

> **Note**
>
> If you were creating a large DLL, you might choose to gather your function declarations into one include file, STATS.H, leaving only the function definitions in STATS.CPP. This include file would be useful to C++ and C programmers who wanted to use the DLL. However, there are only two functions in this DLL and you plan to use it from VB, so leave the declarations in STATS.CPP. It will be helpful to keep all the declarations together at the top of the file.

Here's the declaration and definition of StdDev(), which calculates the standard deviation of the numbers in the array:

```
extern "C" __declspec( dllexport ) double __stdcall
                StdDev( double* numbers,int count);

__declspec( dllexport ) double __stdcall
            StdDev( double* numbers, int count)
{
    double mean = Mean( numbers, count);
    double squaresum = 0;
    for ( int i = 0; i < count; i++)
    {
        squaresum += pow(numbers[i] - mean,2);
    }
    return sqrt(squaresum/(count-1));
}
```

If you don't remember the formula for standard deviation or are lucky enough to have never taken a statistics course, you may find this code hard to read. The heart of the calculation is *the sum of the squares of the differences.* numbers[i]-mean is the difference between this number and the mean or average. Each of these differences is squared, and the for loop calculates the sum of the squares of the differences. To determine the standard deviation, divide the sum by one less than the count and take the square root. You can find this formula and an explanation of it in any statistics textbook.

The functions pow() and sqrt() are part of the math library provided with the Visual C++ compiler. At the top of STATS.CPP, add this line:

```
#include <math.h>
```

There! You have two working functions. Before you build the DLL, just add one nice touch. At the beginning of each function, add the following lines:

```
if (count == 0)
{
return 0;
}
```

This simple check prevents run-time errors in your functions. In Mean(), if count is zero, the last line will divide by zero. In StdDev(), if count is zero, the last line will take the square root of a negative number because count-1 will be –1, so squaresum/(count-1) will be negative.

Build the DLL by clicking the Build icon on the Standard toolbar or choosing <u>B</u>uild, <u>B</u>uild STATS.DLL. When the build completes successfully, your DLL is ready to use. (STATS.DLL is on the CD that comes with this book.)

Putting Your DLL to Work

At the end of this chapter, you'll actually use this DLL to test the OCX control, so at the moment a very simple-minded test should suffice.

In Visual Basic, build a simple form with three text boxes on the left and two on the right. Call the left-hand boxes In1, In2, and In3. Call the right-hand boxes Avg and Dev. Add the following lines to the General declarations area:

```
Private Declare Function Mean Lib
➥"p:\msdev\projects\stats\debug\stats.dll"
➥Alias "_Mean@8" (Numbers As Double, ByVal Length As Long)
➥ As Double

Private Declare Function StdDev Lib
➥"p:\msdev\projects\stats\debug\stats.dll"
➥Alias "_StdDev@8" (Numbers As Double, ByVal Length As Long)
➥ As Double

Dim Numbers(3) As Double
```

There are six important parts to each of these `Declare` statements. For `Mean()`, they are as follows:

- `Private Declare Function` starts the declare. `Mean` is a function because it returns a value.

- `Mean` is the name of the function, as you will use it in your VB application.

- `Lib "p:\msdev\projects\stats\debug\stats.dll"` tells VB where to find the DLL. Make sure you change this to the pathname and file on your computer.

- `Alias "_Mean@8"` is the name of the function inside the DLL, as discussed earlier.

- `(Numbers As Double, ByVal Length As Long)` describes the arguments to the function. `Numbers` is passed as an address, and `Length` is passed by value.

- `As Double` describes the return type from the function.

Each of the three text boxes should do essentially the same thing when the number in it is changed. The following is the code for `In1_Change`:

```
Private Sub In1_Change()
Numbers(0) = In1.Text
Avg.Text = Mean(Numbers(0), 3)
Dev.Text = StdDev(Numbers(0), 3)
End Sub
```

Calling `Mean()` and `StdDev()` is like calling any other VB function. By passing the address of the first element of `Numbers`, you give the DLL the address of the start of the array, which is just what it expects to be given.

Copy this code to In2 and In3 and change the object references to In2 and In3 in the first two lines, and the index into `Numbers`: In2 should set `Numbers(1)` and In3 should set `Numbers(2)`. Figure 10.2 shows this application running. It reports that the average of one, two, and three is two, which is correct. You can check the standard deviation using a spreadsheet program, such as Excel, or a hand calculator. You can test with other numbers too. This application is on the CD that comes with this book: the project name is STATTEST.VBP.

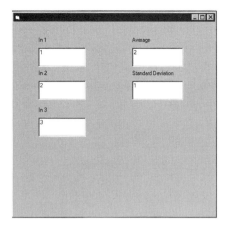

Fig. 10.2
TestStat is a simple
Visual Basic applica-
tion that tests
STATS.DLL.

An OLE Automation DLL is easier to call from VB than an ordinary DLL, such as STATS.DLL, because it exposes its methods with OLE. Strings can be passed, modified, and returned far more easily. Other arguments, including arrays, are also easier to handle as parameters. The DLL is harder to write, but easier to use. For the power of OLE as well as a visual interface, OLE Custom Controls are the way to go.

Creating an OCX

OCX is the common or slangy name for OLE Custom Controls, which are kept in files with the extension .OCX. Like VBX controls before them, OCX controls allow programmers to extend the control set provided by the compiler. The original purpose of VBX controls was to allow programmers to provide unusual interface controls to their users. Controls that looked like gas gauges or volume knobs became easy to develop. But almost immediately, VBX programmers moved beyond simple controls to modules that involved significant amounts of calculation and processing. In the same way, many OCX controls are far more than just controls; they are *components* that can be used to build powerful applications quickly and easily.

VBX controls are being left behind by Microsoft. A 32-bit implementation is not planned. If you want to write 32-bit custom controls for Visual Basic, Visual C++, Access, and other Microsoft products, then you will have to write OCX controls. Luckily, it's not hard.

Don't be scared off by the word OLE. You may have had experience using OLE with large and complex applications like Word or Excel—experience that would surely make you think OLE is slow. Alternatively, you may have tried to write your own OLE programs from scratch, something that is so difficult it could lead you to swear off OLE forever. But developing an OCX with Visual C++ 4.0 is not difficult at all: the OLE aspects are all taken care of for you. And OCX controls are very, very fast. OCX controls are as small and fast as VBX controls, but they can do far more—thanks to the portable, open standard represented by OLE.

A nice simple control that illustrates the basic OCX concept is a die: one of a pair of dice. Imagine a picture of a cubic die with the familiar pattern of dots indicating the current value between one and six. When the user clicks on it, a new number, chosen randomly, is shown. You might implement one or more dice into any game program.

The following is a blueprint for the construction of this simple OCX:

1. Build an OCX shell.

2. Add code to display the current value as a digit.

3. Arrange to handle a mouse click.

4. Add code to "roll" the die.

5. Add code to display dot patterns.

6. Allow the user to choose digit or dot display.

7. Allow the user to set colors.

Let's get started!

Building an Empty OCX

Visual C++ 4.0 makes creating OCX controls even easier than it was with Visual C++ 2.x. That's because the Control Developers Kit (CDK) has been integrated into Visual C++. Now Microsoft's AppWizard will create an empty OCX shell for you.

From within Visual C++, choose File, New. From the list that appears, choose Project Workspace and click OK, or double-click Project Workspace. Click OLE Control Wizard in the list at the left of the dialog, and fill in a project name at the top, then click Create. Figure 10.3 shows this dialog as I completed it with the project name die.

Fig. 10.3
AppWizard makes
creating an OCX
control simple.

After you click Create on this first AppWizard dialog, a second one appears asking a few simple questions. You want to create one control; you don't need to implement run-time licensing; you want comments added to the code that AppWizard writes for you; and you don't plan to include help with your control. After you have completed the dialog, click Next.

The second and final step in the AppWizard process allows you to set the features of the new control. Make sure that Activates When Visible, Available in "Insert Object" Dialog, and Has an "About Box" are selected, then click Finish. AppWizard summarizes your settings in a final dialog. Click OK, and AppWizard creates eighteen files for you and adds them to a project to make them easy to work with. These files are ready to compile, but they don't do anything at the moment. You have an empty shell and it is up to you to fill it.

This simple, visually oriented control receives input from the user (a mouse click), provides output to the user (a representation of the current number between one and six), and performs a calculation ("rolling" the die to get a new current number). You will code these three aspects of the control in turn.

Displaying the Current Value as a Digit

Before you can display the value, the control must have a value to display. That involves adding a *property* to the control. OCX controls have four types of property:

■ *Stock:* These are standard properties supplied to every control, such as font or color. The developer must activate stock properties, but there is little or no coding involved.

■ *Ambient:* These are properties of the environment that surrounds the control of the container into which it has been placed. These cannot be changed, but the control can use them to adjust its own properties.

For example, it can set the control's background color to match the container's background color.

- *Extended:* These are properties that will be handled by the container, typically involving size and placement on the screen.

- *Custom:* These are properties added by the control developer.

Add a custom property called Number using the Visual C++ ClassWizard. Choose Visual C++, View ClassWizard and click the OLE Automation tab. Make sure that the two drop-down boxes across the top of the dialog are set to the correct project and class. The project name should be die (unless you chose a different name when building the control with AppWizard), and the class name should be CDieCtrl. There are only two classes to choose from: the other describes the Property Page for this control.

Click the Add Property button and fill in the dialog. Type **Number** into the External Name Combo box, and notice how ClassWizard fills in suggested values for the variable name and notification function boxes. Select short for the type; short is equivalent to Visual Basic's Integer data type. The dialog should resemble figure 10.4. Click OK to complete the Add Property method and OK to close ClassWizard.

Fig. 10.4
ClassWizard simplifies the process of adding a custom property to your die rolling control.

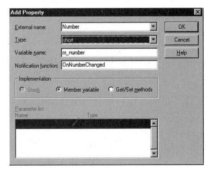

Now, before you can write code to display the value of this property, it needs to have a value. OCX properties are initialized in a method called DoPropExchange(). This method actually implements *persistence*; that is, it allows the control to be saved as part of a document and read back in when the document is opened. Whenever a new control is created, the properties cannot be read from a file, so they are set to the default values provided in this method.

AppWizard generated a skeleton `DoPropExchange()` method that looks like the following:

```
void CDieCtrl::DoPropExchange(CPropExchange* pPX)
{
    ExchangeVersion(pPX, MAKELONG(_wVerMinor, _wVerMajor));
    COleControl::DoPropExchange(pPX);

    // TODO: Call PX_ functions for each persistent custom property.

}
```

Take away the TODO comment that AppWizard left for you, and add the line:

```
        PX_Short( pPX, "Number", m_number, (short)3 );
```

`PX_Short()` is one of many property exchange functions that you can call—one for each property type that is supported. The parameters you supply are as follows:

- The pointer that was passed to `DoPropExchange()`

- The external name of the property as you typed it on the ClassWizard Add Property dialog

- The member variable name of the property as you typed it on the ClassWizard Add Property dialog

- The default value for the property (later you can replace this hardcoded three with a random value)

The code to display the number belongs in the `OnDraw()` method of the control. This function is called automatically whenever Windows needs to repaint the part of the screen that includes the control. AppWizard generated a skeleton of this method too, and it looks like this:

```
void CDieCtrl::OnDraw(CDC* pdc, const CRect& rcBounds,
                      const CRect& rcInvalid)
{
    // TODO: Replace the following code with your own drawing code.
    pdc->FillRect(rcBounds,
        CBrush::FromHandle((HBRUSH)GetStockObject(WHITE_BRUSH)));
    pdc->Ellipse(rcBounds);
}
```

This draws a white rectangle throughout the space occupied by your control, `rcBounds`, and then draws an ellipse inside that rectangle using the default foreground color. Although you can keep the white rectangle for now, rather than draw an ellipse on it, draw a character that corresponds to the value in

Number. Here's how to do that. Replace the last line in the skeletal OnDraw()
with these:

```
char val[6]; //character representation of the short value
sprintf(val, "%i",m_number);
pdc->ExtTextOut( 0, 0, ETO_OPAQUE, rcBounds, val, NULL );
```

These convert the short value in m_number (which you associated with the
Number property on the Add Property dialog) to a character variable called val.
The function ExtTextOut() draws a piece of text (the character in val) within
the rcBounds rectangle. At the moment, that number will always be three.
The next step is to allow the user to request a roll of the die.

Reacting to a Mouse Click

There are actually two things you want your control to do when the user
clicks the mouse on the control: to inform the container that the control has
been clicked, and to roll the die and display the new internal value.

Let's tackle container notification first, using the stock event Click
that is already provided for you. Bring up ClassWizard by choosing View
ClassWizard, and click the OLE Events tab. Click the Add Event button and
fill in the Add Event dialog. The external name is Click: choose it from the
drop-down box, and notice how the internal name is filled in as FireClick.
Click OK to add the event, and your work is done. Now when the user clicks
the control, the container class will be notified. So, if you are writing a backgammon game, for example, the container can respond to the click by using
the new value on the die to evaluate possible moves or do some other
backgammon-specific task.

The second part of reacting to clicks involves actually rolling the die and
redisplaying it. Not surprisingly, ClassWizard is going to help implement this.
It should still be up, but if not, bring it up. Select the Message Map tab this
time, and make sure your control class, CDieCtrl, is selected in the Class
Name Combo box. Scroll through the Messages list box until you find the
WM_LBUTTONDOWN message, which is generated by Windows whenever the left
mouse button is clicked over your control. Click Add Function to add a function that will be called automatically whenever this message is generated—
in other words, whenever the user clicks your control. This function must be
named OnLButtonDown(), and ClassWizard has made an empty one for you.
Click the Edit Code button to close ClassWizard, and look at the new
OnLButtonDown() code:

```
void CDieCtrl::OnLButtonDown(UINT nFlags, CPoint point)
{
    // TODO: Add your message handler code here and/or call default

    COleControl::OnLButtonDown(nFlags, point);
}
```

Replace the TODO comment with a call to a function you will write in the next section:

```
m_number = Roll();
```

To force a redraw, add this line next:

```
InvalidateControl();
```

Leave the call to COleControl::OnLButtonDown() at the end of the function: it takes care of the rest of the work of processing the mouse click.

Rolling the Die

To add Roll() to CDieCtrl, first add declaration lines to DIECTL.H right before the end of the class definition:

```
public:
    short Roll(void);
```

This will be a *public* function so that other objects can roll the die. At the end of DIECTL.CPP, add an empty function definition:

```
short CDieCtrl::Roll(void)
{

}
```

What should Roll() do? It should calculate a random value between one and six. The C++ function that returns a random number is rand(), which returns an integer between zero and RAND_MAX. Dividing by RAND_MAX + 1 gives a positive number that will always be less than one, and multiplying by six gives a positive number that is less than six. The integer part of the number will be between zero and five, in other words. Adding one produces the result you want: a number between one and six. The code looks like this:

```
short CDieCtrl::Roll(void)
{
    double number = rand();
    number /= RAND_MAX + 1;
    number *= 6;
    return (short)number + 1;
}
```

> **Note**
>
> If RAND_MAX+1 isn't a multiple of six, this code will roll low numbers slightly more often than high ones. A typical value for RAND_MAX is 32,767, which means that one and two will come up on average 5,462 times in 32,767 rolls, but three through six will come up on average 5,461 times. You're neglecting this inaccuracy.

The random number generator must be seeded before it is used, and it's traditional (and practical) to use the current time as a seed value. In DoPropExchange(), add the following line before the call to PX_Short():

```
srand( (unsigned)time( NULL ) );
```

Instead of hard coding the start value to three, call Roll() to determine a random value. Change the call to PX_Short() so that it reads:

```
PX_Short( pPX, "Number", m_number, Roll());
```

At this point you should have a working OCX control. It is initialized to a random value; it displays its current value as a numeral at all times; and it changes its value when clicked. If you can't resist the temptation, why not test it?

You'll add this control to the Control Palette in Visual Basic, so you'll need to have an icon to represent it. Actually, AppWizard created one for you already, but it just says "OCX." You can create your own with AppStudio. Click the ResourceView tab of the Project Workspace window, click the + next to Bitmap, and double-click IDB_DIE(English(US)). You can now edit the bitmap one pixel at a time. Figure 10.5 shows the icon I designed for the die.

Fig. 10.5
The ResourceView of Visual C++ allows you to build your own icon to will be added to the control palette in Visual Basic.

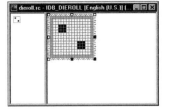

Build the project by choosing Build Build die.ocx. Then open Visual Basic with a blank form and choose Tools, Custom Controls. A dialog appears listing available insertable objects and controls. Click the box next to die OLE Control module to select it and click OK. A die appears on the control palette. Drop a die onto the form, and the control should display as a white rectangle with a number in the upper-left corner. Click it once, and the number should change. Play with it a little—make sure that you can resize it, move it, and so on. Click it over and over, and make sure that the number changes each time, that it never displays zero or seven, and so on. Figure 10.6 shows the control embedded in a new Visual Basic form.

> **Tip**
>
> If the control won't resize properly, remember to set the SizeMode property to Stretch.

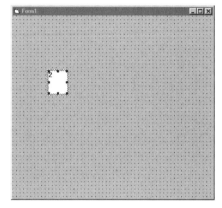

Fig. 10.6
The die rolling control is put into action in a simple Visual Basic application.

Displaying Dots

Well, your control has brains now—all the brains it will ever have—but it's a little short on beauty. You want it to look like a die. A nice three dimensional effect with part of the other sides showing is beyond the reach of an illustrative chapter like this one, but you can at least display a dot pattern.

The first step is to set up a switch statement in OnDraw(). Comment out the three drawing lines, and add the switch statement so that OnDraw() looks like the following:

```
void CDieCtrl::OnDraw(
                CDC* pdc, const CRect& rcBounds, const CRect& rcInvalid)
{
    pdc->FillRect(rcBounds,
        CBrush::FromHandle((HBRUSH)GetStockObject(WHITE_BRUSH)));
//      char val[6]; //character representation of the short value
//      sprintf(val, "%i",m_number);
//      pdc->ExtTextOut( 0, 0, ETO_OPAQUE, rcBounds, val, NULL );

    switch(m_number)
```

```
        {
        case 1:
            break;
        case 2:
            break;
        case 3:
            break;
        case 4:
            break;
        case 5:
            break;
        case 6:
            break;
        }
    }
```

Now all that remains is to add code to the case 1: block that draws one dot, to the case 2: block that draws two dots, and so on. If you happen to have a real die available to you, take a look at it closely. The width of each dot is about $1/4$ the width of the whole die face. Dots near the edge are about $1/16$ the die width from the edge. Figure 10.7 shows the layout for a roll of five. All the other rolls except six are contained within the layout for five anyway: for example, the single dot for one is in the same place as the central dot for five.

Fig. 10.7
The dot layout for a standard die, fills a grid 16 units by 16 units.

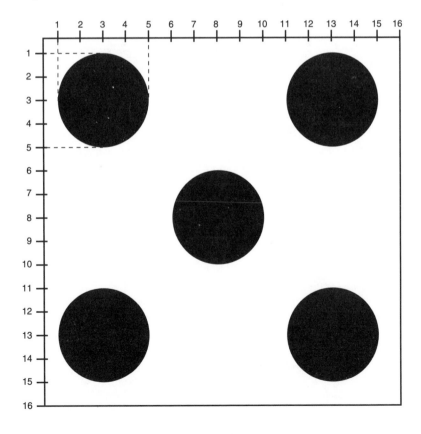

The second parameter of OnDraw(), rcBounds, is a CRect that describes the rectangle occupied by the control. It has member variables and functions that return the upper-left coordinates, width, and height of the control. The default code that AppWizard generated called CDC::Ellipse()to draw an ellipse within that rectangle. Your code will call Ellipse() too, passing a small rectangle within the larger rectangle of the control. Your code will be easier to read—and will execute slightly faster—if you work in units that are $1/16$ of the total width or height. Each dot will be four units wide or high. Add the following code before the switch statement:

```
int Xunit = rcBounds.Width()/16;
int Yunit = rcBounds.Height()/16;

int Top = rcBounds.top;
int Left = rcBounds.left;
```

Before drawing a shape by calling Ellipse(), you need to select a tool to draw with. Because these circles should be filled in, they should be drawn with a brush. This code creates a brush, and tells the *device context* pdc to use it, while saving a pointer to the old brush so that it can be restored later:

```
CBrush Black;
Black.CreateSolidBrush(RGB(0x00,0x00,0x00)); //solid black brush
CBrush* savebrush = pdc->SelectObject(&Black);
```

After the switch statement, add this line to restore the old brush:

```
pdc->SelectObject(savebrush);
```

Now you're ready to add lines to those case blocks to draw some dots. For example, rolls of two, three, four, five, or six all need a dot in the upper-left corner. This dot will be in a rectangular box that starts one unit to the right and down from the upper-left corner, and extends to five units right and down. The call to Ellipse looks like this:

```
pdc->Ellipse(Left+Xunit, Top+Yunit,
             Left+5*Xunit, Top + 5*Yunit);
```

The coordinates for the other dots are determined similarly: check figure 10.7 if you need to see where some of the numbers come from. The switch statement ends up as:

Listing 10.1   10LIST01.TXT—Switch Statement

```
switch(m_number)
{
case 1:
    pdc->Ellipse(Left+6*Xunit, Top+6*Yunit,
                 Left+10*Xunit, Top + 10*Yunit); //center
```

(continues)

Listing 10.1 Continued

```
        break;
case 2:
        pdc->Ellipse(Left+Xunit, Top+Yunit,
                    Left+5*Xunit, Top + 5*Yunit);    //upper left
        pdc->Ellipse(Left+11*Xunit, Top+11*Yunit,
                    Left+15*Xunit, Top + 15*Yunit); //lower right
        break;
case 3:
        pdc->Ellipse(Left+Xunit, Top+Yunit,
                    Left+5*Xunit, Top + 5*Yunit);    //upper left
        pdc->Ellipse(Left+6*Xunit, Top+6*Yunit,
                        Left+10*Xunit, Top + 10*Yunit); //center
        pdc->Ellipse(Left+11*Xunit, Top+11*Yunit,
                    Left+15*Xunit, Top + 15*Yunit); //lower right
        break;
case 4:
        pdc->Ellipse(Left+Xunit, Top+Yunit,
                    Left+5*Xunit, Top + 5*Yunit);    //upper left
        pdc->Ellipse(Left+11*Xunit, Top+Yunit,
                    Left+15*Xunit, Top + 5*Yunit);  //upper right
        pdc->Ellipse(Left+Xunit, Top+11*Yunit,
                    Left+5*Xunit, Top + 15*Yunit);  //lower left
        pdc->Ellipse(Left+11*Xunit, Top+11*Yunit,
                    Left+15*Xunit, Top + 15*Yunit); //lower right
        break;
case 5:
        pdc->Ellipse(Left+Xunit, Top+Yunit,
                    Left+5*Xunit, Top + 5*Yunit);    //upper left
        pdc->Ellipse(Left+11*Xunit, Top+Yunit,
                    Left+15*Xunit, Top + 5*Yunit);  //upper right
        pdc->Ellipse(Left+6*Xunit, Top+6*Yunit,
                    Left+10*Xunit, Top + 10*Yunit); //center
        pdc->Ellipse(Left+Xunit, Top+11*Yunit,
                    Left+5*Xunit, Top + 15*Yunit);  //lower left
        pdc->Ellipse(Left+11*Xunit, Top+11*Yunit,
                    Left+15*Xunit, Top + 15*Yunit); //lower right
        break;
case 6:
            pdc->Ellipse(Left+Xunit, Top+Yunit,
             Left+5*Xunit, Top + 5*Yunit);    //upper left
            pdc->Ellipse(Left+11*Xunit, Top+Yunit,
             Left+15*Xunit, Top + 5*Yunit);  //upper right
            pdc->Ellipse(Left+Xunit, Top+6*Yunit,
             Left+5*Xunit, Top + 10*Yunit);  //center left
            pdc->Ellipse(Left+11*Xunit, Top+6*Yunit,
               Left+15*Xunit, Top + 10*Yunit); //center right
            pdc->Ellipse(Left+Xunit, Top+11*Yunit,
             Left+5*Xunit, Top + 15*Yunit);  //lower left
            pdc->Ellipse(Left+11*Xunit, Top+11*Yunit,
             Left+15*Xunit, Top + 15*Yunit); //lower right
            break;
    }
```

Build the OCX again, and try it out in Visual Basic. You should see something like figure 10.8, which actually looks like a die!

Fig. 10.8
Your rolling die control now looks like a die.

If you're sharp-eyed or if you stretch the die very large, you might notice that the pattern of dots is just slightly off-center. That's because the height and width of the control are not always an exact multiple of 16. For example, if Width() returned 31, Xunit would be one and all the dots would be arranged between positions zero and 16—leaving a wide blank band at the far right of the control. Luckily the width is typically far more than 31 pixels, and so the asymmetry is less noticeable. If it bothers you, declare XUnit and YUnit as double variables rather than int, and cast to int only after multiplying (by six or 11 or 15) within the switch. Your code will be a little less readable with 76 casts, but your die will look more balanced.

Choosing Digit or Dots

It's a simple enough matter to allow the user to choose whether to display the current value as a digit or a dot pattern. Simply add a property that indicates this preference, and use the property in OnDraw(). The user can set the property using the property page.

First, add the property using ClassWizard. Bring up ClassWizard, select the OLE Automation page, and add a property with the external name Dots and the internal name m_dots. The type should be BOOL, because Dots can be either TRUE or FALSE. Click OK to complete the Add Property method, and OK to close ClassWizard.

To initialize Dots and arrange for it to be saved with a document, add the following line to DoPropExchange() after the call to PX_Short():

```
PX_Bool( pPX, "Dots", m_dots, TRUE);
```

In OnDraw(), uncomment those lines that displayed the digit. Wrap an if around them so the digit is displayed if m_dots is FALSE, and dots are displayed if it is TRUE:

```
void CDieCtrl::OnDraw(
             CDC* pdc, const CRect& rcBounds, const CRect& rcInvalid)
{
    pdc->FillRect(rcBounds, CBrush::FromHandle((HBRUSH)GetStockObject
    ➥(WHITE_BRUSH)));

    if (!m_dots)
    {
            char val[6]; //character representation of the short value
            sprintf(val, "%i",m_number);
            pdc->ExtTextOut( 0, 0, ETO_OPAQUE, rcBounds, val, NULL );
    }
    else
    {
        //dots are 4 units wide and high, one unit from the edge
        int Xunit = rcBounds.Width()/16;
        int Yunit = rcBounds.Height()/16;

        int Top = rcBounds.top;
        int Left = rcBounds.left;

        CBrush Black;
        Black.CreateSolidBrush(RGB(0x00,0x00,0x00)); //solid black brush

        CBrush* savebrush = pdc->SelectObject(&Black);

        switch(m_number)
        {
        case 1:
                …
        }
        pdc->SelectObject(savebrush);
    }
}
```

How will the user set Dots? Through a property page, which you build in AppStudio as though it was any other dialog. Click the Resource View tab in the Project Workspace window, then click the + next to Dialog. The OCX has two dialogs: one for the About box and one for the property page. Double click IDD_PROPPAGE_DIE to open it. Remove the static control with the TODO reminder, add a check box labeled Display Dot Pattern, and change its resource ID to IDC_DOTS. Figure 10.9 shows the dialog after these changes are made.

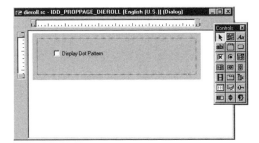

Fig. 10.9
You building the
property page for
DIE.OCX like any
other dialog.

When the user brings up the property page and clicks to set or unset the
check box, that does not directly affect the value of m_dots or the Dots property. To connect the dialog to member variables, use ClassWizard as always.
Bring it up while AppStudio is still open, and select the Member Variables
tab. Make sure that CDiePropPage is the selected class, and click the Add Member Variable button. Fill in m_dots as the name and BOOL as the type, and fill
in the Optional OLE Property Name Combo box with Dots. Click OK, and
ClassWizard generates code to connect the property page with the member
variables in CDiePropPage::DoDataExchange().

Build the OCX and test it in a new VB form. To change the properties, right-
click the control and choose Properties: your own property page appears.
Prove to yourself that the control displays dots or a digit depending on the
setting on this page.

You might want to display that number in a font that's more in proportion
with the current width and height of the control and centered within the
control. That's a relatively simple modification to OnDraw(), which I'll leave
for you to investigate.

User-Selected Colors

At the moment, your die always has black dots on a white background. Giv-
ing the user control over this is remarkably simple. First, you need to add two
stock properties: BackColor and ForeColor. Bring up ClassWizard, select the
OLE Automation page, make sure that CDieCtrl is the selected class, and click
Add Property. Choose BackColor from the top Combo box, and click OK.
Then add ForeColor in the same way.

You can use a stock property page for these colors. Look through DIECTL.CPP for a block of code like this:

```
/////////////////////////////////////////////////////////////////
//////////
// Property pages

// TODO: Add more property pages as needed.
// Remember to increase the count!
BEGIN_PROPPAGEIDS(CDieCtrl, 1)
    PROPPAGEID(CDiePropPage::guid)
END_PROPPAGEIDS(CDieCtrl)
```

Remove the TODO reminder, change the count to 2, and add another PROPPAGEID so that the block looks like this:

```
/////////////////////////////////////////////////////////////////
//////////
// Property pages

BEGIN_PROPPAGEIDS(CDieCtrl, 2)
    PROPPAGEID(CDiePropPage::guid)
    PROPPAGEID(CLSID_CColorPropPage)
END_PROPPAGEIDS(CDieCtrl)
```

Now when the user brings up the property page, there will be a color one as well as the general page you already created. Both ForeColor and BackColor will be available on this page, so all that remains to be done is to use the values that the user sets.

In OnDraw(), access the background color with GetBackColor(). It returns an OLE_COLOR, which you translate to a COLORREF with TranslateColor(). You can pass this COLORREF to CreateSolidBrush() and use that brush to paint the background. Access the foreground color with GetForeColor() and give it the same treatment. (Use SetTextColor() in the digit part of the code.) Here's how OnDraw ends up (with most of the switch statement cropped out):

```
void CDieCtrl::OnDraw(CDC* pdc, const CRect& rcBounds,
                      const CRect& rcInvalid)
{
    COLORREF back = TranslateColor(GetBackColor());
    CBrush backbrush;
    backbrush.CreateSolidBrush(back);
    pdc->FillRect(rcBounds, &backbrush);

    if (!m_dots)
    {
        char val[6]; //character representation of the short value
        sprintf(val, "%i",m_number);
        pdc->SetTextColor(TranslateColor(GetForeColor()));
        pdc->ExtTextOut( 0, 0, ETO_OPAQUE, rcBounds, val, NULL );
    }
}
```

```
        else
        {

            //dots are 4 units wide and high, one unit from the edge
            int Xunit = rcBounds.Width()/16;
            int Yunit = rcBounds.Height()/16;

            int Top = rcBounds.top;
            int Left = rcBounds.left;

            COLORREF fore = TranslateColor(GetForeColor());
            CBrush forebrush;
            forebrush.CreateSolidBrush(fore);

            CBrush* savebrush = pdc->SelectObject(&forebrush);

            switch(m_number)
                    …
        }
    }
```

Build it and try it out again—this is turning into a nice little control.

Putting Your OCX to Work

Perhaps you're curious about whether the die you've created is a "true" die; that is, whether it has an equal chance of rolling each of the six numbers. (It should, in theory, but it never hurts to test.) One simple test is to roll it a number of times and average the rolls. For example, if you rolled a true die 6,000 times, you should get 1,000 of each number. These would average 3 ½, because 1+2+3+4+5+6 is 21, and 21 ÷ 6 is 3 ½. If the average over a large number of rolls was three, you would know the die rolled low numbers more often than high ones. Why not combine your die-rolling OCX with your array-averaging DLL to create a test application?

Open a new Visual Basic application, and drop a die called Die and a text box called Avg onto the form. Label the text box "Average Roll." Add these lines to the General declarations area:

```
Private Declare Function Mean
➥Lib "p:\msdev\projects\stats\debug\stats.dll"
➥Alias "_Mean@8" (Numbers As Double, ByVal Length As Long)
➥As Double
Dim Rolls() As Double
Dim Size As Integer
```

Here's the code called when the die is clicked:

```
Private Sub Die_Click()
Size = Size + 1
ReDim Preserve Rolls(Size)
Rolls(Size-1) = Die.Number
Avg.Text = Mean(Rolls(0), Size)
End Sub
```

This enlarges the `Rolls` array (note the `Preserve` keyword) and adds the current die roll at the end of the array. It then calls `Mean()` and stores the value in `Avg.Text`. Figure 13.10 shows this application after many rolls of the die. This application is on the CD that comes with this book: the project name is ROLLAVG.VPJ.

Fig. 13.10
ROLLAVG is a simple Visual Basic application to test the die OCX. The average of a large number of rolls of a true die should be 3.5.

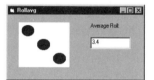

Summary

Both the examples in this chapter have been simple illustrations of the power of Visual C++ and how it can be accessed from Visual Basic. If either (or both) of them inspire you to create your own DLLs or OCX controls, you might want to start by enhancing these first. The statistics DLL could have a great number of functions added to it. You'll find inspiration (and the formulas) in any statistics book, but here's a start:

- *Median*—Half the numbers are above, and half below it.

- *Mode*—The number (or range of numbers) that is most common.

- *Percentiles*—The *n*th percentile is the value that n% of the numbers are below.

- *Geometric Mean*—A weighted mean calculated using logarithms.

- *Harmonic Mean*—The reciprocal of the average of the reciprocals. It's useful for quantities like speed.

- *Range*—The difference between the highest and lowest number.

- *Variance*—The square of the standard deviation.

- *Coefficient of Variation*—The standard deviation divided by the mean.

The die rolling control may seem complete, but it too could be made better. For example, in many dice games, you can only roll the die when it is your turn. At the moment, this control rolls whenever it is clicked, no matter what. Buy adding a custom property called `RollAllowed`, you can allow the container to control the rolling. When `RollAllowed` is FALSE, `CDieCtrl::OnLButtonDown` should just return without rolling and redrawing. Perhaps `OnDraw` should draw a slightly different die (gray dots?) when `RollAllowed` is FALSE. You decide, it's your control.

And why restrict yourself to six-sided dice? There are dice (see fig. 10.11) that have 4, 8, 12, 20, and even 30 sides—wouldn't they make an interesting addition to a dice game? You'll need to get one of these odd dice so that you can see what it looks like and change the drawing code, then change the hard-coded six in `Roll()` to a custom property: an integer with the external name `Sides` and a member variable `m_sides`. Don't forget to change the property page to allow the user to set `Sides`, and add a line to `CDieCtrl::DoPropExchange()` to make `Sides` persistent and initialize it to six.

> **Tip**
>
> There is such a thing as a two sided die as well: it's commonly called a coin.

Now, if you're writing a backgammon game, you need two dice. One approach would be to embed two individual die controls. But how would you synchronize them so that they both rolled at once with a single click? Why not expand the control to be an *array* of dice? The number of dice would be another custom property, and the control would roll them all at once. The `RollAllowed` flag would apply to all of them, as would `Sides`, so that you could have two six-sided dice or three twelve-sided dice, but not two four-sided dice and a twenty-sider. `Number` would become an array.

Fig. 10.11
Dice are available
with many
different numbers
of sides.

As you can see, it's quick to get started writing DLLs and OCXs. And once you know how much power they can add to your Visual Basic applications, you'll want to make them a regular part of your programming toolkit. They shouldn't be intimidating, but instead exciting. Why not start tapping their power with your very next project?

Chapter 11

VBX versus OCX

by Michiel de Bruijn

Michiel lives in Rotterdam, The Netherlands, and is co-owner of VBD Automatiseringsdiensten, where he is the designer and lead programmer of the Network Communications System, a Windows-based messaging system written almost entirely in Visual Basic. In his spare time, he is a section leader in the VBPJ Forum on CompuServe (GO VBPJFO) and tries to help out people in the Microsoft Basic forum (GO MSBASIC). For the latter efforts, he received a Microsoft Most Valuable Professional (MVP) Award. Contact Michiel on CompuServe at 100021,1061 or on the Internet at mdb@vbd.nl.

The latest release of Microsoft Visual Basic introduces an entirely new implementation of the custom controls that played such a large part in making the earlier releases so successful. You might wonder why the decision was made to move away from VBX controls and what the real advantages are of the new OCX architecture.

In this chapter, we'll cover the following:

- ■ The decision to move away from controls

- ■ The real advantages of the new OCX architecture

- ■ The cool new OCX features in VB4

Unlike many explanations of OCX controls, there's not much OLE or C++ terminology in this chapter. This means that, although my explanations may not always be 100 percent "technically correct," you should be able to satisfy your curiosity about the new controls anyway, without having to refer to other sources first.

Why a New Custom Control Architecture?

Though you may never have experienced this, the underlying architecture of the VBX controls that you know and love has a large number of limitations. To understand the reasons for these limitations, it helps to know something about how these controls evolved.

Windows 3.0 introduced the so-called "custom controls" that allowed users of the Windows Software Development Kit (SDK) to create and use their own controls in addition to the ones that were already supported by the operating system (such as the text box, combo box, and check box).

An application that wanted to use a custom control (the "host") communicated with it by using window messages, which it sent by using the SendMessage API call and received through a callback procedure or by continuously issuing GetMessage calls. The application programmer needed to know the names and purposes of all messages used beforehand: there was no way to "ask" the control which functionality it supported and there was no high-level interface that implemented properties and events (in fact, those terms weren't being used yet when talking about custom controls). Property values were set or retrieved by sending window messages to the control (for example, WM_SETTEXT to alter the contents of a text box); events were implemented as WM_COMMAND messages sent by the control to its host. The values for these messages were hard-coded into the application through the use of C header files and if the programmer made a mistake in the usage or the parameters passed with these messages, the application would simply not work or even crash.

The VBX control specification addressed most of these problems: apart from defining special data structures (called the Control Model) to describe the properties and events supported by the control, it added a clean interface to change control data through the use of two special window messages called VBM_GETPROPERTY and VBM_SETPROPERTY. Other messages, such as VBM_LOADPROPERTY and VBM_SAVEPROPERTY enabled the control to keep its property values, something that was also not supported by the Windows custom controls. The process of sending notifications from the control to its host was streamlined through the VBFireEvent call, defined in the VB API provided in a library file that was part of every VBX control. Figure 11.1 shows the relationship between these different components.

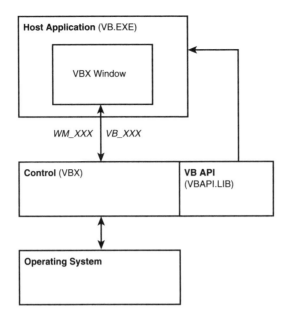

Fig. 11.1
The relationship
between a VBX
and its host. Note
the dependency of
the VBX on the
host application
(in this case, Visual
Basic).

Nothing but Problems

All these neat messages and calls are one part of the problems faced by the
VBX architecture. If you take a look at the C header file that defines the VB
API (aptly called `vbapi.h`), you'll find the definitions for the data structures
used to describe properties and events. Several member variables are of type
BYTE, which, for example, limits the property list to 256 entries. This amount
may be sufficient for the "better text box" that custom controls were originally designed for, but for a more-complicated component (like a full-
featured chart control), this could be a severe restriction. Also, all pointers
are 16-bit "based pointers," which means they only include the offset portion
of the more common `segment:offset` address. This was never a problem in
16-bit environments and helped keep data structure sizes down. When using
32-bit code, though, this kind of pointer is unusable. Changing the VBX
specification to work in such environments would amount to redesigning
it from the ground up.

The most severe problem with VBXs, though, is that they rely on the host
environment for some important functions, such as reading and writing control properties from and to a file. The controls were originally designed for
use with Visual Basic only, so this made perfect sense at that time. However,

when VBXs became so popular and widespread that other applications started adding support for them too, such implementations proved to be very hard. So hard, in fact, that even other Microsoft programming tools (such as Visual C/C++) today only support the very first revision of the VBX specs, and none of the extensions that were added in later versions. Other vendors (Borland, PowerSoft) experienced similar problems.

Starting from the Ground Up

When the VB team at Microsoft started thinking about a new custom control architecture, it was well aware of these problems, as well as the fact that VBXs had created a whole new market with a significant volume: component software. Because existing 16-bit VBX controls would have to undergo huge changes anyway in order to work with the (then upcoming) 32-bit operating systems, the decision was made to forget about backward compatibility, and design a completely new component architecture. Apart from solving most existing problems with VBXs, this would enable Microsoft to make developing components significantly easier, especially for components that don't really fit in the old user-interface-related custom control model. Microsoft had already done extensive work on a framework called OLE (then still expanded as Object Linking and Embedding), which was used to build "smart documents," composed of several objects. The decision was made that the new component architecture for VB (and many other Microsoft applications) was to be based on the OLE specifications. The new components were called OCXs, for OLE Custom Controls (the X was retained to point out the similarity to the well-known VBXs). Figure 11.2 shows the new component architecture: note that the controls no longer rely on a particular application (such as Visual Basic), but interface directly to the OLE libraries, which can be considered part of the operating system, especially in a 32-bit Windows environment.

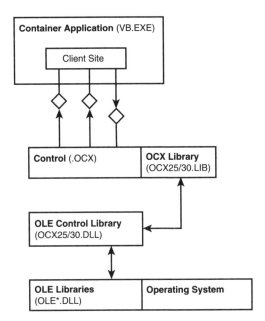

Fig. 11.2
How an OCX control works with its environment. The component is only dependent on the OCX runtime and the operating system, not on the container (host application).

Introduction to the OCX Architecture

Like VBXs, OCXs are regular Windows DLLs with a special extension that follow a certain convention. Where VBXs conform to the VB Control API, OCXs are a special form of OLE (version 2) servers. As you probably know, OLE is Microsoft's implementation of its architecture called the Component Object Model that defines how software components function under Windows. OLE servers can be used by ("expose their functionality to") other applications, called OLE clients. OLE servers can be full servers (most typically implemented as complete applications, such as Microsoft Excel), mini-servers (apps that can't run stand-alone, such as the WordArt applet that comes with many Microsoft products) or in-process servers (which are only usable by the process that loads them). OCXs fall into the latter category, which is a good thing: whereas regular OLE servers communicate with their clients by using the Lightweight Remote Procedure Call (LRPC) mechanism, in-process servers use direct function calls, which is much more efficient.

OCX controls can be used by any OLE 2 container application: it is perfectly legal to embed the Tab control (TABCTL16.OCX) that comes with VB, for example, in a Microsoft Word for Windows document. Though the control will display just fine, Word of course doesn't know how to handle control properties or events. To do anything useful with the control, you will need to embed it in a container application that implements the new OCX-specific interfaces (through the OLE Automation mechanism), such as VB 4. OCX controls are different from regular OLE objects in one more aspect: they are implemented "inside-out." A regular OLE object, like a Word document, will normally remain inactive until the user activates it, for example, by double-clicking it. An OCX object will become active as soon as it is visible (which in VB means when the form the control is on is loaded) and will remain in that state until it is unloaded. The only state transitions most OCX controls will see are from active to "UI-active" (which is the OLE term for getting the focus) and vice-versa.

The fact that you can embed an OCX control in a Word document already shows an important advantage of using the OLE architecture. The OLE and OLE control libraries (which should be seen as an important part of the Windows operating system) provide a number of important services to the control:

General OLE Support

The General OLE services enable the OCX control to "be a good OLE citizen," i.e., support Linking, Embedding, and In-Place activation, and thus act as a component that can be inserted in a compound document. Having this support available (which also includes a number of low-level services, such as memory management and coordinate transformation) is an enormous advantage to the control developer: it means there's much less standard code left to write and that the focus can be on control functionality right from the beginning.

Connectable Object and Event Support

Through the Object Connection and Event mechanisms, the OCX control can perform two functions essential for custom controls: establishing links with other components (and containers) and notifying a container application (fire events). For each interface (for example, a certain function) that a control wants to be usable by other components, it creates a "connection point." A component that wants to use such an interface can subsequently create a "sink" and link that to the connection point. The OCX also supports a special interface that enumerates all available connection points, allowing other objects to query an OCX about its interfaces. Events are implemented through outgoing connection points, to which a container interested in responding to events can connect through a sink.

Property Change Notifications and Property Pages

Getting and setting properties is done through OLE Automation, which is a standard part of OLE that implements all actions needed by OCX controls, except for one: change notification. It can be important for a control to notify its container application that it changed its own properties. A good example is the Database List (DBLIST) control, which displays data from an external source and needs to be updated if the underlying data changes. The OCX specifications define a special interface for this (implemented by using connection points, just like normal event notifications).

The OCX libraries also provide minimal support for a user interface to set properties at design time. Whereas VBXs relied solely on the host environment to provide this interface, every OCX should let the user modify settings through a "property page" interface. This has no real advantages if you're used to the Visual Basic design environment, but should make it easier to implement the controls in other applications. Also, some controls, such as the Windows 95 user interface controls included with VB, offer an extended interface through these pages that would have been impossible to implement using the standard Visual Basic property window.

The OCX libraries also offer help for implementing a number of standard properties and events, much like the older VBX API did. The OCX support is more extensive, though, and divides the control properties and events into four categories:

Stock—Stock properties, events and methods are implemented by the OCX control runtime (OC25.DLL or OC30.DLL, depending on whether you're using 16-bit or 32-bit controls) and provide basic functionality like the `BackColor`, `Caption`, and `hWnd` properties and the `Click` and `DblClick` events. Among the stock methods provided is a blank about box and support for empty property pages: the actual content for these elements is provided by the control.

Ambient—Ambient properties are read-only and provide information about the container a control is embedded in, such as its color and size. This information can be used by the control to fit better into its environment. All properties are implemented by the container: for obvious reasons there are no such things as ambient events or methods.

Custom—Custom properties, events, and methods are the actual reasons for writing a control: they implement the functionality that's unique to an OCX and are implemented inside the control itself.

Extended—Properties, events, and methods of the type "extended" appear to the user to be regular control properties, but are actually provided by the container application. For example, a development environment that allows the user to lock the size and position of controls in a document might add a "Locked" extended property to each control.

The concept of a control supporting "methods" is also new for the OCX architecture: it allows custom methods (functions) with or without parameters. The latter functions are similar in concept to VB 4.0's new Property Get/Let/Set features.

To describe which properties, events, and methods an OCX supports, it can include a special binary resource called a "type library." This type library is generated from a definition written in the Object Definition Language (ODL) and tagged onto the control by a utility called MKTYPLIB and the linker used to generate the OCX library module. The type library can be used by a container application to validate usage of the control interfaces and also to present a complete overview of control capabilities to the user. The OCX programmer can also include constant values used by the control in a type library.

Type libraries aren't necessarily linked into an OCX control: they can also be distributed as separate files, typically with the extension TLB. You could, for example, create a type library for the Win32 API, which could then be used by users of a development environment that provides "object browser" functionality as described before. Visual Basic 4 is such a development environment: it also allows you to directly use methods (functions) and constants contained in a type library, eliminating the need for `Declare` and `Const` statements. So, because the standard VB type library is always present, you can use code like

```
If MsgBox("Run the log file viewer now?", vbYesNo) = vbYes Then
    Shell "logview.exe", vbNormalFocus
End If
```

without having to include a bulky CONSTANT.TXT file in your project or waste your time performing search/copy/paste operations on that file.

Visual Basic also uses the type library to perform "early binding"; even before you actually use a control, the environment is aware of all properties and methods and parameters supported by a control. This is significantly faster than having to find out about all this at runtime, and also allows for better error checking (for example, using a nonexistent property will already be flagged at compilation time). When you first use VB4, it may seem that error checking is actually worse than in previous versions, as many errors only pop up after you've started running your program. In most cases, this will be because the "Compile On Demand" feature is turned on, and VB is not compiling (or error-checking) your code until it really needs to execute it. Turning off Compile On Demand (Tools/Option menu, Advanced tab) or choosing Run/Start With Full Compile will make VB behave the way you're used to.

Storage Support

OLE defines a standard file format that OCX controls use to store their property values and (if desired) other information about the control. In the VBX architecture, the host application (Visual Basic, most of the time) was responsible for retrieving or setting all properties for each control on a form each time it was loaded or saved; when dealing with an OCX, the container can simply use the "stream from/to persistent storage" interfaces available for every OLE object to do this work. Both the regular (binary) OLE file format as well as a text format are supported by this interface; the control can decide which one to use. For most controls, the binary format will be overkill, as it adds too much overhead. This is probably the reason why Visual Basic 4 finally ditches the not-too-stable (non-OLE) binary format previously used to save form and module files and always uses the text format.

Auto-Registration Support

As we'll see later, every OCX control needs to be registered with the system's Registry in order to be available to other components. Previously, OLE components were typically registered by distributing a REG file along with them, and using that file as an input file for the Registry editor. (The REG file contains some essential information about the control, which allows the operating system and other components to find and activate it— for example, the "CLSID" value that uniquely identifies a control. The long hex numbers you see in the Registry Editor are CLSIDs.) This process is clearly a bit cumbersome, and has another disadvantage, too. For example, if the REG file associated with an OCX gets lost (or is just not copied when moving the OCX to another system), the control becomes useless.

To address these issues, the OCX specifications introduce the concept of "self-registering servers." Any OLE server (whether it's an OCX, a DLL, or an EXE) that includes a certain string in its version information table (inside the executable file header) and implements two special functions

(DllRegisterServer and DllUnregisterServer) can be automatically registered by the container application as soon as it's loaded for the first time. The DllRegisterServer function adds the information (that used to be in the REG file) to the Registry: DllUnregisterServer removes it again. Since VB4 is based on OLE internally, its runtime files need to be registered too using this mechanism. This may have some implications for the program or toolkit you currently use to write your setup programs: if it doesn't support (auto)registering DLLs, you will not be able to install your program on systems that don't contain the full VB4/OLE runtime yet.

Other Extensions

This category contains a number of functions specifically designed for programming environments, such as toolbar images and licensing and versioning information. The toolbar images are traditionally stored as resource icons in the control file. This is still true for OCX controls, but instead of relying on fixed resource names, Registry entries are used to identify the right resources.

Ever since custom controls (in their VBX form) became popular, it has been a big problem to make sure that a target system had the right version of a control to run a certain application. The OCX specifications contain some guidelines to help solve these problems, but they certainly won't make them go away. The biggest help for versionitis-plagued programmers will be the Win32 environment—as all processes are separated here (instead of running in one and the same process space, as under Windows 3.x), clashes between custom controls can be easily resolved. If two applications use two different, incompatible, versions of the module SPIN, for example, the clashing files can simply be loaded from an application-private directory (for example, the \APP\SYSTEM directory), instead of from a shared location. Windows 3.x would refuse to load a second copy of SPIN (after all, it's already in memory), but Win32 will do this just fine. The downside to this method, though, is that a Win32 system will require more memory, especially when running multiple applications.

The OCX libraries (and the Microsoft MFC class libraries included with their C++ compiler) include extensive support for setting up a licensing scheme, or, in other words, determining if a component may be used on a certain system, and if so, in which mode (runtime only or also in design mode). Most VBX controls already implement license-checking schemes, in which the presence of a LIC file with certain (encrypted) information indicates a valid design-time license. OCX controls use a similar method, but store license information in the Registry, which, apart from helping reduce system-directory clutter, is also supposed to make it harder for the casual OCX control pirate to copy the information.

OCX controls also specifically allow for localization (adapting to different country-specific settings) of property, event, and method names. For example, a control running on a system with the country set to Canada might want to implement its Color property as Colour. With a VBX, you'd have to compile a different version of the control, whereas an OCX can contain multiple sets of localized terms. Whether controls (and programming languages in general) should be localized is a continuing debate. Whereas most "real programmers" don't seem to want it, end-users of a programmable application that supports custom controls might have an entirely different opinion on this subject.

OCX Implementation in Visual Basic 4

Now that you should have a good idea of how the OCX architecture works, let's take a look at how VB 4 implements these controls. There have been a number of changes in the VB design environment, some to make it easier for you to work with, some to expose the new functionality the OCX controls have to offer. A change in the first category is that you no longer add controls to your project by file, but that you can select them from a descriptive list, as shown in figure 11.3. After choosing Tools/Custom controls from the VB menu (or pressing Ctrl-T), you get a list of all controls and insertable objects (OLE objects exposed by applications) registered on your system. If you're not interested in the latter category, you can exclude them by setting the check boxes in the "Show" frame. If you want to insert a control that has not yet been registered, you can use the "Browse" command button to specify the name of the file that contains the control—if it contains an auto-registration function, VB will register it for you on the spot.

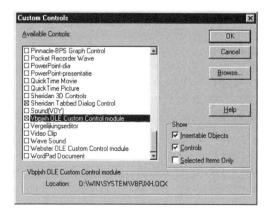

Fig. 11.3
The Custom Controls dialog, used to add or remove components to and from your VB project.

Where does VB get the information required to build this list? As already mentioned while discussing the OCX architecture, Windows maintains a list of controls in the Registry. If you fire up REGEDIT (or REGEDT32, if you're running Windows NT) and take a look at the HKEY_CLASSES_ROOT section, you'll find that all classes are listed here. Note that it also contains other information—only the keys that have a CLSID subkey qualify as insertable objects. The default value for a key describing an object is its "friendly" name, as displayed in VB's Custom Control dialog. The CLSID is a unique identifier, which refers to more information about a control, as stored in the HKEY_LOCAL_MACHINE\SOFTWARE\Classes\CLSID section of the registry. As you can see in figure 11.4, this entry provides information about the location of the control, its toolbox bitmaps, Type Library, and versioning information.

Fig. 11.4
The Registry entries for the THREED custom controls (16- and 32-bit versions) as shipped with VB.

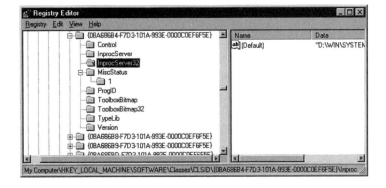

The first time you add an OCX control to a project, Visual Basic will generate an OCA file with the same base name as the control. This file contains various information extracted from the control (the most important part being its type library), allowing VB to load it faster in the future. Until you actually execute a part of your program that uses the OCX, VB only needs to load the OCA file in order to validate property use, etc. This little trick speeds up project loading significantly. Note that this OCA file is used only by the VB development environment—you don't gain anything by distributing it with your finished application.

New Custom Control Features

When you've added an OCX control to your form, it appears in the toolbox and you can use it in the same way you used your VBX controls. If you take a look at the property list, you'll notice a new property for most controls— "Custom." If you select it and click on the associated "..." button, you'll be able to view and set property values through the standard UI that the OCX libraries define for this purpose—the property pages. Figure 11.5 shows the interface used by the Sheridan 3D-control (THREED16/32.OCX) included with VB. Though some controls have a rather poor implementation of these pages (for example, not all available properties are present), other controls (such as Microsoft's COMCTL32, which we'll take a look at later) allow you to do very nifty things here.

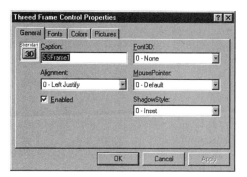

Fig. 11.5
The property pages for the Frame user interface element contained in THREED 16/32.OCX.

Except for those controls that offer an extended user interface through this mechanism, property pages won't be too exciting for most VB programmers. Another addition to the design environment, the Object Browser, is much more interesting. This browser (accessible through the View/Object Browser menu or by pressing F2) replaces the "View Procedures" dialog from VB3 and allows you to view all information contained in the type library for a control, in addition to similar information about your VB modules, forms, and classes. If you activate the browser, it will by default show the latter information. To access other categories, pull down the "Libraries/Projects" combo box and select the desired entry—for example, the `Threed - Sheridan 3D Controls` shown in figure 11.6.

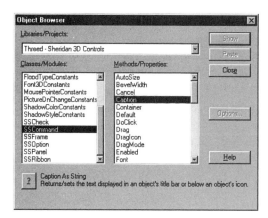

Fig. 11.6
Browsing the Type Library information supplied by THREED 16/32.OCX.

The captions used by the Object Browser to label its list boxes are extremely confusing. As you will notice, the Classes/Modules list contains much more than that (forms, groups of constants and controls, among others) and the contents of the Methods/Properties box will also vary depending on what you're viewing. For constant groups, for example, it will contain the actual constant values. One note on constants—due to the magic of the type libraries, you can use these constants without assigning them first. Just click the "paste" button to insert the name in your code and use it happily thereafter.

If you're not completely sure about the meaning or usage of a certain method, property, or constant, just select it from the browser and click the "?" button. Provided the supplier of the type library included a reference to a help file, you'll be automatically transferred to WinHelp with the right file and topic loaded.

Visual Basic lists all type libraries (called "object libraries" by the printed documentation and electronic help files) for the controls and parts of VB you're using. You can include additional type libraries by using the Tools/References menu and selecting "Browse" to specify the type library file name. Using the references dialog, you can also remove unused type libraries (which can significantly reduce the runtime requirements of your program) and set the order in which they're referenced. The latter may seem unimportant, but it isn't. If a symbol (let's say, a constant named X) is defined in both type libraries Y and Z, your application will use the value from the library that's referenced first. If Y and Z both define the same value for X, this is not a problem, but if the libraries happen to define different values (which is perfectly possible and legal), the outcome of your program can depend on the reference order.

Which Control Fits Where?

Unlike previous versions of Visual Basic, which knew only about one type of custom control (the 16-bit VBX), VB 4 supports multiple types of controls. It works with 16-bit VBX and OCX controls and with 32-bit OCXs, depending on which version of VB you use (16-bit or 32-bit, regardless of the operating system it runs on). Of these new controls, the 32-bit OCXs, only usable from within the 32-bit version of VB (VB32.EXE), are probably the most important, as these enable you to fully exploit the features of the 32-bit Windows versions (Windows 95 and Windows NT). The 16-bit version of VB 4 (VB.EXE) works with both the older VBX modules as well as with the 16-bit OCX controls. Neither of these control types is usable in VB32.

This means that in order to create 32-bit programs, you should upgrade all your VBX controls to their 32-bit OCX equivalents. For controls that have been designed to maintain compatibility with the VBX version (such as all the Microsoft controls shipping with VB 4), this should be a relatively painless process—just edit your project's MAK file (with any ASCII text editor) and replace the line that loads the VBX with the path to the OCX. For controls that use a different class name in the 32-bit version, you'll also have to edit all your forms and change the "begin" lines that contain the old control name to reference the new one. For controls that changed part of their interface (either because it was needed due to differences between the Win16 and Win32 APIs or because new functionality was desired), major rewrites can be necessary.

For the VBXs that used to come with VB itself, Microsoft offers an option to automatically do the upgrading for you. The controls eligible for this process are listed in VB.INI, in the [VBX Conversions16] and [VBX Conversions32] sections. An entry in these sections looks like this:

```
VBXfile=CLSID#versioninfo#0;OXCfile
```

VBXfile is the name of the VBX file to be upgraded (for example, `THREEED.VBX`); the string to the right of the equal sign uniquely identifies the control the VBX should be replaced with (CLSID, file version and full path to the custom control file). Every time VB loads a project that contains one or more VBX controls identified in the appropriate conversion section of VB.INI, it will display a dialog box offering to replace them. Conversion from VBX to OCX files is permanent—there is no way to reverse the process, except by manually editing the project files.

The Standard Controls in Visual Basic 4

The Professional and Enterprise Editions of Visual Basic 4 ship with OCX equivalents of all VBX controls that were part of VB 3 Professional, with the exception of OLE2.VBX. The functionality of this control is now integrated into the VB environment, and the OLE control can be used without explicitly adding it to your project. There are no spectacular changes in the controls. In fact, the ANIBUTTON, GAUGE, GRAPH, GRID, MCI, MSMASKED PICCLIP, and SPIN controls have not changed at all, except that they're now implemented as an OCX instead of a VBX. A few minor changes that affect all controls shipped with VB 4. Four nice ones are as follows:

- The `FontSize` and `FontBold`/`FontItalic`/`FontUnderline`/`FontStrikethru` properties are no longer listed separately in the design-time property list. Instead, they're accessible through a "Font" common dialog box that appears after selecting the "..." button associated with the Font property. The runtime interface also supports this new way of setting font properties through the Font object—you can now use a syntax like SSCheck1.Font.Bold = True, though the old SSCheck.FontBold = True is also still supported for obvious reasons of backward compatibility. This new feature may cause you to go and clean your system, though: if you've got lots of fonts installed, the new dialog can take ages to load.

■ The default control names now match the control class names. In previous VB versions, a new instance of a SScheck (3D check box) control was by default called Check3D1. The default name generated by VB 4 is SScheck1.

■ You can now set multi-line values for controls like text boxes and list boxes by selecting the control value in the property window and using Control+Enter to separate the line values.

■ One of the advantages of VB4's heavy reliance on OLE is that you can now also access the standard OLE types, such as StdFont, the default font used by the system. If you add the "Standard OLE Types" type library (from either OC25.DLL or OC30.DLL, depending on your environment) to your project and put two labels on a form, the following code will allow you to change the font properties of both labels with just one statement:

```
'//Initial font setup, will change label font
'//to the default system font
Dim fntLabel As New StdFont
'//Note that you could also do this here:
'//  fntLabel.Name = "Times New Roman"
Set Label1.Font = fntLabel
Set Label2.Font = fntLabel

'//Now, change all labels to the desired user font
'//by just changing the font properties of the
'//first label
Label1.FontName = "Arial"
Label1.FontSize = 10
Label1.FontBold = False
```

Let's take a look at the (minor) changes to the other controls.

CMDIALOG

The CommonDialog control will, when you use the 32-bit version on Windows 95 or Windows NT 3.51 or higher, display the new common dialogs used by those operating systems. Your code should be prepared to handle the long file names these functions might return. Also keep in mind that it's legal for such file names to contain spaces and other characters that used to be illegal in the DOS 8.3 file system. If you're looking at the common dialog-related sections of your application anyway, you might want to upgrade all code that uses the 'Action' property to use the new ShowColor, ShowFont, ShowHelp, ShowOpen, ShowPrinter and ShowSave methods, which helps improve readability. One minor annoyance that remains with this control is that the DialogTitle property is ignored for all dialogs except the file open and file save boxes. So, the following code will still just give you a dialog box with a boring "Color" caption (or the localized equivalent):

```
CommonDialog1.DialogTitle = "Pick your favorite color"
CommonDialog1.ShowColor
```

CRYSTAL

There are no obvious changes to the Crystal Reports control itself, but the report designer that comes with it has been much improved since the previous release of VB. Version 3 of the Crystal Reports for Visual Basic has a number of user interface improvements, as well as an expanded set of field formulas. If you're really serious about reports, though, it's a good idea to upgrade to the current commercial release of Crystal Reports, Version 4, instead of waiting for VB 5 to get your hands on it.

KEYSTAT

The good news about the MhState control is that it no longer causes a General Protection Fault when you use it in two or more VB apps that happen to be running at the same time. The bad news is that it's still a good candidate for the title "most useless control on earth," as the entire functionality of the control can be easily implemented in native Visual Basic code, using just two Windows API calls. The following code shows you how to toggle the state of the Caps Lock key—implementing a class to get and set the value of any other key is left as an exercise to the reader.

```
'//This should be part of the (declarations) section of your form or module.
'//Check compiler constant to determine environment:
#If Win32 = True Then
    Private Declare Sub GetKeyboardState Lib "User32" (lpKeyState As Any)
    Private Declare Sub SetKeyboardState Lib "User32" (lpKeyState As Any)
#Else
    Private Declare Sub GetKeyboardState Lib "User" (lpKeyState As Any)
    Private Declare Sub SetKeyboardState Lib "User" (lpKeyState As Any)
#End If
```

```
'//This is the main code for toggling the Caps Lock key
Const VK_CAPITAL = &H14
Const VK_NUMLOCK = &H90
Const VK_SCROLL = &H91

ReDim KeyBuf(256) As Byte

'//Get keyboard state map
GetKeyboardState KeyBuf(0)

'//Test value of the Caps Lock key
If KeyBuf(VK_CAPITAL) And 1 Then
    '//If it's on, turn it off...
    KeyBuf(VK_CAPITAL) = 0
Else
    '//...and vice versa
    KeyBuf(VK_CAPITAL) = 1
End If

'//Finally, set the new keyboard state
SetKeyboardState KeyBuf(0)
```

MSCOMM

The MSComm control is a slightly updated copy of the original version, and fixes some problems at high speeds (which even for the 32-bit OCX still means 19,200 bps). One problem remains, though—the default setting of the RTSenable property. If you're not using hardware handshaking (i.e., the Handshaking property is set to a value below 2), this property should be set to True instead of False to prevent problems with most high-speed modems (which will seem to receive everything you send to them, but refuse to respond).

MSMAPI

The two MAPI-related custom controls (MAPISession and MAPIMessage) don't bring much in terms of new functionality (surprise!), but *do* fix a longstanding bug that made the VBX version almost unusable—it's no longer required for each system that runs a VB executable that contains the controls to support the MAPI interface. As soon as you actually start using the controls, it is, of course, required, but you can now at least check whether the system you're running on has mail support and disable mail-related menu items if it hasn't.

MSOUTLIN

The outline control used to be buggy and have a limited run-time interface—in the OCX incarnation, only the limited interface is left. This means the control will now safely run on systems that are configured to use more than 256 colors. Also, general video driver problems (resulting in hard-to-track-down GPFs) should have been eliminated. To MSOutlin's credit, the control is quite fast—faster, actually, than any other outline control on the market.

THREED

The only, but very welcome, news for the Sheridan 3D controls is that THREED16.OCX and THREED32.OCX no longer conflict with the widely distributed "hacked" version of THREED.VBX that had incorrect versioning information, causing it not to be overwritten by most setup programs. This resulted in programs failing to start up with a `THREED.VBX is Out of Date` error message or made 3D panels turn out white instead of gray. Unless someone decides to do something similar to the OCX versions, VB apps should be safe from this from now on.

Note that using these controls probably won't be necessary in new projects, because the new form `Appearance` property can be set to "3D" and all Windows 95 controls already have a 3D-look anyway. If you're going to port your programs to the 32-bit version of VB, planning to phase out this control might be a good idea.

New Controls in VB 4

In addition to these existing controls, the Professional edition of Visual Basic 4 comes with a number of new controls. Let's take a brief look at those.

DBGRID

DBGrid is a data-aware version of the existing Grid control. This means that if you use the Data control to access your databases, you can set this as the data source for the DBGrid. If you're familiar with the default format Microsoft Access uses to let you edit data, you'll find the DBGrid control very familiar.

DBLIST

The DBLIST16/32.OCX file contains the DBList and DBCombo controls, which are data-aware versions of their similarly named counterparts. Welcome additions to these controls are the `Matchentry` property that lets you choose between basic or extended matching and the `IntegralHeight` property that allows you to create list boxes and combos with a height that's not evenly divisible by the line height. The latter property is also available for regular list box and combo controls.

TABCTL

TABCTL16/32.OCX brings the Sheridan Tab control, which allows you to easily implement a property page-like interface in both your 16-bit and 32-bit applications. For 32-bit apps, you'll probably want to use the COMCTL32 control for this purpose (though this control is a little easier to use, as it is a full container that allows you to place controls on its pages without further tricks).

RICHTX32

The RichText box control works only with the Windows 95 or Windows NT (version 3.51 or higher) operating system and only with the 32-bit version of VB. It's more a mini-application than a control. It allows the user to edit text and use all kinds of styles and colors, and it supports both regular and RTF-formatted text for input and output. The sample application that's on the CD shows how easy it is to implement a small editor using this control.

COMCTL32

The COMCTL32 control contains all the cool new Windows 95-style user interface elements. We'll be taking an in-depth look at it later in this chapter.

SYSINFO

The new Microsoft 32-bit operating environments offer extensive support for dynamic changes to the system environment. This support was added in response to new kinds of hardware, such as PCMCIA cards, which can be inserted and removed at any time, but also the user need for "on the fly" reconfiguration of many aspects of the system, such as screen resolution. This means your application should be able to respond to such changes and adapt itself to the new situation. The SYSINFO control helps do this. At the end of this chapter, we'll take a brief look at how it works.

Note that SYSINFO is an "unsupported control" (which means Microsoft doesn't want you to complain about it—it seems to work fine, though) which is not included in the regular VB 4 installation: you'll need to copy it from the CD manually.

MSRDC32.OCX

The Enterprise Edition of VB 4 contains one additional control for accessing remote databases. It's similar to the Data control built into all versions of VB, but is based on the new Remote Data Object and offers powerful features to access SQL Server (and other server-based) databases. For more information, see Chapter 18, "Using Remote Data Objects," and Chapter 19, "Remote Automation."

Is OLE Slow?

One big question you're likely to have about all these new OCX controls is, "How fast are they?" If you've experimented with embedding OLE controls from full servers (such as Word for Windows and Excel) on a VB form, you probably weren't very impressed by the performance. OCX controls are very different from these kinds of objects, though. As described in the section on OCX architecture, these components are implemented as in-process (or "in-proc") servers, which don't use the relatively slow Remote Procedure Call mechanism to communicate with their clients. Also, the OCX support libraries are optimized for fast property access and event notification and method execution. The actual OLE libraries have been optimized a lot as well. One note on VB4 performance testing: *always* compile the projects you want to analyze into an .EXE file before paying attention to performance. In previous versions of VB, there was not much difference in execution speed between the development and the runtime environment, whereas in VB4 it can be significant.

Still, OCX controls will *always* be slower than their VBX counterparts, for the simple reason that more layers of software are involved. Setting a property in a VBX control simply amounts to a `VBM_SETPROPERTY` message being sent to a window; doing the same for an OCX control requires a number of function calls between the application, the OCX, the OCX runtime library, and the OLE libraries. So, how bad is it? Considering the flexibility of the OCX architecture, not very. In a very simple property-setting benchmark I ran on a pre-release version of VB 4, I found that my (worst-case) OCX test program was about three times slower than the VBX equivalent. Here's the code I used, on a form with one Sheridan 3D Check box (the OCX version, `SSCheck1`):

```
Private Sub Form_Load()

Dim a As Integer, btime As Long

btime = Timer

For a = 1 To 10000
    SSCheck1.Caption = "First Caption"
    SSCheck1.Caption = "Second Caption Text"
Next a

MsgBox "Took " & Format(Timer - btime) & " seconds"

End Sub
```

I subsequently removed the check box and THREED16.OCX from the project and added THREED.VBX (as well as a new check box). Because of the different default control name, I had to change the loop code to:

```
For a = 1 To 10000
    Check3D1.Caption = "First Caption"
    Check3D1.Caption = "Second Caption Text"
Next a
```

As this code ran nearly three times faster, I was curious if there were some easy optimizations to make the OCX version run better. After switching from

a THREED.VBX to a THREED16.OCX check box again, I used the new VB
'With/End With' construct inside the loop:

```
For a = 1 To 10000
    With SSCheck1
        .Caption = "First Caption"
        .Caption = "Second Caption Text"
    End With
Next a
```

This code ran a little faster, but not significantly. When setting a lot of properties for one control, though, the speed gain should be more substantive.

The next thing I did was run the same test on the 32-bit version of VB, which
meant I could use only THREED32.OCX. It turned out to be about two times
as slow as its 16-bit counterpart, which should not be too surprising, as a 32-
bit control has two times as much data to shuffle around. Timings for other
controls showed roughly the same pattern.

I encourage you to run these simple tests yourself (just remember: compile
before you perform your timings). The results you get should be different,
because the released version of VB 4 will more than probably have been optimized for speed in these areas. Before deciding that OCX controls are too
slow to use, keep in mind that setting a property 10,000 times is not exactly a
real-world application. As long as you adhere to the following simple rules,
the effect of the decreased property access speed on your application can be
kept to a minimum:

- When accessing properties in a loop, always use a variable of the most
  efficient type (for example, an integer) to "cache" property values or to
  store intermediate results, if possible.

- If setting a lot of properties for the same control, use the With/End With
  construction. It not only saves you some typing, but also will speed up
  your code.

- Try to identify whether there are parts of your program which access
  certain control properties extensively. Try to rewrite that code to use
  cached property values or defer certain property updates. (If you're
  updating an on-screen value in a loop, for example, doing so once each
  second or so should be perfectly acceptable to the user and can make
  your code run much faster.)

Implementing a Windows 95-Compliant User Interface with COMCTL32.OCX

When the Windows 95 preview hit the streets, a question that popped up often was, "How can I use these exciting new user interface controls from my VB app?" For Visual Basic 3, the answer had to be, "Sorry, you can't," but with the release of VB 4 and the COMCTL32 control (which only works on Windows 95 and Windows NT 3.51 and higher), you can use all new UI elements in your own projects. That's one part of the good news. The other part is that it's surprisingly easy to do so. Let's take a look at the various controls that are part of COMCTL32.

ImageList

The ImageList is quite similar to the older PictureClip control—it stores images of the same size. Unlike PictureClip, though, an ImageList can store both icon and bitmap images and allow you to add/remove individual images (technically, an ImageList is a collection of `ListImage` objects) instead of requiring one large bitmap.

You'll most probably be using the ImageList control a lot. Every other COMCTL32 control that uses pictures one way or another will want to get these from this control. The design-time interface for the ImageList is as easy as it gets. If you activate its property pages (through the "custom" item in VB's property list or by means of the menu you get when you right-click on the control), you'll be able to insert and remove image files easily, as shown in figure 11.7.

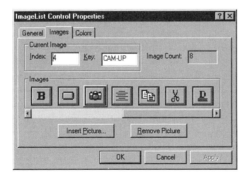

Fig. 11.7
Assigning images to the ImageList control. An ImageList can contain icons or bitmaps, which all need to be the same size.

ToolBar

Every Real Application has a toolbar these days. And guess what—with the new Toolbar control, your app can have one too, easily. Using the design-time interface to this control, as shown in figure 11.8, you can set up a complete toolbar within minutes. Most properties available here explain themselves pretty much. For others (like "Key"), it's handy to remember that a Toolbar is really a collection of Button objects.

When you run your program, the toolbar you just designed will be fully functional immediately, including tooltips (the yellow boxes that pop up, explaining a button's purpose in life), toolbar wrapping (if after resizing a form the toolbar no longer fits, it resizes itself to have multiple rows), and modification by the user (double-clicking on an empty part of the toolbar brings up a Customize Toolbar dialog). If you don't like any of these features, you can turn them off through the toolbar properties. Figure 11.9 shows an example of a completed toolbar. Note that it's very well possible to design one that doesn't look like the standard "Microsoft Office" issue.

Unfortunately, the version of COMCTL that made it into the released version of VB 4 is not entirely bug-free. You might encounter some problems with toolbar icons dropping off when you run your program (try a different sequence of assigning the images at design time), Microsoft-supplied "Windows 95" toolbar images with wrong background colors (use a paint program to correct these) and other things. The UIdemo sample project included on the CD shows how to work around some of these problems and design issues.

Fig. 11.8

Setting up the ToolBar control through its property pages. The ToolBar is a prime example of a control with a good design-time interface.

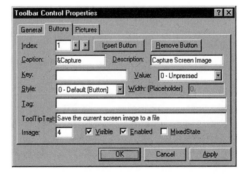

StatusBar

Once you've got a toolbar, you'll probably want a status bar for your application, too. The ToolBar control should work quite nicely. The ToolBar has an extremely easy-to-use design-time interface that allows you to set up the various parts (panels) of the status bar. A panel can contain a maximum of 16 panels, which can be set up to contain text (act like a label), the state of the Caps Lock, Num Lock, Scroll Lock, or Insert Key (which is automatically updated) and the current date or time. The ToolBar is a collection of Panel objects, which you can use to manipulate the individual toolbar parts at runtime.

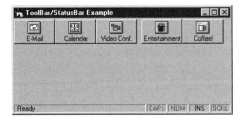

Fig. 11.9
A completed ToolBar/StatusBar combo. Unless you disable this functionality, the user can rearrange the buttons on the ToolBar.

ProgressBar

The ProgressBar is a pretty simple control that can be used to indicate the progress of an operation to the user. After placing it on a form, there's nothing more left to do than set its "Value" property at runtime. By default, this is a percentage, but you can use the Min and Max properties to define any range you want. An example of a ProgressBar control is shown in figure 11.10.

Fig. 11.10
A dialog box using the ProgressBar. You can also use the ProgressBar control on a status line.

Slider

The Slider control is also a pretty basic control, but it looks much better than using a scrollbar to let the user set values. Like the ProgressBar control, it has Value, Min, and Max properties, but also a number of properties to set its appearance (like TickFrequency and TickStyle). A Slider can have either a horizontal or a vertical orientation. Figure 11.11 shows an example of the first case.

Fig. 11.11
Using a Slider
control, which is
now finally a part
of the standard
Windows controls.

TreeView

The TreeView control, which you probably know from the Windows 95 Explorer shell or otherwise can check out in figure 11.12, can be used to easily display tree structures (such as a disk directory structure). It takes care of all user interface action (such as scrolling, expanding and collapsing nodes, and even editing the labels) automatically. The only thing you have to do is set some appearance properties (the TreeView control gets its images from an ImageList control; the last parameter in the Nodes.Add statement is the index into this list) and set up the tree nodes from code. Here's an example of how easy this is:

```
'//Set up array of nodes to add to TreeView control
Dim nodItem(6) As Node

'//Set some general properties
TreeView1.ImageList = ImageList1
TreeView1.LineStyle = tvwRootLines
TreeView1.Font.Size = 12

'//Add the actual nodes
Set nodItem(1) = TreeView1.Nodes.Add(, , , "VB Demo Projects", 1)
Set nodItem(2) = TreeView1.Nodes.Add(nodItem(1), tvwChild, ,
➡"Communications-related", 2)
Set nodItem(3) = TreeView1.Nodes.Add(nodItem(2), tvwChild, ,
➡"VBTERM", 3)
Set nodItem(4) = TreeView1.Nodes.Add(nodItem(1), tvwChild, , "Data
➡Access-related", 2)
Set nodItem(5) = TreeView1.Nodes.Add(nodItem(4), tvwChild, ,
➡"BROWSER", 3)
Set nodItem(6) = TreeView1.Nodes.Add(nodItem(4), tvwChild, ,
➡"VISDATA", 3)
```

Fig. 11.12
The result of the
sample TreeView
code. Normally,
you'll probably
want to use small
(16×16) icons
instead of the
32×32 icons used
here.

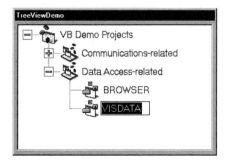

ListView

The ListView is an extremely sophisticated control. Like the TreeView control, you only have to build a collection of items to be shown (unlike the TreeView, the ListView control displays flat, not hierarchical, data). A ListView control supports four different views (all of which you can find back in the Windows 95 Explorer shell):

Icon—Similar to the view presented by the Windows 3.1 Program Manager. Contains a 32×32 icon and a short textual description (label).

Small Icon—Similar to Icon, but uses 16×16 icons in order to show more data.

List—Similar to Small Icon, but contains only one item on each line.

Report—Full-blown view of all data. Similar to List, but adds column headers and all other information (sub-items) available for each line.

The ListView control in figure 11.13 was set up by using the following code:

```
Dim clmHeader(2) As ColumnHeader
Dim itmItem(6) As ListItem
Dim a As Integer

ListView1.Icons = ImageList1
ListView1.SmallIcons = ImageList2

Set clmHeader(1) = ListView1.ColumnHeaders.Add()
clmHeader(1).Text = "Project name"

Set clmHeader(2) = ListView1.ColumnHeaders.Add()
clmHeader(2).Text = "Description"

Set itmItem(1) = ListView1.ListItems.Add()
With itmItem(1)
    .Icon = 1
    .SmallIcon = 1
    .Text = "BROWSE"
    .SubItems(1) = "BIBLIO.MDB Database Browser"
End With

Set itmItem(2) = ListView1.ListItems.Add()
With itmItem(2)
    .Icon = 1
    .SmallIcon = 1
    .Text = "VISDATA"
    .SubItems(1) = "Visual Data Sample Application"
End With
```

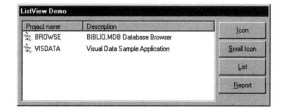

TabStrip

The final control in the Windows 95 User Interface element collection, the TabStrip, is a tab control (which you've probably used before) with a difference: it's not a container control. TabStrip just displays the actual tabs—hence the last part of its name—and leaves it up to you to make changes to the controls displayed on-screen in response to the selection of a different tab. This may seem like a severe limitation, but the implementation of a "real" tab control (basically, stacking container controls, such as picture boxes, on top of each order and changing the Z-order to display the right container) is quite simple: just take a look at the Uidemo project included on this book's CD to see how it's done.

TabStrip is really two controls in one: by changing its Style property from Tabs (the default) to Buttons, the result is something that closely resembles the Windows 95 Taskbar. For both styles, full design time support is available for adding and deleting tabs and setting their properties. Figure 11.14 shows both TabStrip styles.

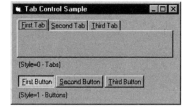

Integrating with the Operating System by Using the SysInfo Control

The dynamic nature of the new Microsoft operating systems bring new responsibilities for your application. For example, where a user typically had to reboot (and thus close/restart all running programs) when making changes to the system configuration under Windows 3.x, Windows 95 allows such changes while the rest of the system continues functioning.

This means that new resources, such as modems, disk drives, etc., can become available (or existing resources can disappear!) during the runtime of your program. Also, the screen can be resized (due to a resolution change or the user switching the Taskbar on or off), or the system colors can change.

How do you keep in touch with such events? The notifications the operating system generates for this can normally not be intercepted by a native VB application. The SysInfocontrol is designed specifically for this purpose. It has a number of properties that allow you to learn more about the system your program is running on, such as `OSPlatform` and `OSBuild`, and the status of that system (such as `ACStatus` and `BatteryLifePercent`, very usable for laptop systems). The dimensions of the usable screen (the physical screen minus the Taskbar) are available through the `WorkAreaXXX` set of properties.

Among the events supported by SysInfo are `DisplayChanged` (the resolution or the color-depth of the screen has changed), `SettingChanged` (the name of the system setting that has changed is passed as a parameter), `DeviceArrival` (the user added a device to the system) and `TimeChanged` (someone changed the system time).

Should you use these properties and events? Most probably, yes. Even if it doesn't seem to make sense at this moment, the increased use of PCMCIA devices and laptops with docking stations and enhanced hardware will make sure your users will expect your application to respond to such changes. If you revise an existing project or start a new one, consider how you could use the SysInfo control here. For example, a communications program would probably want to respond to changes in the hardware configuration (`DeviceArrival` and `DeviceRemoveComplete` events) and rescan the systems for modems after such an event. A database application might want to prevent a user from suspending the system during a critical update (by returning a True value when the `PowerSuspendQuery` event fires), etc.

Use all this new power to your advantage!

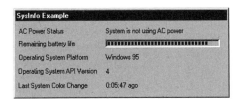

Fig. 11.15

An overview of some of the possibilities of the SysInfo control.

Summary

The latest release of Microsoft Visual Basic introduces an entirely new implementation of the custom controls that played such a large part in making the earlier releases so successful. You might wonder why the decision was made to move away from VBX controls and what the real advantages are of the new OCX architecture.

In this chapter, you covered the decision to move away from controls, the real advantages of the new OCX architecture, and the cool new OCX features in VB4. Unlike many explanations of OCX controls, there's not much OLE or C++ terminology in this chapter. This means that, although my explanations may not always be 100 percent "technically correct," you should be able to satisfy your curiosity about the new controls anyway, without having to refer to other sources first.

Chapter 12

Porting Your Existing Apps to Visual Basic 4

by Frank Sommer

Frank is the Vice President of VideoSoft Consulting, a company that creates custom Windows applications for its clients using Visual Basic. Frank may be reached on CompuServe at 76002,426, or at VBGuy@MSN.com.

Version 4.0 of Visual Basic (VB4) is easily the most significant upgrade to the Visual Basic programming language since Visual Basic 1.0. In this chapter, you will learn how to take projects you have created under Visual Basic 3.0 (VB3) and move them forward to VB4. For most projects, this will be a trivial exercise. However, for many of them this will be but the first step in a migration, the end goal of which is an application that can display the Windows 95 logo.

Windows 95 migration need not necessarily be the cause for moving to VB4. Indeed, even if you intend to spend the rest of your days writing applications for a pure Windows 3.1 environment, you may very well want to write them in VB4 for the many new features this new version of Visual Basic offers.

This chapter deals with getting your VB3 project to run and behave properly under VB4. Although you will not encounter some of the issues raised here unless you are running VB4 under Windows 95, for the most part I will not cover Windows 95 user interface (UI) issues.

As mentioned above, getting most VB3 projects to run under VB4 is not a big job. However if you have used some sloppy programming practices in the past (shame) or have made use of the Windows API (good for you), there are a few factors you should be aware of, and we will look at them.

In the narrowest sense, the goal of this chapter is to simply get your VB3 application to run under VB4. Microsoft did such a good job with backwards compatibility that this would be a very short chapter indeed if I kept strictly to that charge. In order to add a bit more meat to the chapter—and to give you a useful tool in the process—I will convert a project that can take advantage of some of the new features of VB4. The project, once converted, will be implemented as an OLE server, and I will show you how to use that OLE server as an add-in to the Visual Basic design-time environment.

In this chapter, you will learn how to do the following:

- Open a VB3 project under VB4

- Modify a project to accommodate VB4 language changes

- Modify a project to accommodate changes in the JET engine

- Modify the UI of a project to harmonize with the Windows 95 environment

- Use VB3 controls in the VB4 environment

- Handle changes necessitated by the Windows 95 operating system

- Convert a project and create a VB4 Add-In application

Opening a VB3 Project under VB4

The procedure you go through to open a project under VB4 is no different from opening it under VB3. The easiest way is to use the File/Open menu item. If this is the first time you are opening the project under VB4, you will be prompted with a dialog informing you that when the project is saved, it will be saved in the new VB4 format. What occurs next depends on whether you are using the 16-bit or 32-bit version of VB4 and whether or not your project uses any VBXs.

For projects that use no VBXs, you will be ready at this point to apply the Forehead Test: bend forward at the waist and smack the F5 key with your forehead. In most cases, your project will be up and running with no further trials or tribulations.

Dealing with VBXs

If your project uses third-party controls (VBXs), you have a few more hurdles to clear. Under VB4/16, you need to decide whether you want to continue to use the VBXs or to replace them with 16-bit OCXs. If you choose VBXs—and assuming the specified VBXs are present in the expected locations—the project is ready to open and run as above (choose File, Open or press F5). A missing VBX causes problems similar to those that occur when a VBX is missing in VB3.

Opening a VBX-laden project for the first time under VB4/32 is a bit more complicated. VBXs can't be used in the 32-bit version of Visual Basic. You must either supply a compatible 32-bit OCX or remove the VBX-based controls and code from your project.

Running with OCXs

OCXs come in two flavors: 16-bit and 32-bit for use in VB4/16 and VB4/32, respectively. Before you can use an OCX control in VB4, it must be registered. Once you have done that, it will reside in the list of available controls in the Custom Control dialog. No longer do you need to go hunting all over your hard disk—or, almost as bad, searching through the system directory—to find the controls you want to add to a project. In VB4, all OCXs are available in one handy list. From the design environment, just press Ctrl+T to see the Custom Controls dialog.

When porting your VB3 apps, you may be able to take advantage of a VB4 facility called *morphing*. This trendy little word refers to the ability of VB4 to automatically substitute compatible OCXs for any VBXs found in your project. The ability to morph depends on entries in your VB.INI file. When you install new OCXs on your system, the installation program should make the required entry for you in the VBX Conversions16 and VBX Conversions32 sections. If the entries are there, VB4 will automatically make the substitution for you. If not, you will have to do it manually.

Summary

In the majority of cases, getting a project to run under VB4 is easy. It is also a major milestone because, in most cases, once a project runs successfully under VB4, the conversion job is complete. The project can be compiled, and it will run error-free (at least as error-free as it ran under VB3). The remainder of this chapter deals mainly with projects that defy this rule and require additional tweaking. Note that this exception automatically includes any mission-critical applications that absolutely have to be delivered last week.

VB4 Language Changes

For the most part, language changes to Visual Basic have been in the form of extensions to the language—not in changes to existing usage. There *are* a few loose ends to look at however. Many of these are in the "shot myself in the foot" category. A few of them are true "gotchas."

Multi-Statement Lines

A prime example of an item in the foot-shooting category is the fact that VB4 treats multi-statement lines differently than they were treated in VB3. A multi-statement line is one such as

```
Print "Foo": Beep: Print "Bar"
```

In this example, space has been saved (at the expense of readability) by placing three lines of code on one line. In VB4, if the first statement on a line consists of a single keyword, that keyword is treated as if it were a line label. Let's look at an example. The following subroutine will work fine in VB3:

```
Sub Command1_Click ()
Dim db As Database
Dim dyn As Dynaset
    Set db = OpenDatabase("biblio.mdb")
    Set dyn = db.CreateDynaset("Authors")
    BeginTrans : dyn.Edit
        dyn("Author") = "Unknown"
        dyn.Update
    CommitTrans
End Sub
```

In VB4, the `BeginTrans` statement is interpreted as a label, and thus a transaction is never initiated. When the `CommitTrans` statement is reached, an error occurs: "`Commit or Rollback without BeginTrans`." Not only has readability suffered from a human standpoint, but it has also suffered from the machine viewpoint. If you are in the habit of concatenating several lines of code into one, now is a good time to break the habit.

String Concatenation

In previous versions of Visual Basic, you could concatenate strings with either a plus sign (+) or an ampersand (&):

```
MyString = "Foo" + "Bar"
```

and

```
MyString = "Foo" & "Bar"
```

produce the same results. The latter method has long been the preferred method as it is both faster (the interpreter can more easily parse it) and less ambiguous (a human can more easily parse it).

The context rules have changed in VB4, and the plus operator now behaves differently in some circumstances when used with strings. The following code works properly under VB3:

```
Sub Command1_Click ()
Dim FBSales
```

```
    FBSales = 3
Print FBSales & " foobars were bought."
Print FBSales + " foobars were sold."
End Sub
```

It produces this output:

3 foobars were bought.

3 foobars were sold.

Under VB4, the second line causes a "Type mismatch" error at run time. There are numerous other related examples that depend on the mix of variable typing and concatenation order. You can try to remember a complex rule matrix, or you can use the ampersand when concatenating strings.

Proper Use of the Bang Operator

In VB1 (that's *One* with a capital *O*), you were taught that the proper way to access a control on another form was as follows:

```
Form1.Text1.Text = "Foo"
```

In VB2, a new syntax was introduced utilizing the Bang (!) operator:

```
Form1!Text1.Text = "Foo"
```

While the previous dot operator was still recognized for compatibility reasons, programmers were encouraged to adopt the bang operator for reasons of "future compatibility." When VB3 arrived, those reasons never materialized, and now here we are with VB4.

Once again, the Holy Grail of future compatibility is being raised, and guess what it says this time. For future compatibility you should use the following form:

```
Form1.Text1.Text = "Foo"
```

The explanation goes something like this. The dot operator is used to denote properties and methods, and the bang operator is used for members of a collection. A control can be accessed as a property of a form using the dot notation, and it can also be accessed as a member of the controls collection through the Item method. The latter syntax is as follows:

```
Form1.Controls.Item("Text1").Text = "Foo"
```

Since the Item method is the default method for a collection and the controls collection is the default property of a form, this can be abbreviated to the familiar

```
Form1!Text1.Text = "Foo"
```

The upshot of this is that when you use the bang syntax, it must be translated internally into the `Controls.Item` syntax with an attendant performance hit. Visual Basic has a specific optimization (read this: exception code) that lets the compiler translate the bang form to the dot form.

It's this optimization that might not be available in future versions of Visual Basic. For this reason, you are encouraged to readopt the dot operator for accessing controls on a form.

64k Limits

Some VB3 programs—that from all other standpoints are fine—may still have trouble running under VB4 due to some 64k limits that are imposed by Visual Basic. These are the 64k limit for amount of code in a single procedure and the 64k limit for the amount of data in a user-defined type structure. The limits themselves haven't changed since VB3, but rather some changes to the language have made it necessary to take another look at them.

The first of these problems is another from the foot-shooting category. If you have anywhere near 64k of code in a single procedure, you are most likely doing something very wrong. At any rate, the fix is easy enough: break your procedure into several smaller procedures. The reason that this problem may arise in porting from VB3 to VB4 is that version 4.0 of Visual Basic is the first one that uses Visual Basic for Applications (VBA) as the underlying engine. VBA generates code that is more generic than that generated by VB3. The generic code, while allowing for a wider range of processors, also makes for a slightly larger procedure.

The second 64k alligator won't bite you unless you use VB4/32. The 32-bit version of Visual Basic stores strings as *Unicode*. Unicode is a double-byte standard that uses two bytes per character to store a string. This allows for unique representation for all of the characters in all of the alphabets in use throughout the world. Because of this, in VB4/32, character strings take up twice as much room as they did under 16-bit Visual Basic. A user-defined type that could hold 64k characters under VB3 will now hold only 32k characters under VB4/32.

Accommodating Changes in the JET Engine

VB4 introduces the JET 3.0 database engine. This is the same engine used by Access 95. It provides gains in speed and efficiency and introduces some exciting new capabilities. Unfortunately, the JET 3.0 engine is 32-bit only and if you want to take advantage of the improvements and features, you have no choice but to use VB4/32. Although this engine makes a lot available to the Visual Basic programmer in terms of power and speed, its presence may also necessitate some changes to your code.

Data Access Objects

If you used VB3 with Access 2.0, at some point you probably installed the Access 2.0 compatibility layer to update the Data Access Object (DAO) model from DAO 1.1 to DAO 2.0 or 2.5. VB4 comes with three versions of the DAO library. The only one that can be used with VB4/16 is the 16-bit DAO 2.5 library. This is the same library that you installed as the Access 2.5 compatibility layer. As such, it presents no problems when porting your VB3 application to VB4/16.

For projects that are migrating to VB4/32, the 16-bit DAO 2.5 library is not available, but you have two others from which to choose. Most likely you will want to use the 32-bit DAO 3.0 object library. This library incorporates a number of changes to the DAO programming model, and many objects from previous DAO libraries have been replaced by improved versions. The easiest way to identify whether your project uses any of the objects that have been replaced is to run your project; the compiler is very efficient at finding them. Don't be surprised when it chokes on such dear and familiar objects as the `Table`, `Dynaset`, and `Snapshot`. The line

```
    Dim MyDyn as Dynaset
```

produces a "`User-defined type not defined`" error.

Microsoft strongly encourages you to replace any outdated DAO syntax with the new syntax, both for reasons of efficiency and for future compatibility.

The number of changes necessary and the effort required can be quite large even for a reasonably sized project. If you are not overly concerned about speed or compatibility or you just need to do a port quickly, Microsoft has provided an easy way out. It lies in the hybrid 32-bit DAO 2.5/3.0 library. This library is fully compatible with existing code and contains all of the new DAO 3.0 functions to boot!

To use DAO 2.5/3.0, you must specify it in the References dialog (see fig. 12.1). This dialog may be reached by choosing Tools, References). The entry you want is listed as the Microsoft DAO 2.5/3.0 Compatibility Library. To use it, place a check mark in the corresponding check box. Also be sure to uncheck the default Microsoft DAO 3.0 Object Library, as only one DAO library can be specified at a time.

Fig. 12.1
The References
dialog.

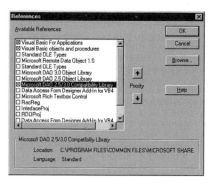

Bookmarks

In VB3, database bookmarks were stored as strings. This has been changed
in VB4, and the bookmark property is now stored internally as a byte array.
Since, in general, you can't compare two arrays directly, you can't compare
two bookmarks directly. The comparison must be done by first offloading the
bookmark property into a string variable and comparing it to another similarly derived string variable. The following code will work in VB3:

```
If MyDynaset.Bookmark = MyClone.Bookmark Then
```

But it must be modified to work under VB4, as follows:

```
MyString1 = MyDynaset.Bookmark
MyString2 = MyClone.Bookmark
If MyString1 = MyString2 Then
```

Property Defaults

The default property for some data access objects has changed. In general, for
any data access object that has a collection as a property, that collection is
now the default property. For example, in VB3 the default property of the
TableDefs object was the Name property, and thus the following code would
load a ListBox with a list of table names:

```
Sub Command1_Click ()
Dim I As Integer
Dim MyDB As Database
    Set MyDB = OpenDatabase("BIBLIO.MDB")
    For I = 0 To MyDB.TableDefs.Count - 1
       List1.AddItem MyDB.TableDefs(I)
    Next
End Sub
```

In VB4, the default property of the TableDefs object is the Fields Collection,
and the above code will produce a "Type mismatch" error. The code can be
fixed by explicitly specifying the Name property, as follows:

```
List1.AddItem MyDB.TableDefs(I).Name
```

Windows 95 GUI Issues

For the most part, I will not cover Windows 95 user interface issues here as Ken will be doing that in Chapter 13, "The New User Interface of Visual Basic 4." However, from a porting standpoint, it should be noted here that if the Windows 95 look is all you are after, you may not even need to convert your VB3 program. A VB3-created executable file running under Windows 95 will automatically inherit many of the UI features of its operating environment. It will have a left-justified form caption with a mini-application icon to the left, and the minimize, resize, and close buttons to the right. It will also inherit some other Windows 95 UI enhancements, such as list boxes with proportionally sized thumb buttons.

Much of the Windows 95 3-D look will come free too. You will automatically get 3-D forms and menus. If your application used the standard (flat) check boxes and option buttons, they too will sport the new 3-D look when running under Windows 95. To get some of the other Windows 95 GUI changes, such as 3-D Combos, text boxes, and list boxes, you will have to open the project in VB4 and do just a bit of tuning (which I'll talk about in the next section).

Using VB3 Controls

For the most part you may continue in VB4 to use the controls that you used in VB3. With the controls that shipped in the VB3 box, Microsoft has gone to great lengths to ensure VB4 compatibility. Third-party controls are an entirely different matter, and will only be dealt with in general terms here.

Standard Controls

Many features of the standard controls that come with Visual Basic were covered in Chapter 11, "VBX versus OCX," but there are issues related to the porting of some standard controls that need to be discussed here.

Caption Wrapping

Several VB4 controls now automatically wrap a long caption property to multiple lines. Standard controls that exhibit this new behavior include the `command button`, `option button`, `check box`, and `label` (see fig. 12.2). A caption that would just barely fit onto a VB3 command button, for instance, may now extend into the wrapping zone. If it does, it will automatically split into a two-line caption. (Under VB3, the 1365 button looks just like the 1380 button.) This may come as a pleasant surprise if the control is tall enough for the extra lines (as in the Tall Button), but as the 1365 button demonstrates, your application will require some adjusting otherwise.

Fig. 12.2
Examples of caption wrapping in VB4.

Fortunately, VB4 does its wrapping intelligently. Break points fall automatically between words. The space character between two words is dropped if it falls into the wrap zone, allowing words to butt right up to the edge of a control. Individual words are not split unless they are too wide to fit even on a line by themselves. Among the four controls, only the label differs from this behavior. Words too wide to fit on a label line by themselves are truncated at the caption margin; the text is not wrapped.

The command button exhibits one additional peculiarity: as in VB3, when a command button gets focus, it also gets a focus rectangle. In VB4, the Caption is rewrapped (if necessary) to fit within this focus rectangle. One would have expected the focus rectangle to lie outside of the wrapping margins—or at least not affect the wrap margins—but this is apparently not the case. The behavior is anomalous enough to be considered a bug (ahem, undocumented feature).

Although disconcerting, the problem is not severe unless the rewrap causes the caption to become too tall to fit on the button. In figure 12.2, the 1380 button will wrap to look like the 1365 button when you click it. When you click any other control, it reverts to its original one-line state. By adjusting caption text and/or button widths at design time, this problem can be prevented. Fortunately, the focus rectangles of the option button and check box do not exhibit this curious behavior. The label control is spared, of course, because it has no focus rectangle in the first place.

The Appearance Property
Standard VB3 controls automatically inherit any new VB4 properties as soon as you open your VB3 project in VB4. For example, VB3 text boxes will inherit Locked and WhatsThisHelpID properties. However, there are some control properties you will need to set yourself if you want to add the new 3-D look to your controls.

As noted earlier, OptionButtons and CheckBoxes in a VB3 executable look great when running under Windows 95. Unfortunately, the same is not true when you take that same VB3 project and recompile it to a new executable under VB4. The result is a Raccoon-eyes effect that looks worse than the original VB3 controls. In a sense, the new 3-D controls in VB4 aren't new controls at all, they are simply the old ones with some new properties. The 3-D look of the controls is due to a new Appearance property.

The Appearance property has two possible values, Flat and 3D. The default value is 3D. Thus, any new controls you draw on your VB4 project will automatically look 3-D. For VB3 projects that are opened in VB4, however, the value of the Appearance property is initially set to Flat. While this seems like a mistake, it actually makes very good sense. VB4 won't force a 3-D look onto your old projects. More importantly, it won't add its own 3-D effects on top of any 3-D look you might have created yourself using drawing methods or a third-party 3-D tool, such as VideoSoft's Elastic. To gain the new 3-D look, you will need to manually change the Appearance property of the desired controls from Flat to 3D.

Windows 95 was pretty clever about this when it comes to handling your VB3-created executables. Since 3-D times two isn't very pretty, it only provides the new 3-D look to those controls that you couldn't have modified yourself with drawing methods or Elastics (CheckBoxes and OptionButtons). Controls that you may have augmented yourself (TextBoxes, etc.) it leaves alone.

Third-Party Controls

With VB4/16, third-party controls need not be a problem. If a compatible OCX is available, use it. If not, simply continue to use the VBX. This scheme will work fine unless a VBX you need was written to take advantage of undocumented internal features of Visual Basic. Since VB4 was completely rewritten from the ground up, those VBXs may rely on features that are no longer available.

As mentioned previously, if you are using VB4/32, you must replace any VBXs with compatible versions of the vendor's 32-bit OCXs.

As used here, *compatible* means that the control vendor has matched the OCX, property for property and event for event, to the VBX. If not, you will have, at a minimum, some tricky find and replace operations ahead of you. Check with your OCX vendors to see if their controls are completely compatible with their VBX forebears.

The Windows 95 Operating System

As mentioned in the introduction to this chapter, a consideration of Windows 95 issues is not strictly necessary for a VB3 to VB4 port. The foregoing notwithstanding, if you run into problems when porting an application from VB3 to VB4, the operating system is the area in which they are most likely to occur. For that reason, this chapter would not be complete without at least a cursory examination of some of these issues.

Windows API Issues

If you are porting code from VB3 to VB4/16, the Windows API calls in your program will not be of concern. If you are porting to VB4/32, they will be a big issue. Most (but not all) 16-bit API calls have 32-bit counterparts. In some cases, all you will need to do is change the library name to its 32-bit counterpart. For instance,

```
Declare Function GetMessageTime Lib "User" () As Long
```

becomes

```
Declare Function GetMessageTime Lib "User32" () As Long
```

Most often though, there are changes to the function type and/or argument types. For instance,

```
Declare Function IsWindow Lib "User" (ByVal hWnd As Integer) As
Integer
```

becomes

```
Declare Function IsWindow Lib "User32" (ByVal hWnd As Long) As Long
```

Not only must you change the declare statement, but you also need to look at each line in your code where a call is being made and determine if the proper data types are being used. If you have used many API calls, the task, while not difficult, can become rather mind-numbing and subject to error. Fortunately, there is help available.

Much of the task can be automated for you by a program called the Upgrade Wizard. This wizard was created by Crescent Software and is being made available at no cost to the VB community. You can locate a copy on the World Wide Web at **http://www.progress.com/crescent**. What the wizard does is search through your project for API declarations and calls. When it finds one, it will either convert it or flag it with a comment. Laudably, the wizard does not modify your original code, but rather works with a copy that it places in a subdirectory.

The wizard will ask you for the name of a project and choice of target platform: 16-bit, 32-bit, or both. There are then some options regarding whether changes should be inserted as code or in the form of comments. Old code can optionally be commented or removed. Once all of the options are set, you can turn the wizard loose and let it work on your code.

The results are quite pleasing. If you request code for both platforms, the wizard will use conditional compilation statements to create a single source code base that can be used to create both 16-bit and 32-bit applications. For example, the profile string declare

```
Declare Function GetPrivateProfileString Lib "Kernel" _

  (ByVal lpAppName$, ByVal lpKeyName$, ByVal lpDefault$, _

  ByVal lpReturnedString$, ByVal nSize%, ByVal lpFileName$) _

  As Integer
```

is converted into

```
#IF WIN32 THEN
  Declare Function GetPrivateProfileString Lib "kernel32" Alias _
    "GetPrivateProfileStringA" (ByVal lpApplicationName As String, _
    ByVal lpKeyName As Any, ByVal lpDefault As String, _
    ByVal lpReturnedString As String, ByVal nSize As Long, _
    ByVal lpFileName As String) As Long
#ELSE
  Private Declare Function GetPrivateProfileString Lib "Kernel" _
    (ByVal lpAppName$, ByVal lpKeyName$, ByVal lpDefault$, _
    ByVal lpReturnedString$, ByVal nSize%, ByVal lpFileName$) _
    As Integer
#ENDIF
```

In addition, every call to the function in your code is flagged with a comment (search on "TODO: "). The comment will warn you to check the parameter typing in the call, and it will include an example of the declaration so that you can make the check without having to search for the original declaration. Thus the following call to profile string:

```
I = GetPrivateProfileString(sect, key, "", value, 128, INIPath)
```

would be converted into

```
#IF WIN32 THEN
  'TODO: Function/Sub GETPRIVATEPROFILESTRING parameters should _
    be checked against the calling convention on the next line.
  'Declare Function GetPrivateProfileString Lib "kernel32" Alias _
    "GetPrivateProfileStringA" (ByVal lpApplicationName As String, _
    ByVal lpKeyName As Any, ByVal lpDefault As String, _
    ByVal lpReturnedString As String, ByVal nSize As Long, _
    ByVal lpFileName As String) As Long
```

```
#ELSE
  I = GetPrivateProfileString(sect, key, "", value, 128, _
    INIPath)
#ENDIF
```

With the Upgrade Wizard, converting your API calls is a snap.

File Dialog Issues

Windows 95 uses long file names, and herein lie several potential problems for your VB3 code. Any assumptions your VB3 code makes that rely on the old 8.3 format of file names will most likely fail under Windows 95. For instance, if your code searches for the first period (.) and assumes that everything to the right is the extension, you will have a problem with foo.bar.bat, which is a perfectly valid Windows 95 file name. Likewise storing filenames in fixed-length, twelve-character strings will create a problem.

If your application uses the File Open/Save Common Dialogs from VB3, VB4 will automatically volunteer to substitute the appropriate OCX into your project. The 16-bit version looks very similar to the VB3 dialog, while the 32-bit version mimics the new Windows 95 dialogs.

In VB3 under Windows 3.1, if you wanted to modify the behavior of the standard File Open/Save dialogs, you could easily create your own dialog that looked just like them using the file system controls. The FileListBox, DirListBox, and DriveListBox controls could be glued together with two lines of code to form a very good substitute. Although this solution will port to VB4 and Windows 95 without change and will work properly, it won't look anything like the Windows 95 dialog. Additionally, the VB4 file system controls are aware of long file names only when they are used in VB4/32. Under VB4/16, they will display "My long filename.txt" as "mylong~1.txt." This is intentional, as it is consistent with other 16-bit behavior.

The ListView control (available only when using VB4/32) is the control that makes up the body of the Windows 95 File Open/Save dialogs. It has quite a bit of functionality, but it will take a lot more than two lines of code to make a custom dialog from it. Further, there is no control provided in VB4 that will easily give you the functionality of the folders drop-down list that appears at the top of the Windows 95 dialog. Custom file dialogs are not a practical consideration under VB4/32, at least not ones that look like the Windows 95 dialogs.

Case Study: Creating a VB4 Add-In

The development environment in VB4 has been opened up to extension by third party products. By exposing a selection of objects, properties, and methods to manipulation by OLE automation, external programs can now directly manipulate the Visual Basic environment. Such a product is called an add-in, and the good news is that you can create them using VB4.

CodeKeep is an application that lets you organize and reuse your VB code, or more specifically subroutines and functions. I'll discuss its operation briefly so that some of the porting issues will make more sense when I cover them later.

If you have programmed for very long, you have probably discovered yourself doing some things over and over. After writing the `CenterForm` subroutine for the umpteenth time, you may decide to save it in a module of commonly used routines that you can add to every project. As the module grows, a different problem arises: for any given project there are more routines in the module that you don't use than there are ones that you do. You can remove the unused ones at the end of the development cycle, but as soon as you do, you are bound to find a need for one of them and have to add it back. Compounding the problem are routines that are not common enough to justify placement in the module, but are truly useful and need to be cataloged nonetheless.

CodeKeep addresses this problem by storing each routine in its own separate file. It then provides an interface in which they can be picked from a list and easily added to a project as they are needed (see fig. 12.3). Routines are added to the list by copying the desired routine to the clipboard and clicking the Save clip button. The program assumes that the first line of the routine following the subroutine declaration is a comment describing the routine. This description for the routine is saved, and the description of the routine that is highlighted in the list appears in a box below the list.

Fig. 12.3
The main screen from CodeKeep.

The subroutine files that make up the list are stored in a directory called \Data that is located just off of the directory that holds CodeKeep. An individual file can be edited if necessary through the Edit Procedure menu entry. This entry calls Notepad (which it expects to find in your \Windows directory) to edit the routine.

The VB3 version of CodeKeep uses a raft of API calls and some messy SendKeys sequences to integrate itself nicely into the Visual Basic development environment. This all works fine, but this is an application just crying out to be rewritten as an add-in. Since VB4 affords you the opportunity, that is just what you will do.

The first step in porting a VB3 project to VB4 is to make a copy of it for safety's sake. This is because, as noted before, once you open a project under VB4 and save it, you will no longer be able to use the source code with VB3. Since you will be using Crescent's Upgrade Wizard, which creates its own copy, this step will be taken care of for you.

The Upgrade Wizard

Like any good wizard, this one will take you step-by-step through the process of converting your API declarations. It will first prompt for a project name and a directory to hold the copy. It will then ask whether you want to create 16-bit code, 32-bit code, or both (see fig. 12.4). The last step is to specify some options for handling the code changes. When you click the start button, the wizard opens your project and makes the specified changes. If it finds problems, it warns you that code in the project was changed and reminds you to search for comments that begin with "ToDo:."

Fig. 12.4
Target Platform screen from the Upgrade Wizard.

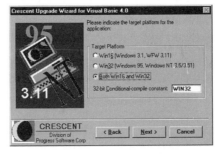

Once the Upgrade Wizard pass is complete, you can run Visual Basic 4.0 by selecting it in the Start Menu and use the File, Open command to select Codekeep.mak. VB4 immediately presents a dialog informing you that the file was saved in a previous version of Visual Basic, and that when it is saved, it will be saved in the new VB4 format. You are already ahead of the game here, so answer this dialog by clicking OK for All. If you click OK, it will show this dialog for each file in the project.

The next dialog you are presented with also comes from opening a VB3 project for the first time. It asks if you want to add a library reference for data access objects to your project. Since this project doesn't use any database access, you should click Don't Add. If you clicked Add, the DAO 3.0 object library would be added by default. If you answer this dialog incorrectly, you can always change the option by choosing Tools, References. If your VB3 project used obsolete objects, such as dynaset and snapshot, you would have to modify your code to be compatible with the new object module, or else choose Tools, References to substitute the DAO 2.5/3.0 compatibility library for the default 3.0 library.

Once you click Don't Add, VB4 will be up and running. Thanks to the conditional compilation statements added by the Upgrade Wizard, the project will compile and run as well. Before you run it, however, you should heed the advice of the Upgrade Wizard and do a text search in the code for lines tagged with the comment "'TODO:." A search shows that the wizard inserted "TODO" references into two code modules: Global and frmMain.

I'll deal with the Global module later and concentrate for now on the frmMain comment that was inserted in a routine that is called when the user clicks the Edit Procedure menu entry: mnuProcEdit_Click. This comment is a warning that although the GetWindowsDirectory API call is still supported in Windows 95, the calling conventions may be different. Conveniently, the Upgrade Wizard has placed the declaration as a comment on the very next line so that you can examine it and determine if any changes need to be made. The pertinent lines of the routine are as follows:

```
Dim Res as Integer

#If Win32 Then
  'TODO: Function/Sub GETWINDOWSDIRECTORY parameters should be _
    checked against the calling convention on the next line.
  'Declare Function GetWindowsDirectory Lib "kernel32" Alias _
    "GetWindowsDirectoryA" (ByVal lpBuffer As String, _
    ByVal nSize As Long) As Long
#Else
    Res = GetWindowsDirectory(Editor, 256)
#End If
```

A quick look reveals that there is indeed a problem. The 32-bit call returns a long, and you have declared Res as Integer. As mentioned previously, this is a common "problem" with 32-bit API calls. In this instance, the quickest fix would be to declare Res as Variant. A more elegant fix is to use a conditional compilation declaration instead, and replace the above lines with the following:

```
#If Win32 Then
    Dim Res as Long
#Else
    Dim Res as Integer
#End If
Res = GetWindowsDirectory(Editor, 256)
```

Note that while you have declared Res twice, no error is generated because the compiler will only see it declared once due to the conditional compilation statement.

You have now done everything that you need to do to run your VB3 project under VB4, but one very big issue remains. CodeKeep is a program that was written to work in close harmony with another program, VB3. Although you have fixed the code of CodeKeep to run under the VB4 language, you need to modify the logic of CodeKeep to navigate in the VB4 development environment. The menu structure of VB4 is different from that of VB3, and so the SendKeys sequences will no longer work. The window structure has changed as well, and so your API calls are now hunting the wrong snark.

This brings us back to the Global module, and the "ToDo" items that you did not fix earlier. Those items are all located in the SetCodeWidow routine and the API declares that support it. SetCodeWidow searches for a VB source code window and sets focus there so that CodeKeep can paste code into it. Your new CodeKeep will use OLE automation to accomplish this task, and so you can delete SetCodeWidow and all of its supporting API calls.

Add-In Basics

An add-in is an OLE server application that uses objects exposed by Visual Basic to extend the functionality of the Visual Basic environment. What you will do now is turn CodeKeep into an OLE server and attach it to a menu item of the Visual Basic design environment.

Add-ins are accessed through menu entries in the Add-Ins menu. Any add-ins that are installed for the current project will appear in the Add-In menu below the Add-In Manager entry. The Add-In Manager is used to add and remove items from the menu. It is activated by clicking the menu entry. This brings up a list of available add-ins. Each item in the list has a check box to indicate if it should appear in the Add-Ins menu. It is the VB.INI file that controls which items should be in the list of available add-ins. Depending on your version of Visual Basic (Standard, Professional, or Enterprise Edition)

and the installation options that you chose, you may or may not initially
have items in your list of available add-ins.

Creating a Connector Class

In order to implement CodeKeep as an add-in, you need to hang a bit of
supporting structure onto it, but there is very little you need to change in the
existing code. One thing that all add-ins must have is a `Public` class module
with two procedures: `ConnectAddIn` and `DisconnectAddIn`. The `ConnectAddIn`
routine is called when the user checks the CodeKeep box in the Add-In Manager, and it is used to perform initialization chores. In your program, it sets a
global object (`MyVBInst`) that keeps track of the Visual Basic instance that
called the add-in. You can run multiple instances of Visual Basic under VB4,
and you need to make sure that CodeKeep talks to the correct one. You also
need a few lines of code to create a menu entry in the Add-Ins menu for your
application.

```
Sub ConnectAddIn(VBDriverInstance As VBIDE.Application)

    'Save the instance of Visual Basic so we can refer to it later.
    Set MyVBInst = VBDriverInstance
    Set AddInItems = VBDriverInstance.AddInMenu.MenuItems

    'Add our menu line to the Visual Basic Add-In menu.
    Set MyMenuLine = AddInItems.Add("&Code Keep")

    'Set the AfterClick handler for the CodeKeep form.
    ConnectID = MyMenuLine.ConnectEvents(Me)

End Sub
```

Similarly, there is a `DisconnectAddIn` routine that is called when Visual Basic is
being closed or the Add-In Manager is removing the add-in.

```
Sub DisconnectAddIn(Mode As Integer)

    'Disconnect the event handlers from the menu lines
    MyMenuLine.DisconnectEvents ConnectID

    'Remove item from Addins menu.
    AddInItems.Remove MyMenuLine
    Unload frmMain

End Sub
```

The final procedure in your connector class is the `AfterClick` routine. It is
called when the user selects your menu line. All it does is make the CodeKeep
UI visible.

```
Public Sub AfterClick()
    frmMain.Show
End Sub
```

In the VB3 version of CodeKeep, when the user clicked the Paste into VB button, the `PasteSelRoutine` procedure was called. It would open the requested data file, read the contents into a string, and place the string on the clipboard. The `SetCodeWindow` routine mentioned previously would then be called to work its API magic, after which `SendKeys` could be used to insert the code. The routine looks like this:

```
Sub PasteSelRoutine ()
'Paste the subroutine highlighted in the list into the current module
Dim FName As String, Proc As String
   'read the procedure from file
   FName = gPI(gPNum).FName & ".TXT"
   FName = FQFilename(gDataPath, FName)
   If ExistWarn(FName) Then Exit Sub

   Open FName For Input As #3
      Proc = Input(FileLen(FName), #3)
   Close #3

   'paste procedure into code module
   If SetCodeWindow() Then
      Clipboard.SetText Proc
      SendKeys "^{End}", True  'move to end of sub
      SendKeys "^v", True      'paste from clipboard
   End If
End Sub
```

In the VB4 version this entire section plus the `SetCodeWindow` routine can be replaced by one line invoking the `InsertFile` method.

```
MyVBInst.ActiveProject.SelectedComponents.Item(0).InsertFile FName
```

This is rather a mouthful by VB3 standards, so let's go through it piece by piece. `MyVBInst` is the global object defined earlier that identifies the particular instance of Visual Basic that is using your add-in. The `ActiveProject` property returns an object representing the active project. The `SelectedComponents` collection is a collection of all of the items in the Project window (forms, code modules, class modules) that are currently selected. Because in VB4 only one component can be selected at a time, this collection implies more latitude than it allows. The `Item` method specifies which member of this collection you are interested in. For the aforementioned reason, the index of `Item` must be zero. The `InsertFile` method inserts the specified file (`FName` in this example) into the selected component (i.e., into the code module).

Note that this model implies that a code window need not even be present on the screen when a paste is executed; the code will go into whichever module is selected in the project window whether its associated code window is displayed or not. This is certainly different from the VB3 model where you had to find an actual code window and set focus to it before you could insert any code.

All that remains are a few clean-up items. In VB3, you provided an Exit button so the user could terminate the program. Now, as an add-in, that chore is handled by the Add-In Manager, and the code behind the Exit button needs to be changed from

```
Unload Me
```

to

```
Me.Hide
```

Similarly, you need to remove the control box from the main form so the user doesn't terminate the application prematurely.

In order to make this application into an OLE server, there is one more step: you need to choose Tools, Options and select the Project tab. On this tab, select Sub Main as the startup form and OLE Server as the start mode.

At this point, you can choose File, Make EXE File and create the OLE server—but it still won't be listed in the Add-In Manager. Before you can go to the Add-In Manager and load it, you need to register it with the VB.INI file. This is done by making an entry in the Add-Ins16 or Add-Ins32 section:

```
CodeKeep.Connector = 0
```

You can make an add-in self-registering by placing code in the Sub Main procedure to look in the VB.INI file and insert the appropriate line if it is not already there. Use Sub Main as the startup since you don't want the UI exposed as soon as the add-in is loaded. You only want to see it when the menu item is clicked.

The CD-ROM that comes with this book contains a complete version of both the VB3 and VB4 source code for this project. Also included is a \Data subdirectory with a few useful subroutines to get you started. If you decide that you would like CodeKeep to always be present in the Add-Ins menu instead of having to add it manually each time you open a project, change the VB.INI line to:

```
CodeKeep.Connector = 1
```

Summary

In this chapter, I have taken a close look at the language, database, UI, and API issues that you need to be aware of when porting an existing VB3 application to VB4. You've seen that, for the most part, there really isn't that much to do.

The detailed look I took at creating an add-in is just one small example of the many new things you can do with a project once you make the port.

Chapter 13

The New User Interface of Visual Basic 4

by Ken Schiff

Ken is president of Productivity Through Technology, Inc., a consultancy he founded to create and promote obvious, discoverable, and usable software. A frequent and popular conference presenter, Ken's clients include some of the largest corporations and commercial software developers in the country, as well as small ISVs, VARs, and system integrators.

The user interface of the integrated design environment (IDE) of Visual Basic 4 has undergone substantial changes due to the new capabilities of Windows 95. Whereas the general top-level design of the IDE has changed little, new components and tools have been added, and the overall usability has been improved.

In the first part of this chapter, we will look at Visual Basic 4 as a program and discuss the changes in its own user interface. We'll look at these areas:

- Right mouse button support

- Using the new and improved Properties Window and Toolbox

- Changes in the menus

- Changes to conform with Windows 95 design standards

- New precision capabilities for sizing and positioning controls

In the second part of this chapter, we'll look at Visual Basic 4 from the viewpoint of the applications we can create with it. Specifically, we'll cover the following:

- Support for Help topics

- 3D and the Appearance property

- Mouse pointers and fonts

- Access keys

- Windows 95 specific custom controls

ToolTips and Mouse Button Support

The ever-so-helpful ToolTips allow us to discover the meaning of the various graphics on the buttons in both the main window's toolbar and the controls tool box. Also new is generous right-mouse pop-up menu support. As I recommend with *any new* application, take some time to explore the program, traversing the menus and clicking the right mouse button over various parts of the application's windows and the various objects in them.

Here's a sampling of right mouse click results germane to Visual Basic 4 (not included are right mouse click results supported by Windows 95 for *all* applications):

Right Mouse Click On:	Gives You a Pop-up Menu with These Choices:
Form	View Code, Menu Editor..., Lock Controls, Properties
Control on a Form	Bring to Front, Send to Back; View Code, Align to Grid; Properties
Project Window	For the selected file: View Form (not available when the selected file is a code or class module), View Code, Save, Save File As..., Add [another] File, Remove File, Print.... When SourceSafe is loaded: Check In and Check Out For the Project window itself: Hide, Always On Top
Toolbox	[Add or Delete or View] Custom Controls..., Hide, Always On Top
Properties Window	Hide, Always On Top
Debug Window	Object Browser..., Procedure Definition; Continue, End; Hide, Always On Top
Code Window	Toggle Breakpoint; Break on All Errors, Break in Class Module, Break on Unhandled Errors; Procedure Definition, Properties

Toolbox

One of the more noticeable on-screen changes is the look of the toolbox. Gone are the flat, two-dimensional controls that typified older versions of Windows and Visual Basic. The three-dimensional controls that required the add-in control set THREED.VBX, are all included in the standard toolbox. Several of the toolbox buttons sport pleasingly soft colors that do not violently commandeer your attention (GUI design tip). As mentioned earlier, helpful ToolTips pop up to let you know the function of the button under the mouse pointer.

As the preceding list shows, a right mouse click on the toolbox displays a context-sensitive pop-up menu whose first item is Custom Controls. Choosing it calls a dialog with a multiselect list box of all the available contols and insertable objects registered with the system. Multiple controls and objects can be added and/or deleted from the toolbox in the same instance of the dialog—a much more convenient way than the old, multi-click add file/delete file process.

Properties Window

At first glance, the Properties window does not appear to have changed much. However, some major improvements come to light as soon as you select the first property. For example, the awkward but familiar edit cell near the top, complete with its Excel-like Cancel ⟨x⟩ and OK ☑ buttons, is gone. Now we have in-cell editing and dialog boxes that make setting and changing property values much easier.

Another change that is evident with many, but not all controls, is a new "property" called *(Custom)*. Not to be confused with a single property, the word in parentheses indicates that a secondary window needs to be opened to see the property's contents. (Custom) is actually a collection of properties in a tabbed property sheet. It is opened by clicking on the button with the ellipsis or by clicking the right mouse button on an object and choosing Properties from the context menu.

Menus

The menus in Visual Basic 4 have been restructured. Gone are the Debug, Options, and Window menus. They were replaced by the Insert, Tools, and Add-Ins menus. Note that these are not just menus renamed; a great number of the menu items have been moved around. Take some time to familiarize yourself with the new menu structures and shortcut keys.

Keystroke Changes

Although VB4 is designed to be one of the "latest and greatest" Windows 95 applications, regretfully there is still no shortcut key to bring up the toolbox, and Ctrl+N is not assigned to File, New Project or any other command.

Bring to Front and Send to Back are no longer supported with Ctrl+ and Ctrl-. These shortcut keys have been changed to Ctrl-J and Ctrl-H, respectively. Finally, the Project window can now be opened with the shortcut key of Ctrl+R, although the toolbox, as already mentioned, still lacks a shortcut key.

Object Browser

The Object Browser is a convenient organizer and locator for the contents of your object libraries. Using a pair of linked list boxes, it is easy to move among the classes and modules and see the methods and properties for each. For a more detailed discussion of the Object Browser, see Chapter 11, "VBX versus OCX."

Color Palette

The Color Palette is an enhancement to the Properties window color selector seen in previous versions of Visual Basic. Not only is it a floating palette with the ability to "Keep on Top," but also it has an area to display the foreground and background colors of the selected form or control and an area to display the foreground and background colors of any text on that form or control. This is especially useful if you are using a lot of color combinations (GUI Tip: please don't!) in your application and you want to see what a particular color conbination looks like.

User Interface Changes Not Embodied in Properties

There are several more changes that affect user interface design but are not embodied in properties of controls.

Command Button Caption Wrap

Command button captions now automatically wrap. It is up to the developer to adjust the height and width of the button to accommodate the caption's text. Since there is no explicit property for word-wrap, this capability cannot be disabled.

Windows 95 Compatibility

The CheckBox control has undergone a visual change, in that the mark for "checked" or *value=vbChecked* is now actually a check ☑ instead of the former X. (This change was made for Windows 95 compatibility and is certainly more in keeping with the model used in Excel editing.)

Also in keeping with the design standards for Windows 95, the default font is still MS San Serif; however, the default font style is now regular or normal, rather than bold.

In previous versions of Windows, there was an obvious visual distinction between the drop-down list box and the drop-down combo box. With the drop-down list box, the drop-down arrow was directly adjacent to the text box, while the drop-down combo box displayed a space between the drop-down arrow and the text box. This visual differentiation has been removed in Windows 95 and VB4 follows suit: the drop-down arrow is always directly adjacent. Now the best way a user can discover which control is a drop-down text box and which one is a drop-down combo box is to place the mouse pointer over the control. When it is over a drop-down list box, the pointer will be an I-beam. When it is over a drop-down combo box, the mouse pointer will be a northwest arrow. Of course, if you click inside the drop-down list box, the list will drop down; if you click inside the drop-down combo box, the text will be selected. There is no change in the functionality of these controls.

New Layout Features in Visual Basic 4

Layout of the form is one of the most critical steps in user interface design. In fine-tuning a form, many programmers have discovered the frustration of trying to move or resize a control in very small increments by using the mouse. Inevitably, controls get moved when attempting to resize and vice versa. Visual Basic 4 has fixed this situation with two enhancements: the ability to use the arrow keys to position and size controls, and the Lock Controls command.

Coax Controls with the Arrow Keys

Although you may have suitable Form Design Grid settings for your project, at times you will want to move and resize controls in such small increments that to do so would be difficult with the mouse. Visual Basic 4 has the ability to use the arrow keys to coax the size and position of a control in increments of one column or row of the Form Design Grid. (The grid is defined by the distance (in twips) between columns and rows. Therefore, the lower the number in the grid settings, the closer the gridlines or the finer the grid.)

Lock Controls

Although the ability to coax the controls stands on its own as a significant improvement, its usefulness is enhanced by the Lock Controls command. Found on the Edit menu, the Lock Controls command disables the dragging capabilities of the mouse. Although you can still select a control, you cannot drag either the resizing handles or the control itself, effectively locking it in place. The visual cue that a form is locked is that the control handles of objects on a locked form are not solid anymore (■) but are "hollow" (□). You can still move and resize the controls on a locked form by changing the appropriate settings in the Properties Window or by using the arrow keys as described earlier. Note that the Lock Controls command works on a form level, allowing you to apply it to a form you have completed, while still permitting the use of the mouse to manipulate controls on a different form.

Visual Basic 4 and the Windows 95 User Interface

The original book, *The Windows Interface—An Application Design Guide* (1992) covered Windows 3.x user interface design, but even as it was being written, there were design changes evolving. As Microsoft introduced new user interface components in its Office suite, user expectations began to change, and developers began to include some of the new ideas into their applications. The design specifications for Microsoft Office (late 1993), embodied in the *Office Developer's Kit*, was the first articulation of the new design features and elements that were to become standards in the Windows 95 user interface. And with the publication of *The Windows Interface Guidelines for Software Design* (which will be referred to from here on as *The Guidelines),* a clear and definitive explication of graphical user interface design for Microsoft Windows applications became available.

Any developer considering developing for Windows 95 should, at a minimum, be familiar with *The Guidelines*. Although mastery of it might best be left to specialists in user interface design, knowledge of the concepts, use, appearance, and behavior of the design elements will greatly contribute to the initial usability and compatibility of the application. *What* the code should cause to happen, not *how* the code should cause it to happen, is at the core of *The Guidelines*.

To comply with the new design guidelines for Windows 95, all of the standard controls in VB4 that are used in user interface design have undergone at least some changes. In addition, two entirely new Visual Basic extensions, COMCTL32.OCX (containing eight new controls), and the RichTextBox control (RICHTX32.OCX) have been added. The rest of this chapter will deal with these changes and additions.

A Little Help for Your Friends

Although you work hard to create an application that is both obvious and discoverable, inevitably, the users need some kind of aid or assistance. Help should be treated as part of the user interface and the same kind of design attention should be paid to it. Visual Basic 4.0 affords easy access to the new Windows 95 contextual user assistance tool: *What's This?*

What's This exists as both a method (ShowWhatsThis and WhatsThisMode) and a property (WhatsThisHelp, WhatsThisHelpID, and WhatsThisButton). This affords you the flexibility to give the user access to What's This context-sensitive help in many places in the program. While the WhatsThisHelp property is limited to the Form and the MDI Form, the What'sThisHelpID property is found on almost all of the controls that have a visual component.

When the user clicks the question-mark button in the upper-right corner of the dialog ![?] (provided by the WhatsThisButton property), the system enters WhatsThisMode and the mouse pointer changes to an arrow with a question mark ![arrow with ?]. The next mouse click indicates the area or control for which help is being sought and a context menu or pop-up window (whose context is provided by the WhatsThisHelpID property) displays the help message. This same process should also be made available when the user clicks the right mouse button over an object and chooses What's This from the context or pop-up menu.

3D or Not 3D...It's No Longer a Question

Back in the "old days" of Windows 3.x, some software was designed with a three-dimensional look and some were created with the 2-D look. Among the native controls in Visual Basic 3, only the command button was inherently 3-D; you had to explicitly set the properties on just about every control to create a 3-dimensional application.

Well, times have changed, and now the reverse is true. All of the Visual Basic 4 controls' default appearance is 3-D. In fact, there is even an Appearance property now (for some 17 standard controls) that will allow you to change between "3-D" or "Flat" effects.

Border to Border

The BorderStyle property in Visual Basic 3 allowed for two kinds of fixed borders (single and double), as well as a sizable border or no border at all. When designing a dialog box, the Maximize and Minimize buttons had to be explicitly turned off. Now with Visual Basic 4, the BorderStyle property options have been expanded. By just choosing the Fixed Dialog setting (3), the Maximize or Minimize buttons are turned off, the window is not resizable, and yet you can still include a Control-menu box and title bar.

For toolbox-style windows, there are two more settings for the BorderStyle property: Fixed ToolWindow (4) and Sizable ToolWindow (5). In both settings, the Maximize and Minimize buttons are not displayed and the title bar caption is shown in a smaller font size. Quite importantly, while it is a form and technically a window, it does *not* appear in the Windows 95 task bar.

Align at a Time

The Align property settings have also been expanded to allow for dockable toolbars. The new settings of Left (3) and Right (4) have been added to the current values of None (0), Top (1), and Bottom (2) to specify to which border of the form the toolbar will "adhere."

All Locked Up

The new Locked property allows a text box to display text while prohibiting the user from editing the text. However, *The Guidelines* stipulate that read-only fields or textboxes should be drawn with the "button-down border style." This is accomplished by setting the BackColor property to light gray and the Appearance property to 3D. If and when you allow the text box to be edited, change the Locked property to False and the BackColor property back to white.

Please note that, even with the Locked property set to True, it is still possible to select the read-only text so that it can be copied to the clipboard. If it is absolutely necessary to prevent the selecting and copying of read-only text (for security reasons, for example) then replace the text box with a Label control of the same size. Set the Appearance and BorderStyle properties to 3D and Fixed Single, respectively. Then copy whatever text is in the text box and place it in the caption of the Label control. The result will be a 3D inset box with a gray background and black text that cannot be selected *or* edited.

Of Mice and Pointers

The mouse pointer is one of the most underused resources in the Windows environment. A source of immediate feedback to the user because the eye is usually focused on it, it typically stays a boring, uninformative northwest arrow. Visual Basic 4 has added three new settings and images:

Arrow		Usage
Arrow and hourglass (13)		Used over any screen location; indicates processing in the background or loading an application, but the pointer is still interactive
Arrow and question mark (14)		Used over most objects; indicates mode contextual help or What's This
Size all (15)		Indicates move mode (should really be called *move*)

A fourth setting (99) gives the developer the opportunity to specify a custom mouse pointer (either a .CUR or .ICO file) in the MouseIcon property.

Fontology 101

In previous versions of Visual Basic, all seven properties that affect the appearance of a font have appeared individually in the Properties Window. Now they have been rolled into one summary Font property, reducing the number of properties in the window. At design time, their individual attributes can be set via the Font common dialog whose Sample pane allows different settings to be tried out before committing them to the control. Of course, font settings can still be changed at run time via code, although the syntax has changed slightly due to the addition of the font object (ObjectName.FontObject.Property). Thus fontbold=true becomes font.bold=true.

The Only Word in English That Starts with mn...

A new property, UseMnemonic has been added to the Label control to allow single ampersands to be interpreted as such rather than as an access key. Setting UseMnemonic to False, it is possible to bind a label control to a field in a recordset where the data includes ampersands. If this property is set to True, the ampersand in the label control is interpreted by Visual Basic to be an access key, it is not displayed, and the letter following it appears underscored. Clicking Alt+ the letter brings focus to the label.

Windows 95 Custom Controls

As mentioned earlier, before the release of Windows 95, Microsoft was continually releasing updates to its Office suite and programmers began to include some of these ideas in their applications. Accomplishing this with native Visual Basic 3 controls was non-trivial and a host of third-party VBXs sprung up. Even then, some design elements were, at best, difficult or tedious to implement.

Most of that has changed with Visual Basic 4. The Professional Edition includes extensions specifically designed to enable you to design applications with the Windows 95 appearance and behavior. These controls will only run on 32-bit systems such as Windows 95 and Windows NT version 3.51 or higher. They are found in COMCTL32.OCX, which is added to the tool box by clicking the right mouse button on the tool box and selecting Custom Controls from the context menu, then selecting Microsoft Windows Common Controls from the Custom Controls list.

StatusBar Control

The StatusBar is used primarily as a mechanism of feedback to the user, although in some applications, it has interactive properties. The leftmost portion of the StatusBar typically displays help messages that change dynamically (`MouseMove` event) as the mouse pointer is moved across the screen.

Since there is considerably more space available in the StatusBar than in a ToolTip, the StatusBar help text can be more verbose. StatusBar messages should be written for toolbar controls as well as menus. They should begin with a verb in the present tense (e.g., "Opens an existing document or template") and should include help for *unavailable* controls and menu items as well. Frequently overlooked by developers, help for unavailable objects should explain *why* the particular control or menu item is unavailable. The user should also have the option to hide or display the StatusBar by choosing the appropriate menu item from the View menu.

Creating a StatusBar in Visual Basic 4 is an easy task. Start by drawing the StatusBar control on a form, setting the `Align` property to `Align Bottom (2)`, and adjusting the height (330 twips seems to work just fine). Then, in the Properties Window, select Custom. The ellipsis indicates that a dialog will follow; clicking it opens the StatusBar Control Properties sheet. You can also click the right mouse button on the StatusBar control. That will display its context menu. Selecting the last item, Properties, will bring up the same dialog.

> **Note**
>
> This style of properties sheet will become familiar to you as you work with the Windows 95 custom controls. The first tab on each sheet is titled General. The remaining tabs change as the controls and properties change, but they will usually contain the majority of the user interface-related properties.

Also note that, in the case of the StatusBar Properties sheet, the PanelProperties property in the Properties Windows will open a subset of the (Custom) property sheet containing one tab titled Panel Properties.

On the Panel Properties page are the controls that enable you to insert and remove panels from the StatusBar as well as vary the individual properties of *each* panel. The Style property allows you to set the text that will be displayed in a panel or choose from seven established styles (CAPS, NUM LOCK, INS, SCROLL, Time, Date, and KANA LOCK). No coding is necessary!

Of particular interest is the AutoSize Property for the Panel Object. This is an important property if you have a resizable form. If you want panel objects on a StatusBar to maintain defined widths regardless of the width of the parent form, the default setting of sbrNoAutoSize should be used. However, if you want any panel objects to resize with the form, you have two setting options. The first, sbrSpring, will cause the panels to adjust their width to occupy additional space as it becomes available, yet the panels will never become narrower than the individual MinWidth setting of each one. The second setting option is sbrContents. Simply stated, the panels resize to fit their contents. If there are any conflicts in dimensions as the panels resize, the panel objects with the Content style take precedence over those with the Spring style. Although the behavior is predictable, the width of the form (and the results) may not be, so test this carefully to avoid "dumb-looking" screens.

ImageList Control

The ImageList control is similar to the Data Control in that they both supply other controls with collections of images and data records, respectively. Neither control stands on its own and both are intended to be convenient and resource conserving. Like the Timer control, neither has a visual component and all three are invisible at run time. The ImageList is included in this discussion because several important visual controls rely on it as the source of their graphic images.

The ImageList is a collection of ListImage objects. Similar to an array, each `ListImage` object in an ImageList control can be referenced by an index. However, since the index can change with the addition and removal of objects from the collection, it makes more sense to use the new `Key` property that, instead of being another integer, is a string and does not change while the program runs unless the change is explicitly made in code. Therefore, referencing the image by its key yields predictable and consistent results. There are four controls that use the ImageList control as the source of their graphic images: TabStrip, Toolbar, TreeView, and ListViewThese will be discussed in turn.

Toolbar Control

The toolbar provides easy access to the most commonly used commands found in the menus, and, in the last few years, has become one of the features that users expect in Windows products. Selecting the (`Custom`) property, opening the Toolbar Control Properties sheet, and clicking the Buttons tab brings you to a dialog that permits you to insert and remove buttons, select the style of each button, set the `Caption`, `ToolTipsText` and `Description`, set the `Visible`, `Enabled`, `MixedState`[1], and `Value` properties.

At first glance, the VB4 toolbar control appears to be limited to buttons, therefore making it difficult to add controls such as drop-down combo boxes and list boxes. Although the toolbar can contain only button objects, the versatility of the button object allows virtually any kind of control to be placed on a toolbar. The key to this flexibility is the `Style` property of the button object. Each style sets specific appearance and behavior attributes for each button object. (Some of this functionality was contained in VB3's 3D Group Push Button control.)

The button object style can be set to any of six values, each style carrying specific appearance and behavior attributes. Table 13.1 summarizes the `Style` property settings in the new version.

[1] *The mixed state is a visual cue that indicates that the selected objects do not share the same value of a particular property. For example, selecting text that is comprised of both italic and non-italic characters, the MixedState property is used. The resulting image in the Toolbar should be displayed as dimmed, but not disabled.*

Table 13.1 Style **Property Settings**

Style **Property** Setting	Description	VB3 Equivalent
tbrDefault	Behaves like normal command or pushbutton	command button
tbrCheck	Toggle; behaves like checkbox control (Bold button in Windows 95 WordPad)	3D Group Push Button in its own group with GroupAllUp = true
tbrButtonGroup	One and only one button in the group must always be pressed (Paragraph alignment buttons in Windows 95 WordPad)	3D Group Push Button with GroupAllowAllUp= false
tbrCheckGroup	One or none of the buttons in the group may be pressed	3D Group Push Button with GroupAllowAllUp = true
tbrSeparator	Fixed width separator (8 pixels)	none
tbrPlaceholder	Variable width separator	none

The last style, tbrPlaceholder, allocates space so that you can place controls such as list boxes and combo boxes on the toolbar. The undocumented trick here is to remember to set the ZOrder of the control being added to zero (0), otherwise it will be hidden by the toolbar. Although the toolbar can be configured to float and dock at any of the four borders of the window, moving an added control (ComboBox box, list box, etc.) along with the toolbar is a non-trivial coding issue. There will be third-party tools that will make this task easy by the time you are reading this chapter.

And regardless of the style of any individual button, the ImageList property allows you to associate a specific group of button images with the toolbar.

From the perspective of the user interface, there are several other properties that should be pointed out. The first one is the AllowCustomize Property. As its name suggests, it prevents or allows the user to customize the toolbar. The surprise is that there is a precoded customization dialog embedded within the control. With the AllowCustomize Property set to True, all the user has to do is double-click on the toolbar and the Customize Toolbar dialog is invoked.

There the user can add, remove, and reorganize the toolbar. This property also enables customization of the toolbar by holding down Shift while dragging the buttons to new positions or even off the toolbar. It's all built in: no code, folks!

Two other properties of the toolbar that are important to the user interface design are ShowToolTips and Wrappable. When ShowToolTips is set to True (default), the text that is specified in the ToolTipText property is displayed in a small rectangular pop-up adjacent to the toolbar. When Wrappable is set to True, the toolbar will wrap its buttons and other controls as the shrinking width of the parent window starts to "crowd" the controls when resizing.

ListView Control

New to Windows 95 is the ability to view files and folders in four different ways: Icon, Small Icon, List, and Report (called Detail View in the Windows 95 Explorer). Each of these views corresponds to the four views found in the Windows 95 Explorer and My Computer. At first glance, it appears that the only difference between the views is the size of the icon and the position of the label. However, on closer look, several more differentiations become evident.

In both Icon and Small Icon views, when the Arrange property is set to None, the objects in the list can be dragged to any location in the view. When the Arrange property is set to AutoArrange, the items line up in rows starting at the top left corner of the area, and filling left to right, top to bottom.

In List and Report views (see figs. 13.1A and 1B), the AutoArrange setting for the Arrange property is unavailable. That is because, by definition, these two views arrange the objects in them in columns. In List view, the columns consist of an icon and a label, and the column "snakes" from top to bottom, left to right, just like newspaper columns. The Report view, on the other hand, shows detail in a multi-column arrangement. There is no "snaking" or wrapping of the columns; if the list is too long for the display area, scrollbars appear. Column headers may be optionally displayed.

The icons, both small and large, are contained in two separate ImageList controls, which are specified on the Images page of the (Custom) Properties sheet.

In addition to the user interface properties just mentioned, the ListView Control also has several properties that address issues of how the user can interact

with the application. `ListFindItemWhere` and `ListFindItemHow` both deal
with searches and how matches are made and are beyond the scope of this
chapter.

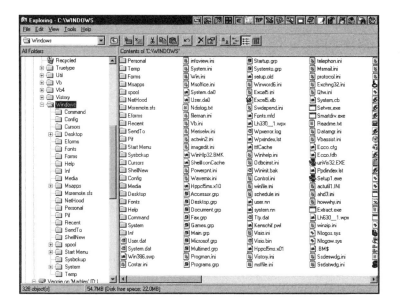

Fig. 13.1A
The ListView
control in
ListView, and the
ListView control in
Detail view with
column headers
enabled.

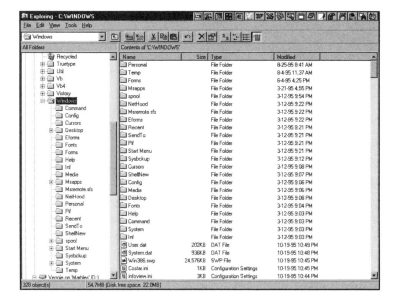

Fig. 13.1B

TreeView Control

The TreeView control, another of the Windows 95 specific controls, allows you to create an indented hierarchical display of objects, expanding and collapsing the outline to reveal greater and lesser amounts of detail. As a developer, you have considerable control over the appearance of the TreeView control. Combinations of text, bitmaps (using the ImageList control), lines, and plus and minus signs are determined by the Style property. To make sure that all the images for the nodes are the same size, each TreeView control can reference only one ImageList at a time. Although it is a highly graphical component of the user interface, the TreeView control robustly supports keyboard control.

Typical uses for the TreeView (see fig. 13.2) are files and directories in a file system, tables of contents, files in a (paper) filing system, etc.

Fig. 13.2

The typical tree view.

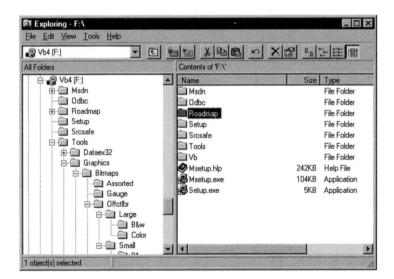

TabStrip Control

Before the advent of the tab metaphor, multiple dialogs (tedious) or multiple child windows (confusing) had to be used to accomplish the many and diverse tasks in some programs. The introduction of the tab metaphor enabled dialogs to have multiple "pages" and allowed switching between "pages" that occupy the same area window without having to trouble with maximizing and minimizing, nor use the Windows menu commands. An immediately obvious navigational tool, it has all but eliminated the multiple dialogs needed to change font settings, user options, formatting, properties, and a myriad of other settings.

The Visual Basic 3 third-party tab controls were containers, and it is important to note that the Visual Basic 4 TabStrip is *not*. Instead, it is a mechanism to switch *between* containers. The controls that are brought in and out of the user's view in the TabStrip's client area must be contained within a picture box or other container control whose width and height are equal to the ClientWidth and ClientHeight and whose placement equals the ClientLeft and ClientTop properties of the TabStrip. From there, you use the SelectedItem property of the TabStrip to determine which tab has been clicked. That known, the appropriate container's visible or position properties can be set or it can be brought to the top by using the Zorder method. A control array for the containers helps tremendously, because each member of the array can be associated with a specific Tab [object].

As a default, the width of the control and the number of tabs determines the number of rows. This default setting then allows the number of rows to increase or decrease if the TabStrip is resized. However, this can be controlled by the TabWidthStyle property. Working in conjunction with other properties, the TabWidthStyle property determines the width of the individual tabs and how the tabs are spaced along the control's width. Set to Fixed, the width and height of each tab are determined by the TabFixedWidth and TabFixedHeight properties, respectively. Set to Justified (see fig. 13.4), each tab accommodates its caption and then pads with spaces so that all the tabs have the same width and extend along the full width of the control. (This property is ignored if the MultiRow property is set to False or if there is only a single row of tabs.) And lastly, a setting of NonJustified (see fig. 13.3) results in each tab being wide enough to accommodate only its caption. This results in tabs of different widths, possibly not extending the entire width of the TabStrip control. This design style is best seen in the Property sheets in Windows 95.

A nice visual variation within the TabStrip control is afforded by the Style property, which has two settings: Tabs and Buttons. This switches the appearance of the TabStrip control from tabs to toggle buttons. Note that with the Buttons style, *only* one, but *always* one button must be in the "pressed" state at all times.

Fig. 13.3
TABOPT-1
(from Microsoft
Windows 95)
Tabstrip with
MultiRow=False.

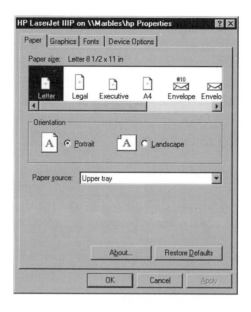

Fig. 13.4
STAT_BAR
(from Microsoft
Word 7.0):
Tabstrip with
MultiRow=True,
TabFixedWidth=
Justified

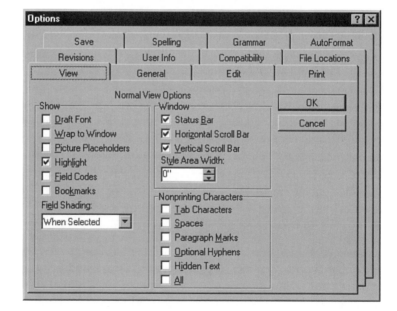

Possible Sidebar for TabStrip Control or GUI Tip

A word here about user interface design with the tab metaphor. On discovering the ability of tabs to pack lots of information into multiple tab sheets, there is a great tendency to overpopulate a screen or dialog with many tabs, arranging them in multiple rows. With two rows of tabs, when the user clicks on the upper row, that row of tabs becomes the lower row, the lower row becomes the upper row, and the user must readjust mentally. It becomes worse with three rows of tabs. There the middle row becomes the bottom row, the top becomes the middle, and the lower becomes the top.

The problem is that the user cannot develop what is known in human factors circles as *motor memory:* the ability to place the hand (or mouse) in a precise location with no visual cue as to the coordinates of that location. We've all had the experience of performing an action in a dialog and, knowing that a confirmation dialog is going to open, placing the mouse pointer on the precise spot where the OK button will appear. Then we click the button before it has even been painted to the screen! This scenario demonstrates the principle of *motor memory*. Think of what it would be like if a dialog that we use frequently appeared at a different place each time—we would not be able to use motor memory to accelerate the pace of our tasks.

What does this have to do with tabs? By configuring multiple rows of tabs, (for instance, three rows), when you select a tab on the top row, the rows shift and all the positions of the tabs change! There's no chance for motor memory to help you.

One solution is to design in such a way that multiple rows of tabs will not be necessary. Previous versions of third-party tab controls have implemented a dog-eared appearance on the right-most or left-most tab to indicate that there are more tabs but that they are not visible. Essentially, they have served as scrollbars. The TabStrip control's implementation of this is to display a horizontal spin control at the upper right corner of the single row of tabs. Inconsistent with Windows 95 conventions, neither arrow of the spin button becomes unavailable when the series of tabs is at either limit, nor do the buttons cause the tabs to wrap[2]. This being said, be cautious when you set the TabStrip's `MultiRow` property to `True`.

Slider Control

With the advent of multimedia, sound cards, and the tremendous variety of system setting and adjustments that a user can make, a new control was necessary that would not only permit the change of settings, but also would indicate the current value and its relationship to the maximum and minimum values. Enter the Slider control.

Included in the Visual Basic 4.0 Professional Edition Windows Common Controls, the Slider (see fig. 13.5) is a graphical tool that can be used to enter data or values. It can be configured to work horizontally or vertically, so keep this in mind when you use it in your program. Unless screen real estate is so critical that it cannot be avoided, try to map the layout of the control so that it fits the mental model of the user. In the following example (from Windows 95's Volume Control), note that a vertical slider is used to control volume, which we think of as being higher or lower, while a horizontal slider is used to control balance, which we perceive as being left or right of center.

Fig. 13.5
The slider is a graphical tool that you can use to enter data or values.

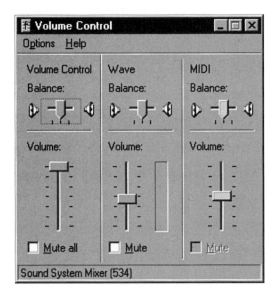

When possible, try to add a Label control whose caption changes as the value of the slider changes. This is an excellent way to give feedback to the user. Following are two examples from the Windows 95 Display Properties Settings sheet (see figs. 13.6 and 13.7). Note the Desktop area group frame and the way the resolution setting is displayed by a label and is changed as the resolution is changed by the position of the horizontal slider.

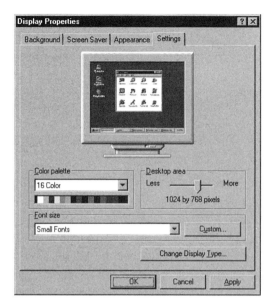

Fig. 13.6
An example from
the Display
Properties sheet.

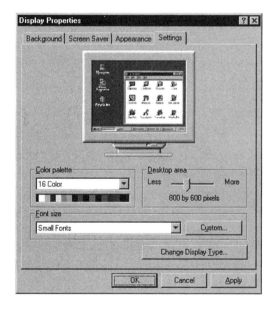

Fig. 13.7
An example from
the Display
Properties sheet.

RichTextBox Control

The RichTextBox control is a text box that went to college. Whereas its undergraduate cousin can handle only simple text editing, the RichTextBox control allows for formatting of style (bold or italic), color, margins and indents, and special effects (super- and subscripts) of any selected text, even down to character-by-character formatting.

The RichTextBox control also supports searching, printing, file opening and saving, dragging and dropping of external text or files into the control, and is not constrained by the same 64K character limit of the text box.

ProgressBar Control

The ProgressBar control (see fig. 13.8) is like the Gauge control in that they are both used to graphically represent the size of a portion in relation to the whole. But whereas the Gauge control can display a variety of bitmaps in a variety of configurations and appearances, the progress bar is specialized to represent the percentage of completion of a process and displays only as a portion of a horizontal bar. The progress bar displays as a series of chunks rather than a smooth expansion of a solid bar. While these chunks are less accurate than the Gauge control, they are sufficient to give the user an indication of progress of a process and the relative amount remaining. Visual Basic 4 Help recommends that "for a chunk size that best shows incremental progress, make a progress bar control at least 12 times wider than its height."

Fig. 13.8
An example of progress bars (from the Windows 95 Resource Meter).

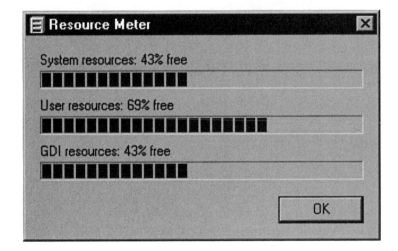

Summary

Accomplished writers distinguish themselves from novice writers by the way they string words together. Mastery of grammar and a good vocabulary are not sufficient in and of themselves. So it is with user interface design. Good software design is marked by the choice of controls, the way they are organized, and the flow of the screens.

This chapter has merely listed some of the elements of Windows 95 user interfaces as they can be implemented in Visual Basic 4. No attempt has been made to actually "string them together" to form an actual user interface. Read *The Guidelines,* look at every example you can find, experiment, and stay open to feedback. You may have a bestseller!

Following is a list of resources that you may find helpful.

User Interface Design and Usability Selected Bibliography and Online Resources List

Compiled by Ken Schiff, Productivity Through Technology, Inc. Updated: 10-95

Microsoft Corporation. *The Windows Interface Guidelines for Software Design.* Microsoft Press: Redmond, WA, 1995. The "official" Microsoft guidelines for creating well-designed, visually and functionally consistent Windows interfaces. With emphasis on Windows 95 (and soon to be Windows NT), the book is illustrated in full color, is full of illustrative screen shots, and is complemented by five appendixes including international word lists for Windows terminology.

Tognazzini, B. *Tog on Interface.* Addison-Wesley: Reading MA. 1992. A classic! Tognazzini's book is based on a series of columns, papers, and correspondence during the development of System 7 for the Macintosh. These essays point out the complexity of GUI design. Tog offers his own set of guidelines on topics ranging from user testing to menu design. Though focused on the Macintosh, many of the guidelines would apply to any GUI platform.

Norman, D. *The Design of Everyday Things.* Doubleday: New York, 1990. *The Design of Everyday Things* provides hundreds of examples of good and bad product design. This book is especially good as a catalyst for getting people to think about design. There is a paperback version of this book in many good bookstores. Other books by Norman that are worthwhile are *Things That Make Us Smart*, and *Turn Signals Are the Facial Expressions of Automobiles.*

Horton, W. *The Icon Book: Visual Symbols for Computer Systems and Documentation*. Wiley: New York, NY, 1994. Everything you ever wanted to know about icon design. *The Icon Book* describes the process for designing icons, provides guidelines for icon design, and gives advice on how to design for international audiences. There is one version of the book that includes a disk with a set of 500 public domain icons. Small companies that can't afford graphic designers might find this set of icons useful.

Horton, W. *Illustrating Computer Documentation: The Art of Presenting Information Graphically on Paper and Online*. Wiley: New York, 1992. Horton presents detailed guidelines on the appropriate use of graphics for computer documentation.

Tufte, E. R. *The Visual Display of Quantitative Information*. Graphics Press: Cheshire, CT, 1983. This is a classic book on the minimalist approach to presenting quantitative information. Tufte provides a language for discussing statistical graphics and suggests many techniques for refining graphics and making them more usable.

Tufte, E. R. *Envisioning Information*. Graphics Press: Cheshire, CT, 1990. *Envisioning Information* is a guide to presenting multi-dimensional data in two dimensions.

Nielsen, J. *Usability Engineering*. Academic Press: Boston, MA, 1993 Nielsen's *Usability Engineering* is highly recommended. The book describes the process by which development groups can create usable applications. The book details how usability issues must be considered throughout the development process and provides techniques for gathering usability data. There is excellent information on low-cost usability testing techniques.

Rubin, J. *Handbook of Usability Testing: How to Plan, Design, and Conduct Effective Tests*. Wiley: New York, 1994. This handbook is a step-by-step guide to effective usability testing. Rubin provides many tips that will benefit both the new and the experienced usability practitioner. The book was written with the assumption that readers won't have human factors training.

Dumas, J. and Redish, J. *A Practical Guide to Usability Testing*. Ablex, Norwood: NJ, 1993. This book provides excellent practical advice for groups that want to initiate usability testing.

Professional Societies

Special Interest Group on Computer and Human Interaction (SIGCHI); Association for Computing Machinery (Member Services)

1515 Broadway
New York, NY 10036
EMAIL: ACMHELP@ACM.org

Human Factors and Ergonomics Society (HFES)
P.O. Box 1369
Santa Monica, CA 90406
(310) 394-1811

Society for Technical Communication (STC)
901 North Stuart Street, Suite 304
Arlington, VA 22203
(703)-522-4114

Usability Professionals' Association (UPA)
10875 Plano Road
Suite 115
Dallas, TX 75238
(214) 349-8841

Association for Software Design
2120 Bonar Street
Berkeley, CA 94702
(800) 743-9415

User Interface Design and Usability Resources Online

Compuserve

Visual Basic Programmer's Journal; User Interface Studio: GO VBPJ

Mailing lists

Usability Testing List: utest@hubcap. clemson.edu   Frequented by usability testing folks, this lively list's topics span UI design, documentation, human factors issues, and others. To join, send an email to listproc@hubcap.clemson.edu with the body of the message subscribe utest YourFirstName YourLastName. The subject can be anything (or blank).

Project on People, Computers, and Design at Stanford   The PCD project currently maintains two lists for distributing notices and one list for open discussion:

pcd-seminar: This list is used for the distribution of abstracts and announcements for the Seminar on Human Computer Interaction held at Stanford (CS547).

pcd-fyi: This list is used for the distribution of information and announcements that may be of general interest to the PCD community including talk and conference announcements. It does not include pcd-seminar announcements. It is not for direct posting, but if you have something you think would be of interest, send it to pcd-person@pcd.stanford.edu.

pcd-discuss: This is an unmoderated discussion list for those interested in discussing issues about people, computers, and design.

For information on how to subscribe or unsubscribe to one of these lists, send lists@pcd.stanford.edu a message with the body (not the subject header) containing: help. For more information about the particular list, send lists@pcd.stanford.edu a message with the body (not the subject header) containing info <listname> (e.g., info pcd-fyi).

For general information on the Project on People, Computers, and Design, send lists@pcd.stanford.edu a message with the body (not the subject header) containing the line info pcd or send human-readable email to pcd-person@pcd.stanford.edu.

For information about the seminar schedule or the Human-Computer Interface program at Stanford on the World Wide Web:

Seminar : <http://www-pcd.stanford.edu/seminar.html>

HCI: <http://www-pcd.stanford.edu/hci.html>

Association for Software Design

Again, there are several lists. Send a message with the body (not the subject header) containing the line:

asd-person @pcd.stanford.edu: a person who responds
asd-members@pcd.stanford.edu: all the members
asd-discuss@pcd.stanford.edu: the discussion list

Newsgroup

comp.human-factors Participants include practitioners as well as academicians; generally interesting, although some threads linger on long after they should have died (IMHO).

Chapter 14

Put Your Code into Overdrive

by Drew Fletcher, Joe Robison,
and Scott Swanson

Drew Fletcher works for Microsoft as a program manager on the Visual Basic team. He has been on the Visual Basic team since version 1.0. Before coming to Microsoft, Drew worked for Boeing Computer Services, several startup companies, and as a freelance classical musician.

Joe Robison. In nearly eight years at Microsoft, Joe has worked on a variety of Microsoft products, including Basic 7.0, PDS, and Microsoft Access. In 1990 he joined a project that eventually became Visual Basic 1.0, and he has worked on every subsequent version. He is currently a program manager working on future products in the Visual Basic group. He can be reached on the Internet at joero@microsoft.com.

Scott Swanson is a product manager working on Visual Basic. He has been writing Visual Basic code since version 1.0. Before that he spent eight years as a systems engineer and instructor designing, installing, and supporting local area networks and client/server environments. Basic Programmer's Guide to the Windows API, How Computer Programming Works, *and the forthcoming* Visual Basic Programmer's Guide to the Win32 API *from Ziff-Davis Press.*

Programmers always want to improve the performance or efficiency of every aspect of their application. Wanting the highest performance out of code is no exception. Fortunately, there are several ways available.

Optimization Philosophy

Optimization is not a single set of tricks or techniques. It's not a simple process you can tack on at the end of your development cycle: "There, it works.

Now I'll speed it up and make it smaller." To create a truly optimized application you must be optimizing it all the time while it is being developed. You choose your algorithms carefully, weighing speed against size and other constraints; you form hypotheses about what parts of your application will be fast or slow, large or compact, and you test those hypotheses as you go.

And you remember that optimization is not always completely beneficial. Sometimes the changes you make to speed up or trim down your application result in code that is hard to maintain or debug. And some optimization techniques fly in the face of structured coding practice, which may cause problems when you try to expand it in the future or incorporate it into other programs (not to mention aggravating fellow programmers if you're working as part of a team).

You can waste a lot of time optimizing the wrong things. This is particularly true in Visual Basic because so much goes on "behind the scenes" and there isn't a true profiler available that would enable you to immediately find the proverbial 10 percent of your code that takes 90 percent of the time or uses 90 percent of the space. (VB4 Professional and Enterprise Editions now come with a profiler that you can use to find that slow code.)

Nevertheless, you can learn an awful lot by stepping through your code and thinking carefully about what's actually happening. It sounds obvious, but I've discovered things in my own code that "seemed like a good idea" when I coded them, but turned out to be amazing memory or CPU hogs in practice. You often forget that setting properties causes events to occur, and if there is a lot of code in those event procedures, an innocuous line of code can cause a tremendous delay in your program.

It's important to throw away your assumptions, especially if you got those assumptions by playing with older versions of Visual Basic. VB4 contains a different language engine than earlier versions, and the techniques for optimizing code may differ.

It's sometimes useful to think of having an "optimization budget." Know where to start. You don't have time to optimize everything, so where do you spend your time to get a maximum return on your investment? Obviously, you want to focus on the areas that seem to be the slowest or fastest. But to maximize the results of your efforts, you want to concentrate on code where a little work will make a lot of difference.

The bodies of loops are a good place to start. Whenever you speed up the operations inside a loop, that improvement is multiplied by the number of times the loop is executed. For loops with a large number of iterations, just one less string operation in the body can make a big difference.

Also, find the place where you can make the most difference. Use a profiling tool to find where your application is really spending its time. (The Enterprise and Pro versions of Visual Basic 4 come with a profiling tool to help in that process, but we won't cover in this chapter how to use that.)

Sometimes things aren't worth optimizing, so you have to know where to stop, too. For example, writing an elaborate but fast sorting routine is pointless if you're only sorting a dozen items. In fact, I've seen programs that sort things by adding them to a sorted list box and then reading them back out in order. In absolute terms this is horribly inefficient, but if there aren't a lot of items it is just as quick as any other method, and the code is admirably simple (if a bit obscure).

There are other cases where optimization is wasted effort. If your application is ultimately bound by the speed of your disk or network, there is little you can do in your code to speed things up. Instead, you need to think about ways to make these delays less problematic for your users. For example, progress bars to tell them your code isn't simply hung, or caching data so they see the delays less often, or yielding so that they can use other programs while they wait, and so on. Remember, to your user, apparent speed is the most important. We've done user tests where an app that actually loads slower, but has some feedback (like a splash screen on startup) is perceived to be faster than one without any feedback.

Tradeoffs

You can optimize your program for many different characteristics:

- Real speed (how fast your application actually calculates or performs other operations)

- Display speed (how fast your application paints the screen)

- Apparent speed (how fast your application appears to run; this is often related to display speed but not always to real speed)

- Size in memory

- Size of graphics (this directly affects size in memory, but often has additional ramifications when working in Microsoft Windows)

- OLE Operations (or communication between EXEs and DLLs using OLE)

Rarely, however, can you optimize for *multiple* characteristics. Typically, an approach that optimizes size compromises on speed; likewise, an application optimized for speed is often larger than its slower cousin. For this reason recommended techniques in one area may directly contradict suggestions in another.

It's also important to remember to step back and make sure you can see the forest. Sometimes it's just better to throw away an entire block of code and start over. One way to determine whether you should be in this "start over" stage is to ask yourself, "Am I really doing the right thing?" If you aren't, then try something different to get around speed problems. Get rid of your ego and don't feel defensive about code you've already written.

Although it isn't often considered, you may want to throw hardware at the problem. Remember, optimizing will help your program only in a few places, but moving from a 100 MHz Pentium to a 133 MHz Pentium will give you a 33 percent increase in speed in all places, not just in the two or three places you'll be able to rewrite. Also, think about repartitioning your application into separate OLE Servers (covered later).

Actual Speed

Unless you're doing things like generating fractals, your applications are unlikely to be limited by the actual processing speed of your code. Typically, other factors, such as video speed, network delays, or disk activities are the limiting factor in your applications. For example, when a form is slow to load, the cause is often the many controls or graphics on the form rather than slow code in the `Form_Load` event. However, you may find points in your program where the speed of your code is the gating factor. When that's the case, you can use the following techniques to increase the real speed of your applications:

- Avoid Variant variables (use Option Explicit and watch out for implicit type conversions)

- Use Integer variables and integer math

- Cache properties in variables

- Use `For...Each` rather than `For(index)...Next`

- Swap-tune your application. (Actually not important anymore in Visual Basic 4, because of internal changes. If you are using earlier versions of Visual Basic, you'll still want to perform swap tuning.)

- For file input/output use binary rather than text or random

- Avoid string copies

- Learn when to use collections versus Arrays

The default data type in Visual Basic is Variant. This is handy for beginning programmers and for applications where processing speed is not an issue. However, if you are trying to optimize the real speed of your application avoid Variant.

While most operations involving the Variant data type in Visual Basic 4 are faster than they were in Visual Basic 3.0, operations involving other simple data types are still faster than Variant equivalents. A good way to avoid Variants is to use Option Explicit (turn on the "Require Variable Declaration" option in the development environment), which forces you to declare all your variables. Be careful, however, and watch for implicit type conversions. For example, if you DIM X, Y, Z as Integer, Visual Basic will only see Z as an Integer and will convert X and Y to a variant.

For arithmetic operations avoid Currency, Single, and Double variables. Instead, use Byte, Integer, and Long integer variables whenever you can, particularly in loops. These are the Intel CPU's native data types, so operations on them are very fast.

It's surprising how much of your programs you can write, using only Integer variables. And you can often tweak things so that you can use integers when a floating point value would otherwise be required.

For example, if you always set the Scalemode of all your forms and Picture controls to either Twips or Pixels, you can use integers for all the size and position values for controls and graphics methods. In a similar vein, it's often possible to modify calculations so that they can be performed entirely with integers (don't forget the integer division operator: \). As an example, Microsoft QuickBasic included a sample program that generated the Mandelbrot set entirely using integer math. If you do need to do math with decimal values, use Double rather than Currency. Double is faster, particularly on machines that have math co-processors (most machines running Windows NT or Windows 95 probably have co-processors).

Variables are generally 10 to 20 times faster than properties of the same type. Never get the value of any given property more than once in a procedure unless you know the value has changed. Instead, assign the value of the property to a variable and use the variable in all subsequent code. For example, code like this is very slow:

```
For i = 0 To 10
    picIcon(i).Left = picPallete.Left
Next I
```

Rewritten, this code is much faster:

```
picLeft = picPallete.Left
For i = 0 To 10
     picIcon(i).Left = picLeft
Next I
```

Likewise, code like this:

```
Do Until EOF(F)
     Line Input #F, nextLine
     Text1.Text = Text1.Text + nextLine
Loop
```

is much slower than this:

```
Do Until EOF(F)
     Line Input #F, nextLine
          bufferVar = bufferVar + nextLine
     Loop
Text1.Text = bufferVar
```

However, this code does the equivalent job and is even faster:

```
Text1.Text = Input(F, LOF(F))
```

Yet another example of a better algorithm being the best optimization.

Collections of objects is a Visual Basic for Applications feature that is new in Visual Basic 4. Collections are very useful, but for the best performance you need to use them correctly. Here's some rules:

■ Use For...Each rather than For...Next.

■ Avoid using Before and After parameters when adding objects to a collection.

■ Use keyed collections rather than arrays for groups of objects of the same type.

Collections allow you to iterate through them by using an integer For...Next loop. However, the new For...Each syntax is more readable and in many cases will be faster. The For...Each iteration is implemented by the creator of the collection so the actual speed will vary from one collection object to the next. However, For...Each will generally never be slower than For...Next because the simplest implementation is a linear For...Next style iteration. In some cases developers may use a more sophisticated implementation than linear iteration so For...Each can be much faster.

It is quicker to Add objects to a collection if you don't use the Before and After parameters. These require Visual Basic to find another object in the collection before it can add the new object.

When you have a group of objects of the same type, you can choose to manage them in a collection or an array (if they are of differing types, a collection is your only choice). From a speed standpoint, which you should choose depends on how you plan to access the objects. If you can associate a unique key with each object, then a collection is the fastest choice. Using a key to retrieve an object from a collection is always faster than traversing an array sequentially. However, if you do not have keys and so will always have to traverse the objects, an array is the better choice. Arrays are faster to traverse sequentially than collections.

Display Speed

Because of the graphical nature of Microsoft Windows, the speed of graphics and other display operations contributes greatly to the *perception* of the speed of your application. In many cases, you can make your application seem faster simply by making your forms repaint faster—even if the actual speed of your application hasn't changed at all (or even gotten slower). There are several techniques you can use to speed up the apparent speed of your application:

- Turn off ClipControls

- Use AutoRedraw appropriately

- Use Image instead of Picture box

- Use Line instead of PSet

- Hide controls when setting properties to avoid multiple repaints

- Use 'PaintPicture' to BitBlt Pictures

Unless you are using graphics methods (Line, PSet, Circle, and Print) you should set ClipControls to False for the form and for all Frame and Picture box controls. When ClipControls is False, Visual Basic does not do the extra work required to avoid overpainting controls with the background before repainting the controls themselves. On forms that contain a lot of controls, the resulting speed improvements are significant.

The right setting for the AutoRedraw property varies, depending on what is being displayed. If you can quickly redraw the contents of the form or picture control, using graphics methods, you should set AutoRedraw to False and perform the graphics in the `Paint` event. If you have a complicated display that doesn't change very often, you should set AutoRedraw to True and allow Visual Basic to do the redrawing for you. Note, however, that when AutoRedraw is True Visual Basic maintains a bitmap it uses to redraw the picture, and this bitmap can take up a considerable amount of memory. Also, anything in Visual Basic that writes to an HDC will need AutoRedraw turned on.

Image controls always paint faster than Picture controls. Unless you need some of the capabilities unique to Picture controls (such as DDE and graphics methods), you should use Image controls exclusively.

Speaking of graphics methods, a little experimentation will demonstrate that the Line method is much faster than a series of PSet methods. Avoid using the PSet method, and batch up the points into a single Line method.

Every repaint is expensive. The fewer repaints Visual Basic must perform, the faster your application will appear. One way to reduce the number of repaints is to make controls invisible while you are manipulating them. For example, suppose you want to resize several List boxes in the Resize event for the form:

```
Sub Form_Resize ()
Dim i As Integer, sHeight As Integer
    sHeight = ScaleHeight / 4
    For i = 0 To 3
        lstDisplay(i).Move 0, i * sHeight, _
            ScaleWidth, sHeight
    Next
End Sub
```

This creates four separate repaints, one for each list box. You can reduce the number of repaints by placing all the List boxes within a picture box, and hiding the picture box before you move and size the list boxes. Then, when you make the picture box visible again, all of the list boxes are painted in a single pass:

```
Sub Form_Resize ()
Dim i As Integer, sHeight As Integer
    picContainer.Visible = False
    picContainer.Move 0, 0, _
        ScaleWidth, ScaleHeight
    sHeight = ScaleHeight / 4
    For i = 0 To 3
        lstDisplay(i).Move 0, i * sHeight, _
            ScaleWidth, sHeight
    Next
    picContainer.Visible = True
End Sub
```

Apparent Speed

Often the subjective speed of your application has little to do with how quickly it actually gets through the meat of its task. To the user, an application that starts up rapidly, repaints quickly, and provides continuous feedback feels "snappier" than an application that just "hangs up" while it churns through its work. You can use the following techniques to give your application that "snap":

- Keep forms hidden but loaded
- Pre-load data you expect to need
- Use timers to work in the background
- Use progress indicators
- Use OLE Callbacks (from Cross-Process Servers. This is covered later in this chapter)

Hiding forms instead of unloading them is a trick that has been around since the early days of Visual Basic 1, but it is still effective. The obvious downside to this technique is the amount of memory the loaded forms consume, but it can't be beat if you can afford the memory cost and making forms appear quickly is of the highest importance.

You can also improve the apparent speed of your application by pre-fetching data. For example, if you need to go to disk to load the first of several files, why not load as many of them as you can? Unless the files are extremely small, the user is going to see a delay anyway. The incremental time spent loading the additional files will probably go unnoticed, and you won't have to delay the user again.

In some applications you can do considerable work while you are waiting for the user. The best way to accomplish this is through a timer control. Use static (or module-level) variables to keep track of your progress, and do a very small piece of work each time the timer goes off. If you keep the amount of work done in each timer event very small, users won't see any effect on the responsiveness of the application and you can pre-fetch data or do other things that further speed up your application.

When you can't avoid a long delay in your program, you need to give the user some indication that your application hasn't simply hung up. Windows 95 uses a standard progress bar to provide this indication to users. You can add this to your applications by using the Progress Bar control in the Microsoft Windows Common Controls included with 32-bit Visual Basic 4. Use DoEvents at strategic points, particularly each time you update the value of the Progress Bar, to allow your application to repaint while the user is doing other things.

First Impressions

Apparent speed is most important when your application starts. Users' first impression of the speed of an application is measured by how quickly they see something after clicking on its name in the Start menu. With the various runtime DLLs that need to be loaded for VBA, OLE controls, and OLE, some delay is unavoidable with any application. However, there are some things you can do to give a response to the user as quickly as possible:

- Use Show in `Form_Load` event

- Use DoEvents after 'Show' in `Form_Load`

- Simplify your Startup form

- Don't load modules you don't need

- Run a small Visual Basic application at startup to preload the runtime DLLs

- Use a Splash Screen

When a form is first loaded, all of the code in the `Form_Load` event occurs before the form is displayed. You can alter this behavior by using the Show method in the `Form_Load` code, giving the user something to look at while the rest of the code in the event executes. Follow the `Show` method with `DoEvents` to ensure that the form gets painted.

```
Sub Form_Load()
    Show
    ' Display startup form.
    DoEvents
    ' Ensure startup form is painted.
    Load MainForm
    ' Load main application form.
    Unload Me
    ' Unload startup form.
    MainForm.Show
    ' Display main form.
End Sub
```

The more complicated a form is, the longer it takes to load. From this observation comes a rule: keep your startup form simple. Most applications for Microsoft Windows display a simple copyright screen at startup: your application can do the same. The fewer controls on the startup form, and the less code it contains, the quicker it will load and appear. Even if it immediately loads another, more complicated form, it gives the user immediate feedback that the application has started.

For large applications you may want to preload the most commonly used forms at startup so that they can be shown instantly when needed. A satisfying way to do this is to display a progress bar in your startup form and update it as you load each of the other forms. Call `DoEvents` after loading each form so that your startup form will repaint. Once all the important forms have been loaded the startup form can show the first one and unload itself. Of course, each form you preload will run the code in its `Form_Load` event, so take care that this doesn't cause problems or excessive delays.

Visual Basic loads code modules on demand, rather than all at once at startup. This means that if you never call a procedure in a module, that module will never be loaded. Conversely, if your startup form calls procedures in several modules then all of those modules will be loaded as your application starts up, which slows things down. For this reason, you should avoid calling procedures in other modules from your startup form.

A large part of the time required to start a Visual Basic 4 application is spent loading the various runtime DLLs for Visual Basic, OLE, and OLE controls. Of course, if these are already loaded none of that time needs to be spent. Thus, users will see your application start up faster if there is another application already running that uses some or all of these DLLs. A way to significantly improve the startup performance of your applications is to provide another small, useful application that the user always runs when starting up Windows.

For example, it is easy to write a small calendar application that uses a calendar OCX and place it in the startup group for Windows. It starts up minimized and is always available, and while it is useful in itself it also ensures that the various Visual Basic runtime DLLs are loaded. Note that Office 95 includes a FastStart application that performs a similar operation for the OLE DLLs. Keep in mind that the runtime DLLs are different between 16 and 32 bits, so an application that loads the 16-bit set will not help improve the startup time of a 32-bit application and vice versa.

Finally, you can divide your application into a main skeleton application and several OLE server executables or DLLs. A smaller main application will load faster, and it can then load the other parts as needed. I discuss this technique in detail later in this chapter.

Keeping It Small

You can reduce the size of your application in memory by:

- Reclaiming space used by strings, arrays, and object variables

- Avoiding Variant variables

- Avoiding fixed-length String variables

- Using dynamic arrays, reclaiming memory by using the Erase statement

- Removing dead code

- Completely unloading forms (set form=nothing)

The space used by (non-Static) local string and array variables is reclaimed automatically when the procedure ends. However, global and module-level string and array variables remain in existence for as long as your program is running. If you are trying to keep your application as small as possible, you should reclaim the space used by these variables as soon as you can. You reclaim string space by assigning the zero-length string to it:

```
SomeStringVar = ""      ' Reclaim space
```

You reclaim the space used by a dynamic array with the Erase statement:

```
Erase LargeArray
```

The Erase statement completely eliminates an array; if you want to make an array smaller without losing all of its contents, you can use the ReDim Preserve statement:

```
ReDim Preserve LargeArray(10, smallernum)
```

Similarly, you can reclaim some (but not all) of the space used by an object variable by setting it to Nothing. For example:

```
Global F As New StatusForm
...
    F.Show 1
    ' Form is loaded and shown modally.
    X = F.Text1.Text
    ' User pressed a button that hides form
    Unload F
    ' Get rid of visual part of form
    Set F = Nothing
    ' Reclaim space (module data).
```

Even if you don't use explicit form variables, you should take care to Unload (rather than simply hide) forms you are no longer using.

Variant variables are another size hog: each Variant takes 16 bytes, compared to two for an Integer or eight for a Double. Variable-length String variables use four bytes plus one per character in the string, but each Variant containing a string takes 16 plus one per character in the string. Because they are so large, Variant variables are particularly troublesome when used as local variables or arguments to procedures, because they quickly consume stack space. Use variants whenever you don't know how large a number you'll get back. The variant can help you thus avoid overflow problems.

You'll rarely exhaust stack space in 32-bit Visual Basic, but in the 16-bit version you may still hit the limit. Visual Basic for Applications uses stack space more efficiently—local fixed-length strings larger than 255 bytes are not placed on the stack like they were in Visual Basic 3, for example—so even in 16-bit stack space is less of an issue.

Sometimes forms will accidentally be kept loaded. Make sure you completely unload your forms by running this code:

```
Unload frmFoo
Set frmFoo = Nothing
```

If you don't do this properly, form information can be left in memory. Before you run through and change all your code to completely unload form information, make sure your application doesn't depend on that information somewhere else.

Oh, and don't worry about testing Literals vs. Constants, because in Visual Basic 4 they are the same speed.

Finally, if your applications are anything like ours, by the time they are close to being finished, parts of them have been rewritten several times. In the process, you've probably left behind variables that you're no longer using, and sometimes even whole procedures that aren't being called from anywhere. Visual Basic does not detect and remove this "dead code," so you have to look for and remove it yourself. There are tools like Whippleware's VB Compress Pro to help with this process.

Cutting Back on Graphics

In many Visual Basic applications, the space used by graphics dwarfs the memory used by everything else combined. However, there are also opportunities to accomplish significant savings by using some simple techniques:

- Reclaim graphics memory with `LoadPicture()` and `Cls`

- Replace Picture box with Image controls

- Load Pictures only when needed, and share pictures and icons

- Use RLE bitmaps or metafiles

- Use RES files to store images, strings, and blobs

Reclaim memory with `LoadPicture()` and `Cls`. If you aren't going to use a Picture or Image control again, don't just hide it: remove the bitmap it contains:

```
Image1.Picture = LoadPicture()
```

Another way to empty a picture, new in Visual Basic 4, is:

```
Set Image1.Picture = Nothing
```

Another technique reclaims the memory used by the AutoRedraw bitmap in forms and picture controls (the AutoRedraw bitmap is the bitmap that Visual Basic uses if you set AutoRedraw to True, or if you reference the Image property of forms or picture controls). You can reclaim this memory, using code like this:

```
mypic.AutoRedraw = True
' Turn on AutoRedraw bitmap.
myPic.Cls
' Clear it.
myPic.AutoRedraw = False
' Turn off bitmap.
```

The Picture controls in many Visual Basic applications exist merely to be clicked, or to be dragged and dropped. If this is all you're doing with a Picture control, you are wasting a lot of Windows resources.

For these purposes, Image controls are superior to Picture controls. Each Picture control is an actual window, and uses significant system resources. The Image control is a "lightweight" control rather than a window, and doesn't use nearly as many resources.

In fact, you can typically use 5 to 10 times as many Image controls as Picture controls. Moreover, Image controls repaint faster than Picture controls. Use a Picture control when you need a feature only it provides, such as DDE, graphics methods, or the ability to contain other controls.

Obviously, you use less memory if you only load pictures as you need them at runtime, rather than storing them in your application at design time. What may be less obvious is that you can share the same picture between multiple Picture controls, Image controls, and forms. If you use code like this you only maintain one copy of the picture:

```
Picture = _
    LoadPicture("C:\Windows\Chess.BMP")
Image1.Picture = Picture
' Use the same picture
Picture1.Picture = Picture
' Use the same picture
```

Contrast that with this code, which causes three copies of the bitmap to be loaded, taking more memory and time:

```
Picture = LoadPicture("C:\Windows\Chess.BMP")
Image1.Picture = _
    LoadPicture("C:\Windows\Chess.BMP")
Picture1.Picture = _
    LoadPicture("C:\Windows\Chess.BMP")
```

Similarly, if you load the same picture into several forms or controls at design time, a copy of that picture is saved with each form or control. Instead, you can place the picture in one form and then share it with the other forms and controls as described above. This makes your application both smaller (because it doesn't contain redundant copies of the picture) and faster (because the picture doesn't have to be loaded from disk multiple times).

You may want to completely avoid storing pictures in forms or controls at design time (that way your graphics aren't loaded until they are needed). Instead, store the pictures as resources in your Visual Basic program and load them as needed at runtime with the `LoadResPicture` function. If you never use all the pictures associated with a form at the same time, this technique saves memory over storing all the pictures in controls on the form. And it can speed up form load because not all the pictures need to be loaded before the form can be shown.

Rather than placing bitmaps in controls, you can use the new `PaintPicture` method to display bitmaps anywhere on forms. This is particularly useful when you want to tile a bitmap repeatedly across a form: you only need to load the bitmap once but you can use `PaintPicture` to draw it multiple times.

Finally, try to use smaller picture data. Several painting and graphics programs allow you to save bitmaps in a standard compressed bitmap format called Run Length Encoded (RLE). RLE bitmaps can be several times smaller than their uncompressed counterparts, particularly for bitmaps that contain large swatches of solid color, and aren't appreciably slower to load or display. The savings found by using metafiles can be even more significant—10 times or more in some cases. Try to use metafiles at their normal size: they are much slower to paint when they have to be stretched larger or smaller.

Increase the Throttle on OLE

Many of you will be playing with OLE features for the first time, now that OLE in Windows 95 and Windows NT is far more robust than in 16-bit operating systems, and also because there are far more OLE Automated applications (Adobe Acrobat, Visio, and Excel are three that come to mind, but even the new Schedule Plus that comes with Office 95 is OLE Automated). Also, with Visual Basic 4, you can now build your own OLE servers, and you can see that spending a few minutes to optimize the OLE parts of your application will result in great speed increases.

We'd like to get one myth out of the way: OLE itself isn't slow. OLE provides a lot of functionality, however, and some techniques you use to harness those features are faster than others. Here's a primer on OLE, and which type you'll want to pick.

Application Partitioning by Using OLE

The OLE features of Visual Basic 4 now enable you to think about the architecture of your application in new ways. Instead of a single, monolithic executable, you can write an application that consists of a core "front-end" executable supported by a swarm of OLE servers. This approach offers several significant optimization benefits:

■ The OLE servers are loaded on demand, and can be unloaded when no longer needed

■ Cross-process OLE servers can be 32-bit executables on Windows 95 or Windows NT, even if other parts of the application are 16-bit applications

■ Remote OLE servers can use the resources of other machines on the network

■ And the OLE servers can be debugged independently and reused in other applications. This may not improve the speed of your application but it may improve your speed in creating the next one

To determine how to best optimize your application by segmenting it by using OLE, you must evaluate the kinds of OLE servers you can create and how they fit into your application. There are three kinds of OLE servers you can create with Visual Basic:

■ Cross-process (which are separate VB4 EXEs).

- In-process (which are VB4's OLE DLLs).

- Remote (separate VB4 EXE's running somewhere on your network). You'll need the Enterprise Edition of VB4 to build and manage Remote OLE Servers.

These three kinds are not exclusive: you could use all three in a single application. But from the standpoint of optimizing your application, they each have very different characteristics.

Cross-Process OLE Servers

A cross-process OLE server is an executable program that offers OLE services to other programs. Like all executables, it starts up and runs with its own stack in its own process space; thus, when a client application uses one of the server's OLE objects, the operation crosses from the client's process space to the server's—hence the name.

Cross-process OLE servers offer some valuable features when compared to the other types:

- Asynchronous operation

- Non-modal forms

- Untrapped error in server won't cause calling app to crash

- Interoperability between 16-bit and 32-bit

Of these, the first and the last points are of particular interest from an optimization standpoint. Because a cross-process OLE server is a separate program, it can operate synchronously with the client. It has a separate process that multitasks with the client program (technically speaking this is not a thread but a separate process; however, conceptually the two are equivalent).

The two programs can communicate via OLE and shared objects, but they run independently. This is particularly useful when your application needs to perform some operation that takes a long time. The client can call the server to perform the operation and then continue responding to the user.

Even when running on a 32-bit system, you may not be able to make your application 32-bit immediately because you rely on 16-bit DLLs or VBXs. However, if you segment your application, using cross-process OLE servers, you can leave some parts as 16-bit programs and recompile the rest in 32-bit.

You can then make one part the core of your application and the rest OLE servers called from that core. This allows you to incrementally take advantage of 32-bit features and performance while preserving your investment in 16-bit components.

But, for all their strengths, cross-process OLE servers have a significant disadvantage: performance. This manifests itself in a couple of ways:

- Startup speed.

- Cross-process call overhead.

A cross-process OLE server is an executable created with Visual Basic 4, so the same startup issues discussed earlier also apply. The good news is that if you are calling a cross-process OLE server written in Visual Basic from another Visual Basic program, almost all the support DLLs will be already loaded.

Having all the OLE stuff already loaded greatly reduces the time required to start the server. And many OLE servers are smaller than your average Visual Basic application, with few or no forms to load, which again improves load time (since many servers aren't meant to be end-user applications, but are meant to run on a server in the closet). Nevertheless, a cross-process OLE server will always be slower to start than an in-process OLE server. (On some tests, this difference can be up to 20-times slower.)

Once it is running, a cross-process OLE server suffers from its very nature: every interaction with the server is a cross-process call.

Crossing process boundaries takes a lot of CPU cycles. So every reference to an object from the cross-process server is much more expensive than an equivalent reference to an object in the client application itself or an in-process server. However, clever coding (discussed later) can reduce the number of necessary cross-process calls and thus reduce the affect of the cross-process call overhead.

In-Process OLE Servers

An in-process OLE server is a DLL that offers OLE services to other programs. Like all DLLs, it starts up and uses its client's stack and process space; thus, when a client application uses one of the server's OLE objects the operation remains in the client's process space—hence the name. Compared to cross-process OLE servers, in-process OLE servers offer a couple of advantages:

- Improved load time

- Greatly improved performance (sometimes up to 20 times faster than cross-process EXEs)

■ No cross-process overhead

■ Doesn't create a new process

Because an in-process server runs as a DLL, no new process needs to be created and none of the runtime DLLs need to be loaded. This can make an in-process OLE server considerably quicker to load compared to an equivalent cross-process server.

And because it is in-process, there is no cross-process overhead when referring to the methods or properties on an object supplied by the server. Objects from the server operate with the same efficiency as objects within the client application itself.

Of course, there are some limitations to in-process OLE servers. Perhaps most significantly they must be 32-bit and can only use modal forms.

Remote OLE Servers

The Enterprise Edition of Visual Basic 4 enables you to create remote OLE servers that execute on a separate machine elsewhere on the network. While network overhead will inevitably exact a toll on application performance, you can make up for it by using the resources of additional CPUs.

This is particularly true when you work with a remote OLE server operating on data that is local to the machine containing the server. Since this data would have to be fetched across the network anyway, an OLE server operating on it locally and returning only the results across the network may actually be more efficient.

For example, you might write an object in an OLE server that can search for files matching a specified criteria on the local hard disk. By making this a remote OLE server and placing a copy on each machine on the network, you can write a distributed file-finder program that searches all the network servers in parallel, using CPU resources of all those CPUs.

Optimizing OLE

As you use more and more OLE objects in your Visual Basic applications, optimizing your use of those objects becomes more and more important. There are several key techniques to making the most efficient use of OLE objects:

■ Use early binding

■ Minimize the dots

- Use `Set` and `With...End With`

- Minimize cross-process calls.

In Visual Basic 3, referencing an OLE Automation object in your code (get/set an object's property, or execute one of its methods) constitutes a cross-process call. Cross-process calls are expensive and you should avoid them if you are concerned about optimizing your application.

Early Binding versus Late Binding

Visual Basic can use objects more efficiently if it can early bind them. An object can be early bound if you supply a reference to a typelib containing the object, and you declare the type of the object:

```
Dim X As New MyObject
```

Or, equivalently:

```
Dim X As MyObject
Set X = New MyObject
```

Early binding enables Visual Basic to do most of the work of resolving the definition of the object at compile time rather than at runtime when it affects performance. This also allows Visual Basic to check the syntax of properties and methods used with the object, and report any errors.

If Visual Basic cannot early bind an object, it must late bind it. Late binding objects is expensive: at compile time you get no error checking, and each reference at runtime requires at least 50 percent more work by Visual Basic.

Generally, you should always early bind objects if possible. The only times you should have to declare a variable `As Object` is if you do not have a TypeLib for the object in question, or you need to be able to pass any kind of object as an argument to a procedure.

Minimize the Dots

When referencing OLE objects from Visual Basic, you use the dot syntax "." to navigate an object's hierarchy of collections, objects, properties, and methods. It is not uncommon to create very lengthy navigation strings. For example:

```
' Refers to cell A1 on Sheet1 in the first
' workbook of an Excel spreadsheet.
Application.Workbooks.Item(1).Worksheets._
    Item("Sheet1").Cells.Item(1,1)
```

In addition to being a rather lengthy string to manually type, this line of code is fairly difficult to read—and it is extremely inefficient.

When calling an OLE Server object from Visual Basic, each "dot" requires Visual Basic to make several calls to OLE (`GetIDsOfNames`, `IDispatch`). To write the most efficient OLE Automation applications, minimize the use of dots when referencing an object.

You can usually make immediate inroads to minimizing the dots by analyzing the objects and methods available to you. For example, the preceding line of code can be shortened by removing the `Item` method (this is the default method for collections anyway, so you'll rarely use it in code) and by using the more efficient `Range` method:

```
' Refers to cell A1 on Sheet1 in the first
' workbook of an Excel spreadsheet.
Application.Workbooks(1).Worksheets_
    ("Sheet1").Range("A1")
```

You can shorten this even further by rewriting the code so that it refers to the active sheet in the active workbook, instead of a specific sheet in a specific workbook:

```
' Refers to cell A1 on the active sheet in the
' active workbook.
Range("A1")
```

Of course, the above example assumes it's OK to refer to cell A1 of any sheet that happens to be active.

You may find that using the `For Each` property instead of the count property to be faster, but you'll need to test this one, since on some OLE Servers, it may be slower.

Use Set and With...End With

Using the `Set` statement also allows you to shorten navigation strings and gives you a bit more control over your code. The following example uses the `Dim` and `Set` statements to create variables that refer to frequently used objects:

```
Dim xlRange As Object
Set xlRange = Application.ActiveSheet._
    Cells(1,1)
xlRange.Font.Bold = True
xlRange.Width = 40
```

Visual Basic for Applications provides the With...End With construct to set an implied object within code:

```
With Application.ActiveSheet.Cells(1,1)
    .Font.Bold = True
    .Width = 40
End With
```

Minimize Cross-Process Calls

If you are using a cross-process OLE server you can't completely avoid making cross-process calls. However, there are several ways to minimize the number of cross-process calls you need to make.

If possible, do not reference OLE objects inside a For...Next Loop. Cache values in variables and use the variables in loops. If you have to call a large number of methods on an object, you can greatly improve the performance of your application by moving the code into the OLE server. This would be a perfect place to use OLE Callbacks (see the article in the October 1995 issue of *Visual Basic Programmer's Journal* on how to do OLE Callbacks).

For example, if the OLE server is Word or Excel you can put a looping macro in a template in Word or a looping procedure into a module in Excel. You then call the macro or procedure from Visual Basic: a single call that launches a looping operation within the server.

If you are writing OLE servers, you can design the objects in the OLE server to be efficient by reducing the cross-process calls required to perform an operation. For example, when you have several interrelated properties, implement a method with several arguments—one for each property.

Calling the method requires a single cross-process call regardless of how many arguments it has, whereas setting each property requires a cross-process call. Likewise, if you anticipate uses of your server where the client will want to call your server in a loop (for example, to sum or average all the values in a list property) you can improve performance by providing methods that do the looping within your object and return the appropriate value.

Summary

One thing we should add is that we don't know it all. You'll see many clever optimizing techniques discussed by other programmers on the VBPJFORUM and MSBASIC forums on CompuServe, and if we find any other techniques, we'll present them at future VBITS conferences, as well as including them on the Microsoft Developer Network and in the VB KnowledgeBase available online. In addition, discussing your code with others at user group meetings will often help you find a new way to optimize your code, which you wouldn't explore on your own. You can find a VB user group by calling 1-800-228-6738.

Chapter 15

Programming the Web

by Chris Barlow

In addition to writing a monthly column for the Visual Basic Programming Journal and speaking at VBITS, Comdex, and TechEd, Chris Barlow is the President of SunOpTech®, Inc.

His background includes a combination of entrepreneurial, management, and computer skills. He earned his undergraduate degree from Dartmouth College with Distinction in Economics & Computer Science and, as a student at Dartmouth, worked as a programmer on some of the later enhancements to the BASIC language with its inventors, Drs. Kemeny and Kurtz. He received his M.B.A degree from Harvard Business School, and worked for Fortune 500 companies in manufacturing and management information systems.

Based in Sarasota, Florida, SunOpTech uses Visual Basic and Visual C++ to develop Windows-based decision support applications for medium to large size manufacturing enterprises.

Reach Chris at SunOpTech, Inc., 1500 West University Parkway, Sarasota, FL, 34243; by telephone at 941-362-1271; by fax at 941-355-4497; and on the Internet at ChrisB@SunOpTech.com.

The World Wide Web is the most exciting place for a Visual Basic programmer! I believe the opportunities are endless and that we are just beginning to exploit the possibilities.

The Internet and the Web

The Web provides a standard way to publish information on a server and distribute it to clients around the world. One of the neatest things is that the clients need only a standard Web Browser—they can get information from any server in the world without any other specialized software. As a programmer, this means you can distribute your application around the world but all the software stays on your server—no setup program needed!

As a beginning Visual Basic programmer, you might find it difficult sometimes to find truly interesting applications to tackle. As hard as it may be to believe, writing programs that interact with Web Servers on the Internet's World Wide Web is easily within your reach.

In this chapter, we'll do the following:

- Take a look at the World Wide Web on the Internet

- Develop some simple applications that exploit the Web's wealth of information

- See how these applications fit into the information needs of an enterprise.

By now I'm sure you're familiar with Mosaic, Netscape, and other Web Browsers. Just a year ago you seldom saw the Internet mentioned in the general press. It used to be that you only heard about the Internet in certain technical magazines. Now it seems you cannot turn on the television or pick up a magazine or newspaper without seeing a story about the Internet. Just about every news program mentions its e-mail address and many have a Web Server to publish information on the Internet. The Internet has grabbed people's imaginations because of its ability to easily link computers all over the world. As someone working with Visual Basic, you should be asking yourself how you can learn more about this hot area.

Although e-mail is by far the largest use of the Internet, the fastest growing part of the Internet is the World Wide Web. If you are familiar with the World Wide Web you know how easy it is with a Web Browser to jump from computer to computer all over the world and view vast amounts of information. Web Browsers, like Mosaic and Netscape, let you jump from one computer to another anywhere on the Internet by using simple point and click hypertext—very much like navigating a Windows Help file. You just point and click and almost immediately your computer is downloading a file from another computer on the other side of the world! Each hypertext jump connects to a Web Server at some location on the Internet, requests a certain file from that computer, and displays that file on the screen.

If you work in an organization with an Internet connection you might start your day with a few exciting minutes of downloading the latest European Union currency cross-exchange rates from a computer in Sweden or viewing the current weather map for Japan. In the space of less than five minutes this morning, I pointed my Web Browser at the primary Web site in Cern, Switzerland (*www.w3.org*), then clicked on a hypertext jump called W3Servers to retrieve another file called *servers.html* from Switzerland that lists all the countries in the world with Web Servers. I clicked on Florida and was connected to the University of Florida in Gainesville and retrieved a file showing all the Web Servers in Florida. I clicked on SunOpTech and retrieved our own web home page file from the Windows NT computer sitting next to me (*www.sunoptech.com*). Then I clicked on Carl & Gary's Visual Basic Page and was connected to Apex Software Corporation in Pennsylvania where Carl Franklin and Gary Wisniewski maintain a Web Server with Visual Basic-related information (*www.apexsc.com/vb*). Whew! I've traveled all over the world and my coffee is still hot!

Unfortunately, then you have to turn away from the outside world and see if you can somehow convince your corporate MIS department that you really do need to know the availability of tools on the shop floor more frequently than getting a stack of computer paper once every morning! Why is it so easy to get information from the other side of the world and so hard to get it from your own shop floor? Why don't more enterprises publish their information internally by using this Web technology? Why don't more enterprises set up their own internal Webs to distribute information to their organizations?

As a Visual Basic programmer, you have the resources to write programs that both gather information from the World Wide Web and publish information, including database information, over the Web. At SunOpTech® we installed our own Web Server to provide information about our company and our affiliates. It turned out to be a relatively easy and inexpensive task.

See the sidebar for more information on SunOpTech's Web Server.

The Components of the Web

To understand the Web, you need to understand three distinct Web components:

- **The Web Server,** which "listens" for requests for files, transmits them, and handles the interface to other programs.

- **The Web files** that contain the data to be transferred between the server and the client.

- **The Web Browser** that requests these Web files from the Web Server, presents them in a formatted display, and manages the hypertext jumps to other Web files.

Web Servers

Web Servers, like the free HTTP program you can download from Cern (*www.w3.org*), or the WebSite® program that you can purchase from O'Reilly & Associates (*www.ora.com*), reside on a computer whose network card is connected on a network running the TCP/IP protocol. Usually, this network card's IP address is associated with the host name "WWW" within a domain. When the Web Server is started, it "listens" on port 80 for a client trying to establish a connection and then responds to a small specific group of commands. The most common command is to GET a file. In response to this command, the Web Server retrieves the specified file and sends it over the TCP/IP connection.

If all a Web Server could do was transmit files, it would still be a quite useful program. But the addition of the capability to pass data to another program and receive results from that program to transmit back to the client greatly expands the utility of the Web.

This interface to other programs is called the Common Gateway Interface (CGI). Until recently, this interface was limited to scripts or C programs on UNIX machines or, on Windows NT machines to C console applications. But O'Reilly Associates' WebSite lets you write a Visual Basic program that can interact through its CGI-WIN interface. For example, you can write a program that searches an Access database and returns the results as a Web File.

Web Files

Any type of file can be transmitted by a Web Server. You can retrieve a ZIP file, an EXE, a graphics file, or a word processing document. But the most common files are simply ASCII text files that contain embedded Hyper Text Markup Language (HTML) codes. This type of file is usually called a Web Page. It is these embedded codes that allow the Web Browsers to display the fancy fonts and formats. These codes also provide the information needed to "jump" to another Web Server and retrieve a different Web File.

The specification for HTML is changing rapidly. Until recently there was no standard HTML code to center text on the screen or to provide for tabular information. The addition of the capability to create and process HTML Forms allows a Web Server to easily capture information from the user and provides an interface for database queries. These forms can be made to look a lot like Visual Basic forms and can contain text boxes, list boxes, combo boxes, check boxes, and labels.

Web Browsers

Any program that can send and receive data over a TCP/IP connection can act as a Web client and communicate with Web Servers. The most common Web clients are the Web Browsers like Mosaic and Netscape. Web Browsers display the data from the files they retrieve from the Web Servers with attractive document formats and hypertext jumps by interpreting the HTML codes embedded in these text files. They interpret the HTML codes to display the text in various font sizes and the positioning of the text.

After the browser retrieves a file that contains embedded graphics files, it sends additional GET commands to the Web Server to retrieve each of these graphics files and displays them in the proper position on the screen.

Finally, the browser interprets the HTML anchors, which indicate the embedded URL jumps to other web pages. They sense a mouse click on these hypertext jumps and establish a connection with the indicated Web Server and issue a GET command to retrieve the indicated file.

Creating Web Files with Visual Basic

Let's begin by seeing how we can use a Visual Basic program to build a Web Page. The first step is to understand a little about HTML files. It is easy to look at one of these HTML text files with Notepad and see the HTML codes.

Some of the HTML codes are paired and some stand alone. For example, a new paragraph is indicated by **<P>** and a horizontal rule by **<HR>**; but, if you want to display text in italics you put an **<I>** at the beginning of the text to start italics font and **</I>** at the end of the text to stop italics font. You can change the font size by using the paired code **<H1></H1>** for the largest font down to **<H6></H6>** for the smaller font. You can even create bulleted or ordered lists by using the **<BL>** or **<OL>** codes.

In addition to using HTML codes to format text, you can enter codes to provide the hypertext jumps to other documents on any Web Server on the Internet. These jumps are in the form of an *anchor* that includes a *uniform resource locator* (URL) followed by the text that will be displayed for the jump. For example, to include a jump with the underlined text SunOpTech Home Page in any HTML document you would insert the following line:

```
<A
href="http://www.sunoptech.com/sunoptec.htm"
>SunOpTech Home Page<
/A>
```

The part following href points to an HTML document (http:) called sunoptec.htm on the Web Server located at the machine called www at the sunoptech.com domain on the Internet. There are several other commands that can follow the href keyword. One particularly useful command is mailto: followed by an e-mail address that pops up a window to type an e-mail message. For example, to add a hypertext link that will send e-mail to me, you can include the following lines:

```
<A
href="mailto:chrisb@sunoptech.com"
>Email Chris Barlow<
/A>
```

Any program that can write ASCII files can create a Web Page. In the past, I have created all my Web Pages by using Notepad and entering the HTML codes myself. But nothing I have tried can beat Microsoft's Internet Assistant. It is an add-on to Microsoft Word 6 that lets you use the Word toolbar to easily format an HTML document. Not only can you create HTML documents but also, if you have an Internet connection, you can browse the Web from inside Word!

Now that these tools have made it so easy to create HTML documents, the challenge is not embedding these codes but getting the data for the document. This is where a Visual Basic program can come in handy!

Let's take a look at a real example of how to use Visual Basic procedures to create an HTML document from a list in an ASCII text file.

On SunOpTech's Web Server, we wanted to have a page listing the e-mail addresses of our personnel. We also wanted to list each person's name as a hypertext jump that would trigger the mailto command so users could send mail to that e-mail address. See figure 15.1 to see how this page looks from Word's Web Browser. Remember, you can open this file directly from most browsers if you don't have a Web Server yet.

We already had an ASCII file containing the names of the personnel. The task was to write the procedures to create the HTML document. When we want to create the HTML document we will run the MAKEHTML program and select the File, Create HTML menu item. This procedure runs the main driver procedure called CreateMailHTML that will get the filename that contains the list of names and places the names in a list box. Then it will get the filename of the HTML document to create, open the file for output (which will erase it if it already exists), and call procedures to write the header, body, and footer of the document.

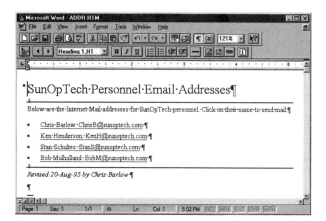

Fig. 15.1
How this page
looks from a
Word's Web
Browser.

The header of the document begins with the code <HTML> to indicate that this is an HTML document, and is followed by the Title within the header beginning and ending codes:

```
Sub WriteHTMLHeader()
Print #1, "<HTML>"
Print #1, "<HEAD>"
Print #1, "<TITLE>Internet Mail Addresses</TITLE>"
Print #1, "</HEAD>"
End Sub
```

We'll divide the writing of the body of the document between two procedures—writing the body text and writing the addresses:

```
Sub WriteHTMLBody()
WriteBodyText
WriteAddresses
End Sub
```

Can you see how organizing your procedures in these small pieces makes it easier to follow the code? At SunOpTech, we try to keep all procedures less than 50 lines of code—most are much less than this maximum!

The body text starts with the keyword <Body> and is followed by the text that we want to display at the top of the document. We can use the heading one font <H1> codes to make this text larger than the regular body text. We will add a horizontal rule <HR>, which is usually displayed as a three-dimensional line across the entire display window and start a new paragraph <P> of normal text:

```
Sub WriteBodyText()
Print #1, "<BODY>"
Print #1, "<H1>SunOpTech Personnel Email Addresses</H1>"
Print #1, "<HR>"
Print #1, "<P>"
```

```
Print #1, "Below are the Internet Mail addresses for SunOpTech personnel."
Print #1, "Click on their name to send mail:"
Print #1, "<P>"
End Sub
```

To write the names and e-mail addresses, we will need to loop through the list box control that we loaded with the names. We want the names to be in an unordered list so we will start with the <UL> code that will automatically indent and add bullets to each item in the list:

```
Sub WriteAddresses()
Dim Nme As Object, i%
Print #1, "<UL>"
For i = 0 To List1.ListCount - 1
   Print #1, MakeMailHTML(List1.List(i))
Next
Print #1, "</UL>"
End Sub
```

Notice how we use a function called MakeMailHTML that creates the e-mail address from the passed name parameter. Let's examine this function step-by-step. First we dimension temporary variables and define Q$ to hold a quotation mark. This will make it easy to embed a quote in the string we will create:

```
Function MakeMailHTML(Nme)
Dim txt$, Q$, addr$, pos&
Q$ = Chr$(34) 'quote
```

Like many companies, SunOpTech uses the first name followed by the first letter of the last name as an e-mail address. So, we will examine the passed name parameter, Nme, and use the InStr function to find the position of the first space and set it equal to Pos&. Then we will use this position to parse the characters to the left of this position (the first name) and use the Mid function to extract the first letter of the last name. Finally we will append our domain name:

```
pos& = InStr(Nme, " ")
addr$ = Left(Nme, pos& - 1) & Mid(Nme, pos& + 1, 1)
addr$ = addr$ & "@sunoptech.com"
```

Now that we have the e-mail address, we can build the HTML string beginning with <LI> to indicate that this line is an item in the list, add the anchor href and the command mailto:, then append the calculated address and finish with the passed name and address:

```
txt$ = "<LI><A href=" & Q$ & "mailto:"
txt$ = txt$ & addr$ & Q$ & ">"
txt$ = txt$ & Nme & ": " & addr$ & "</A>"
MakeMailHTML = txt$
End Function
```

The last step is to write the footer, beginning with a horizontal rule and the revision date in italics. Remember to use an international date format with a three-letter month—your Web page might be accessed from all over the world!

```
Sub WriteHTMLFooter()
Print #1, "<HR>"
Print #1, "<I>Revised " & Format(Now, "dd-mmm-yy") & " by Chris Barlow</I>"
Print #1, "</BODY>"
Print #1, "</HTML>"
End Sub
```

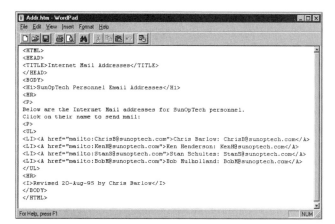

Fig. 15.2
The HTML
Document

Exploring the Web

When you see the graphics, rich text formats, and hypertext jumps in browsers like Netscape and Mosaic, it is hard to believe that a small Visual Basic program could actually be more useful.

One of the strengths of these browsers is their ease of use. For example, users only have to point and click to jump to a new site. This is wonderful for "surfing," but it can become a real burden when you're trying to retrieve a specific piece of information. How many times have you used a browser and watched thousands of bytes of graphics being transferred just so you could look up a single piece of information? This is where a small Visual Basic program can help.

The Internet's World Wide Web is built on the standard Internet TCP/IP protocol and is available from Windows through the WinSock DLL. There are several controls that wrap the winsock functions and make it easier to use. I will follow Carl Franklin's lead and use Stephen Cramp's `dsSocket` control available in both VBX and OCX versions. This control makes it simple to send and receive data over a TCP/IP connection including Port 80—the Web port. The neat thing is you don't have to worry about a polling routine—this control triggers a normal Visual Basic event whenever data arrives at this socket.

Writing a Web Client

Let's start with an example that Carl Franklin wrote—NEWS. This Visual Basic program retrieves a summary of today's news from a server. See the complete code in Listing 15.1. Start a new Project and add a text box called txtNews to your form. Then drag and drop `dssocket.vbx` from File Manager to your toolbox (don't you love this new Visual Basic 4 interface?). In the code window, define a variable called nConnected that will be set by the Connect event of the socket control and one to hold the text from the server (see fig. 15.3).

Fig. 15.3
The News Window. Notice how you can easily display HTML formatted info in a text box by using Carl Franklin's *szStripHTML* procedure.

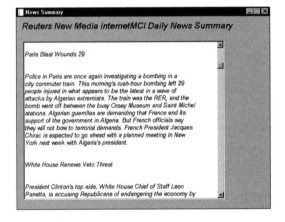

```
Option Explicit
'-- Used to tell us when we've connected
Private nConnected As Integer
'-- Stores received data
Private szNews As String
```

The code in the following Form_Load event will make the connection to the Web Server on Port 80. In the full listing, I include code to return an error if the connection fails. Note that making the connection is simple—just set the RemoteHost and RemotePort property and set the Action property of the socket control to a value of Connect:

```
'-- Connect to the internetMCI server
    DSSocket1.RemotePort = 80
    DSSocket1.RemoteHost = "www.fyionline.com"
    On Error Resume Next
    DSSocket1.Action = 2
```

Then we will wait in a loop until the connection succeeds:

```
nConnected = False
Do
        DoEvents
Loop Until nConnected
```

When we're connected, we'll initialize the variable to hold the news text and use the Send method to request the HTML document that contains the news. We request a Web File from a Web Server by using the GET command followed by the full path to the file. I always append a couple of carriage return linefeeds to signal the end of line to the Web Server:

```
            szNews = ""
            DSSocket1.Send = "GET /infoMCI/update/NEWS-MCI.html" & _
                    vbCrLf & vbCrLf
    End If
End Sub
```

At this point, the code under the Receive event takes over and builds up the szNews string as it receives the file over the Internet from the Web Server and places it in the text box. We'll use the szStripHTML function to remove all HTML codes from the file and just display the raw text:

```
Private Sub DSSocket1_Receive(ReceiveData As String)
    szNews = szNews & ReceiveData
    txtNews = szStripHTML(szNews)
End Sub
```

That's it! See the complete code in Listing 15.2 . Can you see how this would fit into an Enterprise Web? Suppose that this code was connecting to the Human Resources department's Web Server for a list of upcoming training seminars or publishing the latest price list to your field sales representatives? Any standard piece of information could be easily retrieved and displayed to any users with access to your Web Server.

Daily Exchange Rates

An interesting Web Server at the Lund University in Sweden allows you to query the daily exchange rates between two currencies. The Web page, whose URL is *www.dna.lth.se/cgi-bin/kurt/rates,* first guides you through selecting two currencies, then runs a query and displays the exchange rate information.

When you use this page from a Web Browser, you can see that it uses the following URL to process a query for the US dollar and Deutsch mark currencies:

```
www.dna.lth.se/cgi-bin/kurt/rates?USD+DEM
```

This process of point-and-click works well for a single query but it would be very time consuming to gather information on five or ten different currencies. The preceding query URL tells us how the Web page queries the currency data. Let's write a Visual Basic program that will automatically make this query for five or ten different currencies and store the information. See the complete code in Listing 15.3.

Start a new Project and add a text box, a grid control like Spread VBX, two command buttons, a panel for help messages, and the `dsSocket` control to your form. Then add column and row headings to the grid control by using the international currency symbols USD = U.S. dollars, DEM = Deutsch Marks, etc. We'll use these row and column headings as the currency arguments to pass to the server (see fig. 15.4).

Fig. 15.4
The Currency Demo. The user can double-click on an individual cell or click the button to retrieve all cells.

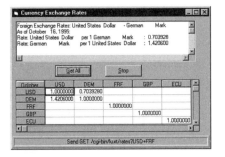

The `dsSocket` `Close`, `Connect`, and `Receive` events will contain essentially the same code as in the News sample. We'll use these procedures to set the value of the `nConnected` variable and build the `szHTML` string from the received data. The `Connect` event sets the public `nConnected` variable to True:

```
Private Sub dsSocket1_Connect()
nConnected = True
HelpLine = "Connected"
End Sub
```

The `Close` event sets the public `nConnected` variable to False:

```
Private Sub dsSocket1_Close(ErrorCode As Integer, ErrorDesc As String)
nConnected = False
HelpLine = "Closed"
End Sub
```

And the `Receive` event accumulates the received data in the `szHTML` string:

```
Private Sub dsSocket1_Receive(ReceiveData As String)
szHTML = szHTML & ReceiveData
HelpLine = "Receive: " & szHTML
End Sub
```

Now let's write a general purpose routine that will connect to a Web Server and retrieve and return an HTML document. We'll pass two arguments—a remote host, like *www.dna.lth.se*, and an HTML Get command, like *GET /cgi-bin/kurt/rates?USD+DEM*. Then we can use this routine in other Web programs.

We'll begin by attempting to establish the connection with the remote host:

```
Private Function szGetHTML(szHost$, szGet$) As String
dsSocket1.RemoteHost = szHost$
dsSocket1.RemotePort = 80
On Error Resume Next
dsSocket1.Action = 2
```

Then we'll loop until we're connected:

```
nConnected = False
Do
        DoEvents
Loop Until nConnected Or nStop
```

Then send the Get command:

```
szHTML = ""
dsSocket1.Send = szGet & vbCrLf
HelpLine = "Send " & szGet
```

And return the receive data after the connection is closed. As before, we'll use the szStripHTML function to return just the text without the embedded HTML codes:

```
Do
        DoEvents
Loop Until (nConnected = False) Or nStop
szGetHTML = szStripHTML(szHTML)
End If
End Function
```

Now we can call this procedure anytime we need to receive a Web Page from a Web Server.

After we've received the text, we'll need to parse the text response from the Web Server to grab the proper exchange rates. This parsing of returned text is one of the biggest problems with automating the Web retrieval process since we are relying on the positions of items in the text. Some of the new HTML standards will make this easier with explicit revision dates and embedded tables. Fortunately, if you're helping to set up an internal Enterprise Web, it is easier to set some standards for automated information retrieval.

The response from this particular server that we need to parse looks like this:

```
Foreign Exchange Rates: US Dollar              - German Mark
As of 02.08.1995 (day.month.year):
Rate: US Dollar              per 1 German Mark          : 0.719682
Rate: German Mark            per 1 US Dollar            : 1.389502
```

We'll write a ParseResponse procedure that uses a standard ParseString routine to parse the date and the two exchange rates from this text. Encapsulating the parsing within this single procedure makes it easier to modify it if the Web Page format changes:

```
Private Function ParseResponse(szResp$, Item%) As Variant
Select Case Item
Case 0:ParseResponse = Mid(ParseString(szResp, "As of", 2), 5, 11)
Case 1:ParseResponse = Left(ParseString(szResp, ":", 5), 11)
Case 2:ParseResponse = Left(ParseString(szResp, ":", 7), 11)
End Select
End Function
```

Now that we've written procedures to retrieve the text and parse it, we need to write code under the Spread control's `double-click` event to call these routines, and make a single query:

```
Private Sub Spread1_DblClick(col As Long, row As Long)
Dim szHost$, szGet$
Dim C1 As Variant, C2 As Variant, i%
Spread1.row = row:Spread1.col = 0:C1 = Spread1.TEXT
Spread1.row = 0:Spread1.col = col:C2 = Spread1.TEXT
szHost = "www.dna.lth.se"
szGet = "GET /cgi-bin/kurt/rates?" & C1 & "+" & C2
Text1 = szGetHTML(szHost, szGet)
```

and load the result into that cell:

```
SpreadSetText Spread1, 0, 0, ParseResponse(Text1, 0)
SpreadSetText Spread1, col, row, ParseResponse(Text1, 1)
SpreadSetText Spread1, row, col, ParseResponse(Text1, 2)
End Sub
```

Rather than having to click on each cell, we'll write a routine to automate the cell double-click process to fill the entire spread when the Get All button is clicked:

```
Private Sub butGo_Click()
Dim col&, row&, MaxRow&
MaxRow = 1
For col = 2 To 5
  For row = 1 To MaxRow
          Spread1_DblClick col, row
  Next
  MaxRow = MaxRow + 1
Next
End Sub
```

The ability to automate Web information retrieval, particularly over a more tightly controlled internal Enterprise Web, is a huge step forward over the "surf, point-and-click" method of information retrieval and truly makes the World Wide Web a practical source for enterprise data.

Serving the Web

So far in this chapter, we've seen how to write a program to create Web Pages and how to write a web client to retrieve Web pages over the Internet. Now let's see how to enhance a Web Server to let it query a database and return the results.

Common Gateway Interface

When the World Wide Web began, it was conceived as a way for scientists to exchange their scientific technical papers. The Web Servers' ability to send a file to a web client met this need quite well. As other users, particularly corporations, began to publish information on the Web, they realized that much of the information they wanted to publish was contained in corporate databases. As the HTML standard was expanded to allow the use of HTML Forms, it became easy to envision using the Web as a distributed database query system.

However, many programmers were stymied by the limited ability of Web Servers to communicate with other programs on the server. Several new Web Servers solve this problem, including O'Reilly Associates' WebSite®.

Using O'Reilly Associates' WebSite as the Web Server, a Visual Basic program can use the CGI-WIN interface to receive a query from the WebSite server, open and search a database, and return a Web Page.

The Common Gateway Interface specifies the data that is passed to the backend application by a Web Server. However, it usually assumes a UNIX environment for passing this information. WebSite passes the data to the CGI-WIN program by using an INI file. When WebSite passes the arguments, it specifies a file for the Visual Basic program to return the results. Then it launches the Visual Basic program with a command line in the following form passing these four arguments:

```
cgi-profile input-file output-file url-args
```

The CGI Profile File

The format of the profile is the same as a Windows INI file with bracketed sections and key/value pairs. There are seven sections in a CGI profile file, [CGI], [Accept], [System], [Extra Headers], [Form Literal], [Form External], and [Form huge]. These sections represent the same information passed by CGI in a UNIX environment.

This INI file provides a wealth of information that may be useful to the developer of a backend server CGI program. For example, the [CGI] section of the INI file contains the following information provided by the Web Server:

```
CGI Version=        The version of CGI spoken by the server
Request Protocol=   The server's info protocol (e.g. HTTP/1.0)
Request Method=     The method specified in the request (e.g., "GET")
Executable Path=    Physical pathname of the back-end (this program)
Logical Path=       Extra path info in logical space
Physical Path=      Extra path info in local physical space
Query String=       String following the "?" in the request URL
```

```
Content Type=       MIME content type of info supplied with request
Content Length=     Length, bytes, of info supplied with request
Server Software=    Version/revision of the info (HTTP) server
Server Name=        Server's network hostname (or alias from config)
Server Port=        Server's network port number
Server Admin=       E-Mail address of server's admin. (config)
Referer=   URL of referring document
From=      E-Mail of client
Remote Host=        Remote client's network hostname
Remote Address=     Remote client's network address
Authenticated Username=   Username if present in request
Authenticated Password=   Password if present in request
Authentication Method=    Method used for authentication (e.g., "Basic")
Authentication Realm=     Name of realm for users/groups
```

The [Form Literal] section translates the data from an HTML Form submitted with the POST method into key/value pairs. For example, if the form has a zip code field called zcode and the user enters 34231, then the INI file would look like this:

```
[Form Literal]
zcode=34231
```

From this point, it is a simple task to read this INI file and use the field information to build a database query. You could use standard API calls or use special functions that are included with WebSite.

WebSite provides a module called CGI.BAS, written by Robert Denny, that can be included in your Visual Basic project to easily work with this CGI interface and read these INI files. Let's look at the source code for a real working CGI program that publishes database information on the Web. See the complete code in Listing 15.4. You can try out this program on Sun Hydraulics' Web Page (*www.sunhydraulics.com*). See figure 15.5.

Fig. 15.5
The Sun Hydraulics' Web Page.

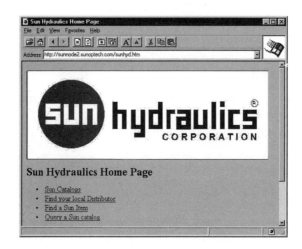

Sun Hydraulics, one of SunOpTech's customers, sells its hydraulics cartridge valves through distributors located around the United States. When customers need one of these parts they must order it through their local distributor. But how do they know how to contact their local distributor? Easy! They connect to Sun Hydraulics' Web Page and click on the hypertext jump `Find your local distributor`. This launches a Visual Basic program that presents a form to the users to get their zip code, then it queries an Access database to find the distributor, and returns a Web Page with the information.

In this example, our CGI-WIN program will be called twice—first to return the entry form and second to return the result form. In the Sun Hydraulics Home Page, `sunhyd.htm`, is an HTML anchor that will launch a program called DISTLIST.EXE:

```
<A HREF="cgi-win/distlist.exe">Find your local Distributor</A>
```

When the program is launched, after certain initialization contained in the Main procedure of the CGI.BAS module, our procedure `CGI_Main` will be called. This procedure will examine the `CGI_RequestMethod` to see if the program was launched from the `POST` method of an HTML Form. If so, we will call a procedure to return the distributor. Otherwise, we'll call a procedure to return an HTML Form.

```
Sub CGI_Main()
If CGI_RequestMethod = "POST"
   ReturnDist
Else
   ReturnForm
End If
End Sub
```

When this program is launched from a normal HTML anchor, as in the example on the Sun Hydraulics Home Page, the `GET` method will be used by the Web Server, so the `ReturnForm` procedure will be called.

`ReturnForm` creates an HTML Form for the users to enter their zip codes and prints the HTML code for the form to the specified output file by using the `Send` procedure.

The first step is to create a normal heading and body for the HTML file. Note how the H1 and H2 codes can be used to generate different font sizes:

```
Sub ReturnForm()
Send "Content-type: text/html"
Send ""
Send ("<HTML><HEAD><TITLE>Distributor Query List</TITLE></HEAD>")
Send ("<BODY><H1>Welcome To</H1>")
Send ("<H2>Sun Hydraulics Distributor Query</H2>")
Send ("Enter your Zip Code for distributor search")
```

Then use the FORM code to identify this as an HTML Form with a POST method and create a single INPUT field with a field name of zcode and a command button to submit the form to the Web Server:

```
Send ("<FORM ACTION=""/cgi-win/distlist.exe"" METHOD=""POST"">")
Send ("      Zip Code: <INPUT SIZE=5 NAME=""zcode"">")
Send ("To start search, press this button: <INPUT TYPE=""submit""")
Send ("VALUE=""Search"">")
Send ("<HR></FORM></BODY></HTML>")
End Sub
```

The Web Server will return this form to the client (see fig. 15.6).

Fig. 15.6

The HTML Form Document

When users enter a zip code and click the Search button, their Web Browser will send a POST command to the Web Server with the requested zip code. Since the POST method is used, the CGI_Main procedure will call the ReturnDist procedure.

First, ReturnDist calls the procedure GetSmallField, part of the CGI.BAS module to retrieve the zip code from the INI file created by WebSite:

```
Sub ReturnDist()
Dim szip As String, sendstr$
Dim db1 As DATABASE, db2 As DATABASE
Dim table1 As TABLE, table2 As TABLE
szip = GetSmallField("zcode")
```

Then it opens the zipcode and distributor databases:

```
Set db1 = OpenDatabase("\ZIPCODE\OBPOSTAL.MDB")
Set db2 = OpenDatabase("\ZIPCODE\OBMASTER.MDB")
Set table1 = db1.OpenTable("ZipCodes")
Set table2 = db2.OpenTable("Locations")
```

And, after appropriate error-checking for invalid or missing zip code, it searches the first database by zip code for the distributor ID. If it finds the distributor ID it searches the second database by ID for the distributor's name and address information:

```
table1.Index = "PrimaryKey"
table1.Seek "=", szip
table2.Index = "Quick"
table2.Seek "=", table1("Distributor")
```

When it finds the distributor information, it builds the header of the resulting HTML document from that database record:

```
Send ("Content-type: text/html")
Send ("")
Send ("<HTML><HEAD><TITLE>Your Sun Distributor is:</TITLE></HEAD>")
Send ("<H1>Your Sun Distributor is:</H1>")
Send ("</HEAD><BODY>")
```

And then it creates the body of the HTML document with the data from the database fields:

```
Send ("<PRE>")
Send (Trim$(table2("Name")))
Send (Trim$(table2("Addr1")))
Send (Trim$(table2("City")) & ", " & _
    table2("State") & ", " & table2("Cntry") & "   " &
table2("Postal"))
Send ("Phone: " & table2("Phone"))
Send ("Fax: " & table2("Fax"))
```

And before closing the databases, adds an H2 font line to encourage the customers to call this distributor to place their orders!

```
Send ("<H2>Please call this distributor to place your order.</H2>")
Send ("</PRE></BODY></HTML>")
table1.Close:db1.Close
table2.Close:db2.Close
End Sub
```

See figure 15.7.

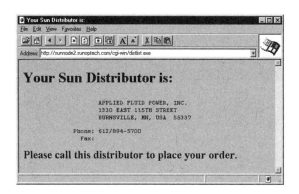

Fig. 15.7
The resulting HTML Document.

That's all there is to it! As you can see, the CGI-WIN interface makes it simple to write a Visual Basic program to publish database information over the World Wide Web.

Chapter Summary

The World Wide Web should not be a mystery to you any longer. You can use Visual Basic to develop Web Pages, to act as a web client and retrieve information from the Web, and to interface with a Web Server to publish database information over the Web.

The SunOpTech® Web Server

Setting up a Web Server has gotten quite easy. Here are the steps we followed to set up our Web Server:

Get a dial-up PPP connection to a local Internet provider.

Have your provider assist in establishing your domain name and IP addresses, ask them to handle the Smarthost and DNS functions, and have them establish a Cname for WWW at your domain address.

Install NT on a 486 or better PC and set up Remote Access to dial your Internet provider and establish a TCP/IP connection.

Download one of the public domain Web Servers that will run as an NT Service and install it with a data directory of C:\HTTP.

In this directory, create your home page HTML document named DEFAULT.HTM.

That's all there is to it!

Listing 15.1 15LIST01.TXT—The Create HTML program. This program creates a properly formatted HTML file from a simple ASCII file.

```
Option Explicit

Sub CreateMailHTML()
Dim FName$, txt$
CommonDialog1.DialogTitle = "Input File Name"
CommonDialog1.Filter = "HTML(*.htm)¦*.htm¦All Files¦*.*"
CommonDialog1.FilterIndex = 2
CommonDialog1.ShowOpen
FName$ = CommonDialog1.filename
```

```
Open FName$ For Input As #1
Do Until EOF(1)
   Input #1, txt$
   List1.AddItem txt$
Loop
Close #1
CommonDialog1.DialogTitle = "HTML Document Name"
CommonDialog1.Filter = "HTML(*.htm)¦*.htm¦All Files¦*.*"
CommonDialog1.FilterIndex = 1
CommonDialog1.filename = "addr.htm"
CommonDialog1.ShowOpen
FName$ = CommonDialog1.filename
Open FName$ For Output As #1
WriteHTMLHeader
WriteHTMLBody
WriteHTMLFooter
Close #1
Open FName$ For Binary As #1
Text1 = Input(LOF(1), #1)
Close #1

End Sub

Sub WriteHTMLHeader()
Print #1, "<HTML>"
Print #1, "<HEAD>"
Print #1, "<TITLE>Internet Mail Addresses</TITLE>"
Print #1, "</HEAD>"
End Sub

Sub WriteHTMLBody()
WriteBodyText
WriteAddresses
End Sub

Sub WriteBodyText()
Print #1, "<BODY>"
Print #1, "<H1>SunOpTech Personnel Email Addresses</H1>"
Print #1, "<HR>"
Print #1, "<P>"
Print #1, "Below are the Internet Mail addresses for SunOpTech
➥personnel."
Print #1, "Click on their name to send mail:"
Print #1, "<P>"
End Sub

Sub WriteAddresses()
Dim Nme As Object, i%
Print #1, "<UL>"
For i = 0 To List1.ListCount - 1
   Print #1, MakeMailHTML(List1.List(i))
Next
Print #1, "</UL>"
End Sub
```

(continues)

Listing 15.1   Continued

```
Function MakeMailHTML(Nme)
Dim txt$, Q$, addr$, pos&
Q$ = Chr$(34) 'quote
pos& = InStr(Nme, " ")
addr$ = Left(Nme, pos& - 1) & Mid(Nme, pos& + 1, 1)
addr$ = addr$ & "@sunoptech.com"
txt$ = "<LI><A href=" & Q$ & "mailto:"
txt$ = txt$ & addr$ & Q$ & ">"
txt$ = txt$ & Nme & ": " & addr$ & "</A>"
MakeMailHTML = txt$
End Function

Sub WriteHTMLFooter()
Print #1, "<HR>"
Print #1, "<I>Revised " & Format(Now, "dd-mmm-yy") & " by Chris Barlow</I>"
Print #1, "</BODY>"
Print #1, "</HTML>"
End Sub


Private Sub mCreate_Click()
   CreateMailHTML
End Sub

Private Sub mExit_Click()
   Unload Me
End Sub
```

**Listing 15.2   15LIST02.TXT—The News Demo program. This
program acts as a web client and queries information over the
Web.**

```
Option Explicit

'-- Used to tell us when we've connected
Private nConnected As Integer

'-- Stores received data
Private szNews As String

Private Function szStripHTML(szString As String) As String

   Dim szTemp As String
   Dim szResult As String
   Dim nPos As Integer
   Dim nMarker As Integer

   '-- Copy the argument into a local
   '    string so the original does not
   '    get whacked.
   szTemp = szString
```

```
'-- Remove HTML codes
Do
        nPos = InStr(szTemp, "<")
        If nPos = False Then
                Exit Do
        Else
                '-- szResult contains the final
                '   product of this routine.
                szResult = szResult & _
                        Left$(szTemp, nPos - 1)
                '-- szTemp is the working string,
                '   which is continuously
                '   shortened as new codes
                '   are found
                szTemp = Mid$(szTemp, nPos + 1)
                nPos = InStr(szTemp, ">")
                If nPos = False Then
                        '-- No complimentary arrow
                        '   was found.
                        Exit Do
                Else
                        '-- Shorten the working
                        '   string
                        szTemp = Mid$(szTemp, _
                                nPos + 1)
                End If
        End If
Loop

'-- Find a marker byte by looking for
'   a char that does not already exist
'   in the string.
For nMarker = 255 To 1 Step -1
        If InStr(szResult, Chr$(nMarker)) _
                = 0 Then
                Exit For
        End If
Next

'-- Remove carriage returns
Do
        nPos = InStr(szResult, Chr$(13))
        If nPos Then
                szResult = Left$(szResult, _
                        nPos - 1) & Mid$(szResult, _
                        nPos + 1)
        Else
                Exit Do
        End If
Loop

 Replace linefeeds with Marker bytes
Do
        nPos = InStr(szResult, Chr$(10))
```

(continues)

Listing 15.2 Continued

```
            If nPos Then
                    szResult = Left$(szResult, _
                            nPos - 1) & Chr$(nMarker) _
                            & Mid$(szResult, nPos + 1)
            Else
                    Exit Do
            End If
    Loop

    '-- Replace marker bytes with CR/LF pairs
    Do
            nPos = InStr(szResult, Chr$(nMarker))
            If nPos Then
                    szResult = Left$(szResult, _
                            nPos - 1) & Chr$(13) & Chr$(10) _
                            & Trim$(Mid$(szResult, nPos + 1))
            Else
                    Exit Do
            End If
    Loop

    '-- Thats all for this routine!
    szStripHTML = szResult

End Function

Private Sub DSSocket1_Close(ErrorCode As Integer, ErrorDesc As String)

    '-- Display the news string after converting
    '   it to straight text
    txtNews = szStripHTML(szNews)

    '-- Re-enable the form and reset the mouse
    '   pointer
    Screen.MousePointer = vbDefault
    Enabled = True

End Sub

Private Sub DSSocket1_Connect()

    '-- Set this flag indicating we've connected
    nConnected = True

End Sub


Private Sub DSSocket1_Receive(ReceiveData As String)
```

```
    '-- Data was received. Add to the module-level
    '   string variable
    szNews = szNews & ReceiveData
    txtNews = szStripHTML(szNews)
End Sub


Private Sub Form_Load()

    '-- Temporarily disable the form and set the hourglass cursor
    Enabled = False
    Screen.MousePointer = vbHourglass

    '-- Show the form
    Show

    '-- Connect to the internetMCI server
    DSSocket1.RemotePort = 80
    DSSocket1.RemoteHost = "www.fyionline.com"
    On Error Resume Next
    DSSocket1.Action = 2

    If Err Then
            '-- There was an error. Re-enable the form
            '   and reset the mouse pointer
            Screen.MousePointer = vbDefault
            Enabled = True

            '-- Display the error
            MsgBox "Error connecting: " & Error
            Exit Sub
    Else
            '-- Wait until we've connected
            nConnected = False
            Do
                    DoEvents
            Loop Until nConnected

            '-- Initialize the szNews module-level variable,
            '   which holds the received data.
            szNews = ""

            '-- Send the command to retrieve the daily news summary
            DSSocket1.Send = "GET /infoMCI/update/NEWS-MCI.html" & _
                    vbCrLf & vbCrLf
    End If

End Sub
```

```
Option Explicit
Private nConnected As Boolean
Private nStop As Boolean
Private szHTML As String
Private Function ParseResponse(szResp$, Item%) As Variant
Select Case Item
Case 0  'date
   ParseResponse = Mid(ParseString(szResp, "As of", 2), 5, 11)
Case 1  'from
   ParseResponse = Left(ParseString(szResp, ":", 5), 11)
Case 2  'to
   ParseResponse = Left(ParseString(szResp, ":", 7), 11)
End Select
End Function
Private Function szGetHTML(szHost$, szGet$) As String
dsSocket1.RemoteHost = szHost$
dsSocket1.RemotePort = 80
On Error Resume Next
dsSocket1.Action = 2
If Err Then
   MsgBox Error$
Else
   nConnected = False
   Do
         DoEvents
   Loop Until nConnected Or nStop
   szHTML = ""
   dsSocket1.Send = szGet & vbCrLf
   HelpLine = "Send " & szGet
   Do
         DoEvents
   Loop Until (nConnected = False) Or nStop
   szGetHTML = szStripHTML(szHTML)
End If
End Function
Private Function szStripHTML(szString As String) As String

   Dim szTemp As String
   Dim szResult As String
   Dim nPos As Integer
   Dim nMarker As Integer

   '-- Copy the argument into a local
   '   string so the original does not
   '   get whacked.
   szTemp = szString

   '-- Remove HTML codes
   Do
         nPos = InStr(szTemp, "<")
```

```
        If nPos = False Then
                Exit Do
        Else
                '-- szResult contains the final
                '   product of this routine.
                szResult = szResult & _
                        Left$(szTemp, nPos - 1)
                '-- szTemp is the working string,
                '   which is continuously
                '   shortened as new codes
                '   are found
                szTemp = Mid$(szTemp, nPos + 1)
                nPos = InStr(szTemp, ">")
                If nPos = False Then
                        '-- No complimentary arrow
                        '   was found.
                        Exit Do
                Else
                        '-- Shorten the working
                        '   string
                        szTemp = Mid$(szTemp, _
                                nPos + 1)
                End If
        End If
Loop

'-- Find a marker byte by looking for
'   a char that does not already exist
'   in the string.
For nMarker = 255 To 1 Step -1
        If InStr(szResult, Chr$(nMarker)) _
                = 0 Then
                Exit For
        End If
Next

'-- Remove carriage returns
Do
        nPos = InStr(szResult, Chr$(13))
        If nPos Then
                szResult = Left$(szResult, _
                        nPos - 1) & Mid$(szResult, _
                        nPos + 1)
        Else
                Exit Do
        End If
Loop

'-- Replace linefeeds with Marker bytes
Do
        nPos = InStr(szResult, Chr$(10))
        If nPos Then
                szResult = Left$(szResult, _
                        nPos - 1) & Chr$(nMarker) _
```

(continues)

Listing 15.3   Continued

```
                                & Mid$(szResult, nPos + 1)
        Else
                Exit Do
        End If
    Loop

    '-- Replace marker bytes with CR/LF pairs
    Do
        nPos = InStr(szResult, Chr$(nMarker))
        If nPos Then
                szResult = Left$(szResult, _
                        nPos - 1) & Chr$(13) & Chr$(10) _
                        & Trim$(Mid$(szResult, nPos + 1))
        Else
                Exit Do
        End If
    Loop

    '-- Thats all for this routine!
    szStripHTML = szResult

End Function

Private Sub butGo_Click()
'get all
Dim col&, row&, MaxRow&
MaxRow = 1
For col = 2 To 5
    For row = 1 To MaxRow
            Spread1_DblClick col, row
    Next
    MaxRow = MaxRow + 1
Next

End Sub

Private Sub butStop_Click()
    nStop = True
End Sub

Private Sub dsSocket1_Close(ErrorCode As Integer, ErrorDesc As String)
nConnected = False
HelpLine = "Closed"
End Sub

Private Sub dsSocket1_Connect()
nConnected = True
HelpLine = "Connected"
End Sub

Private Sub dsSocket1_Receive(ReceiveData As String)
szHTML = szHTML & ReceiveData
HelpLine = "Receive: " & szHTML
End Sub
```

```
Private Sub Spread1_DblClick(col As Long, row As Long)
'get the row and col header
Dim szHost$, szGet$
Dim C1 As Variant, C2 As Variant, i%
Spread1.row = row
Spread1.col = 0
C1 = Spread1.TEXT
Spread1.row = 0
Spread1.col = col
C2 = Spread1.TEXT
'built query
   szHost = "www.dna.lth.se"
   szGet = "GET /cgi-bin/kurt/rates?" & C1 & "+" & C2
'connect and send get
   Text1 = szGetHTML(szHost, szGet)
   SpreadSetText Spread1, 0, 0, ParseResponse(Text1, 0)
   SpreadSetText Spread1, col, row, ParseResponse(Text1, 1)
   SpreadSetText Spread1, row, col, ParseResponse(Text1, 2)

'receive and build response
'on close parse and update
End Sub
```

Listing 15.4   15LIST04.TXT— DistList CGI-WIN   This program interfaces with a CGI-WIN-capable server to query a database and return a Web Page.

```
DISTMOD.BAS Module
Option Explicit
Sub CGI_Main()
If CGI_RequestMethod = "POST" Then 'If it came in with a POST
➥method
    ReturnDist                                    ' Return zip
                                                  ➥code
    Beep                                          '
➥Announce to server's owner
  Else
➥' If not "submit"-ed (GET Method)
    ReturnForm                                    ' Send back
                                                  ➥request form

  End If
End Sub

Sub ReturnDist()
Dim szip As String, sendstr$
Dim db1 As DATABASE, db2 As DATABASE
Dim table1 As TABLE, table2 As TABLE
szip = GetSmallField("zcode")
Set db1 = OpenDatabase("\ZIPCODE\OBPOSTAL.MDB")
Set db2 = OpenDatabase("\ZIPCODE\OBMASTER.MDB")
Set table1 = db1.OpenTable("ZipCodes")
Set table2 = db2.OpenTable("Locations")
```

(continues)

Listing 15.4 Continued

```
table1.Index = "PrimaryKey"
table1.Seek "=", szip
If table1.NoMatch Then
   Send ("Content-type: text/html")
   Send ("")
   Send ("<HTML><HEAD><TITLE>Distributor</TITLE></HEAD>")
   Send ("<H1>Zip Code Not Found</H1>")
   Send ("</HEAD><BODY>")
   Send ("ZipCode Not Found")
   Send ("</BODY></HTML>")
   Exit Sub
End If
table2.Index = "Quick"
table2.Seek "=", table1("Distributor")
If table2.NoMatch Then
   Send ("Content-type: text/html")
   Send ("")
   Send ("<HTML><HEAD><TITLE>Distributor</TITLE></HEAD>")
   Send ("<H1>Distributor Not Found</H1>")
   Send ("</HEAD><BODY>")
   Send ("<H2>Distributor Not Found.  Please call Sun Hydraulics
   ➥for assistance.</H2>")
   Send ("</BODY></HTML>")
   Exit Sub
End If
Send ("Content-type: text/html")
Send ("")
Send ("<HTML><HEAD><TITLE>Your Sun Distributor is:</TITLE></HEAD>")
Send ("<H1>Your Sun Distributor is:</H1>")
Send ("</HEAD><BODY>")
Send ("<PRE>")
Send ("                            " & Trim$(table2("Name")))
If table2("Addr1") <> "" Then
   Send ("                            " & Trim$(table2("Addr1")))
End If
If table2("Addr2") <> "" Then
   Send ("                            " & Trim$(table2("Addr2")))
End If
If table2("Addr3") <> "" Then
   Send ("                            " & Trim$(table2("Addr3")))
End If
Send ("                            " & Trim$(table2("City")) & ", "
& _
   table2("State") & ", " & table2("Cntry") & "  " & table2("Postal"))
Send ("")
Send ("                   Phone: " & table2("Phone"))
Send ("                      Fax: " & table2("Fax"))
Send ("")
Send ("<H2>Please call this distributor to place your order.</H2>")
Send ("</PRE>")
Send ("</BODY></HTML>")
table2.Close
table1.Close
db2.Close
```

```
db1.Close
End Sub

Sub ReturnForm()
   '
   Send "Content-type: text/html"
   Send "" ' Header-document separator
      '
      ' Now send the sign-in form document
      '
   Send ("<HTML><HEAD><TITLE>Distributor Query List</TITLE></HEAD>")
   Send ("<BODY><H1>Welcome To</H1>")
   Send ("<H2>Sun Hydraulics Distributor Query</H2>")
   Send ("Enter your Zip Code for distributor search")
   Send ("<FORM ACTION=""/cgi-win/distlist.exe"" METHOD=""POST"">")
   Send ("<PRE>")
   Send ("   Zip Code: <INPUT SIZE=5 NAME=""zcode"">")
   Send ("")
   Send ("</PRE>")
   Send ("To start search, press this button: <INPUT TYPE=""submit""")
   Send ("VALUE=""Search"">")
   Send ("<HR>")
   Send ("</FORM></BODY></HTML>")

End Sub

CGI.BAS Module
'---------------------------------------------------------------------
'     **********
'     * CGI.BAS *
'     **********
'
' VERSION: 1.7  (March 18, 1995)
'
' AUTHOR:   Robert B. Denny <rdenny@netcom.com>
'
' Common routines needed to establish a VB environment for
' CGI "scripts" that run behind the Windows Web Server.
'
' INTRODUCTION
'
' The Common Gateway Interface (CGI) version 1.1 specifies a minimal
' set of data that is made available to the back-end application by
' an HTTP (Web) server. It also specifies the details for passing this
' information to the back-end. The latter part of the CGI spec is
' specific to UNIX-like environments. The NCSA httpd for Windows does
' supply the data items (and more) specified by CGI/1.1, however it
' uses a different method for passing the data to the back-end.
'
' DEVELOPMENT
'
' Windows httpd requires any Windows back-end program to be an
' executable image. This means that you must convert your VB
' application into an executable (.EXE) before it can be tested
' with the server.
'
```

(continues)

Listing 15.4   Continued

```
' ENVIRONMENT
'
' The Windows httpd server executes script requests by doing a
' WinExec with a command line in the following form:
'
'   prog-name cgi-profile input-file output-file url-args
'
' Assuming you are familiar with the CGI specification, the above
' should be "intuitively obvious" except for the cgi-profile, which
' is described in the next section.
'
' THE CGI PROFILE FILE
'
' The Unix CGI passes data to the back end by defining environment
' variables which can be used by shell scripts. The Windows httpd
' server passes data to its back end via the profile file. The
' format of the profile is that of a Windows ".INI" file. The keyword
' names have been changed cosmetically.
'
' There are 7 sections in a CGI profile file, [CGI], [Accept],
' [System], [Extra Headers], and [Form Literal], [Form External],
' and [Form huge]. They are described below:
'
' [CGI]                       <== The standard CGI variables
' CGI Version=              The version of CGI spoken by the server
' Request Protocol=         The server's info protocol (e.g. HTTP/1.0)
' Request Method=     The method specified in the request (e.g., "GET")
' Executable Path=  Physical pathname of the back-end (this program)
' Logical Path=            Extra path info in logical space
' Physical Path=        Extra path info in local physical space
' Query String=            String following the "?" in the request URL
' Content Type=            MIME content type of info supplied with request
' Content Length=    Length, bytes, of info supplied with request
' Server Software= Version/revision of the info (HTTP) server
' Server Name=             Server's network hostname (or alias
from config)
' Server Port=             Server's network port number
' Server Admin=            E-Mail address of server's admin.
                           ➥(config)
' Referer=                 URL of referring document (HTTP/1.0
                           ➥draft 12/94)
' From=                       E-Mail of client user  (HTTP/1.0
                           ➥draft 12/94)
' Remote Host=             Remote client's network hostname
' Remote Address=     Remote client's network address
' Authenticated Username=Username if present in request
' Authenticated Password=Password if present in request
' Authentication Method=Method used for authentication (e.g.,
➥"Basic")
' Authentication Realm=Name of realm for users/groups
' RFC-931 Identity=        (deprecated, removed from code)
'
' [Accept]                 <== What the client says it can take
' The MIME types found in the request header as
```

```
'  Accept: xxx/yyy; zzzz...
' are entered in this section as
'  xxx/yyy=zzzz...
' If only the MIME type appears, the form is
'  xxx/yyy=Yes
'
' [System]                    <== Windows interface specifics
' GMT Offset=                  Offset of local timezone from GMT,
                               ➥seconds (LONG!)
' Output File=                 Pathname of file to receive results
' Content File=                Pathname of file containing request
                               ➥content (raw)
' Debug Mode=                  If server's back-end debug flag is set
                               ➥(Yes/No)
'
' [Extra Headers]
' Any "extra" headers found in the request that activated this
' program. They are listed in "key=value" form. Usually, you'll see
' at least the name of the browser here.
'
' [Form Literal]
' If the request was a POST from a Mosaic form (with content type of
' "application/x-www-form-urlencoded"), the server will decode the
' form data. Raw form input is of the form "key=value&key=value&...",
' with the value parts "URL-encoded". The server splits the key=value
' pairs at the '&', then spilts the key and value at the '=',
' URL-decodes the value string and puts the result into key=value
' (decoded) form in the [Form Literal] section of the INI.
'
' [Form External]
' If the decoded value string is more than 254 characters long,
' or if the decoded value string contains any control characters,
' the server puts the decoded value into an external tempfile and
' lists the field in this section as:
'  key=<pathname> <length>
' where <pathname> is the path and name of the tempfile containing
' the decoded value string, and <length> is the length in bytes
' of the decoded value string.
'
' NOTE: BE SURE TO OPEN THIS FILE IN BINARY MODE UNLESS YOU ARE
'     CERTAIN THAT THE FORM DATA IS TEXT!
'
' [Form Huge]
' If the raw value string is more than 65,536 bytes long, the server
' does no decoding. In this case, the server lists the field in this
' section as:
'  key=<offset> <length>
' where <offset> is the offset from the beginning of the Content File
' at which the raw value string for this key is located, and <length>
' is the length in bytes of the raw value string. You can use the
' <offset> to perform a "Seek" to the start of the raw value string,
' and use the length to know when you have read the entire raw string
' into your decoder. Note that VB has a limit of 64K for strings, so
'
' Examples:
```

(continues)

Listing 15.4 Continued

```
'
' [Form Literal]
' smallfield=123 Main St. #122
'
' [Form External]
' field300chars=C:\TEMP\HS19AF6C.000 300
' fieldwithlinebreaks=C:\TEMP\HS19AF6C.001 43
'
' [Form Huge]
' field230K=C:\TEMP\HS19AF6C.002 276920
'
' =====
' USAGE
' =====
' Include CGI.BAS in your VB project. Set the project options for
' "Sub Main" startup. The Main() procedure is in this module, and it
' handles all of the setup of the VB CGI environment, as described
' above. Once all of this is done, the Main() calls YOUR main procedure
' which must be called CGI_Main(). The output file is open, use Send()
' to write to it. The input file is NOT open, and "huge" form fields
' have not been decoded.
'
' (New in V1.3) If your program is started without command-line args,
' the code assumes you want to run it interactively. This is useful
' for providing a setup screen, etc. Instead of calling CGI_Main(),
' it calls Inter_Main(). Your module must also implement this
' function. If you don't need an interactive mode, just create
' Inter_Main() and put a 1-line call to MsgBox alerting the
' user that the program is not meant to be run interactively.
' The samples furnished with the server do this.
'
' If a Visual Basic runtime error occurs, it will be trapped and result
' in an HTTP error response being sent to the client. Check out the
' Error Handler() sub. When your program finishes, be sure to RETURN
' TO MAIN(). Don't just do an "End".
'
' Have a look at the stuff below to see what's what.
'
'-------------------------------------------------------------------------
' Chris:   Robert B. Denny <rdenny@netcom.com>
'              June 7, 1994
'
' Revision History:
'   26-May-94 rbd    Initial experimental release
'   07-Jun-94 rbd    Revised keyword names and form decoding per
'                         httpd 1.2b8, fixed section name of Output File
'   13-Dec-94 rbd    Move FreeFile calls to just before opening files.
'   04-Feb-94 rbd    Fix Authenticated User -> Username, added new
'                         variables Referer, From and Authentication Rea
'                         Removed RFC931 stuff (deprecated)
'   11-Feb-95 rbd    Added Inter_Main() support and stub.
'   01-Mar-95 rbd    Add support for password pass-through, clean
'                         up HTML in error handler. Add SendNoOp().
```

```
'                              Add Server: header to error handler msg.
'    17-Mar-95 rbd   Fix error handler to remove deprecated
'                              MIME-Version header. Add GMT offset, new CGI var.
'                              Add WebDate() function for producing HTTP/1.0
'                              compliant date/time. Add Date: header to error
'                              messages.
'    18-Mar-95 rbd   Add CGI_ERR_START for catching CGI.BAS defined
'                              errors in user code. Decode our "user defined:
'                              errors in handler instead of saying "User
'                              defined error".
'----------------------------------------------------------------------
Option Explicit
'
' ==================
' Manifest Constants
' ==================
'
Const MAX_CMDARGS = 8        ' Max # of command line args
Const ENUM_BUF_SIZE = 4096  ' Key enumeration buffer, see GetProfile()
' These are the limits in the server
Const MAX_XHDR = 100                  ' Max # of "extra" request headers
Const MAX_ACCTYPE = 100      ' Max # of Accept: types in request
Const MAX_FORM_TUPLES = 100 ' Max # form key=value pairs
Const MAX_HUGE_TUPLES = 16  ' Max # "huge" form fields
'
'
' =====
' Types
' =====
'
Type Tuple                        ' Used for Accept: and "extra" headers
   key As String                  ' and for holding POST form key=value pairs
   value As String
End Type

Type HugeTuple                        ' Used for "huge" form fields
   key As String                  ' Keyword (decoded)
   offset As Long                 ' Byte offset into Content File of value
   length As Long                 ' Length of value, bytes
End Type
'
'
' ================
' Global Constants
' ================
'
' -----------
' Error Codes
' -----------
'
Global Const ERR_ARGCOUNT = 32767
Global Const ERR_BAD_REQUEST = 32766               ' HTTP 400
Global Const ERR_UNAUTHORIZED = 32765        ' HTTP 401
Global Const ERR_PAYMENT_REQUIRED = 32764    ' HTTP 402
Global Const ERR_FORBIDDEN = 32763           ' HTTP 403
Global Const ERR_NOT_FOUND = 32762           ' HTTP 404
```

(continues)

Listing 15.4   Continued

```
Global Const ERR_INTERNAL_ERROR = 32761     ' HTTP 500
Global Const ERR_NOT_IMPLEMENTED = 32760   ' HTTP 501
Global Const ERR_TOO_BUSY = 32758           ' HTTP 503 (experimental)
Global Const ERR_NO_FIELD = 32757           ' GetxxxField "no field"
Global Const CGI_ERR_START = 32757          ' Start of our errors


' ====================
' CGI Global Variables
' ====================
'
' --------------------
' Standard CGI variables
' --------------------
'
Global CGI_ServerSoftware As String
Global CGI_ServerName As String
Global CGI_ServerPort As Integer
Global CGI_RequestProtocol As String
Global CGI_ServerAdmin As String
Global CGI_Version As String
Global CGI_RequestMethod As String
Global CGI_LogicalPath As String
Global CGI_PhysicalPath As String
Global CGI_ExecutablePath As String
Global CGI_QueryString As String
Global CGI_Referer As String
Global CGI_From As String
Global CGI_RemoteHost As String
Global CGI_RemoteAddr As String
Global CGI_AuthUser As String
Global CGI_AuthPass As String
Global CGI_AuthType As String
Global CGI_AuthRealm As String
Global CGI_ContentType As String
Global CGI_ContentLength As Long
'
' -----------------
' HTTP Header Arrays
' -----------------
'
Global CGI_AcceptTypes(MAX_ACCTYPE) As Tuple     ' Accept: types
Global CGI_NumAcceptTypes As Integer                ' # of
➥live entries in array
Global CGI_ExtraHeaders(MAX_XHDR) As Tuple   ' "Extra" headers
Global CGI_NumExtraHeaders As Integer            ' # of live
➥entries in array
'
' -------------
' POST Form Data
' -------------
'
```

```
Global cgi_FormTuples(MAX_FORM_TUPLES) As Tuple ' POST form key=value pairs
Global CGI_NumFormTuples As Integer                    ' # of live entries in array
Global CGI_HugeTuples(MAX_HUGE_TUPLES) As HugeTuple ' Form "huge tuples
Global CGI_NumHugeTuples As Integer                    ' # of live entries in array

'
' ----------------
' System Variables
' ----------------
'
Global CGI_GMTOffset As Variant            ' GMT offset (time serial)
Global CGI_ContentFile As String          ' Content/Input file pathname
Global CGI_OutputFile As String           ' Output file pathname
Global CGI_DebugMode As Integer           ' Script Tracing flag from server
'
'
' =======================
' Windows API Declarations
' =======================
'
' NOTE: Declaration of GetPrivateProfileString is specially done to
' permit enumeration of keys by passing NULL key value. See GetProfile().
'
#If Win32 Then
Declare Function GetPrivateProfileString Lib "kernel32" Alias
➥"GetPrivateProfileStringA" (ByVal lpApplicationName As String,
➥ByVal lpKeyName As Any, ByVal lpDefault As String, ByVal
➥lpReturnedString As String, ByVal nSize As Long, ByVal lpFileName
➥As String) As Long
#Else
Declare Function GetPrivateProfileString Lib "Kernel" (ByVal
➥lpSection As String, ByVal lpKeyName As Any, ByVal lpDefault As
➥String, ByVal lpReturnedString As String, ByVal nSize As Integer,
➥ByVal lpFileName As String) As Integer
➥#End If
'
'
' ==============
' Local Variables
' ==============
'
Dim CGI_ProfileFile As String                ' Profile file pathname
Dim CGI_OutputFN As Integer                  ' Output file number
Dim ErrorString As String


'-------------------------------------------------------------------------
'
'    ErrorHandler() - Global error handler
'
' If a VB runtime error occurs dusing execution of the program, this
' procedure generates an HTTP/1.0 HTML-formatted error message into
' the output file, then exits the program.
'
```

(continues)

Listing 15.4 Continued

```
' This should be armed immediately on entry to the program's main()
' procedure. Any errors that occur in the program are caught, and
' an HTTP/1.0 error messsage is generated into the output file. The
' presence of the HTTP/1.0 on the first line of the output file causes
' NCSA httpd for WIndows to send the output file to the client with no
' interpretation or other header parsing.
'.......................................................................
Sub ErrorHandler(code As Integer)

   On Error Resume Next     ' Give it a good try!

   Seek #CGI_OutputFN, 1    ' Rewind output file just in case
   Send ("HTTP/1.0 500 Internal Error")
   Send ("Server: " + CGI_ServerSoftware)
   Send ("Date: " + WebDate(Now))
   Send ("Content-type: text/html")
   Send ("")
   Send ("<HTML><HEAD>")
   Send ("<TITLE>Error in " + CGI_ExecutablePath + "</TITLE>")
   Send ("</HEAD><BODY>")
   Send ("<H1>Error in " + CGI_ExecutablePath + "</H1>")
   Send ("An internal Visual Basic error has occurred in " +
   ➥CGI_ExecutablePath + ".")
   Send ("<PRE>" + ErrorString + "</PRE>")
   Send ("<I>Please</I> note what you were doing when this problem
   ➥occurred,")
   Send ("so we can identify and correct it. Write down the Web
   ➥page you were using,")
   Send ("any data you may have entered into a form or search box,
   ➥and")
   Send ("anything else that may help us duplicate the problem.
   ➥Then contact the")
   Send ("administrator of this service: ")
   Send ("<A HREF=""mailto:" & CGI_ServerAdmin & """>")
   Send ("<ADDRESS>&lt;" + CGI_ServerAdmin + "&gt;</ADDRESS>")
   Send ("</A></BODY></HTML>")

   Close #CGI_OutputFN

   '======
   End                      ' Terminate the program
   '======
End Sub


'---------------------------------------------------------------------
'
'   GetAcceptTypes() - Create the array of accept type structs
'
' Enumerate the keys in the [Accept] section of the profile file,
' then get the value for each of the keys.
'.......................................................................
Private Sub GetAcceptTypes()
  Dim sList As String
  Dim i As Integer, j As Integer, l As Integer, n As Integer
```

```
    sList = GetProfile("Accept", "") ' Get key list
    l = Len(sList)
                                                        ' Length incl trailing null
    i = 1                                               ' Start at 1st character
    n = 0                                               ' Index in array
    Do While ((i < l) And (n < MAX_ACCTYPE)) ' Safety stop here
            j = InStr(i, sList, Chr$(0))            ' J -> next null
            CGI_AcceptTypes(n).key = Mid$(sList, i, j - i) ' Get Key, then value
            CGI_AcceptTypes(n).value = GetProfile("Accept", CGI_AcceptTypes(n).key)
            i = j + 1                                   ' Bump pointer
            n = n + 1                                   ' Bump array index
    Loop
    CGI_NumAcceptTypes = n                          ' Fill in global count

End Sub

'-------------------------------------------------------------------------------
'
'   GetArgs() - Parse the command line
'
' Chop up the command line, fill in the argument vector, return the
' argument count (similar to the Unix/C argc/argv handling)
'-------------------------------------------------------------------------------
Private Function GetArgs(argv() As String) As Integer
  Dim buf As String
  Dim i As Integer, j As Integer, l As Integer, n As Integer

  buf = Trim$(Command$)                              ' Get command line

  l = Len(buf)                                       ' Length of command line
  If l = 0 Then                                      ' If empty
          GetArgs = 0
          ➥' Return argc = 0
          Exit Function
  End If

  i = 1
  ➥' Start at 1st character
  n = 0
  ➥' Index in argvec
  Do While ((i < l) And (n < MAX_CMDARGS)) ' Safety stop here
          j = InStr(i, buf, " ")                    ' J -> next space
          If j = 0 Then Exit Do                     ' Exit loop
                                                    ➥on last arg
          argv(n) = Trim$(Mid$(buf, i, j - i)) ' Get this token,
          ➥trim it
          i = j + 1
          ➥' Skip that blank
          Do While Mid$(buf, i, 1) = " "      ' Skip any additional
          ➥whitespace
                  i = i + 1
          Loop
          n = n + 1
          ➥' Bump array index
  Loop
```

(continues)

Listing 15.4 Continued

```
    argv(n) = Trim$(Mid$(buf, i, (l - i + 1))) ' Get last arg
    GetArgs = n + 1
➥' Return arg count

End Function

'------------------------------------------------------------------------
'
'   GetExtraHeaders() - Create the array of extra header structs
'
' Enumerate the keys in the [Extra Headers] section of the profile file,
' then get the value for each of the keys.
'------------------------------------------------------------------------
Private Sub GetExtraHeaders()
    Dim sList As String
    Dim i As Integer, j As Integer, l As Integer, n As Integer

    sList = GetProfile("Extra Headers", "") ' Get key list
    l = Len(sList)
➥' Length incl. trailing null
    i = 1
➥' Start at 1st character
    n = 0
➥' Index in array
    Do While ((i < l) And (n < MAX_XHDR))    ' Safety stop here
            j = InStr(i, sList, Chr$(0))         ' J -> next null
            CGI_ExtraHeaders(n).key = Mid$(sList, i, j - i) ' Get Key, then value
            CGI_ExtraHeaders(n).value = GetProfile("Extra Headers",
CGI_ExtraHeaders(n).key)
            i = j + 1
    ' Bump pointer
            n = n + 1
    ' Bump array index
    Loop
    CGI_NumExtraHeaders = n                          ' Fill in global count

End Sub

'------------------------------------------------------------------------
'
'   GetFormTuples() - Create the array of POST form input key=value pairs
'
'------------------------------------------------------------------------
Private Sub GetFormTuples()
    Dim sList As String
    Dim i As Integer, j As Integer, k As Integer
    Dim l As Integer, n As Integer
    Dim s As Long
    Dim buf As String
    Dim extName As String
    Dim extFile As Integer
    Dim extlen As Long

    n = 0
```

```
➥' Index in array

'
' Do the easy one first: [Form Literal]
'
sList = GetProfile("Form Literal", "")  ' Get key list
l = Len(sList)                                       ' Length incl. trailing null
i = 1
' Start at 1st character
Do While ((i < l) And (n < MAX_FORM_TUPLES)) ' Safety stop here
        j = InStr(i, sList, Chr$(0))            ' J -> next null
        cgi_FormTuples(n).key = Mid$(sList, i, j - i) ' Get Key, then value
        cgi_FormTuples(n).value = GetProfile("Form Literal", cgi_FormTuples(n).key)
        i = j + 1                                         ' Bump pointer
        n = n + 1
        ➥' Bump array index
Loop
'
' Now do the external ones: [Form External]
'
sList = GetProfile("Form External", "") ' Get key list
l = Len(sList)
➥' Length incl. trailing null
i = 1
➥' Start at 1st character
extFile = FreeFile
Do While ((i < l) And (n < MAX_FORM_TUPLES)) ' Safety stop here
        j = InStr(i, sList, Chr$(0))            ' J -> next null
        cgi_FormTuples(n).key = Mid$(sList, i, j - i) ' Get Key,
        ➥then pathname
        buf = GetProfile("Form External", cgi_FormTuples(n).key)
        k = InStr(buf, " ")                               ' Split
        ➥file & length
        extName = Mid$(buf, 1, k - 1)                ' Pathname
        k = k + 1
        extlen = CLng(Mid$(buf, k, Len(buf) - k + 1)) ' Length
        '
        ' Use feature of GET to read content in one call
        '
        Open extName For Binary Access Read As #extFile
        cgi_FormTuples(n).value = String$(extlen, " ") ' Breathe
        ➥in...
        Get #extFile, , cgi_FormTuples(n).value 'GULP!
        Close #extFile
        i = j + 1
        ➥' Bump pointer
        n = n + 1
        ➥' Bump array index
Loop

CGI_NumFormTuples = n                          ' Number of
                                               ➥fields decoded
n = 0                                          ' Reset counter
'
' Finally, the [Form Huge] section. Will this ever get executed?
'
sList = GetProfile("Form Huge", "")       ' Get key list
```

(continues)

Listing 15.4   Continued

```
      l = Len(sList)
   ➡' Length incl. trailing null
      i = 1
   ➡' Start at 1st character
      Do While ((i < l) And (n < MAX_FORM_TUPLES)) ' Safety stop here
              j = InStr(i, sList, Chr$(0))              ' J -> next null
              CGI_HugeTuples(n).key = Mid$(sList, i, j - i) ' Get Key
              buf = GetProfile("Form Huge", CGI_HugeTuples(n).key) '
              ➡"offset length"
              ➡'k = InStr(buf, " ")
              Delimiter
              CGI_HugeTuples(n).offset = CLng(Mid$(buf, 1, (k - 1)))
              CGI_HugeTuples(n).length = CLng(Mid$(buf, k, (Len(buf) - k + 1)))
              i = j + 1                                  ' Bump pointer
              n = n + 1                                  ' Bump array index
      Loop

      CGI_NumHugeTuples = n                              ' Fill in global count

  End Sub


  '-----------------------------------------------------------------------------
  '
  '    GetProfile() - Get a value or enumerate keys in CGI_Profile file
  '
  ' Get a value given the section and key, or enumerate keys given the
  ' section name and "" for the key. If enumerating, the list of keys for
  ' the given section is returned as a null-separated string, with a
  ' double null at the end.
  '
  ' VB handles this with flair! I couldn't believe my eyes when I tried this.
  '-----------------------------------------------------------------------------
  Private Function GetProfile(sSection As String, sKey As String) As String
     Dim retLen As Integer
     Dim buf As String * ENUM_BUF_SIZE
     If sKey <> "" Then
             retLen = GetPrivateProfileString(sSection, sKey, "",
             ➡buf, ENUM_BUF_SIZE, CGI_ProfileFile)
     Else
             retLen = GetPrivateProfileString(sSection, 0&, "",
             ➡buf, ENUM_BUF_SIZE, CGI_ProfileFile)
     End If
     If retLen = 0 Then
             GetProfile = ""
     Else
             GetProfile = Left$(buf, retLen)
     End If

  End Function


  '-----------------------------------------------------------------------------
  '
  ' Get the value of a "small" form field given the key
  '
```

```
' Signals an error if field does not exist
'
'----------------------------------------------------------------
Function GetSmallField(key As String) As String
   Dim i As Integer

   For i = 0 To (CGI_NumFormTuples - 1)
         If cgi_FormTuples(i).key = key Then
                 GetSmallField = Trim$(cgi_FormTuples(i).value)
                 Exit Function              ' ** DONE **
         End If
   Next i
   '
   ' Field does not exist
   '
   Error ERR_NO_FIELD
End Function


'---------------------------------------------------------------------------
'
'   InitializeCGI() - Fill in all of the CGI variables, etc.
'
' Read the profile file name from the command line, then fill in
' the CGI globals, the Accept type list and the Extra headers list.
' Then open the input and output files.
'
' Returns True if OK, False if some sort of error. See ReturnError()
' for info on how errors are handled.
'
' NOTE: Assumes that the CGI error handler has been armed with On Error
'---------------------------------------------------------------------------
Sub InitializeCGI()
   Dim sect As String
   Dim argc As Integer
   Static argv(MAX_CMDARGS) As String
   Dim buf As String

   CGI_DebugMode = True     ' Initialization errors are very bad

   '
   ' Parse the command line. We need the profile file name (duh!)
   ' and the output file name NOW, so we can return any errors we
   ' trap. The error handler writes to the output file.
   '
   argc = GetArgs(argv())
   CGI_ProfileFile = argv(0)

   sect = "CGI"
   CGI_ServerSoftware = GetProfile(sect, "Server Software")
   CGI_ServerName = GetProfile(sect, "Server Name")
   CGI_RequestProtocol = GetProfile(sect, "Request Protocol")
   CGI_ServerAdmin = GetProfile(sect, "Server Admin")
   CGI_Version = GetProfile(sect, "CGI Version")
   CGI_RequestMethod = GetProfile(sect, "Request Method")
   CGI_LogicalPath = GetProfile(sect, "Logical Path")
```

(continues)

Listing 15.4 Continued

```
    CGI_PhysicalPath = GetProfile(sect, "Physical Path")
    CGI_ExecutablePath = GetProfile(sect, "Executable Path")
    CGI_QueryString = GetProfile(sect, "Query String")
    CGI_RemoteHost = GetProfile(sect, "Remote Host")
    CGI_RemoteAddr = GetProfile(sect, "Remote Address")
    CGI_Referer = GetProfile(sect, "Referer")
    CGI_From = GetProfile(sect, "From")
    CGI_AuthUser = GetProfile(sect, "Authenticated Username")
    CGI_AuthPass = GetProfile(sect, "Authenticated Password")
    CGI_AuthRealm = GetProfile(sect, "Authentication Realm")
    CGI_AuthType = GetProfile(sect, "Authentication Method")
    CGI_ContentType = GetProfile(sect, "Content Type")
    buf = GetProfile(sect, "Content Length")
    If buf = "" Then
            CGI_ContentLength = 0
    Else
            CGI_ContentLength = CLng(buf)
    End If
    buf = GetProfile(sect, "Server Port")
    If buf = "" Then
            CGI_ServerPort = -1
    Else
            CGI_ServerPort = CInt(buf)
    End If

    sect = "System"
    CGI_ContentFile = GetProfile(sect, "Content File")
    CGI_OutputFile = argv(2)
    CGI_OutputFN = FreeFile
    Open CGI_OutputFile For Output Access Write As #CGI_OutputFN
    buf = GetProfile(sect, "GMT Offset")
    CGI_GMTOffset = CVDate(CDbl(buf) / 86400#) ' Timeserial offset
    buf = GetProfile(sect, "Debug Mode")      ' Y or N
    If (Left$(buf, 1) = "Y") Then                  ' Must start with Y
            CGI_DebugMode = True
    Else
            CGI_DebugMode = False
    End If

    GetAcceptTypes             ' Enumerate Accept: types into tuples
    GetExtraHeaders           ' Enumerate extra headers into tuples
    GetFormTuples              ' Decode any POST form input into tuples

End Sub

Sub Inter_Main()
    'say it is a CGI program and exit.
    MsgBox "This is a CGI-WIN Program. It is called from WebSite."
End Sub

'------------------------------------------------------------------
'
'   main() - CGI script back-end main procedure
'
```

```
' This is the main() for the VB back end. Note carefully how the error
' handling is set up, and how program cleanup is done. If no command
' line args are present, call Inter_Main() and exit.
'----------------------------------------------------------------
Sub Main()
  On Error GoTo ErrorHandler
  If Trim$(Command$) = "" Then     ' Interactive start
        Inter_Main                                 ' Call inter-
                                                ➥active main
        Exit Sub                                       ' Exit
        ➥the program
  End If
  InitializeCGI       ' Create the CGI environment

  '===========
  CGI_Main                          ' Execute the actual "script"
  '===========


Cleanup:
  Close #CGI_OutputFN
  Exit Sub                                           ' End
  ➥the program
'------------
ErrorHandler:
  Select Case Err                           ' Decode our "user
                                        ➥defined" errors
        Case ERR_NO_FIELD:
                ErrorString = "Unknown form field"
        Case Else:
                ErrorString = Error$     ' Must be VB error
  End Select

  ErrorString = ErrorString & " (error #" & Err & ")"
  On Error GoTo 0                          ' Prevent recursion
  ErrorHandler (Err)                       ' Generate HTTP error
                                        ➥result
  Resume Cleanup
'------------
End Sub


'------------------------------------------------------------------------
'
'  Send() - Shortcut for writing to output file
'
'------------------------------------------------------------------------
Sub Send(s As String)
  Print #CGI_OutputFN, s
End Sub


'------------------------------------------------------------------------
'
'   SendNoOp() - Tell browser to do nothing.
'
```

(continues)

Listing 15.4 Continued

```
' Most browsers will do nothing. Netscape 1.0N leaves hourglass
' cursor until the mouse is waved around. Enhanced Mosaic 2.0
' oputs up an alert saying "URL leads nowhere". Your results may
' vary...
'
'------------------------------------------------------------------------
Sub SendNoOp()

  Send ("HTTP/1.0 204 No Response")
  Send ("Server: " + CGI_ServerSoftware)
  Send ("")

End Sub

'------------------------------------------------------------------------
'
'   WebDate - Return an HTTP/1.0 compliant date/time string
'
' Inputs:   t = Local time as VB Variant (e.g., returned by Now())
' Returns:  Properly formatted HTTP/1.0 date/time in GMT
'------------------------------------------------------------------------
Function WebDate(dt As Variant) As String
  Dim t As Variant

  t = CVDate(dt - CGI_GMTOffset)    ' Convert time to GMT
  WebDate = Format$(t, "ddd dd mmm yyyy hh:mm:ss") & " GMT"

End Function
```

Chapter 16

The Leszynski Naming Conventions for Microsoft Visual Basic

by Stan Leszynski

Stan Leszynski founded Leszynski Company, Inc., in 1982 to create custom PC database applications, and since that time the firm has created database-centric solutions for hundreds of clients, including Microsoft. The company has also written retail products sold by Microsoft, Microrim, Qualitas, and Kwery with a user base of several million people. Successful products include the OLE Calendar controls shipped with Access 95 and Access 2, the 386MAX memory manager, and four R:BASE developer tools. The company currently specializes in Access, Visual Basic, SQL Server, and Visual C++ applications.

Stan's second company, Kwery Corporation, shipped the first Access add-in, Access To Word, and the first OLE controls—Kwery Control Pak 1. Stan is the author of the Leszynski Naming Conventions for Microsoft Visual Basic, *a standard used by thousands of developers and Microsoft's own documentation team. He is a frequent writer on VB, VBA, and Access, and speaks regularly at developer conferences in North America, Europe, and Australia. Stan is the author of* Access Expert Solutions *published by Que Corporation. You can contact Stan on CompuServe (71151,1114).*

Cartoon Chaos

"I learned the value of naming conventions years ago. Before I was at Microsoft, I was working on an accounting application for a client and needed to hire a contractor to do some of the work on the project. At the time, I didn't have any formal naming conventions, nor a specific structure or style that I wanted the code to look like—I

(continued)

just wanted the app to work. Well, the contract coder did his part of the application, and it seemed to work fine. Some time later, however, I had to modify the application, and I couldn't figure out what the code did. For example, his code looked like this:

```
Barney = 500
Do While Fred < Barney
...
   Fred = Wilma + 1
...
Loop
```

My confusion stemmed from the fact that he had named all of his objects and variables after cartoon characters, and they had no consistency or link to the application at all!"

Tod Nielsen, General Manager, Microsoft Access Business Unit

Developers by nature have this "love/hate thing" about naming conventions. Such standards are often seen as slowing the development process, increasing the size of object names and files, and stifling true programming creativity. And yet, without order, the laws of entropy invariably draw every project toward incoherent "spaghetti code" and/or "spaghetti objects." Thus, few developers would argue against the need for an ordered approach to development, but they want the system that is least intrusive.

Sorry, but you can't have it both ways! A system that is comprehensive, and applied consistently, will also by nature be mildly intrusive. If you want to apply a naming convention to your objects, you will incur a penalty of a few keystrokes everytime you type an object name. However, the small pain of extra keystrokes certainly produces a large gain.

Creating your own naming conventions takes research, group effort, and testing. To complicate matters, there are several different approaches you can take when naming objects. For a complete discourse on designing your own naming conventions, see the book *Access Expert Solutions* by Stan Leszynski, from Que Corporation.

In this chapter, I detail for you the *Leszynski Naming Conventions* ("LNC"), a set of standardized approaches to naming objects during Visual Basic ("VB") development. These naming conventions were born of necessity, since some members of my staff spend all day in VB development, year after year. They were also born of a different need—a void that existed in the marketplace due to a lack of consensus about development styles among leading VB developers.

Our Visual Basic conventions are tightly linked with our Access/Jet conventions (now also called *LNC*, formerly called *L/R*). The *L/R* conventions were distributed broadly, with over 500,000 copies in print, and have become the most widely used such conventions in the Access community. Over the last few years, we have received feedback about *L/R* from hundreds of developers and companies, and have tried to accommodate some of their input, as well as our ongoing experiences, into *LNC* documents for both Access and Visual Basic.

LNC assumes that most VB developers also work with other Microsoft development tools: Access, Excel, SQL Server, and others. Microsoft development products have more in common in their '95 versions than in any previous iterations. Consequently, this VB style dovetails with the *LNC* development style detailed in the *Leszynski Naming Conventions for Microsoft Solution Developers*, a separate document which covers all of Microsoft's application development products.

This document includes Jet conventions and examples in recognition of the fact that the Jet has become the default database engine for many VB developers. More detailed style information for working with Access and Jet is found in the *Leszynski Naming Conventions for Microsoft Access* document.

I use the terms *naming conventions*, *style*, and *LNC* interchangeably throughout this chapter.

Naming Conventions—A Primer

Naming conventions are one of the foundation elements of your overall development style. We developed our naming conventions primarily to achieve four objectives:

- To be able to quickly understand an application's structure and code by making object names more informative.

- To simplify team development of applications by creating a standardized vocabulary for all team members.

- To improve our ability to work with VB and Jet objects, including enforcing object name sort orders, creating self-documenting program code, and enhancing find and replace capabilities.

- To increase our ability to create tools for our VB development work, and to create code libraries across various VBA platforms.

To meet these objectives, we create and apply consistent naming conventions to the VB application objects shown in Listing 1.

Listing 16.1   16LIST01.TXT—Target Objects for Naming Conventions

```
Class modules
Forms
Form controls
Modules
Procedures
Variables
Constants
User-defined types
Database¹ tables
Database table fields
Database queries
```

Object names are the foundation upon which your entire application is built, so they are almost impossible to change once development has begun in earnest. Therefore, you will probably not find it cost- or time-efficient to retrofit these conventions into your existing applications. For new applications, however, you should apply these naming conventions consistently from the moment you create your first object in a new project file.

LNC relies primarily on leading tags—several characters placed before an object's name (for example, frmCust). This approach is sometimes referred to as "Hungarian Notation." Leading tags provide several benefits:

- The first thing you see about an object when you see its name is the leading type tag, which is often more important than the name itself.

- Leading tags drive the ordering of object names in Access, Jet, VB, and VBA object lists, sorting by type and then by base name.

- Leading tags are consistently located in the same place in an object's name, making them easier to find by parsers and other tools.

If you are averse to Hungarian Notation for some reason and prefer trailing tags, *LNC* will still work for you. However, *LNC* prescribes no standard for locating and punctuating trailing tags. You will have to decide if they are offset with an underscore (Order_fmdi), or by capitalization (OrderFMdi), or by some other technique. Remember also that you should be consistent throughout your style, so if you use trailing tags for objects, you will need to use them when writing VB code as well.

For purposes of this chapter, we have created the standardized terminology in Table 16.1 for grouping objects. We will use these group names when discussing naming conventions.

Table 16.1 Object Groupings		
VB Objects	**VBA Objects**	**Database Objects**
Class modules	Procedures	Tables
Forms	Variables	Table fields
Form controls	Constants	Queries
Modules	User-defined types	

Structuring Object Names

In *LNC*, object names are constructed by using this syntax:

> [prefix(es)] tag [BaseName] [Qualifier] [Suffix]

The brackets indicate optional syntax elements. Notice that the *tag* element is required even though the *BaseName* is not in some cases. These options will be explained later in this chapter. Note in the syntax diagram that the case of each element reflects its case in actual use. The element *tag* is in lowercase since the tags themselves are always lowercase.

Table 16.2 shows sample object names using these constructions.

Table 16.2 Object Names Constructed in LNC Format					
Object Name	**Prefixes**	**Tag**	**BaseNam**	**Qualifier**	**Suffix**
frmCust		frm	Cust		
qsumSalesPerfBest WA_		qsum	SalesPerf	Best	WA
plngRecNumMax	p	lng	RecNum	Max	
ialngPartNum	ia	lng	PartNum		

What Is a Prefix?

A *prefix* is an identifier that precedes a tag and clarifies it narrowly. Prefixes describe one or more important properties of an object. For example, a Long variable that is public in scope (declared `Public`) has a prefix p, as in `plngRecNumMax`. Prefixes are one or two characters long and in lowercase. Multiple prefixes can be used together on one object, as in `ialngPartNum`, where i and a are both prefixes.

What Is a Tag?

A *tag* is a multi-character string placed against an object base name to characterize it. In object-oriented programming terms, the tag is basically an identifier for the *class*. Note that the word *class* here refers to a naming convention construction, not an exact object model construction. For example, there is only one `Query` (or `QueryDef`) class object in Jet, and the data action (delete, update, etc.) is determined by its SQL statement, not its class. *LNC* prescribes several tags for this one Jet class.

Tags are three or four characters long for readability and to allow for the hundreds of combinations necessary as the Microsoft Office object model grows over time. They are always to the left of the base name and in lowercase, so that your eye reads past them to the beginning of the base name.

A tag is created to mnemonically represent the word it abbreviates, such as "frm" for "form." However, some tags may not seem fully mnemonic for three reasons. First, the perfect (i.e., obvious) tag for a particular new object may already be assigned to another object in a product that existed previously. Second, where common objects (objects with similar properties and usage) exist in multiple Microsoft applications, the tag for one may be used to represent similar objects in other products, even if the names are different. For example, Visual Basic Shape objects and Access Rectangle objects share the tag `shp` in *LNC*, since they are very similar objects structurally. Finally, there may not be such a thing as an "obvious" tag, so a suitable one may be chosen from a body of several reasonable candidates.

What Is a Base Name?

The *base name* is the starting point when you name a particular object—the name you would use anyway if you had no naming conventions. The *LNC* guidelines for creating base names are driven by a set of rules stated in the sections that follow.

What Is a Qualifier?

A *qualifier* is an extension following the base name that provides context to the specific use of an object. Unlike prefixes, which detail properties of the object (for example, that the variable has public scope), qualifiers describe how the object is being used in a context. For example, `plngRecNumMax` is obviously the maximum record number, in an application that could also have variables for the minimum (`plngRecNumMin`) and current (`plngRecNumCur`) record numbers. Qualifiers are short and written with mixed upper- and lowercase, as in the examples in Table 16.3.

Table 16.3 Some Suggested LNC Qualifiers	
Qualifier	**Usage**
Curr	Current element of a set
Dest	Destination
First	First element of a set
Hold	Hold a value for later re-use
Last	Last element of a set
Max	Maximum item in a set
Min	Minimum item in a set
Next	Next element of a set
New	New instance or value
Old	Prior instance or value
Prev	Previous element of a set
Src	Source
Temp	Temporary value

What Is a Suffix?

Suffix elements provide specific information about the object and are used only as "tie-breakers" when more detail is required to differentiate object names that could otherwise legitimately be identical. Suffixes are the only element in the syntax diagram where our naming conventions do not suggest standardized values. You will create suffix items as needed by your company, development team, or application. For example, a series of queries that summarized the best sales performance by state would need the state name in each object name to properly qualify it, as in `qsumSalesPerfBest_AK`. Placing the state name at the very end of the name as a *suffix* item allows the entire collection of related queries to sort together, like this:

```
qsumSalesPerfBest_AK
qsumSalesPerfBest_AL
...
qsumSalesPerfBest_WY
```

Since the suffix is the last piece of information on a name, it can be easier for the eye to find if delimited from the rest of the object name with an underscore, as above, but this convention is optional.

Naming Conventions for VB Objects

The building blocks of your application are its objects. When creating base names for VB objects, careful consideration should be given to the purpose of the object, the approaches used to name associated objects, and the rules of thumb in this chapter for naming objects.

Tags for Project Objects

Your Visual Basic project can consist of many files, and good development style often dictates that you keep all files for a project in the same directory. However, with the advent of long file names, I have found it helpful to give each project a unique abbreviation and apply the characters as a tag for files in the project. This helps me to:

- Track project files that might become intermingled with other files

- Delineate project files from other application files in the same directory

- Differentiate project-specific files from company library files in the same project

- Create a server tag that can be used if the application becomes an OLE server

Tags for Module Objects

Table 16.4 lists the tags for Visual Basic module objects.

Table 16.4 Visual Basic Module Object Tags	
Object	**Tag**
Class module	cls
Standard module	bas

Tags for Form Control Objects

VB applications usually consist of many forms. While it is acceptable to tag every form with `frm`, *LNC* provides the opportunity to be more specific about the nature of each form, as seen in Table 16.5. While object name sort order is not enforced in the Project window (*Dear Microsoft, I wish you treated object names with greater importance than file names in the Project window...*), viewing forms through the Object Browser *is* easier with meaningful object tags.

Table 16.5 Visual Basic Form Object Tags	
Object	**Tag**
Form	frm
Form (dialog)	fdlg
Form (lookup table)[2]	flkp
Form (menu/switchboard)	fmnu
Form (message/alert)	fmsg
Form (wizard main)	fwzm
Form (wizard subform)	fwzs
MDI form	fmdi
MDI child form	fmdc

Table 16.6 lists the tags for control objects on forms, and Table 16.7 provides tags for critical OLE control types. VBA code written behind forms using this convention will reflect a control's type in its event procedure names (for example, `cboState_AfterUpdate`). The automatic sorting provided by this notation in the VB IDE can be very helpful during development. All control tags are three characters long.

Table 16.6 Form Control Object Tags				
Control	**Tag**	**Constant Prefix**	**VB 4 Docs**	**Class**
AniButton	ani	ani	none	AniButton
CheckBox/3D	chk/chk3	none/ss	chk	CheckBox

(continues)

Table 16.6   Continued

Control	Tag	Constant Prefix	VB 4 Docs	Class
ComboBox	cbo	none	cbo	ComboBox
CommandButton/3D	cmd/cmd3	none/ss	cmd	CommandButton
CommonDialog	cdlg	cdl	none	CommonDialog
Communications	com	com	none	Communications
Control (generic)	ctl	none	none	n/a
Data	dat	vb	dat	Data
DBCombo	dcbo	dbl	dbc	DBCombo
DBGrid	dgrd	dbg	dbg	DBGrid
DBList	dlst	dbl	dbl	DBList
DirListBox	dir	none	dir	DirListBox
DriveListBox	drv	none	drv	DriveListBox
FileListBox	fil	none	fil	FileListBox
Frame/3D	fra/fra3	none/ss	fra	Frame
Gauge	gau	gau	none	Gauge
Graph	gph	gph	none	Graph
Grid	grd	none	grd	Grid
GroupPushButton	gpb3	ss	none	GroupPushButton
HScrollBar	hsb	vb	hsb	HScrollBar
Image	img	none	img	Image
KeyStatus	key	key	none	KeyStatus
Label	lbl	none	lbl	Label
Line	lin	none	lin	Line
ListBox	lst	none	lst	ListBox
MAPIMessage	mpm	map	none	MAPIMessage
MAPISession	mps	map	none	MAPISession
MaskedEdit	msk	msk	none	MaskedEdit

Constant Control	VB 4 Tag	Prefix	Docs	Class
MCI	mci	mci	none	MCI
Menu	mnu	vb	mnu	Menu
Menu (shortcut)	mct	n/a	none	Menu
OLEContainer	ole	vb	ole	OLEContainer
OptionButton/3D	opt/opt3	none/ss	opt	OptionButton
Outline	out	out	none	Outline
Panel	pnl3	ss	none	Panel
PictureBox	pic	vb	pic	PictureBox
PicClip	clp	none	none	PicClip
RemoteDataControl	rdc	rd	none	RemoteData Control
Report	rpt	none	none	Report
Shape	shp	vb	shp	Shape
SpinButton	spn	spn	none	SpinButton
Tab	tab	ss	none	Tab
TextBox	txt	none	txt	TextBox
Timer	tmr	none	tmr	Timer
VScrollBar	vsb	vb	vsb	VScrollBar

The trailing *3* on the tags above for 3D controls is included for backward compatibility with VB3 projects using THREED.VBX, but is not required by LNC for controls in new VB4 projects.

Some conventions attempt to catalog or create tags for third-party VBX and OLE controls. Such an effort is beyond the scope of this chapter—I take responsibility here only for helping you use controls that are part of a VB developer's standard tool set or are created by my company. A starting point if you are interested in tags for third-party controls is the document "Microsoft Consulting Services Naming Conventions for VB" on the Microsoft Developer Network CD subscription.

Table 16.7 OLE Control Object Tags for Windows 95, VB, Access, and Kwery Controls

Control	Tag	Source	Filename	Classname
Calendar	cal	Access	MSACAL70.OCX	MSACal70
Kwery Calendar	kcal	Kwery	KCCAL32.OCX	KCCalendar
Kwery Clock	kclk	Kwery	KCCLOK32.OCX	KCClock
Data Outline	dout	ADT	DBOUTL32.OCX	DataOutline
Kwery Gauge	kgau	Kwery	KCGAGE32.OCX	KCGauge
Image List	ilst	VB	COMCTL32.OCX	ImageList
List View	lvw	VB	COMCTL32.OCX	ListView
Kwery Preview	kpvw	Kwery	KCPRVW32.OCX	KCPreview
Progress Bar	pbr	VB	COMCTL32.OCX	ProgressBar
Rich Text Box	rtf	VB	RICHTX32.OCX	RichTextBox
Slider	sld	VB	COMCTL32.OCX	Slider
Status Bar	sbr	VB	COMCTL32.OCX	StatusBar
Tab Strip	tabs	VB	COMCTL32.OCX	TabStrip
Toolbar	tbr	VB	COMCTL32.OCX	Toolbar
Tree View	tvw	VB	COMCTL32.OCX	TreeView
Kwery Wheel	kwhl	Kwery	KCWHL32.OCX	KCWheel

Naming Menus

Most VB coders use a standard menu naming convention already, which consists of the tag `mnu` before a menu control base name built of the menu's options, as in `mnuFileExit`. This technique will cause menu options to sort in a very distinct order in the property dialog, and is acceptible for *LNC*.

In addition to standard bar and drop-down menu combinations, you can create pop-up or "shortcut" menus in VB4. *LNC* suggests that you prefix these objects with the `mct` tag to keep the menu items grouped together when sorted. "Shortcut" is the term used by Windows 95 for context menus, so I prefer using it over the terms "pop-up menu" and "context menu" used in the VB documentation.

Naming Conventions for VBA Objects

When creating base names for VBA objects, remember that the base name must be descriptive even in the absence of its tag. For some programmers, the syntax `Dim I As Integer` for a loop variable is quite acceptable. Within *LNC*, however, the variable named `I` would become `iintLoop`—an index integer variable to control a loop. Single character variable names, especially without tags, are not allowed. Instead, create a list of short and standardized work variables to handle common daily needs. See Table 16.11 later in this document.

Rules for VBA Object Base Names

Crafting VBA object base names involves creating and following simple rules such as these:

1. Spaces are not allowed in any object name. Spaces create a multitude of problems with consistency, readability, and documentation. Where the readability of a space is required, use an underscore instead.

2. Object names begin with a letter and should only include letters, digits, and underscores.

3. Object names use mixed uppercase and lowercase to add readability to the name.

4. The only syntax element that can have multiple capital letters is the base name. A qualifier or suffix begins with a single capital letter and then contains only lowercase letters, unless it is an abbreviation, as in `qsumSalesPerfBestUSA`. If you need to clearly see the elements of a name (prefixes, tag, base name, qualifier, and suffix), *LNC* allows for—but does not require—underscores as separators, as in `qsum_SalesPerf_Best_USA`.

5. Object names are usually singular (`Widget`) rather than plural (`Widgets`).

6. An object's base name should include the base names of any objects it is built on, if practical.

Note that Rule 6 requires a reference in variable names to objects of any type that they relate to. For example, a `Recordset` variable created on `tblCust` should be named `rstCust`. Also, if a string array variable of part numbers `astrPartNum` had an Integer index variable, it should include the array's base name in its own sans tagging: `iaintPartNum`.

VBA Object Base Name Lengths

There is no *LNC* guideline limiting variable name length, but common sense dictates that variable names longer than 15 or 20 characters waste a lot of keystrokes at each use. For procedure names, the VBA module editor by default shows the first 30 characters of a procedure name, so this number is suggested as the target maximum procedure name length.

Abbreviate VBA object base name elements wherever possible using a standardized abbreviation table such as the one in the section "Standardized Abbreviations" later in this chapter. You can extend *LNC* by creating your own standard abbreviations. You should also create and use standardized terminology in your applications wherever possible; for examples see the section "Standardized Terminology."

Compound VBA Object Base Names

Procedure base names should follow the construction *ObjectVerb*, where the *Object* portion describes the primary object type affected (often the same as the primary argument), and *Verb* describes the action. This style sorts functions and subs by their target object when shown in ordered lists:

> FormCtlHide
>
> FormCtlShow
>
> FormPropAdd
>
> FormPropGet
>
> FormPropSet

We find this sort order much more appealing than the more common alternative with *VerbObject* construction:

> AddFormProp
>
> GetFormProp
>
> HideFormCtl
>
> SetFormProp
>
> ShowFormCtl

Using Tags with VBA Objects

In *LNC*, tags are required for the following VBA objects:

- Variables

- Type structures

- Constants

Optional tags also are available for some types of procedures.

In the syntax diagram earlier we noted that base names are optional in some constructions. When programming in VBA, the *tag* element is always required, but the *base name* is optional for local variables only. For example, a procedure that declares only one form object variable can legitimately use the variable name `frm`, which is a tag without a base name. Normally, however, I prefer more detail. Type structures, constants, and variables that have module-level or public scope must have both a tag and base name.

Tags for Variables

VBA variable tags are noted in Tables 16.8 through 16.10, grouped by type of variable.

Table 16.8 Tags for VBA Data Variables	
Variable Type	**Tag**
Boolean	bln
Byte	byt
Conditional Compilation Constant	ccc
Currency	cur
Date[3]	dtm
Double	dbl
Error	err
Integer	int
Long	lng
Object	obj
Single	sng
String	str
User-Defined Type	typ
Variant	var

In the previous table, note that Conditional Compilation Constant, Error, and User-Defined Type are not true data types (created with `Dim` *name* `As` *datatype*), but rather programming concepts. A Conditional Compilation Constant variable is a flag of type Boolean, an Error variable is a Variant created with the `CVErr()` function, and user-defined types are unique constructs.

Table 16.9 Tags for VBA Object Variables

Object	Tag
AddInManager	add
App	n/a
Application	app
Button	btn
Buttons	btns
Clipboard	n/a
Collection	col
Column	clm
Columns	clms
ColumnHeader	chd
ColumnHeaders	chds
Component	cmp
Components	cmps
Control	ctl
Controls	ctls
ControlTemplate	ctp
ControlTemplates	ctps
Debug	n/a
Err	n/a
FileControl	flc
Font	fnt
Form	frm
Forms	frms

Object	Tag
FormTemplate	ftpl
ListImage	lsi
ListImages	lsis
Menu	mnu
MenuItem	mni
MenuItems	mnis
MenuLine	mnl
Node	nod
Nodes	nods
Panel	pnl
Panels	pnls
Picture	pic
Pictures	pics
Printer	prn
Printers	prns
ProjectTemplate	tpl
Property	prp
Properties	prps
RowBuffer	row
Screen	n/a
SelBookmark	sbk
SelBookmarks	sbks
SelectedComponents	scms
SelectedControlTemplates	scts
SubMenu	msub
Tab	tab
Tabs	tabs

Table 16.10   Tags for Data Access Object Variables

Object	Tag
Container	con
Containers	cons
DBEngine	dbe
Database (any type)	dbs
Database (Btrieve)	dbtv
Database (dBASE)	ddbf
Database (Excel)	dxls
Database (FoxPro)	dfox
Database (Jet)	djet
Database (Lotus)	dwks
Database (ODBC)	dodb
Database (Paradox)	dpdx
Database (SQL Server)	dsql
Database (Text)	dtxt
Databases	dbss
Document	doc
Documents	docs
Dynaset	dyn
Error	err
Errors	errs
Field	fld
Fields	flds
Group	gru
Groups	grus
Index	idx
Indexes	idxs
Parameter	prm

Object	Tag
Parameters	prp
Properties	prps
QueryDef (any type)	qdf
QueryDef (Btrieve)	qbtv
QueryDef (dBASE)	qdbf
QueryDef (Excel)	qxls
QueryDef (FoxPro)	qfox
QueryDef (Jet)	qjet
QueryDef (Lotus)	qwks
QueryDef (ODBC)	qodb
QueryDef (Paradox)	qpdx
QueryDef (SQL Server)	qsql
QueryDef (Text)	qtxt
QueryDefs	qdfs
Recordset (any type)	rst
Recordset (Btrieve)	rbtv
Recordset (dBASE)	rdbf
Recordset (dynaset)	rdyn
Recordset (Excel)	rxls
Recordset (Fox)	rfox
Recordset (Lotus)	rwks
Recordset (ODBC)	rodb
Recordset (Paradox)	rpdx
Recordset (snapshot)	rsnp
Recordset (SQL Server)	rsql
Recordset (table)	rtbl

(continues)

Table 16.10   Continued

Object	Tag
Recordset (text)	rtxt
Recordsets	rsts
Relation	rel
Relations	rels
Snapshot	snp
Table	tbl
TableDef (any type)	tdf
TableDef (Btrieve)	tbtv
TableDef (dBASE)	tdbf
TableDef (Excel)	txls
TableDef (FoxPro)	tfox
TableDef (Jet)	tjet
TableDef (Lotus)	twks
TableDef (ODBC)	todb
TableDef (Paradox)	tpdx
TableDef (SQL Server)	tsql
TableDef (Text)	ttxt
TableDefs	tdfs
User	usr
Users	usrs
Workspace	wsp
Workspaces	wsps

In Tables 16.9 and 16.10 above, tags for collection variables are made by adding s after the tag for the object type stored in the collection, as in usr for User and usrs for Users. The tags dyn, snp, and tbl for Dynaset, Snapshot, and Table objects are directly relevant to users of Jet 1 and Jet 2. Starting with

Jet 3, these object types are allowed only as a subtype of recordset variables, thus the recordset tags `rdyn`, `rsnp`, and `rtbl`.

Even though we noted previously that a tag by itself is a legitimate variable name, a few variable tags shown (such as `int`) are VBA reserved words and will not compile in your procedures. Such tags require a base name.

Instead of using I and J as work variable names, use names that are still short but meaningful. For example, even `iintI` and `iintJ` are more descriptive than I and J, although I'd never use them. Instead, I try to keep a short list of handy work variables and reuse these variables where practical. Table 16.11 suggests the *LNC* approach to commonly used variables.

Table 16.11   Standardized LNC Work Variables

Variable	Description
blnRet	Captures a True/False return value from a function call
cccDebug	A conditional compilation constant for turning conditional debugging on and off
intErr	Preserves the value of Err
iintLoop	A counter for For...Next loops
intMsg	Captures a return value from a MsgBox function call
intResult	Holds the result of math operations (also dblResult, lngResult, etc.)
intRet	Captures a numeric return value from a function call (also dblRet, lngRet, etc.)
intWork	Used for any temporary work (also dblWork, lngWork, etc.)
strMsg	Used to build long message box strings
strOrder	Used to build long SQL ORDER BY strings
strSQL	Used to build long SQL strings
strWhere	Used to build long SQL WHERE clauses

Creating OLE Automation Variables

Table 16.12 lists entry points for common OLE server applications.

Table 16.12 Tags for OLE Object Variables	
Object	**Tag**
Access.Application	accapp
DAO.DBEngine	daodbe
Excel.Application	xlsapp
Excel.Chart	xlscht
Excel.Sheet	xlssht
Graph.Application	gphapp
MAPI.Session	mpsmps
MSProject.Application	prjapp
MSProject.Project	prjprj
OfficeBinder.Binder	bndbnd
PowerPoint.Application	pptapp
SchedulePlus.Application	scdapp
SQLOLE.SQLServer	sqlsvr
Word.Basic	wrdbas

Note that variables for objects in the object hierarchy of a referenced type library can be dimensioned directly by class, as in this line:

```
Dim xlsapp As Excel.Application
```

Alternatively, if the variable is created with *late binding* (i.e., as a generic object) rather than *early binding*, the prefix o is added to denote an object variable:

```
Dim oxlsapp As Object
Set oxlsapp = CreateObject("Excel.Application")
```

The naming convention for entry points into OLE server applications follows this syntax:

```
applicationtag [entrypointtag] primaryobjecttag BaseName
```

The item *applicationtag* is a three-character notation for the server application, and *entrypointtag* is three characters denoting the entry point used. The *entrypointtag* is optional and should be used when clarification is necessary (when variables for several entry points are declared in the same procedure), or when the entry point is not the standard Application object. The *primaryobjecttag* describes the ultimate class of the object (the one you intend to address with the variable). The *BaseName* is optional and clarifies the use of the variable, as with other VBA variables.

For example, the following code creates an Excel Range object and manipulates it.

```
Sub SalesCheck()
  Dim xlswksSales As Excel.Worksheet
  Dim xlsrngYTD As Excel.Range
  Set xlswksSales = GetObject("C:\Data\Sales.Xls", "Excel.Sheet")
  Set xlsrngYTD = xlswksSales.Range("YTDSales")
  If xlsrngYTD.Value < 100000 Then
    MsgBox "Sales are lame.", vbOKOnly, "Get to Work!"
  End If
  Set xlswksSales = Nothing
End Sub
```

In this example, the Range object is technically several layers deep in the application hierarchy, and a purely accurate combination of tags and code structure would yield this line of code, which actually runs:

```
Set xlsappwkbwksrngYTD = _
    xlsapp.ActiveWorkbook.Worksheets("Sales").Range("YTDSales")
```

In practice, of course, such nomenclature is unwieldy, and the shorter style is accurate but more friendly.

I prefer to show the server name in the variable declaration for clarity of code. While both lines below will run, the second is less ambiguous:

```
Dim xlsrng As Range
Dim xlsrng As Excel.Range
```

See the section "Creating Your Own Tags" further in this chapter for more discussion of OLE syntax. See the *Leszynski Naming Conventions for Microsoft Solution Developers* document for a complete listing of tags for Microsoft OLE servers and objects.

Tags for Remote Data Objects

The capabilities of the Remote Data Objects and the RemoteData control in VB4 to work with ODBC data sources, and the structure of the objects themselves, make it tempting to compare RDO and Jet objects. While there are many commonalities, there are also enough differences that we opted to create separate tags for use with RDO, as shown in Table 16.13.

Table 16.13 Tags for Remote Data Objects	
Object	**Tag**
rdoColumn	rdclm
rdoColumns	rdclms
rdoConnection	rdcnn
rdoConnections	rdcnns
rdoEngine	rdeng
rdoEnvironment	rdenv
rdoEnvironments	rdenvs
rdoError	rderr
rdoErrors	rderrs
rdoParameter	rdprm
rdoParameters	rdprms
rdoPreparedStatement	rdprs
rdoPreparedStatements	rdprss
rdoResultset	rdrsl
rdoResultsets	rdrsls
rdoTable	rdtbl
rdoTables	rdtbls

Prefixes for Variables

The prefixes for VBA variables can be categorized into two groups: prefixes for scope, and all other prefixes. Since the model for variable scope has changed somewhat in VB4, I will discuss scope prefixes first. The prefixes below are ordered by increasing (broader) scope.

Use no prefix for variables that are local to a procedure.

s   Place this prefix before variables that are declared locally to a procedure with a `Static` statement.

m   Use this prefix for module-level variables that are declared with `Dim` or `Private` statements in the `Declarations` section of a module.

p   Use this prefix to denote variables declared as `Public` in the `Declarations` section of a module. This prefix is new to the '95 conventions and supplements the *g* prefix.

g   Use this prefix to denote variables declared as `Public` or `Global` in the `Declarations` section of a standard module. Such variables are truly global and may be referenced from procedures in the current or other projects.

When used, scope prefixes always begin a variable name and precede any other prefixes.

In addition to scope, there are other characteristics of variables that can be identified by prefixes, as listed below.

a   Use this prefix to denote a variable that is declared as an array, including a `ParamArray` argument to a function.

c   This prefix is placed before constants defined with the `Const` statement.

e   Use this prefix for a variable that is an element of a collection. Such variables are usually part of a `For Each...Next` loop structure.

i   Use this prefix to denote a variable (usually of type Integer) that serves as an index into an array or an index counter in a `For...Next` loop.

o   This prefix is placed before object variables that reference OLE Automation servers through late binding (an Object variable), where the tag denotes the type of server.

r   Use this prefix for variables that are arguments (parameters) passed in to a procedure and declared as `ByRef`, or not declared as either `ByRef` or `ByVal` (including a `ParamArray`), which implies `ByRef`.

t   Use this prefix to describe a variable that is declared as a user-defined Type structure. The variable should inherit the base name from the original declaration for the type.

v   Use this prefix for variables that are arguments (parameters) passed in to a procedure and declared as `ByVal`.

A prefix provides a very detailed description of a variable. The number of allowable prefix combinations is limited, as shown in Table 16.14.

Table 16.14 Allowable Prefix Combinations	
Any One of These...	**...Can Come Before This**
s, m, p, g, r, v	a
m, p, g	c
s, m, p, g, r, v	e
s, m, p, g, r, v	i
s, m, p, g, r, v	ia
s, m, p, g, r, v	o
m, p, g	t

Variables require a unique prefix when declared Public in a widely distributed application to prevent name contentions. See the "Tags and Prefixes for Procedures" section later for more information.

Naming Constants

VB4 introduced some changes in the area of constants. The changes most relevant to naming conventions include these:

- A constant can now be assigned a data type when it is defined.

- All constants have been renamed and carry a tag of ac, db, or vb to identify their primary functional area (Access, Jet, and VBA respectively).

- Constants can now be created with the Variant data type.

When creating constants, use a scope prefix (if appropriate), the prefix c, and the suitable tag for the constant's data type. To properly synchronize the tag, the data type, and the value, do not let VB assign the type; always use the full "**Const** *name* **As** *datatype*" syntax.

Constants require a unique prefix when declared Public in a widely distributed application to prevent name contentions. See the "Tags and Prefixes for Procedures" section that follows for more information.

Tags and Prefixes for Procedures

Whether and how to prefix and tag procedure names is a debatable subject. In general, this style neither requires nor encourages placing characters before a procedure name except in the following situations.

Prefixes for Procedures

Procedures can have scope similar to that of variables—s (`Static`), m (`Private`), p (`Public`), or g (global `Public`). *LNC* allows, but does not encourage, the use of these scope prefixes on function names if they solve a particular need, and are used consistently throughout an application.

If you are creating code libraries for retail sale, for inclusion in the public domain, or for broad distribution in some other manner, *LNC* recommends that you prefix Public variables, constants, and procedures with a unique prefix identifying you, your company, or the application. The prefix consists of two to four unique characters (optionally followed by an underscore), and prevents your object names from conflicting with object names in the host project, or in other referenced or referencing applications on a user's machine. To create an author prefix, use your personal or company initials. For example, author prefixes for my companies are *lci_* for Leszynski Company, Inc. and *kwc_* for Kwery Corporation. Before using your selected prefix, make an effort to determine if the prefix is already widely in use.

Tags for Procedures

With the large number of methods and properties listed in the Object Browser for most objects, differentiating built-in attributes of objects from those added during development can be a challenge. Procedure tags in class or form modules add a high degree of order to working with user-defined elements in the Object Browser (and other sorted lists), by clearly grouping custom procedures, methods, and properties apart from built-in object attributes.

On the other side of the coin, some developers feel strongly that procedure names should not have tags, especially in OLE Automation server applications. Before you blindly accept or condemn the use of tags in this context, try it awhile and then decide for yourself.

The *LNC* style prescribes the following naming convention tags for procedures:

cbf   Use this tag on procedure names for general code inside a class module or form.

mtd   Use this tag on custom method procedures defined for class modules.

prp   Use this tag on Property procedure names defined in class modules with `Property Get`, `Property Let`, and `Property Set` statements.

LNC does not require or suggest assigning a data type tag to functions to reflect their return value. However, if you have a specific need to tag procedures to reflect their return value type, use the appropriate tags from the "Tags for Variables" section and apply them consistently to all procedures in an application.

VBA Object Name Examples

Table 16.15 shows examples of VBA variables applying the various conventions in this section.

Table 16.15 VBA Variable Name Examples	
Declaration	**Description**
Dim oxlsappBudget As Object	Excel.Application
Function lci_ArraySum (ParamArray ravarNum() As Variant) As Double	Company identifier
Public giaintPartNum As Integer	Global index into array
Const clngCustNumMax As Long = 10000	Const for max CustID
Function FileLock (ByVal vstrFile As String) As Boolean	ByVal argument

Naming Conventions for JET Objects

The data building blocks of many data-centric VB applications are JET database objects. Creating names for database objects is no less important than creating VB application object names.

Rules for Base Names

The rules for database object base names are similar to those for VBA objects expressed earlier. Follow these rules when developing a base name for a new database object:

1. Spaces are not allowed in any object name. Where the readability of a space is required, use an underscore instead.

2. Object names begin with a letter and should include only letters, digits, and underscores. The use of special characters in object names is disallowed in order to comply with the naming rules of both VBA and Microsoft SQL Server. This allows your Basic variable names to include database object base names, and your entire schema to be easily upsized to the more powerful SQL Server platform.

3. Object names use mixed uppercase and lowercase to add readability to the name. (Previously, some developers used all lowercase names to allow for upsizing to Microsoft SQL Server. Starting with version 6, that product is now installed case-insensitive and allows you to maintain uppercase and lowercase in object names that are moved to the server from Jet.)

4. The only non-abbreviated syntax element that can have multiple capital letters is the base name. For example, CustAddr is allowed as a base name, but not as a qualifier or suffix. However, WA is allowed for all three.

5. Object names are usually singular rather than plural. By implication, tables, queries, and forms are plural, since they usually work with more than one record, so why restate the obvious?

6. An object's base name should include the base names of any table objects it is built on, if practical. Table base names should propagate into the names of dependent objects.

Rules 1 and 2 also apply to the other naming convention elements: prefixes, tags, qualifiers, and suffixes. These elements should never include spaces or special characters.

You should abbreviate object base name elements wherever possible, using a standardized abbreviation table such as the one in the section "Standardized Abbreviations" later in this chapter. You can extend *LNC* with your own standard abbreviations as well. You should also create and use standardized terminology in your applications wherever possible. For examples, see the section "Standardized Terminology" later.

Base Name Length Limits

LNC includes some constraints and suggestions for object name lengths.

We *target* our table name length at 15 characters maximum, for two reasons:

- Short names (15 characters or less) fully display within the default column width of the Access query design grid, in case you use Access to build and maintain your Jet objects.

- Query and form names usually include the base name(s) of the primary table object(s) they relate to, and will be unusably long if the table base names are long.

Beyond the 15-character target, we *absolutely limit* our table name lengths to 30 characters, which maintains compatibility with the table name length limit in SQL Server. For other objects, we *target* a 30-character limit as well, because the Access and VB interfaces show no more than the first 30 characters of object names in the default width of any lists or property grids.

Compound Base Names

The name of an object that is driven by a table must include the base name of the table. Thus, for the `tblCust` table, the primary query would be `qryCust`, the primary form `frmCust`, and so forth. Queries and forms that are sourced from multiple tables should reflect the base names of all the tables if it is practical. If not, you must decide which tables are the primary tables and list as many as possible in the name. Generally, in a multi-table query or form, the most "important" tables are not necessarily the first and second, but more often the first and last. So, a query joining `tblCust` to `tblAddr` to `tblPhone` to get the phone numbers for customers, would be named `qryCustAddrPhone` if the address information is included in the query result, or simply `qryCustPhone` if the address information is used to join to the phone numbers and is not displayed.

Bound control base names on forms are always equivalent to the base name of the bound field (the ControlSource). For example, a text box tied to the `LastName` field is named `txtLastName`.

Field Base Names

As part of standardizing terminology, we adhere to the concept of an "integrated data dictionary." This principle dictates that any fields in the data structure that have the same name must have the same properties and data purpose. For example, if the `LastName` field in `tblCust` is of type Text 30, and holds the customer last name, any other field named `LastName` in the same application must have the same type, length, properties, and purpose. If your application needs last name fields for both customers and dealers, this philosophy dictates that you name them differently (such as `CustLastName` and `DlrLastName`).

Applying the integrated data dictionary principle also means that table fields do not get leading prefixes or tags, since I prefer my data dictionaries to be platform-neutral. That way, a field does not have to be renamed if data is "upsized" or ported to a platform with different data types. A table is still called a *table* in SQL Server, so moving `tblCust` there from JET would require no table rename. However, if `tblCust` had a field `lngCustID` defined as a Long Integer in JET, moving the database to SQL Server would require a field rename to `intCustID`, since SQL Server uses the data type name Integer to mean the same as JET's Long Integer. Since renaming fields affects all dependent objects and code, it should be avoided at all costs, so I would call the field simply `CustID` from the start.

Qualifiers and suffixes are acceptable in field names, however, because they describe the object's data purpose and not its type, and the purpose does not change between platforms.

Ordering Base Name Elements

Object base name elements should be ordered from left to right with respect to their importance, readability, and desired sort order. In the example from the previous section, `CustLastName` is a better name than `LastNameCust`, because the group name portion (`Cust` or `Dlr`) carries greater weight in an object's name than the specific item name (`LastName` or `PhoneNum`). Think of `Cust` as the name of a collection of customer-related items and this rule becomes clear—what you are really saying is that `CustLastName` is analogous to `Cust(LastName)` or `Cust.LastName` in *Collection.Object* terminology.

Some of you will naturally carry this example to its extreme and say that the Customers collection really has a Names collection with multiple elements, including Last, thus the representation of that idea as `Cust.Name(Last)` would lead to the field name `CustNameLast` instead. Such a construction model still fits within the rules of *LNC*, and we won't debate you against using it. In practice, however, such names often become fairly unreadable, even if they are accurate.

Tags for JET Objects

In *LNC*, tags are required for JET table and query database objects. Table 16.16 lists the tags for JET database objects.

Table 16.16 JET Database Object Tags	
Object	**Tag**
Query	qry
Query (form source)	q[obj]
Query (append)	qapp
Query (crosstab)	qxtb
Query (data definition)	qddl
Query (delete)	qdel
Query (form filter)	qflt
Query (lookup table)[3]	qlkp
Query (make table)	qmak
Query (select)	qsel
Query (SQL pass-through)	qspt
Query (union)	quni
Query (update)	qupd
Table	tbl
Table (attached Btrieve)	tbtv
Table (attached dBASE)	tdbf
Table (attached Excel)	txls
Table (attached Fox)	tfox
Table (attached Lotus)	twks
Table (attached ODBC)	todb
Table (attached Paradox)	tpdx
Table (attached SQL Server)	tsql
Table (attached text)	ttxt

Object	Tag
Table (lookup)[3]	tlkp
Table (audit log)	tlog
Table (many-to-many relation)	trel
Table (summary information)	tsum

These tags provide rich detail about the objects and sort objects with similar attributes together. For example, lookup tables and their maintenance forms are often used over and over in multiple applications. The tags `tlkp`, `qlkp`, and `flkp` clearly identify these objects, making it easy for you to import them from an existing database into a new one or manipulate them together in other ways. However, if a particular database does not warrant rich detail, you have generic tags to use as well (for example, `qry` instead of `qsel`).

The conventions prescribe a single character tag added to the front of the full object name (including the tag) of the related object in one special case above. This situation occurs where a query is created solely to serve as the data source for one particular form, as in `qfrmCust`.

Prefixes for Database Objects

The list below describes the database object prefixes and their usage.

_(underscore)   Use this prefix for objects that are incomplete and under development. When the Database window is sorted by object name, this prefix sorts objects to the top where they are immediately recognized as unfinished and unusable. When the object is ready for testing or deployment, remove the underscore. This prefix is not used with form controls.

zh   Use this prefix to denote "system" objects, which are for use by developers and application code only, and which should be hidden from the user by default. System objects provide the infrastructure for an application but are not meant for user interaction. For example, you would use this prefix on a form's hidden text box that is used to compute a value, or on a hidden table that provides message strings to your VBA code. Note that Access has its own prefix—`USys`—with a similar meaning. Items prefixed with

USys are also not for user interaction and are not displayed in the Database window by default. In past versions of Access, it was necessary to use USys instead of zh to prevent the display of system objects in the Database window. With Access 95, you can use the zh prefix combined with setting the object's Hidden property to True to achieve this result. If the system object should not be hidden, use the zs prefix instead.

zs   Use this prefix to denote displayed "system" objects, which are for use by developers and application code only and should be displayed in the Database window. If the system object should be hidden, use the zh prefix instead.

zt   Use this prefix for temporary objects that are created programmatically. For example, a query written out from VBA code, used in code, and then deleted by the code, would have a zt prefix. Any database object labeled with zt showing in the Database window should be deleted during administrative sweeps of a database (before each repair and compact), since by definition it is probably left over from an abnormally terminated process that did not clean up after itself.

zz   This prefix denotes backup copies of objects that you keep in the Database window for reference or possible re-use. Items with this prefix should be periodically reviewed to determine their value, and deleted if not needed.

Note that most of these database object prefixes use "z" as the first character. Database objects with such prefixes sort to the bottom of the Database window, below the user-oriented objects that are accessed more frequently.

Database Object Name Examples

Table 16.17 shows examples of database objects, applying the various conventions in this section.

Table 16.17   Database Object Naming Convention Examples

Object	Description
zhtxtUser	Hidden system text box
zttfoxCustHist	Temporary Fox table attachment
qupdCustBal_Dlr	Update customers that are also dealers
trelCustAddrPhone	Link many addresses to many phones

Creating Your Own Tags

What do you do when *LNC* doesn't address a particular object naming need? First, contact us and let us know why, so that we can improve the style for the benefit of all users. Second, consider if what you are trying to do is covered by the style in some other way. For example, in your development team you call tables that link two other tables in a many-to-many relationship "linking" tables, and you want to create a new table tag `tlnk` as a result. However, on examination of all table tags, you would find `trel` already exists, defined as "Table (many-to-many relation)," which is the correct tag for what you need. Even though the nomenclature is not exactly what you might use, it is better to use an existing tag than create another one.

Finally, when other options are exhausted, you can create a custom tag to address your need. When creating a custom tag, these should be your guidelines:

1. Do not redefine an existing tag. No matter how badly you really want the three or four character combination for your own purpose, never re-use a defined tag.

2. Do not change the rule for tags. Stay within the three to four character range followed by *LNC*.

3. Use the conventions in existing tags as your guide for the new one. For example, all table tags start with `t`, all query tags with `q`, and so forth. Any new tags you make for these objects should begin with the correct letter. See Table 16.18 for guidelines on standard tag components. Note that some of the examples are from the Office version of *LNC*. Tag components that can be easily inferred from the tags above are not listed in the table (for example, the component `fox` for FoxPro can be inferred from the tags `tfox` and `dfox`).

When creating a new tag, it should be mnemonic enough to uniquely shorten the word it represents, and should only use characters from the root word or a generally accepted shorthand (see Table 16.18).

Table 16.18	Some Standard Tag Components		
Item	**Segment**	**Examples**	**Location**
bar	br	mmbr, pbr,tbr	anywhere
database/databound	d	dcbo, dgrd, dlst	leading
form	f	fdlg	leading
MAPI	mp	mpm	leading
module	b	bas	leading
query	q	qsel	leading
set	st	rst	anywhere
table	t	tdf	leading
view	vw	lvw, tvw	anywhere

To create tags for object variables pointing to OLE Automation server applications, start with a three-character application prefix that is unique and applicable. Add to the application abbreviation a three-character tag for the entry point of the application, such as bas for "Basic" in "Word.Basic."

For example, to create a tag for OLE Automation with Shapeware's Visio program, which is an OLE server, use either vsd (the data file extension) or vis (a mnemonic for Visio) as the basis for the tag, then add app for Application, because the entry point to Visio's automation engine is a call to "Visio.Application." Thus the tag and its use in variable declarations would look like this:

```
Dim ovisapp As Object
Dim ovisappDoc As Object
Set ovisapp = CreateObject("Visio.Application")
Set ovisappDoc = ovisapp.Documents.Open("C:\VISIO\HOUSE.VSD")
```

VBA Coding Conventions

In addition to object naming conventions, *LNC* suggests several standardized coding conventions for VBA procedures.

Common Practices

Common coding practices in VB coding that are supported by LNC include:

■ Use indents of two characters to show nesting program structures (I find the default of four spaces produces too much white space and too many truncated code lines).

■ Use Option Explicit in each module to force declaration of variables before use.

■ Declare all necessary variables at the top of each procedure.

■ Place comments and error handling in each procedure.

Code Comments

There are as many in-line Basic code commenting styles as there are Basic coders. Whatever convention you use, the keys are to (a) be terse yet descriptive, and (b) be consistent.

LNC suggests placing the following minimum set of comments at the beginning of each procedure:

Purpose	Briefly describe the purpose of the procedure
Arguments	List the arguments to a function and how they are to be used
Returns	Describe what the return value of a function signifies
Authors	Name the creator, the date created, the last editor, and the date last edited

Comments placed on the same line as code should be separated from the code by two spaces. Comments placed on their own line should be no longer than 60 characters so they are displayed in full in the default module design view size. Some developers like to keep a change log in procedures as a comment block; if so, I suggest keeping it at the bottom rather than the top, since it is less frequently accessed than the code it displaces.

Trapping Errors

Every procedure that can fail, which is virtually every procedure with more than a few simple lines, should have an error trap. Error traps are created by placing this line at the beginning of the procedure, after the header comments and before any other statements:

```
On Error GoTo procname_Err
```

The marker *procname* above should be replaced with the full procedure name. The error handler is placed at the bottom of the procedure, denoted with the label procname_Err:. At the end of the error handler, control is returned somewhere in the procedure, usually to a line label name procname_Exit that precedes a block of code immediately above the error handler.

To allow you to turn off error trapping during program debugging, *LNC* suggests that you place the On Error statement inside a conditional compilation directive, like this:

```
#If pcccDebug Then
   On Error Goto 0
#Else
   On Error Goto procname_Err
#Endif
```

Before running an application, you can enable or disable error trapping by setting the value of pcccDebug to -1 (True) or 0 (False) in the "Conditional Compilation Arguments" text box on the Module tab of the Options dialog.

We use the procname_label structure rather than the label_procname structure preferred by many coders in order to maintain our *ObjectVerb* construction metaphor described above. Some developers prefer to place the qualifier of the label first, as in Err_*procname*, but philosophically the phrases Err_, Exit_, and so forth are not class tags, they are qualifiers for the line label object, thus they belong at the end like any other qualifier. This argument becomes more compelling when you remember that you can also create line labels for GoSub and GoTo statements in VBA, and thus creating many different combinations of leading characters, as if they were tags, becomes problematic.

Standardized Abbreviations

Table 16.19 lists some of our standard abbreviations used when building object names.

Table 16.19 Standardized Object Name Abbreviations	
Abbrev.	**Description**
Acct	account
Actg	accounting
Addr	address
Admin	administration
Agmt	agreement

Abbrev.	Description
Amt	amount
Anal	analysis
Apvd	approved
Arch	archive
Arvl	arrival
Asst	assist(ant)
Atty	attorney
Auth	authorized
Avg	average
Beg	beginning
Bilg	billing
Bldg	building
Busn	business
Char	character
Comm	comment
Cont	contact
Corp	corporate, corporation
Ctrl	control
Ctry	country
Cty	county
Cur	currency
Curr	current
Cust	customer
Dept	department
Desc	description
Det	detail, details

(continues)

Table 16.19 Continued	
Abbrev.	**Description**
Devlpmt	development
Disc	discount
Dlr	dealer
Empe	employee
Engrg	engineering
Exec	executive
Extd	extend, extended
Extn	extension
Fin	finance, financial
Genl	general
Glbl	global
Int	interest
Intl	international
Inv	inventory
Invc	invoice
Loca	location
Mfg	manufacturing
Mgmt	management
Mgr	manager
Mkt	market
Mktg	marketing
Mon	month
Mtg	meeting
Mtl	material
Mtls	materials
Num	number
Ofc	office

Abbrev.	Description
Ofcr	officer
Op	operation
Ops	operations
Ordr	order
Othr	other
Perd	period
Pers	personal, personnel
Phon	phone
Phys	physical
Pmt	payment
Prim	primary
Prnt	print
Proj	project
Pros	prospect, prospective
Qty	quantity
Rec	record
Recd	received
Rem	remark
Schd	schedule, scheduled
Secy	secretary
Seq	sequence
Srce	source
Stat	status
Stats	statistics
Std	standard
Sum	summary, summaries, summation

(continues)

Table 16.19 Continued	
Abbrev.	**Description**
Super	supervise, supervisor
Svc	service
Titl	title
Tran	transaction
Ttl	total
Var	variable
Ver	version
Whse	warehouse
Whsl	wholesale
Xsfr	transfer
Xsmn	transmission
Xsmt	transmit

Standardized Terminology

When creating code comments, object names, help files, and system documentation, it is important to use terms that have an accepted and non-ambiguous meaning. You should build a list of standardized terms for your specific industry or application to ensure consistency. Table 16.20 provides a short sample list of standardized terminology. These terms are not a feature of *LNC*, they are only examples as a starting point for your efforts.

Table 16.20 Examples of Standardized Terminology	
Term	**Description**
Add	To create a new record. You should select one of: Add, Create, Enter, and New and be consistent.
Beg	Beginning, the start of a process
Close	To close an open object
Comment	A more familiar term for text originating with a human than Remark or Notes

Term	Description
Desc	A description, often a long text string
Edit	To change or modify
Editor	The last person to change a record
End	The end of a process
Flag	A programming item with fixed set of values, usually True/False (a Boolean)
Key	A unique index used to find a record
Max	The maximum, better than Most
Min	The minimum, better than Least
Open	To open
Owner	The creator of a record, process, or object
Save	To commit a record
User	The person currently running an application

[1] *The term database in this table refers to using VB against Jet and SQL Server data. While Jet is discussed in this document, naming conventions for NT SQL Server are documented in the Leszynski Naming Conventions for Microsoft Solution Developers paper.*

[2] *A lookup table has records that map short codes to full text values, like state abbreviations to states, and is used to populate combo and list boxes, validate fields, and so forth.*

[3] *Many developers use dat as a tag for date objects, but this conflicts for us with the tag for Visual Basic's Data control.*

Summary

You can get copies of this chapter from Kwery Corporation. The following additional information is also available: the *Leszynski Naming Conventions for Microsoft Solution Developers* document, the *Leszynski Naming Conventions for Microsoft Access* document, Windows Help file versions of each *LNC* document, and *LNC* programmers' tools. Contact Kwery via the order line at 1-800-ATKWERY, or on the product information line at 206-644-7830. Kwery can also be reached via CompuServe at 71573,3261 or by fax at 206-644-8409.

I welcome your feedback on these conventions, including your likes, dislikes, stories, and suggestions.

Chapter 17

Creating Visual Basic Naming Conventions

by Stan Leszynski

Stan Leszynski founded Leszynski Company, Inc., in 1982 to create custom PC database applications. Since that time the firm has created solutions for hundreds of clients, including dozens of applications for Microsoft. The company has also written retail products sold by Microsoft, Microrim, Qualitas, and Kwery with a user base of several million people. Successful products include the OLE calendar controls shipped with Access 2 and Access 95, the 386MAX memory manager, and four R:BASE developer tools. The company currently specializes in Access, Visual Basic, SQL Server, and Visual C++.

Stan's second company, Kwery Corporation, shipped the very first Access add-in—Access To Word—and the first OLE controls for Access—Kwery Control Pak 1.

Stan is the author of Access Expert Solutions *from Que. He speaks regularly at Access conferences in the U.S., Canada, and Europe, and is consistently one of the top-rated Access speakers. You can contact Stan on CompuServe (71151,1114).*

Character Development

In the early years of developing in Visual Basic (versions 1 and 2), we used naming conventions derived from styles we had created over many years of working in xBASE and R:BASE. Deriving our VB conventions from a DOS world, limited by eight-character file and object names, produced mostly single-character tags. As a result, our early VB style was incomprehensible to anyone but us.

Then, in 1993, a beacon shone through the fog—Microsoft published an "Object Naming Conventions" section in Chapter 3 of the Visual Basic 3 documentation. In it,

(continues)

(continued)

they recommended attaching three-character type tags to control names. We felt suddenly freed from shackles of bondage—we now had *three full characters* of information with which to classify objects! We lengthened all of our VB object tags to three characters and never looked back.

(Forgive the tangent, but numerologists in the audience will note the eerie preponderance of the number 3 in the preceding paragraph, as in: 1993 plus Chapter 3 plus VB 3 yielded three-character tags. Does this mean that some strange alignment of planets caused us to all be using three-character object tags instead of two characters or four? Probably not. A more reasonable explanation is that three-character identifiers have been a feature of the computer world since the early days, thanks to acronyms like DEC, IBM, and MVS....)

While most serious developers live and die by their programming conventions, some are casual about issues like consistent object naming. To find out if the issue of naming conventions is important to you, take the following test.

In the Project window in figure 17.1, can you identify:

- Which form is for customer entry and which is for customer editing?

- Which form is for maintenance of lookup tables?

- Which forms are modal dialogs?

- Which forms involve customer records?

Fig. 17.1
These form names do not provide adequate information.

If you found it frustrating that the object names in figure 17.1 were not very descriptive, you will get value from this chapter. For me, an application filled with names like the ones above is as difficult to navigate through as a messy garage!

To continue the illustration of the value of naming conventions, next consider the Project window in figure 17.2. The objects are the same as in figure 17.1, but the names follow standardized conventions, both for base names and leading characters. Even if you don't know the specific naming conventions used, I'll bet you can infer from the object names a lot about each object's important properties, and identify the items on my bulleted list above.

Fig. 17.2
These form names follow specific naming conventions.

The specific conventions used in the figure are described in the previous chapter, but whether or not you know my conventions, you probably determined quite easily what the major characteristics are for each form.

Notice that two types of naming conventions were applied in figure 17.2. The first, and most obvious, convention is the standardization of the object base names. The use of the different terms C, Cust, and Customer in the form names to mean the same thing were all standardized to Cust. The Cust portion of the names was moved to the beginning of the base name so the customer objects would each sort with their peers in the Object Browser. Also, the random use of singular and plural was stopped, and the names were made more descriptive. The second, and equally important, convention applied is the addition of leading characters denoting the type of the forms. Many VB naming conventions have in common the standardization of the base object name and the addition of descriptive information on one or both ends of the base name.

The example provided by the contrasting form names above is equally applicable to the other named elements of a VB project. Any object in your application that you will view or refer to frequently—database objects stored in a Jet database, forms and their controls, procedure names, and Basic variables—is a candidate for naming conventions. The fact that you may see and use a particular object's name dozens or hundreds of times throughout a development project further accentuates the need for devising good rules for naming objects. Any name you see and use over and over should be both informative and familiar (as some say, "easy on the eyes").

In this chapter, you'll explore and discover answers to these questions:

- Why are object naming conventions important?

- What are the guidelines for creating naming conventions?

- What are the components of a naming convention?

- How are naming convention components assembled and applied?

I will use the terms *naming conventions* and *style* interchangeably throughout this chapter. Naming conventions and other key development foundation items are each a part of your overall development style.

Why Use Naming Conventions?

The motivation to create naming conventions for working with your development tools usually derives from specific problems or situations you encounter. However, there are other, and more compelling, reasons for developing and using naming conventions in an application. A description of each of the most important ones follows.

Reverse Engineering an Application

When you look at an application written by someone else, or revisit your own after some period of time, the overall structure should make sense to you almost immediately. If not, you will waste time researching and reviewing it, or chasing down documentation, if it even exists. Although good naming conventions cannot help you to immediately infer the complex workings of an SQL statement, or help you read an intricate code module if you don't speak Basic, they give you at least an immediate treetop view of an application's architecture.

Suppose I'm at a client site and they need me to discuss the feasibility of my company supporting and modifying an accounting application they've written. In a perfect world, they would sit their developer down with me and step me through the facets of the application. In the *real* world, however, they will place me in front of a computer and give me only a few hours to review their application, understand their situation, and make a recommendation (because whatever objective they have was probably due yesterday). If this client's programming staff has followed good naming conventions, I can learn much about the composition of the application in a short time by analyzing its object names. (Even better, if the hypothetical client used *my* naming conventions, reading through the application would be quite familiar and friendly for me.) If the application object names have no consistency, as shown in figure 17.1 previously, my job is harder.

Figure 17.3 shows the Object Browser view of the objects shown in figure 17.2. Thanks to naming conventions, I immediately know the composition of the objects in this application with respect to:

- Customer objects versus dealer objects

- Pop-up dialog forms versus database maintenance forms

- The MDI parent form and its MDI child forms

- Class modules versus standard forms

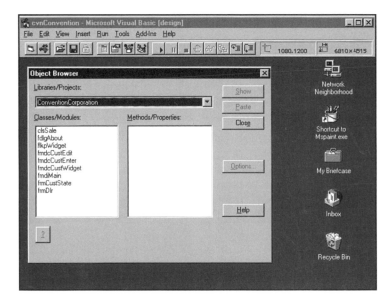

Fig. 17.3
This application's makeup can be inferred from the Object Browser.

Team Development

When multiple developers are working on the same project, having a common methodology helps to pull them together as a team. A stated set of standards and objectives allows individuals to work together more effectively:

- Predefined standards remove the variability introduced by individual styles, and prevent the "turf wars" that can occur when champions of conflicting styles get together.

■ Predefined standards ensure that objects are interchangeable among team members. Developers can share objects created by each other and understand them easier through their knowledge of the standards applied to the objects during development.

■ New team members feel less intimidated when the expectations for them are clearly defined (as in "Please code to this written standard"). Existing team members can be reassigned to new responsibilities with an equally clear sense of direction.

■ Departing team members can be replaced with less expense because their replacements can quickly understand the inherited application's architecture and code.

When creating application development standards, including naming conventions, the expected benefit for team development can be summarized this way: *Any member of the team should be able to quickly navigate and comprehend the application's object and program structure as if it were his or her own.*

The code shown in Listing 17.1 provides an illustration of these points. When you read this code for the first time, you see immediately what the author intends for the code to do (to sum up data items from a transaction table). Not only are the base names descriptive, but also the prefixes in front of the variable names allow the reader to always know the context of a variable when seeing it anywhere in the code routine.

Listing 17.1   17LIST01.TXT—The Dim statements in this procedure are very specific

```
Public Function CustOrderSum() As Integer

Dim dbs As Database
Dim dblOrderSum As Double
Dim lngCustID As Long
Dim rstOrderSum As Recordset
Dim varValidTest As Variant
Dim wsp As Workspace

Set wsp = Workspaces(0)
Set dbs = wsp.OpenDatabase("C:\Conven\Conven.Mdb")
Set rstOrderSum = dbs.OpenRecordset("tblCustOrder", dbOpenDynaset)
rstOrderSum.MoveFirst

Do While Not rstOrderSum.EOF
...
```

Making VB Easier to Use

New users of naming conventions and similar standards often complain that the conventions require extra time to implement, and slow down the pace of development. While it is true that any new system involves an investment of time to learn, good standards will always save time in the long run, not cost time.

Consider the Object Browser in VB4. When you create a new form and view it in the Object Browser dialog, you'll see exactly 77 built-in methods and properties listed for the form. The list is quite crowded before you've written one line of code. After you have written several code procedures in the form module, using the Object Browser to find those procedures among the dozens of method and property items listed can be very time consuming. Figure 17.4 shows two code procedures (`Validate` and `WidgetCost`) aligned alphabetically with other items in the Object Browser.

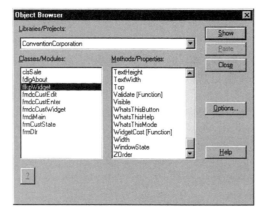

Fig. 17.4
Two functions sorted in the Object Browser by name.

Now, let's apply a simple naming convention to the two procedures in figure 17.4. Because these are form module procedures (often called *code behind forms*), we will prefix all the form's functions (and subs) with `cbf`. Placing these characters before the name sorts all form procedures with this naming convention together in the Object Browser. Figure 17.5 shows how the new sort order makes it much easier to go quickly to a specific routine, or to find a routine when you don't know its precise name, because all the form's procedures will group together.

Fig. 17.5

Two functions
sorted in the
Object Browser
by type.

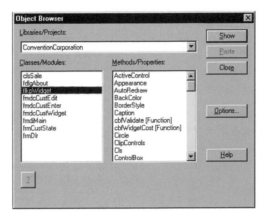

As a further example, consider what happens when you rename a form (or control, database table, or any other object) in an application, for example changing *Widget* to *Gadget*. You will have to globally find and replace every reference to the original name *Widget* in all of your code. When you do so, the name may occur in other contexts than as a form name, making for a slow replacement process as you read through each match and check the context. For example, in the code snippet in Listing 17.2, you would only want to change one of the six references to *Widget*—the one that is a form reference—during your replace operation:

Listing 17.2   17LIST02.TXT—Basic function with multiple occurrences of the word Widget

```
Function WidgetArchive() As Integer
' Flag all widget records for archive that have no
' transactions for 300 days
' Widget records are archived during weekly maint. routine

Dim dbs As Database
Dim rstWidget As Recordset
...
Set rstWidget = dbs.OpenRecordset("Widget", dbOpenDynaset)
Widget.lblWaiting.Caption = "Archiving, please wait..."
```

If however, a unique naming convention was applied so that the form in the last line above was named frmWidget, the code in Listing 17.2 would have only one reference to the target string, not six. Your find and replace operation would be more precise and more rapid.

Leveraging Your Techniques

The final benefit in the list of naming convention justifications is the ability to extend your development environment and techniques by leveraging your naming conventions. Good object naming habits should enhance your ability to document an application, create tools and utilities, create reusable code libraries, and otherwise increase your productivity.

For example, assume you use a common set of forms in most of your applications, and this set of forms includes dialogs (such as a login form and an About dialog), as well as lookup forms for your common database tables. You might keep a project template (a repository filled with your reusable objects), and write an application wizard to create new projects from your template. Such a wizard would begin the process of creating a new project by opening your template project and saving it under a new name. Your wizard would then ask you if the new project will include a Jet database component or not. If you answer in the negative, the wizard will identify the lookup forms in the new project (based on the leading `flkp` characters in each form's name) and remove them from the project. It is easy for your wizard code to identify a class of objects if your naming conventions are applied consistently to each object.

Even if you don't create your own tools, naming conventions facilitate better use of the VB development environment itself. For example, in the introductory section of this chapter, I demonstrated standardizing the abbreviation for `Customer` to `Cust` throughout a particular application. With this kind of standardization in place, all references to customer tables, forms, and other objects in a project should have the string `Cust` in their base name somewhere. (In fact, in my world, even VBA variables that worked with the customer-related objects would have `Cust` somewhere in their name.) Therefore, if you were looking for a particular set of program routines in your application, you could use the VB search engine to search all modules for the string `Cust`. You would be quite successful at finding all code routines for customer objects if you used such a convention consistently. Applying naming conventions to your daily work this way can be quite a time saver.

Naming Convention Considerations

I summarized in the preceding section the objectives I think of as most important when developing a naming convention. Before choosing or developing a style of your own, first list out your own objectives if they are different from mine. Next, decide what considerations will affect the development of your conventions.

To help you create a style, following are four considerations to keep in mind:

■ **Be Consistent.** If you take the trouble to create a naming style, apply it uniformly over a long period of time. Don't change elements of the style every time someone lobs a criticism or suggestion at it. The reason you create a style is to guide your long-term development strategy and to provide a foundation of common elements across multiple projects and applications. Therefore, your naming conventions should be more like a foundation of rock than of sand.

For example, I've used Apvd as an abbreviation for Approved in database structures for at least 10 years. In our dBASE and R:BASE days, when names were very short, we needed the real estate. Now, VB lets us use longer names, but we still use Apvd. Why? Because consistency makes our lives better. When clients call and say "We'd like to create a status report driven by approval date, where do we start?", I don't have to think hard, or dig for their documentation, or restore their application from a tape. Instead, I can tell them immediately to look in their database structure for the field ApvdDate. Whether their application is one year old or ten, I know the answer without looking it up because we've always used that name and spelling, and we probably always will.

Of Hobgoblins and Brain Size

While my efforts over the past several years to help standardize Basic naming conventions have met with mostly favorable reception, there have been a few detractors as well. And, much to my amusement, a large portion of the people that tirade against naming conventions include this same quote in their messages, year after year: *Consistency is the hobgoblin of small minds.*

I wonder if people who use this quote for their purposes truly believe what it says? Do they really conclude that all people who choose to drive consistently on the right side of the road, and stop at red lights, have small minds? Do they think in their hearts that things like on-time airline arrivals and departures are a sign of low intellect among airline pilots and FAA personnel?

I could go on, but obviously from my perspective, consistency is in no way an evil thing. Using naming conventions faithfully does not imply that you are *not* a free thinker. Quite the opposite—it shows that you are smart enough to create repeatable systems to automate your mundane tasks, in order to free up your rather *large* mind to float unhindered toward higher purposes!

(As a footnote, I find it equally amusing that not one person who has used this quote against my naming conventions has actually used the exact quote correctly, which reads: *A foolish consistency is the hobgoblin of little minds (Ralph Waldo Emerson)*. Notice that Emerson wasn't against consistency, only the *foolish* use of it. But, of course, people who twist this quote for their own purposes can't be expected to quote him *consistently*, right?)

■ **Plan Ahead.** If you know where the feature sets of your development products are going, or have a long-term development strategy, let such information influence your naming conventions. Ideally, you never want to be forced to rename objects or rewrite code in a production application over its lifespan.

For example, despite Microsoft's suggested three-character prefixes (tags) shown in the VB3 documentation, it was tempting to use one or two characters instead, as many developers were doing at the time. However, we expected that someday other Microsoft Office applications would have much of the same capabilities as VB, so we used three characters for all our tags, to give ourselves room to grow. Now, several years later, our VB naming conventions are used in or must coexist with objects, procedures, and variables in Excel, Access, and so forth. One-character and two-character tags would now be too limiting to develop a cross-application style for so many products, so we're glad we planned ahead.

■ **There Is No Single Correct Answer.** Different developers have different goals. Different users have different needs. Consequently, there are many ways to approach development styles, and no specific naming convention is *the* correct one. What you are looking for is a tool that works for you now and later, not an answer to philosophical programming questions. As you will see later, naming conventions can be short or long, lead and/or follow object names, use many characters or few, and so forth. There is no single approach that works for every-one — there are as many approaches to naming conventions as there are creative thinkers.

In my dBASE and R:BASE days, there were few published styles and little debate on the subject, so we just used a style that worked best for us and kept it to ourselves. However, the VB and VBA worlds present a different situation. Since the publication of our original naming conventions in 1992, we have received hundreds of e-mail and telephone suggestions, and have reviewed more than a dozen other naming conventions, some derived from ours and others completely different. Developers, and even casual users, seem very interested in the subject and have widely differing opinions.

■ **Making the Build vs. Borrow Decision.** With many people interested in the subject, there are obviously several standards from which to choose. The one proposed in the next chapter has unique merits that will be described later, but it may not have value to you specifically. If not, you are left at a fork in the road, facing the age-old *Build vs. Borrow* decision.

Up one fork of the road is the hard task of creating your own naming conventions. You can do this from scratch, using the objectives, considerations, and techniques learned in this chapter. Or you can review other published conventions and extract from them parts that meet your needs, filling in the gaps and creating a hybrid.

Up the other fork in the road is the decision to take an existing convention and apply it as is. If you are new to VB development, this route may be the easiest. You can ask other developers for suggestions on what style they use. Also, you can check the Basic forums on CompuServe (search for the keyword *naming*), browse other books by VB developers, and review the major VB periodicals.

With a foundation laid of objectives and considerations, let's delve into the specific mechanics of naming conventions. You will want to consider each of the topics in the remainder of this chapter when developing your style.

Creating Object Base Names

If you used no naming conventions at all, each object would still have a name of some sort. For forms and other objects, these names are usually descriptive, such as `Salespeople` or `FriendsOfMine`. For program variables, programmers are usually more economical—the classic `Dim I As Integer` statement for loop variables comes to mind. We could call this starting point (`Salespeople`, `FriendsOfMine`, or `I`) the *initial name*, *primary name*, *base name*, or perhaps *root name*. For our purposes here, I'll use the term *base name* to describe the starting point when you name a particular object.

A strategy for selecting, abbreviating, capitalizing, and organizing object base names is, in and of itself, a naming convention. Thus if you do nothing more than create a consistent approach to base names, you have authored a development style for yourself. What topics would you include in a convention for base names? Let's examine the needs of specific VB objects.

Because the majority of my applications—and probably yours also—include a Jet or SQL Server database component, I ascribe database objects the same weight as Visual Basic objects for the rest of this chapter.

> ### Tip
>
> If you use Access to create Jet databases for your VB applications, or to create application components such as reporting modules in mixed-platform solutions, read my white paper "The Leszynski Naming Conventions for Microsoft Access" or my book *Access Expert Solutions* from Que for an expanded discussion of Access and Jet object naming conventions.

Table Base Names

When naming data tables, your standard should specify a desired target length for names. Some developers prefer things very terse, and use the shortest name they can read (although that doesn't ensure that others can read it!). One naming convention I reviewed suggested limiting table names to eight characters to be compatible with dBASE and FoxPro formats! I find such short names to be totally non-intuitive to read, and would not recommend such a restrictive approach unless you routinely move your data from Jet or SQL Server to a platform with shorter name restrictions. I spent a decade working on products with eight character names and am happy to be free of that bondage. While most users can infer that `CustInfo` is the customer information table, far fewer will recognize that `InStTxSl` is the table for "in-state taxable sales," since it could just as easily be the "internal structure of Texas silos."

At the other end of the spectrum, some developers prefer longer names that are fully descriptive. Long names may even refer to the source or range of the data. Examples include: `MainEuropeanCustomerData`, `north region sales summary from db2`, and `WidgetProductionStatisticsFirstQuarter1994`. While these names are valid in Jet, they become rather unwieldy when you use them in your application, whether in SQL code from VB or building your database using the Access query grid.

For table names, as with most things in life in general, moderation is probably the best approach. If you create a set of standard abbreviations for your development (see later in this chapter), and remove extraneous words, you

can create table names that are not overly long and yet are fully descriptive.
I prefer to keep table names to 15 characters or less through the use of standard abbreviations. At most, I use a 30-character absolute limit for my Jet
table names so they can "upsize" eventually to SQL Server without breaking
that product's length limitation.

Another justification for modest table name lengths is that table names often
become part of the base name for other objects that depend on them, thus
long table names breed even longer names for queries, forms, and reports. For
example, a table `Customer` would probably have several queries based on it,
like `CustomerSalesSummary`, `CustomerByRegion`, and so forth. The longer the
table name, the longer the names derived from it.

The final consideration affecting table name length is a very pragmatic one.
If you are using Access to create your Jet database, the Access user interface
provides limited real estate in property pages, combo boxes, and other objects
that list table names. Table names wider than the display space provided by
Access are difficult to view and work with in the user interface. Table 17.1
shows the default width in average characters displayed by the Access 95 user
interface in various places. As you can see from the different widths listed,
table names longer than 30 characters will always be truncated, and even
those longer than 15 characters will sometimes be truncated.

Table 17.1 Default Average Display Width of Table Names	
User Interface Item	**Default Width (Chars.)**
Form Record Source Property	30
Form/Report Wizard Source Object	25
Query Design Grid Field List	15
Query Design Grid Table Combo	17

Coincidentally, lists of tables and other objects in the various SQL Server
dialogs (such as the Manage Tables and Object Permissions dialogs) also trun-
cate names longer than 30 characters.

In addition to the areas listed in Table 17.1 previously, table names appear in
your query SQL statements and in your Basic code as `Recordset` sources and
SQL parameters. Table names are among the most widespread object names
in a typical data management application. Something that gets that much
usage deserves a few moments of your quality thought when you give it a
name.

Finally, I prefer to keep my table names singular (`Customer`) rather than plural (`Customers`). By implication, a table is always plural since it contains more than one record, so why waste one or more characters (to pluralize the name) everywhere you use its name? Whether you prefer singular or plural names, remember to pick one approach and apply it uniformly. I frequently see other developers mix and match singular and plural object names, and some confusion can arise when users try to decide if they should enter more than one record in tables with singular names, or only in tables with plural names.

Whether or not to use capitalization and punctuation schemes in your table names will be discussed in the "Capitalization and Punctuation" section later in this chapter. The use of prefixes and suffixes to further clarify table names will also be discussed later in this chapter.

In the preceding discussion of table name length, I noted three sample table names that were long enough to be problematic for us. I'll now restate those names, along with a suggestion of how I would rename them based upon the factors we've just considered:

- **MainEuropeanCustomerData.** I would find `CustEurope` equally effective. `Main` and `Data` seem redundant (what else would be in a table but data?), and I can apply an abbreviation to `Customer`.

- *`North region sales summary from db2`.* I much prefer mixed case names without spaces, so I would use `tsumNRegionSaleDB2` instead. I can abbreviate *`North`*, use one of my standard tags (`tsum`) for summary tables to convey the fact that this is not raw data, and eliminate *`From`* to save keystrokes with no loss of meaning.

- *`WidgetProductionStatisticsFirstQuarter1994`.* I can use my standard abbreviation to shorten *`Statistics`*, assume that most users know it's a production-oriented database and drop `Production`, and shorten the year and period. That leaves me with the name `WidgetStats94Q1`. Why did I move the quarters after the year? See the section "Sorting Object Names" for an explanation.

An object naming convention rarely stops with base names, but if you have no need for more elaborate conventions, simply applying the forethought described in this section to table names will allow you to develop standards for good base names and make your application development and use more pleasant.

Table Field Base Names

The considerations discussed in the "Table Base Names" section previously apply to any discussion of field names as well, including:

■ Keep the names short but readable

■ Use standardized abbreviations

■ Be consistent in applying singular versus plural

Because a table holds many different types of information, but a field holds only one, it is easier to shorten field names than table names. Whatever target you select for table name length, your field name standard length should be less than or equal to, but not longer than, the standard for table names. Like table names, field names appear in the VB and Access user interfaces in property dialogs, the query grid, the Data Manager, and so forth, and each of these areas has display-width limitations for object names. You will find that sticking with field names around 20 characters long removes most of the annoying truncations in the user interface of your tools.

One common discussion that arises during the development of field naming conventions involves the order of compound elements in the name. Some compound name ordering questions are easily resolved—LastName is a more readable field name than NameLast. Other names are equally adequate in any order, such as date field names like ClosedDate versus DateClosed. And because field names usually appear in the Access user interface in natural order rather than sorted, the ordering decision does not have a large impact on your development. If you opt for the style ApvdDate and ClosedDate, you are placing more weight on the important part of the base name rather than the data type. If you opt instead for DateApvd and DateClosed, you are placing more emphasis on the type of field. I view this latter style as the more dangerous of the two, because when you carry it out to its logical conclusion, you should use names like CommentMgr instead of MgrComment, because Comment is essentially the field type. This construction becomes essentially unworkable beyond date and time fields.

Whether or not to use capitalization and punctuation schemes in your field names will be discussed in the "Capitalization and Punctuation" section later in this chapter. The use of prefixes and suffixes to further clarify field names will also be discussed later.

Query Base Names

As already noted in the "Table Base Names" section, many query (SQL Server uses the term "view") names are built around the primary table in the query.

Thus, query names are longer on average than table names. One of the reasons I suggested 15-character table names previously is so that query names built around that table names would also be reasonable. Recall from the discussion earlier that the Access 95 and SQL Server 6 interfaces never give you more than 30 characters of table name display space by default. In most cases, the user interface areas that display table names can display query names as well, so in order to try to keep query names to 30 characters, you must build them around shorter table base names.

Having decided on a target length for query names, applying the standard can become a challenge. It is harder to be terse with query names than table names, because queries perform actions on data or change the presentation of data. A good query name must express the actions it performs on the data. To solve this problem without being verbose, I prefer to use prefix and suffix characters placed around the query base name to express the query's actions succinctly, rather than including action information in the base name. For example, a query to delete all dormant sales prospects could have a base name like `Cold Prospects Delete`, or perhaps `DeleteDormantSalesProspects`. For my tastes, these are both too wordy and they marry the action too closely to the base name. My preferred approach would be to keep the base name simple—`SalesProsCold`, and describe the action using a prefix or suffix. Using this approach, the base name describes a group of records independent of the action, so it can be reused in various related objects. Adding an action prefix or suffix to this query would allow for multiple "flavors" of the same base name: `qselSalesProsCold`, `qdelSalesProsCold`, and `qupdSalesProsCold`.

Finally, I prefer to keep my query names singular (Customer) rather than plural (Customers), because a query usually is always plural by its nature. Select a pluralization scheme for your queries and tables and apply it uniformly.

Whether or not to use capitalization and punctuation schemes in your query names will be discussed in the "Capitalization and Punctuation" section later in this chapter. The use of prefixes and suffixes to further clarify query names will also be discussed later.

Form and Class Module Base Names

Because form and class module names are widespread throughout your application and the VB user interface, you will want to use names that are descriptive but not intolerably long. VB allows object names up to 40 characters long, but few people find that such long names are usable in practice.

You may decide to also establish a name length standard for form and class module names. Forms are often based on a source table in a database, and the object name can be derived from the source table name. Thus, I would suggest using the same name length guidelines you establish for query names as your form name guidelines. More important than the discussion of length is the establishment of rules for constructing the names of these objects.

There can be many different flavors of forms. Forms can be dialogs, switchboard menus, data entry screens, record edit screens, record selection lists, floating (popup) text or utilities, and more. Thus, how to convey a form or class module's purpose in the Project window without being wordy should be the primary focus of your conventions for these objects.

Consider a form to edit customer orders. It is possible to create a form with customer records bound to one data control, customer orders bound to another, and order details tied to a third. The driving table for the form is the customer table, but the primary purpose of the form is to get to the order details. So, is the form's base name `Customer`, `CustomerEdit`, `CustomerOrder`, `Customer Order Detail Edit`, or one of a dozen other possibilities? This is an example of the type of problems you should think through clearly as you create your naming conventions. Good conventions should help you and your co-developers approach such problems with ease.

How would I solve this specific dilemma? Our conventions require that the base name of the primary table be a part of the form or report name. The *primary table* here is the one that is most important to the purpose of the entire form (`CustOrdrDet`), not the one driving the main form (`Cust`). Thus I would name the form `frmCustOrdrDet`; if there were two varieties of the form I'd use `frmCustOrdrDetAdd` and `frmCustOrdrDetEdit`.

Whether or not to use capitalization and punctuation schemes in your form and report names will be discussed in the "Capitalization and Punctuation," section later in this chapter. The use of prefixes and suffixes to further clarify form and report names will also be discussed later.

Control Base Names

When you create a data bound control on a form, consider using the field name of the bound control's source as its base name. This technique is commonly used and virtually without debate, unless you need even more detail in your style. For example, since multiple data controls can serve a form, perhaps you want the data control object's name, or the underlying table's name, included in the control's base name.

For unbound controls, determining the approach for base names is not quite so obvious. An unbound control usually displays the result of an expression or a message string value. Because the unbound control holds data, it is analogous to a temporary table field (a "virtual field") in memory. Thus my recommendation would be to apply the same logic stated previously for naming table fields. For example, if your naming convention would produce a field name of `LastName` rather than `NameLast`, you would use the same rules to produce an unbound control base name `FullName`, as opposed to `NameFull`.

Module Base Names

Module names are quite subjective, and follow the convention that is most convenient for the developer(s) of the application. Your coding standards may already dictate how related procedures will be grouped into modules. In such a case, the module name will or should reflect the procedures it contains. You and fellow developers should be able to quickly determine the most logical module to look in to find a specific code routine; to accomplish this, your module names will generally be longer and more specific than names of other objects, for example `basAPIRoutines_FromTechNet` and `basAPIRoutines_Library`.

Whether or not to use capitalization and punctuation schemes in your module names will be discussed in the "Capitalization and Punctuation" section later in this chapter. In general, since module names can be lengthy, they are difficult to read without some uppercase letters mixed in for emphasis. The use of prefixes and suffixes to further clarify module names will also be discussed later.

Procedure Base Names

Naming Basic code procedures (functions and subs) is often a whimsical task. Some applications involve hundreds of procedures and thousands of lines of code, yet the average developer gives no more than a second or two of thought to naming a new procedure. Procedure names are often repeated ("called") in many other procedures, so they are annoying to type if they are quite long. On the flip side, procedure names usually cannot be descriptive in a mere ten or fifteen characters. Your naming convention should prescribe techniques to find a balance point between names that are too long and too short. The use of abbreviations can increase brevity in your procedure names.

Some developers create a naming convention of leading or trailing characters to delineate functions from subs. You should consider if this technique is useful for you or not. In practical application, I write very few subs, and those that I do create often become functions later (as subs expand in purpose or scope I often need them to return a value to the calling procedure). Thus, I don't identify the type of a procedure in the name (such as `subLogin`), but it would be a legitimate thing to do if it served some purpose.

It may also be useful for you to formalize the construction of your procedure names. Consider these three function names, which could all describe the same function:

```
UserName()

GetUserName()

UserNameGet()
```

There is nothing inherently wrong with any of these names. However, the function name UserName() is too broad for my liking, because I can't tell by looking if it retrieves or sets a user name. The second option, GetUserName(), is better because the leading action verb tells me more specifically what the function does. However, if I consistently apply the philosophies in this chapter, I should arrive at a preference for the name UserNameGet(). This name begins by describing the object, then the action. Because I prefer my object names to achieve some end result with respect to sorting, this convention causes similar routines to sort by target object (User). UserNameGet() and UserNameSet() would sort together in procedure lists, while the alternate construction GetUserName() and SetUserName() would cause them to sort farther apart, by action. In general, I prefer to place the object name first, then the verb, when naming procedures.

Whether or not to use capitalization and punctuation schemes in your procedure names will be discussed in the "Capitalization and Punctuation" section that follows. In general, most developers tend to use mixed upper and lower case in procedure names for readability. The use of prefixes and suffixes to further clarify procedure names will also be discussed later.

Capitalization and Punctuation

On the surface, it would seem nonsensical to ask the question: "Who doesn't use uppercase and lowercase mixtures in their object names?" The answer, however, may surprise you.

Before version 6, SQL Server's default installation mode made it case sensitive with respect to object names, including table and field names. This fact led VB developers who prototype in Jet, then migrate the database schema to a server later, to prefer lowercase names for tables and fields. Otherwise, when the application was "upsized" to the server, mixed-case object names had to be changed to lower case, and supporting objects and code sometimes had to be modified to reflect the rename. With SQL Server 6.0 however, the default (and preferred) installation mode is case insensitive, making it easier to "upsize" Jet databases to the product without any name changes.

Also, I have met many developers who are religious about economizing keystrokes. Such people often work with lowercase object names, to save their "pinkie" fingers thousands of visits to the Shift key on the keyboard each day. Conversely, developers exist who cut their teeth in the years before personal computers and can remember terminals that had no lowercase letters. They work mostly in uppercase out of habit.

With these points considered, it is true that the majority of developers work with mixed-case when naming objects. Each independent part of an object's name is treated as a proper name, with the initial letter capitalized. Thus customer personal information goes into a form named `CustomerPersonalInformation` or perhaps `frmCustInfoPers`.

There are two caveats to consider with this simple capitalization rule:

- Other elements of your naming conventions do not automatically use mixed-case simply because your base names do.

- Some people can't read object names clearly with only mixed-case; punctuation is required.

Simply because your base names use upper and lower case does not automatically mean that your naming conventions should be mixed-case, as in the tag `frm` in the previous paragraph. Some naming convention elements (leading items) are actually more effective in lower case. See the section "Applying Naming Conventions to Your Work" later in this chapter for a discussion of this point.

Also, mixing case may not automatically make object names readable. Some developers prefer to use additional punctuation to further improve readability. The first and most obvious option is to add spaces to names, which VB does not allow but Jet allows for database objects. Thus some developers drift into the habit of using spaces to punctuate table and query names. Evaluate carefully whether or not this is a good option for your application and/or your overall style. Adding spaces to object names means that you will have to bracket the names (for example, `[Customer Info]`) when working with the objects in VB code. It also removes the ability to easily upsize the application to a server platform, since virtually none of them support embedded spaces in object names. Finally, spaces in names will make it more difficult for you to create tools or Data Access Object routines that involve any string parsing (separating component items), since you will have to look for both brackets and multiple spaces in object names when grabbing them from inside a string or string variable.

In addition to spaces, I am basically sour on any kind of punctuation in database object names except for underscores. This ensures that I can move data from a Jet database to other platforms without a rename. For example, SQL Server allows only letters, digits, $, #, and underscores in names. Visual FoxPro is even more restrictive, allowing only letters, digits, and underscores. I also frown on using characters in one context that have a different meaning in another context, I would rather be more consistent even if Jet doesn't require me to be. For example, the apostrophe is a comment marker in VB code, and if I see apostrophes in an object name, I think that the part of the name after the apostrophe is a comment! You will have to decide just how restrictive to make your naming conventions in this respect.

When punctuating names by using underscores, consider if they should be allowed anyplace, or only in certain contexts. While a form named `frm_Customer_Info_Edit` is certainly readable, I don't want to spend my life adding that many underscores to all object names as I type. However, in the discussion of qualifiers and suffixes later in this chapter, you will see that underscores may be of great value in specific contexts.

Abbreviating Object Names

You discovered earlier that using standardized abbreviations can be useful to shorten object names without a loss of meaning. Typically, when the design phase of an application is completed and table and field names are being finalized, you should look for opportunities to apply your standard abbreviations or to create new ones needed for the project. The tables in the "Standardized Terminology" section in the preceding chapter show a list of some of the standardized abbreviations my company has created and used consistently over the years.

Abbreviations that we use ourselves tend to fall in the three to five character range, although some variances occur for clarity. Few words require more than five characters to convey the original word with no loss of readability or meaning. Also note how many characters can be eliminated in an object name when abbreviations are used—in the case of "admin" as a short form of "administration," nine characters are saved.

When creating standard abbreviations, some developers establish restrictive rules for abbreviating. For example, I've seen conventions using a rule like this: "Remove all vowels past the first character until five characters remain. If the abbreviation is less than five characters, add back vowels from left to right until a five character length is achieved." Table 17.2 shows a few of our standard abbreviations, and the revised abbreviation using the stricter rule I just stated.

Table 17.2 Leszynski Company Abbreviations Contrasted with Five-Character Consonant-Centric Abbreviations		
Term	**Our Abbrev.**	**Revised Abbrev.**
accounting	Actg	Accnt
administration	Admin	Admns
approved	Apvd	Apprv
authorized	Auth	Athrz
beginning	Beg	Bgnnn
building	Bldg	Bldng
record	Rec	Recrd

Witness the dramatic difference in abbreviations using the harsh rule. The revised abbreviations are, in my opinion, less obvious than our original versions in four of the six cases. Abbreviating "beginning" as "bgnnn" is particularly silly. As opposed to a firm abbreviation rule, our approach to abbreviating is more pragmatic: "Using as few characters as possible, convey the full term using characters from the term or an acceptable shorthand." (The "acceptable shorthand" clause lets us use commonly accepted contractions like "xsfr" for "transfer.")

This example serves to drive home an important point about abbreviations, and by inference about naming conventions in general: Your rules for naming objects should be flexible enough to serve the ultimate objectives, not restrictive for their own sake.

Sorting Object Names

At this point in the chapter, you've wallowed through the philosophy of object base names, how to shorten them, and how to standardize abbreviations. With a strategy for shorter and meaningful base names in place, the remaining piece of the puzzle is a sequence for ordering the components of base names.

In the field name discussion earlier, I noted the improvement in readability of the field name `LastName` over `NameLast`. I also showed the example of shortening the table name `WidgetProductionStatisticsFirstQuarter1994` to `WidgetStats94Q1`. Why did I select this particular order for segments of the name? I did it with sorting in mind.

By default, the Object Browser, and various combo box lists in VB, sort object names alphabetically. When I name related objects (those with similarities in the base name), I want them to sort close together so that they appear consecutively in ordered lists. So, the first rule I apply is to start with the most important part of the name at the left. If every object dealing with widgets begins with `Widget`, the objects will sort together. Next would come the second most important part of the name, then the third, and so forth.

Notice also that I changed the trailing `FirstQuarter1994` portion of the example table name to `94Q1`, a convention that ensures that similar object names will sort by year, then quarter, producing a list like this:

```
WidgetStats94Q3

WidgetStats94Q4

WidgetStats95Q1

WidgetStats95Q2
```

Figure 17.6 shows a well-ordered class module, where consideration has been given to making the procedure names sort in a logical sequence.

Fig. 17.6

These procedure names sort in a logical sequence.

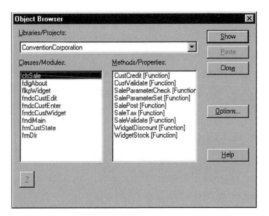

Developing Naming Convention Tags

With conventions firmly in hand for object base names, you can proceed to creating the wrappers around the base name that provide extra information and capabilities. The most important, in my view, are "tags."

Fig. 17.7
The form controls in this list are easily identified by their three-character tags.

Several years ago, a Microsoft programmer named Charles Simonyi wrote a paper titled "Program Identifier Naming Conventions," which some point to as the beginning of formalized C language naming conventions. Actually, Simonyi's article was narrowly defined to (non object-oriented) C programming, and concentrated on philosophical as well as pragmatic issues. Nevertheless, it was one of the first times in print that the issue of variable names was analyzed broadly. The paper also popularized the terms *tag* (a short prefix) and *qualifier* (a scope limiter placed after the tag), which are still in common use today. (Although, before the terms existed, programmers were still using the concept. For example, we used one-character variable tags in our dBASE and R:BASE work as far back as 1984.)

For our purposes here, I'll use *tag* to mean "a set of characters placed against an object base name to characterize it." In object-oriented programming terms, the tag is somewhat analogous to an identifier for the *class*. The biggest challenges for you as you define your naming style are to define: whether or not to use tags, where they should be placed, the size for the tags in number of characters, and the specific tags themselves. (I discuss *qualifiers* in the "Using Qualifiers and Suffixes" section later in this chapter.)

Tags can be placed before (as in `qryCust` or `qdelCustClosed`, see figure 17.8) or after (as in `CustQry` or `CustClosed_QDel`, see figure 17.9) an object's base name. As examples throughout this chapter betray, I have standardized on tag placement before the object name. To be fair, however, I will discuss both placements in the next section. Placing tags in front of object names is sometimes called "Hungarian Notation," a reference to Charles Simonyi's nationality.

Fig. 17.8
These Jet queries have leading tags and sort by type.

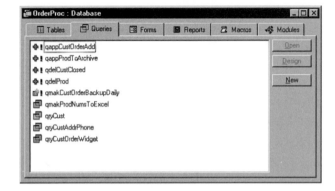

Fig. 17.9
These Jet queries have trailing tags and sort by base name.

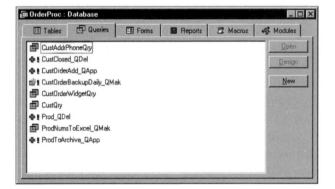

Why Use Tags on Names?

Why use tags at all? In an environment like VB, where terms like *Object*, *Class*, and *Property* are becoming more and more important, a base name by itself does not convey enough information for many developers. It can be very convenient to encapsulate within an object's name information about the type of the object (i.e., its class and/or primary characteristics).

For example, reading through VB code that executes a saved query in a Jet database, you would have to look at the database with Access to determine the type of the query if only its base name were used. However, a query name with a type tag on its base name, such as `qdel` for a delete query, is instantly recognizable as to its type, purpose, or features. This can provide programming benefits like enhanced program readability and less coding errors.

In addition to these advantages for Basic programmers, here are a few other benefits of tags:

- General leading tags on objects cause them to sort by the type (the tag) first, and the name second, grouping items by their class/properties.

- Highly detailed leading tags on objects cause them to sort by subtype within their type group (for example, all `fdlg` forms, then all `flkp` forms, and so forth).

- Highly detailed `trailing` tags on objects provide object type information with a minimum of extra characters and no penalty on sort order.

- Tags on form controls remove ambiguity (they differentiate the control name from a reference to its bound field in a recordset).

- Tags on program variables remove any need to review a variable's `Dim` statement to discern its type. They also remove the danger of assignment errors (where a variable's value is affected unintentionally through math with or assignment to a non-identical type).

- Leading tags on Jet tables and queries cause them to sort by object type in lists where these objects are combined (for example, all `qry`-tagged objects sort before all `tbl` objects).

As the examples above imply, you can have tags that are broad (`frm` for form) or detailed (`fdlg` for dialog form). You must weigh the advantage of the detailed versions—they are more informative—against the added cost of creating, learning, using, and maintaining a larger number of tags.

The placement of tags can become a hotly debated issue as you standardize: "Are tags that precede a name better for us than those that follow the name?" As the listings in various figures shown in this chapter point out, leading tags on objects in sorted lists cause them to sort by type before name. However, many programmers prefer to scan an object list and see the base name as the primary sort order. With such individuals around, you might opt for trailing tags. To recap, programmers who are more interested in an object's properties than its name will opt for a leading tag scheme, while coders who are focused on base names will place tags after that element.

If you have decided to use tags and where to place them, you next need to determine which objects should be tagged. Consider each of the following objects as candidates for tags, and note the order:

- Program variables and structures

- Form controls

- Database Queries/Views

- Forms

- Database Tables

- Modules

- Procedures

- Database Fields

I have ordered the preceding list based on my experience reviewing many different conventions and talking with developers; the list is ordered from the most frequently to the least frequently used object naming conventions. In other words, most developers who use tags use them in Basic program code, while very few developers who use tags use them on table fields. Below, I give a short summarization of each item on the list.

Program variable and structure tags are the most widely used tags. As I mentioned earlier, the Microsoft FoxPro documentation even suggests variable type tags for FoxPro users. Most C programmers have used type tags for many years (some influenced by the Charles Simonyi paper I referred to earlier). As C and FoxPro coders become, or work with, VB developers, they influence the acceptance of tags for VB variables and structures (used here to mean arrays, constants, and type definitions). The overwhelming majority of programmers who use tags in Basic coding place them in front of the base name. See figure 17.10 for an example of leading variable tags.

Fig. 17.10
Visual Basic code
with variable
declarations using
type tags.

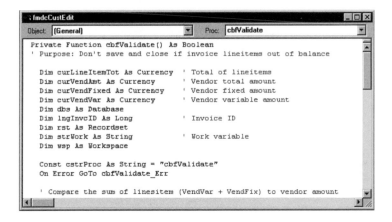

Form control tags help to distinguish the control's name from its data source (if any), eliminating ambiguous references that can occur in Basic code. Leading control tags also sort the events for controls by control type in the code behind forms (see fig. 17.11).

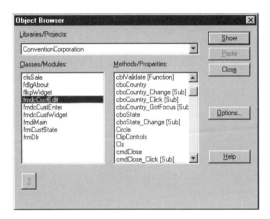

Fig. 17.11
Tags on control names cause their events to sort by the tags first.

Database query/view tags are also commonly used by advanced developers using Jet or SQL Server. Because queries perform actions (delete, update, etc.), their type is vitally important, so tags on query names (see fig. 17.12) usually convey the underlying action. The other reason cited by most developers for query tags is to differentiate them from tables in certain lists and SQL statements (as noted in an early example in this chapter).

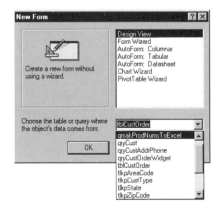

Fig. 17.12
Tags on query names cause them to sort separately from tables in the Access interface.

Form tags help to differentiate the various styles of forms that can be created in VB. Different developers prefer different levels of detail in their form and class module tags, but most that use tags distinguish data bound forms (entry/edit) from navigation forms (switchboard menus and dialogs) (see fig. 17.13).

Fig. 17.13
These form tags provide a high degree of specific information about the type of form.

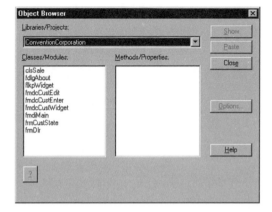

Database table tags are lauded by developers who use them, since different types of tables are often singled out for different treatments. For example, all summary tables (with a `tsum` tag) in an application might be deleted each night by program code and rebuilt from mainframe data. Some developers, however, prefer to keep their table names "pure," and use tags elsewhere in the application but not for tables (see fig. 17.14).

Fig. 17.14
Leading table tags group these tables by the type of data they contain or their role in the database.

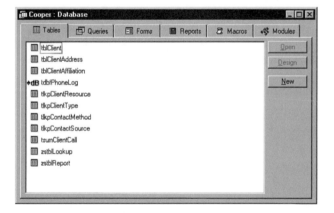

Module tags are one of the least necessary elements of an object naming strategy, since they are never referenced in code. Most developers tend to give modules descriptive names as a matter of practice, and tags may not be necessary in such a scenario. If tags are used to add additional detail, they tend to prescribe the type of procedures found in the module, as in the example in figure 17.15, and help the procedures to sort in the Object Browser.

Fig. 17.15
Module tags should describe the functions grouped in the module.

Procedure tags are not frequently used. Descriptive function and sub names usually do not need clarification. One exception is my use of the tag cbf to group procedures in code behind forms distinctly from event procedures (see figure 1.16.). A few developers will prefix function names to designate a procedure's scope or return value; although this practice is not common, you should at least consider whether it has value in your situation.

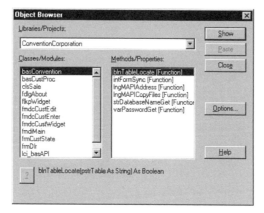

Fig. 17.16
Procedure tags can classify a procedure's type.

Database field tags are also infrequently implemented. Tagging a field name with the field's data type is favored by some developers, but this strategy has a dangerous inherent risk and I dislike it. If the data type of a field changes, for example from Integer to Long Integer as the users' needs expand, the field name must be changed throughout the application when the data type (and tag) changes. This includes changing all related queries, forms, reports, macros, and code—very difficult process. An alternate scheme to field data type tags used by some developers is to create a unique tag for each table in the database, for example `cu_` for `tblCustomer`, and attach the tag to each field in that table. This strategy makes tables and their queries more self documenting, and those who use it believe strongly in it. I do not use the table name tag approach, however, since I tend to design databases more around the concept of an integrated data dictionary. This concept states that a field name must represent the same data type and data content in all tables that contain it, thus counteracting the use of field tags that represent table names. (While Jet does not strictly enforce a data dictionary, you can apply the concept yourself through good schema design techniques.)

Choosing Tag Length and Placement

Some developers use tags that are as short as a single character. While this certainly economizes on keystrokes, such tags are not very intuitive except in limited cases. For example, there are 11 standard variable types in VB4 (not including the Data Access Objects, user-defined types, and specific object types), few enough that you could conceivably create a single-character tag for each.

I feel that one-character tags are too obscure and limiting (the limit is the 26 letters of the alphabet, which doesn't allow enough room for growth). For an example of single character tags, see the Microsoft Visual FoxPro documentation, which shows suggested single-character variable tags for FoxPro developers (see Table 17.3). In the FoxPro convention, the tag c is used for Character variables, and the letter y denotes Currency types. Conceivably, you could create a VB naming convention to dovetail with this FoxPro model. However, most users would not find this notation intuitive at first glance (does y clearly indicate Currency to you?).

Table 17.3 Single-Character Variable Tags Recommended by Microsoft in the Visual FoxPro Documentation	
Variable Type	**Tag**
Array	a
Character	c
Currency	y
Time	t
Date	d
Double	b
Float	f
General	g
Logical	l
Numeric	n
Object	o
Unknown	u
Window	w

Many developers find that single-character, and even double-character, pre-fixes are not intuitive enough to serve as tags, and that three and four char-acter tags are more useful. This tag length is the most prevalent across the majority of published Windows Basic development styles, although users of this style admit that it introduces quite a few extra keystrokes into develop-ment efforts. If you're not averse to even more keystrokes, your style could conceivably use more than four characters for tags.

Be aware that you cannot use reserved words as object names, so cases where a tag is also a reserved word may cause problems. Only the second syntax below is legal as a naming convention in VB:

```
Dim int As Integer
Dim intWork As Integer
```

Table 17.4 shows several different tags for selected VB and Jet objects, culled from various naming convention documents that have been sent to me by developers over the previous two years. Note that none of the tags exceed five characters in length.

Table 17.4 Selected Tags From Various VB/Jet Naming Conventions	
Object Type	**Tag**
QueryDef Variable	q
QueryDef Variable	q_
QueryDef Variable	qd
QueryDef Variable	qdf
QueryDef Variable	qdf_
QueryDef Variable	qry
String Variable	s
String Variable	s_
String Variable	str
String Variable	str_
String Variable	sz
TextBox Control	otxt_
TextBox Control	t_
TextBox Control	tbx
TextBox Control	txt
TextBox Control	txt_

As was noted in the preceding section, tags can be placed before (as in qryStateCapitol) or after (as in StateCapitol_qry) the base name. The majority of developers place them at the front, but there are some naming conventions where tags trail the name. Both the primary benefit and the primary liability of leading tags are the same: the sort order of objects is affected. In my experience, the best approach to decide on a placement strategy for yourself is to create two small, similar applications. Use the leading tag convention in one, and the trailing tag convention in the other. Have a meeting of your development team and compare the pluses and minuses of the two approaches after actually using them in a hands-on experiment; this produces the best input for making your decision.

Creating Object Tags

At this point you may have debated and decided on a tagging strategy that includes length and placement. With such guidelines in place, the tags themselves need to be created. Below are four rules of thumb that I suggest you apply to the process.

■ **Abbreviations Must Be Intuitive.** In the previous section "Abbreviating Object Names," I proposed guidelines for creating abbreviations. The discussion is appropriate to creating tags as well. The general rule propounded in that section was: "Your rules for naming objects should be flexible enough to serve the ultimate objectives, not restrictive for their own sake." I'll restate the rule here with tags in mind: "To create tags, begin with the full word that the tag will abbreviate, or a generally accepted shorthand of the word. Remove non-essential characters until the target length is reached and the remaining tag is the clearest representation of the original word."

For example, if you had targeted three characters as a tag length, removing the vowels from *table* to produce `tbl` is the obvious choice for creating a tag, since `tbl` is probably more recognizable to a majority of users as *table* than `tab` or `tbe` or `tle` would be. The example gets more complex, however, with the word *check box*. Removing characters to produce a viable three-character tag would produce both `chk` and `cbx` as logical and usable choices. Thus you need more rules to break the tie.

■ **Follow the Crowd When It Suits You.** Unless you have a legitimate need to be unique, your conventions should probably lean toward one or more of the existing popular conventions. That way, the other convention(s) can be your guide through the gray areas if you so desire. In the check box example just mentioned, the tag `chk` would be a preferable choice over `cbx` if you factored in that Microsoft has used `chk` as a sample tag in their Visual Basic manuals for several years.

■ **Remember What Problem You Are Solving.** We explored previously how naming conventions should always fit the objectives you designate for them. For example, if object sort order is a primary objective for your tags, you would favor tag characters that fed this objective over all others. Assume that you have created unique tags for each type of query (`qapp` for Append, `qdel` for Delete, and so forth). In this model,

Select queries using `qsel` or `qry` tags would sort below most other types of queries. If your stated objective for query tags is to have most primary (Select) queries at the top of each query list, your tag for select queries would need to sort above `qapp`, which is alphabetically the first query tag. Therefore, you would need a Select query tag of `q_ry` or `qaaa` or a similar device to suit this purpose. As a second example, if your objective for form object tags was specifically to group forms by *base name* in the Object Browser and other sorted lists, a trailing tag scheme would be required. You could use `_f` after form names and `_c` after class modules to achieve your stated objective—you would have no need of longer, more descriptive tags.

- **Define the Big Picture.** Your naming convention may need to dovetail into other conventions in your organization. For example, if you are creating an Access naming convention in a company where a Visual Basic naming convention already exists, objects in Access that are common to both products (check boxes, for example) would inherit the existing Visual Basic tags. (I can think of nothing more chaotic in a development team than multiple, different conventions.) Also, your naming convention may need to allow for a growth path into conventions for other platforms. See the section "Considering Other Platforms" further on for a more detailed discussion of this objective.

If you've gotten the impression that there is no single, simple rule for creating tags, you're right. The process is unique to your needs and experience as an individual developer or development team.

Using Prefixes to Clarify Tags

By definition, a tag describes the type of the object. However, some objects can have attributes (essentially properties) other than their type that give them additional capabilities. For example, a VB variable can have a scope, `Public` or `Private`, in addition to its data type. Further, it may be helpful to you to denote static variables with a prefix in front of the tag, like this:

```
Static sintSubtotal As Integer
```

In your naming convention, you should consider whether or not it is important to add such identifiers to your tags to describe scope and similar attributes. I call an identifier that precedes a tag a *Prefix*, which you could essentially define as "a clarification tag placed on an object tag."

How you use and define prefixes depends on your needs. There are several places in VB and Jet where extra qualification of a tag can be useful, and prefixes are obviously helpful in such cases. Table 17.5 lists examples. There may be other areas where your own needs and development style lead you to create specific prefixes for specific needs.

Table 17.5 Areas in VB/Jet Where Tag Prefixes Are Useful	
Object Type	**Prefix Use**
Forms	To denote form characteristics like bound/unbound, MDI parent/child, and class module.
Tables	To denote specific table characteristics such as system tables, archive copies, work in progress, etc.
Queries	Same as for tables.
Modules	To designate specific attributes of the module. For example, you could create specific prefixes to denote modules containing only API calls, constant declarations, company library routines, and so forth.
Controls	To designate more specific information about generic controls. For example, an OLE Container Control can hold various kinds of OLE objects. You could create prefixes to differentiate PaintBrush picture object frames (`pole`) from Excel worksheet object frames (`xole`).
Procedures	To designate procedure scope (`Public` vs. `Private` vs. `Static`). Also, when creating public library routines, some developers use a unique prefix (in our case, `lci_` for Leszynski Company Inc.) to clearly designate such routines.
Variables	To designate variable scope (`Public` vs. `Private` vs. `Static`), or the type of variable passed as a parameter (`ByRef` vs. `ByVal`).

Because a prefix often equates to an object property, any object that can have multiple properties can legitimately have multiple prefixes. Thus your conventions will need to prescribe ordering rules for using multiple prefixes. For example, your program code requires a global (a `g` prefix) string array (an `a` prefix) of parts. The two options for prefix order are `gastrPart` or `agstrPart`. However, creating an integer variable used to index this array is a bit more problematic, since it would require three prefixes: `g` for global, `a` for array, and `i` for index. Thus there are six combinations of prefix orders that you could create from these prefixes, including `gaiintPart`, `giaintPart`, and `aigintPart`.

Your convention should detail how to decide which prefix order is appropriate when such compounding occurs.

Using Qualifiers and Suffixes

A qualifier is a naming extension that provides context to the specific use of an object. Unlike prefixes, which detail properties of the object (for example, that the variable has public scope), qualifiers describe how the object is being used in context. For example, assume you need three Basic variables to track movement through an array: the first item, the current item, and the last item. You could consider using the qualifiers First, Cur, and Last at the end of the object names to make the names unique and their purpose obvious, while retaining the same base name:

    iaintPartCur

    iaintPartFirst

    iaintPartLast

Placing the qualifier after the base name like this allows the object base names (Part) to sort together (for example, in the Watch pane). An alternate construction would place the qualifiers after the tags and before the base name, to drive the sort order differently:

    iaintCurPart

    iaintFirstPart

    iaintLastPart

If qualifiers in your style always came at the end of the object name, they would actually be a type of *suffix*. However, the term *qualifier* is superior to *suffix* since it is location-neutral. Further, you may want your naming convention to include both qualifiers *and* suffixes. This construction can get slightly complicated for its users, but the qualifier would still describe the use, and the suffix would designate still other information about the object.

For example, your application creates separate queries on a per-state basis so that state sales managers can review their employees' performance daily. While this operation could be done with parameter queries, your company has specific reasons to make a different saved query for each state. Your naming convention could dictate that state abbreviations are legitimate suffixes, so that your queries could look like the list below. Note that the names in the list also include the qualifiers Best and Worst:

```
qsumSalesmanPerfBest_AK

qsumSalesmanPerfBest_AL

...

qsumSalesmanPerfBest_WY

qsumSalesmanPerfWorst_AK

qsumSalesmanPerfWorst_AL

...

qsumSalesmanPerfWorst_WY
```

In the example above, I use underscores to offset the suffix from the qualifier. The reason is that I want the qualifiers `Best` and `Worst` to be separated from the suffixes and easily recognized when the names are read, since the difference between the meaning of these two qualifiers is substantial. Some developers also prefer to use underscores before all *qualifiers* and all suffixes, to pull them further from the base name. You should consider whether or not this is a good strategy for your style.

Considering Other Platforms

Your naming convention may legitimately be able to exist in a vacuum. If you are an independent developer and expect to be working only in VB for many years, you could create a development style that was VB-centric. However, most developers use a variety of tools (for example, with the inclusion of Jet in VB, most VB developers use Access to some degree), which introduces both a problem and an opportunity.

The problem is that developing multiple styles can be time-consuming, learning the styles and keeping them separated at development time can be challenging, and styles with overlapping elements can breed confusion. For example, what if the same tags in two different platforms have two different meanings, for a perfectly good reason?

The opportunity presented is for you to create a style that transcends products and dictates how you deal with common objects wherever they may reside. This task becomes easier with each release of Microsoft Office, as the suite of products begins to have more features and objects in common.

For example, in addition to Visual Basic, you can create `CheckBox` controls in Access, Excel, PowerPoint, Visual FoxPro, and Word. As you created naming conventions for each of these tools, you would be best served by standardizing your tag for CheckBox across all these products. Your developers would only have to remember one CheckBox tag for all of their Office and VBA applications.

On the other hand, Access, Excel, Visual Basic, and Visual FoxPro all have a Label control type, while PowerPoint calls the same control the StaticText control, and Word calls it the Text control. When you create a naming convention that must cover several of these products, and account for the disparate control names these products give to the same object, you have a significant problem to solve. Four solutions are available to you:

1. **The Product Majority Rules.** You can decide to use one convention for all products you consider relevant, such as Microsoft Office, Microsoft Project, Visual Basic, and Visual FoxPro. The single convention will be the one that is most appropriate for the majority of the products.

2. **Your Majority Rules.** If you use only a subset of the tools listed in item 1, select a convention that is most appropriate for the products that you actually use on a regular basis.

3. **Different Products, Different Standards.** You could also make a compelling case for using the exact terminology of each product in its conventions. Thus different names across products for the same object would result in different tags.

4. **Predict the Future.** If you can make an educated or informed guess as to the direction of the majority of tools you must use, build the convention for the future, not now. For example, if you thought most controls in the products listed a few paragraphs back would eventually use the same control types as Visual Basic now does, you would let your VB conventions dictate the conventions for other products.

The best argument in favor of cross platform conventions is the ability to move your code from host to host, and to create common code libraries. Since VBA is standardized across most of the Office suite, some VBA code is now quite portable across the products. For example, though Word does not yet include Visual Basic for Applications, you may want to apply your VBA naming conventions to your work in Word Basic now, so that when VBA comes, your Word code will look and feel like your other VBA code already and need only minor upgrades. As another example, if your company does work in both Visual FoxPro and Access 95, having a fairly common set of naming conventions across these platforms will make it easier to move an application from one of the platforms to the other.

Applying Naming Conventions to Your Work

In this chapter, I have identified five possible components that you may use in your naming conventions:

Prefixes

Tags

Base names

Qualifiers

Suffixes

These components are most commonly arranged in some derivative of the following form:

[prefix(es)] tag [BaseName] [Qualifier] [Suffix]

The brackets indicate optional syntax elements, and the spaces between components are added for readability and are not part of the actual usage. Notice in the syntax diagram that the tag is required even though the base name is not. Once you adopt a naming convention that uses tags, you cannot mix and match such usage. Either every object has a tag, or none do—you should not break this model. Therefore, the tag becomes more critical than the base name, and in a case where the tag is unambivalent, it can be used by itself. For example, in the code snippet below, there is only one database object and one recordset in the procedure. While a base name on each variable, especially `Cust` on the `Recordset` variable, would make the code more clear, the tag is obviously even more useful:

```
Dim dbs As Database
Dim rst As Recordset
...
Set rst = dbs.OpenRecordset("tblCust", dbOpenDynaset)
rst.MoveFirst
```

Table 17.6 provides a syntax chart of the various combinations of these components. The chart will help you understand that some combinations of components can be nonsensical, like putting a puzzle piece in the wrong place. Of course, the terms used for these components and the component layout described in this chapter are suggestions only, derived from my experience. Your naming convention components may not resemble those in the table in every respect. (The spaces between components are not part of the actual usage.)

Table 17.6   Object Name Component Logical Combinations

Components	Description
BaseName	Without a naming convention, this is all you have.
tag BaseName	The simplest and most common construction.
BaseName Tag	An alternate approach, to sort by base name.
prefix BaseName	This construction would only be useful if you were not ever using any tags.
prefix tag BaseName	Provides more detail on the object.
BaseName Prefix Tag	An alternate approach, to sort by base name.
prefix tag BaseName Qualifier	Provides the most detail on the object.
prefix tag qualifier BaseName	A variation on the qualifier location.
BaseName Prefix Tag Qualifier	An alternate approach, to sort by base name.

To each of the items in the table, a suffix could also be added, subject to the discussion in the "Using Qualifiers and Suffixes" section earlier in this chapter.

Notice also in the table the careful use of uppercase and lowercase as applied to the components. I use lowercase tags, prefixes, and qualifiers when they begin the object name, but mix the case on them, as well as qualifiers and suffixes, when they trail the base name. When prefixes and tags begin the object name, I want to read past them quickly to get to the first (uppercase) character of the base name. For example, I find the name `fmdcCust` easier to read than either `FMdcCust` or `FMDCCust`. When any naming conventions, whether prefixes, tags, qualifiers, or suffixes, trail the base name, they may be more readable when mixed-case is used. For example, `intCustFirst` is a more friendly variable name than `intCustfirst`.

If you adopt or create a set of naming conventions, should you apply it retroactively to any existing applications? The answer depends on these two questions:

> **What is the longevity of the system?** If an application has a potential lifespan of one or two years, retrofitting a naming convention into it is not very cost-effective. Since the benefits of naming conventions accrue more to developers than users, a system that has already

been deployed to users should not normally be modified retroactively to include developer features.

Can you afford it? A naming convention retrofit can take a hundred hours of work or more in a substantial application, so there must be development time and money available to cover the effort. If you decide to retrofit, the most cost-effective approach is to include the renaming of objects and rewriting of code as part of a major application upgrade, since there will already be resources budgeted into the upgrade cycle to re-test the application. Since name changes are very pervasive in an application, strong testing after the rename process is crucial.

Summary

This chapter included many thought-provoking questions for you and your development team. If you intend to standardize naming conventions as a result of this discussion, you may want to answer the questions and prototype a naming convention style now. Alternatively, you can review Chapter 16, "The Leszynski Naming Conventions for Microsoft Visual Basic," which describes in detail the answers my company came up with to the questions posed in this chapter. Chapter 16 is the current update of the most widely published naming convention style for Windows Basic.

Chapter 18

Using Remote Data Objects

by Jeffrey Smith

Jeffrey Smith is a consultant with Clarity Consulting, Inc. Jeff holds a degree in biomedical engineering from Northwestern University. He has written articles for several technical journals, including Visual Basic Programmer's Journal. *Jeff can be reached via the Internet at jdsmith@claritycnslt.com and via fax at (312) 266-1006.*

Many applications deployed today require some sort of interaction with a database. A database might be used to store day-to-day sales information for a company, to provide month-end rolled-up data for reporting purposes, or simply to provide a list of users who are permitted to use an application. In all of these scenarios, in order to use the data stored within the database, we must first connect to it.

Once we have connected to the server, we need a service that will allow us to manipulate this data as well as exploit the database's powerful processing features. Choosing a service that provides these features may determine the success or failure of your application as its user base begins to grow. The choice of a service should be a careful one.

In this chapter, we will do the following:

- Look at the criteria that should be used when selecting a method for accessing the remote data services

- Review some of the common ways available to Visual Basic applications to gain access to the data services

- Look at the underlying architecture and the details of connecting to RDBMSs, using the most robust of the access methods, Visual Basic's Remote Data Objects

Data Access Methods

The three-tier application architecture relies on the ability of the business services to connect to and manipulate data provided by the data services tier. Since version 3 of Visual Basic, one of its most distinguishing features has been its ability to provide a number of options for establishing this connection and accessing the underlying data.

Taking the time to select the appropriate data access method for the application will pay off in the long run. Don't make the common mistake of choosing a data access method without thinking about the long-term position of the application being developed. The following section outlines criteria that are important to consider when selecting a data access method.

What to Look For

When selecting your data access method, be sure to take into account the full life cycle of the application. All too often, applications that start out with a user base consisting of five people will balloon into an application that supports 50-100 users. If the method used to access the data in the initial version does not support this increase in volume, or is not easily modified to do so, the application will have to be rewritten.

When choosing a method to access the enterprise data services, there are four main characteristics that you should be insistent upon. They are as follows:

- Object based access—It is easier for application developers to learn an object hierarchy and its interfaces than it is to learn an API.

- Solid performance—Providing the throughput that is required by the application now and into the future.

- Support for advanced database features—Support for DBMS-specific features such as server-based cursors.

- Database independence—The ability to operate against multiple DBMSs.

As we will see in the next section, only one data access method is available to Visual Basic that provides all of these features in a manner that can be utilized within a three-tier application.

Popular Data Access Methods

Unlike many development tools on the market, Visual Basic's open environment has allowed third-party vendors to develop mechanisms to access data sources from within a VB application. While this provides for a flexible development environment, it also makes choosing an enterprise-wide data access method a more difficult decision.

In this section, we will discuss several common ways that can be used to access data from within a Visual Basic application. For each method, we will also examine the advantages and disadvantages of each.

Jet/DAO

The Microsoft Jet database engine and its Data Access Objects (DAO) is probably the most common method for accessing relational data from Visual Basic. The Jet engine ships with Visual Basic and is also the database engine used in Microsoft Access.

DAO, as the name implies, provides an easy to understand object-based interface for accessing relational data. The application developer retrieves and updates data by setting and reading object properties and executing the data access object methods. The Jet engine also makes use of ODBC, allowing Jet/DAO to provide access to multiple DBMSs ranging from personal productivity database systems, like dBASE and Paradox, to larger enterprise databases, such as Oracle and SQL Server. However, Jet can utilize the Open Database Connectivity (ODBC) API to connect to a data source, but it requires a large amount of information about the data source itself. This information is requested each time a query is submitted, which adds a lot of overhead to each transaction and decreases overall performance.

The downfall of Jet/DAO comes in terms of performance and support for large systems with multiple concurrent users. Because DAO is based on the Jet database engine, regardless of the actual back-end database, the application will still rely on Jet's ability to process the query. As we learned in the previous paragraph, Jet performance is often slow, and therefore, does not make Jet the best choice as an enterprise-wide data access method.

Data Bound Controls

The Visual Basic data bound control is by far the simplest means for accessing data from within a Visual Basic application. The data controls used in Visual Basic 4 have been improved over those used in version 3 through performance increases and additional data bound controls.

Using the data control in conjunction with bound controls reduces the amount of application code that is required to access data. Aspects such as moving from one record to another through the result set and updating records are handled for you by the control. However, these advantages do have their limitations.

Not all of the data manipulation procedures are handled inherently by the data control. For example, there is no support for adding or deleting records using the data control. These two functions must be handled through additional VB code. The data control also makes it difficult to control the manner in which transactions are processed because the record edit and update process is handled automatically. This means that verifying data prior to commitment is difficult.

While data bound controls work well in small applications, application developers often run into problems when the application is suddenly supporting 50 users across the network. One problem that is frequently encountered is an increase in the record contention due to the locking mechanism used by the data control. When 50 users attempt to access common database tables at once, errors occur.

Because the data control relies on Jet to access data, it permits access to multiple back-end data sources through the use of ODBC. But, just as we see with DAO, a performance hit usually occurs. This degradation in performance is a result of the fact that the data control must utilize the Jet engine to access. This requires additional information about the database being accessed, thus adding an additional application layer.

Data bound controls are also designed to work with an end user, requiring that GUI controls be present. In the three-tier environment, all of the data access is handled through the business servers. Business servers often do not possess any GUI elements. This aspect alone eliminates the data control as an option when developing three-tier applications.

VBSQL/DB-LIB

The Programmer's Toolkit for SQL Server, also known as VBSQL, provides Visual Basic application developers with the ability to utilize SQL Server's call-level interface, DB-LIB. DB-LIB is a set of C APIs that handles opening connections, formatting and submitting queries, executing stored procedures, and other operations that can be performed against a Microsoft SQL Server database.

VBSQL offers optimal performance when working with SQL Server databases because it provides the most direct route to the data. Rather than utilizing Jet or some other access layer to get at the data, VBSQL talks directly with the SQL Server API. VBSQL allows you to access SQL Server-specific features, such as BCP, that cannot be accomplished from Jet or bound data controls. VBSQL also provides a custom control that can be used to access data so that the developers don't have to learn the API itself. While this is not as easy as learning an object model, it is certainly easier than learning the API interface.

While VBSQL provides improved performance over Jet, it does not match the flexibility of other options. VBSQL only provides access to database servers that support the DB-LIB API: Microsoft and Sybase SQL Server. This means that VBSQL is an option only in an environment that exclusively utilizes SQL Server databases. If you plan to use a data source other than SQL Server, DB-LIB is no longer an option.

Oracle Objects

As part of its Workgroup/2000 suite of client/server development tools, Oracle has provided Oracle Objects for OLE: an object-based mechanism for accessing data residing in an Oracle database. Oracle Objects exposes a data access object hierarchy that is similar to the DAO objects exposed by the Jet database engine. A developer familiar with DAO should not have a problem coming up to speed using Oracle Objects in a short amount of time.

Oracle Objects provides connectivity across multiple network protocols using its built-in SQL*Net technology. This permits developers to access the advanced features of the Oracle 7 database server. However, it does not provide the ability to access back-end data sources other than Oracle. This means that, similar to DB-LIB, Oracle Objects provides a solid mechanism for accessing data stored in an Oracle database. However, if you plan to utilize a data source other than Oracle in your enterprise-wide applications, you can quickly rule out Oracle Objects.

The ODBC API

Microsoft's ODBC API provides the ability to access multiple DBMS back-ends, exploit the advanced features of each of these independent database back-ends, as well as providing solid data access performance. Microsoft's goal when creating ODBC was to provide a standard mechanism by which applications could operate against multiple back-end databases without requiring front-end coding changes.

Because it's a low-level API, the ODBC API provides a great deal of flexibility. Its support for multiple database back-ends makes it a good solution for applications that require portability. For example, you can create an application that runs against an Access back-end using ODBC. You can then use the identical source code to access a SQL Server or Oracle database back-end. In addition, since ODBC talks directly to the data source, the data access operations are fast.

The greatest disadvantage of directly accessing the ODBC API is the fact that developers must learn a low-level API and often have to create wrapper procedures to limit the number of API calls they make. The ODBC API lacks an object-based interface that developers can use to access enterprise data. At least this has been true prior to Visual Basic 4.

RDO

Visual Basic 4 introduces a new data access method that combines the performance and multiple database support of ODBC with an easy-to-learn object interface similar to that of Jet's Data Access Objects. Visual Basic's Remote Data Objects, or RDO, is an object interface layer similar to the existing DAO objects. The interface "sits" on top of the existing ODBC API architecture. This thin application layer exposes the features of the ODBC API to application developers without requiring an intimate knowledge of ODBC itself. Instead, application developers need only learn an intuitive object interface.

RDO's biggest advantage over DAO is that it does not rely on Jet. Jet makes the database engine part of the application. This affects overall performance as well as limiting the number of back-ends accessible from the application. RDO instead uses the ODBC API to pass the data requests to an ODBC data source. This allows you to connect to any ODBC-compliant data source, as well as the ability to access many of the advanced features of the database you are connecting to, such as server-side cursors and stored procedures. RDO is implemented as a thin wrapper around the ODBC API, ensuring that performance degradation over the ODBC API is a minimum.

RDO provides all of the desired characteristics of an enterprise data access method. Because of this, it is the focus of the remainder of this chapter. We will start by developing a high-level understanding of the underlying ODBC architecture, and then go into the details of accessing an ODBC-complaint database using RDO.

Understanding ODBC

ODBC is one of the key components of Microsoft's WOSA architecture. *WOSA* (Windows Open Services API) is a set of standard application interfaces for accessing all aspects of the enterprise from data services to electronic mail. Since its introduction, ODBC is well on its way to becoming the *de facto* standard for cross-vendor database access mechanisms.

ODBC is the framework upon which many of the data access methods mentioned in the previous section of this chapter are built. In this section, we will discuss the basic architecture that ODBC utilizes as well as the process of defining an ODBC data source.

Architecture Overview

The ODBC architecture is divided into three levels that work together to provide the application with access to information contained in the data source. These layers consist of the following:

- The ODBC driver manager

- The ODBC driver

- The data source itself, as shown in figure 18.1.

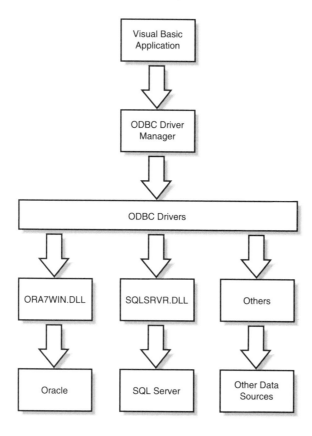

Fig. 18.1
The various layers
of the ODBC
architecture.

When an application requests data or submits a query, the ODBC Driver Manager takes the request and communicates with the specific ODBC driver associated with the data source. The ODBC driver then reformats the request so that it can be handled by the database. The reformatting process will be discussed in more detail later in the chapter. The result of the request—a result set or query completion status—is returned to the ODBC driver, which in turn passes it to the Driver Manager. The Driver Manager takes the results and passes them back to the client application.

Most of the work to submit a request is handled by the ODBC driver. All ODBC drivers provide two basic types of functionality:

- The ability to install, set up, and remove ODBC data sources: the named connections used by applications.

- The ability to manage queries and SQL statements from client applications to database servers, return of result sets and completion status from a database server to a client application, and the return of error messages generated by a data source or ODBC driver to the client application.

ODBC passes all SQL statements and queries to the database using the same method. First, ODBC uses a standard set of functions to translate the ANSI SQL queries submitted to the ODBC Driver Manager into the SQL dialect specific to the RDBMS. This translation from ANSI SQL to DBMS-specific syntax is handled by the ODBC driver. ODBC also provides the ability to pass SQL statements already written to the RDBMS dialect directly without translation through the use of the SQLPassThrough method. This can help to improve database performance at the risk of generating errors.

All ODBC drivers are classified as being a member of one of two categories:

- *Single-tier drivers*—These are developed for DBMSs that do not have the ability to process SQL statements themselves. These drivers translate SQL operations passed by a client application into the low-level instructions necessary to operate directly on the database files themselves. Microsoft Access, FoxPro, and Paradox are examples of single-tier ODBC drivers.

- *Multiple-tier drivers*—These are developed for DBMSs that have a query engine capable of processing SQL statements themselves. These drivers translate the SQL operations passed from client applications into the dialect support by the database server. The instruction set is then passed along to the server for processing. Oracle and Microsoft SQL Server are examples of multiple-tier ODBC drivers.

In addition to falling into one of these two levels of classification, each ODBC driver adheres to one of the three ODBC conformance levels:

- *Core drivers*—These provide the ability to connect to a database, prepare and execute SQL statements, retrieve query result sets, support transaction processing using commit and rollback, and retrieve error messages.

- *Level 1 drivers*—These provide all of the features available in the Core level plus the ability to connect to a data source using driver-specific dialogs, get and set connection options, and the ability to obtain information about ODBC driver and data source capabilities.

- *Level 2 drivers*—These provide all of the features available in Level 1 drivers plus the ability to list and browse current data source connections, retrieve query results in any format, and utilize scrollable cursors.

Most of the ODBC drivers conform to Level 1 specification and many add aspects of Level 2 drivers (such as scrollable cursors).

Setting Up an ODBC Data Source

As mentioned in the previous section, in order for an application to connect to a database using ODBC, the appropriate ODBC driver must be installed on the machine. In addition, a data source must be defined for the database to which you plan to connect. ODBC drivers and data sources can be created manually through the ODBC Manager applet installed in the Windows Control Panel group. Additionally, you can create ODBC data sources programmatically using the data access methods.

The ODBC Manager applet found in the Control Panel provides the ability to install new ODBC drivers as well as create new data sources. When the ODBC Manager is started, the Data Sources dialog box is displayed. From this dialog box, you can add, remove, or modify data sources, as well as add or remove ODBC drivers.

To install or remove an ODBC driver, select the drivers button from the Data Sources dialog box. This will bring up the Driver dialog box, illustrated in figure 18.2, which displays all of the ODBC drivers currently installed on the machine.

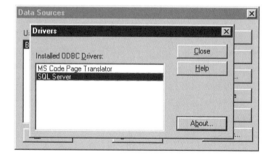

Fig. 18.2
ODBC Drivers
dialog box.

You can then click the Add button and locate the directory where the ODBC driver you wish to add is located. It is worthwhile noting that at the time of publication, the 32-bit version of the ODBC Administrator is incapable of adding new ODBC drivers. Instead, you will need to add the driver using an installation application provided by the vendor.

To create a new ODBC data source, click the Add button in the Data Sources dialog box. This will bring up the Add Data Sources dialog box, which contains a list of the ODBC drivers currently installed. Select the driver that you wish to use for the new data source. For example, if you wanted to create a data source for a SQL Server database, you would select the SQL Server database driver. After selecting the ODBC driver, click the OK button to continue. This displays the ODBC Setup dialog box, which is shown in figure 18.3.

Fig. 18.3
The ODBC Setup
dialog box.

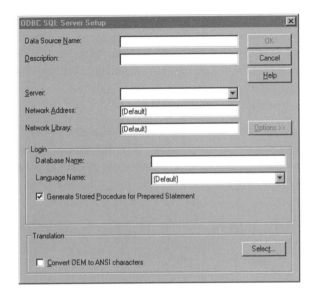

The ODBC Setup dialog is specific to the ODBC driver that is being used. Figure 18.3 shows the SQL Server Setup dialog. In the SQL Server setup dialog, you need to specify a name for the data source and the name of the SQL Server to which you will be connecting. You can use the Options button to display the login and other optional information that can be specified when creating an ODBC data source. Other ODBC Setup dialogs, such as those for Oracle and Access, require similar information. Access, for example, requires you to locate the .MDB file you plan to access.

After completing the information in the Setup dialog box, the data source has been defined. You are now ready to access the database using ODBC or an ODBC-compliant data access method (like RDO).

Understanding Remote Data Objects

In this section we will discuss the remote data object (RDO), which is the new method of data access provided by Visual Basic 4. As we learned earlier in this chapter, RDO is a set of OLE objects that provides the ability for applications to access remote data stored in a variety of databases. RDO is implemented as a thin layer that sits on top of the ODBC API.

To help gain a better understanding of RDO, we will first discuss the functionality that is supported within RDO and the object model it exposes. Once we have an understanding of RDO's high-level features, we will discuss the specifics of the individual objects and how the objects can be used to access data from within a Visual Basic application.

Features of RDO

RDO supports the data access features that are desirable in a robust data access method. These include the following:

- Access to ODBC data sources
- Support for server-specific functionality
- Asynchronous query execution
- Minimal memory requirements
- Utilization of an object model for data access

The following sections of this chapter will discuss each feature in detail.

Access to ODBC Data Sources

Since RDO is implemented as a layer on top of the ODBC API, RDO provides the ability to access any ODBC-compliant data source. This includes server-based RDBMSs like Microsoft SQL Server and Oracle, as well as file-based DBMSs like Microsoft Access and Orlando's Paradox.

When accessing a server-based database, RDO will utilize the server's query engine to increase the performance of remote queries. From a performance perspective, RDO outperforms nearly all ODBC data access methods. Its performance is rivaled only by the ODBC API itself in addition to the database-specific APIs like the DB-LIB API for Microsoft SQL Server.

You should keep in mind that if your application relies heavily upon some vendor-specific implementation of a database feature, your source code may have to be modified slightly when accessing different ODBC data sources. This will be explained in more detail later in this section.

Server-Specific Functionality

Since RDO is built upon ODBC, it also supports server-specific functionality like stored procedures, multiple result sets, and the limiting of result set size. However, as we have noted in the previous section, you should take great care when using vendor-specific implementations of server-specific functions if you plan to allow your client application to communicate with multiple DBMSs.

Many server-specific features, such as stored procedures, are handled the same way by ODBC no matter which DBMS you are accessing. As we will see later in this chapter in the section, "Using Prepared Statements," the methods used to access Oracle stored procedures using RDO are identical to the methods used to access SQL Server stored procedures.

The following sections describe several server-specific features that are supported by RDO.

Stored Procedure Support. RDO provides the applications with the ability to access stored procedures when supported by the RDBMS. The support for stored procedures works for database server stored procedures like those found in Microsoft SQL Server and Oracle, as well as stored queries found in file-based database systems like Microsoft Access.

The functionality that can be placed within the stored procedures is dependent upon the database engine. For example, Microsoft SQL Server supports returning result sets from stored procedures while Oracle only supports the ability to return a single row through the use of output parameters. When developing applications that will support multiple back-end databases, the functionality of all supported engines should be considered. For example, an application that uses SQL Server stored procedures to retrieve result sets will not work against an Oracle database without requiring modifications to the application's code.

Multiple Result Set Support. When supported by the database server and the ODBC driver, RDO allows applications to manage multiple result sets from a single query. This provides an increase in performance because a single query can obtain the information needed to populate multiple lists in a client application.

Govern Result Size. Often it is desirable to limit the number of rows that the client application is allowed to retrieve. RDO provides a query governor that can limit the amount of data returned to the client application. This allows the developer to better manage the resources of the server and workstations.

Server-Side Cursor Support. Many server database engines like SQL Server and Oracle support the ability to create cursors on the server instead of the client workstation. Creating cursors on the server can greatly improve performance because the cursor's key does not have to be sent to and from the client workstation.

RDO provides the ability to specify where the ODBC library will create cursors. A cursor can always be created on the client workstation. This is referred to as an ODBC library cursor. ODBC library cursors usually offer the best performance when working with small result sets. Performance of ODBC library cursors degrades quickly as result size increases. Many DBMSs, such as SQL Server, permit the creation of server-side cursors. Server-side cursors can be created with RDO and generally offer improved performance when dealing with large result sets. Finally, driver-dependent cursors can be created. Driver-side cursors allow the ODBC driver to determine where a cursor will be created. The driver will create server-side cursors when supported by the ODBC data source and ODBC library cursors when they are not.

Asynchronous Query Support

When executing a query that takes an extended period of time to complete, an application should have the ability to perform other functions as well as allow the user to cancel the query. RDO provides the asynchronous query option that permits applications to do just that.

When a query is executed, using the asynchronous option, RDO returns control back to the client application while the query is executing. This allows the application to perform other tasks. In addition, you can program your application to allow a user to cancel a query that has not yet completed.

Minimal Memory Requirements

The machine running the client application often has a limited amount of RAM memory. Because of this, RDO was developed to use a smaller amount of RAM and workstation resources than other data access methods that are available. For example, RDO does not require local memory or disk space to implement its lowest-level cursors. By better utilizing your system's resources, RDO can help to improve your overall application performance.

Object Model Data Access

RDO provides access to data within the database through an easy to understand object model. And object model interface is desirous because it is much simpler to learn than an API interface. The specifics of the RDO object model will be discussed in the next section.

RDO Object Model

As the name implies, RDO provides a series of objects that allow applications to access data stored in relational databases. Every object exposes an interface, which consists of properties, methods, and events, that can be manipulated from Visual Basic applications. Before you can develop applications using RDO, you must have an understanding of the objects that exist. Figure 18.4 shows the RDO object hierarchy.

Fig. 18.4
The RDO Object
Model.

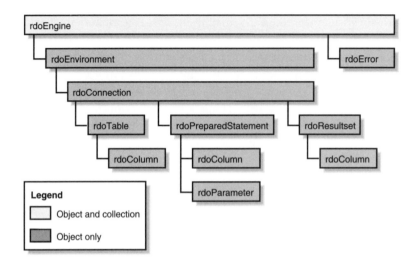

The RDO object hierarchy is the framework applications used to manipulate aspects of a remote ODBC database. The relationships between the objects represent the logical structure of the database, making it easier for developers new to the interface to understand it. For example, the rdoTable object is analogous to a table in a database. Within the rdoTable object exists the rdoColumn object, which is analogous to a column within a database table. The object hierarchy used by RDO is also similar to the DAO object hierarchy exposed by Jet. This makes it easier for application developers who have used DAO in the past to more easily make the transition to RDO.

The RDO framework consists of two series of objects: those that manage the connections to the remote data sources, and those that allow the application to interact with and manipulate the data provided by the data sources.

An application uses the rdoEngine and rdoEnvironment objects to set up the properties of the rdoConnection object. The rdoConnection object represents a physical link to a database. The rdoConnection object allows an application to create rdoResultset and rdoPreparedStatement objects, which return and manipulate the data.

The next sections of this chapter will describe in detail the objects that are exposed by RDO and detail how each of these objects is used when developing an application that will access a relational database.

Connecting Through RDO

Now that we have an understanding for the functionality provided by RDO, and the architecture that it is built upon, we will look at the specific objects within the RDO object hierarchy used to establish a connection to a remote data source. To use RDO with Visual Basic, a reference must first be established by using the <u>T</u>ools <u>R</u>eferences dialog box.

After specifying the reference, you can use the `rdoEngine`, `rdoEnvironment`, and `rdoConnection` objects to connect to an ODBC-compliant database. The use of these objects is detailed in the next few sections.

The `rdoEngine` Object

The highest object in the RDO hierarchy, the `rdoEngine` object, represents a remote data source. The `rdoEngine` object is created automatically the first time that a reference is made to RDO. Since `rdoEngine` is a pre-defined object created automatically when RDO is referenced, an application is not allowed to create an additional instance of the object.

Because `rdoEngine` is the top-level object in the RDO hierarchy, all other objects and collections within the RDO hierarchy are exposed by it. This does not, however, mean that all RDO objects must be specified in application code using the `rdoEngine` object. For example, the following statements will produce the same results.

```
Print rdoEngine.rdoVersion
Print rdoVersion
```

Instead, it means that you must first use the `rdoEngine` object when creating a connection to a database.

The `rdoEngine` object is used to set the data source parameters, as well as the parameters used to define the default `rdoEnvironment` settings. Table 18.1 lists the properties that are exposed by the `rdoEngine` object and a description of what they represent.

Table 18.1   The Properties of the `rdoEngine` Object

Property	Description
rdoDefaultCursorDriver	Type of cursor to be created; ODBC, server-side, server-side if supported or else ODBC
rdoDefaultErrorThreshold	Value of the ErrorThreshold property used by rdoPreparedStatement objects

(continues)

Table 18.1 Continued	
Property	**Description**
rdoDefaultLoginTimeout	Number of seconds ODBC driver will wait when attempting to connect to a data source. This property is the default for all connections, but is overridden if a value is specified in the LoginTimeout property of the rdoEnvironment object.
rdoDefaultPassword	Password used when creating a new rdoEnvironment if no password is supplied
rdoDefaultUser	UserId used when creating a new rdoEnvironment if no userid is supplied
rdoVersion	5-character RDO library version number

The rdoDefault properties are used when creating a new rdoEnvironment or rdoConnection object if the corresponding arguments of the methods are not specified.

Table 18.2 lists the methods exposed by the rdoEngine object and a description of their function.

Table 18.2 The Methods Exposed by the rdoEngine Object	
Method	**Description**
rdoCreateEnvironment	Creates a new connection to the remote data source and an rdoEnvironment object
rdoRegisterDataSource	Registers data source connection information into the Windows Registry

When the rdoEngine object is created, the default environment object, rdoEnvironment(0), uses the rdoDefault parameters. When the application needs settings other than those specified in the default properties, it can change the default values of rdoEnvironment(0) or rdoEngine before creating the connection.

Although the rdoEngine object is shared by the applications that use it, the default properties of the rdoEngine are not shared. Each instance of the application has its own default values that do not affect any other applications using RDO.

As mentioned earlier, ODBC data sources can be defined programatically. This is done by using the rdoEngine's rdoRegisterDataSource method. This method only needs to be executed once to create the data source. Once the data source has been created, it will be displayed in the ODBC Administrator. Setup applications can utilize this method to create the ODBC data source that applications will be expecting.

The rdoRegisterDataSource method takes four arguments:

- *dsName* — Name used in the OpenConnection method that refers to the name that will be used to identify the new data source.

- *driver* — Name of the ODBC driver, not the ODBC DLL file.

- *silent* — Boolean value indicating if the ODBC dialog box which prompts for driver-specific information should be displayed.

- *attributes* — String listing the keywords that are added to the ODBC.INI file.

For specific details on registering an ODBC data source, see the documentation that accompanies your ODBC-compliant database driver.

The rdoEnvironment **Object**

The rdoEnvironment object represents a set of database connections for a specific user ID. The rdoEnvironment object has a logical correspondence to an ODBC environment. A single rdoEnvironment object can support multiple database connections. Since ODBC only supports one environment handle per application, actual ODBC connections only occur when an rdoConnection object is opened.

When multiple connections are made, using a single environment, the rdoEnvironment properties like UserName and Password are shared between the connections. As mentioned in the previous paragraph, in order to open a connection using a different UserName, a new rdoEnvironment object must be created and added to the collection.

rdoEnvironment objects are created by using the rdoCreateEnvironment method of the rdoEngine object. For example, the following code could be used to create a new ODBC environment. In this example, the rdoEngine object is not specified because it is assumed when referring to one of its methods or collections. To help track your rdoEnvironment objects within the collection, you can supply a unique name. In our example, we will name the new environment "Test Environment." In addition, you supply the default user ID and password to be used when subsequent connections are created.

```
Dim objEnv as rdoEnvironment
Set objEnv = rdoCreateEnvironment("Test Environment",
➥"MyUser", "MyPassword")
```

Within an application, the `rdoEnvironment` object can manage the transactions being performed. When transactions are managed at the environment level, executing the `CommitTrans` method will commit the pending transactions in all of the open `rdoConnections` associated with that `rdoEnvironment` object. This type of commit, known as a one-phase commit, should not be confused with what is referred to as a two-phase commit operation. A one-phase commit informs all pending transactions to commit, regardless of the success of each individual transaction. A two-phase commit insures that all transactions in the first phase are committed before transactions in the second phase can be committed.

Managing transactions at the environment level links all transactions occurring within the same environment together. Remember that a single `rdoEnvironment` can support multiple connections, including connections to different databases. To process multiple transactions independently of one another, the application must create a separate `rdoEnvironment` object.

ODBC and RDO do not support nested transactions. This means that within an `rdoEnvironment` object, a second `BeginTrans` cannot be issued until the initial transaction is either committed or rolled back. However, SQL statements can be used to implement nested transactions when it is supported by the data source.

Table 18.3 describes all of the properties that are exposed by the `rdoEnvironment` object.

Table 18.3 The Properties of the `rdoEnvironment` Object	
Property	**Description**
Count	Number of rdoEnvironment objects that exist within the collection
CursorDriver	Type of cursors that can be created; ODBC, server-side, dependent upon ODBC driver support
hEnv	ODBC environment handle that can be passed to the ODBC API
LoginTimeout	Number of seconds the ODBC driver manager will wait before timeout occurs when establishing a connection

Property	Description
Name	Name associated with the rdoEnvironment
Password	Write once property containing password used to create the rdoEnvironment
UserName	Write once property containing the username of the rdoEnvironment object user

Table 18.4 lists all of the methods associated with the rdoEnvironment object and a description of their functionality.

Table 18.4 The Methods of the rdoEnvironment Object	
Method	**Description**
BeginTrans	Begins a new transaction
Close	Closes an rdoEnvironment and any open rdoConnections, rolling back, and pending transactions
CommitTrans	Completes current transactions, saving any changes that were made
Item	Returns the specified member of the rdoEnvironments collection
OpenConnection	Opens a connection to an ODBC data source, returning an object representing that database
RollbackTrans	Completes the current transactions, undoing any changes that were made

The OpenConnection method is used to establish the actual connection to the data source. This method has the following four arguments:

- *dsName*—Specifies the name of the registered data source to which an application will connect.

- *prompt*—Specifies whether the user is allowed to supply additional arguments through the ODBC connect dialogs. Specifying rdDriverNoPrompt prevents the user from seeing the ODBC dialogs.

- *readonly*—Specifies if the user expects to update data using this connection.

- *connect*—String that specifies parameters to the ODBC driver manager; these parameters differ between data sources.

The following example, shown in listing 18.1, demonstrates how to use the OpenConnection method to establish a connection to the data services. In this example, the application is using integrated security so there is not a requirement for additional *connect* information. The example also uses a data source named "My Database".

Listing 18.1 18LIST01.TXT — The creation of a connection to an ODBC-compliant data source

```
'set up default environment
rdoEngine.rdoDefaultUser = UserId
rdoEngine.rdoDefaultPassword = Password
'open a connection to the database
Set db = rdoEngine.rdoEnvironments(0).OpenConnection( _
            "My Database", _
            rdDriverNoPrompt, _
            False)
```

When using integrated or mixed security, the userid and password parameters of the connect argument should be left blank, as in the previous example. Under this security model, Windows NT will pass a user's NT logon ID and password to the data source. This eliminates the need for the application to have any knowledge of the current userid and password when connecting to the data sources.

rdoConnection

The rdoConnection object represents a physical link to a data source. An rdoConnection object is created as the result of the rdoEnvironment's OpenConnection method discussed in the previous section.

Table 18.5 describes the properties and methods that are exposed by the rdoConnection object.

Table 18.5 The Properties of the rdoConnection Object

Property	Description
AsyncCheckInterval	Number of milliseconds RDO will wait before checking the completion status of an asynchronous query
Connect	Read-only string containing the ODBC connect string value used with the OpenConnection method
Count	Number of rdoConnection objects currently in the collection

Property	Description
hDbc	The ODBC connection handle corresponding to this rdoConnection object
Name	Data source name used for the connection
QueryTimeout	Number of seconds the ODBC driver manager will wait before causing a timeout error during query execution
RowsAffected	Number of rows affected by the most recent Execute method
StillExecuting	Boolean indicating if the query is still running
Transactions	Boolean indicating if the rdoConnection object supports transactions
Updatable	Boolean indicating if changes can be made to the object
Version	Version of the data source associated with this object

Remember from our discussions about the rdoEngine object that transactions can also be managed at the connection level. In this implementation, the commit or rollback of a transaction affects only the current connection, not all connections within a specified environment. This level of transaction monitoring is accomplished by executing the CommitTrans and BeginTrans methods of the rdoConnection object instead of the rdoEnvironment object. A transaction statement issued at the environment level will still affect transactions specified at all connections.

Table 18.6 lists the methods exposed by the rdoConnection object and a description of their functionality.

Table 18.6 The Methods of the rdoConnection Object

Method	Description
BeginTrans	Begins a new transaction
Cancel	Cancels a query that is running in asynchronous mode
Close	Closes the specific connection
CommitTrans	Ends the current transaction, saving the changes
CreatePreparedStatement	Creates a new rdoPreparedStatement object

(continues)

Table 18.6 Continued	
Method	**Description**
Execute	Runs an action query or SQL statement that does not return any rows
Item	Returns a member of the rdoConnections collection
OpenResultSet	Creates a new rdoResultSet object. Used to execute queries and SQL statements that will return data.
RollbackTrans	Ends the current transaction, undoing any changes

In addition to representing a connection to a remote data source, the rdoConnection object provides the methods and properties used to manipulate underlying data. This includes the CreatePreparedStatement, Execute, and OpenResultSet methods. The rdoConnection objects also expose several dependent objects and collections, such as the rdoTable and rdoTables objects. The remainder of this chapter will discuss how these objects and methods can be used to access and update data.

Accessing Remote Data

Now that we have discussed the steps taken to establish a connection to a remote data source using RDO objects, we can look at the objects beneath the rdoConnection object in the RDO object hierarchy. It is these lower-level objects that allow an application to programatically manipulate data. RDO supports data access through result set objects, as well as the use of stored procedures. In this section we will focus on the rdoResultset objects, using cursors, and executing stored procedures.

The rdoTable Object

An rdoTable object represents the definition of a table or view within a database. Each rdoTable object is a member of the rdoTables collection, which contains information on all the rdoTable objects that exist within the database. The rdoTables and rdoTable objects are dependent objects of the rdoConnection object. This means that they cannot be created directly from a Visual Basic application. You must first create an rdoConnection object to access the underlying rdoTable objects.

For performance reasons, the rdoTables collection is not populated when a connection is made to the database. Instead, the collection must be populated using the .Refresh method of an rdoConnection object. After invoking the method, individual rdoTable objects can be accessed.

The `rdoTable` object provides applications with the ability to examine the definition of a table within the database. Additionally, applications can examine the data stored within these tables. The definition is read-only and cannot be changed through RDO. To modify the definition of a database table, add a new table definition, or to modify data within a table, the application must generate the SQL statements necessary to do so. The application can also create an `rdoResultset` object that can be used to modify the data, as well as an `rdoPreparedStatement` object. Modifying data using an `rdoPreparedStatement` object is discussed later in this chapter in the section "Using Prepared Statements."

The `rdoTable` object exposes the `rdoColumns` collection. This collection contains the definition of each individual column within a specified table. The `rdoColumn` object will be discussed in more detail later in this chapter in the section "The `rdoColumn` Object."

Table 18.7 lists all of the properties that are exposed by the `rdoTable` object.

Table 18.7   The Properties of the `rdoTable` Object. Note That the `rdoTable` Object Is Not Often Used with RDO.

Property	Description
Count	The number of rdoTable objects present in the collection
Name	The database table name associated with the rdoTable object
RowCount	The number of rows that exist within the database table
Type	String that represents the object type; table, view, alias, and so on
Updatable	Boolean indicating if the table can be changed

The `rdoTable` object exposes an `OpenResultset` method that allows the application to create an `rdoResultset` object based on all of the rows within the table. Since this method does not provide any means for filtering the results, it is not the recommended way to create a result set.

Instead, `rdoTable` objects should be used to examine statistics and make-up of database tables only. When you need to modify or examine data, you should utilize the `OpenResultset` method of the `rdoConnection` object, described later in this chapter in the section "Creating an `rdoResultset` Object."

Table 18.8 lists all of the methods exposed by the `rdoTable` object.

Table 18.8 The Methods Exposed by the `rdoTable` Object	
Method	**Description**
Item	Returns a specific member of the rdoTables collection
OpenResultSet	Creates a new rdoResultset object containing all rows from the rdoTable object
Refresh	Retrieves the list of table names from the database and repopulates the rdoTables collection

Creating an `rdoResultset` Object

When a query or SQL statement that returns records from the database is executed, these records are stored in an `rdoResultset` object. The `rdoResultset` represents all of the rows that were returned from the select query or statement. The `rdoResultsets` collection contains all of the open `rdoResultset` objects that are associated with a specific `rdoConnection`. Each `rdoResultset` object is made of rows and columns just like database tables. The rows represent each record that satisfied the selection criteria and the columns correspond to the elements of the select list.

An `rdoResultset` object is created by using one of following methods:

- Invoking the `OpenResultset` method of the `rdoConnection` object

- Invoking the `OpenResultset` method of an `rdoTable` Object

- Invoking the `OpenResultset` method of an `rdoPreparedStatement` object

Remember during our discussion of the `rdoTable` object that creating a result set with the `OpenResultset` method of the `rdoTable` object is not recommended because the table object's result set does not provide a means for filtering. For this reason, the `rdoTable` object's `OpenResultset` method will not be discussed in this section.

Result sets should generally be used to hold records that have been retrieved from the database. Although result sets also permit you to update the data within them, it should be avoided when possible. If you need to update or modify data in your database, it is a good idea to use prepared statements. Discussed later in this chapter in the section, "Using Prepared Statements," prepared statements often provide a performance increase when modifying data.

Using the `rdoConnection` Object

The `OpenResultset` method of the `rdoConnection` object allows you to create a result set utilizing an existing table in the database, a stored procedure in the database, or through dynamic SQL. In each case, the `OpenResultset` method has the following syntax:

```
Set rdoResultset = rdoConnection.OpenResultset(source[, type[,lockType[,
   options]]])
```

Where `rdoResultset` is an object declared as type `rdoResultset` and `rdoConnection` is any existing `rdoConnection` object.

The source argument specifies the source that will be used to create the result set. This is a string containing the name of a table or stored procedure in the database. It can also be a string containing an ANSI-compliant SQL statement.

when creating a new `rdoResultset` object, the type argument of the `OpenResultset` method specifies the type of result set object to be created. Specifically, the type of argument specifies the type of cursor that is created to access the data. The four type options are:

- *Forward-Only*—Rows of the results set can be accessed and updated using a row pointer that can only move toward the end of the result set. A forward-only result set is not a cursor.

- *Static-Type*—A copy of the rows in the result set is used. Static result sets can be updatable when using ODBC or server-side cursors depending upon the ODBC driver and data source support.

- *Keyset-Type*—A dynamic result set that can be used to add, update, or delete rows from the database tables. Specifying keyset type allows unrestricted movement through the result set. The rows that belong to the result set are fixed.

- *Dynamic-Type*—A dynamic result set that can be used to add, update, or delete rows from the database tables. The rows that belong to the result set are not fixed.

Table 18.9 shows the main differences between the features supported by each `rdoResultset` object type. This table compares the ability to move between the rows contained in the cursor, the visibility to cursor data, ability to update the cursor data, and the ability to refresh the cursor selection.

Table 18.9 Feature Differences Between Each Type of rdoResultset				
rdoResultset Type	Updatable	Record Selection	Row Visibility	Movement
Forward-only	Driver Dependent	Fixed	One	Forward
Static	Driver Dependent	Fixed	All	Anywhere
Keyset	Yes	Fixed	All	Anywhere
Dynamic	Yes	Dynamic	All	Anywhere

The locktype argument specifies the type of concurrency control that will be used when the result set is modified. The locktype argument accepts any one of the values shown in table 18.10:

Table 18.10 The Available Locking Mechanisms of an rdoResultset Object	
rdoResultset LockType	Concurrency
rdoConcurLock	Pessimistic
rdoConcurReadOnly	Read-only (Default)
rdoConcurRowVer	Optimistic, based on row-id
rdoConcurValues	Optimistic, based on row values

Last, the rdoResultset object accepts an options argument, which can be used to specify asynchronous retrieval of the result sets data. This option allows an application to continue processing on the foreground while the database continues to retrieve data in the background. Asynchronous retrieval is specified by passing the rdAsyncEnable constant **rdoResultset**.

Navigating and Updating Data within the rdoResultset Object. After creating an rdoResultset object, the data returned to it can be manipulated by using the rdoResultset object's properties and methods. The properties and methods allow you to perform such actions as adding new records to a database, updating existing records, and moving through result sets.

When working with a result set, the current row is positioned at the first row of the rdoResultset object when it is created, assuming that at least one row was returned. If no rows are returned, the *RowCount* property is set to zero, and the *BOF* and *EOF* properties are both set to True. The Move methods, MoveFirst, MoveLast, MoveNext, and MovePrevious of the rdoResutset object can be used to change row positions within the result set.

When a select query returns multiple result sets, they must be processed in a serial manner, meaning that the first result set contained in the rdoResultset object must be processed before the second can be used. The *MoreResults* method will discard the rows associated with the current result set, and activate the next rdoResultset. This method can be repeated until the *MoreResults* method returns false, signaling no more result sets to process.

An rdoResultset is an object representation of a database cursor. In some cases, the ability to update records within the cursor is dependent upon the functionality of the data source or the ODBC driver being used. You can determine if an rdoResultset object is updatable by checking its Updatable property. If the Updatable property is true, the rdoResultset object can be modified using the AddNew, Delete, Edit, and Update methods.

Table 18.11 lists the properties that are exposed by the rdoResultset object.

Table 18.11 The Properties of the rdoResultset Object	
Property	**Description**
AbsolutePosition	Zero-based value indicating the ordinal position within the keyset, dynamic, or static rdoResultSet. Can be used to move to the specific location, or determine the current location within the result set.
BOF	Boolean value indicating if the current row is the first row in the result set
Bookmark	Returns/Sets a bookmark that identifies the current row within the result set. Used to quickly move to a specific row.
Bookmarkable	Boolean value indicating if the rdoResultset object supports bookmarks
Count	Returns the number of rdoResultset objects in the collection
EOF	Boolean value indicating if the current row is the last row in the result set
hStmt	Corresponds to an ODBC statement handle
LastModified	Returns a bookmark to the last modified or changed row

(continues)

Table 18.11   Continued

Property	Description
LockEdits	Boolean value indicating the type of locking used during editing
Name	String containing the first 256 characters of the SQL query used to populate the result set
PercentPosition	Indicates or changes the approximate location of the current row based on the number of rows in the result set. To ensure that the rdoResultset is fully populated, use the MoveLast method before accessing this property.
Restartable	Boolean indicating if the rdoResultset object supports the Requery method
RowCount	Number of rows accessed in the result set
StillExecuting	When created using rdAsyncEnable, Boolean value indicates if the query has finished processing the results. The rdoResultset object cannot be accessed until the property is set to False.
Transactions	Boolean value indicating whether the rdoResultset supports transactions
Type	Read-only value indicating the Type argument that was specified when creating the rdoResultset object
Updatable	Boolean indicating if the result set contains updatable rows

Table 18.12 lists all of the methods exposed by the rdoResultset object.

Table 18.12   The Methods of the rdoResultset Object

Method	Description
AddNew	Prepares a new row that can be edited and added to the database, for updatable result sets. Changes are saved using the Update method; moving to a new row without issuing an Update will cause changes to be lost.
Cancel	Cancels any pending results associated with the rdoResultset object
CancelUpdate	Cancels any pending updates to the rdoResultset object by clearing its copy buffer

Method	Description
Close	Removes the rdoResultset object from the rdoResultsets collection
Delete	Deletes the current row from an updatable result set. The delete occurs immediately in the database, and the current row pointer must be moved to a new location before it can be accessed again.
Edit	Places a copy of the current row of an updatable result set into the copy buffer where editing can occur. Changes are not saved until the Update method is called.
GetRows	Copies multiple rows from a result set into a two-dimensional array
Item	Returns a specific rdoResultset object from the rdoResultsets collection
MoreResults	Prepares the next result set for processing, clearing the previous result set
Move	Positions the current row *Rows* records from the *Start* row. If *Rows* is positive the current position is moved forward; if it's negative the current position is moved backwards.
MoveFirst	Places the current row pointer in the first row in the result set
MoveLast	Places the current row pointer at the last row in the results set
MoveNext	Places the current row pointer at the next row in the result set
MovePrevious	Places the current row pointer at the previous row in the result set
Requery	Re-executes the query used to create the result set, repopulating the rdoResultset object
Update	Save the changes to the current row that are present in the copy buffer

The rdoColumn Object

The rdoColumn object represents a column of data present in a database table. The rdoColumn object's properties contain the specifications that were used to create the table in the database, as well as the value that is present for the current row.

The `rdoColumn` object, exposed by the `rdoResultset` and `rdoPreparedStatement` objects, is used to obtain and update the values of the data columns of the current row. The `rdoColumn` object exposed by the `rdoTable` object provides only the definition of the data column within the database. This information can be used to view the structure of the database table, but cannot be updated through RDO properties and methods.

All `rdoColumn` objects are included in the `rdoColumns` collection of an `rdoTable` object. The `rdoColumn` object can be referenced within the `rdoColumns` collection using its `Name` property. This name is the same as the column name that was specified during the creation of the table, or the SQL query that produced the result set.

When exposed by an `rdoResultset` object, the data for the current row is accessible through the `rdoColumn` object's `Value` property. The following code fragment shows how an `rdoColumn` within an `rdoResultset` can be used to affect a table's data:

```
rsltMyresultSet.rdoColumns("DATA_COLUMN").Value = 100
```

In the preceding expression, `rsltMyResultSet` is a result set created using one of the methods described in the previous section. The `rdoColumns` collection is a collection of all columns in the result set. We have specified DATA_COLUMN as the column we will modify. Finally, we use the `Value` property of the `rdoColumn` object to change the columns value.

Since the `rdoColumns` collection is the default collection of the `rdoResultset` object, it is often not referenced directly. The following two code fragments bear the same results:

```
rsltMyresultSet.rdoColumns("DATA_COLUMN").Value = 100
rsltMyresultSet.rdoColumns("DATA_COLUMN") = 100
```

Table 18.13 lists all of the properties exposed by the `rdoColumn` object.

Table 18.13 The Properties and Methods of the `rdoColumn` Object

Property/Method	Description
AllowZeroLength	Boolean indicating if a zero length string is valid for the Value property of the column. If set to false, zero length strings must be inserted as NULLS.
Attributes	Indicates characteristics of the column like fixed length, auto increment, updatable, etc.

Property/Method	Description
ChunkRequired	Boolean indicating if the GetChunk method must be used to retrieve data from this column
Count	Number of rdoColumn objects that exist in the collection
Name	Database column name
OrdinalPosition	Returns the ordinal position within the rdoColumns collection
Required	Boolean indicating if this column requires a non-Null value
Size	Indicates the maximum number of characters the column will accept for string columns, and the maximum number of bytes the column will accept for numeric columns
SourceColumn	Name of the column that is the original source of the data in the column object
SourceTable	Name of the table that is the original source of the data in the column object
Type	Data type of the column object
Updatable	Boolean indicating if the value of the column can be changed
Value	Current data held in the column object
AppendChunk	Append data to a column of type rdTypeLONGVARBINARY or rdTYPELONGVARCHAR
ColumnSize	Returns the number of bytes in an `rdoColumn` object that requires AppendChunk/GetChunk to access its value
GetChunk	Returns all or part of an rdoColumn object with the ChunkRequired property set to true

Using Prepared Statements

The ability to use stored procedures to interact with a data source provides applications with a performance increase over the use of embedded SQL statements. This increase in performance comes about because stored procedures are pre-compiled SQL statements that the database engine has already created an execution plan for. Thus, when a stored procedure is executed, the database is not required to parse a SQL string and formulate an execution plan. The result is an increase in performance over dynamic SQL statements when accessing or updating data.

RDO provides a series of objects that allow an application to utilize stored procedures when working with a remote data source. These are:

- The `rdoPreparedStatement` object

- The `rdoParameter` object

Both the `rdoPreparedStatement` object and the `rdoParameter` object are described in detail in the following sections.

The `rdoPreparedStatement` Object

The `rdoPreparedStatement` object represents a stored query definition within the database. It can also be used to store SQL statements that will be repetitively executed from an application. This is one of the most flexible and important aspects of an `rdoPreparedStatement` object.

As a developer, you can create a library of prepared statements that represent both stored procedures and dynamic SQL statements. As we will see later in this section, the ability to define prepared statements will help you to make your application more portable by minimizing its dependence on the back end. It will also improve your application's performance when accessing the database. The `rdoPreparedStatements` collection contains all of the `rdoPreparedStatement` objects that exist within a given rdoConnection.

Stored procedures, as well as dynamic SQL statements, often require a user to pass one or more parameters. These parameters can be used to better define the set of data to be retrieved or acted upon. To facilitate this, the `rdoPreparedStatement` object supports both static SQL statements and what are often referred to as "parameter" queries. A parameter query allows the application to create a SQL procedure that accepts values at run-time that affect the actions of the query. The use of the parameter object will be discussed later in the chapter.

Creating a Prepared Statement

As we have learned, a prepared statement is created in one of two ways: utilizing an existing stored procedure in the database, or creating a dynamic SQL statement that performs an action on the database or returns rows from the database. Both types of prepared statements are created using the same syntax:

```
Set rdoPreparedStatement =
    rdoConnection.CreatePreparedStatement (name, sqltext)
```

where *rdoPreparedStatement* is an `rdoPreparedStatement` object, *rdoConnection* is an `rdoConnection` object that has been previously created, and *name* is an optional name you supply to identify the new `rdoPreparedStatement` object in the `rdoPreparedStatements` collection.

The final argument, *sqltext*, is a string containing either a call to an existing stored procedure in the database, or string containing valid SQL text.

The following is an example of the SQL text that would be used to call an existing stored procedure. The procedure is named `sp_delete_names`. The general syntax for calling an existing stored procedure is as follows:

```
{call procedurename (?, ?, ...)}
```

where *procedurename* is the name of the stored procedure as it appears in the database. The question marks represent bound parameters for the query. Parameters are discussed later in this chapter. In our example, the name of our stored procedure is `sp_delete_names`. We will assume the `sp_delete_names` procedure takes no parameters. Our sqltext argument would look like the following:

```
{call sp_delete_names }
```

When we declare the prepared statement, we will include this as our sqltext. We can also supply a name for the stored procedure that will allow us to access the `rdoPreparedStatement` in the `rdoPreparedStatements` collection. For our example, we will give the prepared statement the same name as it appears in the database, `sp_delete_names`.

Now that we have all of our arguments, we can create the prepared statement. To do so, we would use the following code:

```
Set rdoPreparedStatement = rdoConnection.CreatePreparedStatement
("sp_delete_names", "{call sp_delete_names}")
```

Suppose we wanted to create a prepared statement that did not execute a stored procedure, but instead executed a SQL statement we created. For our example, we will use a simple SQL statement that retrieves rows from a table named MY_RECORDS. To return all records from the table, we would use the following SQL text:

```
SELECT * FROM MY_RECORDS
```

This will become our *sqltext* argument.

For our *name* argument, we will use the text "RetrieveRecords." Notice in this example that the name you assign to a prepared statement can be any valid string and does not have to be a reproduction of the database name. To create our prepared statement, we would use the following code:

```
Set rdoPreparedStatement = rdoConnection.CreatePreparedStatement
("RetrieveRecords", "SELECT * FROM MY_RECORDS")
```

Executing a Prepared Statement

Once the prepared statement has been created, we can execute it using the Execute method or OpenResultset method of the rdoPreparedStatement object. If the prepared statement does not return any rows (it is an action query), the code would look like the following:

```
rdoPreparedStatement.Execute
```

where *rdoPreparedStatement* is a previously created rdoPreparedStatement object. When the Execute method is invoked, the appropriate database action is carried out. After the statement has completed, you can check the RowsAffected of the rdoPreparedStatement object to determine how many rows were affected by the action query.

If the prepared statement returns a result set, the following code would be used:

```
Set rdoResultset = rdoPreparedStatement.OpenResultset
```

where *rdoResultset* is an object declared as type rdoResultset and *rdoPreparedStatement* is a previously declared rdoPreparedStatement object. The OpenResultset method creates a new rdoResultset object that can be manipulated just as any other rdoResultset object can. For more information of result sets, see the section, "Using Result Sets," earlier in this chapter.

Closing Prepared Statements

If a prepared statement will be used repetitively in an application, such as a prepared statement used to write a new order to the database in an order processing application, you may want to declare it at a global or modular level so that you do not have to re-create it each time you want to use it. When you have completed using the prepared statement, you need to close to free all resources used by it. Closing the prepared statement will remove the temporary procedure created on the database and will remove the rdoPreparedStatement object from the rdoPreparedStatements collection. To remove the prepared statement, you use the Close method:

```
rdoPreparedStatement.Close
```

where rdoPreparedStatement is a previously declared prepared statement object. It is good programming practice to close prepared statements once your application no longer needs them.

Performance Benefits

We have already discussed how a stored procedure pre-compiled in the database can help to improve the performance of your application when accessing data. The performance boost comes about because the database does not have to parse a SQL string each time the procedure is called. The database server will also generate an execution plan for the query which determines the optimal method for executing the procedure.

When an `rdoPreparedStatement` object is created, a temporary stored procedure is created. This temporary stored procedure is parsed by the server. The server also creates an execution plan for the query. Since a prepared statement is compiled only once by the database server, it provides a performance increase of the use of the same embedded SQL statement over and over. This is true even for dynamic SQL statements used to create an `rdoPreparedStatement` object. This makes the use of prepared statements in an application ideal.

Naming Prepared Statements

When you create a new `rdoPreparedStatement` object, you are given the opportunity to include a name for the new prepared statement when referring to it in the `rdoPreparedStatements` collection. The name can be any valid string expression. This gives you, as a developer, a chance to give your procedures more descriptive names than perhaps the database will allow.

For example, in an earlier example, we created a prepared statement that retrieved all of the records from a table named MY_RECORDS. To do this, we created a `SELECT` statement and assigned it to a prepared statement. When we created the `rdoPreparedStatement` object, we gave it the name RetrieveRecords. We could have given it any name we wanted, including Select Record or GetRecords.

We can access any `rdoPreparedStatement` from the `rdoPreparedStatements` collection using the name we give it. For example, we could execute the `RetrieveRecords` prepared statement using the following syntax:

```
Set rdoResultset = rdoPreparedStatements -- can break
here("RetrieveRecords").OpenResultset
```

Providing a name like RetrieveRecords for the prepared statement made it more obvious what the function of the prepared statement was.

When you create new prepared statements, you can give the statements verbose, meaningful names that will help other developers to understand what the function of the procedure is or what effect it has on the database. This will make utilizing stored procedures simpler for all persons involved in a project.

Managing Prepared Statements

As previously mentioned, prepared statements can be used with database stored procedures as well as embedded SQL statements. This means that applications which use the same SQL statement multiple times within the application can create an `rdoPreparedStatement` object for the SQL statement, allowing it to be accessed, using a more meaningful name.

A set of prepared statements, therefore, can define all of the elementary data functions of the data service, whether they are actually stored procedures or dynamic SQL statements. These data functions need not be elementary to a single application; they may define the elementary data functions for many applications in the enterprise. The preparation of the prepared statements can be encapsulated in an OLE automation server. The OLE server could expose a method which takes an `rdoConnection` object as a parameter. This method could add the appropriate `rdoPreparedStatement` to the `rdoPreparedStatements` collection of the calling application and allow the calling application to make subsequent calls to the prepared statements added. This allows multiple business servers to dynamically link to the elementary data functions provided. This OLE server could also be placed into a logical "tier" containing other business logic and functions pertinent to your application.

By placing the code necessary to prepare data functions in a separate tier, you will allow yourself to more easily make modifications to the data server and subsequently pass those changes on to your entire user base. For example, suppose you decided to change the name of a stored procedure in your database. If you defined all of your prepared statements in the client application that was distributed to end-users, you would need to re-code and then re-distribute the application for your changes to take effect. In the meantime, end-users would either be unable to use the stored procedure, or you would need to maintain two separate versions of the database until all end-users had obtained a copy of the updated app.

On the other hand, if prepared statement preparation was encapsulated in an OLE server and placed on a file server that could be accessed by all end-users, you would need to make the change in only one place. The change would be instantly realized by all end-users without requiring redistribution of your application.

For more information on creating multitiered applications and encapsulating business logic in OLE servers, read *Visual Basic Enterprise Development*, available from QUE publishing (ISBN 0-7897-0099-9).

The `rdoPreparedStatement` Properties and Methods

Table 18.14 lists the properties associated with the `rdoPreparedStatement` object.

Table 18.14 The Properties of the `rdoPreparedStatement` Object	
Property	**Description**
BindThreshold	Largest column that will be automatically bound under ODBC, thus not requiring the GetChunk/ AppendChunk functions
Connect	Read-only string that contains connection information used to create the rdoConnection object
Count	Number of rdoPreparedStatement objects that exist within the rdoPreparedStatements collection
ErrorThreshold	Determines the severity level which triggers a fatal error
hStmt	ODBC statement handle
KeysetSize	Specifies the number of rows in the keyset buffer
LockType	Indicates the type of record concurrency handling to be used
LogMessages	Location of the ODBC trace file used by the ODBC driver to record its operations
MaxRows	Maximum number of rows that can be returned by a query; a value of -1 sets no limit on the number of rows returned
Name	Name used in the CreatePreparedStatement method for this object
QueryTimeout	Number of seconds the ODBC driver waits before generating a timeout error while waiting for a query to complete

(continues)

Table 18.14 Continued	
Property	**Description**
RowsAffected	Number of rows affected by the last Execute method
RowsetSize	Number of rows of the keyset cursor that will be buffered by the application
SQL	SQL statement used to define the query that is executed
StillExecuting	Boolean value indicating if a query run with the rdAsyncEnable option has completed
Type	Indicates if the query is a select, action, or procedural query
Updatable	Indicates if the result set being created is updatable

Table 18.15 lists all of the methods exposed by the rdoPreparedStatement object.

Table 18.15 The Methods of the rdoPreparedStatement Object	
Method	**Description**
Cancel	Cancels an asynchronous query
Close	Removes the rdoPreparedStatement object from the collection
Execute	Executes a query or SQL statement that does not return any rows
Item	Returns a specific rdoPreparedStatement object from the collection
OpenResultSet	Creates a new rdoResultset object that is appended to the rdoResultsets collection

The rdoParameter Object

The rdoParameter object provides the mechanism by which the application developer can set query parameters before running a query. This requires that a rdoPreparedStatement be defined using parameter markers.

For example, one of the most powerful aspects of result sets over tables is that while a table contains all data in the database object, a result set can contain a filtered subset of the data. This subset may be more manageable in an application, and may improve overall performance by requiring fewer data operations to be carried out.

In a previous example, we created a result set that returned all records from a table named MY_RECORDS. Let's assume that the MY_RECORDS table contains a list of customers, including their first and last names. What if we wanted to create a result set containing all the customers with the last name Jones? We could create this filtered result set using parameters.

In the following code segment a prepared statement is created and is defined to accept one parameter: a person's last name:

```
Set lprepGetCustomers = gconConnection.CreatePreparedStatement( _
                            "GetCustomers", _
                            "SELECT * FROM MY_RECORDS WHERE
LAST_NAME = ?")
Set lprepGetCustomers = gconConnection.CreatePreparedStatement( _
    "GetCustomers","SELECT * FROM MY_RECORDS WHERE LAST_NAME = ?")
```

We can then use the rdoParameters collection to select a value for the last name parameter. In our example, we would use the following syntax to return only the customers whose last name is Jones:

```
lprepCustomers.rdoParameters(0) = "Jones"
```

As you can see, like all RDO collection objects, the ordinal position of the collection begins with zero. When the prepared statement is executed using the OpenResultset method, a result set containing only the customers whose last name is Jones would be returned.

Parameters can also be bound to prepared statements that call stored procedures. In an earlier section, we created a prepared statement that called the stored procedure sp_delete_names. We did not pass any parameters to the query. This time, let's assume that we need to pass the ID of the record we want to delete. The stored procedure in the database has been created to accept a single parameter: ID.

To create the rdoPreparedStatement object, we could use the following syntax:

```
Set lprepGetCustomers = gconConnection.CreatePreparedStatement
("sp_delete_names","{call sp_delete_names (?)}")
```

To execute the prepared statement, we would first specify our parameter using the rdoParameters collection:

```
lprepCustomers.rdoParameters(0) = 100
```

And then execute the prepared statement:

```
lprepCustomers.Execute
```

Note that not all ODBC drivers support bound parameters. In this case, you can still specify parameters, but you will need to use dynamic SQL when specifying your SQL text. For example, instead of using the dynamic SQL text we specified earlier in this section:

```
"SELECT * FROM MY_RECORDS WHERE LAST_NAME = ?"
```

We would use the following:

```
"SELECT * FROM MY_RECORDS WHERE LAST_NAME = " & lsParam1
```

Where `lsParam1` is a string variable you have declared in your application. By changing the value of `lsParam1` in your application you can change the SQL string that is sent to the database and thus change the filtering criteria of your result set. Prepared statements calling stored procedures in the database must always use bound parameters.

RDO supports both input and output parameters. The `rdoParameter`'s `Direction` property is used to determine if the parameter is an input, output, input/output, or return value. Output parameters are common when working with data sources like Oracle that do not support the ability to return result sets from a stored procedure.

When a procedure uses a return value to pass data back to the calling application, the `rdoParameter`'s `Direction` should be set to `rdParamRetunValue`. While using `rdParamOutput` will work, to ensure compatibility with future versions of RDO, it is recommended that the more specific directional indicator be used.

When working with parameters that have a direction of anything other than `rdParamInput`, the default, the Direction property must be set before the procedure is executed. This ensures that the ODBC driver handles the parameter correctly.

Table 18.16 lists all of the properties associated with the `rdoParameter` object.

Table 18.16 The Properties of the rdoParameter Object	
Property	**Description**
Count	Returns the number of rdoParameter objects that are present in the collection
Direction	Indicates how the parameter is used by the query
Name	Name assigned to the parameter
Type	Data type expected by the parameter
Value	The default property which specified the value of the parameter

Cursors

When an `rdoResultset` object is created, RDO implements a cursor or a cursor-like object depending on what type of result set you request. The *Type* argument of the `OpenResultset` method determines the type of cursors/result set that is created. The different cursor implementations and result set types primarily affect the manner in which the application is allowed to move through the cursor, at which location the cursor is created, and how often the data within the cursor is updated.

The `OpenResultset` method provides four types of cursors:

- Forward-only
- Static
- Keyset
- Dynamic

When working with cursors, choosing the right type of cursors for your application can impact the performance of the application. In this section, we will look at the different options available when creating cursors using RDO, and the types of applications that each is best suited for.

Forward-only Cursors

Although it does not actually create a cursor, forward-only `rdoResultset` objects act like a cursor and provide increased performance over an actual cursor. This is because they eliminate the overhead that is associated with creating a cursor.

Creating a forward-only result set works well when the application needs to quickly retrieve data and see only one row at a time. If the application needs the ability to move around within the cursor then the forward-only result set will not provide the needed functionality.

If you do not specify which type of cursor you want when you create a result set, a Forward-only cursor is created.

Static Cursors

Static cursors are similar to the Jet snapshot object. Data within a Static cursor appears to be static. The rows contained within the cursor, and the order and values in the result set are set when the cursor is opened. Any updates, deletions, or inserts that occur to the database while the cursor is open are not visible to the cursor or result set until they are closed and reopened.

Static cursors themselves are not updatable either. This means that methods such as `AddNew` or `Edit` will produce errors when used on result sets of type `Static`. `Static` result sets can be quickly retrieved and moved through because the application is not required to re-poll the database periodically to determine if changes have occurred.

Keyset Cursors

Keyset cursors, like static cursors, remain unchanged from the time the cursor is opened. A keyset cursor contains the key value for each row contained within the cursor. When the application requests a row, the key value is used to obtain the remaining data from the data source.

Keyset cursors can be set up to build the cursor on the client, an ODBC library cursor, or on the server, a server-side cursor. The ability to create server-side cursors is dictated by the features of the data source.

Dynamic Cursors

Dynamic cursors perform differently from those previously mentioned and also result in the greatest amount of overhead. A dynamic cursor is created in the same manner as a keyset cursor except that it constantly checks the data source to ensure that all rows which meet the selection criteria are included in the cursor.

For example, if another application changes the data to the point where an additional record meets the criteria of the cursor, a dynamic cursor will add the additional record to the result set. Keyset and static cursors will only pick up the additional record if the cursor is closed and reopened. Even though they require a large amount of overhead, dynamic cursors are faster than keyset cursors at the initial build of the cursor.

Choosing a Cursor Type

The type of cursor you use depends upon the functionality of the application being developed. For example, an application that requires optimal speed might use forward-only result sets because of their speed and the fact that the business server only needs to see one row of the result set at a time. Other applications may need to move forward and backward within a result set, and require updated information. In this case, a dynamic cursor, while slower than a forward-only result set, will provide the functionality that is necessary without the application developer writing additional code.

When creating cursors, the location of the cursor itself also affects its performance. Server-side cursors will generally operate faster because they are located on more powerful server machines, and are not required to load all of the cursor information down to the client machine. The ability to create a server-side cursor is dependent upon the data source that is being used.

The `rdoDefaultCursorDriver` property of the `rdoEngine` object or the `rdoEnvironment`'s `CursorDriver` property allows you to specify the location of the cursor that is to be created. As mentioned earlier in the chapter, these properties can be set to create ODBC cursors, server-side cursors, or driver dependent cursors, meaning that a server-side cursor is created if the ODBC driver supports it.

Handling Transactions

A transaction refers to an operation performed against a database. Transaction management is the process of grouping these transactions into logical units of work, whereby either all of the operations are completed or none of them are completed.

For example, when creating an order in an order processing application, the program might first insert a record into an order header table containing information such as customer ID, name, and address. The program might then insert the individual line items of the order—containing information such as product ID, cost, and quantity—into a line items table. This entire operation needs to occur as a single transaction. If the line item insert fails, then the order header should be removed from the table.

The remainder of this section will explain how to maintain consistent data in your application using transactions, and how to manipulate record locking when processing transactions.

Ensuring Database Consistency

RDO provides a number of methods for the `rdoConnection` and `rdoEnvironment` objects that allow applications to effectively manage transactions.

To mark the start of a transaction, the application calls the `BeginTrans` method. Once this method is called, all database operations that are performed will be part of this transaction.

To signal the end of a transaction, the application calls either the `CommitTrans` or `RollbackTrans` methods. The `CommitTrans` method is called after the operations that make up the transaction have completed successfully. `CommitTrans` will save all of the changes made to the database and end the transaction.

The RollbackTrans method, on the other hand, is used when an error has occurred during one of the operations within the transaction. For example, suppose a one-line item of an order was rejected by the database when the order processing application attempted to insert it. The RollbackTrans method could be invoked to end the transaction and undo any changes that were made to the database since the BeginTrans method was executed. In this case, the database is returned to the state it was in at the time the BeginTrans method was issued.

The following code, shown in Listing 18.2, shows the implementation of a transaction used while updating orders in a fictional order processing application. In this example, the existing orders are first deleted, and the current values contained in an Order object are inserted into database tables. If for some reason the inserts fail, the transaction will be rolled back, restoring the old order information.

Listing 18.2   18LIST02.TXT—A sample transaction-based function that removes and inserts records into a database. If any phase of an insert fails, the transaction is rolled back.

```
Public Function UpdateOrders() as Boolean

Dim qryDeleteOrder As rdoPreparedStatement
Dim qryAddOrder As rdoPreparedStatement
Dim qryAddLineItem As rdoPreparedStatement

Dim OrderIdx As Long
Dim LineItemIdx As Long
Dim NextLineItem As LineItem

'1) Delete all orders and line item keys in the original collection
'2) Insert all orders and line items in current collection,
'    ignoring those orders marked RemoveFlag="Y"
' if an isert of an odrer header or the line items within an
' order are unsuccessful, rollbakc the transaction and return
' false

' db is an rdoConnection object that we have created previously
db.BeginTrans

'open a handle to the delete orders stored procedure
' the delete orders stored procedure is a stored procedure in the
' database which accepts one argument - the ID of the order you
' wish to delete
Set qryDeleteOrder = db.CreatePreparedStatement( _
                          "sp_Delete_OrderHdr", _
                          "{call sp_Delete_OrderHdr (?)}")

'delete orders
' This is done by supplying the ID parameter to the
```

```
' sp_delete_orderhdr stored procedure (which has been
' referenced by the qryDeleteOrder object)
OrderIdx = 0
Do
    OrderIdx = OrderIdx + 1
    qryDeleteOrder.rdoParameters(0).Value = Me.Item(OrderIdx).OrderID
    qryDeleteOrder.Execute
' We are actually performing this operation within a class module
' that represents a collection. The collection has a Count method.
' Thus, to determine how many orders we need to delete, we can invoke
' the Count method of our collection object
Loop Until OrderIdx >= Me.Count

'close the delete orders PreparedStatement handle
' This will remove it from the rdoPreparedStatements
' collection of the db object
qryDeleteOrder.Close


'open a handle to the add order stored procedure
' The add order procedure accepts four arguments:
' OrderID, CustomerID, Date of the Order, and an
' indicator as to whether or not the order has been shipped.
Set qryAddOrder = db.CreatePreparedStatement( _
                            "sp_Add_OrderHdr", _
                            "{call sp_Add_OrderHdr (?, ?, ?, ?)}")
' Specify the direction of each parameter
qryAddOrder.rdoParameters(0).Direction = rdParamInputOutput
qryAddOrder.rdoParameters(1).Direction = rdParamInput
qryAddOrder.rdoParameters(2).Direction = rdParamInput
qryAddOrder.rdoParameters(3).Direction = rdParamInput

'open a handle to the add line item stored procedure
' The procedure accepts five arguments:
' Order ID, LineItem ID, Product ID, Order Qty,
' and Shipped Qty.
Set qryAddLineItem = db.CreatePreparedStatement( _
                            "sp_Add_LineItem", _
                            "{call sp_Add_LineItem (?, ?, ?, ?, ?)}")

'reload all of the order currently in the orders collection
OrderIdx = 0
Do
    OrderIdx = OrderIdx + 1
    'only add if not marked for removal
    If Me.Item(OrderIdx).RemovedFlag = "N" Then
        With Me.Item(OrderIdx)
            ' Place appropriate values into the rdoParameters collection
            ' of the rdoPreparedStatement object
            qryAddOrder.rdoParameters(0).Value = .OrderID
            qryAddOrder.rdoParameters(1).Value = .CustomerID
            qryAddOrder.rdoParameters(2).Value = .OrderDate
            qryAddOrder.rdoParameters(3).Value = CStr(.ShippedFlag)
            qryAddOrder.Execute
```

(continues)

Listing 18.2 Continued

```
    ' After the execute, check the rdoError object. If an
    ' error occurred in the procedure, we must rollback the
      ➥transaction
    ' and exit the function
    If rdoError.SQLRetCode <> rdSQLSuccess Then
  db.Rollback
  UpdateOrders = False
      qryAddOrder.Close
      qryAddLineItem.Close
  Exit Function
    End If

    'update order id which was set by SP
    ' Again, we are in a collection object. By referring
    ' to the Item method of our object, we can reference a
      ➥specific
    ' item in our collection and update its ID property
    Me.Item(OrderIdx).OrderID =
  ➥qryAddOrder.rdoParameters(0).Value
End With

'add the line items
LineItemIdx = 0
Do
    LineItemIdx = LineItemIdx + 1
    Set NextLineItem =
  ➥Me.Item(OrderIdx).LineItems.Item(LineItemIdx)
    With NextLineItem
    ' Place appropriate values into the rdoParameters
      ➥collection
        qryAddLineItem.rdoParameters(0).Value =
      ➥Me.Item(OrderIdx).OrderID
        qryAddLineItem.rdoParameters(1).Value = LineItemIdx
        qryAddLineItem.rdoParameters(2).Value = .ProductId
        qryAddLineItem.rdoParameters(3).Value = .OrderQty
        qryAddLineItem.rdoParameters(4).Value = .ShipQty
        qryAddLineItem.Execute

    ' After the execute, check the rdoError object. If an
    ' error occurred int he procedure, we must rollback the
      ➥transaction
    ' and exit the function
    If rdoError.SQLRetCode <> rdSQLSuccess Then
            db.Rollback
            UpdateOrders = False
            ' close the prepared statements
            qryAddOrder.Close
            qryAddLineItem.Close
            Exit Function
    End If

    End With
Loop Until LineItemIdx >= Me.Item(OrderIdx).LineItems.Count
```

```
        End If

    Loop Until OrderIdx >= Me.Count

    'close the PreparedStatement handles
    qryAddOrder.Close
    qryAddLineItem.Close

    'commit the transaction
    db.CommitTrans

    Set prvOrders = Nothing

    UpdateOrders = True

    End Function
```

In the previous example, as we insert new records into the database, if an error occurs the transaction will be rolled back and the original order data is restored. If we do not roll back, we risk losing a line item within an order, or losing an entire order. Code of this type can be applied to any transaction-based system requiring two phases of an action to complete before a transaction can be committed to the database.

Manipulating Record Locking

Another aspect of transactions that needs to be understood is the concept of locking records. RDO supports the two types of record locking found in most data sources: pessimistic and optimistic.

Most relational databases store data in conceptual chunks known as pages. Many databases consider a page to be as many rows that can be stored in a 2K memory space. Other RDBMSs allow you to specify page size. As you can see, it is often difficult to predict in which page a record or records lie.

When you update a record, you actually lock the record's page. This means that the record being updated, as well as all other records contained within the records 2K page, are unavailable for updating by other processes. If your database table is "thin," that is if the table has a small number of rows that each consumes very little space, you may lock up many rows.

Under pessimistic locking, the database page containing the record being updated is locked and no other process is allowed to access it from the time it is selected until the changes have been committed to the database.

Optimistic record locking, on the other hand, locks the database page containing the record to be updated only while the actual update is taking place. Other processes are allowed to access the record after it has been selected and before the update takes place.

The type of record locking is specified using the LockEdits property of the rdoResultset object. When LockEdits is set to True, the default, pessimistic locking is used. Using this option, the database page is unavailable to other users from the time the record is placed in edit mode using the *Edit* method until the *Update* method has been executed.

Setting LockEdits equal to False uses optimistic record locking. In this case, the database page is still available to other users when the record is placed in edit mode. The database page is unavailable only while the Update method is being executed.

The type of record locking that is used for an application depends upon the number of concurrent updates that will be taking place within the system.

Asynchronous Queries

RDO provides an rdAysncEnable option, which allows applications to process queries in an asynchronous fashion. When this option is specified, RDO will initiate a query, and immediately return control back to a calling application before a result set is built, or an action query is completed. The rdAsyncEnable option is available when creating a result set using the OpenResultset method or when running an action query using the Execute method.

During an asynchronous operation, the application is allowed to perform other tasks that do not involve the result set that was requested. The application is responsible for checking the StillExecuting property of the rdoResultset object to determine when the query has completed. RDO will periodically pool the database to determine if a query has completed and then update the StillExecuting property. You must then programatically and periodically check the StillExecuting property. The AsyncCheckInterval property of the rdoConnection object allows you to indicate the interval at which RDO will query the database to check for completion.

When rdAsyncEnable is used while creating an rdoResultset object, the result set is not available until the StillExecuting property has been set to false. In addition, your application must wait until all query processing has stopped before it receives control. If your application executes queries that require a large amount of processing time, you may force your users to bear long, un-productive pauses. Using the rdAsynchEnable option ensures that your users will always perform optimally.

A second advantage of queries executed asynchronously is that they can be stopped by using the Cancel method of the rdoResultset object. This method will stop the execution of a query, including any aspects of the query which may have already returned data. This feature can be very helpful when your application generates queries that may return large data sets to a user. If users feel that they have waited too long for a result set to return, they can cancel the operation and begin another without wasting additional overhead or impacting database performance.

When the `rdAsyncEnable` option is not used, Visual Basic does not allow any other tasks to be performed within the application until the first row of the result set has been retrieved. Only the current Visual Basic application is blocked; other Windows applications are allowed to continue execution.

Caution should be used when implementing asynchronous queries. For example, if you do not place a limit on the number of asynchronous queries that a user can execute concurrently, you may inadvertently grind your database to a halt. If a user begins to run too many queries at the same time, huge amounts of record locking may occur or processor time may not be handed out appropriately.

In addition, you should keep in mind that asynchronous operations require an additional level of management that is often taken for granted in synchronous operations. You may need to disable or hide option buttons on a form, for example, when a query is executing asynchronously. Suppose you had developed an order processing application that required a user to select several products from the database to place on an order. Once the products had been selected, an end-user could submit the order for shipping. If you create an asynchronous query to retrieve the product IDs, and did not disable the button used to submit an order, a user might inadvertently submit an order without products. This might cause errors farther down the line on your application.

Handling Errors

Any statement that uses RDO can cause an error or multiple errors to occur. The `rdoError` object and `rdoErrors` collection provide the information about all errors associated with the most recent RDO operation.

Each `rdoError` object within the collection represents a specific error that occurred during the operation. Unlike most collections, the `rdoError` objects are not appended to the collection, but instead are added based on their severity or detail.

For example, if an application attempts to create a result set, and an ODBC error occurs, the first object in the `rdoErrors` collection will contain the most specific, or lowest level ODBC error. The remaining errors in the collection represent the ODBC errors that were generated in the other layers of ODBC, the driver manager and driver for example.

To determine the cause of an error, the application can examine the rdoErrors(0) object since it contains the lowest level error.

When an error occurs during an RDO operation, the rdoErrors collection is cleared, and all of the errors that result from the operation are placed into the collection. Each error that occurs is represented by an individual rdoError object within the rdoErrors collection.

The rdoDefaultErrorThreshold setting determines whether or not the error is severe enough to generate a run-time error within the application. When a run-time error is generated, the application execution will fork into the error handling routine. Using the properties listed in Table 18.17, the error handler can determine what action should be taken.

Table 18.17 The Properties of the rdoError Object	
Property/Method	**Description**
Count	Returns the number of errors currently in the rdoErrors collection
Description	Text message that describes the error
HelpContext	Windows Help file context ID associated with the error code
HelpFile	Path to the Windows Help file
Number	Error number
Source	Indicates the source of the error, often the object class where the error occurred
SQLRetCode	Status code from the last RDO operation, indicates completion status; rdSQLSucess, rdSQLError, etc.
SQLState	String corresponding to the X/Open and SQL Access Group SQL error standard, containing the error class and subclass value
Clear	Resets the rdoErrors collection
Item	Returns a specific rdoError object from within the rdoErrors collection

Summary

In this chapter, we discussed the powerful new data access method introduced in Visual Basic 4, the Remote Data Object. RDO allows you to quickly and easily connect to multiple ODBC-compliant data sources and exploit the powerful functions inherent to those data sources. In addition, RDO offers improved performance over other data access methods such as Jet or bound data controls.

After reading this chapter, you should understand the hierarchy of the RDO object model, how to establish a connection to an ODBC-compliant database using RDO, and how to manipulate data using the `rdoResultset` and `rdoPreparedStatement` objects.

Chapter 19

Remote Automation

by James Schmelzer

James Schmelzer is a consultant with Clarity Consulting, Inc. Jay has architected a number of enterprise client/server solutions with tools such as Visual Basic, PowerBuilder, SQL Server, and Oracle. Jay is coauthor of Que's Visual Basic Enterprise Development *(ISBN: 0-7897-0099-9).*

Visual Basic 4 Enterprise Development provides the ability to not only create OLE Automation servers, but also to control OLE objects that physically reside on another machine located across the network. This is accomplished by using a technology known as *Remote Automation.*

In this chapter, you will learn the following:

- ■ The capabilities of Remote Automation

- ■ How Remote Automation works behind the scenes, specifically its interaction with the registry

- ■ How Remote Automation is used when creating three-tier applications

- ■ How to use the tools provided with Visual Basic to manage remote objects

Overview of Remote Automation

Remote Automation is a standard that defines how OLE Automation can operate transparently over a network. In this architecture, neither the client nor the server knows or cares where the other object is physically located.

Before we take a look at how remote automation works, let's take a look at how local automation works. When two processes communicate via OLE automation, they do so via a proxy/stub combination. This is called *single machine remoting.* See figure 19.1.

Fig. 19.1
Single machine remoting (local automation).

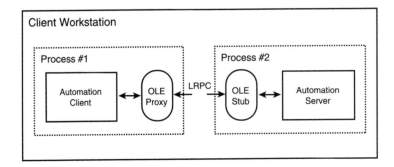

Remote automation introduces an additional component, the remote Automation Manager, which replaces the original proxy/stub combinations with the capability to communicate over a network. This is called *cross machine remoting*. See figure 19.2.

Fig. 19.2
Cross machine remoting (remote automation).

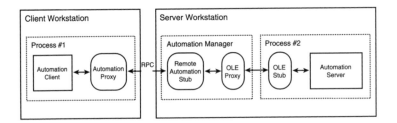

The automation proxy replaces the standard OLE proxy on the client machine. The Automation Manager residing on the server marshals requests across the network—it manages RPC calls for the OLE stub. Neither the client controller nor the OLE server is aware that the communication is being remoted.

The OLE automation relationship is a client/server relationship. The controlling application, or client, makes requests of the server. These requests are in the form of standard OLE automation interface calls, such as properties, methods, and collections. The OLE server, in turn, processes these interface requests.

This relationship can be reversed as well. For example, the client application can expose its own properties and methods that the server can invoke. This technique is often referred to as a *callback*. For example, application A (the client) may invoke a method on application B (the server) that searches the Internet for a document. When application B finds the document, it invokes a method in application A. This invocation reverses the relationship: application B is acting as the OLE client, and application A is acting as the OLE automation server.

The registry setting on the client computer determines whether the client uses the standard OLE proxy or the remote automation proxy. Although the proxy and stub are handled automatically by OLE, the Automation Manager must first be running on the server machine before clients can instantiate objects.

Applications written for remote automation will continue to run unmodified when remote automation is superseded by the Distributed Component Object model (DCOM).

OLE and the Registry

Now that we have an understanding of what Remote Automation is and how it works behind the scenes, we need to become familiar with the mechanism Remote Automation uses to determine where to find the remote OLE servers. This is done by using the Registry.

Data in the registry is stored in the form of hierarchical trees. Each node in the tree is called a key. The registry hierarchy is analogous to a file system in that each key can contain both subkeys (analogous to directories) and data entries (analogous to files).

Applications use the registry in Windows 95 and Windows NT much the way they used INI files in Windows 3.x: as a centrally located database where information about the computer is stored.

Each key has zero or more values associated with it. A value has multiple attributes:

- *Name.* Identifies the value.
- *Type.* Defines the type of data stored in the particular value, such as string, binary, or DWORD.
- *Data.* Specifies the data associated with the value.

There are a number of predefined entry or top-level points to the registry, called *hives*. For example, OLE class information is contained subordinate to the *HKEY_CLASSES_ROOT* hive. This handle is actually an alias for *HHEY_LOCAL_MACHINE\Software\Classes*.

Configuration Files

There are many types of files that relate to the registry: .VBR, .REG, .OLB, .TLB, .EXE, .DLL, and .OCX files.

.EXE and .DLL files can be OLE automation servers. .EXE files are out-of-process servers, while .DLL files are in-process servers. Often, these are all you need to register the server in the registry—they contain the special registry resource information. For example, an .EXE file is often self registering, and a .DLL file can often be added as a reference to the Object Browser. Likewise, .OCX files may contain interface information as well.

A .REG file is a text file that contains information about what entries need to be written to the registry. When you run a .REG file as a command-line argument with REGEDIT, it reads this "script" to determine what entries it should make to the registration database. Most applications no longer use .REG files, because they can "self-register" at startup. An example of self-registering applications are Visual Basic Automation Server's, Office 95 applications, and MFC OLE applications written with AppWizard.

.OLB, and .TLB files are type libraries. These files expose the object's interface without actually requiring the object to be present on the system.

VBR files are special types of .REG files that are used for Remote Automation.

For more information on OLE and the registry, see the following:

- Microsoft Developer's Network (MSDN), which contains *Inside OLE 2*.

- The OLE Programmer's Reference from Microsoft Press.

Registering Objects

Now that you are familiar with the Registry and how it is used by OLE and remote automation, we can discuss the process of registering an object. Registering an object means placing the appropriate information about the object into the registry. This information addresses questions like the following:

- Where is the object file located?

- Should the object be executed locally or remotely?

- If remotely, what protocol and security should be used?

- Where can interface information about the class be found?

Conversely, the process of unregistering a class involves removing the class information from the registry.

In general, components will be registered automatically for you, either when the component is executed or with some of the utilities, like the Component Manager, described in this chapter. Likewise, components should be unregistered with these tools as well.

Sometimes, however, an errant program will cause the registry to become corrupted. For example, the registry might contain duplicate CLSID entries or CLSID entries with no class parent. In these cases, the registry editor is useful for debugging and correcting the situation.

Developing Remote Automation Applications

Now that you have an understanding of what remote automation is and how it works, we can discuss the new types of applications that can be developed by using Visual Basic and Remote Automation.

In this section, we will first look at the new class of applications that can be developed: three-tier applications. After discussing what these applications are, we will look at related performance issues that need to be kept in mind when designing and developing these applications. Later in the chapter, we will look at techniques for debugging an application that utilizes remote automation.

Overview of the Three-Tier Services Model

Databases, development tools, and corporations are moving toward a three-tiered application architecture to overcome the limitations of the two-tiered architecture.

The three-tier services model adds an additional tier between the client and data services tiers of the more traditional two-tier architecture. This middle tier, known as the business services tier, provides an explicit layer for the business rules that sit between what used to be called the front-end and the back-end.

Table 19.1 shows a summary of the tiers of services in a three-tiered architectural approach.

| | Service | | Responsible | |
Tier	Type	Characteristics	For	Tools
1. User Services	Client Applications	GUI interface	Presentation & Navigation	4gls, desktop applications
2. Business Services	Business Servers	Businges Policies, objects, properties and methods	Business policy enforcement, security, business integrity	Some 4gls, COBOL, C
3. Data Services systems, systems,	Data Servers	Raw database managers	Data integrity and reliability, data storage and retrieval, low-level services	Databases, imaging messaging others data

Table 19.1   A Summary of the Three Tiers

In the Visual Basic documentation, Microsoft correctly refers to client applications as *user services* because they directly interact with end-users.

In the three-tier services model, a tier communicates with its parent, child, or sibling, which means that it can make requests and return answers to a process within its own tier, immediately above its tier, or immediately below its tier. Usually, the only communication that doesn't occur is a client application communicating directly with a data service.

In a traditional layered architecture, a layer can communicate only with another layer directly above or below. In the services architecture, however, the user services, business services, and data services can communicate with themselves. This model is known as the *services* model because, unlike a layered model, any service may invoke another service within its tier.

An example of this model would be an order business server that uses a customer and product business server to help fulfill an order, without the client application having visibility to the business servers' interaction.

So, a single client application request can involve many business servers. Because such a request involves more than a single data and business server interaction, this request is often referred to as an *n-tier* architecture. The terms three-tier, n-tier, and services model are often thought of as equivalent terms.

A client application request to update an order, for example, may be asked directly of an order processing business server, which in turn requests a shipment business server to schedule shipments, which both use an underlying database service. In this example, a single client application request involved two business servers and one data server.

Remember, these tiers do not necessarily correspond to physical locations on a network. Rather, they are logical layers that give the developer flexibility to deploy the particular service to wherever is best.

Just as there is confusion over the exact definition of two-tier client/server computing, there also is confusion over the exact definition of three-tier. This chapter refers to a three-tier client/server architecture (or services model) as simply an architecture that is logically partitioned into user service, business service, and data service layers.

The details of designing and developing applications using this services model is beyond the scope of this chapter. For more information about creating three-tier applications using Visual Basic read Que's *The Visual Basic 4 Enterprise* (QUE, ISBN: 0-7897-0099-9).

Now that you have a basic understanding of the types of applications that can now be created using Visual Basic and remote automation, let's look at some specific considerations that need to be kept in mind when designing these applications.

Performance Issues

Although an object reacts identically, whether controlled locally or across the network, remote automation introduces several performance considerations. If an object is to be used remotely, then, reality dictates that you should consider performance issues when deigning the OLE server.

For example, a lengthy in-process OLE call might take <0.1 second. A lengthy out-of-process call, which adds context switching, might take 1 second. A lengthy remote OLE automation call, which adds network RPC overhead, might take 3 seconds.

These numbers aren't scientific, they're just presented to give you a feel for the performance differences between in-process, out-of-process, and remote OLE automation calls.

As you may guess, then, the biggest impact on performance in a three-tier system will be the remote automation calls. Each OLE "dot" operation is an OLE automation call. Therefore, each "dot" operation makes a request across the network.

OLE automation objects that are going to be deployed remotely, then, should be designed so they can be used with minimal dot operations. Likewise, client applications should be designed so that they minimize the use of the server's dot operations.

The following design techniques are useful for improving the speed of remote automation. These techniques are also useful for local out-of-process servers.

Methods versus Properties

Setting a property represents an OLE call, and thus an RPC call. Commonly, client applications need to set multiple properties. If several properties need to be set, it is often useful to create a special method that is capable of taking multiple property values and setting them internally.

Likewise, controllers often need to read multiple property values. A special method that takes multiple optional parameters can be implemented in the server that enables the client to read multiple property values.

For example, if an object has three properties, *customer*, *product*, and *quantity*, instead of making three separate property set calls, the server would implement a *PropertySet* procedure that takes optional *customer*, *product*, and *quantity* parameters. The following code example demonstrates how this could be implemented for the previous example.

```
Public Sub PropertySet(Optional Customer As Variant, _
                       Optional Product As Variant, _
                       Optional Quantity As Variant)

    'determine which properties are to be set
    If IsMissing(Customer) = False Then
        prvCustomer = Customer
    End If
    If IsMissing(Product) = False Then
        prvProduct = Product
    End If
    If IsMissing(Quantity) = False Then
        prvQuantity = Quantity
    End If

End Sub
```

Instance Managers

Techniques for pooling object instance on the server can improve performance of remote automation. For example, servers that need to communicate with other servers can be designed in-process to each other.

An instance manager is merely a tool for managing your own custom server objects, usually business services. Most of the functionality of a particular instance manager will probably be useful for all objects. Instance managers are powerful, necessary tools for managing server objects.

In the future, DCOM and TP monitors will most likely incorporate all of the features of today's instance manager. However, until that day comes, they are an important tool for increasing the performance of your application.

Returning Arrays

OLE servers often expose collections of objects. If a client application needs to access all or many property elements of the object, it will need to make an OLE automation call for each element.

For example, an *Order* object might expose a collection of *LineItem* objects. The client application may commonly need to read all of the line items at once, to place in a grid control for example. Instead of making an OLE call to read each line item object's properties (such as the *PropertyGet* example mentioned above), the *LineItems* collection (not object) might implement a *CollectionGet* method that takes a two-dimensional array as a parameter, and returns an array of property values for the entire collection with a single OLE call.

32-Bit

Automation servers operate much more efficiently if they are built as 32-bit OLE automation servers.

Visual Basic Remote Automation Tools

To make Remote Automation even easier for the application developer to use, Visual Basic ships with tools that assist in the installation and configuration of remote OLE Automation servers. In this section, we will these tools, and the functionality that they provide.

Component Manager

One of the primary benefits of the three-tier architecture is code reuse at the component level. For example, multiple client applications should be able to reuse an *Order Manager* business component.

In complex systems with many components, the developer and end-user needs to be able to locate and install the various components that make up a system. The Component Manager is a tool that ships with VB Enterprise that addresses this need.

The Component Manager and its associated Component Catalog databases are the central, shareable repository that manage distributed components. The Component Manager is useful for managing all OLE server components, not just those created in Visual Basic.

The Component Manager uses a Component Catalog database to store this information. A Component Catalog is just a set of tables that reside in a database. The database can either be a Microsoft Access .MDB file or an ODBC data source such as SQL Server or Oracle.

A single Component Manager application can maintain references to multiple Component Catalogs. For example, a user might want to keep references to two catalogs when running the Component Manager: an order processing catalog that contains *Order Manager*, *Product Manager*, and *Customer Manager* component references; and a purchasing catalog that contains *Vendor Manager* and *Inventory Manager* component references.

The Component Manager application is stored in the \CLISVR directory of the VB directory. The filename is CMPGR32.EXE.

A Catalog of Objects

Before we talk about how to maintain and modify a Component Catalog with the Component Manager, we will walk through exactly how to use an existing Component Manager Component Catalog.

The Component Manager is divided into three main panes. See figure 19.3. The *Scope* pane on the left shows the Component Catalog databases the application currently references. The *Criteria* pane on the top shows which components for the selected catalog are currently displayed. The *Results* pane on the right shows the components in the currently selected catalog in the Scope pane that match the criteria last searched in the Criteria pane.

Fig. 19.3

The three main panes of the Component Manager: The Scope pane on the left, the Results pane on the right, and the Criteria pane on the top.

For example, when the Component Manager is executed for the first time after VB is installed, the Scope pane shows only one Component Catalog: The Sample Components Component Catalog. The Tags in the Criteria pane are empty by default. Because the Criteria pane is empty, and thus no filter criteria has been set, the Results pane shows all of the components in the Sample Components catalog.

Using the Results Pane. The Results pane displays a list of the available components in the selected catalog in the Scope pane. For components created in Visual Basic, the component name corresponds to the VB project name.

Under each component (accessed by double-clicking the component name) is a list of available classes. For components created in VB, the class name corresponds to the name of the public class module.

Under each class is the interface of the class: the properties, methods, member objects, and collections.

The outline, then, is hierarchically structured like this:

```
Component item
     Class item
          Interface item
Component item
     Class item
          Interface item
          Interface item
     Class item
          Interface item
          Interface item
```

To view the properties of a component, class, or interface item, highlight the item, click the right mouse button, and select *Properties*. Alternatively, you can select the *Results..Properties* menu item.

A property sheet for the select item appears. The property sheet contains four tabs of property information on the item: *Description, Property Tags, Details,* and *Associated Files.*

Like any property sheet, each tab has an *Update* and *Close* button. The *Update* button immediately saves any changes made. The *Close* button closes the property sheet without saving any changes.

Filtering & Searching Components. Now that you know how to browse the results pane, you're ready to learn how to manipulate the components, classes, and interface items displayed in the Results pane.

Why is this useful? As components proliferate in your organization, a typical Component Catalog may contain hundreds of components and associated classes. Since business rules are never repeated, you may have to search through hundreds of components to find the exact piece of business functionality you need.

The Criteria pane at the top is used to filter, sort, and find specific components. See figure 19.4.

Fig. 19.4

The results of a find and sort specified in the Criteria pane on the Sample Components Component Catalog.

The Criteria pane lists the properties of the currently selected catalog in the Scope pane. For example, the Sample Components Component Catalog has four properties: *Sample Type, Technology, Comp Type, and 3-Tier Layer*.

Each of the properties combo boxes can be used to either filter or sort on the associated property. To select a filter for a property, choose a property tag from the property's drop down combo box.

To sort by a particular property, select the sort order with the numeric buttons next to the property combo box.

Once the property filter and sort criteria have been chosen, pressing the *Find Result Now* button or choosing the *Search..Find Results Now* menu item will update the *Results* pane to reflect the search criteria.

For each level of sort criteria specified, the *Results* pane will add a level corresponding to the sort criteria. For example, if you specify to sort by *Comp Type* and *3-Tier Layer*, two levels will be added on top of the component, class, and interface hierarchies—one for each sort criteria. Since these layers are not components, classes, or interfaces, you cannot view their properties.

The Component Manager also lets you specify a filter on the item's full text or file date. To filter on the item's full text *Usage Notes* (described earlier), specify the text string in the *Text Search* combo box. Likewise, to filter on the component's file date, specify a date range in the *Date* text boxes.

Often, you will want to erase the last applied filter and sort criteria and reload the entire Component Catalog into the Results pane. This can be accomplished quickly by pressing the *Clear Search Criteria* button or selecting *Search..Clear Search Criteria* from the menu, and then pressing the *Find Results Now* button again.

Grouping Components. Within a Component Catalog you may find that you frequently apply the same filter criteria to obtain a list of related components. Or you may find that all you ever use is a single class from a complicated component that contains many classes.

The Component Manager allows you to create predefined groups of component, class, and interface items. In the Component Manager, these are called *Named Collections* (not to be confused with OLE object collections).

Viewing Named Collections. To view a list of predefined Named Collections, select the Show *Collection Lists* button or choose *View..Show Collection Lists* from the menu. The *Criteria* pane will change to the *Named Collections* pane. Like the *Criteria* pane, the *Named Collections* pane allows you to change the items displayed in the *Results* pane.

A list of predefined Named Collections is displayed in the list box. Selecting an item in the list box changes the Results pane to reflect the items in the Named Collection.

Adding Named Collections. To create a new group of components, click the right mouse button over the Named Collections text box, and select *Add* from the menu.

A dialog box will prompt for a new collection name. Enter the name of the new named collection. When finished, the newly created empty named collection will appear in the list of named collections.

Modifying Named Collections. To modify the items contained a named collection, select the collection, click the right mouse button, and then choose *Edit* from the pop-up menu. The *Edit Named Collections* window will appear. See figure 19.5.

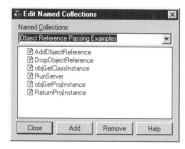

Fig. 19.5
The Edit Named Collections window, where items within a named collection can be added and removed.

This window is not a dialog. That is, it is not modal—it is related back to the Component Manager's main window.

To add an item to the named collection, select the item you would like to add from the Component Manager's *Results* pane. Remember, because the *Edit Named Collections* window isn't modal, you can browse the *Results* pane while it remains open—even applying new filters. Once the proper item is selected, switch back to the *Edit Named Collections* window and press the *Add* button.

Alternatively, the items from the Results pane can be dragged and dropped into the *Edit Named Collections* window.

To remove an item from the named collection, select the item in the *Edit Named Collections* window and press the Remove button.

Remember, named collections are just logical groupings of components in the component catalog. When an item is removed from a named collection it is not removed from the component catalog.

Installing Components

Now that you're familiar with how to maneuver through the Component Manager and find the appropriate component, you're ready to learn how to install them, using the Component Manager.

To install a component, first select a component in the Results pane. Make sure to select a component, not a class item, interface item, or sort grouping item. Click the right mouse button and select *Install*.

A dialog similar to figure 19.6 appears.

Fig. 19.6
Installing a
component.

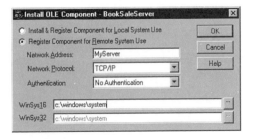

The Component Manager allows you to install the component either for local use or remote use. In this context, local and remote refer to whether the component will execute on the workstation (run from either the local hard disk or on a network share), or whether the component will run on another machine via remote automation, such as an application server over the network.

Don't confuse this local and remote terminology with the location of the component catalog. You can install a component for remote use from a local catalog, just as you can install a component for local use from a remote catalog.

The *WinSys16* text box specifies the path to the 16-bit Windows system directory, if one is installed on the machine. If it is in the same directory as the 32-bit system directory, then specify the 32-bit system path.

The *WinSys32* text box specifies the path to the 32-bit Windows system directory, if one is installed on the machine.

The 16-bit and 32-bit paths have different behavior, depending on whether or not you're running the 16-bit or 32-bit version of the Component Manager. Let's walk through the 32-bit Component Manager scenario first.

The 16-bit path tells the 32-bit version of the Component Manager where to find the path to the 16-bit proxy stub (which cannot reliably be found programatically). If the 16-bit path is specified, the 32-bit Component Manager will register the server for access by both 16-bit and 32-bit apps. If it isn't, the 32-bit Component Manager will only register the server for access by 32-bit clients. The 32-bit path will automatically be filled in by the 32-bit Component Manager and cannot be changed by the user.

The 16-bit Component Manager works analogously to the 32-bit version just described—just reverse 16-bit and 32-bit in the preceding description.

Local Installation. To select the component for local use, select the top radio button. When selected, the remote component is copied to the local system. The component and its related files, by default, are placed in the \WINDOWS\OLSVR directory. The registry is updated to point all references to the OLE server to the local copy.

This option is appropriate in a number of scenarios:

■ For performance reasons, the OLE server needs to be run locally

■ The OLE server is an in-process server that can't be run via remote automation

■ The OLE server is a user service and, in general, user services are physically deployed on the client workstation

■ The user is a disconnected laptop user who needs to run all three tiers on the same laptop CPU

Remote Installation. To select the component for remote use (via remote automation), select the bottom radio button. When selected, the registry is updated to point to the remote server—no files are copied locally since no additional process needs to execute on the client workstation.

A few additional parameters need to be specified when installing a component for remote use, so that the client can find and communicate with the remote server over the network:

- *Network Address.* The network address of the system where the server component is located. You can enter the name of the remote server with or without preceding backslashes (\\). For example, you can enter either \\MYSERVER or MYSERVER. In addition, you can specify an IP address for TCP/IP connections.

- *Network Protocol.* The network protocol that the client and server systems use to communicate with each other.

- *Authentication.* The RPC (remote procedure call) authentication to use for communication. Authentication is a tool used to ensure data privacy and integrity.

Remote automation will be covered in detail later in this chapter.

This option is appropriate in a number of scenarios:

- You wish to lock up and deploy business servers on powerful server machines.

- Client PCs don't have the resources to execute anything more than user services.

- You want to offer services over the Internet.

Switching Between Local and Remote. It might be helpful to switch between local and remote components frequently. For example, for many reasons you may want to develop servers locally but frequently test them remotely—the way they will be deployed in production.

The Component Manager can safely reinstall components on top of each other. Therefore, to switch between local and remote you need only reinstall the component with the appropriate settings.

Automation Manager

As mentioned throughout this chapter, the Automation Manager manages the RPC connection on the remote automation server. The program is installed in the \WINDOWS\SYSTEM directory and is AUTMGR32.EXE.

The Automation Manager is a multi-threaded application, so the single Automation Manager application process can service multiple clients simultaneously. Even though it is multi-threaded, though, OLE servers are single-threaded. So if you need multiple clients to be simultaneously served by the same OLE object, you must consider the instancing of that object. For example, the object should be Creatable Single-Use.

The Automation Manager adds little overhead beyond OLE and RPC. It does not automatically start up in response to a client request, so in general, on a server machine, it should be configured to start up when the machine boots.

If your application implements asynchronous notification or call-backs to the client machine, the client machine will automatically start the Automation Manager to handle such requests. Under this scenario in Windows 95, the Automation Manager will run invisibly.

Remote Automation Connection Manager

The Remote Automation Connection Manager is a utility that ships with VB to help manage remote automation configuration. It accomplishes two things:

- Enables the controller to switch between pointing to local or remote servers

- Configures the server security options

The Remote Automation Connection Manager is somewhat confusing in that it is useful for administering both server machines and client machines.

So, when should the Remote Automation Connection Manager be used? On a client machine, it is used to point to either a local or remote server. On the server machine, it is used to determine what OLE servers can be automated remotely and by whom.

What's the difference between the Component Manager and the Remote Automation Connection Manager? The Component Manager is used for installing and managing component catalogs, while the Remote Automation Connection Manager is used only *after* the server has been installed. In addition, the Remote Automation Connection Manager can set server security options.

When the Remote Automation Connection Manager is started, you will see two main panes. On the left is an *OLE Classes* pane which lists all of the OLE classes currently in the registry, and on the right is the *Client Access* and *Server Connection* tabs used to administer servers and clients respectively.

Server Connections

The Server Connection tab is used to administer the way clients point to servers. See figure 19.7.

Fig. 19.7

The Remote Automation Manager's Server Connection tab.

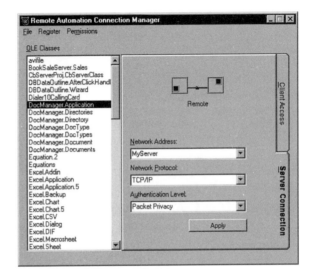

On the left, the OLE Classes list box enables you to select a previously installed class to administer. The OLE classes listed come from the machine's registry. As classes are selected, their configurations are shown on the right.

The icon at the top indicates whether the currently selected class is installed for remote or local use. To change the installation between remote and local use, move the mousepointer over the OLE class item, click the right mouse button, and click the Remote or Local menu items.

When the class is installed remotely, the right pane indicates how the client connects to the server. The three options, *Remote Name*, *Network Protocol*, and *Authentication Level* are identical to the options in the Component Manager, described in the previous section.

Security/Client Access

The Client Access tab is used to administer the way clients are allowed to access the server. See figure 19.8.

The System Security Policy radio buttons administer the way security is applied to all classes on the server. Specifically, it enforces which classes can or cannot be instantiated by controlling applications. Some security policies allow more granularity than others.

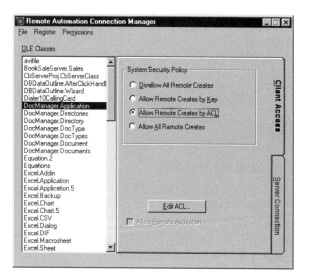

Fig. 19.8
The Remote
Automation
Manager's Client
Access tab.

Allow All Remote Creates. This policy allows any client machine to instantiate *any* class on the server. This is not a recommended configuration, because it essentially gives others free reign to run applications on the server. It can be useful in a test or development environment, however.

Disallow Remote Creates. This policy prohibits all client applications from instantiating objects on the server machine. This is useful for machines that aren't going to be remote automation servers and is the default setting.

Allow Remote Creates by Key. This policy enables you to turn on remote automation selectively by key. When this policy is set, the Allow Remote Activation check box is enabled. As classes are selected in the list box on the left, this check box indicates whether or not the class supports remote automation.

This is useful in an open, unsecured environment when the server only wants to make certain classes public. For example, Microsoft Office OLE servers such as Excel should not allow remote automation.

It is also useful in a non-integrated Windows NT security environment—if users don't log on to an NT domain, for example.

Allow Remote Creates by ACL. This policy lets you enable remote automation by user for each class. When this policy is set, the edit ACL (access control list) button is enabled. As classes are selected in the list box on the left, this button allows you to assign access by user and group.

This is the most robust security method, but requires that the server run on a Windows NT machine. This is most useful in a production environment where you need to selectively assign different class permissions to different users.

A workstation can be both a remote automation client and a server. That is, a workstation can reference objects on other machines while other machines are referencing its objects.

Client Registration Utility

The Client Registration Utility is basically a command line version of the Remote Automation Manager that also allows you to install and uninstall a remote automation class in the registry. It is located in the \CLISVR directory off the VB directory, and is called CLIREG32.EXE.

The Client Registration Utility is used by the VB Setup Toolkit to register servers for remote use. But it also helpful for organization's that need to install servers in batch or as a part of their own custom setup applications.

The utility uses the Remote Support (.VBR) and Type Library (.TLB) files that Visual Basic produces when it compiles the OLE server's .EXE file and the Remote Server Support Files check box is selected.

The complete syntax is:

```
CLIREG[32][.EXE] vbrfile -s {s} ¦ -p {p} ¦ -a {a} ¦ -t {t} ¦ -u ¦ -
q ¦ -1 ¦ -nologo ¦ -[h ¦ ?]
```

Table 19.2 Describes these command line parameters in detail.

Table 19.2 Client Registration Utility Command Line Parameters	
Option	**Description**
-s {s}	Specify network address {s}.
-p {p}	Specify network protocol {p}.
-a {a}	Specify security authentication level {a}; valid range is from 0 to 6.
-t {t}	Specify TypeLib file {t}.
-u	Quiet mode: no information dialogs or error messages.
-l	Log error information to file "CLIREG.LOG".
-nologo	Do not display copyright information.
-[h ¦ ?]	Display the Help dialog box that presents command line options.

Debugging Remote Automation

Setting up remote automation for the first time can be overwhelming, especially if things don't work: there are a lot of pieces that need to work together. Usually, the errors aren't specific enough to identify where the problem is.

The following methodical installation and debugging procedure will help you isolate where problems are occurring. The philosophy behind this method is that before remote automation can work, local automation needs to work. These procedures outline a manual approach that will enable you to identify exactly where the problem lies.

In these steps the *client workstation* is the workstation you intend to run the remote automation controller on, and the *server workstation* is the workstation you intend to run the OLE server on. The *controlling application* is the OLE test client, and the *OLE server* is the OLE server application.

Step 1: Unregister Components

The server should be installed into fresh registry entries. So, the first step is to unregister the OLE server with the /UNREGSERVER command line parameters.

This should be executed on both the client workstation and the server workstation.

If an error occurs on the client or server, there is a problem with the registry. It may be corrupt, for example. You may need to go into the registry with the Registry Editor or another utility and try to clean up the corrupt registry entries.

Step 2: Register Components

The next step is to register the OLE sever component for local use on both the machines. To do this, run the OLE server with the /REGSERVER command line parameter on both the client workstation and the server workstation.

Make sure that you are using the same .EXE. Compiling from the same OLE server project is not good enough: when you compile the OLE server project a different CLSID may be generated. It is not good enough to have just the same class names registered on the client workstation and server workstation, they must also have the same CLSIDs. The safest way to insure this is to register the components from the same OLE server .EXE.

If a problem occurs in this step, the registry or OLE server .EXE may be corrupted.

Step 3: Test Local

Before we switch to remote automation, we need to make sure local automation of the OLE server works on both the client workstation and the server workstation.

To test this, run the controlling application once on the client workstation and once on the server workstation.

If an error occurs in this step, it must be related to the way in which the controlling application and OLE server are communicating.

Step 4: Configure Server Workstation for Remote Automation

The server needs to be prepared for remote automation requests. The first step is to make sure security won't hinder the connection. To do this, run the Remote Automation Connection Manager on the server workstation. Set the security policy to allow all creates. This should be just a temporary setting for debugging purposes.

Now execute the Automation Manager so that the server workstation is prepared to marshal client requests.

If an error occurs in this step, you may have a problem with your server workstation network configuration.

Step 5: Configure Client Workstation for Remote Automation

Now that the server workstation is ready to receive requests and we have verified that the OLE server runs locally on both machines, we are ready to point the client workstation's controlling application to the server workstation's OLE server.

To do this, execute the Remote Automation Connection Manager on the client workstation. Select the OLE server class. Type in the server name, select the appropriate protocol, and select No Authentication.

Step 6: Test Remote

Everything should be set up at this point. Execute the controlling application on the client workstation.

If it fails at this point, most likely the problem is with the network connection. Make sure the client workstation has visibility to the server workstation through other services. For example, test to see if the client workstation can access a file share on the server workstation.

Or try experimenting with other protocols. Or try accessing the server from another workstation, or even reversing the client/server relationship.

If things work well, try re-implementing security on the server workstation and authentication on the client workstation.

As you become more familiar with remote automation you will begin to recognize and associate common errors with common configuration problems.

As you may have concluded from reading this section, it's always a good idea to have a simple test controlling application for every remotely deployed OLE server for just such debugging scenarios.

Summary

At this point, you have an understanding of what remote automation is, how is works, the types of applications that can be developed using this technology, and common performance issues that need to be addressed when using it. You are now ready to learn how to design and develop a three-tier application. For more information about designing and developing three-tier applications, read Que's *Visual Basic Enterprise Development* (ISBN: 0-7897-0099-9).

Index

Symbols

S

If you try to use Visual Basic 4.0 *without* Choreo to build client/server applications, you'll be missing an *essential* technical component:

Cool Stuff.

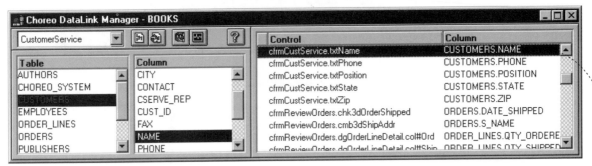

The DataLink Manager makes it easy to develop 32-bit client/server applications. The DataLink Manager lets you drag and drop field names onto standard *or* third-party controls to create *DataLinks*. DataLinks tell Choreo to automatically place the data into the designated control at run time.

The Navigation ToolBar lets the user navigate easily through records. This includes the ability to insert, update and delete records, create and use bookmarks and search for records using Query by Example (QBE). You get all of this with *no code!*

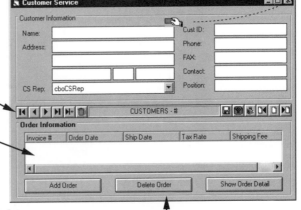

The Choreo DataGrid enables the user to display and edit data in tabular format. Use Drag-and-Drop to specify what columns to display.

32-bit Choreo DataDrivers are *faster* than ODBC and *smarter* than RDO since they spare you all of the coding headaches thanks to *Data Choreography*. Just select a driver, log in and go!

The Choreo API gives you the capability to create custom solutions when you need to push the envelope. You can even use CAL API calls to create OLE servers, leveraging Choreo's 32-bit power across the enterprise.

So get the Cool Stuff. Call 1-800-4-CHOREO

and find out how Choreo can help you quickly and easily build powerful 32-bit client/server applications that run at *lightning* speed.

CHOREO for Visual Basic 4.0.
Cool Stuff!

CENTERVIEW
SOFTWARE INCORPORATED
651 Gateway Blvd. Suite 105C
South San Francisco, CA 9408
(415) 266-7060

About Clarity Consulting, Inc.

Clarity Consulting, Inc., is a Chicago-based consulting firm that specializes in the design and implementation of client/server information systems. The corporation's primary business objective is to help organizations achieve clear, logical, and well-planned solutions to modern business and information system problems.

Clarity has extensive experience in custom application development, strategic planning, technical design, and project management within the Fortune 500 community. The corporation utilizes leading edge client/server technologies including Visual Basic, Powerbuilder, Visual C++, SQL Server, Oracle, Sybase, DB2, Access, OLE, Windows NT, and UNIX, as well as enabling technologies involving the Internet, voice processing, imaging, and hand-held devices.

Clarity is a Microsoft Solution Provider. Applications developed by Clarity consultants have won industry awards and been featured in national publications. Clarity's consultants are dedicated to continued education and maintain high profiles within the developer community. They are full-time, salaried employees committed to the success of the company and client engagements.

If you have project work that might benefit from Clarity's services, or if you are interested in joining Clarity, you can reach Clarity via the Internet at info@claritycnslt.com, or via fax at (312) 266-1006.

Gregory Consulting Limited

Software development in Visual C++

- Internet programming
- Internet-enabling your applications
- porting from C to C++
- OCX design and development

Training

- C++
- Unix
- Business use of the Internet

Technical Writing

- Online Help
- User Manuals
- Books

Consulting

- Using the Internet
- Developing an Internet presence
- Remote work
- Effective C++

Kate Gregory is a partner in Gregory Consulting Limited, a software development and consulting company founded in 1986. Gregory Consulting is happily located in rural Ontario, Canada, with clients across North America. Most projects are done as contracts, as short as a few weeks or as long as a year.

For more information, please contact us:

Voice: (705) 277 1861
Fax: (705) 277 9193
Email: info@gregcons.com

Michael McKelvy is the owner of McKelvy Software Systems of Birmingham, Alabama. His firm develops custom programs and business solutions for a variety of businesses, and specializes in the development of PC-based database applications. Some of these applications include:

- Member and activity tracking system for health clubs. This program keeps up with a club's clients, their workout activities, and progress toward fitness goals. The program also includes contact tracking for the clubs.

- Restaurant management system. This system handles operations of a restaurant including order tracking, total sales, food inventory, and employee time-keeping.

- Membership information system for churches. This system keeps track of the names, addresses, and phone numbers of members. The system also keeps up with birthdays, anniversaries, dates joined, etc. for all members. In addition, the system helps the church track the attendance of its members. A related program helps youth groups keep track of their members and activities.

- Fuel cost accounting system. This system was designed to track the costs of nuclear fuel for an electric utility. The system keeps up with material inventories, vendor invoices, and material requirements. The system also prepares budget information for the utility.

In addition to his work on the VBPJ Guide to Visual Basic, Mike is the author of Que's "Using Visual Basic 4," and the co-author of "Special Edition Using Visual Basic 4" and "Visual Basic Expert Solutions."

Mike can be contacted at:

McKelvy Software Systems
P.O. Box 380125
Birmingham, Alabama 35238

Fax: (205) 980-9816

CompuServe: 71477,3513

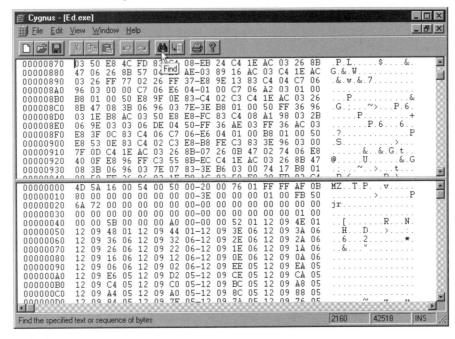

- Based in Sarasota, Florida, SunOpTech uses Visual Basic and Visual C++ to develop decision support applications for manufacturing enterprises.

- SunOpTech's systems, which are now operating in the United States, Germany, and Great Britain, are oriented to multi-location, multi-national enterprises which operate in an environment of continuous change that requires rapid response.

- SunOpTech develops *mentor systems* which empower an enterprise by distributing information to people enabling them to make proactive business decisions, to effectively utilize their resources over time, and to reduce hassle-factor

ObjectBank System	ObjectJob System
An electronic safekeeping place, the ObjectSafe, using patented technology to store objects including spreadsheet files, word processing documents, graphic files, fax files, CAD files, and database files. These files can be easily deposited and withdrawn with the ObjectTeller and automatically replicated to other ObjectSafes using the ObjectWire. Easily integrates with other applications through an OLE interface.	A general purpose order scheduling system for mission-critical tasks which have finite resources. Uses a cube paradigm with axes of time, resources, and space. Attempts to muster resources at a space and time to complete a task based on user-defined rules. Ideal for distributed workcells because it uses OLE messaging between Resource Objects to share schedules and requirements.

For information contact:
Chris Barlow, President & CEO
chrisb@SunOpTech.com

SunOpTech, 1500 West University Parkway, Sarasota, FL, 34243-2290
Phone: (941) 362-1270; Fax (941)362-1296
www.SunOpTech.com.

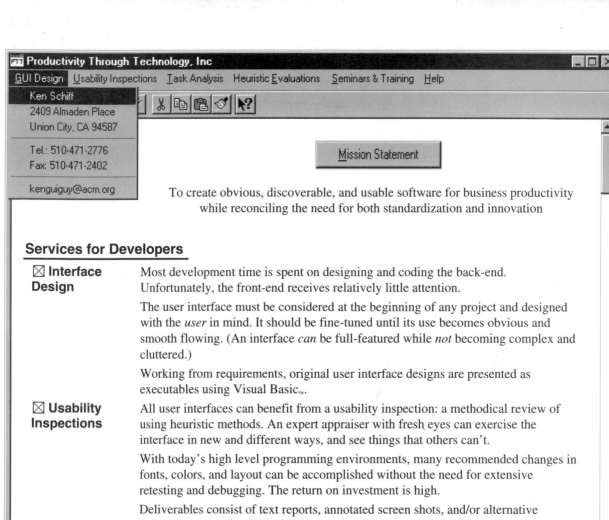

Productivity Through Technology, Inc

GUI Design   Usability Inspections   Task Analysis   Heuristic Evaluations   Seminars & Training   Help

Ken Schiff
2409 Almaden Place
Union City, CA 94587

Tel.: 510-471-2776
Fax: 510-471-2402

kenguiguy@acm.org

> **Mission Statement**
>
> To create obvious, discoverable, and usable software for business productivity while reconciling the need for both standardization and innovation

Services for Developers

☒ Interface Design

Most development time is spent on designing and coding the back-end. Unfortunately, the front-end receives relatively little attention.

The user interface must be considered at the beginning of any project and designed with the *user* in mind. It should be fine-tuned until its use becomes obvious and smooth flowing. (An interface *can* be full-featured while *not* becoming complex and cluttered.)

Working from requirements, original user interface designs are presented as executables using Visual Basic™.

☒ Usability Inspections

All user interfaces can benefit from a usability inspection: a methodical review of using heuristic methods. An expert appraiser with fresh eyes can exercise the interface in new and different ways, and see things that others can't.

With today's high level programming environments, many recommended changes in fonts, colors, and layout can be accomplished without the need for extensive retesting and debugging. The return on investment is high.

Deliverables consist of text reports, annotated screen shots, and/or alternative prototypes created in Visual Basic™.

☒ Demo Review

Many demos have actually scuttled sales! In an effort to demonstrate every conceivable thing a program or tool can do, demo screens are frequently rendered unreadable due to clutter and inappropriate use of colors, fonts, and 3D effects. A good demo should be designed with the same criteria as a good user interface.

Reviews consist of text reports and annotated screen shots.

———— 8 ————

Clients (partial list)

ProBusiness, Inc.
Prism Solutions, Inc.
NetFRAME Systems, Inc.
Caere Corporation
Blyth Software
Wells Fargo Bank
Charles Schwab Company

Pacific Gas & Electric Company
Visa International
Bank of America
Summit Integration Group
Windows Magazine
Consumer Market Analysts
Vision Software, Inc.

Conference Presenter

WinDev East
DBExpo East
WinDev West
DBExpo West
Windows Solutions
Blyth International

Creating obvious and discoverable software for business productivity.   CAPS   NUM   INS   8-24-95   12:01 AM